*Political Development
and Social Change*

Political Development
and Social Change

JASON L. FINKLE
University of Michigan

RICHARD W. GABLE
University of California, Davis

John Wiley & Sons, Inc.   NEW YORK · LONDON · SYDNEY

Preface

Karl Polanyi characterized the collapse of nineteenth-century civilization as *The Great Transformation*. In his classic analysis, Polanyi examined the four major institutions he saw as the basis of nineteenth-century civilization and, employing the insights of several scholarly disciplines, traced the forces which led to the downfall of these institutional foundations. But the civilization Polanyi analyzed was of the Western world; the events he scrutinized were no longer in the process of change; and a distinct stage in history had come to a close.

Far greater transformations are taking place in the twentieth century, not just in one civilization, but in virtually every society in the world. As compared to the changes in the nineteenth century, these great transformations affect the lives of far more people in more profound ways, involve many more institutions, are more complex and difficult to comprehend—and their outcomes are unknown. In assembling this book, we have tried to provide a meaningful conceptual framework for understanding and analyzing the contemporary process of political development and its relationship to other societal transformations. It is this theme, the relationship of political development to social change, which gives unity to our volume.

Our objective has been to bring some degree of order to the plethora of terms and concepts, approaches and theories, constructs and models which abound in an emerging field. If the modernizing countries could develop as rapidly as the literature on them is expanding, their developmental problems might soon be solved.

The decision to treat the problems of political development in combination with social change, we feel, is amply justified throughout the following pages. The multiple and interrelated transformations in all of the systems by which man organizes his life and society constitute the general process of modernization. However, an attempt to account for so great a range of phenomena involves the risk of accounting for nothing in a satisfactory way. To help avert this pitfall, we have utilized a systems approach viewing society as a "master" social system made up of political, economic, religious and other subsystems which are constantly undergoing change. We have sought to focus attention on those elements of the social system which impinge more or less directly on the polity—the social changes most likely to be consequential for political development.

v

The emerging countries are engaged in the task of political development and nation-building and their success in this undertaking is largely dependent on the rate, direction, and quality of social change that they can effect. Thus, at least until the developing nations have achieved an ability to generate and absorb persistent transformation and have attained the stability, legitimacy, and unity that is concomitant with nationhood, there shall remain compelling reasons for political scientists to examine modernization with an acute sensitivity to the multiplicity of interconnected factors involved in social change. As political scientists ourselves, the wide range of ideas, approaches, and empirical research we have collected here has produced a book which might be classified as political sociology rather than orthodox political science.

The scope of this undertaking has obviously imposed constraints on us which warrant explanation, especially as many of the outstanding contributions to the scholarly literature on modernization and development have been omitted. These omissions, for the most part, are not a result of oversight but are due to the agonizing choices which confront editors suffering under the economic hardship of word and page limitations. Having made the decision to reproduce entire articles, complete with footnotes (except for seven excerpts from longer works because we felt their integrity and coherence could endure compression), we found that these limitations required us to adopt a number of guidelines for selecting articles to include in this volume: (1) whenever possible, we chose articles which contained a strong theoretical orientation combined with empirical research; (2) we chose the shorter article when confronted with two of approximately equal quality; (3) with but a few notable exceptions, we attempted to select a recent article on a subject, particularly when the newer article incorporated or alluded to ideas and findings contained in earlier research efforts; (4) we attempted to avoid articles with a single-country focus, and decided to include such articles when they introduced concepts and methodologies that were applicable to developing nations generally; (5) although not a prime consideration, we attempted to select articles with illustrations and analyses from widely varied areas and countries, so that the Far East, South and South East Asia, the Middle East, Africa, and Latin America are represented as well as such individual countries as Japan, China, Indonesia, Cambodia, Burma, Ceylon, India, Turkey, Tunisia, Ethiopia, Ghana, Uganda, Mexico, and Guatemala; and finally (6) we have included a small group of articles (which we shall not specify) whose intellectual content seemed so overwhelmingly attractive or provocative that we simply could not omit them, notwithstanding any or all of our guidelines.

It may be maintained that one criterion of a "developed" society is the ability of its members to voluntarily cooperate with one another. By this standard, we found the academic community to be highly developed. The authors whose works we have reprinted were gracious collaborators even when, in a few cases, we had to perform cruel surgery on their writings for the purpose of conciseness. We wish to acknowledge the helpful advice and comments received from the many graduate students at the University of Southern California and the University of Michigan who participated in the seminars in which this reader took shape.

Before expressing our indebtedness for the generous and constructive criticisms and suggestions made by a number of colleagues, we should like to exonerate them from the final product because each in his own way indicated that he would have compiled a different book. Our own confidence was sustained by the fact that no two of our very able critics envisaged the same book. We extend our particular gratitude to Douglas E. Ashford, Karl W. Deutsch, Alfred Diamant, S. N. Eisenstadt, Samuel P. Huntington, Warren F. Ilchman, Gayl Ness, John H. Kautsky, Fred W. Riggs, Edgar L. Shor, and Robert E. Ward. In addition, we wish to acknowledge the encouragement and assistance received from the School of Public Administration, University of Southern California, where we were colleagues for much of the time when this volume was being prepared.

JASON L. FINKLE
RICHARD W. GABLE

Contents

PART V. THE POLITICS OF DEVELOPMENT AND NATION-BUILDING

*Political Development
and Social Change*

PART I

A SYSTEMS APPROACH
TO POLITICAL DEVELOPMENT

INTRODUCTION

Political development in the newly independent or less industrialized countries is a cause as well as a consequence of other types of social change. To understand how and why political development occurs, it seems necessary to view the polity within a conceptual framework capable of accounting for significant changes elsewhere in the social system. We begin, then, with the assumption that the political system is functionally related to nonpolitical elements of the social system and that the attempt to understand this relationship and its properties constitutes a meaningful approach to the study of political development.

While any social system, the preindustrial traditional society as well as the industrialized societies of the West, can be better understood from this perspective, there are significant and important reasons why this approach is essential for analyzing the processes of change occurring today in the traditional and transitional societies of Asia, Africa, and Latin America. Without desiring to engage in a discourse on the merits of a "multidisciplinary approach," our judgment is that the developing nations at this time do not possess institutions sufficiently autonomous and differentiated from one another to warrant the perpetuation of disciplinary purity in the social sciences. The formidable boundaries separating the traditional academic disciplines must be crossed if there is to be progress in this field. Economists have sought answers to questions about entrepreneurship and managerial skills by utilizing the theories and methods of psychology; political scientists have invaded the preserve of anthropology and sociology to explain authority relationships; psychologists have borrowed from the fields of economics and political science to deepen their analyses. In short, social scientists concerned with the processes of modernization in the developing nations are increasingly likely to utilize multidisciplinary skills to examine the dynamics of development and change.

To give a brief example, in carrying out research on advanced industrial society like that of the United States, one might or might not take cognizance of family structure in the study of economic and political behavior, but in investigating developing societies it is *mandatory* to be systematically alert to kinship patterns. The phenomena being observed in developing societies, and particularly the process of political development, require that a broader range of methodological techniques and approaches be marshalled in an analytical framework capable of relating political variables to a full range of social and other variables. While those things we call political and those things we call social may be treated as distinct at the analytical level, the distinction breaks down at the empirical level where the points of articulation between them are frequent, numerous, and intense.

A final justification for dealing with political development in a context of social change should be stressed. Despite the energy and talent currently being brought to bear on the problems of political development, social scientists are profoundly aware of gaps and uncertainties in their analysis of this process. Even though students of industrial societies experience short-comings in their work, their problem is one of achieving a deeper under-standing of the variables relevant to their interests. The student of political development, on the other hand, is at this stage of history engaged in a search for those variables that are relevant to political development. The difference is between knowing more about something and trying to identify what it is you should know more about. Therefore, to view societies as systems and to approach political development within the framework of social change creates a higher level of sensitivity to a broader range of possible variables and to their interrelationships.

One word of caution! The points of articulation between political and social phenomena are obviously not uncharted in our studies of industrial societies. However, it would be erroneous to assume that our understanding of the interaction between political and social variables in an industrial society is easily transferrable to preindustrial societies. Furthermore, our knowledge of political development in the industrialized nations unfortunately lags behind our ability to explain other aspects of Western political systems.

While there is considerable need for students of the politics of developing nations to appreciate the reciprocal relations between political and non-political variables, there is a comparable need to do so, when possible, in a systematic way employing full methodological rigor. Systems models and systems analysis are useful in achieving this objective. Systems analysis pro-vides a comprehensive frame of reference, yet it is sufficiently rigorous to facilitate ordering, integrating, and relating disparate aspects of the social system. By regarding society as a social system comprised of subsystems, such as the political and the economic subsystems, it is possible to make these analytical distinctions without falling into the trap of assuming that com-parable distinctions exist in the empirical world.

The initial article in this volume, by Robert Chin, introduces the reader to the major concepts relevant to the use of system and developmental models as a mode of analysis. A common criticism of systems theory, to which Chin refers, is that it assumes that systems return to "equilibrium" or a "steady state" so that the theory does not satisfactorily account for change and development.

Chin maintains that the *developmental model*, while deficient in other respects, is aptly suited to account for changes in a system over time.

Francis X. Sutton continues with the theme of societies as social systems; he introduces and integrates into his discussion three additional concepts and forms of analysis which will recur throughout this book: (1) structural functional analysis; (2) the dichotomous "pattern variables" that were formulated by Talcott Parsons, although they have long historical antecedents in sociological analysis; and (3) a typology of societies that contrasts agricultural society with modern industrial society based on pattern-variable analysis.

In spite of the difficulties and limitations of structural functional analysis, it is exceptionally useful for comparative research. One pitfall of the institutional approach of traditional political science was the tendency to associate particular functions with particular structures. Structural functional analysis permits us to identify "functional equivalents," that is, to identify equivalent functions which may be performed by different structural units.

Pattern variables facilitate the process of contrasting traditional society with modern society, but, like any dichotomous classification, they distort reality by overemphasizing the differences. Wilbert Moore has reminded us: "The dichotomous classification in the analysis of social change . . . relies primarily on 'comparative statics' rather than on processes and procedures, rates and sequences."[1]

The utility of structural functional analysis for understanding social change and modernization is ably demonstrated by Neil J. Smelser, who, like Sutton, sees economic development as involving fundamental alterations in the social structure. These social changes, in turn, influence the rate and quality of economic development. While Smelser is undoubtedly sensitive to the empirical world in his theoretical analysis, he stresses that he is primarily concerned with presenting an "ideal type" construct, in the sense the term was employed by Max Weber.

The three key concepts Smelser discusses are differentiation, integration, and the discontinuities between differentiation and integration. An appreciation of the meaning of these concepts is fundamental to an understanding of the stresses and strains of social development. When the family system is no longer capable of satisfying the needs of economic production and new structural forms emerge to engage in production, adjustment between the old and new structures becomes necessary. While these adjustments are generally recognized as inevitable concomitants of economic development, they in turn produce new problems concerning the relationship of these differentiated structures to one another. Government, particularly in industrial societies, is likely to play a prominent role as the integrative mechanism, but it is by no means the only social unit to perform the function. The appearance of numerous differentiated structures in a society experiencing modernization does not mean that integrative mechanisms capable of

[1] Wilbert Moore, "Introduction: Social Change and Comparative Studies," *International Social Science Journal*, **15**, 522, 1963.

resolving relationships between these structures will emerge. Thus, social change, in developing societies, even under the best of circumstances, is likely to be uneven, discontinuous, and characterized by acute disturbances.

The three articles which comprise the next chapter, by Gideon Sjoberg, Phillip Hauser and David Apter, explore the characteristics and forces for change within those societies we type as "traditional" and "transitional." Any abstraction tends to blur some of the significant details of reality, yet these typologies are the analytical tools of social science, and no better substitute has been found except to refine these constructs. A classic characterization of traditional society is Robert Redfield's portrayal of "folk society,"[2] an analysis based upon empirical research in Mexico and the theoretical insights of Maine, Tönnies, and Durkheim. Redfield's presentation has become an inspiration and a point of departure for students of sociology and anthropology who continue to use and refine it.

Sjoberg suggests that the folk typology, however useful, most nearly corresponds to "primitive" society and is inadequate for understanding and interpreting the more complex, developing societies in Asia, Europe, and even Latin America. He designs a model of "feudal" society, not in its historical sense, but as a construct more suitable to the complex social systems that are not yet industrial but no longer qualify as folk societies.

Hauser describes what he feels are the significant cultural and personal characteristics of the peoples of South and Southeast Asia that constitute obstacles to their economic development. He is not writing within the framework of a theoretical or classificatory scheme, but rather attempts to extrapolate the factors that he observed impeding economic development in a number of transitional societies. One of his five major obstacles to economic development resulting from colonial heritage is "over urbanization." Other students of national development have found a statistical correlation between urbanization, on one hand, and social and political development, on the other. Hauser does not identify the point at which urbanization becomes "over urbanization" and is dysfunctional.

In an imaginative study combining theory and empiricism, David Apter considers the functional implications of traditionalism for political development. Apter's article is based on research in Ghana and Uganda, but the analytical scheme he employs and the problems he discusses have broader applicability. He poses the question, why do some traditional systems innovate more easily than others? In answering the question, Apter demonstrates that traditionalism may differ between societies, and some forms of traditionalism are more easily amenable to innovation and may, therefore, lend themselves to the tasks of nation-building and political modernization. However, it is not the form of traditionalism itself that may determine the outcome, but the kind of political structure imposed on a traditional society that may influence

---

[2] Robert Redfield, "The Folk Society," *The American Journal of Sociology*, **52**, 293–308, January 1947.

whether traditionalism will be enlisted in the service of innovation or will remain an impediment.

The complex character of the development process itself is reflected in the lack of consensus on the parameters and ingredients of political development and its linkage to social change. A graphic way to highlight the complexity of the problem is to conceive of a community—for example, a village in India—as a social system with economic and political subsystems. External and internal inputs into this village social system have often yielded higher standards of living, better educational facilities, a higher rate of literacy, and countless other increments in the quantitative indicators associated with social and economic modernization.

Yet numerous reports emanating from such community development projects in India indicate that the kinds of transformation generally associated with political development have not occurred. Community development assistance has often been administered through traditional elites—caste and class leaders—and has had the consequence of reinforcing their hold on village political life despite the introduction of new and higher standards of living and qualitative improvements in the way of life. In many cases there has been no greater equality, no increase in political participation, no expansion in the capacity of the political system to resolve its own village problems, and no greater differentiation in political roles. Thus, social change was not accompanied by political development, thereby suggesting that social and economic development may have lasting effects on the community without corresponding change in the political system. This example does not tell us what political development is, but it does suggest that sociodemographic and structural indices of modernization may not be able, either separately or together, to tell us what we desire to know about political development.

The last three articles in this part deal with the nature of the political system and the meaning of political development. The diverse attempts to provide definitions of political development are described by Lucian W. Pye. He does not presume to reconcile these differences, bu he does seek to illuminate the semantic confusion which he feels impedes the purposes and understanding of those concerned with political development. Pye finds three meaningful themes which prominently recur in the literature on political development: (1) a general spirit or attitude toward equality, (2) an increase in the capacity and capabilities of the political system per se, and (3) increased differentiation, specialization, and integration of structures, with all that is implied in these concepts. He concludes by suggesting that the "problems of political development revolve around the relationships between the political culture, the authoritative structures, and the general political process."

Alfred Diamant's analysis of the nature of political development is representative of the views of several students of the developing nations, namely, S. N. Eisenstadt and Fred W. Riggs, who would agree with Diamant that it is not analytically useful to think of the process of political development as having a specifically definable end product nor as requiring the creation of particular kinds of political institutions. Development is mainly an issue of system capabilities rather than of institutional form or normative policy. "Political development is a process by which a political system acquires an increased capacity to sustain successfully and continuously new types of goals and demands and the creation of new types of organizations."

The seminal article by Gabriel A. Almond deserves particular attention because it is the result of a long and prolific concern with the problem of political development by one whose writings are unsurpassed in influencing students of this field. He confronts a number of the criticisms directed toward systems theory in general and in his own earlier writings by attempting to "adapt systems theory in a developmental direction." Political development is discussed in terms of the interrelations of three kinds of political functions: capabilities, conversion functions, and system maintenance and adaptation functions. This complex and closely reasoned article constitutes an appropriate conclusion to Part I, utilizing many of the theories and methods discussed in the previous articles and expanding on them.

Chapter 1

Societies as Systems

THE UTILITY OF SYSTEM MODELS AND DEVELOPMENTAL MODELS

Robert Chin

All practitioners have ways of thinking about and figuring out situations of change. These ways are embodied in the concepts with which they apprehend the dynamics of the client-system they are working with, their relationship to it, and their processes of helping with its change. For example, the change-agent encounters resistance, defense mechanisms, readiness to change, adaptation, adjustment, maladjustment, integration, disintegration, growth, development, and maturation as well as deterioration. He uses concepts such as these to sort out the processes and mechanisms at work. And necessarily so. No practitioner can carry on thought processes without such concepts; indeed, no observations or diagnoses are ever made on "raw facts," because facts are really observations made within a set of concepts. But lurking behind concepts such as the ones stated above are assumptions about

SOURCE. Robert Chin, "The Utility of System Models and Developmental Models for Practitioners," in W. G. Bennis, K. D. Benne, and R. Chin, eds., *The Planning of Change* (New York: Holt, Rinehart, and Winston, 1961), pp. 201–214. Copyright (c) 1961 by Holt, Rinehart, and Winston, Inc. Reprinted by permission of the editors and publisher.

how the parts of the client-system fit together and how they change. For instance, "Let things alone, and natural laws (of economics, politics, personality, etc.) will work things out in the long run." "It is only human nature to resist change." "Every organization is always trying to improve its ways of working." Or, in more technical forms, we have assumptions such as: "The adjustment of the personality to its inner forces as well as adaptation to its environment is the sign of a healthy personality." "The coordination and integration of the departments of an organization is the task of the executive." "Conflict is an index of malintegration, or of change." "Inhibiting forces against growth must be removed."

It is clear that each of the above concepts conceals a different assumption about how events achieve stability and change, and how anyone can or cannot help change along. Can we make these assumptions explicit? Yes, we can and we must. The behavioral scientist does exactly this by constructing a simplified *model* of human events and of his tool concepts. By simplifying he can analyze his thoughts and concepts, and see in turn where the congruities and discrepancies occur between these and actual events. He becomes at once the

7

observer, analyzer, and modifier of the system[1] of concepts he is using.

The purpose of this paper is to present concepts relevant to, and the benefits to be gained from, using a "system" model and a "developmental" model in thinking about human events. These models provide "mind-holds" to the practitioner in his diagnosis. They are, therefore, of practical significance to him. This suggests one essential meaning of the oft-quoted and rarely explained phrase that "nothing is so practical as a good theory." We will try to show how the "systems" and "developmental" approaches provide key tools for a diagnosis of persons, groups, organizations, and communities for purposes of change. In doing so, we shall state succinctly the central notions of each model, probably sacrificing some technical elegance and exactness in the process. We shall not overburden the reader with citations of the voluminous set of articles from which this paper is drawn.

We postulate that the same models can be used in diagnosing different sizes of the units of human interactions— the person, the group, the organization, and the community.

One further prefatory word. We need to keep in mind the difference between an "analytic" model and a model of concrete events or cases. For our purposes, *an analytic model* is a constructed simplification of some part of reality that retains only those features regarded as essential for relating similar processes whenever and wherever they occur. *A concrete model* is based on an analytic model, but uses more of the content of actual cases, though it is still a simplification designed to reveal the essential features of some range of cases. As Hagen[2] puts it: "An explicitly defined analytic model

helps the theorist to recognize what factors are being taken into account and *what relationships among them are assumed* and hence to know the basis of his conclusions. The advantages are ones of both exclusion and inclusion. A model lessens the danger of overlooking the indirect effects of a change of a relationship" (our italics). We mention this distinction since we find a dual usage that has plagued behavioral scientists, for they themselves keep getting their feet entangled. We get mixed up in analyzing "the small group as a system" (analytic) and a school committee as a small group (concrete) or a national social system (analytic) and the American social system (concrete) or an organizational system (analytic) and the organization of a glue factory (concrete). In this paper, we will move back and forth between the analytic usage of "model" and the "model" of the concrete case, hopefully with awareness of when we are involved in a semantic shift.

The "System" Model

Psychologists, sociologists, anthropologists, economists, and political scientists have been "discovering" and using the system model. In so doing, they find intimations of an exhilarating "unity" of science, because the system models used by biological and physical scientists seem to be exactly similar. Thus, the system model is regarded by some system theorists as universally applicable to physical and social events, and to human relationships in small or large units.

The terms or concepts that are a part of the system model are "boundary," "stress or tension," "equilibrium," and "feedback." All these terms are related to "open system," "closed system," and "intersystem" models. We shall first define these concepts, illustrate their meaning, and then point out how they can be used by the change-agent as aids in observing, analyzing, or diagnosing —and perhaps intervening in—concrete situations.

---

[1] "System" is used here as any organized and coherent body of knowledge. Later we shall use the term in a more specific meaning.

[2] E. Hagen, chapter on "Theory of Social Change," unpublished manuscript.

THE MAJOR TERMS

System. Laymen sometimes say, "you can't beat the system" (economic or political), or "he is a product of the system" (juvenile delinquent or Soviet citizen). But readers of social science writings will find the term used in a rather more specific way. It is used as an abbreviated term for a longer phrase that the reader is asked to supply. The "economic system" might be read as: "we treat price indices, employment figures, etc., as if they were closely interdependent with each other and we temporarily leave out unusual or external events, such as the discovery of a new gold mine." Or in talking about juvenile delinquency in "system" terms, the sociologists choose to treat the lower-class values, lack of job opportunities, ragged parental images, as interrelated with each other, in back-and-forth cause-and-effect fashion, as determinants of delinquent behavior. Or the industrial sociologist may regard the factory as a "social system," as people working together in relative isolation from the outside, in order to examine what goes on in interactions and interdependencies of the people, their positions, and other variables. In our descriptions and analyses of a particular concrete system, we can recognize the shadowy figure of some such analytic model of "system."

The analytic model of system demands that we treat the phenomena and the concepts for organizing the phenomena as if there existed organization, interaction, interdependency, and integration of parts and elements. System analysis assumes structure and stability within some arbitrarily sliced and frozen time period.

It is helpful to visualize a system[3] by drawing a large circle. We place elements, parts, variables, inside the circle as the

[3] A useful visual aid for "system" can be constructed by using paper clips (elements) and rubber bands (tensions) mounted on a peg board. Shifting of the position of a clip demonstrates the interdependency of all the clips' positions, and their shifting relationships.

components, and draw lines among the components. The lines may be thought of as rubber bands or springs, which stretch or contract as the forces increase or decrease. Outside the circle is the environment, where we place all other factors which impinge upon the system.

Boundary. In order to specify what is inside or outside the system, we need to define its "boundary" line. The boundary of a system may exist physically: a tightly corked vacuum bottle, the skin of a person, the number of people in a group, etc. But, in addition, we may delimit the system in a less tangible way, by placing our boundary according to what variables are being focused upon. We can construct a system consisting of the multiple roles of a person, or a system composed of varied roles among members in a small work group, or a system interrelating roles in a family. The components or variables used are roles, acts, expectations, communications, influence and power relationships, and so forth, and not necessarily persons.

The operational definition of *boundary* is the line forming a closed circle around selected variables, where there is less interchange of energy (or communication, etc.) *across* the line of the circle than *within* the delimiting circle. The multiple systems of a community may have boundaries that do or do not coincide. For example, treating the power relationships may require a boundary line different from that for the system of interpersonal likes or dislikes in a community. In small groups we tend to draw the same boundary line for the multiple systems of power, communications, leadership, and so on, a major advantage for purposes of study.

In diagnosing, we tentatively assign a boundary, examine what is happening inside the system and then readjust the boundary, if necessary. We examine explicitly whether or not the "relevant" factors are accounted for within the system, an immensely practical way of deciding upon relevance. Also, we are free to limit ruthlessly, and neglect some factors temporarily, thus reducing the number of considerations necessary to be kept in mind at one time. The variables left outside the system, in the "environment" of the system, can be introduced one or more at a time to see the effects, if any, on the interrelationship of the variables within the system.

Tension, Stress, Strain, and Conflict. Because the components within a system are different from each other, are not perfectly integrated, or are changing and reacting to change, or because outside disturbances occur, we need ways of dealing with these differences. The differences lead to varying degrees of tension within the system. *Examples:* males are not like females, foremen see things differently from workers and from executives, children in a family grow, a committee has to work with a new chairman, a change in the market condition requires a new sales response from a factory. To restate the above examples in conceptual terms: we find built-in differences, gaps of ignorance, misperceptions, or differential perceptions, internal changes in a component, reactive adjustments and defenses, and the requirements of system survival generating tensions. Tensions that are internal and arise out of the structural arrangements of the system may be called *stresses and strains* of the system. When tensions gang up and become more or less sharply opposed along the lines of two or more components, we have *conflict*.

A word of warning. The presence of tensions, stresses or strains, and conflict within the system often are reacted to by people in the system as if they were shameful and must be done away with. Tension reduction, relief of stress and strain, and conflict resolution become the working goals of practitioners but sometimes at the price of overlooking the possibility of increasing tensions and conflict in order to facilitate creativity, innovation, and social change. System analysts have been accused of being conservative and even reactionary in assuming that a social system always tends to reduce tension, resist innovation, abhor deviancy and change. It is obvious, however, that tension and conflict are "in" any system, and that no living system exists without tension. Whether these facts of life in a system are to be abhorred or welcomed is determined by attitudes or value judgments not derivable from system theory as such.

The identification of and analysis of how tensions operate in a system are by all odds *the* major utility of system analysis for practitioners of change. The dynamics of a living system are exposed for observation through utilizing the concepts of tension, stress and strain, and conflict. These tensions lead to activities of two kinds: those which do not affect the structure of the system (dynamics), and those which directly alter the structure itself (system change).

Equilibrium and "Steady State." A system is assumed to have a tendency to achieve a balance among the various forces operating within and upon it. Two terms have been used to denote two different ideas about balance. When the balance is thought of as a fixed point or level, it is called "equilibrium." "Steady state," on the other hand, is the term recently used to describe the balanced relationship of parts that is not dependent upon any fixed equilibrium point or level.

Our body temperature is the classic illustration of a fixed level (98.6° F.), while the functional relationship between work units in a factory, regardless of the level of production, represents a steady state. For the sake of simplicity, we shall henceforth stretch the term "equilibrium" to cover both types of balance, to include also the idea of "steady state."

There are many kinds of equilibria. A *stationary equilibrium* exists when there is a fixed point or level of balance to which the system returns after a disturbance. We rarely find such instances in human relationships. A *dynamic equilibrium* exists when the equilibrium shifts

to a new position of balance after disturbance. Among examples of the latter, we
can observe a *neutral* type of situation.
Example: a ball on a flat plane. A small
push moves it to a new position, and it
again comes to rest. *Example:* a farming
community. A new plow is introduced
and is easily incorporated into its agricultural methods. A new level of agricultural
production is placidly achieved. A *stable
type of situation* exists where the forces that
produced the initial equilibrium are so
powerful that any new force must be
extremely strong before any movement to
a new position can be achieved. *Example:*
a ball in the bottom of a goblet. *Example:*
an organization encrusted with tradition or
with clearly articulated and entrenched
roles is not easily upset by minor events.
An *unstable type of situation* is tense
and precarious. A small disturbance
produces large and rapid movements
to a new position. *Example:* a ball balanced on the rims of two goblets placed
side by side. *Example:* an organization
with a precarious and tense balance between two modes of leadership style.
A small disturbance can cause a large
swing to one direction and a new position of equilibrium. *Example:* a community's balance of power between ethnic groups may be such that a "minor"
disturbance can produce an upheaval
and movement to a different balance of
power.

A system in equilibrium reacts to outside impingements by: (1) resisting the
influence of the disturbance, refusing to
acknowledge its existence, or by building
a protective wall against the intrusion,
and by other defensive maneuvers.
Example: A small group refuses to talk
about a troublesome problem of unequal
power distribution raised by a member.
(2) By resisting the disturbance through
bringing into operation the homeostatic
forces that restore or re-create a balance.
The small group talks about the troublesome problem of a member and con-
vinces him that it is not "really" a

problem. (3) By accommodating the
disturbances through achieving a new
equilibrium. Talking about the problem
may result in a shift in power relationships
among members of the group.

The concepts of equilibrium (and steady
state) lead to some questions to guide a
practitioner's diagnosis.

1. What are the conditions conducive
to the achievement of an equilibrium in
this case? Are there internal or external
factors producing these forces? What is
their quality and tempo?

2. Does the case of the client-system
represent one of the typical situations
of equilibrium? How does judgment on
this point affect intervention strategy?
If the practitioner feels the situation is
tense and precarious, he should be more
cautious in intervention than in a situation
of stable type.

3. Can the practitioner identify the
parts of the system that represent greatest
readiness to change, and the greatest
resistance to and defense against change?
Can he understand the functions of any
variable in relation to all other variables?
Can he derive some sense of the direction
in which the client-system is moving, and
separate those forces attempting to restore
an old equilibrium and those pushing
toward a new equilibrium state?

Feedback. Concrete systems are never
closed off completely. They have inputs
and outputs across the boundary; they
are affected by and in turn affect the
environment. While affecting the environment, a process we call output, systems
gather information about how they are
doing. Such information is then fed back
into the system as input to guide and steer
its operations. This process is called feedback. The "discovery" of feedback has
led to radical inventions in the physical
world in designing self-guiding and self-
correcting instruments. It has also become
a major concept in the behavioral sciences, and a central tool in the practitioner's social technology. *Example:* In

reaching for a cigarette we pick up tactile and visual cues that are used to guide our arm and finger movements. *Example:* Our interpersonal communications are guided and corrected by our picking up of effect cues from the communicatees. *Example:* Improving the feedback process of a client-system will allow for self-steering or corrective action to be taken by him or it. In fact, the single most important improvement the change-agent can help a client-system to achieve is to increase its diagnostic sensitivity to the effects of its own actions upon others. Programs in sensitivity training attempt to increase or unblock the feedback processes of persons; a methodological skill with wider applicability and longer-lasting significance than solving the immediate problem at hand. In diagnosing a client-system, the practitioner asks: What are its feedback procedures? How adequate are they? What blocks their effective use? Is it lack of skill in gathering data, or in coding and utilizing the information?

OPEN AND CLOSED SYSTEMS

All living systems are open systems —systems in contact with their environment, with input and output across system boundaries. What then is the use of talking about a closed system? What *is* a closed system? It means that the system is temporarily assumed to have a leak-tight boundary—there is relatively little, if any, commerce across the boundary. We know that no such system can be found in reality, but it is sometimes essential to analyze a system as if it were closed so as to examine the operations of the system as affected "only by the conditions previously established by the environment and not changing at the time of analysis, plus the relationships among the internal elements of the system." The analyst then opens the system to a new impact from the environment, again closes the system, and observes and thinks out what would happen. It is, therefore, fruitless to debate the point; both open and closed system models are

useful in diagnosis. Diagnosing the client as a system of variables, we have a way then of managing the complexity of "everything depends upon everything else" in an orderly way. Use of system analysis has these possibilities: (1) diagnosticians can avoid the error of simple cause-and-effect thinking; (2) they can justify what is included in observation and interpretation and what is temporarily excluded; (3) they can predict what will happen if no new or outside force is applied; (4) they are guided in categorizing what is relatively enduring and stable, or changing, in the situation; (5) they can distinguish between what is basic and what is merely symptomatic; (6) they can predict what will happen if they leave the events undisturbed and if they intervene; and (7) they are guided in selecting points of intervention.

INTERSYSTEM MODEL

We propose an extension of system analysis that looks to us to be useful for the problems confronting the change-agent. We urge the adoption of an intersystem model.

An intersystem model involves two open systems connected to each other.[4] The term we need to add here is *connectives*. Connectives represent the lines of relationships of the two systems. Connectives tie together parts (mechanics) or imbed in a web of tissue the separate organs (biology); connectives in an industrial establishment are the defined lines of communication, or the leadership hierarchy and authority for the branch plants; or they represent the social contract entered into by a therapist and patient; or mutual role expectations of consultant and client; or the affective ties between family members. These are conjunctive connectives. But we also have conflicts between labor and

---

[4] A visualization of an intersystem model would be two systems side by side, with separately identified links. Two rubber band-paper clip representatives can be connected with rubber bands of a different color, representing the connectives.

management, teenage gang wars, race conflicts, and negative emotional responses to strangers. These are disjunctive connectives.

Why elaborate the system model into an intersystem model? Cannot we get the same effect by talking about "subsystems" of a larger system? In part we can. Labor-management conflicts, or interpersonal relations, or change-agent and client relationships can each be treated as a new system with subsystems. But we may lose the critical fact of the autonomy of the components, or the direct inter-actional or transactual consequences for the separate components when we treat the subsystems as merely parts of a larger system. The intersystem model exaggerates the virtues of autonomy and the limited nature of interdependence of the interactions between the two connected systems.

What are some of the positive advantages of using intersystem analysis? First, the external change-agent, or the change-agent built into an organization, as a helper with planned change does not completely become a part of the client-system. He must remain separate to some extent; he must create and maintain some distance between himself and the client, thus standing apart "in another system" from which he rerelates. This new system might be a referent group of fellow professionals, or a body of rational knowledge. But create one he does and must. Intersystem analysis of the change-agent's role leads to fruitful analysis of the connectives—their nature in the beginning, how they shift, and how they are cut off. Intersystem analysis also poses squarely an unexplored issue, namely the internal system of the change-agent, whether a single person, consultant group, or a nation. Helpers of change are prone at times not to see that their own systems as change-agents have boundaries, tensions, stresses and strains, equilibria, and feedback mechanisms which may be just as much parts of the problem as are similar aspects of the client-systems. Thus, relational issues are

more available for diagnosis when we use an intersystem model.

More importantly, the intersystem model is applicable to problems of leadership, power, communication, and conflict in organizations, intergroup relations, and international relations. *Example:* Leadership in a work group with its liaison, negotiation, and representation functions is dependent upon connectives to another group and not solely upon the internal relationships within the work group. Negotiators, representatives, and leaders are parts of separate systems each with its own interdependence, tensions, stresses and feedback, whether we are thinking of foreign ministers, Negro-white leaders, or student-faculty councils.

In brief, the intersystem model leads us to examine the interdependent dynamics of interaction both within and between the units. We object to the premature and unnecessary assumption that the units always form a single system. We can be misled into an utopian analysis of conflict, change-agent relations to client, and family relations if we neglect system differences. But an intersystem model provides a tool for diagnosis that retains the virtues of system analysis, adds the advantage of clarity, and furthers our diagnosis of the influence of various connectives, conjunctive and disjunctive, on the two systems. For change-agents, the essence of collaborative planning is contained in an intersystem model

Developmental Models

Practitioners have in general implicitly favored developmental models in thinking about human affairs, while social scientists have not paid as much attention to these as they have to system models. The "life sciences" of biology and psychology have not crystallized nor refined their common analytic model of the development of the organism, despite the heroic breakthroughs of Darwin. Thus, we are forced to present only broad and rough categories of alternative positions in this paper.

Since there is no standard vocabulary for a developmental model, we shall present five categories of terms that we deem essential to such models: direction, states, forces, form of progression, and potentiality.

THE MAJOR TERMS

Developmental Models. By developmental models, we mean those bodies of thought that center around growth and directional change. Developmental models assume change; they assume that there are noticeable differences between the states of a system at different times, that the succession of these states implies the system is heading somewhere, and that there are orderly processes which explain how the system gets from its present state to wherever it is going. In order to delimit the nature of change in developmental models we should perhaps add the idea of an increase in value accompanying the achievement of a new state. With this addition, developmental models focus on processes of growth and maturation. This addition might seem to rule out processes of decay, deterioration, and death from consideration. Logically, the developmental model should apply to either.

There are two kinds of "death" of concern to the practitioner. First, "death" or loss of some part or subvalue, as a constant concomitant of growth and development. Theories of life processes have used concepts such as katabolic (destructive) processes in biology, death instincts in Freud's psychology, or role loss upon promotion. On balance, the "loss" is made up by the "gains," and thus there is an increase in value. Second, "death" as planned change for a group or organization—the dissolution of a committee or community organization that has "outlived its purpose and function," and the termination of a helping relationship with deliberateness and collaboration of participants—is properly included as part of a developmental model.

Direction. Developmental models postulate that the system under scrutiny —a person, a small group, interpersonal interactions, an organization, a community or a society—is going "somewhere"; that the changes have some direction. The direction may be defined by (1) some *goal* or end state (developed, mature), (2) the *process* of becoming (developing, maturing), or (3) the degree of achievement *toward* some goal or end state (increased development, increase in maturity).

Change-agents find it necessary to believe that there is direction in change. *Example:* self-actualization or fulfillment is a need of the client-system. When strong directional tendencies are present, we modify our diagnosis and intervention accordingly. A rough analogy may be helpful here. A change-agent using a developmental model may be thought of as a husbandman tending a plant, watching and helping it to grow in its own natural direction of producing flowers. He feeds, waters, and weeds. Though at times he may be ruthless in pinching off excess buds, or even in using "grafts," in general he encourages the plant to reach its "goal" of producing beautiful flowers.

Identifiable State. As the system develops over time, the different states may be identified and differentiated from one another. Terms such as "stages," "levels," "phases," or "periods" are applied to these states. *Example:* psychosexual definition of oral, and anal stages, levels of evolution of species, or phases of group development.

No uniformity exists in the definition and operational identification of such successive states. But since change-agents do have to label the past, present, and future, they need some terms to describe successive states and to identify the turning points, transition areas, or critical events that characterize change. Here, system analysis is helpful in defining how parts are put together, along with the tensions and directions of the equilibrating processes. We have two polar types of the shifts of states: (1) small, nondiscernible steps or increments leading to a qualitative jump (*example:* black hair gradually turning gray, or a student evolving into a scholar); (2) a cataclysmic or critical event leading to a sudden change (*example:* a sickness resulting in gray hair overnight, or an inspirational lecture by a professor.) While the latter type seems more frequently to be externally induced, internal factors of the system can have the same consequence. In other words, the internal disequilibration of a balance may lead to a step-jump of the system to a new level. Personality stages, group stages, and societal phases are evolved and precipitated from internal and from external relations.

Form of Progression. Change-agents see in their models of development some form of progression or movement. Four such forms are typically assumed. First, it is often stated that once a stage is worked through, the client-system shows continued progression and normally never turns back. (Any recurrence of a previous state is viewed as an abnormality. Freudian stages are a good example: recurrence of a stage is viewed as regression, an abnormal event to be explained.) Teachers expect a steady growth of knowledge in students, either in a straight line (linear) or in an increasingly accelerating (curvilinear) form.

Second, it is assumed that change, growth, and development occur in a *spiral* form. *Example:* A small group might return to some previous "problem," such as its authority relations to the leader, but now might discuss the question at a "higher" level where irrational components are less dominant.

Third, another assumption more typically made is that the stages are really phases which occur and recur. There is an oscillation between various states, where no chronological priority is assigned to each state; there are cycles. *Example:* Phases of problem-solving or decision-making recur in different time periods as essential to progression. Cultures and societies go through phases of development in recurrent forms.

Fourth, still another assumption is that the form of progression is characterized by a branching out into *differentiated* forms and processes, each part increasing in its specialization, and at the same time acquiring its own autonomy and significance. *Example:* biological forms are differentiated into separate species. Organizations become more and more differentiated into special task and control structures.

Forces. First, forces or causal factors producing development and growth are most frequently seen by practitioners as "natural," as part of human nature, suggesting the role of genetics and other inborn characteristics. At best, environmental factors act as "triggers" or "releases," where the presence of some stimulus sets off the system's inherent growth forces. For example, it is sometimes thought that the teacher's job is to trigger off the natural curiosity of the child, and that growth of knowledge will ensue. Or the leadership of an organization should act to release the self-actualizing and creative forces present in its members.

Second, a smaller number of practitioners and social scientists think that the response to new situations and environmental forces is a coping response which gives rise to growth and development. Third, at this point, it may be useful to remind ourselves of the earlier discussion of the internal tensions of the system, still another cause of change. When stresses and strains of a system become too great, a disruption occurs and a set of forces is released to create new structures and achieve a new equilibrium.

Potentiality. Developmental models vary in their assumptions about potentialities of the system for development, growth, and change. That is, they vary in assumptions about the capabilities, overt or latent, that are built into the original or present state so that the necessary conditions for development may be typically present. Does the "seed"—and its genetic characteristics—represent potentialities? And are the supporting conditions of its environment available? Is the intelligence or emotional capability or skill-potential sufficient for development and change in a social and human process?

Change-agents typically assume a high degree of potentiality in the impetus toward development, and in the surrounding conditions that effectuate the potential.

UTILITY TO PRACTITIONERS

The developmental model has tremendous advantages for the practitioner. It provides a set of expectations about the future of the client-system. By clarifying his thoughts and refining his observations about direction, states in the developmental process, forms of progression, and forces causing these events to occur over a period of time, the practitioner develops a time perspective which goes far beyond that of the more here-and-now analysis of a system-model, which is bounded by time. By using a developmental model, he has a directional focus for his analysis and action and a temporal frame of reference. In addition, he is confronted with a number of questions to ask of himself and of his observations of the case: Do I assume an inherent end of the development? Do I impose a desired (by me) direction? How did I establish a collaboratively planned direction? What states in the development process may be expected? What form of progression do I foresee? What causes the development? His diagnoses and his interventions can become strategic rather than merely tactical.

The Change-Agent and Models

The primary concern of this paper has been to illustrate some of the major kinds of analytic models and conceptual schemas that have been devised by social scientists for the analysis of change and of changing human processes. But we need to keep in mind that the concern with diagnosis on the part of the social scientist is to achieve understanding, and to educe empirically researchable hypotheses amenable to his methods of study. The social scientist generally prefers not to change the system, but to study how it works and to predict what would happen if some new factor were introduced. So we find his attention focused on a "theory of change," of how the system achieves change. In contrast, the practitioner is concerned with diagnosis: how to achieve understanding in order to engage in change. The practitioner, therefore, has some additional interests; he wants to know how to change the system, he needs a "theory of changing" the system.

A theory of changing requires the selection, or the construction, by theoretically minded practitioners, of thought-models appropriate to their intended purpose. This has to be done according to explicit criteria. A change-agent may demand of any model answers to certain questions. The responses he receives may not be complete nor satisfactory since only piecemeal answers exist. At this period in the development of a theory of changing, we ask four questions as our guide lines for examining a conceptual model intended for the use of change-agents.

The first question is simply this: does the model account for the stability and continuity in the events studied at the same time that it accounts for changes in them? How do processes of change develop, given the interlocking factors in the situation that make for stability? Second, where does the model locate the "source" of change? What place among these sources do the deliberate and conscious efforts of the client-system and change-agent occupy? Third, what does the model assume about how goals and directions are determined? What or who sets the direction for movement of the processes of change? Fourth, does the model provide the change-agent with levers or handles for affecting the direction, tempo, and quality of these processes of change?

A fifth question running through the other four is this: How does the model "place" the change-agent in the scheme of things? What is the shifting character of his relationship to the client-system, initially and at the termination of relationship, that affects his perceptions and actions? The questions of relationship of change-agent to others needs to be part and parcel of the model since the existential relationships of the change-agent engaged in processes of planned change become "part of the problem" to be investigated.

The application of these five questions to the models of systems and models of development crystallizes some of the formation of ingredients for a change-agent model for changing. We can now summarize each model as follows:

A "system" model emphasizes primarily the details of how stability is achieved, and only derivatively how change evolves out of the incompatibilities and conflicts in the system. A system model assumes that organization, interdependency, and integration exist among its parts and that change is a derived consequence of how well the parts of the system fit together, or how well the system fits in with other surrounding and interacting systems. The source of change lies primarily in the structural stress and strain externally induced or internally created. The process of change is a process of tension reduction. The goals and direction are emergent from the structures or from imposed sources. Goals are often analyzed as set by "vested interests" of one part of the system. The confronting symptom of some trouble is a reflection of difficulties of adaptability (reaction to environment) or of the ability for adjustment (internal equilibration). The levers or handles available for manipulation are in the "inputs" to the system, especially the feedback mechanisms, and in the forces tending to restore a balance in the system. The change-agent is treated as separate from the client-system, the "target system."

The developmental model assumes constant change and development, and growth and decay of a system over time. Any existing stability is a snapshot of a living process—a stage that will give way to another stage. The supposition seems to be that it is "natural" that change should occur because change is rooted in the very nature of living organisms. The laws of the developmental process are not necessarily fixed, but some effects of the environment are presumably necessary to the developmental process. The direction of change is toward some goal, the fulfillment of its destiny, granting that no major blockage gets in the way. "Trouble" occurs when there is a gap between the system and its goal. Intervention is viewed as the removal of blockage by the change-agent, who then gets out of the way of the growth forces. Developmental models are not very sharply analyzed by the pure theorist nor formally stated, usually, as an analytic model. In fact, very frequently the model is used for studying the unique case rather than for deriving "laws of growth"; it is for descriptive purposes.

The third model—a model for "changing," is a more recent creation. It incorporates some elements of analyses from system models, along with some ideas from the developmental model, in a framework where direct attention is paid to the induced forces producing change. It studies stability in order to unfreeze and move some parts of the system. The direction to be taken is not fixed or "determined," but remains in large measure a matter of "choice" for the client-system. The change-agent is a specialist in the technical processes of facilitating change, a helper to the client-system. The models for changing are as yet incompletely conceptualized. The intersystem model may provide a way of examining how the change-agent's relationships, as part of the model, affect the processes of change.

We can summarize and contrast the three models with Table 1. We have varying degrees of confidence in our categories, but, as the quip says, we construct these in order to achieve the laudable state of "paradigm lost." It is the readers' responsibility to help achieve this goal!

TABLE 1. *Assumptions and Approaches of Three Analytic Models*

MODELS OF CHANGE

ASSUMPTIONS AND APPROACHES TO:	SYSTEM MODEL	DEVELOPMENTAL MODEL	MODEL FOR CHANGING
1. *Content*			
Stability	Structural integration	Phases, stages	Unfreezing parts
Change	Derived from structure	Constant and unique	Induced, controlled
2. *Causation*			
Source of change	Structural stress	Nature of organisms	Self and change-agent
Causal force	Tension reduction		Rational choice
3. *Goals*			
Direction	Emergent	Ontological	Deliberate selection
Set by	"Vested interests"		Collaborative process
4. *Intervention*			
Confronting symptoms	Stresses, strains, and tensions	Discrepancy between actuality and potentiality	Perceived need
Goal of intervening	Adjustment, adaptation	Removal of blockages	Improvement
5. *Change-Agent*			
Place	Outside the "target" system	Outside	Part of situation
Role	External diagnoser and actor	External diagnoser and actor	Participant in here and now

The Limitations

It is obvious that we are proposing the use of systematically constructed and examined models of thought for the change-agent. The advantages are manifold and—we hope—apparent in our preceding discussion. Yet we must now point out some limitations and disutility of models.

Models are abstractions from the concreteness of events. Because of the high degree of selectivity of observations and focus, the "fit" between the model and the actual thought and diagnostic processes of the change-agent is not close. Furthermore, the thought and diagnostic processes of the change-agent are not fixed and rigid. And even worse, the "fit" between the diagnostic processes of the change-agent and the changing processes of the "actual" case, is not close. Abstract as the nature of a model is, as applied to the change-agent, students of the change-agent role may find the concepts of use. But change-agents' practices in diagnosing are not immediately affected by models' analyses.

Furthermore, there are modes of diagnosing by intervening, which do not fall neatly into models. The change-agent frequently tries out an activity in order to see what happens and to see what is involved in the change. If successful, he does not need to diagnose any further, but proceeds to engage in further actions with the client. If unsuccessful, however, he may need to examine what is going on in more detail.

The patch work required for a theory and model of changing requires the suspension of acceptance of such available models. For this paper has argued for some elements from both the system models and the developmental models to be included in the model for practitioners, with the use of a format of the intersystem model so as to include the change-agent and his relationships as part of the problem. But can the change-agent wait for such a synthesis and emerging construction? Our personal feeling is that the planning of change cannot wait, but must proceed with the available diagnostic tools. Here is an intellectual challenge to the scientist-scholar of planned change that could affect the professions of practice.

ANALYZING SOCIAL SYSTEMS

F. X. Sutton

...I assume that general sociological theory has some interest and utility to the political scientist. Its tools are in any case needed for application in later discussion and I supply a brief primer...[in the first section]. General theory alone will hardly suffice...and my...[next two sections] offer a more concrete view of the structure and typology of societies.... In many places I maintain a general perspective, but I give special attention to modern industrial societies and their problems of transition from earlier forms.

The General Analysis of Social Systems

The elaborate complexity of human societies has evoked a variety of responses from scholars. Historians in particular have been mistrustful of generalized

approaches to the intricate and delicate interdependences they saw in society and have accordingly put their trust in exhaustive scholarship and intuitive, "humanistic" procedures. Other scholars, with a very different cast of mind, have sought to lift themselves above detail and devise very general theories as guides through complexity. Across a broad spectrum of methodological difference there seems nevertheless to have been the common assumption that societies display some kind of intelligible coherence. The development of modern sociology has brought a growing explicitness and clarity about this assumption. Conceptions of *social systems* and *societies* now exist in reasonably orthodox forms and provide the base for general bodies of sociological theory. Since I shall view political systems as social systems of a particular kind, it will be useful to recall some fundamentals in the theory of social systems.[1]

The notion of a system implies an orderly patterning in the parts of the system; this is to say that any system, and a social system in particular, has a *structure*.

SOURCE. Excerpted from F. X. Sutton, "Social Theory and Comparative Politics," in Harry Eckstein and David E. Apter, eds., *Comparative Politics: A Reader* (New York: The Free Press of Glencoe, 1963), pp. 67–81; using only pp. 67–72. Reprinted by permission from *Comparative Studies in Society and History*, **2**, 1, October 1959.

The proper description of structure is thus an essential part of the study of social systems. It provides the setting for and the statement of problems. For if one is to get beyond description into analysis, the orderly patterning of systems must be taken as problematical. The notion of *function* provides the bridge to analysis; it signifies a point of view in which parts and aspects of the system are scrutinized with reference to their significance in the persistence of the system. The acuity and depth of discussion that Professors Parsons, Merton, and Levy have recently addressed to structural-functional analysis have given it a rather difficult and esoteric flavor. I do not think it need or should have this flavor. Like any useful mode of scientific analysis it is "played by ear" all the time, and a working competence in it is certainly not difficult to achieve. [2]

The structural description of social systems requires some specification of elements. A little reflection will show that this specification is not altogether easy and straightforward. It is evident that human action takes place in a physical and biological setting and in a cultural tradition. Any global view of a distinguishable set of action patterns must thus include numerous and heterogeneous elements. (A very able attempt to do this may be found in Chester Barnard's "theory of cooperative systems." [3]) To envisage social systems in such inclusive terms seems necessary, but it threatens to be awkward. If we are to gain a convenient focus of analysis, it is necessary to seek out the more peculiarly "social" in any system of action. This requires a slight step beyond common sense. An attentive person may have noted that I have thus far avoided any talk about social "groups." I have done this deliberately because I am concerned that we recognize a distinction between concrete individuals and their participation in any given social system. The doctrines that "the whole man goes to work in our fair city" or that "militants give the whole of their lives to the Party" are species of

dubious sociology. It seems better to seize upon the evident fact that the action of individuals in any social setting responds to *expectations* peculiar to that setting. Hence, the sociologist's preoccupation with *roles* and his use of them rather than personalities or concrete individuals as structural units in social systems. In this view, any social system, say a parliament, is not just a collection of concrete individuals. It is a system of action built around a set of interlocking roles. The members of a parliament bring their personalities into the chamber, and what they do there will depend in some respects on their personalities. But they will also play the roles expected of them as members, and the coherence of the parliament as a social system (different from others in which the same individuals also play roles) depends on this fact.

Social systems exist in complicated relations to other social systems. [4] A parliament, e.g., contains subsystems in its committees, party caucuses, etc.; it also has multifarious linkage to other social systems through its members' other roles, its constitutional authority, etc. A structural description of any social system usually must take into account its subsystems and some other systems as well. Since a role is always a role in a particular system there will be role-structures corresponding to each subsystem and to each overlapping or linked system.

All of this no doubt sounds distressingly complicated but there are compensations; many of the most interesting problems in social analysis arise from the juxtapositions of different roles and systems.

In the terminology I favor, a *society* is a particular kind of social system, viz., one comprehensive and differentiated enough to be self-sufficient (with respect to the diverse functional needs of its members). [5] (Parsons sometimes speaks of "total social systems" to cover the same idea. [6]) In the section headed *The Structure of Societies* I shall specialize the discussion to societies, but for the present I shall remain on the general level and consider the analysis of any social system.

A general theory of social systems must rest on standard ways of describing social structure and of surveying functional problems. A very useful approach on the structural side is provided by what Parsons now calls "pattern variable" analysis. This approach has, of course, been a part of the working equipment of sociologists since the pioneer work of Maine and Toennies. It derives from the observation that there are recurrent and contrasting patterns which turn up in the norms of social systems. Thus, Toennies saw a contrast between the expected behavior in families and local communities on the one hand, and organizations like modern business firms and markets on the other; his famous categories *Gemeinschaft* and *Gesellschaft*, emerged to become a general tool of analysis for any social system. The discernment of patterns in this fashion has often proceeded very intuitively and unsystematically. Thus Ruth Benedict found patterns of culture among the Zuni, Kwakiutl, Dobuans, Japanese, Thai, and Rumanians; but each society posed new problems, and it was not her interest or talent to forge a standard set of tools for handling any society or social system. Those with a more systematic turn of mind have tried to clarify just what was being patterned, and to discover a standard, exhaustive array of types of patterns. Parsons has worked at this problem over the past two decades. He has, I think, shown conclusively that simple dichotomies such as Maine and Toennies used are not satisfactory; instead of a single dichotomy or variable several must be used. The quest of a definitely exhaustive list has proven to be very difficult, and Parsons' latest work indicates the possible addition of a sixth variable to the five that have been standard in his work for some years. Clarification in this area is certainly one of the most important problems now facing sociological theory, but I am sure that we do not have to await further theoretical advance to make good use of existing

tools. The variables Parsons has recently utilized seem to me to have demonstrated their usefulness in many ways. This is not the place for an extended discussion of their nature and I shall confine myself to listing them with brief, illustrative comments. His list is as follows: [7]

1. Affectivity-affective neutrality: A distinction exemplified in the obligations to love one's wife but to be "businesslike" with one's secretary.

2. Self-orientation—collectivity orientation: Classically exemplified in the contrast of business firms and governments.

3. Universalism-particularism: The formula that laws should operate "without regard to persons" is a universalistic formula. Kinship behavior, by contrast, tends to be particularistic.

4. Ascription-achievement: This is Linton's well-known distinction. Parsons has interpreted it as resting on emphases on *qualities* or *performances*, and has substituted these terms in recent writings.

5. Specificity-diffuseness: The contrast between the bounded obligations of a contract and the undefined range of obligations between close kinship roles.

In later sections of this paper I shall make considerable use of these variables and I hope to offer some concrete evidence of their interest for the study of comparative politics. [8]

The basic virtue of these pattern variables is that they give a standard means of describing the role-expectations and value-standards in *any* social systems. One can by this means identify quickly similarities and differences that are important in comparative analysis, and the technique is applicable from the broadest to the narrowest types of comparison. The same tools can tell us something about the differences between President Eisenhower and Suleiman the Magnificent as well as the differences between President Eisenhower and the spouse of Mrs. Eisenhower.

I might also emphasize that pattern variable analysis is directly applicable to social systems and their interrelationships. Thus we say, e.g., that a bureaucracy is built on universalistic and achievement norms, or that the contractual relations among business firms are ruled by norms of specificity. The application of these variables at the social system level is again perfectly general; they may be used to discuss international relations, or the place of a clique in a local party organization.

Turning now from structure to function, we find systematic problems of great difficulty. The great generality of the notion of social system makes it evident that generality is necessary in conceiving functional problems.[9] Parsons and Bales seem to have been the hardiest explorers in this tenuous atmosphere. I shall dodge around the formidable difficulties of their systematic treatment and confine myself to a rougher sort of general orientation. The simplest starting point is provided by Bales' array of four functional problems, the "adaptive," the "instrumental," the "expressive," and the "integrative,"[10] which "stated" against a background of preoccupation with small discussion groups. The first relates to the fact that social systems exist in situations to which they must adapt. In a total society, there is evidently the problem of adaptation to the physical environment with all that this implies in terms of "maintenance" activities and technology. The second recognizes the goal orientation of human action and the necessity of contriving action patterns with an appropriate instrumental significance in relation to goals. The third recognizes the fact that the human actors in any social systems have psychological states that require maintenance and symbolic expression. The fourth notes the requirement of internal adjustment and coordination of the system as it meets its other functional problems. Whether or not this scheme represents a tight and exhaustive categorization of functional problems for any social system is, of course, a problem deserving the closest attention, but

we cannot stop to wrestle with it here. My hope is that this list gives a sufficient sense of the range of functional problems the sociologist keeps in mind to provide a setting for the special focus of attention to follow.

One of the assumptions of this general approach is that any concrete social system copes with a multiplicity of functional problems. There is no simple correspondence of differentiated social structures to functional problems. If there were, the task of the social scientists would be much simplified, but we must resign ourselves to complexity. In our particular subject of interest here we must not expect that those institutions we call political will have a unique functional significance, or that the "political problem" can be nicely localized in any system. Specialization of social structures about particular functional problems nevertheless does occur in some degree. . . .

The Structure of Societies

The study of societies is a more specialized subject than the general study of social systems. While the general theory of social systems has direct applications to the problems of comparative politics and other special fields of social science, we obviously need additional, more specialized approaches. In particular, we need morphologies for the description of societies. In every-day science work we all use structural categories when we talk of kinship systems or bureaucracies or caste systems. These are categories arising in empirical observation of the gross anatomy of societies, and some set of categories of this type seems to me indispensable. I believe it would be very unfortunate, in the field we are here concerned with, if a revulsion against the sterility of formal institutional description should lead to a neglect of careful structural setting of problems. The contemporary social science literature contains many works that seem to me to involve regrettable distortion because the authors did not see their problems in the relevant structural setting.[11] Unfortunately, there is at present no evidence that the requisite categories can be drawn out of the first principles of a general theory. They have a loose kind of relationship to the general functional problems of societies, but the complications of empirical societies have thus far thwarted efforts at systematic derivation of useful categories.[12]

For the broad comparison of societies, there seem to be two general strategies one might follow in structural analysis. On the one hand, one might try to classify substructures of particular sorts across the range of all societies. In comparative politics, Weber's famous system of ideal types (of patrimonialism, bureaucracy, etc.) is an outstanding venture. The field of kinship probably offers the best developed model, and illustrates the long and patient development that is necessary in this type of work.[13]

Another possibility is to classify societies and develop analysis within the resulting typology. Since the demise of evolutionary theories, this has been an unpopular procedure, but it has special attractions in the subject of comparative politics. The point of view I take throughout this paper is quite in accord with that expressed by the report from the 1952 SSRC Seminar on Comparative Politics;[14] this is a field in which the separation of a special set of institutions from their total social context threatens to be very damaging. One is thus led to investigate the possibility of setting comparative problems in a typology of total societies. The scope of the venture is dismaying but there is encouragement to be found in the literature. Durkheim made the discrimination of different "types" of societies one of the rules of sociological method,[15] and Radcliffe-Brown has subscribed to this rule.[16]

I cannot here perform the labors of generations and present a good general typology of societies. I believe it is possible, however, to sketch the basic features of two broad types that are especially important for the study of comparative politics in the present-day world. Social philosophers from Henry Adams to Mr. Oppenheimer have made the sharpness and rapidity of change the crucial feature of the modern world. A proper focus on this massive fact of rapid change seems to require discrimination of types of change. Societies in which modern science and technology have been institutionalized are intrinsically changing societies, but much of the change they induce goes on without alteration of basic social structure. The transition brought on at the beginning of industrialization appears to be a more fundamental type of social change. One is thus led to seek out a specification of the end-points of the transition.[17]

We now talk freely of "modern industrial society" as a type. I believe it is possible to describe this type in some detail without inviting great controversy. The predecessors of modern industrial society on the other hand seem very heterogeneous. In the perspective of modern industrial society, many of them nevertheless show much in common, as Professor Levy has persistently argued.[18] Professor Redfield's "folk society" is doubtless the best-known model for these societies, and its success offers encouragement that useful models are possible. For our purposes I shall sketch out a related type of society based on intensive agriculture that seems to be a reasonable abstraction from the empirical societies that have existed prior to industrialization over much of the world. When juxtaposed against modern industrial societies, it provides a typology akin to Redfield's scheme of "folk" and "urban" societies.

Before plunging into description of these two types of society, I want to restate what I am doing in the hope of clarification. Following Durkheim, I take the view here that comparative politics and other forms of comparative social science need a classification of types of societies. To approach comparison of the French and German political systems with nothing more than a conception of societies in general seems too meager an equipment. One needs a more specialized conception of the type of society that these cases presumably represent, and this type of society will be different from that underlying a comparison between a West African kingdom and an Indian state. The typology I present here is a very crude one, but it will be serviceable in later discussion of political systems. It may also serve to illustrate a sociological perspective on societies and the use of pattern variable analysis.

A Typology of Societies

Two broad types of societies will be distinguished as "intensive agricultural" and "industrial" societies. This grounding of my typology on the "means of production" has great empirical importance, but I do not stress the technological in the actual definitions. I shall stress social structural features without detailed attention to how they may depend on or derive from modes of production.

An "agricultural" society[19] has the following essential characteristics:

1. Predominance of ascriptive, particularistic, diffuse patterns.
2. Stable local groups and limited spatial mobility.
3. Relatively simple and stable "occupational" differentiation.
4. A "deferential" stratification system of diffuse impact.

Some of these brief general characterizations should be immediately comprehensible. Others will require comment and illustration. Ascriptive norms imply stable patterns in the assignment of individuals to roles by birth, sex, age, etc. Continuities of status implies continuity in access to facilities and rewards, and hence strong ties to locality. In the great agricultural societies of the world, stable local communities have been the familiar rule—the demands of agriculture in most places have been such as to require the continuous attention of people who are functionally specialized as cultivators or husbandmen. The villages or scattered local settlements in which these cultivators and their kin groups have lived have been highly particularistic groupings. They have been marked off from outsiders, and matters within the local community have been ruled by norms appropriate to small numbers of people in permanent and intimate association. Urban agglomerations have occurred in all the great agricultural civilizations, but they have been the homes of a minority of the population; of necessity, the modal pattern has been that of the small, agricultural community.

The role differentiations corresponding to our occupations that occur in these societies may be quite numerous (witness India). By comparison with a modern industrial society they are, however, on a lower level of differentiation. Ascriptive patterns of recruitment also mean that these "occupations" are not subject to the generalizing influences that tend to reduce them to a common character in industrial societies. Instead of having a loose connection to other roles held by an individual, and hence a well-defined character in themselves, the analogues of our occupational roles have disparate qualities and accretions.

In conformity with this relatively weak differentiation of "occupational" roles, class stratification has a diffuse significance and an occupationally concrete character. Land-owners not actively engaged in cultivation but living from rents (in some form) tend to occupy a definite class status that typically has other related occupational features. (Military roles, as in the Western medieval world, are one common example.) The linkage of class status with a limited array of occupational status has led people to speak of "estates" or "Staende," whether or not these have means of corporate expression or action.[20]

I have called the typical class stratification system "deferential." By this I mean that class status has a diffuse character and unless expressly excluded is presumed to be a reference point for interaction.[21] The contrasting form of class status I call "egalitarian"; in this sort of system, familiar in our own society, universalistic norms require the avoidance of class as a normal reference point in interaction. Tocqueville and many lesser observers have pointed to the "deferential" character of class stratification in the older structure of the West, and there are ample grounds for thinking that this type of stratification is general to the type.

One might follow Weber and add "traditionalism" to the characterization of this type of society, but I believe that insofar as it is relevant here, this quality is implied by the prevalence of ascription.

As essential sociological features of a *modern industrial society* I suggest the following:

1. Predominance of universalistic, specific, and achievement norms.
2. High degree of social mobility (in a general—not necessarily "vertical"—sense).
3. Well-developed occupational system, insulated from other social structures.
4. "Egalitarian" class system based on generalized patterns of occupational achievement.
5. Prevalence of "associations," i.e., functionally specific, nonascriptive structures.

I trust that a few comments will serve to illuminate this list and make the necessary explanations of technical terms. The prevalence of universalistic and achievement norms implies a marked restriction of the significance of kinship systems. These norms also act as a kind of solvent to barriers among local, ethnic, and other groups. Spatial mobility is facilitated and stimulated by legitimate access to different possible statuses. A highly differentiated occupational system is governed by universalistic and achievement norms. Holding some sort of occupational role becomes a normal expectation for adult men and for those women for whom kinship duties do not take precedence. This is one sense in which the occupational system becomes

generalized in the society. There is another sense. Occupational roles have the common features of (1) demanding relatively continuous application, (2) being the principal "instrumental role" activity of the incumbent, (3) money remuneration, which in the typical case is the principal source of income of the jobholder. These common features and the criteria that make any qualified person the potential incumbent of any occupational role serve to produce an effective generalization. Occupations can be and are in fact compared with one another. On the basis of such comparisons individuals choose their jobs and measure their attainments or satisfactions. Sociologists have shown that in several countries of the modern world a scale of prestige rankings of occupation can be elicited with good reliability.[22] These prestige rankings have an intimate connection with the scale provided by the money remuneration of occupations and there are pressures to bring the two scales into close conformity.

The weakness of ascription in modern industrial societies provides scope for the flourishing of a type of social structure scarcely to be found in many societies. These are commonly called "associations" and have as their leading characteristic specificity of purpose and participation. Business firms, governmental agencies, hospitals, universities are "associations" built around occupational participation; the rich array of groupings we call "voluntary associations" (Protestant churches, patriotic organizations, etc.) are another class built primarily on more limited participation of their members. I stress particularly the nonascriptive and specific character of "associations." New "associations" may be contrived to meet needs as they arise, and individuals may participate in them in the very limited and segmental way made possible by norms of specificity. It is, of course, one of the more remarkable and important features of our own and other modern industrial societies that "associations" are possible.

The importance of occupations and the prevalence of universalistic norms impose limitations on the possible types of class structure in these societies. The prestige ranking of occupations and the associated differences in personal income make for a ranking of kin groups in a class structure. But this class structure lacks sharp discontinuities, and "egalitarian" norms restrict its impact. In the class systems of agricultural societies there are notable discontinuities in values across the various strata: a military aristocrat is expected to be bold, self-assured, and perhaps "cultivated" but not necessarily industrious; the ideal of a peasant cultivator in the same society usually contains contrasting virtues of industry and deferential submissiveness. But in a developed industrial society, the different class statuses tend to be strung out on a chain of common values in conformity with the universalistic expectation that everybody be judged on the same fundamental bases. The occupational sphere carries many strict hierarchical rankings (as in a typical bureaucratic structure); but these are *specific* to the occupational sphere, and universalism forbids their easy extension into "private" lives. The drawing of clear lines of division in the class structure by organizations specifically based on class status is also inhibited by universalistic values. These "egalitarian" class systems thus tend to have an inconspicuous and restrained character that has led some people to argue that countries like the United States have no class system at all.

Weber stressed the prevalence of rationality as a norm for the guidance of social behavior in modern industrial societies. This sort of norm is, I believe, implied by the norms of universalism and achievement. It means a continuous scrutiny of received ways of doing things in terms of their suitability for a similarly scrutinized set of goals. A modern industrial society cannot be a static society; by giving legitimacy to rational criticism from the realm of technology to the intimacies of family life, it is constantly stimulating change and coping with the unforeseen consequences of these changes.

The major societies of the modern world show varying combinations of the patterns represented in the ideal types I have sketched out. Some stand close to the model of industrial society; others are in various transitional states that hopefully may be understood better by conceptions of where they have been and where they may be going.

We are now prepared to turn to a particular feature of social systems and societies that will lead us into the domain of the political. . . .

NOTES

[1] Radcliffe-Brown gives Montesquieu and Comte credit for first emphasizing the systematic interconnections in social action. The line of more recent theoretical development that is most familiar to me starts in neoclassical, general equilibrium economics. It was there that Pareto first got the notion of a society as a system. Walras' idea of an economy as an interdependent system provided the framework for Pareto's own works as an economist and the model for his effort (in *The Mind and Society*) to treat total societies as systems. When L. J. Henderson expounded Pareto to a generation at Harvard, he did so with a characteristically stern insistence on the notion of a social system. The recent work of Talcott Parsons grows out of this heritage. His is the system of social theory I grew up on and I shall use it in much of what follows. *Structure and Function in Primitive Society* (New York: The Free Press, 1952) pp. 4–5.

There now exists a Society for the Advancement of General Systems Theory, organized by L. v. Bertalanffy, Kenneth Boulding, Ralph W. Gerard, and Anatol Rappaport. Boulding's recent emphasis on action at the boundaries of systems converges closely with Parsons' treatment of the economy as a social system in his recent (unpublished) Marshall Lectures.

[2] Good general discussion of the method, however, is certainly difficult. I have had a great deal of instruction from the writings alluded to, and I do not mean to disparage the importance of this work.

[3] *Functions of the Executive*, Part I.

[4] Cf. the discussion by Parsons, Bales, and Shils in *Working Papers in the Theory of Action* (New York: The Free Press, 1953), Ch. 5, pp. 190–194.

[5] An attempt at careful definition may be found in D. F. Aberle *et al.*, "The Functional Prerequisites of a Society," *International Journal of Ethics*, January 1950. Marion Levy has pursued the question further in his *Structure of Society* (Princeton, N.J., 1952).

[6] Talcott Parsons and Edward A. Shils, *Toward a General Theory of Action* (Cambridge, Mass., 1951), p. 196.

[7] *Ibid.*, p. 77.

[8] One need not, of course, attempt to use precisely this set of variables for all purposes. I do not in fact confine myself to them in this paper, and Professor Levy has used a somewhat different set in his *Structure of Society*. Special problems may call for emphasis on a particular variable (like the representation-autonomy distinction I use later) that does not appear in Parsons' array. If his (or any other array) is truly exhaustive, then all such variables should prove to be "compounds" of the basic variables. This does not mean they should not be used but it will obviously facilitate the advance of knowledge if we can get along with a few basic variables.

[9] At one point the author and others thought the full generality of social systems too forbidding and made an effort to treat the special case of a total society. Aberle, *et al.*, *op. cit.*

[10] *Interaction Process Analysis*, Ch. 2, pp. 49 ff. and Ch. 5.

[11] The field of national character studies blossoms with examples. I would cite Henry Dicks' studies of Russian refugees and Margaret Mead's study of authority patterns in Russia. For want of explicit recognition that much of the behavior they describe occurs in bureaucracies both of these capable analysts are kept from distinguishing things which reflect the problems of bureaucracies and things traceable to a distinctive Russian character.

[12] Talcott Parsons' effort in *The Social System* (New York: The Free Press, 1951, Chs. 2, 4) is the most sophisticated one known to me. He in effect breaks off the systematic derivation in Ch. 5, and takes a new stance to discuss the structure of actually existing societies.

[13] The present state of the subject may be grasped from G. P. Murdock's *Social Structure* (1949) or Radcliffe-Brown's long introduction to *African Systems of Kinship and Marriage* (1950). Systematic work in this field may be dated from Morgan's great study, *Systems of Consanguinity and Affinity* (1870).

[14] *American Political Science Review*, Vol. **47**, September 1953, pp. 641–675.

[15] Durkheim, *op. cit.*, pp. 76–88.

[16] It gives me comfort to quote Radcliffe-Brown:

"The immense diversity of forms of human society must first be reduced to order by some sort of classification. By comparing societies one with another we have to discriminate and define different types. Thus the Australian aborigines were divided into some hundreds of separate tribes, each with its own language, organization, customs, and beliefs; but an examination of a sufficient sample shows that beneath the specific diversities there are such general similarities that we can constitute and describe in general terms an Australian type. The type . . . is an abstraction only a little way removed from the concrete reality. When a number of such types have been adequately defined they in turn can be compared one with another and a further step in abstraction can be made. By such a process, obviously requiring the labour of many students over many years, we may reach classifications and abstract concepts more precisely defined and more exactly representing empirical reality than the concepts indicated by such phrases as 'primitive society,' 'feudal society,' 'capitalist society,' that occur so abundantly in contemporary writing." Introduction to *African Political Systems* (1940), pp. xi–xii.

[17] Recognizing, of course, that neither end point need be rigidly static.

[18] Much of what follows grows out of discussions in recent years with Marion Levy, John Pelzel, David Landes, David Aberle, and Lloyd Fallers. Most of this group participated in a 1953 SSRC seminar on the comparative analysis of societies.

[19] I shall not preserve the qualifying adjective "intensive," but I mean it to be understood. Hunting and gathering and transhuman pastoral societies are of course excluded from this type. So also are societies practicing agriculture in casual or auxiliary forms, and probably those practicing a shifting "slash-and-burn" type of cultivation. The boundaries are naturally obscure, but clearly a great many primitive societies are excluded.

[20] The nobility in France after the procedures of admission became regularized, and especially after it became hereditary, is an excellent example. Cf. Marc Bloch, *La societé féodale*, Vol. II.

[21] This distinction of class systems is discussed more fully in a paper "Achievement Norms and the Motivation of Entrepreneurs,"

which I presented in a conference at the Center for Entrepreneurial History, Cambridge, Mass., in November 1954.

[22] Alex Inkeles and Peter Rossi have recently shown a close agreement among these scales for the United States, Great Britain, New Zealand, Japan, and Germany. "Cross National Comparisons of Occupational Ratings," *American Journal of Sociology*.

MECHANISMS OF CHANGE AND ADJUSTMENT TO CHANGE[1]

Neil J. Smelser

Introduction

A thorough analysis of the social changes accompanying economic development would require an ambitious theoretical scheme and a vast quantity of comparative data. Because I lack both necessities—and the space to use them if I possessed them— I shall restrict this exploratory statement in two ways. (1) Methodologically, I shall deal only with ideal-type constructs, in Weber's sense; I shall not discuss any individual cases of development, or the comparative applicability of particular historical generalizations. (2) Substantively, I shall consider only modifications of the social structure; I shall not deal with factor-allocation, savings and investment, inflation, balance of payments, foreign aid, size of population, and rate of population change—even though these variables naturally affect, and are affected by, structural changes. These omissions call for brief comment.

Max Weber defined an ideal-type construct as a

one-sided accentuation . . . by the synthesis of a great many diffuse, discrete, more or less present and occasionally absent *concrete individual* phenomena,

which are arranged . . . into a unified *analytical* construct. In its conceptual purity, this mental construct cannot be found anywhere in reality.[2]

The analyst utilizes such ideal constructs to unravel and explain a variety of actual historical situations. Weber mentions explicitly two kinds of ideal-type constructs— first, "historically unique configurations," such as "rational bourgeois capitalism," "medieval Christianity," etc.; and second, statements concerning historical evolution, such as the Marxist laws of capitalist development.[3] While the second type presupposes some version of the first, I shall concentrate on the dynamic constructs.

"Economic development" generally refers to the "growth of output per head of population."[4] For purposes of analyzing the relationships between economic growth and the social structure, it is possible to isolate the effects of several interrelated technical, economic, and ecological processes that frequently accompany development. These may be listed as follows: (1) In the realm of technology, the change *from* simple and traditionalized techniques *toward* the application of scientific knowledge. (2) In agriculture, the evolution *from* subsistence farming *toward* commercial production of agricultural goods. This means specialization in cash crops, purchase of non-agricultural products in

SOURCE. Neil J. Smelser, "Mechanisms of Change and Adjustment to Change," in Bert F. Hoselitz and Wilbert E. Moore, eds., *Industrialization and Society* (The Hague: UNESCO and Mouton, 1963), pp. 32–54.

the market, and often agricultural wage-labor. (3) In industry, the transition *from* the use of human and animal power *toward* industrialization proper, or "men aggregated at power-driven machines, working for monetary return with the products of the manufacturing process entering into a market based on a network of exchange relations."[5] (4) In ecological arrangements, the movement *from* the farm and village *toward* urban centers. These several processes often, but not necessarily, occur simultaneously. Certain technological improvements—e.g., the use of improved seeds—can be introduced without automatically and instantaneously causing organizational changes;[6] agriculture may be commercialized without any concomitant industrialization, as in many colonial countries;[7] industrialization may occur in villages;[8] and cities may proliferate even where there is no significant industrialization.[9] Furthermore, the specific social consequences of technological advance, commercialized agriculture, the factory, and the city, respectively, are not in any sense reducible to each other.[10]

Despite such differences, all four processes tend to affect the social structure in similar ways. All give rise to the following ideal-type structural changes, which have ramifications throughout society: (1) Structural differentiation, or the establishment of more specialized and more autonomous social units. I shall discuss the occurrence of this process in the different spheres of economy, family, religion, and stratification. (2) Integration, which changes its character as the old social order is made obsolete by the process of differentiation. The state, the law, political groupings, and other associations are particularly salient in this integration. (3) Social disturbances—mass hysteria, outbursts of violence, religious and political movements, etc.—which reflect the uneven advances of differentiation and integration, respectively.

Obviously, the implications of technological advance, agricultural reorganiza-tion, industrialization, and urbanization differ from society to society, as do the resulting structural realignments. Some of the sources of variation in these ideal patterns of pressure and change are described in the next paragraphs.

1. Variations in premodern conditions. Is the society's value system congenial or antagonistic to industrial values? How well integrated is the society? How "backward" is it? What is its level of wealth? How is the wealth distributed? Is the country "young and empty" or "old and crowded"? Is the country politically dependent, newly independent, or completely autonomous? Such pre-existing factors shape the impact of the forces of economic development.[11]

2. Variations in the impetus to change. Do pressures to modernize come from the internal implications of a value system, from a wish for national security and prestige, from a desire for material prosperity, or from a combination of these? Is political coercion used to form a labor force? Or are the pressures economic, as in the case of population pressure on the land or that of loss of handicraft markets to cheap imported products? Or do economic and political pressures combine, as, for example, when a tax is levied on peasants that is payable only in money? Or are the pressures social, as they are when there is a desire to escape burdensome aspects of the old order? Factors like these influence the adjustment to modernization greatly.[12]

3. Variations in the path toward modernization. Does the sequence begin with light consumer industries? Or is there an attempt to introduce heavy, capital-intensive industries first? What is the role of government in shaping the pattern of investment? What is the rate of accumulation of technological knowledge and skills? What is the general tempo of industrialization? These questions indicate elements which affect the nature of structural change and the degree of discomfort created by this change.[13]

4. Variations in the advanced stages of modernization. What is the emergent distribution of industries in developed economies? What are the emergent relations between state and economy, religion and economy, state and religion, etc.? While all advanced industrialized societies have their "industrialization" in common, uniquely national differences remain. For instance, "social class" has a different social significance in the United States than in the United Kingdom, even though both are highly developed countries.

5. Variations in the content and timing of dramatic events during modernization. What is the import of wars, revolutions, rapid migrations, natural catastrophes, etc., for the course of economic and social development?

These sources of variation render it virtually impossible to establish hard and fast empirical generalizations concerning the evolution of social structures during economic and social development.[14] Therefore, my purpose here is not to search for such generalizations, but rather to outline certain ideal-type directions of structural change that modernization involves. On the basis of these ideal types, we may classify, describe, and analyze varying national experiences. Factors like those indicated above determine, in part, a nation's distinctive response to the universal aspects of modernization; but this in no way detracts from their universality. While I shall base my remarks on the vast literature of economic development, I can in no sense attempt an exhaustive comparative study.

Structural Differentiation in Periods of Development

The concept of structural differentiation can be employed to analyze what is frequently termed the "marked break in established patterns of social and economic life" in periods of development.[15] Simply defined, "differentiation" is the evolution from a multifunctional role structure to

several more specialized structures. In illustration, we may cite here three typical examples. During a society's transition from domestic to factory industry, the division of labor increases, and the economic activities previously lodged in the family move to the firm. As a formal educational system emerges, the training functions previously performed by the family and church are established in a more specialized unit, the school.[16] The modern political party has a more complex structure than do tribal factions, and the former is less likely to be fettered with kinship loyalties, competition for religious leadership, etc.

Formally defined, then, structural differentiation is a process whereby

> *one* social role or organization ... differentiates into *two or more* roles or organizations which function more effectively in the new historical circumstances. The new social units are structurally distinct from each other, but taken together are functionally equivalent to the original unit.[17]

Differentiation concerns only changes in role structure. It must not be confused with two closely related concepts. The first of these involves the cause or motivation for entering the differentiated role. Someone may be motivated to engage in wage-labor, for instance, by a desire for economic improvement, by political coercion, or indeed by a wish to fulfil traditional obligations (e.g., to use wages to supply a dowry). These "reasons" should be kept conceptually distinct from differentiation itself. The other related concept concerns the integration of differentiated roles. For example, as differentiated wage-labor begins to emerge, there also appear legal norms, labor exchanges, trade unions, and so on, that regulate—with varying degrees of success—the relations between labor and management. Such readjustments, even though they sometimes produce a new social unit, should be considered separately from role specialization in other functions.

Let us now inquire into the process of differentiation in several different social realms.

DIFFERENTIATION OF ECONOMIC ACTIVITIES

In underdeveloped countries, production typically is located in kinship units. Subsistence farming predominates; other industry is supplementary but still attached to kin and village. In some cases, occupational position is determined largely by an extended group, such as the caste.[18]

Similarly, exchange and consumption are deeply embedded in family and village. In subsistence agriculture, there is a limited amount of independent exchange outside the family; thus production and consumption occur in the same social context. Exchange systems proper are still lodged in kinship and community (e.g., reciprocal exchange), and stratification systems (e.g., redistribution according to caste membership), and in political systems (e.g., taxes, tributes, payments in kind, forced labor).[19] Under these conditions, market systems are underdeveloped, and the independent power of money to command the movement of goods and services is minimal.

As the economy develops, several kinds of economic activity are removed fom this family-community complex. In agriculture, the introduction of money crops marks a differentiation between the social contexts of production and of consumption. Agricultural wage-labor sometimes undermines the family production unit. In industry, several levels of differentiation can be identified. Household industry, the simplest form, parallels subsistence agriculture in that it supplies "the worker's own needs, unconnected with trade." "Handicraft production" splits production and consumption, though frequently consumption takes place in the local community. "Cottage industry," on the other hand, often involves a differentiation between consumption and community, since production is "for the market, for an unknown consumer, sold to a wholesaler who accumulates a stock."[20] Finally, manufacturing

and factory systems segregate the worker from his capital and not rarely from his family.

Simultaneously, similar differentiations emerge in the exchange system. Goods and services, previously exchanged on a non-economic basis, are pulled progressively more into the market. Money now commands the movement of increasingly more goods and services; it thus begins to supplant—and sometimes undermine—the religious, political, familial, or caste sanctions which had hitherto governed economic activity.[21] This is the setting for the institutionalization of relatively autonomous economic systems that exhibit a greater emphasis on values like "universalism," "functional specificity," and "rationality."[22]

Empirically, underdeveloped economies may be classified according to the respective distances they have moved along this line of differentiation. Migratory labor, for instance, may be a kind of compromise between full membership in a wage-labor force and attachment to an old community life. Cottage industry introduces extended markets but retains the family-production fusion. The employment of families in factories maintains a version of family production. The expenditure of wages on traditional items, like dowries, also manifests the half-entry into the more differentiated industrial-urban structure.[23] The causes of such partial differentiation may lie in resistance on the part of the populace to give up traditional modes, in the economics of demand for handmade products, in systems of racial discrimination against native labor, or elsewhere.[24] In any case, the concept of structural differentiation provides a yardstick for discerning the distance that the economic structure has evolved toward modernization.

DIFFERENTIATION OF FAMILY ACTIVITIES

One consequence of the removal of economic activities from the kinship nexus is the family's loss of some of its previous functions, and its thereby becoming a more specialized agency. As the family ceases to be an economic unit of production, one or more members leave the household to seek employment in the labor market. The family's activities become more concentrated on emotional gratification and socialization. While many halfway houses, such as family hiring and migratory systems, persist, the trend is toward the segregation of family functions from economic functions.[25]

Several related processes accompany the differentiation of the family from its other involvements. (1) Apprenticeship within the family declines. (2) Pressures develop against nepotism in the recruitment of labor and management. These pressures often are based on the demands of economic rationality. The intervention frequently persists, however—especially at the managerial levels—and in some cases (e.g., Japan), family ties continue to be a major basis for labor recruitment. (3) The direct control of elders and collateral kinsmen over the nuclear family weakens. This marks, in structural terms, the differentiation of the nuclear family from the extended family. (4) An aspect of this loss of control is the growth of personal choice, love, and related criteria as the foundation for courtship and marriage. Structurally, this is the differentiation of courtship from extended kinship. (5) One result of this complex of processes is the changing status of women, who generally become less subordinated economically, politically, and socially to their husbands than they had been under earlier conditions.[26]

In such ways, structural differentiation undermines the old modes of integration in society. The controls of extended family and village begin to dissolve in the enlarged, complicated social setting which differentiation creates. Thereupon, new integrative problems are posed. We shall inquire presently into some of the lines of integration.

DIFFERENTIATION OF RELIGIOUS SYSTEMS

Because of Max Weber's monumental thesis linking ascetic Protestantism and

capitalism,[27] a disproportionate amount of attention has been devoted to the initiating role that *formal* religious values play in economic development. Although much excellent work has been done in this area,[28] insufficient emphasis has been given to the important role of secular nationalism in the industrial takeoff.

With the world organized as it is, nationalism is a *sine qua non* of industrialization, because it provides people with an overriding, easily acquired, secular motivation for making painful changes. National strength or prestige becomes the supreme goal, industrialization the chief means. The costs, inconveniences, sacrifices, and loss of traditional values can be justified in terms of this transcending, collective ambition. The new collective entity, the nation-state, that sponsors and grows from this aspiration is equal to the exigencies of industrial complexity; it draws directly the allegiance of every citizen, organizing the population as one community; it controls the passage of persons, goods, and news across the borders; it regulates economic and social life in detail. To the degree that the obstacles to industrialization are strong, nationalism must be intense to overcome them.[29]

In fact, nationalism seems in many cases to be the very instrument designed to smash the traditional religious systems—those like, e.g., the classical Chinese or Indian—which Weber himself found to be less permissive than Protestantism for economic modernization.

On the other hand, nationalism, like many traditionalistic religious systems, may hinder economic advancement by "reaffirmation of traditionally honored ways of acting and thinking,"[30] by fostering anticolonial attitudes after they are no longer relevant,[31] and, more indirectly, by encouraging passive expectations of "ready-made prosperity."[32] We can distinguish among these contrasting forces of "stimulus" and "drag" that such value systems bring to economic development by using the logic of differentiation in the following way.

In the early phases of modernization, many traditional attachments must be modified to permit more differentiated institutional structures to be set up. Because the existing commitments and methods of integration are deeply rooted in the organization of traditional society, a very generalized and powerful commitment is required to pry individuals from these attachments. The values of ascetic and this-worldly religious beliefs, xenophobic national aspirations, and political ideologies (like, e.g., socialism), provide such a lever. Sometimes these diverse types of values combine into a single system of legitimacy. In any case, all three have an "ultimacy" of commitment, in whose name a wide range of sacrifices can be demanded and procured.

The very success of these value systems, however, breeds the conditions for their own weakening. In a perceptive statement, Weber notes that, at the beginning of the twentieth century, when the capitalistic system was already highly developed, it no longer needed the impetus of ascetic Protestantism.[33] By virtue of its conquest of much of Western society, capitalism had solidly established an institutional base and a secular value system of its own—economic rationality. Its secular economic values had no further need for the "ultimate" justification they had required during the newer, unsteadier days of economic revolution.

Such lines of differentiation constitute the secularization of religious values. In the same process, other institutional spheres—economic, political, scientific, etc.—become more nearly established on their own. The values governing these spheres are no longer sanctioned directly by religious beliefs, but by an autonomous rationality. In so far as this replaces religious sanctions, secularization occurs in these spheres.

Similarly, nationalistic and related value systems undergo a process of secularization as differentiation proceeds. As a society moves increasingly toward more complex social organization, the encompassing demands of nationalistic commitment give way to more autonomous systems of rationality. For instance, the Soviet Union, as its social structure grows more differentiated, is apparently introducing more "independent" market mechanisms, "freer" social scientific investigation in some spheres, and so on.[34] Moreover, these measures are not directly sanctioned by nationalistic or communistic values. Finally, it seems reasonable to make the historical generalization that, in the early stages of a nation's development, nationalism is heady, muscular, and aggressive; as the society evolves to an advanced state, however, nationalism tends to settle into a more remote and complacent condition, rising to fury only in times of national crisis.

Hence there is a paradoxical element in the role of religious or nationalistic belief systems. In so far as they encourage the breakup of old patterns, they may stimulate economic modernization. In so far as they resist their own subsequent secularization, however, these same value systems may become an impediment to economic advance and structural change.

DIFFERENTIATION OF SYSTEMS OF STRATIFICATION

In analyzing systems of stratification, we concentrate on two kinds of issues.

1. Are ascribed qualities subject to ranking? Ascription focuses primarily on those aspects of the human condition that touch the biological and physical world—kinship, age, sex, race or ethnicity, and territorial location. To what extent is status determined by birth in a certain tribe? in a certain family? in a certain ethnic group? in a certain place—a region of the country or "the wrong side of the tracks"? Some ascription exists in all societies, since the infant in the nuclear

family always and everywhere begins with the status of his parents.[35] The degree to which this ascribed ranking extends beyond the family varies from society to society. In our own ideology, we minimize the ascriptive elements of class and ethnic membership; but in practice these matter greatly, especially for Negroes.

2. The degree to which all positions in society (occupational, political, religious, etc.) are consequences of status ascribed from birth. For example, the American egalitarian ideology places a premium on the maximum separation of these positions from ascribed categories; but in fact, family membership, minority-group membership, etc., impinge on the ultimate "placing" of persons. In many non-industrialized societies, the link between ascription and position is much closer. Criteria like these reveal the degree of openness, or social mobility, in a system.

Under conditions of economic modernization, structural differentiation increases along both dimensions discussed. Other evaluative standards intrude on ascribed memberships. For instance, McKim Marriott has noted that, in the village of Paril in India,

> Personal wealth, influence, and mortality have surpassed the traditional caste-and-order alignment of kind groups as the effective bases of ranking. Since such new bases of ranking can no longer be clearly tied to any inclusive system of large solidary groupings, judgments must be made according to the characteristics of individual or family units. This individualization of judgments leads to greater dissensus [*sic*].[36]

Of course, castes, ethnic groups, and traditional religious groupings do not necessarily decline in importance *in every respect* during periods of modernization. As political interest groups or reference groups for diffuse loyalty, they may become even more significant.[37] As the sole bases of ranking, however, ascriptive

standards become more differentiated from economic, political, and other standards.[38]

Individual mobility through the occupational hierarchies increases. This is indicative of the differentiation of the adult's functional position from his point of origin. In addition, individual mobility is frequently substituted for collective mobility. Individuals, and no longer whole castes or tribes, compete for higher standing in society. The phenomenon of growing individual mobility seems to be one of the universal consequences of industrialization. After assembling extensive empirical data on patterns of mobility in industrialized nations, Lipset and Bendix conclude that "the overall pattern of [individual] social mobility appears to be much the same in the industrial societies of various Western countries."[39] Patterns of class symbolization and class ideology may, however, continue to be different in industrialized countries.

One of Emile Durkheim's remarkable insights concerned the role of integrative mechanisms during periods of growing social heterogeneity. Attacking the utilitarian view that the division of labor would flourish best without regulation, Durkheim demonstrates that one concomitant of a growing division of labor is an *increase* in mechanisms for coordinating and solidifying the interaction among individuals whose interests are becoming progressively more diversified.[40] Durkheim locates this integration largely in the legal structure; however, similar kinds of integrative forces can be discerned elsewhere in society.

Differentiation, therefore, is not by itself sufficient for modernization. Development proceeds as a contrapuntal interplay between differentiation (which is divisive of established society) and integration (which unites differentiated structures on a new basis). Paradoxically, however, the course of integration itself produces more *differentiated* structures—e.g., trade unions, associations, political parties, and a mushrooming state apparatus. Let us illustrate this complex process of integration in several institutional spheres.

ECONOMY AND FAMILY

Under a simple kind of economic organization, like subsistence agriculture or household industry, there is little differentiation between economic roles and family roles. All reside in the kinship structure. The *integration* of these diverse but unspecialized activities also rests in the local family and community structures, and in the religious traditions which fortify both.

When differentiation has begun, the social setting for production is separated from that for consumption; and the productive roles of family members are isolated geographically, temporally, and structurally from their distinctively familial roles. This differentiation immediately creates integrative problems. How is information about employment opportunities to be conveyed to working people? How are the interests of families to be protected from market fluctuation? Whereas such integrative exigencies had been faced by kinsmen, neighbors, and local largesse in premodern settings, modernization creates dozens of institutions and organizations designed to deal with the new integrative problems—labor recruitment agencies and exchanges, labor unions, government regulation of labor allocation, welfare and relief arrangements, cooperative societies, savings institutions.[41] All these involve agencies which specialize in integration.

COMMUNITY

When industrialization occurs only in villages, or when villages are built around paternalistic industrial enterprises,[42] many ties of community and kinship can be maintained under the industrial conditions. Urbanization, however, frequently creates more anonymity. As a result, in expanding cities there often emerge voluntary associations—churches and chapels, unions, schools, halls, athletic clubs, bars, shops, mutual-aid groups, etc. Sometimes the

growth of these integrative groupings is retarded because of the movement of migratory workers,[43] who "come to the city for their differentiation" and "return to the village for their integration." In cities themselves, the original criterion for associating may have been the common tribe, caste, or village; this criterion sometimes persists or is gradually replaced by more "functional" groupings based on economic or political interest.[44]

POLITICAL STRUCTURE

In a typical premodern setting, political integration is closely fused with kinship position, tribal membership, control of the land, or control of the unknown. Political forms include chieftains, kings, councils of elders, strong landlords, powerful magicians and oracles, etc.

As social systems grow more complex, political systems are modified accordingly. Fortes and Evans-Pritchard have specified three types of native African political systems. These, listed in terms of their respective degrees of differentiation from kinship lineages, are as follows: (1) small societies in which the largest political unit embraces only those united by kinship—thus political authority is conterminous with kinship relations, (2) societies in which the political framework is the integrative core for a number of kinship lineages, and (3) societies with a more formal administrative organization. Such systems move toward greater differentiation as the society's population grows and economic and cultural heterogeneity increases.[45] In colonial and recently-freed African societies, political systems have evolved much further; parties, congresses, pressure groups, and even "parliamentary" systems have emerged.[46] In describing the Indian village, Marriott speaks of the "wider integration of local groups with outside groups."[47] Sometimes such wider political integration is, like community integration, based on extension and modification of an old integrative principle. Harrison has argued that modern developments in India have changed the significance of caste from the "traditional village extension of the joint family" to "regional alliances of kindred local units." This modification has led to the formation of "new caste lobbies" which constitute some of the strongest and most explosive political forces in modern India.[48] We shall mention some of the possible political consequences of this persistence of old integrative forms later.

We have indicated the ways in which differentiation in society impinges on the integrative sphere. The resulting integrative structures attempt, with more or less success, to coordinate and solidify the social structure which the forces of differentiation threaten to fragment. In many cases, the integrative associations and parties are extremely unstable: labor unions turn into political or nationalistic parties, religious sects become political clubs, football clubs become religious sects, and so on.[49] This fluidity indicates the urgent need for reintegration during rapid, irregular, and disruptive processes of differentiation. The initial response is a trial-and-error type of reaching for many kinds of integration at once.

We have outlined some structural consequences of technological advance, agricultural commercialization, urbanization, and industrialization. We have analyzed these consequences in terms of differentiation and integration. The structural changes are not, one must remember, a simple function of industrialization alone. Some of the most far-reaching structural changes have occurred in countries where industrialization has hardly begun. For instance, colonialism or related forms of economic dominance create not only an extensive differentiation of cash products and wage-labor, but also a vulnerability to world price fluctuations in commodities.[50] Hence many of the structural changes already described, and the consequent social disturbances to be described presently, are characteristics of societies which are still technically pre-industrial.

Discontinuities in Differentiation and Integration: Social Disturbances

The structural changes associated with modernization are disruptive to the social order for the following reasons:

1. Differentiation demands the creation of new activities, norms, rewards, and sanctions—money, political position, prestige based on occupation, etc. These often conflict with old modes of social action, which are frequently dominated by traditional religious, tribal, and kinship systems. Traditional standards are among the most intransigent obstacles to modernization; and when they are threatened, serious dissatisfaction and opposition to the threatening agents arise.

2. Structural change is, above all, *uneven* during periods of modernization. In colonial societies, for instance, the European powers frequently revolutionized the economic, political, and educational frameworks; but they simultaneously encouraged or imposed a conservatism in traditional religious, class, and family systems.

> The basic problem in these [colonial] societies was the expectation that the native population would accept certain broad, modern institutional settings . . . and would perform within them various roles—especially economic and administrative roles—while at the same time, they were denied some of the basic rewards inherent in these settings . . . they were expected to act on the basis of a motivational system derived from a different social structure which the colonial powers and indigenous rulers tried to maintain.[51]

In a society undergoing post-colonial modernization, similar discontinuities appear. Within the economy itself, rapid industrialization—no matter how coordinated—bites unevenly into the established social and economic structures.[52] And throughout the society, the differentiation occasioned by agricultural, industrial, and urban changes always proceeds in a see-saw relationship with integration: the two forces continuously breed lags and bottlenecks. The faster the tempo of modernization is, the more severe the discontinuities. This unevenness creates *anomie* in the classical sense, for it generates disharmony between life experiences and the normative framework which regulates them.[53]

3. Dissatisfactions arising from conflict with traditional ways and those arising from *anomie* sometimes aggravate each other upon coming into contact. *Anomie* may be partially relieved by new integrative devices, like unions, associations, clubs, and government regulations. However, such innovations are often opposed by traditional vested interests because they compete with the older undifferentiated systems of solidarity.[54] The result is a three-way tug-of-war among the forces of tradition, the forces of differentiation, and the new forces of integration.[55] Under these conditions, virtually unlimited potentialities for group conflict are created.[56]

Three classic responses to these discontinuities are anxiety, hostility, and fanatasy. If and when these responses become collective, they crystallize into a variety of social movements—peaceful agitation, political violence, millenarianism, nationalism, revolution, underground subversion, etc.[57] There is plausible—though not entirely convincing—evidence that the people most readily drawn into such movements are those suffering most severely under the displacements created by structural change. For example:

[Nationalism appeared] as a permanent force in Southeast Asia at the moment when the peasants were forced to give up subsistence farming for the cultivation of cash crops or when (as in highly colonized Java) subsistence farming ceased to yield a subsistence. The introduction of a money economy and the withering away of the village as the unit of life accompanied this development and finally established the period of economic dependence.[58]

Other theoretical and empirical data suggest that social movements appeal most to those who have been dislodged from old social ties by differentiation without also being integrated into the new social order.[59]

Many belief systems associated with these movements envision the grand, almost instantaneous integration of society. Frequently, the beliefs are highly emotional and unconcerned with realistic policies. In nationalistic movements in colonial societies, for instance, "the political symbols were intended to develop new, ultimate, common values and basic loyalties, rather than relate to current policy issues within the colonial society."[60] Furthermore, belief systems of this kind reflect the ambivalence that results from the conflict between traditionalism and modernization. Nationalists alternate between xenophobia and xenophilia; they predict that they will simultaneously "outmodernize" the West in the future and "restore" the true values of the ancient civilization; they argue both for egalitarian and for hierarchical principles of social organization at the same time.[61] Nationalism and related ideologies unite these contradictory tendencies in the society under one large symbol. If these ideologies are successful, they are then often used as a means to modernize the society and thus to erase those kinds of social discontinuity that caused the initial nationalistic outburst.

Naturally, early modernization does not inevitably produce violent nationalism or other social movements. Furthermore, when such movements do arise, they take many different forms. Below are listed the five factors which seem most decisive in the genesis and molding of social disturbances.

1. The scope and intensity of the social dislocation created by structural changes. "The greater the tempo of these changes ... the greater the problems of acute malintegration the society has to face."[62]

2. The structural complexity of the

society at the time when modernization begins. In the least developed societies, where "the language of politics is at the same time the language of religion," protest movements more or less immediately take on a religious cast. In Africa, for instance, utopian religious movements apparently have relatively greater appeal in the less developed regions; whereas the more secular types of political protest, like trade union movements and party agitations, have tended to cluster in the more developed areas.[63] The secularization of protest increases, of course, as modernization and differentiation advance.

3. The access that disturbed groups have to channels that influence social policy. If dislocated groups have access to those responsible for introducing reforms, agitation is usually relatively peaceful and orderly. If this avenue is blocked—because of either the isolation of the groups or the intransigence of the ruling authorities—demands for reform tend to take more violent, utopian, and bizarre forms. This is the reason that fantasy and unorganized violence are likely to cluster among the disinherited, the colonized, and the socially isolated migrants.[64]

4. The overlap of interests and lines of cleavage. In many colonial societies, the social order broke more or less imperfectly into three groupings: (*a*) the Western representatives, who controlled economic and political administration, and who were frequently allied with large local landowners; (*b*) a large native population who —when drawn into the colonial economy— entered it as tenant farmers, wage-laborers, etc.; (*c*) a group of foreigners—Chinese, Indians, Syrians, Goans, Lebanese, etc.— who fitted between the first two groups as traders, moneylenders, merchants, creditors, etc. This view is oversimplified, of course; but several colonial societies approximated this arrangement.[65] The important structural feature of such an arrangement is that economic, political, and racial-ethic memberships *coincide* with each other. Thus, *any* kind of conflict is likely to assume

racial overtones and to arouse the more diffuse loyalties and prejudices of the warring parties. Many colonial outbursts did, in fact, follow racial lines.[66] In so far as such "earthquake faults" persist after independence has been attained, these societies will probably be plagued by similar outbursts.[67] If, on the other hand, the different lines of cleavage in the society crisscross, the society is more nearly able to insulate and manage specific economic and political grievances peacefully.[68]

5. The kind and amount of foreign infiltration and intervention on behalf of protest groups.

Structural Bases for the Role of Government

Many have argued, on economic grounds, for the presence of a strong, centralized government in rapidly modernizing societies. Governmental planning and activity are required, for example, to direct saving and investment, to regulate incentives, to encourage entrepreneurship, to control trade and prices, etc.[69] To their arguments, I should like to add several considerations that emerge from the analysis of structural change during periods of rapid development.

1. Undifferentiated institutional structures frequently constitute the primary social barriers to modernization. Individuals refuse to work for wages because of traditional kinship, village, tribal, and other ties. Invariably, a certain amount of political pressure must be applied to loosen these ties. The need for this pressure increases, of course, in proportion to the rate of modernization desired.

2. The process of differentiation itself creates conditions demanding a larger, more formal type of political administration. Thus, another argument in favor of the importance of strong government during rapid and uneven modernization is based on the necessity to accommodate the growing cultural, economic, and social heterogeneity, and to control the political

repercussions of the constantly shifting distribution of power accompanying extensive social reorganization.

3. The probability that periods of early modernization will erupt into explosive outbursts creates delicate political problems for the leaders of developing nations. We shall conclude this essay on the major social forces of modernization by suggesting the kinds of government that are likely to be most effective in such troubled areas. First, political leaders can increase their effectiveness by openly and vigorously committing themselves to utopian and xenophobic nationalism. This commitment is a powerful instrument for attaining three of their most important ends. (*a*) They can enhance their own claim to legitimacy by endowing themselves with the mission of creating the nation-state. (*b*) They can procure otherwise unobtainable sacrifices from a populace which may be committed to modernization in the abstract, but which resists making concrete breaks with traditional ways. (*c*) They can use their claim to legitimacy to repress protests and to prevent generalized symbols, such as communism, from spreading to all sorts of particular grievances. However, these political leaders should not take their claim to legitimacy too literally. They should not rely on their nationalistic commitment as being strong enough to enable them to ignore or smother grievances completely. They should "play politics," in the usual sense, with aggrieved groups, thus giving these groups access to responsible political agencies, and thereby reducing the conditions that favor counterclaims to legitimacy. One key to political stability seems to be, therefore, the practice of flexible politics behind the façade of an inflexible commitment to a national mission.

Conclusion

I have attempted to sketch, in ideal-type terms, the ways in which economic and social development are related to the social structure. I have organized the discussion around three major categories: differentiation, which characterizes a social structure that is moving toward greater complexity; integration, which in certain respects balances the divisive character of differentiation; and social disturbances, which result from the discontinuities between differentiation and integration.

Four qualifications must be added to this analysis. (1) I have not tried to account for the determinants of economic development itself. In fact, the discussion of differentiation, integration, and social disturbances has presupposed a certain attempt to develop economically. However, these three forces condition the *course* of that development once it has started. (2) For purposes of exposition, I have presented the three major categories in the order restated above. However, this ordering must not be inferred to mean that any one of the forces assumes causal precedence in social change. Rather, they form an interactive system. Disturbances, for instance, may arise from discontinuities created by structural differentiation; but these very disturbances may shape the course of future processes of differentiation. Likewise, integrative developments may be set in motion by differentiation; but they, in their turn, may initiate new lines of differentiation. (3) Even though the forces of differentiation, integration, and disturbances are closely linked empirically, we should not "close" the "system" composed of the relationship among the three forces. Differentiation may arise from sources other than economic development; the necessity for integration may emerge from conditions other than differentiation; and the sources of social disturbances are not exhausted by the discontinuities between differentiation and integration. The "all-at-once" character of the transition from less differentiated to more differentiated societies should not be exaggerated. Empirically, the process evolves gradually and influences the social structure selectively. This essay has emphasized various halfway arrangements and compromises in order to illustrate this gradualness and irregularity.

NOTES

[1] I am grateful to Professors William Petersen, Herbert Blumer, Reinhard Bendix, and Kingsley Davis of the University of California, Berkeley, for critical comments on an earlier version of this essay.

[2] Max Weber, *The Methodology of the Social Sciences* (Glencoe, Ill., 1949), pp. 90, 93.

[3] *Ibid.*, pp. 93, 101–103.

[4] W. A. Lewis, *The Theory of Economic Growth* (Homewood, Ill., 1955), p. 1.

[5] M. Nash, "Some Notes on Village Industrialization in South and East Asia," *Economic Development and Cultural Change*, 3, 271.

[6] W. H. Becket, for instance, distinguishes between "technical improvement" and "organizational improvement" in agriculture. See "The Development of Peasant Agriculture," in P. Ruopp (ed.), *Approaches to Community Development* (The Hague, 1953), pp. 138–143. For an analysis of the interplay between technological advance and productive reorganization during the Tokugawa period in Japan, see H. Rosovsky, "Japanese Economic Development and the Western Model" (mimeographed), pp. 7–17.

[7] For example, J. H. Boeke, *The Structure of the Netherlands Indian Economy* (New York, 1942), pp. 76–89.

[8] Nash, *op. cit.*; T. Herman, "The Role of Cottage and Small-Scale Industries in Asian Economic Development," *Economic Development and Cultural Change*, 4, 356–370; H. G. Aubrey, "Small Industry in Economic Development," in L. W. Shannon (ed.), *Underdeveloped Areas* (New York, 1957), pp. 215–225.

[9] T. Hodgkin, *Nationalism in Colonial Africa* (New York, 1957), Ch. 2.

[10] B. F. Hoselitz, "The City, the Factory, and Economic Growth," *American Economic Review*, 45, 166–184; K. Davis and H. H. Golden, "Urbanization and the Development of Pre-Industrial Areas," *Economic Development and Cultural Change*, 3, 6–26; Nash, *op. cit.*, p. 277.

[11] S. Kuznets, "Problems in Comparisons of Economic Trends," in S. Kuznets, W. E. Moore, and J. J. Spengler (eds.), *Economic Growth: Brazil, India, Japan* (Durham, N.C., 1955), pp. 14–19; Kuznets, "International Differences in Income Levels: Some Reflec-

tions on Their Causes," *Economic Development and Cultural Change*, 2, 22–23; A. Gerschenkron, "Economic Backwardness in Historical Perspective," and R. Linton, "Cultural and Personality Factors Affecting Economic Growth," both in B. Hoselitz (ed.), *The Progress of Underdeveloped Areas* (Chicago, 1952), pp. 3–29, 80 ff.; H. G. J. Aitken (ed.), *The State and Economic Growth* (New York, 1959).

[12] E. Staley, *The Future of Underdeveloped Areas* (New York, 1954), pp. 21–22; W. W. Rostow, *The Stages of Economic Growth: A Non-Communist Manifesto* (Cambridge, 1960), pp. 26–35; W. E. Moore, *Industrialization and Labor* (Ithaca and New York, 1951), Chs. 1–4, Hoselitz, "The City, the Factory," pp. 177–179.

[13] United Nations, Department of Economic and Social Affairs, *Processes and Problems of Industrialization in Underdeveloped Countries* (New York, 1955), Ch. 1; C. P. Kindleberger, *Economic Development* (New York, 1958), pp. 184–185, 315–316; N. S. Buchanan and H. S. Ellis, *Approaches to Economic Development* (New York, 1955), p. 275 ff.; Kuznets, "International Differences," pp. 21–22.

[14] For instance, Blumer has questioned the generalization that "early industrialization, by nature, alienates and disaffects workers, makes them radical, and propels them to protest behavior." He even concludes that "industrialization . . . is neutral and indifferent to what follows in its wake" (H. Blumer, "Early Industrialization and the Laboring Class," *The Sociological Quarterly*, 1, 9). If one searches for specific generalizations like those Blumer has rejected, of course, he will inevitably be disappointed. One must not conclude, however, that the establishment of ideal-type constructs about the consequences of industrialization, and their use in interpreting national experiences are fruitless.

[15] Kuznets, "International Differences," p. 23.

[16] N. J. Smelser, *Social Change in the Industrial Revolution* (Chicago, 1959), Chs. 9–11.

[17] *Ibid.*, p. 2.

[18] Boeke, *op. cit.*, pp. 8–9, 32–34; E. E. Hagen, "The Process of Economic Development," *Economic Development and Cultural Change*, 5, 195; B. K. Maden, "The Economics of the Indian Village and Its Implications in Social Structure," *International Social Science Bulletin*, 3, 813–821; D. F. Dowd, "Two-thirds of the World," in Shannon, *op. cit.*, pp. 14 ff. For qualifications on the degree to which caste dominates occupation in India, see K. Davis, *The Population of India and Pakistan* (Princeton, N.I., 1951), pp. 163 ff.

[19] K. Polanyi, C. M. Arensberg, and H. W.

Pearson (eds.), *Trade and Market in the Early Empires* (Glencoe, Ill., 1957); N. J. Smelser, "A Comparative View of Exchange Systems," *Economic Development and Cultural Change*, 7, 173–182; Boeke, *op. cit.*, pp. 36–39; M. R. Solomon, "The Structure of the Market in Underdeveloped Economies," in Shannon, *op. cit.*, pp. 131 ff.

[20] These "levels," which represent points on the continuum from structural fusion to structural differentiation, are taken from Boeke, *op. cit.*, p. 90.

[21] F. G. Bailey, *Caste and the Economic Frontier* (Manchester, 1957), pp. 4–5.

[22] M. J. Levy, Jr., "Some Sources of the Vulnerability of the Structures of Relatively Non-Industrialized Societies to Those of Highly Industrialized Societies," in Hoselitz, *The Progress of Underdeveloped Areas*, pp. 116–125. The pattern variables of T. Parsons are also relevant (discussed in *The Social System* [Glencoe, Ill., 1951], pp. 58–67). For applications of the pattern variables to economic development, see G. A. Theodorson, "Acceptance of Industrialization and Its Attendant Consequences for the Social Patterns of Non-Western Societies," *American Sociological Review*, 18, 477–484; and B. F. Hoselitz, "Social Structure and Economic Growth," *Economia Internazionale*, 6, 52–77.

[23] Examples of these compromises may be found in Moore, *op. cit.*, pp. 29–34; *idem.*, "The Migration of Native Laborers in South Africa," in Shannon, *op. cit.*, pp. 79 ff.; A. I. Richards (ed.), *Economic Development and Tribal Change* (Cambridge, n.d.), Ch. 5; C. A. Myers, *Labor Problems in the Industrialization of India* (Cambridge, Mass., 1958), pp. 52, 175; S. Rottenberg, "Income and Leisure in an Underdeveloped Economy," in Shannon, *op. cit.*, pp. 150–151; Aubrey, "Small Industry in Economic Development," in Shannon, *op. cit.*, pp. 215 ff.; A. Doucy, "The Unsettled Attitude of Negro Workers in the Belgian Congo," *International Social Science Bulletin*, 6, 442–451; G. Balandier, "Social Changes and Social Problems in Negro Africa," in C. W. Stillman (ed.), *Africa in the Modern World* (Chicago, 1955), pp. 60–61; Smelser, *Social Change*, Ch. 9; Herman, *op. cit.*, pp. 357–358.

[24] Noneconomic barriers are discussed at length in Moore, *Industrialization and Labor*, Chs. 2–4. On the persistence of handicrafts, see A. L. Minkes, "A Note on Handicrafts in Underdeveloped Areas," *Economic Development and Cultural Change*, 1, 156–158; Herman, *op. cit.*, pp. 362–365; T. Uyeda, *The Small Industries of Japan* (Shanghai, 1938), pp. 84–112.

[25] For case studies, see M. J. Levy, Jr., *The Family Revolution in Modern China* (Cambridge, Mass., 1949), and Smelser, *Social Change*.

[26] Kindleberger, *op. cit.*, pp. 59 ff.; Moore, *Industrialization and Labor*, pp. 29–34, 71–75; E. F. Frazier, "The Impact of Colonialism on African Social Forms and Personality," in Stillman, *op. cit.*, pp. 76–83; UNESCO, *Social Implications of Industrialization and Urbanization South of the Sahara* (Geneva, 1956), pp. 108–109, 115–117, 187, 216–220, 369–372, and 616 ff.; K. El Daghestani, "The Evolution of the Moslem Family in the Middle Eastern Countries," *International Social Science Bulletin*, 6, 442–451; B. J. Siegel, "Social Structure and Economic Change in Brazil," and S. J. Stein, "The Brazilian Cotton Textile Industry, 1850–1950," both in Kuznets, *et al.*, *Economic Growth*, pp. 388 ff., 433–438; W. Elkan, *An African Labour Force* (Kampala, Uganda, 1956), Ch. 5; Myers, *op. cit.*, p. 177; Linton, *op. cit.*, pp. 83–84; H. Belshaw, "Some Social Aspects of Economic Development in Underdeveloped Areas," in Shannon, *op. cit.*, pp. 88 ff., 191 ff.; G. St. J. Orde Browne, *The African Labourer* (London, 1933), pp. 100–105.

[27] Weber's relevant works include *The Protestant Ethic and the Spirit of Capitalism* (London, 1948); *The Religion of China* (Glencoe, Ill., 1951); and *The Religion of India* (Glencoe, Ill., 1958). For secondary treatments, see T. Parsons, *The Structure of Social Action* (New York, 1937), Chs. 14–15; and R. Bendix, *Max Weber* (New York, 1959), Parts I and II.

[28] R. N. Bellah, *Tokugawa Religion* (Glencoe, Ill., 1957); C. Geertz, *The Social Context of Economic Change* (Cambridge, Mass., 1956).

[29] K. Davis, "Social and Demographic Aspects of Economic Development in India," in Kuznets *et al.*, *Economic Growth*, p. 294; Gerschenkron, *op. cit.*, pp. 22–25; Rostow, *op. cit.*, pp. 26–29.

[30] B. F. Hoselitz, "Non-Economic Barriers to Economic Development," *Economic Development and Cultural Change*, 1, 9.

[31] Cf., for example, the Indonesian expulsion of needed Dutch teachers and engineers. It has been maintained that the upsurge of regionalism in India has led to a deterioration of English as a linguistic medium for education in Indian universities. See S. E. Harrison, *India: The Most Dangerous Decades* (Princeton, N.J., 1960), pp. 60–95.

[32] J. van der Kroef, "Economic Developments in Indonesia: Some Social and Cultural Impediments," *Economic Development and Cultural Change*, 4, 116–133.

[33] *The Protestant Ethic and the Spirit of Capitalism*, pp. 181–182.

[34] E. Crankshaw, "Big Business in Russia," *Atlantic*, **202**, 35–41. For discussion of the balance among political and other elements in Soviet society, see R. A. Bauer, A. Inkeles, and C. Kluckhohn, *How the Soviet System Works* (Cambridge, Mass., 1957), Part II.

[35] K. Davis, *Human Society* (New York, 1957), Ch. 14, T. Parsons, "An Analytical Approach to the Theory of Social Stratification," *Essays in Sociological Theory* (rev. ed.; Glencoe, Ill., 1954), Ch. 4.

[36] Marriott, "Social Change in an Indian Village," *Economic Development and Cultural Change*, **1**, 153; UNESCO, *op. cit.*, p. 152; J. S. Coleman, *Nigeria: Background to Nationalism* (Berkeley and Los Angeles, 1958), pp. 70–73.

[37] In some cases, these ascriptive pegs become the basis for political groupings long after the society has begun to modernize. See E. H. Jacoby, *Agrarian Unrest in Southeast Asia* (New York, 1949), pp. 27–28, 50, 76, 91–93, 123–125, and 248; Coleman, *op. cit.*, pp. 332–367. Harrison has argued that the present significance of caste in India is "if anything, stronger than before," but that this significance appears as competitiveness in the new political arena of the country (Harrison, *op. cit.*, Ch. 4; also Davis, *Population of India*; p. 171). William Petersen has suggested that, in the advanced society of Holland, a process of "pillarization" has occurred, in which semi-ascribed religious groups have become the major focus of political and social competition ("Dutch Society *vs.* Mass Society," University of California Public Lectire, May 9, 1960).

[38] For a study of the cross-cultural similarity in the ranking of industrial occupations in developed countries, see A. Inkeles and P. H. Rossi, "National Comparisons of Occupational Prestige," *American Journal of Sociology*, **61**, 329–339.

[39] S. M. Lipset and R. Bendix, *Social Mobility in Industrial Society* (Berkeley and Los Angeles, 1959), pp. 13 ff. Of course, the transition from collective to individual mobility is not instantaneous. See Marriott, *op. cit.*, p. 153; and Davis, "Social and Demographic Aspects," pp. 308–313.

[40] E. Durkheim, *The Division of Labor in Society* (Glencoe, Ill., 1949), Chs. 3–8. A recent formulation of the relationship between differentiation and integration may be found in R. F. Bales, *Interaction Process Analysis* (Cambridge, Mass., 1950).

[41] Smelser, *Social Change*, Chs. 12–13; T. Parsons and N. Smelser, *Economy and Society* (Glencoe, Ill., 1956), Ch. 3; also Nash, *op. cit.*, p. 275; A. Mehta, "The Mediating Role of the Trade Union in Underdeveloped Countries," *Economic Development and Cultural Change*, **6**, 20–23.

[42] Smelser, *Social Change*, pp. 99–108; Myers, *op. cit.*, pp. 52–54; Stein, *op. cit.*, pp. 433 ff.

[43] Orde Browne, *op. cit.*, pp. 112–116; Doucy, *op. cit.*, pp. 446–450; Elkan, *op. cit.*, Chs. 2–3.

[44] UNESCO, *op. cit.*, pp. 84–85, 105, 120–121, 128–130, 220–221, 373–377, and 469–473; D. Forde, "The Social Impact of Industrialization and Urban Conditions in Africa South of the Sahara," *International Social Science Bulletin*, **7**, 119–121; Hodgkin, *op. cit.*, pp. 85 ff.; Hoselitz, "The City, the Factory," p. 183; Coleman, *op. cit.*, pp. 73–80; Harrison, *op. cit.*, pp. 330–332.

[45] M. Fortes and E. E. Evans-Pritchard (eds.), *African Political Systems* (London, 1940), pp. 1–25.

[46] D. Apter, *The Gold Coast in Transition* (Princeton, 1956); Hodgkin, *op. cit.*, pp. 115–139; G. A. Almond and J. S. Coleman, *The Politics of Developing Areas* (Princeton, 1960).

[47] Marriott, *op. cit.*, p. 152.

[48] Harrison, *op. cit.*, pp. 100 ff.

[49] Hodgkin, *op. cit.*, pp. 85 ff.

[50] Jacoby, *op. cit.*, Ch. 1; R. Emerson, L. A. Mills, and V. Thompson, *Government and Nationalism in Southeast Asia* (New York, 1942), pp. 135–136; S. A. Mosk, *Industrial Revolution in Mexico* (Berkeley and Los Angeles, 1950), pp. 3–17.

[51] S. N. Eisenstadt, "Sociological Aspects of Political Development in Underdeveloped Countries," *Economic Development and Cultural Change*, **5**, 298.

[52] P. T. Bauer and B. S. Yamey, *The Economics of Underdeveloped Countries* (Chicago, 1957), p. 64.

[53] E. Durkheim, *Suicide* (Glencoe, Ill., 1951), Book II, Ch. 5.

[54] Davis, "Social and Demographic Aspects," pp. 296 ff.

[55] E.g., M. A. Jaspan, "A Sociological Case Study: Community Hostility to Imposed Social Change in South Africa," in Ruopp, *op. cit.*, pp. 97–120.

[56] E.g., the conflict between migratory workers and full-time resident workers; see Elkan, *op. cit.*, pp. 23–24.

[57] For theoretical discussions of this relationship between strain and disturbance, see T. Parsons, R. F. Bales, *et al.*, *Family, Socialization, and Interaction Process* (Glencoe, Ill., 1955), Chs. 2, 4; Smelser, *Social Change*, Chs. 2, 9–10.

[58] Jacoby, *op. cit.*, p. 246.

[59] Emerson, *et al.*, *op. cit.*, pp. 25–29; Eisenstadt, *op. cit.*, pp. 294–298; W. Kornhauser, *The Politics of Mass Society* (Glencoe, Ill., 1959), Parts II and III; S. M. Lipset, *Political Man* (Garden City, N.Y., 1960), Ch. 2; M. Watnick, "The Appeal of Communism to the Underdeveloped Peoples," in Hoselitz, *Progress of Underdeveloped Areas*, pp. 152–172.

[60] Eisenstadt, *op. cit.*, p. 294.

[61] M. Matossian, "Ideologies of Delayed Industrialization," *Economic Development and Cultural Change*, **6**, 217–228.

[62] Eisenstadt, *loc. cit.*, J. S. Coleman, "Nationalism in Tropical Africa," in Shannon, *op. cit.*, pp. 42 ff.; Hodgkin, *op. cit.*, p. 56.

[63] Hodgkin, *op. cit.*, pp. 95–150; Coleman, "Nationalism in Tropical Africa," pp. 38 ff.

[64] B. Barber, "Acculturation and Messianic Movements," *American Sociological Review*, **6**, 663–669; H. R. Niebuhr, *The Social Sources of Denominationalism* (New York, 1929); J. B. Holt, "Holiness Religion: Cultural Shock and Social Reorganization," *American Sociological Review*, **5**, 740–747; B. G. M. Sundkler, *Bantu Prophets in South Africa* (London, 1948); P. Worsley, *The Trumpet Shall Sound* (London, 1957).

[65] Emerson *et al.*, *op. cit.*, pp. 136–140; Hodgkin, *op. cit.*, pp. 60–75; C. Robequain, *The Economic Development of French Indo-China* (London, 1944), pp. 79–88; J. S. Furnivall, *Colonial Policy and Practice* (Cambridge, 1948), pp. 116–123; F. Machlup, "Three Economic Systems Clash in Burma," *Review of Economic Studies*, **3**, 140–146.

[66] Emerson *et al.*, *op. cit.*, pp. 141–143; Jacoby, *op. cit.*, Ch. 8.

[67] J. M. van der Kroef, "Minority Problems in Indonesia," *Far Eastern Survey*, **24**, 129–133, 165–171; Harrison, *op. cit.*, Chs. 3–6.

[68] Lipset, *Political Man*, Ch. 3.

[69] J. J. Spengler, "Social Structure, the State, and Economic Growth," in Kuznets *et al.*, *Economic Growth*, pp. 370–379.

Chapter 2

Traditional and Transitional Societies

FOLK AND "FEUDAL" SOCIETIES

Gideon Sjoberg

Until the past decade sociologists in the United States directed only a small portion of their efforts toward a comparative study of society. As a result, the distinctions between folk and feudal orders and the differential effects of the process of industrialization and urbanization on the two kinds of society have been little perceived. This oversight is, of course, understandable in the light of American history; only incipient forms of "feudalism" have been evidenced in this country. Attention therefore was not turned toward feudalism, even on the world scene. Recent political changes, however, have placed the United States in a position of world leadership; reform programs are being carried out in many "backward" countries. Through failure to interpret correctly the functionings of other societies, a number of these plans have been naïvely conceived. At the same time, sociologists and anthropologists are becoming increasingly concerned with the comparative study of sociocultural systems; a critical evaluation, therefore, of present-day perspectives is requisite.

The primary purpose of this paper is to formulate a typology of the feudal social system in contradistinction to that of the folk order. Then, through an analysis of the differential effects on folk and feudal societies of social change resulting from the industrial-urban process, justification is offered for their separation. Although other sets of typologies are logically possible, the study should contribute toward the development of a comparative sociology.

It is not suggested here that the concept "folk society" should be discarded. Actually it serves many useful purposes. Yet its indiscriminate application to communities in all nonindustrialized areas has given rise to serious misinterpretations of existing conditions. Although no one society need correspond exactly to the constructed type, the value of the "model" for understanding and interpreting social action is enhanced if it does not diverge too widely from reality.

Redfield,[1] employing the ideal-type method, has provided us with one of the most careful and logically consistent formulations of the folk order. This is a small, isolated, nonliterate, and homogeneous society with a strong sense of solidarity.

SOURCE. Gideon Sjoberg, "Folk and 'Feudal' Societies," *American Journal of Sociology*, **58**, 231–239, November 1952. Reprinted by permission of The University of Chicago Press. Copyright 1952 by The University of Chicago Press.

[1] Robert Redfield, "The Folk Society," *American Journal of Sociology*, **52** (1947), 293–308; see also Alvin Boskoff, "Structure, Function, and Folk Society," *American Sociological Review*, **14** (1949), 749–758.

The primary group ties—those of kinship in particular—are of crucial importance to its effective functioning. Furthermore, a minimum of division of labor is present, from which it can be deduced that stratification in terms of social classes is unknown. Finally, the value orientation is sacred, and the actions of the members tend toward strict conformance to the norms of the folk.

The so-called "primitive" societies most nearly correspond to this folk typology; some isolated tribal communities fit the constructed type rather well. On the other hand, the concept is much less meaningful for interpreting complex societies in Asia, Europe, and even Latin America. Although a few writers[2] have recognized certain distinctions between "folk and peasant" and "nonliterate and literate" societies, no systematic presentation of these differences and their implications for social change seems to be extant.

The Feudal Society

Both feudal and folk societies are static and have sacred-value orientations; consequently, the action patterns of their members are clearly defined. But the feudal society is far more heterogeneous and complex than is the folk order. Their essential differences can best be stated in terms of the respective social structures. The feudal order is characterized by rigid class or caste-like stratification and complex state, educational, and economic institutions—all of which necessitate an extensive division of labor. Furthermore, it has a relatively large population and an extended territorial base.

It should be noted before proceeding, however, that the concept "feudalism" has been used in several ways. Historians conventionally have taken as their criteria certain restricted institutional patterns of

medieval Europe, especially the lord-vassal relationship.[3] Although this structural arrangement may have existed at times in other societies also,[4] the application of the concept in this manner is too limited for sociological analysis. The formulations of Boeke, Weber, and Rüstow,[5] although quite incomplete, more nearly fulfil our requirements. The more inclusive meaning given herein to the concept "feudalism" avoids the pitfalls of historicism and the resultant emphasis on uniqueness.

The structural arrangement of the feudal society is outlined below. In order to demonstrate a degree of empirical plausibility for this typology, brief references are made to social situations which correspond rather closely to its criteria.[6]

Typically, feudalism is predicated on a large peasant population. These individuals live in small village settlements and gain their livelihood primarily from intensive cultivation of the soil through the use of a

---

[2] See, e.g., A. L. Kroeber, *Anthropology* (rev. ed.; New York: Harcourt, Brace & Co., 1948), p. 284, and Robert Bierstedt, "The Limitations of Anthropological Methods in Sociology," *American Journal of Sociology*, **54** (1948), 22–30.

[3] F. L. Ganshof, *Qu'est-ce que la Féodalité?* (2nd ed., Neuchâtel: Éditions de la Baconnière, 1947); Otto Hintze, "Wesen und Verbreitung des Feudalismus," *Sitzungsberichte der Preussischen Akademie der Wissenschaften, philosophisch-historische Klasse* (1929), pp. 321–347; Carl Stephenson, *Mediaeval Feudalism* (Ithaca; Cornell University Press, 1942).

[4] Ch'i Ssu-ho, "A Comparison between Chinese and European Feudal Institutions," *Yenching Journal of Social Studies*, **4** (1948), 1–13.

[5] J. H. Boeke, *The Interests of the Voiceless Far East* (Leiden: Universitaire Pers Leiden, 1948), pp. 1–8; Max Weber, *Wirtschaft und Gesellschaft* (Tübingen: J. C. B. Mohr, 1925), **3**, Part 2, 724 ff.; Alexander Rüstow, *Ortsbestimmung der Gegenwart: Eine universalgeschichtliche Kulturkritik*. I: *Ursprung der Herrschaft* (Erlenbach-Zürich: Eugen Rentsch Verlag, 1950).

[6] In constructing any typology, a mass of descriptive material is essential. Many sociologists fail to recognize that Weber, the popularizer of the ideal-type method, relied heavily upon a great accumulation of historical materials for his typologies. The author has avoided constructing types about merely one historical situation; special study was made of China, Japan, India, and France, and surveys of other areas were read to check the generalizations offered.

simple technology. Scattered about the countryside, they form the backbone of the feudal system. But the peasant villages, significantly, are not isolated from one another. Field studies which have focused strictly upon the local community have often lost sight of the total sociocultural setting.

Unlike the members of a folk order, the peasants provide sufficient surplus food to sustain a limited number of population concentrations—the focal points of the feudal society. Towns spring up as political, religious, and trading centers, and although only a small portion of the total populace inhabit these communities, their social significance extends far beyond mere numbers. That these towns are quite unlike industrial cities is obvious: feudal towns do not exhibit the social disorganization and individualization commonly associated with present-day industrial-urban centers.[7] However, it must not be inferred that life in the feudal town is not distinct from that in the feudal village. These towns, moreover, are linked to one another. But inasmuch as transportation and communication still are relatively undeveloped, the contacts between the various communities are not comparable to those in industrial-urban societies.

Within the towns reside many of the elite, particularly its most important members. The ruling stratum is at the very least composed of a governmental bureaucracy and a priestly and/or scholar group. In addition, a nobility, a landlord group, and militarists or warriors, among others, may be present in various combinations. The unique cultural-historical development of a given social order determines the exact com-

position of the elite; it varies not only among societies but from time to time within a society.

But the significant feature of the stratification pattern is its bifurcation—a small minority supported by and "exploiting" a large subservient populace which passively accepts its role. The traditional Chinese society evidenced this most strikingly. To be sure, hierarchical gradations occur in both the upper stratum and the masses, but these are slight when compared to the basic cleavage within the society as a whole. The upper class is differentiated in terms of its monopoly of power and authority, the "correct" kinship groupings, and the highly valued achievements. Particularly important in this context are institutionalized differences in personal attributes. Distinctive dress, speech, and manners render the elite easily recognizable at all times.[8] And inasmuch as an individual's status within the elite or the masses is ascribed, social mobility is minimized.

A closer examination of the ruling minority is essential. As noted, political functionaries are one of the constituent elements. For in a feudal society a complex and highly institutionalized state system extends its control directly or indirectly over the masses. Among other forms, this state system may be a monarchy or possibly a theocracy such as existed in medieval Europe. Aside from exerting legal control, the political functionaries exact some kind of tribute from the peasantry. This serves to perpetuate the elite and support such groups as an army, which protects the society from external aggression. Political functionaries are recruited from the upper class and thus reflect an inherently conservative tradition which is gauged to preserve the status quo.

Scholars and priests are another integral

[7] See, e.g., Morton H. Fried, "Some Preliminary Considerations of Larger Units in Chinese Social Organization," *Transactions of the New York Academy of Sciences*, Ser. 2, **11** (1949), 121–126; Roger Le Tourneau, *Fès: Avant le Protectorat* (Casablanca: Société Marocaine de Librairie et d'Édition, 1949). The latter study, which has received no formal recognition by sociologists in this country, is a most detailed description of a feudal city.

[8] An illuminating discussion of personal attributes in a feudal order may be found in Cornelius Osgood, *The Koreans and Their Culture* (New York; Ronald Press Co., 1951), Ch. 8. This discusses the city of Seoul at the end of the nineteenth century.

element of the elite. Usually they merge into one group, for the educational and religious institutions are characteristically identical. In addition, some of these individuals may be political bureaucrats. The scholar's prime qualification is his knowledge of the sacred writings and traditions of the past; these govern the actions of the present. Memorization and understanding of the ancient thought-ways are preconditions for his assumption of a role in the highly institutionalized educational system. Scholarship is notable for its compiling and preserving qualities and not for any degree of originality. This aspect of the typology is empirically attested by the characteristics of such groups as the Chinese literati, the Indian Brahmins, and the medieval European clergy.

The scholar-priests perform an important function as official carriers of the classical written tradition which provides the social system with a sophisticated and elaborate justification for its existence and continued survival. Inconsistencies (present in all societies) are explained away. Through the sacred writings a continuity is achieved and the past more easily retained. This is not possible among the folk, whose history is perpetuated solely by oral transmission. The ideology of the sacred writings, by standardizing the action patterns of the elite, also establishes solidarity over a broad geographic area. As a result, the homogeneity of the upper class is typically greater than that of the masses.[9] Finally, the scholar-priests' existence as members of the elite brings about a striking divergence of their religious actions from those of the masses, who comprehend little of the philosophical basis of the religion they practice.

Landlords often constitute part of the elite class—for example, in China and in medieval Europe. But the landlord fac-

tion per se is not an essential component of feudalism as conceived herein. At times the political bureaucrats assume functions similar to those of the landlords; this occurred in India before the arrival of the British. The strength of the landlord stems from his direct control over the peasantry and concomitantly over the surplus food supply. Finally, other special groups may comprise the elite; for example, in Japan prior to the Meiji Restoration the topmost position of prestige and power was commanded by the military, or *samurai*, but some of these also doubled as governmental leaders.

Economically and politically the elite class dominates the mass populace. The latter supply the ruling minority with food, goods, and services but receive little in return. The trading relations of the city, therefore, are not with the countryside but with other towns, sometimes in quite distant regions. The relationship between the upper stratum and the masses is not entirely one-sided, however. Guidance is offered in the "moral" or religious sphere—the elite's ideal patterns are those emulated by the masses. Protection from outside attack and conquest is also the responsibility of the upper stratum. But more concrete functions may be performed—for example, the Chinese bureaucrats had an important duty in water control, chiefly for purposes of irrigation.

The peasants are not the only components of the masses. Characteristic of a feudal economic system is handicraft manufacturing based on a household economy. This requires skilled artisans. Most typically they reside in the towns, although some may be village-dwellers, where commonly they are also part-time farmers. The characteristic organizational units of artisans in the towns are guilds, each of which embraces a different occupational grouping: potters, weavers, metal workers, and carpenters, among others.

Not only do the guilds maintain a monopolistic control over recruitment through the apprenticeship system, but they also establish the norms of work. Furthermore, the actions of the members

---

[9] On this point see E. Shouby, "The Influence of the Arabic Language on the Psychology of the Arabs," *Middle East Journal*, 5 (1951), 284–302, and Gerald F. Winfield, *China: The Land and the People* (New York: William Sloane Associates, Inc., 1948), p. 184.

are prescribed down to the family level; in time of crisis the guild functions as a welfare agency. The artisans are instrumental in providing the elite with the luxury goods and services for the "conspicuous consumption" which clearly differentiates the latter from the disadvantaged members in the society.

Finally, another group within the feudal order must be considered. Typically, a small minority (or minorities) reside in the feudal society but occupy a marginal position, not being fully integrated into the social system. These persons are ranked even lower than peasants and artisans. Feudal orders often have scorned the merchant: he usually has too much contact with foreigners and is therefore a transmitter of "dangerous" ideas. Other outsiders have been slaves, the "untouchables" of India and the Eta class of Japan. These groups provide special goods and perform those services considered degrading by members of the morally valued occupations. In this way, they are functionally important to the entire society, particularly the elite.

To recapitulate: folk and feudal societies are similar in that both are relatively static and possess a sacred-value orientation. As such, the action patterns of their members are predictable, for there exists a minimum of internal conflict and disorder. In their structural arrangements, however, they differ perceptibly.

Implications for Social Change

What are the implications of separating folk and feudal societies for sociological in-terpretation? A clearer understanding of contemporary social change follows from treating these as distinct social systems.

That industrial urbanization is bringing about change in the sociocultural organization of many societies is obvious.[10] But the resistance of the feudalistic structure to this process has been equally significant. Recent evidence for this is overwhelming: only a few exemplary cases are presented here. Authorities on China have often commented on how the elite in that country during the twentieth century has held firmly to the Confucianist ideology, the feudalistic governmental structure, the traditional family system, and even the feudal economic organization, although the forces making for change have been formidable.[11] (That the present Chinese regime will eradicate the feudalistic past is most doubtful.) And the tenacity of feudalism in Europe has only recently come to public consciousness. France is a case in point, although other countries (e.g., Germany and Italy) might also be cited. Despite the fact that France has experienced industrial urbanization for over a century, many feudalistic institutions have survived: a kind of handicraft system is still an important element in the economy, the pro-monarchical group continues to reassert itself in one form or another, and the feudalistic church and family systems are still in evidence.[12] All this has fostered the schisms and conflicts so typical of France since the Revolution.

Even the material coming to light on Russia reveals that the Soviets, though

[10] The industrial-urban process is not the only factor which has induced change in "backward" areas. The state system per se, including colonial government, could be considered. Yet, to deal primarily with industrialization and urbanization is not unreasonable, even though these are being carried forward by the state. It is the industrial factor which makes the present-day state so potent.

[11] See, e.g., Marion J. Levy, Jr., and Shih Kuoheng, *The Rise of the Modern Chinese Business Class* (New York: Institute of Pacific Relations, 1949), pp. 8–17, 34 ff.; John King Fairbank, *The United States and China* (Cam-bridge: Harvard University Press, 1948), pp. 240 ff.; *Far Eastern Culture and Society* ("Princeton University Bicentennial Conferences," Ser. 2, Conference 7) (Princeton: Princeton University Press, 1946), p. 21.

[12] For two excellent discussions of this subject see: Edward Mead Earle (ed.), *Modern France* (Princeton: Princeton University Press, 1951), esp. John E. Sawyer, "Strains in the Social Structure of Modern France," Ch. 17; Donald C. McKay, *The United States and France* (Cambridge: Harvard University Press, 1951), Chs. 7 and 8.

using forceful persuasion, have found it difficult to subdue at least one of the feudalistic subsystems within their borders —a Moslem group in Central Asia. The persistence of the Moslem religion, with its month of fasting (Ramadan), and the latent power of the old aristocracy have served as stumbling blocks to the efficient industrialization of this regime.[13] (As a matter of fact, the Soviet power complex is itself a reincarnation, loosely speaking, of the feudal regime which existed prior to the 1917 revolution.) Evidence for the survival of feudalistic patterns in the Middle East and India[14] is also readily obtainable.

On the other hand, the rapid disintegration and, at times, loss of cultural identity of folk, or "primitive," societies is common knowledge. Examples can be found in the Americas and in Australia, Africa, and various parts of Asia. Specifically, India comes to mind. There the feudal order has maintained itself, whereas the tribal units, much to the concern of many anthropologists and government officials, are being "detribalized."[15]

[13] Mark Alexander, "Tensions in Soviet Central Asia," *The Twentieth Century*, **150** (1951), 192–200.

[14] See, e.g., Lewis V. Thomas and Richard N. Frye, *The United States and Turkey and Iran* (Cambridge: Harvard University Press, 1951); Halford L. Hoskins, "Point Four with Reference to the Middle East," *Annals of the American Academy of Political and Social Science*, **268** (1950), 85–95; J. A. Curran, Jr., *Militant Hinduism in Indian Politics: A Study of the R.S.S.* (New York: Institute of Pacific Relations, 1951); Radhakamad Mukerjee *et al.*, *Inter-Caste Tensions: A Survey under the Auspices of UNESCO* (Lucknow, India: Lucknow University Press, 1951); Kingsley Davis, *The Population of India and Pakistan* (Princeton: Princeton University Press, 1951), *passim*.

[15] D. N. Majumdar, *Races and Cultures of India* (2nd rev. ed.; Lucknow, India: Universal Publishers, Ltd., 1950), pp. 97, 179, 187; J. H. Hutton, "Primitive Tribes" in L. S. S. O'Malley (ed.), *Modern India and the West* (London: Oxford University Press, 1941), pp. 415–444; and various issues of the *Eastern Anthropologist*, published in Lucknow, India, esp. Vol. 3, September 1949.

The question now arises: How is the feudalistic social structure able to survive in the face of industrial urbanization? For one thing, the elite strives to retain its traditional advantages at all cost. The elite is assumed to have "everything to lose and nothing to gain" from social change. The following discussion points to some of the conditions which make this resistance possible.

The upper stratum's ability to ward off the consequences of industrial urbanization first arises from its command of technical intelligence. To insure the continuance of the society, positions in the complex governmental and educational institutions must be staffed; the alternative is chaos. A modicum of order must be maintained by all ruling groups if they are to preserve their positions of power (this is true even of revolutionary elements). Reliance upon the feudal functionaries who possess the necessary knowledge to sustain a degree of efficient organization is therefore mandatory. As a result, feudal political or educational bureaucrats, because of this strategic location, are able to veto (either formally or informally) any proposed radical change.[16]

The survival of the elite, particularly within governmental and educational and/ or religious institutions, is greatly enhanced by the prevailing language patterns. The speech of the upper class markedly differs from that of the folk. But more important is the nature of the written language—the medium by which officialdom conducts its affairs. It may be a completely different one from that spoken by the masses—for example, Latin in medieval Europe—or, as

[16] An interesting situation has evolved in the case of colonial rule. Inasmuch as members of the elite have commanded the important governmental and educational posts, their contact with the foreign rulers has been far more extensive than that of the masses. The upper-class individuals, especially those who are able to accommodate somewhat, gain access to the implements of the foreigner's power—education, technological knowledge, etc. Actually, this reinforces their status and increases their possibilities for survival; this in turn aids in the preservation of feudal traits.

in the case of the Chinese and Japanese scripts, most difficult to master. In any event, knowledge of the literary language requires much leisure—the prerogative of the elite. Few of the folk are able to gain access to the sacred knowledge possessed by the political and intellectual leaders; thus, criticism or rejection of the elite's moral ideals is quite unlikely. Through this monopoly of the written language the elite seals itself off from the masses. And these written languages have a remarkable survival quality. Latin is a striking example. In addition, the Arabic literary language and the Chinese and Japanese scripts display an inflexibility which assures their continued usage for some time to come, despite the various attempts at reform.[17]

The written tradition, especially as embodied in the sacred literature, is the product of the privileged group. As such, it prescribes the ideal action patterns in family, religious, and interpersonal situations. Many of these rules are carried over into the urban-industrial society through enacted legislation. For example, many of the law norms which are applied to the contemporary industrial-urban communities of India stem from the sacred writings of the Hindus and thus perpetuate the ideal norms not of the lower castes but of the Brahmins.[18] This pattern has no correlate in folk orders. Among the folk, once the oral traditions are lost, they can never be recovered.

Although it is difficult to express the following in strictly objective terms, research reveals that the superiority-inferiority structure is tenacious. Possibly one reason for this is the rationalization it receives in the religious writings. Yet, whatever the explanation, empirical materials lend credence to the "toughness" of this structural nexus in a society. In Japan after World War II, lower-class individuals when asked by pollsters for their opinions would refer the interviewer to upper-class leaders who would speak for them.[19] Employer-employee relations in feudal countries now undergoing industrialization also reflect the continuance of earlier traditions. In southeast Asia, China, and Japan, the employer-laborer relationship exhibits a direct correspondence to the elite-mass system of feudalism.[20] And the prestige of the European nobility has died slowly, even in a country as democratic as England.

Up to this point, only resistance to the industrial-urban complex has been examined. An objection could be raised: Did not the elite in Japan actually instigate the industrialization of the nation? The rebuttal to such an argument is that industrial urbanization was only partially accepted. Many of the value orientations and structural arrangements which ordinarily are correlated with it were summarily rejected. The feudalistic ruling group who retained control of the governmental bureaucracy impeded the "modernization" of women's role in society and the development of a small-family system. Consequently, an overpopulation problem was fostered which may ultimately threaten the whole industrial-urban structure. Furthermore, the state was able to perpetuate many feudal traditions by maintaining rigid control over the educational system and by keeping the workers in a position of subservience.[21]

[17] Shouby, *op. cit.*; John De Francis, *Nationalism and Language Reform in China* (Princeton: Princeton University Press, 1950).

[18] Benjamin Lindsay, "Law," in O'Malley, *op. cit.*, pp. 107–137; Dinshah Fardunji Mulla, *Principles of Hindu Law* (10th ed.; Calcutta: Eastern Law House, Ltd., 1946). Ch. 2.

[19] Frederick S. Hulse, "Some Effects of the War upon Japanese Society," *Far Eastern Quarterly*, 7 (1947), 37.

[20] See, e.g., Bruno Lasker, *Human Bondage in Southeast Asia* (Chapel Hill: University of North Carolina Press, 1950), *passim*; John Campbell Pelzel, "Social Stratification in Japanese Urban Economic Life" (unpublished Ph.D. dissertation, Harvard University, Department of Social Relations, 1950); Shih Kuo-heng, *China Enters the Machine Age* (ed. and trans. Hsiao-tung Fei and Francis L. K. Hsu) (Cambridge: Harvard University Press, 1944), pp. 116 ff.

[21] Some works discussing the persistence of feudalism in Japan and its effects are: Nobutaka Ike, *The Beginnings of Political Democracy in Japan* (Baltimore: Johns Hopkins Press, 1950), Parts III and IV; Hugh Borton (ed.); *Japan*

Recent happenings in a number of folk orders testify to the significance of an elite class. The ability of "primitive" societies to adjust to, or frequently combat, industrial urbanization and the kind of social organization which ordinarily accompanies it is dependent upon the development of an elite which is sufficiently trained to comprehend the implications of what is transpiring. This is strikingly evident in Negro Africa. In the Belgian Congo the government contributed toward the formation of an educated *noire élite*; only then did formal resistance to "modernization" arise.[22] And the incipient opposition of the natives in South Africa and in British West Africa[23] is being led by the educated among them. Only these are able to utilize such mediums as books, newspapers, and the radio—and thus publicize the "evils" of the prevailing social change. In other words, the growth of an institutional apparatus, one not found among the folk, is essential if this society is to preserve its identity. Interestingly enough, anthropologists may place themselves in a position of a "neo-elite" when studying "primitive" peoples. For only after the folk customs have been recorded is it possible for governments to make adjustments in their policies to prevent the disappearance of those groups which lack an educated and political elite.[24]

Among the masses in the feudal order the artisans or craftsmen constitute a group which has a vested interest in keeping the situation stabilized. Although in some countries their resistance has not been noticeably effective, nevertheless the artisans play a role in checking the diffusion of the industrial-urban complex. For if and when it occurs, it does so at the expense of this group. Should a society desire to maintain a minimum of order, the artisans must not be destroyed too rapidly. Furthermore, they are at times active in repelling the intrusion of the new type of economic system.[25]

Second, modern feudal societies are typically overpopulated. In contrast, folk societies are by nature small and are not faced with this problem. Kingsley Davis[26] has offered what is perhaps the most plausible set of explanations showing how overpopulation acts as a deterrent to industrial-urban expansion. Overpopulation, for one thing, focuses economic effort on consumption goods rather than on heavy industry, discounting future for present advantage. The situation of low capitalization is apparent first in agriculture, where land becomes increasingly scarce and expensive. Moreover, a high ratio of farm population to agricultural resources results in the production of food crops for sustenance rather than export crops for investment surplus. As a result of overpopulation, labor is immediately cheaper than machinery, which discourages the rationalization of industry. Finally, rapid population growth implies a high fertility and a somewhat lower, though still high, death rate. This creates an unusually heavy burden of young dependents.

One of the most crucial problems now

[*footnote 21 continued*
(Ithaca: Cornell University Press, 1950), esp. Chs. 7 and 12; Warren S. Thompson, "Future Adjustments of Population to Resources in Japan," in *Modernization Programs in Relation to Human Resources and Population Problems* (New York: Milbank Memorial Fund, 1950), pp. 142–153.

[22] See recent issues of the journal *La Voix du Congolais*, particularly Vol. **6** (1950).
[23] Ellen Hellmann (ed.), *Handbook on Race Relations in South Africa* (Cape Town: Oxford University Press, 1949), Ch. 20; also see various issues of the journal *Race Relations* (published

in Johannesburg, South Africa), esp. Vol. **16**, No. 3 (1949), and Vernon McKay, "Nationalism in British West Africa," *Foreign Policy Reports*, **24** (1948), 2–11.
[24] This is apparent in the United States government-sponsored surveys of nonliterate peoples of Oceania after World War II, as well as in studies of American Indians during the last fifty years.
[25] Levy and Shih Kuo-heng, *op. cit.*, p. 35; R. G. Kakade, *A Socio-Economic Survey of Weaving Communities in Sholapur* (Poona: Gokhale Institute of Politics and Economics, 1947), *passim*.
[26] Davis, *op. cit.*, pp. 218–219.

faced by many countries, especially those in Asia, is how to combat the great inertia inherent in overpopulation. This is further complicated by the resistance of the feudal elite, who impede the process of industrial urbanization sufficiently to facilitate a progressive increase in the population.

An ideal typology has been constructed in contradistinction to that of the folk. One essential of the former is the two-class system—a small elite supported by a large peasant population. Even more significant are the existent and highly developed state and educational and/or religious institutions—through dominant positions in these structures the elite class controls the society. The feudal manufacturing system is much more elaborate than that within the folk order: for example, handicraft workers are present. All this implies an extensive division of labor. Although both feudal and folk societies have a sacred-value orientation and exhibit a minimum of internal change, their social structures are markedly divergent. An understanding of the effects of the industrial-urbanization process in many areas of the world is possible only if these two typologies are separated; too often the distinctions have not been emphasized.

Other implications stem from the foregoing discussion; only a few are mentioned here. First, many sociologists and anthropologists have given undue emphasis to the local community, especially when this is a mere segment of the larger sociocultural setting. Community-bound research stresses the family unit and neglects the study of governmental and educational institutions, through which the family necessarily must work in order to achieve its power and influence. From this it follows that, methodologically, the lumping-together of folk and feudal societies is often not justified. Doubts might legitimately be expressed concerning the validity of such a technique as the "cross-cultural survey" when generalizations are attempted beyond the area of family or kinship system.

Finally, more attention needs to be devoted to the effects of industrial urbanization upon feudalistic societies. Few problems are of greater significance. In Asia, particularly, conflicts of great magnitude have been evidenced as the industrial-urban complex has spread into that region. Europe has been experiencing a similar fate for many decades.

Obviously, despite the resistance of the feudal structure, the industrialization and urbanization process has been moving forward. However, instead of encompassing the whole society (which is now almost the case in the United States), in the feudal order the industrial-urbanized society will in all probability be superimposed upon the existing structure, with the latter remaining to some degree intact. Bifurcation within the society would therefore still persist, although in quite different form and with quite different effects. This possibility has found empirical expression in such countries as France and Italy, where enclaves of peasants still perpetuate the feudal organization. Overpopulation combined with the resistance to change inherent among the elite have contributed to this situation. A similar co-existence of two societies was deliberately planned by the Netherlands government in its rule over the Netherlands East Indies. The Dutch envisaged a "plural" economy, which also meant a bifurcated social structure.[27] Industrial urbanization has thus led to a modification rather than a destruction of feudal societies (folk orders, in contrast, seem to be disappearing). Though any attempt at generalization is fraught with difficulties, such an adjustment in feudal countries is not unlikely for a long time to come. But whatever the outcome, the imposition of the industrial-urban society upon an already highly developed social organization such as that found in feudalism will unquestionably be accompanied by disorganization, severe strains, and conflict.

[27] J. S. Furnivall, *Netherlands India* (Cambridge: Cambridge University Press, 1939), esp. pp. 446 ff.

SOME CULTURAL AND PERSONAL CHARACTERISTICS OF THE LESS DEVELOPED AREAS

Philip M. Hauser

Perhaps the most significant development of our generation, transcending in its import even the control of nuclear energy, has been the emergence of an almost universal aspiration for higher levels of living, together with a diversity of programs for accelerating economic development in the less developed areas of the world. The efforts of the economically backward nations, many of which have only recently gained or regained their independence, to achieve these objectives hold forth what can be exciting opportunities for research into social change. One way to approach this general problem is suggested by the title of this paper. For an analysis of cultural and personal impediments to economic development constitutes one way of focusing on the cultural and personal aspects of the economically less developed societies to establish benchmarks against which change can be observed and analyzed.[1]

SOURCE. Philip M. Hauser, "Cultural and Personal Obstacles to Economic Development in the Less Developed Areas," *Human Organization*, 18, 78–84, Summer 1959. Reprinted by permission of The Society for Applied Anthropology. This article was an invited paper presented at the annual meeting of the American Sociological Society, September 1956, Detroit, Michigan.

[1] The materials which follow are intended more to serve as a basis for setting forth hypotheses for intensive study rather than to report definitive findings. Much of what is presented is based on observations made over a period of some five years, during which the writer spent approximately two years on specific technical assistance assignments and in general travel in the less developed parts of the world, especially in South and Southeastern Asia.

Cultural and personal obstacles in the less developed areas of South and Southeast Asia to the achievement of national aspirations to raise levels of living may be considered in two categories—namely, as elements of the colonial heritage of a number of the countries, and as elements of their indigenous cultures.

The Colonial Heritage

Aspects of the colonial heritage of many of the countries in South and Southeast Asia which appear to impede economic development, include (1) truncated social orders, (2) pluralistic societies, (3) over-urbanization, (4) resurgent nationalism, and (5) mass disillusionment in respect of the timing of economic development.

TRUNCATED SOCIAL ORDERS

Most of the countries in South and Southeast Asia which gained political independence since the end of World War II have in common not only political orders but, also, economic and social orders which have in large part been stripped of their previous leadership. Independence has necessarily meant a change in political and governmental leaders. But the exodus of previous heads of political and governmental agencies has in considerable measure also been accompanied by an exodus of leaders in a broad range of economic and social spheres. These countries have with independence suddenly become bereft of leaders in industry, commerce, education; and in professional and technical fields, in general, as well as of a major part of their experienced governmental and political personnel.

Although there is considerable variability among the nations in South and Southeast Asia in this respect, all of them are greatly handicapped by the dearth of adequately trained and experienced leadership. The situation is worse in the areas which have won independence from the French: Viet-Nam, Laos, and Cambodia; and the Dutch: Indonesia, than in the areas which have achieved liberation from the British: India, Burma, Pakistan, and Ceylon and from the United States: the Philippines.

It may be pointed out that none of these countries has ever had adequate numbers of highly trained and experienced personnel to meet the needs generated by their present national aspirations. The leadership in economic and social, as well as political, affairs provided from the outside under the colonial system, however, constituted a large proportion of total national leadership and virtually all the leadership in these sectors of society associated with Western civilization. In consequence, with the expulsion of leaders identified with the colonial system, the nations of South and Southeast Asia are in the main ill-prepared for the conduct of their own affairs and particularly so for the undertaking of extensive programs of economic development. Since it requires at least a human generation to produce a *cadre* of well-trained and experienced personnel, even when adequate resources and facilities for such training are available, it is probable that the less developed areas in South and Southeast Asia will be badly handicapped for many years to come by the absence of such human resources.

PLURALISTIC SOCIETIES

A number of countries in this region, and especially the countries on the Southeastern Asian peninsula, contain relatively large exogenous population groupings which have never been assimilated—culturally, economically, or politically. This is particularly true, of course, of large numbers of Chinese and Indian emigrants.[2]

The nations in this area tend to be pluralistic in several senses. Disparate social orders are to be found not only in the existence of unassimilated immigrants but also often in the diversity of the indigenous ethnic, linguistic, and religious groupings. Moreover, the immigrants may themselves be split into diverse social orders on ethnic or religious grounds as, for example, in the case of the Indians in Burma who include both the Hindu and the Muslim. Pluralism may also be said to exist in an economic sense. This is evident generally both in the great gap between such Western communities as still remain in this part of the world and the remainder of the economy; and in the gap among the indigenous groups between those who participate in the monetary, as distinguished from the subsistence, sectors of the economy.[3]

Pluralism is manifest in the structure and organization of the Asian city.[4] The large

2 E.g., Cora DuBois, "Cultural Facets of South Asian Regionalism," Phillips Talbot (ed.), *South Asia in the World Today*, University of Chicago Press, Chicago, 1950; E. H. G. Doby, *Southeast Asia*, Wiley & Sons, New York, 1950, especially Part III; Cora DuBois, *Social Forces in Southeast Asia*, University of Minnesota Press, St. Paul, 1949.

3 J. H. Boeke, *Economics and Economic Policy of Dual Societies*, New York, 1953; see also Benjamin Higgins, "The 'Dualistic Theory' of Underdeveloped Areas," *Economic Development and Cultural Change*, 4 (January 1956), 99–115.

4 UNESCO, *Report by the Director-General at the Joint UN/UNESCO Seminar on Urbanization in the ECAFE Region*, UNESCO/SS/10, Paris, December 1956, pp. 8 ff and pp. 19 ff; Institute of Social Research, University of Indonesia, "Djakarta, A Study of Urbanization," in UNESCO, *The Social Implications of Industrialization and Urbanization*, UNESCO Research Center, Calcutta, 1956; H. J. Heeren, "Human and Social Aspects of Urbanization in Asia: Some Socio-Cultural Effects of Urbanization in Djakarta," UNESCO/SS/Conf. Urb/8; E/CN.11/Urb/8, prepared for Joint UN/UNESCO Seminar on Urbanization in the ECAFE Region, Bangkok, August 1956.

city in South and Southeast Asia tends, in a fundamental sense, to be a composite or an agglomeration of discrete worlds. There is, to begin with, a major and quite apparent unbridged gap between that part of the city which is Western built and that built by the native population. The difference in physical structures represented by Western-type masonry and by indigenous construction of bamboo and thatch materials is a highly visible index of disparate worlds.

Within the framework of this visible physical dichotomization of the city are to be found a congeries of quite separate social and population groupings. The disparate character of these social worlds transcends the usual conception of "segregation" in the Western metropolis. The indigenous population groupings in the Asian city often comprise village groups which in many respects retain their "folk" characteristics. The large city in Asia, unlike its Western counterpart, is in large measure an agglomeration of folk societies and is thus inconsistent with prevalent Western dichotomizations of "folk" and "urban" society.[5]

By reason of the pluralistic character of many of these Asian nations, collective behavior toward common goals is often difficult. The newly independent nations are faced with the need for achieving unification and nationhood in fact, as well as in political form, as a prerequisite to unified and effective action toward their national economic and social aspirations.

OVERURBANIZATION

Nations in South and Southeast Asia, particularly the smaller ones, tend to have a "great" or "primate" city, often five or ten times the size of the second city. The great primate cities were developed as entrepots serving as a link between the imperial Western power and the local population in the colonial system.[6] Thus, in contrast with the West, the large city in Asia is not a product of national industrialization. The large population concentrations in the great city, as well as in the lesser cities, in this part of the world are more the result of "push" factors due to the low level of rural living or conditions of physical insecurity, than as in the Western experience of "pull" factors represented by job opportunities and higher levels of living.[7]

Many of the cities in Asia are today swelled with populations streaming to them because of the low land-population ratio and rural poverty, or the disruption and disorganization produced by the last war and its aftermath. Asian cities are choked with refugees who have swelled their populations out of proportion to their economic development.

Asian nations may be said to be overurbanized in the sense that larger proportions of their populations live in urban places than is justified by their degree of economic development. At comparable stages in economic development, the more developed Western countries had smaller proportions of their population in cities; or at comparable levels of urbanization the Western nations had much greater proportions of their labor force engaged in nonagricultural occupations.[8]

Overurbanization tends to impede economic development in a number of ways. For one thing, it tends to call for great

[5] Philip M. Hauser, "World and Asian Urbanization in Relation to Economic Development and Social Change," UNESCO/SS/Conf. Urb/10; E/CN.11/Urb/10, prepared for Seminar on Urbanization in the ECAFE Region, Bangkok, August 1956, pp. 38–39.

[6] Mark Jefferson, "The Law of the Primate City," *Geographical Review* (April 1939); Norton S. Ginsburg, "The Great City in Southeast Asia" in Philip M. Hauser (ed.), *World Urbanism*, special issue of *American Journal of Sociology*, **60** (March 1955), 452–462.
[7] UNESCO, *Report by the Director-General, op. cit.*, pp. 18 ff.
[8] E.g., see Kingsley Davis and Hilda Hertz Golden, "Urbanization and the Development of Pre-Industrial Areas," *Economic Development and Cultural Change*, **3** (October 1954), 16 ff.

capital outlays in urban overhead, including housing, utilities, sanitation, and transport and communication—at a level incommensurate with the degree of economic development. Second, it tends to result in undue concentration of industrialization in the great cities at the cost, perhaps, of potential diseconomies. Third, it tends to result in disproportionate allocation of limited resources to developments in urban areas relative to rural areas when agricultural development should perhaps have priority in the total plan of economic development.

Thus, the city in the less developed areas of Asia, unlike its Western counterpart, may operate as an obstacle to, rather than being a symbol of, economic development. Indeed, economic development is required to provide the Asian city with a sound economic base, in contrast to the situation in the West where the city is the product of economic development.[9]

RESURGENT NATIONALISM

Newly won independence, in most cases after long years of bitter political struggle and in some cases after bloody revolutions, has resulted in widespread and intense nationalistic feelings in South and Southeast Asia. This resurgent nationalism carries with it some manifestations which undoubtedly operate to retard the desired advance in levels of living.

It is understandable, in light of the experience of many of these countries as subjugated colonies, that their exultation in achieving independence is accompanied by attitudes of hostility, suspicion, and distrust toward the Western powers and, often, toward what has been a dominant and sometimes domineering white race. Anticolonial and anti-Western feelings,

moreover, are accompanied by attempts to rid themselves of vestiges of Western imperialism, which are in some instances actually obstructing their efforts to achieve higher levels of living. The understandable tendency, for example, to use their own language and to drop the foreign language, English, Dutch, or French, as the case may be, tends to retard higher education. The training of professional, technical, and other leaders is impeded because the Oriental languages generally do not contain the scientific and technical vocabulary of Western civilization, and because, usually, neither the basic works of research nor textbooks are available in the Asian languages. In a number of countries, college students are already showing signs of being handicapped in their efforts to pursue higher education because Western languages have been relegated to relatively minor places in elementary and secondary education.

Strong nationalistic feelings, curiously enough, have also directly tended to impair the achievement of national unity. Dominant national groups which have taken over the political leadership in the new and independent countries have tended to favor their own ethnic or religious elements, sometimes at the expense of their indigenous minority groups as well as of foreign immigrants. Such attitudes, and often discriminatory behavior in respect of employment, foreign trade licenses, contract awards, business permits, and the like, tend to reinforce the perpetuation of the pluralistic society and impede unified collective effort toward their common economic development goals.

Finally, it may be observed that resurgent nationalism is often accompanied by a nostalgic romanticism—a desire to restore the past. Although efforts to revert to the precolonial state are generally restricted to traditional, cultural, religious, and artistic and aesthetic forms of behavior, traditional value systems, which are not always consonant with economic development goals, tend to be reinforced.

[9] UNESCO, *Report of Director-General, op. cit.*, pp. 4 ff. Also ECAFE Secretariat, "Economic Causes and Implications of Urbanization in the Recent Experience of Countries in Asia and the Far East," UNESCO/SS/Conf. Urb/2; E/CN.11/Urb/2.

MASS DISILLUSIONMENT

As another obstruction to economic development, traceable to the colonial heritage, the increasingly evident mass disillusionment of the population with the rate of economic progress may be cited. The peoples of the less developed areas of the world have for a number of decades been led to believe by their leaders that the collapse of the colonial system, with its attendant national autonomy, would mean rapid increases in economic development and levels of living. A number of these countries have had their independence now for almost a decade and the leaders, as well as the mass populations, are showing increasing signs of disillusionment with the anticipated rapidity of development. It is being learned, the hard way, that the path to higher levels of living is not an easy one, and that the obstacles to national aspirations for economic advance include a great many things other than the imperial system.[10]

Disappointment with the rate of progress in economic development may itself tend further to retard such development. There is a tendency, for example, for governments, in response to political pressures, disproportionately to allocate their limited resources to forms of "social" investment rather than "productive" investment— that is, to such things as health programs, improved housing, education, and consumer goods, rather than to improvements in agricultural technology, industry, and the like. The line of demarcation between social investment and productive investment, to be sure, is not always a clear one. However, to the extent that resources are allocated to meet the current needs of poverty-stricken populations or to develop labor-intensive industry instead of modern industrial plants, such allocations retard the

improvement of long-run productivity and hence retard economic development itself.

Elements of Indigenous Culture

Barriers to the achievement of national economic aspirations in the countries in South and Southeast Asia are also found in their indigenous cultures. Among the more important of these elements are (1) value systems which conflict with material aspirations, (2) highly stratified societies with a relatively small but powerful elite and minimal social mobility, (3) age prestige and deference, (4) prescientific mentality, (5) atomism in interpersonal and intergroup relations, and (6) actual or potential demographic imbalance.

VALUE SYSTEMS

The traditional value systems of the peoples in South and Southeast Asia are in the main carried in the Hindu, Islamic, or Buddhist religiocultural systems. Despite the impact of colonialization and the presence of a limited veneer of Western technology and culture, the mass populations of this area have in the main retained their traditional values. The ingredients of the value systems are in apparent conflict with the new national aspirations for economic advancement. For example, some of the cultural elements which appear to be in conflict with technological development and the attainment of higher levels of living are: the emphasis on spiritual rather than material values; the stress laid on the importance of after-life or future existences, as compared with the present existence; the pressure for conformance with, and often intolerance with deviations from, traditional patterns of thought and action; the relatively rigid definitions of roles of members of the family, the village, and the social order at large; the parochialism of the diverse racial, ethnic, linguistic, and territorial groups; the familistic orientation; the tendency to place savings in traditional channels of investments, including non-productive investments like jewels and precious stones; and the allocation of

[10] E.g., Justus M. van der Kroef, "Economic Development in Indonesia: Some Social and Cultural Impediments," *Economic Development and Cultural Change,* **4** (January 1956), 116–133.

relatively large amounts of life-space and energy to traditional cultural and religious rituals, ceremonies, and festivals.

The traditional value systems do not provide the population with incentive for material gain or expectations of advancement based on merit and application. The prestige vocations and occupations tend to be those in government, religion, and agriculture—not the types of occupations identified with economic development. That is, occupations in commerce, industry, and many of the professions and the services have yet to achieve prestige and attract competent people. Moreover, the traditional value systems do not provide the person with general orientation of the type necessary in a monetary, as distinguished from a subsistence, economy, including conceptions of work as a segmental area of activity requiring fixed time, place, and an employer-employee nexus.

Although these and other elements of the value systems of the Eastern cultures may well retard economic development, it must be recognized that there is a tendency among Western students, perhaps, to over-emphasize the extent to which this may be the case. For example, the conclusion that the nonexistence of certain Western values is probably an explanation of the relatively low level of technical development, is undoubtedly based on tenuous assumptions. There is a long gap between finding certain values identified with Western forms of technological and economic organization and the assumption that such values are prerequisites for economic development in South and Southeast Asia.

More specifically, it is often contended that basic differences in outlook, ideology, and values in the Protestant ethic, and the Hindu, Buddhist, and Islamic traditions are of paramount importance in accounting for differences in the economic development of the West and the East.[11] The Western outlook as embodied in the Protestant ethic has been characterized as consisting essentially of rationalism, willingness to defer immediate for greater future gratification, stress on achievement and success rather than on status and prestige, a cosmopolitan rather than a parochial outlook, and an utilitarian and impersonal rather than sentimental and personal basis for interpersonal relations. It is, of course, a moot question as to whether the Western outlook, so characterized, is a consequence or antecedent of economic development or, as is likely the case, something of both; and also as to whether these elements really are necessary conditions of economic development. It is conceivable that economic development in the East may be possible with, or may produce, a quite different outlook; and that much of what has been written by the Western student on this subject may be a form of ethnocentrism or the result of premature generalization based on limited observation restricted to Western experience. Certainly this is an area which is rich in its opportunity for additional research.

STRATIFIED SOCIETIES

The countries in South and Southeast Asia have highly stratified social orders, the most complex of which is the caste system in India, now legally, if not actually, abolished. The societies tend to be divided into an upper and lower economic class, with a very small or virtually nonexistent middle class. At the top is a small but very powerful elite; at the bottom the predominant portion of the population—in general,

[11] E.g., Bert F. Hoselitz, "Non-Economic Barriers to Economic Developments," *Economic Development and Cultural Change*, No. 1 (March 1952), 14 ff. The classic treatment of this question is to be found in Max Weber, *The Protestant Ethic and the Spirit of Capitalism* (translated by Talcott Parsons), George Allen & Unwin, Ltd., London, 1930. See also Talcott Parsons, *The Structure of Social Action*, The Free Press, Glencoe, Ill., 1945, pp. 500–578. For a criticism of some aspects of the literature, see Philip M. Hauser, *op. cit.*, p. 41 and footnote 58; and Milton Singer, "Cultural Values in India's Economic Development," *The Annals of the American Academy of Political and Social Science* (May 1956), 81–91.

a mass peasant population together with a relatively small proportion of urban residents. These societies evidence very little social mobility. The social, economic, and political status of the person tends to be primarily a function of birth and tradition.

The relatively rigid stratification of Asian society seems to retard economic development in a number of ways. First, it undoubtedly has an adverse effect on individual incentive conducive to economic advance. Second, it tends to restrict the access of persons with ability to education, training, and opportunity consonant with effective utilization of human resources. There is a widespread tendency to restrict education, technical training, and the better vocational opportunities to members of the elite. In consequence, such limited opportunities as exist for training both domestically and abroad through various scholarship, fellowship, and technical assistance programs are often made available on a nepotistic familial, village, ethnic, religious, or personal basis rather than strictly on merit.

Emphasis on democracy in a number of the newly independent nations is tending to undermine the traditional stratified order. During a transitional period which may include some decades to come, however, there is little doubt that rigid stratification and social immobility will tend to retard economic advance.

AGE DEFERENCE

Societies in South and Southeast Asia uniformly place a great premium on age. Seniority is often a major basis for status and prestige. The older person is regarded as a repository of the experience and knowledge of society and is treated with the utmost respect and deference. The privileges and priorities of seniority are in the main rigidly fixed and rarely impaired. This is particularly in evidence in those nations in which a government civil service has been established. A younger man must wait his turn for advancement. Greater competence on his part or incompetence

on the part of a senior officer is rarely an adequate basis for the replacement of an older by a younger person. As a result, the scarcity of skilled human resources to which reference has been made above is often made even more acute by inability of the culture to utilize such skills as are available.

There is increasing evidence that training and competence are taking priority over seniority and age, but it may be anticipated that for some time to come the relatively rigid age grading in the social orders of this part of the world will continue to operate as a barrier to effective utilization of human resources.

PRESCIENTIFIC MENTALITY

Not only the mass populations but, to a large extent, also the elite, including many who have been subjected to Western influence, have not acquired what might be termed a scientific outlook. That is, the culture of many of the nations in South and Southeast Asia carries in it notions inconsistent with the procedures and findings of science.

Among the mass populations adherence to ancient tradition and superstitious ways often directly interferes with economic advance. Widespread beliefs, fears, inhibitions, and behaviorisms generated by living in a universe deemed to be controlled by astrological, numerological, magical, animistic, and supernatural forces often preclude or compete with forms of thought and behavior consistent with technological and economic advance and a general orientation prepared to accept the methodology and fruits of science.

This prescientific mentality, however, it should be noted, often becomes compartmentalized in a manner so as not to interfere with the scientific outlook—even in the same person. But, belief in one's destiny, as foretold by the astrologer, palmist, or other type of seer may or may not be consistent with the development of incentive for economic advancement. Moreover, the amount of time and energy devoted to consultations, propitiations, or other prescientific behavior designed to influence or to control the universe is frequently a deterrent to persistent or effective productive activity.

ATOMISM

Another barrier to economic advance exists in the atomistic or "loose structure"[12] of some of the societies in this part of the world. Despite the widespread tendency to characterize preindustrial orders with relatively little urbanization as cohesive and integrated societies possessing "mechanical" solidarity, a number of the societies in South and Southeast Asia give evidence of individuation and the absence of group consciousness and solidarity. In societies in which the family, the village, the ethnic, religious, or linguistic group are much in evidence such an observation seems paradoxical. Yet, the atomism of some of these societies has been observed by others, as well as by the writer, and is manifest, often, in extremely egocentric behavior and the utter disregard for others or for the social order. Embree in his study of the Thai culture and Ryan and Straus in their investigation of Sinhalese society have been impressed with this same phenomenon. Embree referred to it as "loose structure"; Ryan and Straus have elaborated upon this concept and utilized it in their work.[13]

Without exploration of its genesis, this atomism or loose structure, which Ryan and Straus and, also, the writer believe to be associated particularly with the societies with Hinayana Buddhism (Ceylon, Burma, Thailand), it may be stated that it is manifest in a number of forms of behavior which tend to obstruct economic development. For example, one acute form of this phenomenon is evident in the extreme competition and often conflict for top position and complete control among the relatively few officials, professional men, or technicians in these societies. In situations where the basic problem is one of an inadequate number of skilled and competent persons and there is more to be done than the available personnel can possibly do, it is not uncommon to see bitter feuds and struggles in efforts to eliminate all competitors. Such struggles are manifest in many walks of life, including government, universities, and political and social organizations, as well as in the business world.

Atomism or loose structure is evident in many other ways. Seventeen specific manifestations of "looseness" are set forth by Embree for Thailand and corroborated by Ryan and Straus for Ceylon.[14] The atomistic behaviorisms which, perhaps, have the greatest retarding influence on economic development include (1) the comparative lack of discipline, regularity, and regimentation especially as they effect labor force activity, (2) the tendency to "mind one's own business" to a point where obligation and responsibility to others is almost completely ignored, (3) the insecurity of physical property as evidenced by widespread theft and "dacoity," (4) the emphasis on personal rather than organizational practice, and (5) the general lack of national or organizational consciousness or imagery.

To the extent that economic development involves corporate action and national and organizational consciousness, the atomistic or "loose" social structure operates as an obstruction to economic advance. The achievement of collective consciousness and the ability to act in a concerted, and team, manner toward common objec-

---

[12] The writer is indebted to Murray A. Straus who, after hearing the writer's oral presentation of this paper using the term "atomistic" society, called his attention to the work of Embree and Ryan and Straus and their use of the term "loose structure."

[13] J. F. Embree, "Thailand—A Loosely Structured Social System," *American Anthropologist*, **52**, 181–193; Bryce F. Ryan and Murray A. Straus, "The Integration of Sinhalese Society," *Research Studies of the State College of Washington*, **22** (December 1954), 179–227.

[14] Ryan and Straus, *op. cit.*, pp. 183 ff. The writer can provide further general support for their observations based on his residence of about one and a half years in Burma.

tives may be a prerequisite to effective economic development in this part of the world. The achievement of a better integrated and more cohesive social order would also provide these newly independent nations with positive bonds, in addition to the at present negative ones—anti-colonialism, anti-West and antiwhite feelings—which in large measure constitute the major elements of their nationalistic feelings today.

DEMOGRAPHIC IMBALANCE

In their efforts to raise levels of living, the countries in South and Southeast Asia are faced, also, with the basic obstacle of demographic transition—that is, with a period of rapidly declining mortality while fertility remains at undisturbed high, or even increasing, levels.[15] The resultant great increase in rate of population growth will variously affect efforts to achieve economic development—but the main effect, and certainly in those countries which already possess high population-to-resource ratios, will be to retard advancement of living levels.

The less developed areas throughout the world, including those in South and Southeast Asia, have both high mortality and fertility. Mortality in most of the less developed areas, and especially in the excolonial countries, has shown some decrease in recent decades as a result of contact with Western technology, public health measures, and medicine. With independence, national programs of economic development, and the technical assistance of the United Nations and the Specialized Agencies and various unilateral programs, the countries of South and Southeast Asia have made, and are making, remarkable strides in the reduction of death rates. In fact, rates of mortality decline in this area exceed those experienced by Western nations at comparable stages of develop-

ment. This is to be expected because the less developed nations today do not have to wait for decades or even centuries, as did Western nations, for a combination of developments conducive to low mortality, including technological advance, improvement in environmental sanitation and personal hygiene, and the maturation of modern medicine, including the availability of the antibiotics. The less developed areas today have access, practically at once, to virtually all of the elements of Western culture which produce low mortality. In consequence, the halving of the mortality rate which took several decades to a century and more among the Western countries[16] can be achieved much more quickly; and it has been accomplished by Ceylon, for example, in about one decade.[17]

Continued rapid decreases in the mortality of the less developed areas may be anticipated. Such decreases will result from a number of factors including not only access to the methods and materials of the West but, also, positive incentives to reduce mortality and the apparent absence of values in the indigenous culture in conflict with this objective. Moreover, the reduction of mortality, to a considerable extent may be managed by governmental and private agencies and institutions with relatively little initiative, decision making, or action required on the part of the mass population.

Finally, practically all the initial efforts toward economic advance, including both domestic programs and the various forms of external technical assistance, have as a first effect the reduction of a number of forms of mortality and especially infant and child mortality and that resulting from the infectious and parasitic diseases. Great gains in the reduction of these forms of mortality are relatively easily and quickly achieved.

[15] United Nations, *Determinants and Consequences of Population Trends*, United Nations, New York, 1953, pp. 262 ff.

[16] *Ibid.*, pp. 50 ff.
[17] *Ibid.*, p. 56. See also United Nations, *Proceedings of World Population Conference Summary Report*, United Nations, New York, 1955, pp. 36 ff.

In contrast, there is no similar prospect for rapid reduction in fertility. There is, as yet, no basis for expecting a reduction in the lag between decreases in mortality and fertility and the attendant explosion in rates of population increase experienced by Western nations. In fact, there is reason to believe that the lag in decline of fertility may be even greater among the less developed areas than was the case in the experience of the more developed areas. The reason for this may lie both in the prevalent value system and in the apparent unsuitability of present Western methods of birth control for the less developed areas. Increased efforts and resources are being devoted to improve techniques of controlling conception but, as yet, no great breakthrough is in sight.[18]

Apart from these technological considerations, however, there are other reasons for expecting decreases in fertility to be slower than decreases in mortality. Chief among these, perhaps, is the necessity for individual couples to achieve values, and knowledge, as well as means, which will enable them to desire and to achieve smaller numbers of children. Changes in value systems and the necessary education of marriage partners may require as much as a generation or more, in contrast to the relatively few years in which appreciable declines in mortality may be effected. Furthermore, there is more apt to be cultural resistance to reduction in fertility than in mortality, government and private agencies are less apt to exert positive leadership to bring about reductions in the birth rate than in the death rate, and, in any case, fertility cannot be as readily controlled by government or private agencies and institutions as can mortality. Pending the development of, at present unknown, techniques of rapidly changing human values, as well as more acceptable contraceptive techniques, it may be expected that the less developed areas will experience great population increases.

Rapid population increase does not necessarily retard economic advance. On the contrary, in the history of North America rapid population growth probably contributed to increased levels of living. In general, where the ratio of population to resources is low, rapid population growth may stimulate or even be a prerequisite to rapid economic development; but where the population-resource ratio is high, rapid population increase may retard economic advance.[19] In countries like India, Indonesia, Pakistan, or Japan, where population-resource ratios are high, great population increases retard increases in levels of living. In the countries where population is not as dense, as in Burma or Thailand, rapid population increase, for the time being, is not likely to be as much of a barrier to advancing living levels. In general, and in oversimplified terms, it may be stated that the level of living can advance only if the rate of increase in aggregate product exceeds the rate of population increase. Rapid population increase calls for relatively great capital outlays and increased productivity merely to provide for additional population, and calls for even greater capital outlays and increased productivity to provide both for new mouths and improved living levels. When rapid population growth stimulates increased productivity through increasing economics of scale, it may help to advance living levels; when it fails to increase productivity, or even decreases product per head under conditions of diminishing returns, it retards economic development. Since most of the less developed areas are characterized by high population-resource ratios, rapid population increases tend to obstruct efforts to raise levels of living.

[18] United Nations, *Determinants and Consequences*, *op. cit.*, Chs. 5 and 15; see also United Nations, *Proceedings of World Population*, *op. cit.*, pp. 48 ff.

[19] United Nations, *Determinants and Consequences*, *op. cit.*, Part III, especially Ch. 13; see also United Nations, *Proceedings of World Population*, *op. cit.*, summary reports of meetings numbers 20, 22, 24, and 26.

Concluding Observations

The various cultural and social obstacles to economic advance which have been discussed above, whether deriving from the colonial heritage or the indigenous cultures of the peoples in South and Southeast Asia, have their counterpart in the person. To a considerable extent economic development is retarded in the less developed areas by the limits imposed by the available human resources, as well as the limits imposed by such things as the availability of savings for investment, capital goods, raw materials, and the like.

Among the characteristics of the persons in the less developed areas which tend to obstruct advances in levels of living, some of the more important ones include: the lack of incentive, illiteracy, the lack of occupational skills, prescientific conceptions of the natural and social orders, the absence of leadership traits, parochialism, nostalgic romanticism, a victim complex in respect of the West, and individuation which hampers or precludes cooperative or team effort, and increasing disillusionment about, and impatience with, the rate of economic advance.

This is not the place to elaborate upon these characteristics or their implications. But it may be noted that they have important implications for the social engineer— the policy-makers and administrators of economic development programs. Such programs must necessarily be as much concerned with the cultural and personal barriers to economic advance as with the purely technological and economic obstacles. This is particularly true because a longer time may be required to develop the necessary cultural changes and human resources than the physical, capital, and technological resources for economic advance.

Apart from their social engineering implications, the observations presented suggest the need for more widespread and intensive studies of the cultures and population characteristics of the less developed areas, in general, as well as those in South and Southeast Asia as points of departure for studies of social change.[20] For, in the various economic development programs of the less developed areas, the sociologist or social anthropologist may find natural laboratory and simulated experimental situations for testing many of the generalizations in the literature on social change based largely on inadequate historical data and restricted frequently to Western culture and experience. Focus on the cultural and personal obstacles to economic development is one of the several ways of initiating such investigations.

[20] The importance of a "social change" framework for the analysis of problems of economic development is discussed by Bert F. Hoselitz in his paper, "Noneconomic Factors in Economic Development" to appear in *American Economic Review* (May 1957).

THE ROLE OF TRADITIONALISM IN THE POLITICAL MODERNIZATION OF GHANA AND UGANDA

David E. Apter

Social analysts have long been preoccupied with those features of traditional culture and belief which affect the direction of change and the receptivity of a society to innovation. In spite of the very considerable literature concerned with acculturation, there have been few efforts to examine different types of traditional systems with respect to the problems they pose for political modernization. We attempt this form of analysis here. The plan is to examine two countries, Ghana and Uganda, which are engaged in the effort to build a national society. Each is experimenting with constitutional forms and each has had to deal with the problem of traditionalism. Indeed, the central problem of those concerned with building national, as distinct from local, political institutions has been to create overarching political parties, voluntary associations, and governmental forms that bridge older parochialisms. Moreover, just as tradition is a source of parochial strengths and social pride, so

its characteristics vary widely. There are some who argue that any understanding of modernity in Africa must be based on an examination of the variants of the traditional systems.

In this article, we shall compare recent political events in Ghana and Uganda, and try to show how they have been shaped by the nature of traditionalism. By this means we can illustrate the implications of two different kinds of traditionalism and the problems they pose for modern nation builders.

Traditionalism

The importance of traditional factors in change was not the discovery of Max Weber, as some have thought. Such antecedent greats as Marx and Coulanges sought to link to the problem of modernization those stable symbols, artifacts, and values transmitted by the people of a society through generations. Marx was particularly concerned with its economic aspects; Coulanges with its religious aspects. Since that time, the study of tradition has been either directly or indirectly brought into the most contemporary concerns. Most recently, Lerner has observed the behavioral consequences and durability of tradition by exploring degrees of participation in mass media of communication. Fallers has dealt with it in terms of bureaucracy. My own concern has focused on the functional implications of traditional political forms for modern ones.[1]

SOURCE. David E. Apter, "The Role of Traditionalism in the Political Modernization of Ghana and Uganda," *World Politics*, 12, 45–68, October 1960. In an earlier form, this article was presented at the Dobbs Ferry Conference of the SSRC Sub-Committee on Comparative Government in 1959.

Research by the author in West Africa was first made possible through the generosity of the Social Science Research Council in 1952. Subsequent work was done in West Africa under the auspices of the West African Comparative Analysis Project, a Carnegie-supported research project that is still under way. Work on Uganda was undertaken in 1955–56 through a Ford Foundation Area Research Training Fellowship. None of these agencies is responsible for the opinions expressed in this article.

[1] See D. Lerner *et al.*, *The Passing of Traditional Society*, Glencoe, Ill., 1958; L. A. Fallers, *Bantu Bureaucracy*, Cambridge, Eng., 1956; and D. E. Apter, *The Gold Coast in Transition*, Princeton, N.J., 1955.

Nor is interest in tradition a peculiarity of social scientists. Politicians, no less than academics, recognize that traditional factors which under some circumstances seem to create immobilities in social structure, and abort or minimize innovation, at other times can open the door to an entirely different range of behaviors. Administrators who in Mali Federation (formerly Senegal and French Sudan) for years sought with only small success to establish effective local units of government, possessing cultural and solidary features satisfying to the population, now find the very same measures enthusiastically taken up by African leaders and interpreted as peculiar to the genius of Africans. Under the ideology of *negritude*, the meaning attached to community development, cooperation, and communalism has been transformed into a living and continuous feature of the African past. By this means, innovation has been "traditionalized" and made comfortable. Change is not strange or foreign, requiring new roles or learning. Traditionalism puts novelty on trial rather than the people that novelty is supposed to serve. The lesson of Mali is that contemporary administrators and political leaders in Africa who can learn to enlist traditionalism in the service of innovation will indeed be contributing to successful political modernization.

Traditionalism, as distinct from tradition, we can define as validations of current behavior stemming from immemorial prescriptive norms. It is not that traditionalist systems do not change, but rather that innovation—i.e., extrasystemic action—has to be mediated within the social system and charged to antecedent values. Modernism, in contrast, presupposes a much remoter relationship between antecedent values and new goals. Modern systems, with their complex and highly differentiated social structures, value change itself.

These distinctions between modernism and traditionalism, valid as they are, leave unanswered the question why some tradi-

tional systems can innovate more easily than others. Answers have been sought in the structural features of traditional societies, while traditionalism has remained a more or less undifferentiated concept.

The discussion here accordingly distinguishes between two types of traditionalism. The first can be called *instrumental*; the second, *consummatory*.[2] Each kind exhibits certain structural tendencies. The combination of value type and structural tendency determines the problems that confront political leaders as they seek to build modern nations. We shall examine these combinations in Ghana and Uganda.

As we are using the term, instrumental systems are those which can innovate easily by spreading the blanket of tradition upon change itself. In such systems, those who are called upon to arbitrate in matters of custom, and to interpret in some

[2] As we are using the terms, "instrumental" systems are those characterized by a large sector of intermediate ends separate from and independent of ultimate ends; "consummatory" systems are those characterized by a close relationship between intermediate and ultimate ends. The terms are derived from Parsons' categories of "cognitive-instrumental meanings" and "expressive-integrative meanings." See T. Parsons *et al.*, *Working Papers in the Theory of Action*, Glencoe, Ill., 1953, p. 105.
In our sense, the difference between instrumental and consummatory values can be illustrated by the following example. Consider two traditional systems, one consummatory and the other instrumental in value type. Both are short-hoe cultures and an effort is made to introduce new agricultural techniques, particularly the use of tractors. In the consummatory system, changing from the short hand-hoe system will so corrupt the ritual of hoe-making, the division of men's and women's work, the religious practices associated with both, and the relationship between agricultural rituals and the authority of chiefs that it would be impossible to consider a tractor only in terms of increasing agricultural productivity. In the instrumental system, by contrast, the tractor would simply be viewed in terms of its ability to expand agricultural output and would not affect the ultimate ends of the system. In the first instance, such an innovation represents a threat to the system. In the second instance, it is far likelier to strengthen the system by increasing farm income.

official capacity, are easily persuaded to find traditional counterparts in contemporary events. Such systems can innovate without appearing to alter their social institutions fundamentally. Rather, innovation is made to serve immemoriality. The characteristic structural expression of instrumental traditionalism is a military type of system, with hierarchical authority stemming from a single king or command figure.[3] Appointive ranks in the system tend to underwrite the king as the central source of authority. A heavy reliance on performance is a characteristic of office and the chief who fails to serve his king loyally and well is subject to removal or death. Religion is decidedly secondary in such a system, whose primary value is service to the king or state. Examples of such systems are Morocco, Ethiopia, and Buganda.[4]

The traditionalism of consummatory systems is much more complex. They were first described by Fustel de Coulanges when, deploring the simplistic interpretations of Greece and Rome as prototypes for modern societies, he wrote that examining the institutions of those two systems without a knowledge of their religious notions left them "obscure, whimsical, and inexplicable." He went on to say: "A comparison of beliefs and laws shows that a primitive religion constituted the Greek and Roman family, established marriage and paternal authority, fixed the order of relationship, and consecrated the right of property, and the right of inheritance. This same religion, after having enlarged and extended the family, formed a still larger association,

the city, and reigned in that as it had reigned in the family. From it came all the institutions, as well as all the private laws, of the ancients. It was from this that the city received all its principles, its rules, its usages and its magistracies."[5]

Thus society, the state, authority, and the like are all part of an elaborately sustained, high-solidarity system in which religion as a cognitive guide is pervasive. Such systems have been hostile to innovation. Change has produced fundamental social upheavals such as migration to towns. Broken are the warmth and intimacy of custom. Not only were ancient Greece and Rome examples of such systems, but so was Ashanti.[6]

Our general hypothesis is that the instrumental-hierarchical type of system can innovate with each until the kingship principle is challenged, at which point the entire system joins together to resist change. In other words, such systems are highly resistant to political rather than other forms of modernization, and in particular cannot easily supplant the hierarchical principle of authority with a representative one.

Consummatory values are most significantly rooted where the structural expression of authority is pyramidal rather than hierarchical. Pyramidal structure means that patterns of subordinacy and superordinacy are limited to such activities as war or court appeals. For most purposes a chief or political leader is

[3] For a discussion of hierarchical authority, see A. Southall, *Alur Society*, Cambridge, Eng., 1956, esp. Ch. 6. See also D. E. Apter, *The Political Kingdom in Uganda: A Study of Bureaucratic Nationalism*, Princeton, N.J. (forthcoming).

[4] The reader should note that the name Uganda refers to the entire country, the Uganda Protectorate, which includes many different tribes; Buganda is a tribe within Uganda; the Baganda are the people (plural) of Buganda; a Muganda is a single member of the Buganda tribe; and Kiganda is the adjective form.

[5] Fustel de Coulanges, *The Ancient City*, New York, Doubleday Anchor Books, n.d., p. 13.

[6] Such systems can innovate, however. Indeed, the philosophy prevailing in Senegal today is similar to that described by Coulanges, but the religious system is pervaded by humanistic socialism. Hence to build upon traditional solidarities, the emphasis on family, corporatism in institutions, personalism, and the like go hand in hand with joint participation in communal economic efforts. By this means, work is ennobled and given new meaning in traditional terms. See, for example, the expression of this point of view by M. Mamadou Dia in *L'Economie africaine*, Paris, 1957, and "Economie et culture devant les élites africaines," *Présence africaine*, Nos. 14–15 (June–September 1957), pp. 58–72.

responsible to his social group rather than to a senior chief or official. The chiefs at each level of the pyramid thus have similar powers and are relatively autonomous of one another. Such a structural form relies heavily on semisegmental kinship relationships. The autonomy of the chief or political leader is thus a reflection of the autonomy of the kinship unit itself.

The consummatory-pyramidal systems are highly resistant to all forms of innovation, and the consequences of change are external political groupings that form as new solidary associations cutting across the older ones. In other words, new social structures with a political focus emerge, with the object of tearing down the older ones. Let us examine these processes in Ghana and Uganda.

Two Traditional Systems

Buganda, one of the most important kingdom states in the lake area of Eastern Africa, was regarded very favorably by Europeans who first came upon the country in the latter half of the nineteenth century. First Arabs, and then British and French missionaries, were welcomed by the king, or *Kabaka*, of Buganda. Kabaka Mutesa I encouraged competitive performances by the three religious groups—Muslim, Catholic, and Protestant. Although he died a pagan, he was intensely interested in Christianity.

To the Baganda, adoption of Christianity came to denote a superior technological and educational status. The older religious system, associated with the institution of clanship which was itself giving way to a hierarchical chieftaincy system, disappeared without producing much internal strain. Christianity easily passed muster as an aid to the Baganda in maintaining their society. The only point of concern was the fact that missionaries, in gaining adherents, tended to usurp the functions of chiefs. Since the latter remained responsible to the Kabaka, while the missionaries were not, a disturbing element was introduced into the political system.

Competition among religions, however, resulted in religious wars. These were eventually resolved by allocating fixed numbers of chieftaincies to Catholics, Protestants, and Muslims. The religious factions became tantamount to political parties within Buganda.

The missionaries themselves commented on how quickly the Baganda took to education and became ardent religionists as well.[7] After British intervention and the establishment of the Protectorate over Uganda, regular Catholic and Protestant school systems were established. The chiefs were the best-educated group in the population. Catholic chiefs were products of Kisubi, the Catholic school, and Protestant chiefs were products of King's College, Budo. Both were modeled after British public schools.

Moreover, freehold land tenure was introduced and 8000 square miles were distributed among 1000 chiefs and notables, who thereby became a kind of squirearchy. The recipients of the land were mainly Catholics and Protestants.

Whatever the innovated structure, whether civil-service chieftaincy, a parliament and council of ministers, modern education, or freehold tenure, it strengthened the system. The instrumental quality of hierarchical kingship was never defeated. The innovations that were most easily accepted were those that strengthened the Buganda government and also facilitated the individual's efficiency within it.

As a result, the organization of political life, which had been the crucial social structure in Buganda, was regarded as continuing from the past, with each innovation simply perfecting and strengthening an established system. All novelty came to be regarded as a device for strengthening tradition. As we shall indicate below, the main form of nationalism which emerged was that of a modernizing autocracy in

[7] See R. P. Ashe, *Chronicles of Uganda*, London, 1894; and A. R. Tucker, *Eighteen Years in Uganda and East Africa*, London, 1908, *passim*.

which the government of the Kabaka and the Kabaka himself represented effective nationalism.

In Ashanti, on the other hand, responses to innovation were relatively complicated. Chieftaincy, despite its tiers of relatively autonomous powers with respect to various units of government, was nevertheless hemmed in with restrictions. Chieftaincy faced inward to the people to whom, by lineage and totem, the chief or headman was related. Instead of the individual atomism of Buganda, which was held together by regard for the Kabaka and the external force of hierarchical authority, the Ashanti chief was linked with an elaborate system of religiously sanctioned self-restraints on behavior. When land alienation began to occur in undue measure, for example, chieftaincy was affected and the stable confines of the social system were undermined. When Christianity was introduced, it helped to weaken the traditions of chieftaincy and removed the control that the dead ancestors exercised over the living. The result was excesses by chiefs, who turned to British authorities for their support. When education was introduced, chiefs had to be ordered to send their children to school. While they could not disobey the orders of district officers, they often sent the children of their slave lineages rather than the children of royal blood. The succeeding generations of chiefs were thus by no means the best educated. The support required for the authority of the chiefs violated customary restraints on behavior. The excesses of the chiefs soon came to be regarded as perversions of traditional society, from which younger and more educated elements began to disaffiliate. Christianity helped ease the process of disaffiliation and there developed, along with an increase in urbanization and the growth of villages, the phenomenon of the urban village Christian and the rural village pagan. Most important, a series of wars between the British and the Ashanti was a token of the inability of Ashanti to absorb those

innovating effects of a system of colonial rule which was basically common to both Buganda and Ashanti. In the end the *Asantehene*, or king of Ashanti, had to be exiled. Indeed, from 1901 to 1935, the Ashanti Confederacy did not exist as such.[8]

Within the context of the term "traditional," both Ashanti and Buganda were traditional systems. Both required validations of current behavior by appeal to immemoriality. Both had myths of origin involving a powerful figure associated with the formation of the society, and with whom the king had claims to ancestry. In the case of the Ashanti, the powers of origin descended to the Golden Stool rather than to a person. In Buganda, descent was reckoned through the line of kings, or Kabakas. That the preservation of power and continuity should reside in an object in the case of Ashanti—as distinct from a person, as in Buganda— is not without significance. For, in Ashanti, those in power serve the present by serving the past. It is a symbol of ancestral concern which is the visible repository of authority. In Buganda the king was, as both Roscoe and Fallers have called him, despotic.[9] While there was—and still is— pomp and ceremony around the king, he was not regarded as a descendant of living ancestors. He was rather the punishing, aggressive, and virile representative of a dynamic people expanding their military hegemony in the Lake Victoria region. Hence the essentially religious and theocratic nature of the Ashanti state, and the more secular and military character of Buganda.

There were other important differences between these societies. In Ashanti, the system of political organization had its prototype in the extended family, which included up to a hundred members, possessing strong solidary affiliations.

[8] J. N. Matson, *Warrington's Notes on Ashanti Custom*, Cape Coast, Prospect Printing Press, 1941 (2nd ed.).

[9] See, in particular, John Roscoe, *The Baganda*, London, 1911, p. 232.

Families lived together in villages and it was unusual for an Ashanti to live alone or with only his immediate family.

In addition, the Ashanti had an elaborate lineage system whereby recruitment to office and the allocation of rights and duties were organized. The core political unit was the village. The largest unit was the division, over which there was a paramount chief. Kumasi, which established a compact with the other Ashanti divisions in a historical episode veiled in mystery and magic, became the center of a Confederacy. An elaborate balance of checks and controls on authority extended from the village level to the division, including restrictions on the exercise of power by the Asantehene, or king of the Ashanti Confederacy.

The system in Buganda was much simpler in one respect, and much more complex in others. Unlike the chief in Ashanti, who was a religious figure, a lineage figure and, moreover, elected to office, the chief in Buganda was appointed by the king, or Kabaka, and was responsible to him. The chief was subject to summary dismissal at the pleasure of the Kabaka. Much closer to the Ashanti pattern was an earlier, pre-Kabaka, clan system which continued to play a part in subsequent periods. The king was both *Sabataka* (head of all the clans) and Kabaka.

Every Muganda is a member of a clan. Clans are hereditary. The elders of clans had responsibilities over the family, the social conduct of individuals, and inheritance. Chiefs, who were appointed, reflected the powers of the Kabaka. Clan elders, who were elected from eligible lineages, reflected religious and immemorial powers. These two principles of authority were in constant conflict. Increasingly, performance in serving the Kabaka and thereby the state became the basis of chieftaincy. Performance and service became readily identifiable since Buganda, as a military system, was in process of expanding at the expense of her neighbors.

The acceptance of hierarchical authority thus was associated with successful national aggrandizement and the pure authority of the Kabaka was not mitigated by any other countervailing principle. Tension within the system was produced by conflicts between clanship and chieftaincy. But the Kabaka represented the central authority in both systems—i.e., Sabataka or head of all the clans, and Kabaka or head of all the chiefs.

Two effects were immediately observable from the twin systems of organization in Buganda united by a system of autocratic and hierarchical kingship. Clans were scattered throughout the country. In any area an individual on the move could find a clansman and receive certain benefits from him. This not only facilitated mobility but also ensured considerable uniformity of custom and behavior throughout the system.

The chiefs, who were territorial governors for the king, were also military leaders. Their followers were loyal to the chief because the chief reflected the Kabaka's authority. This military-administrative system of organization included a massive network of military roads converging, radially, upon the center or capital. Yet the capital itself was often moved, so that there was no "center" and "hinterland."

The result was a "suburban" pattern of life in which clanship counterpoised chieftaincy in daily life, but each man's eyes centered upon the king. In time of war, which was often, the military administrative system required almost no modification. The necessary mobilizations took place under the chiefs. Food continued to be produced, and family life managed to go on quite well. In contrast, Ashanti had to shift to a quite different military formation in time of war, and then returned to their peacetime pyramidal organization when war was over.[10]

[10] Ashanti had a complex hierarchy of chiefs. At the pinnacle of the hierarchy was the *omanhene*, or divisional chief. Independent in his sphere of authority, he was nevertheless

What were some of the controversial issues which the Kiganda system was unable to absorb? The most characteristic one was an inability to adjust to any permanent limitation on the power of the Kabaka. Whether a Muganda were chief or peasant, educated or not, he maintained the same unabashed veneration for the office of the Kabaka. Or, to put the matter another way, the principle of national aggrandizement was never lost, and the Kabaka was its symbol. Each of the major conflicts which aroused the Baganda and posed serious problems for the Protectorate government centered around possible dangers to the autonomy of Buganda or diminutions of the authority of the Kabaka.

In contrast to Ashanti, then, the Baganda have instrumental values. Ends are relatively well defined and essentially patriotic.

Both Baganda and Ashanti developed their own forms of tribal parochialism. The former were adept in retaining considerable political autonomy, and the Uganda Agreement of 1900, which stipulated the relations between Baganda and British, became a legal bulwark of ethnic nationalism and political parochialism. In Ashanti, where no such constitutional relationship existed, internal conflict was widely manifested throughout the entire area, creating instabilities which eventually led to mass nationalism. In more contemporary terms, in Buganda nationalist politicians have so far been able to make little headway and are regarded by the Buganda government as malcontents and ne'er-do-wells. One finds there an absorb-

ing situation, in which the British authorities are anxious to see nationalist political parties develop on an all-Uganda pattern as the solution to building a modern state.[11] In Ghana, the party nationalists have become tantamount to the state itself, regarding chiefs dimly, to say the least. Not only have they taken active steps to break the chief's power, but the Asantehene, the paramount chief of Ashanti, has been their particular target. In the last encounter between the Asantehene and the party government, it was the former who had to admit defeat. The quasireligious character of traditional society has been replaced by the quasireligious character of modern nationalism in Ghana. We can analyze these developments more closely.

Contrasting Efforts at Political Modernization

Uganda and Ghana are in the process of modernization. Practically, this has meant establishing parliamentary institutions by means of which the whole country is governed. Ghana achieved the level of political development in 1950 which Uganda now hopes to achieve. In other respects as well, Ghana has developed more rapidly. National income per head in Ghana is double that of Uganda. More effective internal transport and trade facilities are found in Ghana and Africans participate actively in all aspects of technical and commercial life. In Uganda, Asians and Europeans still monopolize the more important sectors of the economy and are the predominant racial groups in the civil service. In contrast, Africanization of the civil service in Ghana is virtually complete, with only a few senior positions and technical services still performed by Europeans, and these mostly on contract.

Ghana is economically well off for an African country.[12] Since 1951, 80 per cent

hedged about with restrictions. His was a religious role symbolizing lineage relationships to ancestors, and only members of a founder's or royal lineage were eligible to be elected to chieftaincy. The same held true for village chiefs and headmen. During war a division chief and others would take a position in the army and a more hierarchical system of authority would come to prevail. See E. Meyerowitz, *The Sacred State of the Akan*, London, 1951, especially Ch. 10.

[11] See *Report of the Constitutional Committee, 1959* (Wild Report), Entebbe, Government Printer, 1959, pp. 33–35.
[12] A population of approximately 5 million in an area of over 90,000 square miles is divided

of its internal savings has been based upon a single cash crop, cocoa. Other sources of income are gold, bauxite, manganese, industrial diamonds, and timber. It has advanced economically under a series of development plans, the first of which was primarily concerned with expanding basic transportation facilities. Railways were extended, a deep-water port built at Takoradi. The principle of a reserve fund for economic contingencies was established early. The first ten-year development plan was launched at the end of World War I. and, except during the period of the world depression, Ghana has been development-conscious. Both under the later stages of colonialism and under her present nationalist government, she has been a social-welfare state.

What was the effect of innovation? Traditional chieftaincy and social organization increasingly became a focus for internal resentments. Bitter conflict over land developed. The pattern of self-restraints on behavior was upset. Land alienation in the form of concessions was common. Considerable friction developed between chiefs who took their seats not only in traditional councils, but on the legislative council and other conciliar bodies set up by the government, and the urban, educated elites which emerged with the spread of modern commerce. Each emerging group thought itself destined to inherit political power. The result was cultural withdrawal which prepared the ground for mass nationalism in Ghana after the Second World War. The chiefs, failing to consider the sources of mass nationalism, regarded it as simply

an event in a long and stable cultural tradition which would only help to restore chieftaincy to its proper role.

The Western-educated elites regarded the nationalists as usurpers of their roles. The British viewed them as dangerous malcontents, subversive of public peace and good order. Such rejection gave fervor to the nationalists of the Convention People's Party (CPP), who by adherence to the party gave a new coherence to Ghana as a national society. They brought about a closer integration of the different peoples making up the territory, and they made economic and political institutions African rather than foreign by using them in the interests of self-government. Politics had already become polarized between traditional and secular authorities during the colonial period. Now the fundamental issues of traditionalism and modernity became wrapped up in more complex conflicts over democracy itself.

The major achievement of the CPP in Ghana was the organization and maintenance of an effective mass political organization. This resulted in centers of communication in the towns and villages, requiring members who could coordinate the activities of others. By building the CPP into a social group, a fraternity of the disadvantaged was encouraged to mold society in its favor by means of national political institutions and political freedom. A widely diverse membership was provided with a feeling of confidence in the future. Self-government was the goal. New opportunities were to be achieved thereby. A vision of a new society which was as vague as it was powerful was the moral claim of the CPP.

Yet in creating a mass political organization devoted to achieving independence, the CPP incorporated elements which had no long-run natural inclinations toward one another. More particularly, traditional groupings formed centers of opposition to Dr. Nkrumah both inside and outside the party. The main source of opposition was Ashanti. The Asantehene and his

[*footnote 12 continued*
into several main tribal groups. The northern peoples are chiefly grouped in Muslim kingdoms. The central group is the seat of the once-powerful Ashanti Confederacy. The southern groups—Fante, Ga, Ewe, and others—have had the longest contact with Western commerce and education. There are old families inhabiting the former "factories" of early traders who intermarried with the local people and established their own family dynasties. See J. Boyon, *Le Ghana*, Paris, 1958, pp. 7–10.

council helped plan the organization of an opposition, the National Liberation Movement (NLM), which itself renewed an old alliance between intellectuals and traditional authorities.[13]

With demands for a federal system of government, the situation rapidly grew dangerous. One Cabinet minister, a leading CPP figure from Ashanti, was ambushed outside his house and his sister killed. Government leaders did not dare to go to Ashanti for almost two years. Moreover, the appearance of successful traditionalism in Ashanti encouraged other opposition groups to form. In Accra, in Nkrumah's own constituency, there was formed an Accra people's movement which was essentially parochial and anti-Nkrumah. Everywhere traditionalism and the natural organization of the ethnic and tribal group seemed the only possible alternative to party rule by the Convention People's Party.

The conflicts over traditionalism and the future of democracy were sharpest during the period just prior to independence. In the general election of 1956, the candidates of seven parties and 45 independents ran for office. In spite of the fact that the NLM was able to put only 39 candidates in the field, and the CPP was well enough organized to contest all 104 seats, the latter received only 398,141 votes and the combined opposition received 299,116. This opposition vote was extremely high, considering the fact that a vote for the CPP was considered a vote for independence. Approximately 50 per cent of the electorate voted. In the post-independence period, the opposition was smashed. A series of acts rushed through Parliament were designed to break the power of traditional authorities. So successful were these efforts that, when elections to the Kumasi Municipal Council were held in February 1958,

the CPP won 17 out of 24 seats—a remarkable achievement.

In attacking traditionalism, movements of the CPP type take on the characteristic of inviolability. They have a tendency to brand splinter groups and the opposition as playing into the hands of the "feudal" elements in society. The idea of party fealty is stressed more than any other.

The pattern which can be clearly seen in this conflict between traditionalism and modernism is thus the continuous affiliation to and disaffiliation from powerful social groupings that each make total claims on the allegiance and support of its members. The clear loser in such a situation is the opposition. In crucial respects, therefore, countries like Ghana find that in attacking tradition and supporting modernity they become one-party systems. It is not that there is no opposition, but that organized party opposition finds itself in difficult circumstances. Traditionalism, which serves the opposition as an effective rallying ground for popular support, is branded as subversive.[14] Indeed, at the Accra African Peoples' Conference in December 1958, tribalism and religious separatism were defined as evil practices by Africa's leading nationalists. It was resolved that "those African traditional institutions whether political, social, or economic which have clearly shown their

---

[13] In 1957 the NLM joined with other tribal parties like the *Ga Shiftimo Kpee* to become the United Party. The former leader of the party, Dr. K. A. Busia, is currently in Holland, Ghana's first real political exile.

[14] At the same time, the parliamentary opposition in Ghana has been effective on occasions. There are times when the CPP backbench threatens to bolt party whips and vote with the opposition. Such a threat has been a useful means of modifying the position of the government on several issues, not the least of which was modification of the Emergency Powers Bill, while the constitutional changes of early 1957 were incorporated under pressure from the opposition. Bitterly contested decisions which often resulted in suspensions of parliamentary sessions have been those involving basic liberties. Three such measures were the Ghana Nationality and Citizenship Bill, the Emergency Powers Bill, and the Deportation Bill. For an excellent study of Ghana's parliament, see D. G. Austin, "The Ghana Parliament's First Year," *Parliamentary Affairs*, **11** (Summer 1958), pp. 350–360.

reactionary character and their sordid support for colonialism be condemned."[15]

What, then, has political modernization meant in Ghana? Attacking tradition has resulted in the development of an "organizational weapon" type of party which, constantly on the attack, probes for weaknesses in the system. It seeks to jostle the public into functionally useful roles for the pursuit of modernization. To prevent the loss of power, and to modernize as rapidly as possible, are the basic goals of those who have inherited the mantle of British power. Modernization has come to require a host of attitudes of mind and social organizations antithetical to traditional ways of doing things. Political modernization therefore attacks head-on traditional ways of believing and acting.

In these respects, the Ghana government has been unable to make use of traditionalism to support innovation. The past has become a dead weight on the present government, which by the use of inducements, and by occasional kicks and blows as well, seeks to drive people toward a new way of life. Because of the government's loss of support in the traditional sectors of society, the burdens of modernization on Ghana have become more intense. Unlike Senegal, where the blending of traditionalism and modernity has eased the transition to new political and economic forms, in Ghana traditionalism has not provided a genuine source of pride and inspiration. Unlike the French African concept of *negritude*, the slogan "African personality" has remained largely devoid of content.[16] Ghana, in assuming the heavy burdens of

[15] All-African Peoples' Conference, Resolution on Tribalism, Religious Separatism, and Traditional Institutions, *Conference Resolutions*, Vol. 1, No. 4, issued by the Conference Secretariat, Accra, 1958.

[16] It is interesting to note that while the term "African personality" is widely attributed to Nkrumah, it is in Nigeria that an effort is being made to give it content. Examples of such efforts are the journals *Black Orpheus* and *Odú*, which, as cultural and literary journals, seek to give a philosophical and cultural significance to the term.

modernization without the supports of traditionalism, has become a relatively autocratic system.

Uganda shows a completely different political pattern. Unlike Ghana, which is a maritime nation, Uganda is situated inland on the shores of Lake Victoria.[17] It is roughly the same size as Ghana, with an area of 80,000 square miles and a population of approximately 6 millions.[18]

By virtue of its superior institutions and successful collaboration with the British, Buganda was made a privileged area. The Uganda Agreement of 1900 formally recognized these privileges, and elsewhere in the country the Kiganda pattern of territorial organization was established— a three-tiered system of local government, each with a chief and a council (*Lukiko*) and ranging in scope from the parish to the county. The British retained an appointive chieftaincy system, but one which followed the practice of a regular civil service, with chiefs being promoted, transferred, and retired. Theirs was the task of maintaining peace and good order, collecting taxes, and otherwise taking care of the areas under their jurisdiction. Buganda, as a province, formed the model for the other ethnic groups to follow in the districts. In more recent times the parliament of Buganda, the Great Lukiko, has been the model for the district councils, which have become the object of considerable tribal parochialism in the districts outside of Buganda.

The three races, African, Asian, and European, live in uneasy proximity. Asians are involved in petty commerce, and increasingly in larger commercial enterprises in urban centers such as Kampala, while Europeans generally remain in charge of

[17] Blessed with an exceedingly good climate and well-distributed rainfall, most of Uganda is fertile agricultural country. To supplement her two main crops, cotton and coffee, she needs more diverse export commodities, and copper and other raw materials are being successfully exploited on an increasing scale.

[18] See *Colonial Report*, Entebbe, Government Printer, 1959. Buganda represents approximately 20 per cent of the population of Uganda.

major commercial operations. Few Europeans were successful in farming in Uganda, where a situation comparable to that of the white settlers in Kenya never developed. Asians and Europeans have always tended to collaborate in representing the commercial interests of the country.[19] Asians were represented on the Legislative Council along with Europeans from the very onset, after World War I. No Africans were represented on the Legislative Council, nor was it regarded as desirable that they should be, until after the Second World War. It was widely held that Buganda's own Lukiko served as her political outlet, and the same situation was thought to prevail in the districts. It was regarded as essential to the interests of Africans that the principle of trusteeship, the mainstay of administration during the interwar period, should be maintained through the Governor and his staff.[20]

Until the present day, nationalism in Uganda was largely expressed through the Buganda government "establishment." There is now stirring the kind of "modern" nationalism which is increasingly inclined to limit the powers of the Kabaka and make of Uganda a united, self-governing nation. But modernism as an ideology is confined to a very few. Indeed, it has been largely pre-empted by the Buganda government. Let us examine the process by which this occurred.

Although the Baganda did not suffer national defeats as did the Ashanti, religious wars in the latter part of the nineteenth century resulted in the deposition and restoration of the Kabaka by Europeans on two occasions. The Baganda have never gotten over that. Given the special position of the Kabaka in the structure of Kiganda society, cavalier treatment of them on the part of the Europeans deeply wounded and aggrieved the Baganda. Even during the period of their closest collaboration with the British (roughly from 1900 to 1926), such grievances were nursed. A singular touchiness has thus characterized relations between the British and the Baganda. Unlike the more typical case in the districts, changes in political organization have, if they originated with the Protectorate government, been stoutly resisted. The Kabaka as a symbol of modern nationalism has been continuously strengthened and now has more power than at any time since British control.

When the Agreement of 1900 was signed, the Lukiko, or African parliament, dominated by the chiefs, was empowered to distribute land on a freehold basis to the most important people in Buganda. The three chief ministers received the largest estates (with the exception of the Kabaka himself), while others were given land according to their chieftaincy rank, or their general status.[21] Few pagans received any land.

Since chieftaincies had been divided up according to religion, both Protestants and Catholics of wealth came to have a considerable stake in the modified system. By fixing the proportions of chieftaincy along religious lines, family wealth and position were distributed in the same manner. Both Protestants and Catholics had some wealthy families in possession of land, and in important positions in the community. The Muslims suffered most of all the religious groups, while paganism quickly disappeared.

Those in the clan system who had been traditionally entitled to certain burial estates or clan lands, and who lost those lands during the parceling-out of freehold, became the first political force in Buganda. The clan system thus formed the "natural" opposition to a government of chiefs. This resulted in considerable internal

---

[19] The Indian Association and the Uganda Chamber of Commerce were instruments of that cooperation.

[20] For a discussion of this period, see K. Ingham, *The Making of Modern Uganda*, London, 1958, *passim*.

[21] Uganda Agreement of 1900, para. 15. See *Laws of the Uganda Protectorate, Native Agreements and Buganda Native Laws*, London, 1936, pp. 1380–1381.

dissension. Gradually the *bataka*, or clan groups, came to represent the *bakopi*, or peasantry. Land holding had become almost synonymous with prestige and social position.[22] Indeed, it appeared for a time that the system would become based on dynastic land-holding families, and the principle of easy access to political office and performance would be eliminated. Yet other innovations helped to prevent this. For example, the expanded educational system, which was enthusiastically supported by the Baganda, did not limit facilities to the children of chiefs, but included peasant children as well. Education was regarded as a major basis for entry into the political hierarchy (which remained the only major social organization throughout Buganda).

The instrumental values of the Baganda, colliding with a threatening monopoly of political roles by families of the senior chiefs who had received land, or by important Protestant and Catholic leaders, prevailed over both elites without altering the autocratic principle of hierarchical kingship. This allowed progressive modification of the Lukiko and greater opportunities to the public as a whole. Unlike the consummatory system of Ashanti, where individuals had virtually to withdraw from the traditional system in order to seek new careers and opportunities in a different kind of society, the Kiganda system was modified in practice, while posing few contradictions in principle.

Although the Buganda government was often in conflict with the peasantry, such conflicts appeared in the guise of govern-

[22] Important in preventing such dissension from assuming proportions of "class conflict" was the fact that peasants could, and did, buy freehold land. Moreover, no landless peasantry was created. Everyone could get a leasehold property at a nominal and fixed rental. This deterred migration to towns, and no urban-rural cleavage developed. Buganda remains a rural "suburbia." See A. W. Southall and P. C. W. Gutkind, *Townsmen in the Making*, East African Studies No. 9, Kampala, East African Institute of Social Research, 1956, *passim*.

ment and its loyal opposition. The British, through a Resident, built up the influence of the chiefs and the ministers of the Buganda government. They regarded them as modern because of the ease and alacrity with which they learned to collect taxes, adapted themselves to methods of bookkeeping, and were able to control the public.

Thus the autocratic principle has prevailed in Buganda until the present. Innovations, it is widely believed, have come not from an alien source, but through the Buganda government itself. With the country's leaders able to maintain social discipline, because to act irresponsibly is to act against the Kabaka, a sense of awe and formality in social relations has helped retain public support. To keep the public "on the alert" and politically conscious, skirmishes against the intervention of the Residency are constantly fought.

As a result, the Baganda have regarded themselves as exceedingly blessed in a state of political autonomy. The Buganda government has been the most successful nationalist "party" in the country. Success in the economic field as well, particularly with the cotton and coffee crops, brought the Baganda considerable wealth as compared with the rest of Uganda. To add to their complacency, they had, by such visible indicators as tin roofs on their houses, number of bicycles, number of laborers from elsewhere working for them, and number of educated people, the highest standard of living in the Protectorate. They were able to absorb new forms of income, and to accept the standards of education, knowledge, skill, and training as requirements for a job such as chieftaincy, while retaining the essential character of their political system.

The freehold system, the chieftaincy system, the method of recruitment, the standards of selection, the acceptance of cash crops, all helped to make Buganda extremely modern in many ways. *But the prerequisite to accepting any modern feature on the political level was that some real or mythical traditional counterpart had to be found for it.* Hence, if the Lukiko was now a regular council with minutes, committees, and a budget, it was nevertheless regarded as an age-old institution. If chiefs were now almost invariably large landowners or related to the original holders of freehold, in custom those responsible for the control over "heads," i.e., over families and soldiers, were found to be the equivalent.

In 1955 several important measures were passed. In the districts, the District Councils Ordinance gave the councils both executive and legislative powers, enabling them to make bylaws on a wide range of subjects.[23] In Buganda, after the deportation of the Kabaka for refusing to cooperate with the Protectorate government (part of his effort to retain autonomy for Buganda), a new Agreement was signed which enhanced the powers of the Lukiko, made the Kabaka in effect a constitutional monarch, and gave the Baganda three new ministries—Health, Education, and Natural Resources—in addition to the three they already had (Prime Minister, Chief Justice, and Treasurer).[24] These reforms in effect gave to Buganda and to the district governments substantive warrants of authority and responsibility to attend to most of the economic and social schemes which are regarded as necessary to modernization. In Buganda the autocratic nature of the system has now come under attack—but the attack is still exceedingly mild. Elsewhere, in the districts, the effort to achieve local autonomy is regarded as the essence of political modernity.

What the system in Buganda cannot resolve are challenges to the principle of autocratic or hierarchical kingship. Resisting the first direct elections to be held in Buganda in 1958, the Baganda saw themselves threatened by devolution of authority to an African national government. Opposed to the nationalism of political parties, they regard representative government on an all-Uganda basis as tantamount to the destruction of their own society. In a pamphlet justifying the position of Buganda, the *Katikiro*, or Prime Minister, recently pointed out that the "peaceful growth of Western democracy in Buganda has been possible because the Baganda's customs and traditions are adaptable to new ideas which do not seek to uproot their fundamental political conceptions. . . . " Yet the pamphlet also warns that "The Baganda cannot exist as a people unless the Kabaka is the Head of the political structure in his Kingdom. Therefore, any constitution which envisages placing any other ruler or any foreign monarch in the position of the Kabaka of Buganda has no other intention but to cause the Baganda to cease to be a nation." More importantly, he concludes: "From time immemorial the Baganda have known no other ruler above their Kabaka in his Kingdom, and still they do not recognize any other person whose authority does not derive from the Kabaka and is exercised on his behalf."[25]

As a result of this position, it is the Protectorate government and British officials who are trying to build a modern national state in Uganda. How well they have succeeded is indicated by the fact that in the first direct elections in 1958, Buganda refused to participate, as did several other districts.[26]

Still more recently, a constitutional committee has recommended the establishment of responsible government at the center, with a legislature possessing 72 elected seats.[27] The Buganda government voiced

[23] See *District Councils Ordinance, 1955*, Entebbe, Government Printer, 1955.
[24] See *Buganda Agreement of 1955*, Entebbe, Government Printer, 1955.

[25] M. Kintu, *Buganda's Position*, Information Department, Kabaka's Government, Kampala, Uganda Printing and Publishing Co., 1960, pp. 1–2.
[26] See C. P. S. Allen, *A Report on the First Direct Elections to the Legislative Council of the Uganda Protectorate*, Entebbe, Government Printer, 1959, Appendix J.
[27] See the Wild Report, *op. cit.*, which anxiously notes the need for political parties in order to create effective central government.

its bitter opposition, but non-Baganda see in it the possibility of a political society not dominated by Buganda. With the Baganda anxious to secede from Uganda entirely if that is necessary to maintain the position of the Kabaka and the Buganda kingdom, there is bitter conflict between the Buganda government, on the one hand, and party politicians allied to British authorities, on the other.

There is now emerging among many Baganda an awareness that the absorptive capacity of the traditional system and its instrumental values has been reached. This is taken by the traditionalists to indicate a need for secession if the system is to be preserved. Younger groups are anxious to build a larger national society, a united Uganda. These are regarded as traitors by the traditionalist. However, the traditionalists are not antimodern. Quite the contrary, as we have seen, they have built up a modern if miniature state in Buganda and now that very modernity is used as a justification for autonomy.

The result is that political parties remain largely ineffective both in Buganda and in Uganda as a whole. Recently, in an effort to gain popular support, several parties induced anti-Asian riots aimed at reducing the economic and commercial power of Indians. But in spite of such efforts, political parties remain weak and the Buganda government continues to be the main source of parochial nationalism. Political party leaders hope that when responsible government develops at the center and the financial resources of the country are allocated on the basis of popular government, the strength of the Buganda government will be diminished. The struggle to obtain parliamentary institutions is less concerned with Britain or the colonial administration than was the case in Ghana. Rather, it is directed against the Buganda government because of its unwillingness to subordinate hierarchical authority to the principle of representative government. Thus the ethnic nationalism of Buganda remains the most important political obstacle to self-

government and has crippled political party growth, rendering the political heart of the country virtually lifeless.[28]

As has been pointed out above, however, non-Baganda groups are developing a new political party that has been launched by recently elected African representatives of the Legislative Council. They seek to make the Legislative Council the crucial political organ in Uganda, and are reluctant to be tied to the tail of Kiganda parochialism. Thus the possibility presents itself that the central conciliar institutions of Uganda will now tend to favor the rest of the country. Grants in aid, development plans, and educational schemes can now become the target of competitive nationalism, fought out in the context of competing parochialisms. In that event, neither the traditional institutions nor their insularity will long be maintained.

Moreover, direct elections to the Buganda Lukiko will bring party politics strongly into the Buganda sphere.[29] It is possible that competitive nationalism can be transformed into federal government at the center. Federal government is a compromise system brought about by conflict among the constituent states, and conflict is necessary for its vitality. What is possible in the Uganda situation is political modernization in a federal system,

[28] It must be pointed out, however, that in Uganda, unlike colonial Ghana, everyone knows that self-government is forthcoming. Lack of such certainty helped to develop an effective nationalist movement in Ghana, where to remain outside the party was tantamount to being procolonialist. In Uganda, all groups know that the country will eventually get self-government, and there is far more effort on the part of each of them to retain and expand their influence and power. Foreknowledge of self-government, in that sense, has helped to diminish the urgency of nationalism.

[29] Already in the new Lukiko, elected in 1959 (without direct election methods), five political parties are represented, a predominantly Catholic party supplying 80 per cent of all party representatives. The Buganda government has accepted the principle of direct elections but has steadfastly refused to implement it.

in which the several traditional states will be allowed to modernize their institutions on their own terms. In the demand for federalism all groups see some hope for their survival. Federalism itself has come to mean political modernism.

Conclusion

In both Ghana and Uganda tribal or ethnic parochialism has persisted with widely varying results. Kiganda parochialism has itself been a form of modernism. Civil-service chieftaincy and bureaucratic norms have bolstered the kingdom. Indeed, the Buganda government is widely regarded as the most progressive force in the country. Hence, for the Baganda, to be modern is to be parochial.

In Ashanti, modernism clashed directly with traditionalism. The religious aspect of the traditional political and social structure was an important part of a network of suitable restraints on behavior. When these were disrupted by innovations in commercial enterprise and colonialism, traditional authority was quickly undermined. Yet because traditional authority was so much a part of daily life and custom, those who broke with tradition found themselves in drastic need of new and powerful social affiliations, for to break with tradition was to break with family, lineage, and ancestral fidelity.

In contrast to Ashanti, Buganda remains the most powerful solidary association possible. Social satisfactions are still achieved within Buganda and its government for all those who belong to the kingdom. In Ashanti the formation of a new political party was itself a process of forming new and powerful symbolic attachments. The Ashanti members of the CPP became fiercely devoted to the organization. The messianic role of the leader was based on the development of a new morality to supplant the old. Hence the deep cleavages in society which remained after self-government had been obtained posed the problem of nation-building after independence rather than before it.

We can summarize some of the more salient points of contrast between the two systems as follows:

1. *Absorption of Innovation.* Ashanti, with its consummatory-pyramidal system, was unable to control the effects of innovation. Ashanti tended to shrink from contact with the modern world. Early missionaries were imprisoned. The Ashanti wars were efforts to expel the British, as a foreign body, from the body politic. The effects of contact loosened the hold of traditionalism, although it remained a powerful force.

Buganda was able to control innovation. The European presence was absorbed and rendered useful. By careful planning and the use of modernizing agencies, the Buganda government increased its autonomy and control as time went on, rather than suffering partial decay.

2. *Internal Divisions and Discontinuities.* What had hitherto been reinforcing social institutions of the consummatory system of Ashanti rapidly broke down into competing power groups and sources of internal antagonism and weakness. Thus the development of conflicts between youth and age, royals and nonroyals, slaves and nonslaves, were all examples of conflict over the continuing strength of particularistic criteria which could be reconciled only so long as older religious and institutional checks were sustained. Such social controls were highly internalized, with authority variously distributed. As soon as the continuity of past and present was disrupted, the various groupings rapidly came to compete.

In Buganda the internal conflict continued, as in the period prior to contact, between clanship and chieftaincy—all, however, under the umbrella of the king as both Sabataka, head of all the clans, and Kabaka, or king. The advantages of appointive chieftaincy had long been apparent in the military undertakings of the kingdom and a secular tendency inherent in the system was simply reinforced by contact with the British. The system was able to modify itself to restrain the old conflicts sufficiently so that the principle of hierarchic kingship did not require substantial alteration. Allegiance did not become confused.

3. *Competition for Affiliations.* Internal conflict in Ashanti produced widespread attitudes of guilt. Cleavages divided the extended and nuclear families. Social breaks which meant modifying one's religious practices and sundering ties with the past (and one's ancestors) led to migration of individuals to urban areas which supported very different patterns of social life. These created more fundamental differences in outlook between urban and rural groups who, within one generation, had grown apart but were still not socially distant. The Ashanti were able to retain affiliations among those who represented orthodoxy. However, breaking such affiliations could not be resolved by the simple acceptance of heterodoxy. Rather a new orthodoxy had to be posed against the old. Thus the new affiliations of the political party assumed the proportions of a militant church movement.

In Buganda, there was relatively easy adaptation of internal cleavage to serve the larger purposes of the state. As a result, no Baganda repudiated their chiefs or the Kabaka. The Buganda government was itself a source of modernism, and no incompatibility between modernism and traditionalism resulted in the enforced disaffiliation of discontented groups. No discontented urban groups emerged, anxiety-ridden and seeking drastic change.

4. *Legitimacy Conflicts.* Just as innovation could not be controlled in Ashanti, so the secular authority of the colonial government was posed against the traditional authority of the chiefs. Immemorial prescriptive rights clashed with concepts of efficiency and performance as a basis of authority. In Buganda, the autocratic principle prevailed and two oligarchies, British and Baganda, worked alongside

one another. They were in constant competition, but they did not challenge each other's legitimacy. Both were oriented to efficiency and performance.

In Ashanti almost any outside activity, by being resisted, posed an ultimate legitimacy problem. So closely interrelated were the elements of social life and belief that they conformed nicely to Durkheim's concept of a fragile and mechanical society. Ultimately all threats were threats against legitimacy. Hence not only was colonialism viewed as a threat to traditional legitimacy, but nationalism was even more so. The conflict between lineage and ancestral sanction (immemoriality) for current acts and secular forces was introduced by colonialism, and helped to produce the nationalism which then had to break the power of traditionalism and its residual hold upon the public. Thus modern nationalism in Ghana is essentially an effort to create a wider legitimacy which introduces some of the same instrumental characteristics which Buganda possessed traditionally. *The result is a growth of an autocratic principle of leadership in Ghana—* the organizational weapon serving as its own justification.

In contrast, in Buganda, the conflict over legitimacy never emerged in sharp form in the colonial-Buganda government relationship. Indeed, even when the Kabaka was exiled, early in the relationship, or more recently when the present Kabaka was deported, the principle of the Kabakaship was not questioned by the Protectorate government authorities.

However, now that the problem of building wider affiliations has been tackled effectively by the Protectorate government, political parties are challenging the principle of hierarchical authority. *They are seeking to supplant hierarchical authority with representative authority* as a means of building a modern nation. They do not, however, need to create attitudes of universalism and performance as the basis of political recruitment since these are already widespread and traditional.

Where the consummatory-pyramidal system prevailed, there developed fierce competitition between traditional and secular leaders to monopolize allegiance. This was expressed by the latter in efforts to build overarching and autocratic institutions which by autocratic means fostered egalitarianism in political recruitment and the exercise of authority. The problem was to prevent social atomism while mobilizing those resources of the society which could capitalize on change itself. This put exceedingly heavy burdens on political nationalists, whose need for organizational control and support became all important.

In the instrumental-hierarchical system prevailing in Buganda, change has aided parochialism and modernism of a local sort, making political modernism of the national state more difficult to achieve. Where consummatory values prevail in the traditional sector, the political leaders lose the advantages of traditionalism. Their need is to find new ways and means of employing it to ease the burdens of political development. Where instrumental values prevail, the local and national forms of modernism need to be brought into some kind of useful identity, so that instrumental traditionalism can reinforce political modernization at the national level.

Ghana shows the effects of a single-party unitary government and its difficulties in modernization. Can a modernizing nation be created through a federal system of government in which the parts will reinforce the whole? In this respect, Uganda represents a potential alternative to the Ghana pattern. Out of regard for instrumental traditionalism, Uganda may find a political compromise proximate to the needs of the public, achieving modernity with both prudence and freedom.

Modernism and traditionalism have become key political issues. Buganda has retained both her tribalism and her separatism, penalizing the political advance of the country as a whole. Ashanti, the last stronghold of tribalism in Ghana, has been defeated by modernism in the form of nationalism. Buganda and Ashanti, Uganda and Ghana, both facing similar problems in different ways, shed some light on the politics of modernization in contemporary Africa.

Chapter 3

The Meaning of Political Development

THE CONCEPT OF POLITICAL DEVELOPMENT

Lucian W. Pye

. . . Western social science was peculiarly unprepared for providing ready intellectual guidance on the problems of political and social development. Indeed, the very stress of contemporary social science that knowledge must be well grounded in empirical investigation caused many social scientists to feel excessively ill-equipped to pass judgments on the prospects of development in strange and unknown societies; thus, paradoxically, men who considered themselves realists above all else often felt it appropriate to drift along with the almost euphorically optimistic view of the possibilities for rapid development in the new state which were so common a few seasons ago. Since many of the guiding considerations which had given a sense of direction and discipline to the social sciences were directly challenged by the emergence of the problems of development, there was an understandable degree of confusion in the field's reactions. Although by now much of this confusion has subsided and there is a general acceptance of the importance of understanding the nature of political development, there is still

considerable ambiguity and imprecision in the use of the term "political development."

Diversity of Definitions

It may therefore be helpful to elaborate some of the confusing meanings which are frequently associated with the expression political development. Our purpose in doing so is not to establish or reject any particular definitions, but rather to illuminate a situation of semantic confusion which cannot but impede the development of theory and becloud the purposes of public policy.

Political Development as the Political Prerequisite of Economic Development. When attention was first fixed on the problem of economic growth and the need to transform stagnant economies into dynamic ones with self-sustaining growth, the economists were quick to point out that political and social conditions could play a decisive role in impeding or facilitating advance in per capita income, and thus it was appropriate to conceive of political development as the state of the polity which might facilitate economic growth.

Operationally, however, such a view of political development tends to be essentially negative, because it is easier to be precise about the ways in which performance of a

SOURCE. Excerpted from Lucian W. Pye, "The Concept of Political Development," *The Annals of the American Academy of Political and Social Science*, **358**, 1–13, March 1965; using only pp. 4–13.

political system may impede or prevent economic development than about how it can facilitate economic growth. This is true because, historically, economic growth has taken place within a variety of political systems and with quite different ranges of public policies.

This leads to the more serious objection that such a concept of political development does not focus on a common set of theoretical considerations, for in some cases it would mean no more than whether a government is following intelligent and economically rational policies while in other situations it would involve far more fundamental considerations about the basic organization of the polity and the entire performance of the society. The problems of political development would thus vary entirely according to the particular economic problems.

Another fundamental difficulty with such a view of political development has become increasingly apparent during the last decade as the prospects for rapid economic development have become exceedingly dim in many of the poor countries. Economies manifestly change far more slowly than political arrangement, and in large numbers of countries substantial economic growth—to say nothing of industrial development—is not likely in our generation although there may still be substantial political change, much of which might, according to other concepts, seem to deserve the label of political development.

Finally there is the objection that in most underdeveloped countries people clearly are concerned with far more than just material advancement, and are anxious about political development quite independently of its effects on the rate of economic growth. Therefore to link political development solely to economic events would be to ignore much that is of dramatic importance in the developing countries.

Political Development as the Poli-
tics Typical of Industrial Societies. A second common concept of political development, which is also closely tied to economic considerations, involves an abstract view of the typical kind of politics basic to already industrialized and economically highly advanced societies. The assumption is that industrial life produces a more-or-less common and generic type of political life which any society can seek to approximate whether it is in fact industrialized or not. In this view the industrial societies, whether democratic or not, set certain standards of political behavior and performance which constitute the state of political development and which represent the appropriate goals of development for all other systems.

The specific qualities of political development thus become certain patterns of presumably "rational" and "responsible" governmental behavior: an avoidance of reckless actions which threaten the vested interests of significant segments of the society, some sense of limitations to the sovereignty of politics, an appreciation of the values of orderly administrative and legal procedures, an acknowledgment that politics is rightfully a mechanism for solving problems and not an end in itself, a stress on welfare programs, and finally an acceptance of some form of mass participation.

Political Development as Political Modernization. The view that political development is the typical or idealized politics of industrial societies merges easily with the view that political development is synonymous with political modernization. The advanced industrial nations are the fashion makers and pace setters in most phases of social and economic life, and it is understandable that many people expect the same to be true in the political sphere. It is, however, precisely the too easy acceptance of this view that agitates the defenders of cultural relativism who question the propriety of identifying industrial, that is, Western, practices as the contemporary and universal standards for all political systems.

Granting this objection, particularly when significance becomes attached to mere fad and fashion, it is still possible to discern in the movement of world history the emergence of certain conventions and even social norms which have increasingly been diffused throughout the world and which people generally feel should be recognized by any self-respecting government. Many of these standards do trace back to the emergence of industrial society and the rise of science and technology, but most of them have by now a dynamic of their own. Mass participation, for example, reflects the sociological realities of industrialized life, but it also has been taken to be an absolute right in the spirit of current world views. Other ideals, such as the demand for universalistic laws, respect for merit rather than birth, and generalized concepts of justice and citizenship, seem now to hold a place above any particular culture and thus reasonably belong to some universal standards of modern political life.

The question immediately arises as to what constitutes form and what is substance in this view of political development. Is the test of development the capacity of a country to equip itself with such modern cultural artifacts as political parties, civil and rational administrations, and legislative bodies? If so, then the matter of ethnocentrism may be of great relevance, for most of these institutions do have a peculiarly Western character. If, on the other hand, importance is attached only to the performance of certain substantive functions, then another difficulty arises in that all political systems have, historically, in one fashion or another, performed the essential functions expected of these modern *and* Western institutions. Thus, what is to distinguish between what is more and what is less "developed"? Clearly the problem of

political development—when thought of as being simply political "modernization"—runs into the difficulty of differentiating between what is "Western" and what is "modern." Some additional criteria seem to be necessary if such a distinction is to be made.

Political Development as the Operations of a Nation-State. To some degree these objections are met by the view that political development consists of the organization of political life and the performance of political functions in accordance with the standards expected of a modern nation-state. In this point of view there is an assumption that, historically, there have been many types of political systems and that all communities have had their form of politics, but that with the emergence of the modern nation-state a specific set of requirements about politics came into existence. Thus, if a society is to perform as a modern state, its political institutions and practices must adjust to these requirements of state performance. The politics of historic empires, of tribe and ethnic community, or of colony must give way to the politics necessary to produce an effective nation-state which can operate successfully in a system of other nation-states.

Political development thus becomes the process by which communities that are nation-states only in form and by international courtesy become nation-states in reality. Specifically, this involves the development of a capacity to maintain certain kinds of public order, to mobilize resources for a specific range of collective enterprises, and to make and uphold effectively types of international commitments. The test of political development would thus involve, first, the establishment of a particular set of public institutions which constitute the necessary infrastructure of a nation-state, and, second, the controlled expression in political life of the phenomenon of nationalism. That is to say, political development is the politics of nationalism within the context of state institutions.

It is important to stress that from this point of view nationalism is only a necessary but far from sufficient condition to ensure political development. Development entails the translation of diffuse and unorganized sentiments of nationalism into a spirit of citizenship and, equally, the creation of state institutions which can translate into policy and programs the aspirations of nationalism and citizenship. In brief, political development is nation-building.

Political Development as Administrative and Legal Development. If we divide nation-building into institution-building and citizenship development we have two very common concepts of political development. Indeed, the concept of political development as organization-building has a long history, and it underlies the philosophy of much of the more enlightened colonial practices.

Historically, when the Western nations came in contact with the societies of the rest of the world, one of the principal sources of tension was the discovery that such societies did not share the same Western concepts about law and the nature of public authority in the adjudication of private disputes. Wherever the European went one of his first revealing queries was: "Who is in charge here?" According to the logic of the European mind, every territory should fall under some sovereignty, and all people in the same geographic location should have a common loyalty and the same legal obligations. Also, in these early clashes of culture the European response was to search for legal redress, and the absence of a recognizable legal order made life uncomfortable for these early Europeans. The Western mind, in groping for a *modus vivendi* to carry out day-to-day relations with what appeared to be exotic and bizarre cultures, naturally turned to the law as a means for achieving order and predictability; and in doing so it estab-

lished the notion that political development rested upon the existence of an orderly legal process.

In time, however, it was discovered that the smooth operation of an explicit and formalized legal system depended upon the existence of an orderly administrative system. The realization of law and order thus called for bureaucratic structures and the development of public administration, and throughout the colonial period the concept of development was closely associated with the introduction of rationalized institutions of administration. And certainly one of the principal heritages of the colonial era for the area of nation-building was that it left behind, in varying degrees, administrative structures which have become the important elements in the infrastructures of now independent nation-states. Indeed, it is now common to evaluate the relative successes of various colonial governments according to the extent to which they succeeded in leaving behind workable administrative systems.

Today the tradition continues, as most newly independent countries consider the strengthening of bureaucracies to be a first task in political development. Much of foreign aid and technical assistance which is conceived to be a value for political development centers on programs in public administrations. Yet recent history, like the longer history of colonialism, has demonstrated that political development involves much more than the building of the authoritative structures of government. More important, when such development moves conspicuously ahead of other aspects of social and political development, it may create imbalances in the system which become in time impediments to nation-building in the full sense. Unquestionably the strengthening of public administration is central in any program of nation-building; the point is only that political development must also cover the nonauthoritative institutions of a polity.

Political Development as Mass Mobilization and Participation. Another aspect of political development involves primarily the role of the citizenry and new standards of loyalty and involvement. Quite understandably, in some former colonial countries the dominant view of what constitutes political development is a form of political awakening whereby former subjects become active and committed citizens. In some countries this view is carried to such an extreme that the effective and mass demonstrational aspect of popular politics becomes an end in itself, and leaders and citizens feel that they are advancing national development by the intensity and frequency of demonstrations of mass political passion. Conversely, some countries which are making orderly and effective progress may, nevertheless, be dissatisfied, for they feel that their more demonstrative neighbors are experiencing greater "development."

According to most views, political development does entail some degree of expanded popular participation, but it is important to distinguish among the conditions of such expansion. Historically, in the West this dimension of political development was closely associated with the widening of suffrage and the induction of new elements of the population into the political process. This process of mass participation meant a diffusion of decision-making, and participation brought some influence on choice and decision. In some of the new states, however, mass participation has not been coupled with an electoral process, but has been essentially a new form of mass response to elite manipulation. It should be recognized that even such limited participation has a role to play in nation-building, for it represents a means of creating new loyalties and a new feeling of national identity.

Thus, although the process of mass participation is a legitimate part of political development it is also fraught with the dangers of either sterile emotionalism or corrupting demagoguery, both of which can sap the strength of a society. The problem, of course, is the classic issue of balancing popular sentiments with public order: that is, the fundamental problem of democracy.

Political Development as the Building of Democracy. This brings us to the view that political development is or should be synonymous with the establishment of democratic institutions and practices. Certainly implicit in many people's view is the assumption that the only form of political development worthy of the name is the building of democracies. Indeed, there are those who would make explicit this connection and suggest that development can only have meaning in terms of some form of ideology, whether democracy, communism, or totalitarianism. According to this view, development only has meaning in terms of the strengthening of some set of values, and to try to pretend that this is not the case is self-deceiving.

As refreshing as it is to find examples of forthright and explicit identification of democracy with development, there is substantial resistance within the social sciences to such an approach. In part this is no doubt the result of a common aspiration within the social sciences to become a value-free science. Even when it is recognized that in an extreme form this aspiration is naive, there is still a sense of propriety which dictates that the categories of social science analysis should reflect reality rather than values.

Also, as a practical matter in the conduct of foreign aid policies Americans have for interesting and revealing reasons believed, probably quite falsely, that it would be easier for us in our relations with underdeveloped countries to talk about "development" rather than "democracy." In this brief survey of attitudes and views we cannot go any deeper into the complex ambiguities which surround the view that development is close to, but not really the same as, democracy. We must instead proceed with our analysis and note that there are those who are equally forthright in asserting that development is fundamentally different from democracy, and that the very attempt to introduce democracy can be a positive liability to development.

Political Development as Stability and Orderly Change. Many of those who feel that democracy is inconsistent with rapid development conceive of development almost entirely in economic or social order terms. The political component of such a view usually centers on the concept of political stability based on a capacity for purposeful and orderly change. Stability that is merely stagnation and an arbitrary support of the status quo is clearly not development, except when its alternative is manifestly a worse state of affairs. Stability is, however, legitimately linked with the concept of development in that any form of economic and social advancement does generally depend upon an environment in which uncertainty has been reduced and planning based on reasonably safe predictions is possible.

This view of development can be restricted mainly to the political sphere because a society in which the political process is capable of rationally and purposefully controlling and directing social change rather than merely responding to it is clearly more "developed" than one in which the political process is the hapless victim of social and economic "forces" that willy-nilly control the destiny of the people. Thus, in the same fashion, as it has been argued that in modern societies man controls nature for his purpose, while in traditional societies man sought mainly to adapt to nature's dictates, we can conceive of political development as depending upon a capacity either to control social change or to be controlled by it. And, of course, the starting point in controlling social forces is the capacity to maintain order.

The problem with this view of development is that it leaves unanswered how much order is necessary or desirable and for what purposes change should be directed. There is also the question of whether the coupling of stability and change is not something which can only occur in the dreams of a middle class, or at least in societies that are far better off than most of the currently underdeveloped ones. Finally, on the scale of priorities there is the feeling that the maintenance of order, however desirable and even essential, stands second to getting things done, and thus development calls for a somewhat more positive view of action.

Political Development as Mobilization and Power. The recognition that political systems should meet some test of performance and be of some utility to society leads us to the concept of political development as the capabilities of a system. When it is argued that democracy may reduce the efficiency of a system there is an implied assumption that it is possible to measure political efficiency; and in turn the notion of efficiency suggests theoretical or idealized models against which reality can be tested.

This point of view leads to the concept that political systems can be evaluated in terms of the level or degree of absolute power which the system is able to mobilize. Some systems which may or may not be stable seem to operate with a very low margin of power, and the authoritative decision makers are close to being impotent in their capacity to initiate and consummate policy objectives. In other societies such decision makers have at their command substantial power, and the society can therefore achieve a wider range of common goals. States naturally differ according to their inherent resource base, but the measure of development is the degree to which they are able to maximize and realize the full potential of their given resources.

It should be noted that this does not necessarily lead to a crude authoritarian view of development as simply the capacity of a government to claim resources from the society. The capacity to mobilize and allocate resources is usually crucially affected by the popular support which the regime commands, and this is why democratic systems can often mobilize resources more efficiently than repressive authoritarian ones. Indeed, in practical terms the problem of achieving greater political development in many societies may involve primarily the realization of greater popular favor —not because of any absolute value of democracy but because only with such support can the system realize a higher degree of mobilization of power.

When political development is conceived of in terms of mobilization and an increase in the absolute level of power in the society, it becomes possible to distinguish both a purpose for development and also a range of characteristics associated with development. Many of these characteristics, in turn, can be measured, and hence it is possible to construct indices of development. Items in such indices might include: prevalence and penetration. of the mass media measured in terms of newspaper circulation and distribution of radios, the tax basis of the society, the proportion of population in government and their distribution in various categories of activities, and the proportion of resources allocated to education, defense, and social welfare.

Political Development as One Aspect of a Multidimensional Process of Social Change. The obvious need for theoretical assumptions to guide the selection of the items that should appear in any index for measuring development leads us to the view that political development is somehow intimately associated with other aspects of social and economic change. This is true because any item which may be relevant in explaining the power potential of a country must also reflect the state of the economy and the social order. The argument can be advanced that it is unnecessary and inappropriate to try to isolate political development too completely from other

forms of development. Although to a limited extent the political sphere may be autonomous from the rest of society, for sustained political development to take place it can only be within the context of a multidimensional process of social change in which no segment for dimension of the society can long lag behind.

According to this point of view, all forms of development are related, development is much the same as modernization, and it takes place within a historical context in which influences from outside the society impinge on the processes of social change just as change in the different aspects of a society—the economy, the polity and social order— all impinge on each other.

The Development Syndrome

There are other possible interpretations of political development—for example, the view common in many former colonies that development means a sense of national self-respect and dignity in international affairs, or the view more common in advanced societies that political development should refer to a postnationalism era when the nation-state will no longer be the basic unit of political life. It would also be possible to distinguish other variations on the theme which we have just presented. For our purposes we have gone far enough to point out, first, the degree of confusion that exists with the term political development and, second, the extent to which behind this confusion there does seem to be a certain more solid basis of agreement. Without trying to assert any particular philosophical orientation or theoretical framework, it may be useful to scan the various definitions or points of view which we have just reviewed in order to isolate those characteristics of political development which seem to be most widely held and most fundamental in general thinking about the problems of development.[1]

[1] The themes basic to the concept of political development which follow reflect the work of

The first broadly shared characteristic which we would note is a general spirit or attitude toward equality. In most views on the subject political development does involve mass participation and popular involvement in political activities. Participation may be either democratic or a form of totalitarian mobilization, but the key consideration is that subjects should become active citizens and at least the pretenses of popular rule are necessary.

Equality also means that laws should be of a universalistic nature, applicable to all and more or less impersonal in their operations. Finally, equality means that recruitment to political office should reflect achievement standards of performance and not the ascriptive considerations of a traditional social system.

A second major theme which we find in most concepts of political development deals with the capacity of a political system. In a sense capacity is related to the outputs of a political system and the extent to which the political system can affect the rest of the society and economy. Capacity is also closely associated to governmental performance and the conditions which affect such performance. More specifically, capacity entails first of all the sheer magnitude, scope and scale of political and governmental performance. Developed systems are presumed to be able to do a lot more and touch upon a far wider variety of social life than less developed systems can. Secondly, capacity means effectiveness and efficiency in the execution of public policy. Developed systems presumably not only do more than others but perform faster and with much greater thoroughness. Finally, capacity is related to ration-

[*footnote 1 continued*
the Committee on Comparative Politics of the Social Science Research Council and will be developed in much greater detail in a forthcoming volume, *The Political System and Political Development*, to be published in the series, "Studies in Political Development," by the Princeton University Press.

ality in administration and a secular orientation toward policy.

A third theme which runs through much of the discussion of political development is that of differentiation and specialization. This is particularly true in the analysis of institutions and structures. Thus, this aspect of development involves first of all the differentiation and specialization of structures. Offices and agencies tend to have their distinct and limited functions, and there is an equivalent of a division of labor within the realm of government. With differentiation there is also, of course, increased functional specificity of the various political roles within the system. And, finally, differentiation also involves the integration of complex structures and processes. That is, differentiation is not fragmentation and the isolation of the different parts of the political system but specialization based on an ultimate sense of integration.

In recognizing these three dimensions of equality, capacity, and differentiation as lying at the heart of the development process, we do not mean to suggest that they necessarily fit easily together. On the contrary, historically, the tendency has usually been that there are acute tensions between the demands for equality, the requirements for capacity, and the processes of greater differentiation. Pressure for greater equality can challenge the capacity of the system, and differentiation can reduce equality by stressing the importance of quality and specialized knowledge.

Indeed, it may, in fact, be possible to distinguish different patterns of development according to the sequential order in which different societies have dealt with the different aspects of the development syndrome. In this sense development is clearly not unilinear, nor is it governed by sharp and distinct stages, but rather by a range of problems that may arise separately or concurrently. In seeking to pattern these different courses of development and to analyze the different types of problems, it is useful to note that the problems of equality are generally related to the political culture and sentiments about legitimacy and commitment to the system; the problems of capacity are generally related to the performance of the authoritative structures of government, and the questions of differentiation touch mainly on the performance of the nonauthoritative structures and the general political process in the society at large. This suggests that in the last analysis the problems of political development revolve around the relationships between the political culture, the authoritative structures, and the general political process.

THE NATURE OF POLITICAL DEVELOPMENT[1]

Alfred Diamant

There is at present no agreement among social scientists on the precise definition of the concept "political development." As has been shown in a previous study, it is quite useless to equate political development or modernization with a kind of rationalizing process by which societies change from traditional political systems into certain forms of democracy as developed in what is loosely called the West. It is obvious that such a conception excludes as irrelevant the political experience of a large number of polities and might lead us to conclude that there has been no form of political development in most parts of the world outside Europe and a few sections of the American hemisphere. We must start with a conception of political development in its most generalized form and then define it more specifically for the large

SOURCE. Alfred Diamant, "The Nature of Political Development," Chapter 2 in "Bureaucracy in Developmental Movement Regimes: A Bureaucratic Model for Developing Societies," a paper prepared for the 1964 Summer Research Seminar of the Comparative Administration Group, American Society for Public Administration, pp. 4–15.

[1] The support of the Ford Foundation, which made possible this seminar as part of a three-year research program in bureaucracy and development, is gratefully acknowledged.

number of polities in Asia, Africa, and Latin America with whose political transformation we are more directly concerned.

Defining the political system, following Gabriel Almond, as the "legitimate, order-maintaining or transforming system in the society,"[2] we find that in the process of modernization the political system undergoes transformation, both in its structure and its functions. In this transformation the relations between polity and society are both autonomous and interdependent. The dynamics of political modernization are at least in part, independent of economic, social, or other forms of change. Furthermore, the political system in a modernizing society comes to deal with an ever wider range of problems— it becomes the generalized problem solver for the entire society. It will be largely unfettered by ascriptive elements which, in a traditional society, restrict the range of problems with which the political system is expected to deal; furthermore, in a traditional system the general level of complexity of problems will be lower than in a modernizing system, so that there is a

[2] "A Functional Approach to Comparative Politics," in Gabriel Almond and James Coleman (eds.), *The Politics of the Developing Areas* (Princeton: Princeton University Press, 1960), pp. 3–64 at 7.

distinction in both the range and complexity of problems between traditional and modernizing societies. The political system becomes not the only problem solver in a modernizing society, but it comes to occupy a dominant role in this respect.

In its most general form, then, political development is a process by which a political system acquires an increased capacity to sustain successfully and continuously new types of goals and demands and the creation of new types of organizations. For this process to continue over time a differentiated and centralized polity must come into being which must be able to command resources from and power over wide spheres and regions of the society. In this most general form political development is certainly a multinormative process, a variety of demands and goals are being pursued simultaneously; as will be pointed out later this ability to process several major demands and goals concurrently marks the "success" or "failure" of modernization. Developing societies want not only a variety of material things, capital as well as consumer goods at the same time, but also desire security, both internal and external, dignity and many other collective and individual goods. Also implied in the criterion of sustaining new goals and demands is the notion that political power be widely distributed and that ultimately all individuals and groups will be entitled to be consulted by the policy makers in some form. There is nothing here to prejudge the form this consultation has to take to be considered "modern"; it may range from democratic elections with alternative programs being offered by competing parties, to a mobilization of nonelites by elites. In fact, even a cursory survey indicates that the latter form occurs quite frequently in societies in which the creation of a comprehensive communications network is still a task to be accomplished.[3]

It must also be stressed that the present conception of political development does not include any notion that this process will have a definable "end product," such as "high mass consumption" which has been defined by W. W. Rostow as the final stage or product of economic development.[4] Rather, political development is conceived as a process of meeting new goals and demands in a flexible manner. It has, in fact, been suggested that flexibility of symbols, of institutions, of establishing and meeting goals and demands, is the central element of the modernization process.[5]

Another explanation which might be in order at this time concerns the juxtaposition of differentiation and centralization in the matter of sustaining political development. The need for centralization in a developing society must be taken to apply chiefly to the earliest stages of modernization when it is necessary to bring together a number of groups, tribes, clans, etc., to create certain minimum conditions for political development to begin and to continue successfully. At the same time it must be added that differentiation as a process does not imply unlimited specialization of functions and creation of specialized institutions, for along with differentiation there goes also a process of integration of newly acquired skills and functions and of new institutions. It might well be that at later stages of political development decentralization, deconcentration, or other processes of dispersal will become significant. Some tantalizing prospects have been opened up on this point with the recent experiences of the Soviet Union and some of the Eastern European Communist countries, but not even the specialists on communist systems can agree on the meaning of the phenomena they observe, not to speak of drawing out of these experi-

---

[3] See the various essays in Lucian Pye (ed.), *Communications and Political Development* (Princeton: Princeton University Press, 1963).

[4] W. W. Rostow, *The Stages of Economic Growth: A Non-Communist Manifesto* (Cambridge [Eng.]: At the University Press, 1960).

[5] S. N. Eisenstadt, "Breakdowns of Modernization," 12 *Economic Development and Cultural Change*, 345–367 (July 1964).

ences some generalizations applicable to very different types of political systems.

In its most general form, the political development process as here defined does not require the creation of particular kinds of political institutions. Though we will subsequently adopt for our use a set of demands or capabilities making up the most common form of developmental goals drawn from the experience of Western political systems, there is no suggestion here that only political institutions we would generally term "Western"—parliament, cabinet executive, etc.—are appropriate for development. The actual patterns of modernization, even as experienced in the West, are so multifarious, and the range of social, political, and economic conditions which characterize societies in Asia, Africa, and Latin America is so wide that we can neither identify nor prescribe a single pattern.

An equally difficult problem of political modernization is that of recognizable stages of development which have to be taken in a specific sequence for a new state to move toward a more developed form of political system. With Almond I would suggest that though there is some common content to the development process, there will not likely be a common outcome; the implications of cultural diffusion and change in general, and those of political change in particular "are far from unilinear."[6] Though it might be impossible to specify "stages of political development," it might still be necessary to develop what might be called the functional equivalents of gradualism. That is to say, where there arise irresistible demands for rapid change we might have to find some mechanisms or procedures that can take the place of "orderly stages." The need for such a functional equivalent

became quite obvious in the Belgian Congo, but if a search was made it certainly was not successful, judging by the history of the Congo (Leopoldville) in recent years.

It must also be stressed that analysis of and experience with recent examples of political development does not support some earlier notions that traditional symbols and institutions cannot be successfully utilized for modernization. Apter's study of Uganda and especially the evidence presented in the recent comparative study of modernization in Turkey and Japan leave little doubt that traditional symbols and institutions can be effective vehicles for political development;[7] to this must be added the thoroughly documented experience of such older Western societies as Great Britain.[8] What seems to be crucial is the flexibility of the traditional symbols and institutions and not simply their presence or absence. France which has been undergoing rapid transformation during the past decade had apparently reached a point of *immobilisme* during the Third Republic and the early years of the Fourth Republic, chiefly because of the inflexibility of the older symbols and institutions. New institutions and symbols had to arise before what Stanley Hoffman has called the "stalemate society" could be overcome.[9] It is not really necessary to resort to the well-worn Marxian gynecological analogy of the new order being conceived in the womb of the old; rather we can say that traditional institutions which can become sufficiently flexible may

[7] David E. Apter, *The Political Kingdom in Uganda: A Study in Bureaucratic Nationalism* (Princeton: Princeton University Press, 1961); Robert E. Ward and Dankwart Rustow (eds.) *Political Modernization in Japan and Turkey* (Princeton: Princeton University Press, 1964). In the latter see especially Ch. 7, "The Civil Bureaucracy," pp. 301–327.

[8] Stanley Rothman, "Modernity and Tradition in Britain," 28 *Social Research*, pp. 297–320 (Autumn 1961).

[9] Stanley Hoffman, "Paradoxes of the French Political Community," in Stanley Hoffman *et al.*, *In Search of France* (Cambridge: Harvard University Press, 1963), pp. 1–117.

[6] Gabriel Almond, "Political Systems and Political Change," 5 *American Behavioral Scientist* 7 (June 1963). For a fuller statement see his "A Developmental Approach to Political Systems," 17 *World Politics* 183–214 (January 1965).

serve as vehicles for modernization and need not be pushed aside abruptly at the inception of the development process.

Finally, it must be noted that the present conception of political development implies nothing about eventual success or failure of the venture. That is to say, the process is not irreversible; modernization having once begun or even after having persisted over a period can stop or even be reversed. There seems to be ample evidence that in a number of new states, Professor Eisenstadt examines Indonesia, Burma, and Pakistan,[10] the process of modernization was halted and that they reverted to a less flexible level of political and social differentiation. In no case did they return to a fully traditional order, but the levels of performance, of differentiation, of flexibility, of being able to meet demands and goals were lowered considerably beyond what had already been achieved.

So far, political development has been defined in broad or generic terms. It has been defined as a process which can occur in any society under a great variety of conditions; there also have been no suggestions about the sort of goals and demands which are posed and which are subsequently processed, more or less successfully. Is it now possible to go a step further and ask: What are the sort of goals and demands originating in the new states of Asia and Africa, as well as in the older states of Latin America and perhaps even in Eastern Europe? A number of attempts have been made to categorize these demands arising in the new states. These will now be examined to see whether it is possible to state more concretely the nature of political development in the new states.

Milton Esman suggests in what he calls his "task oriented" approach that "contemporary public policy in these societies is addressed in large measure to two fundamental and interrelated goals: na-

tion-building and socioeconomic progress." The former he defines as the "deliberate fashioning of an integrated political community within fixed geographic boundaries" with the nation-state as the dominant political institution; the latter, as one might expect, simply means improvement in social and material welfare.[11] These two interrelated goals are the tasks which the elites of the new states are trying to achieve. Esman then goes on to suggest that the elites attempt to accomplish these tasks with the help of certain "doctrines" and "action instruments." The difficulty with Esman's categories is that they attempt to cover too much and thus do not cover enough. The "doctrine" category is little more than the reformulation of the notion of political development in ideological garb. The "action instruments" are identified as political organization, the administrative system, associational interest groups, and the mass media. These would seem to be the instrument any elite would use, including elites in fully developed societies. Esman seems to have succumbed to the same sort of temptation as did Joseph Spengler and Howard Wriggins: to attempt a catalog of "tasks" which governments of developing states must accomplish in order to become fully developed. An inspection of Esman's catalog will reveal that like Wriggins and Spengler[12] he has simply specified the tasks that *any* government must be able to meet successfully. Not surprising, then, that the action instruments for these tasks turn out to be little different from the action instruments of

[10] See Eisenstadt, "Breakdowns of Modernization," *op. cit.*, p. 345.

[11] Milton J. Esman, "The Politics of Development Administration," in William J. Siffin and John D. Montgomery (eds.), *Administration and Development: Theory and Strategy* (New York: McGraw-Hill Book Co., in press).

[12] Joseph J. Spengler, "Economic Development: Political Preconditions and Political Consequences," 22 *Journal of Politics*, pp. 387–416 at 406–414; Howard Wriggins, "Foreign Assistance and Political Development," in Robert Asher, *et al.*, *Development of the Emerging Countries: An Agenda for Research* (Washington: The Brookings Institution, 1962), pp. 39–44 at 41.

any polity, developing or fully developed—with the possible exception of a handful of traditional oligarchies. Though I do not find Esman's present formulation fully satisfactory, he must be credited with having moved in the right direction and for having begun to specify what sort of goals, demands, and tasks are being processed in developing polities.

A better defined, more analytical, and yet less concrete attack on the problem of what sorts of goals and demands get is that of Gabriel Almond.[13] He conceives of political development as the acquisition by political systems of "a new capability, in the sense of a specialized role structure and differentiated orientations which together give a political system the possibility of responding efficiently, and more or less autonomously, to a new range of problems." All political systems, Almond argues, must acquire the capability to deal with four sets of problems: (1) integrative capability—the creation of national unity and a centralized bureaucracy, (2) international accommodative capability—ability to engage in international contacts of various sorts, (3) participation capability—creation of a political culture of civic obligation and of a democratic political structure, (4) welfare or distribution capability—widespread dissemination of welfare standards and accommodation between political and social structures.[14]

With a possible demurrer on point (3) which takes in more than the present generalized concept of political development can accommodate (nothing has been specified about forms of participation), the remainder of this statement fits well with what has been suggested so far. The ability of a system to acquire these performance capabilities would indicate that political development is proceeding effectively and that the new demands, especially participation and welfare, are being met successfully. There might well be failures or breakdowns of development when too many of these capabilities have to be acquired at the same time, France during the Third and Fourth Republic, and Italy and Germany after 1870 would be excellent Western examples of the consequences of the simultaneity of demands; the experience of many of the new states in Asia and Africa could be similarly classified. Almond can tell us little about the institutional aspects of acquiring new capabilities, but his identification of types of demands is preferable to Esman's catalog, or even those of Wriggins and Spengler. On balance, Almond's "theoretical insight," as he calls it, has several attractive features; it stresses problem-solving capability, it calls attention to participation and centralization, and, most important, it links new capabilities to new role structures and personal identifications (political culture).

In drawing together the evidence about political modernization in Turkey and Japan, Rustow and Ward add a dimension to the problem of development too often left aside:

The problems which a country confronts in setting out to modernize its political system seem to us to be of two main types: (1) those which are set or predetermined in such a manner as to be wholly or largely beyond the control of the leaders of the modernizing society, and (2) those which are amenable to some significant degree of influence or control by these leaders.[15]

Among the former are three: geopolitical problems—location, resources, etc., of the modernizing country; then there is the problem of timing, the point in the country's evolution when change is initiated as well as the general level of political development of the outside world which impinges on the modernizing society; and finally, the nature of the country's traditional

[13] Almond, "Political Systems and Political Change," *op. cit.*
[14] *Ibid.*, p. 8.

[15] Ward and Rustow, "Conclusion," in Ward and Rustow, *Political Modernization in Japan and Turkey, op. cit.*, pp. 434–468 at 465.

heritage which, differing widely from country to country, profoundly affects the rate and even the direction of development. These, Ward and Rustow point out, are largely intractable as far as the modernizing groups are concerned. The second set of problems, however, can be managed to a certain degree by the modernizing groups. The seven problems or crises identified by Ward and Rustow follow closely the four types of system capabilities developed by Almond; they also recognize the possibilities inherent in using traditional institutions for modernizing purposes. Rustow and Ward suggest that political development begins during some form of traditional rule and proceeds to some form of mass society, either democratic or authoritarian. The range of public services expands and at the same time the individual is called upon for a variety of services, including military:

> The very concepts of public service and civic duty ... are among the vital prerequisites of modern politics. The tendency, moreover, is for services and obligations to become universal. ... Hence political modernization clearly has egalitarian tendencies.[16]

[16] Rustow and Ward, "Introduction," in *ibid.*, pp. 3–13 at 5.

To sum up, we understand by political development a generic process of successfully sustaining new demands, goals, and organizations in a flexible manner. In the case of the "developing nations" it means the meeting of particular goals and demands. Certain of these are given for each society, depending on its ecology, traditional institutions, and time and manner of entering into the "development stream." Other demands and goals of a particular sort involving nation-building and socioeconomic progress can be processed provided the system acquires certain system capabilities. The widening range of demands implies an egalitarian mass society, though nothing can be specified about its democratic or non-democratic character. Though it is possible to state what are the characteristics of a modernized polity,[17] it is almost impossible to state with equal specificity those of a modernizing or developing system. ...

[17] *Ibid.*, pp. 6–7. The characteristics specified by Rustow and Ward include the usual features of a modern society: differentiated and specific system of government; high degree of integration within government system; rational and secular procedures for making political decisions; popular identification with national identity of state; widespread interest and involvement in politics, etc.

A DEVELOPMENTAL APPROACH TO POLITICAL SYSTEMS

Gabriel A. Almond

During the past decade two tendencies have come to dominate the field of comparative politics. One of these is the concern for theoretical explication and methodological rigor, and the second is the emphasis on field studies of the "emerging," "new,"

SOURCE. Gabriel A. Almond, "A Developmental Approach to Political Systems," *World Politics,* **17,** 183–214, January 1965.

and "non-Western" nations. The theoretical tendency has largely taken the form of applications of "systems" theory to the study of politics, and the chief criticism of this approach has been that it is a static theory, not suitable for the analysis and explanation of political change.

The great output of empirical studies of contemporary politics in the new and emerging nations and the relative decline in the volume of European political studies have similarly been criticized. Here the argument is that the relative neglect of Western political studies, and particularly of their historical dimension, handicaps us in our efforts to work out the developmental theories and approaches which we need for our research on the new and emerging nations.

Both of these criticisms have great cogency. Systems theory does have a static, "equilibrium" bias; and the stress on the politics of the new and emerging nations gives us an inadequate sampling of man's experience with social and political change. The only answer to this criticism is that this seems to be the way sciences develop—not by orderly, systematic progression, but in a dialectical process involving overemphases and neglects. If we are to come to grips more effectively with political change, we shall have to redress this imbalance, adapt systems theory in a developmental direction, and utilize historical knowledge of Western political development (but not only Western history) in elaborating theories of political systems and political change.

This article represents a move in this direction, an effort on the part of one political systems theorist to define what political development consists of and to take into account the variables which affect it.[1]

System and Function

The term "system" has become increasingly common in the titles of texts and monographs in the field of comparative politics. Older texts tended to use such terms as "governments" or "foreign powers." Something more is involved here than mere style in nomenclature. The use of the concept of system reflects the penetration into political theory of the anthropological and sociological theory of functionalism. The chief social theorists whose names are associated with functionalism are the anthropologists Malinowski and Radcliffe-Brown and the sociologists Parsons, Merton, and Marion Levy.[2] Though they differ substantially in their concepts of system and function, what these men have been saying is that our capacity for explanation and prediction in the social sciences is enhanced when we think of social structures and institutions as performing *functions* in *systems*.

The point being made here is both simple and important. A circulatory system in an organism makes little sense by itself. When we view it as serving a purpose or set of purposes for the functioning of the organism as a whole, we can begin to comprehend its significance. Similarly, political parties or administrative agencies mean little by themselves. Their significance becomes clear when we see them as interacting with

[1] Whatever merit this contribution to the theory of political change may have is due to a long series of polemics which began with my paper, "Comparative Political Systems" (*Journal of Politics*, **17** [August 1956], 391–409), and became somewhat more lively after the appearance of my introductory essay in Almond and Coleman, eds., *The Politics of the Developing Areas* (Princeton, 1960). An early and partial version of some of the ideas contained here appeared in Almond, "Political Systems and Political Change," *American Behavioral Scientist*, **6** (June, 1963), 3–10. The polemics were in part with myself, in part with graduate students in seminars, in part with reviewers, and in most substantial part with my friends and colleagues of the Committee on Comparative Politics. These ideas were partly formulated during two

summer workshops which the Committee held, one in 1962 and the second in 1963. Sidney Verba spent several weeks during both of these summers discussing "input-output" and "capabilities" theory with me. I am deeply in his debt for these formulations.

[2] Bronislaw Malinowski, *Magic, Science, and Religion* (Anchor Books, Garden City, N.Y., 1954); A. R. Radcliffe-Brown, *Structure and Function in Primitive Society* (Glencoe, 1957); Talcott Parsons, *Essays in Sociological Theory Pure and Applied* (Glencoe, 1949); Parsons, *The Social System* (Glencoe, 1951); Talcott Parsons and Edward Shils, eds., *Toward a General Theory of Action* (Cambridge, Mass., 1951); R. K. Merton, *Social Theory and Social Structure* (Glencoe, 1957); Marion Levy, Jr., *The Structure of Society* (Princeton, 1952).

other institutions to produce public policies and enforcements of public policies in the domestic or international environments.

Functional-system theory as formulated by such writers as Talcott Parsons and Marion Levy implies three conditions: functional requisites, interdependence, and equilibrium. A particular system, whether it be an organism, a machine, or a family, has to behave in particular ways, perform a set of tasks, in order to "be" the particular organism, machine, or family. Levy calls these requirements "functional requisites," and lists nine activities as essential to the existence of any society. To illustrate, Levy includes among these requisites adaptation to the natural environment, differentiation of and recruitment to social roles, the maintenance of a common body of knowledge and beliefs, the socialization of the young, and the control of disruptive behavior.[3] Parsons speaks of four "imperatives of any system of action," including adaptation, goal gratification, integration, and latent pattern maintenance and tension management.[4] These and other writers also make the point that, for a system to continue in operation, these functions must be performed in certain ways. When a function is performed in such a way as to maintain the equilibrium of the system, the performance of the function by the agency or structure is referred to as "functional" (or *eufunctional*, in Marion Levy's formulation). When the performance upsets the equilibrium, then it is referred to as "dysfunctional." We shall come back to this concept of functionality-dysfunctionality at a later point.

We need to elaborate a little on the other two assumptions of systems theory—*interdependence* and *equilibrium*. By the interdependence of the parts of a system, we mean that when the properties of one component in a system change, all the

others, and the system as a whole, are affected. Thus if the rings of an automobile erode, we speak of the car as "burning oil"; the functioning of other systems deteriorates; and the power of the car declines. Or, in the growth of organisms there are points, for example, when some change in the endocrine system affects the overall pattern of growth, the functioning of all the parts, and the general behavior of the organism. In political systems, the emergence of mass parties or mass media of communication changes the performance of all the other structures of the political system, and affects the general capabilities of the system in its domestic and foreign environments. In other words, when one variable in a system changes in magnitude, or in quality, the others are subjected to strains and are transformed, and the system changes its pattern of performance; or the dysfunctional component is disciplined by regulatory mechanisms, and the equilibrium of the system is reestablished. Parsons and Shils argue that social systems tend toward equilibrium;[5] i.e., families, economies, churches, polities tend to preserve their character through time, or to change slowly. Hence the analytical scheme which they propose for generalized use in the social sciences is this concept of system, implying the interdependent interaction of structures performing functions in such a way as to maintain the social system in equilibrium.

Even in this starkly simple form, the generic system model has value for the study of politics. The concept of function pushes us into realism and away from normative or ideological definitions. To answer functional questions we have to observe what a particular social system actually is and does. The concepts of functionality and dysfunctionality sensitize us to the factors making for social stability and social change, and enable us to perceive them in an orderly and thorough way. The concept of interdependence forces us

[3] Levy, *Structure of Society*, 149 ff.
[4] Talcott Parsons, *Economy and Society* (Glencoe, 1956), 16 ff.

[5] Parsons and Shils, eds., *Toward a General Theory of Action*, 107 ff.

to examine the performance of any structure or institution systemically; i.e., in all of its ramifications and interdependencies. We can no longer be contented with describing a single institution or looking at bilateral interactions. Our research must assume interdependence and interaction among all components.

Critique of Functional Theory

The introduction of functionalism into the social sciences has stirred up a good deal of controversy and polemic.[6] Among the critics of functional theory, the logician Hempel has raised questions about the scientific status of functionalism, arguing that its exponents fail to provide operational criteria of function and dysfunction, and of the kind of interaction among variables which maintain a system in equilibrium. Gouldner's principal criticism is that the concept of system and function has come from biology and mechanics, and that there has been a tendency to attribute the properties of organismic and mechanical systems to social systems. He points out that interdependence and equilibrium may be of a radically different character in social systems. The autonomy of the components of social systems—i.e., the extent to which they may vary without significantly affecting other variables and the system as a whole—may be far greater than in mechanical and organismic systems.

Gouldner also argues that there is a static tendency in systems theory, a tendency to stress the functionality of institutions and the equilibrium of social systems. The distinction as formulated in anthropological and sociological theory tends to be dichotomous; i.e., structures perform either functionally or dysfunctionally. He argues that they should be

viewed as continua, since without specification and measurement it is impossible to say what kind and degree of performance by given structures and institutions produce what kind of social equilibrium. Here Gouldner and Hempel would agree that what we need is a model of interaction of components in which the relations among variables and their consequences for system performance are left open to empirical investigation.

A further valuable criticism is Gouldner's argument that there is a tendency to treat each component in a social system as having a value equal to each of the others. Actually the significance and autonomy of the various parts of social systems may be quite unequal. Thus one may argue that the bureaucracy in differentiated political systems is in some sense the central structure of these systems, and that all other structures are significant by virtue of the way in which they affect the performance of the bureaucracy. Here again we need system models more appropriate for social and political phenomena.

Finally Gouldner argues that such a social system theorist as Parsons does not give sufficient stress to the special character of the interaction of social systems with their environments. He may attribute too great an impermeability to the boundaries of social systems. Thus political systems are quite porous, so to speak. The exchanges and movements which take place between political systems and their societies or their international environments, particularly in the modern world, are quite massive. It is impossible to account for either equilibrium or change in political systems without observing the volume and kind of their interactions with their social and international environments.

The main burden of these criticisms is that social system theory is still too much under the influence of biological and mechanical analogies, and that it fails to specify operational indices for such concepts as functionality, interdependence, and equilibrium. The criticisms have merit,

[6] See *inter alia* Carl G. Hempel, "The Logic of Functional Analysis," and Alvin W. Gouldner, "Reciprocity and Autonomy in Functional Theory," in Llewellyn Gross, ed., *Symposium in Sociological Theory* (New York, 1959), 241 ff.

but they should not obscure the importance of the original insights of the social system theorists. What we are engaged in here is simply an elaboration and adaptation of their work.

Before we drop the generic system concept and turn to the special characteristics of political systems, we need to deal with one or two other terms. Intrinsic to the concept of system is the notion of boundary and of exchanges or actions across boundaries. A system starts somewhere and stops somewhere. In dealing with an organism or a machine, it is relatively easy to locate the boundary and specify the interactions between it and its environment. The gas goes into the tank; the motor converts it into revolutions of the crankshaft and the driving wheels; and the car moves on the highway. In dealing with social systems, of which political systems are a class, the problem of boundary is not that easy. We may speak of what separates a social system from its environment as a boundary, but what we mean by this is not at all clear. Social systems are not made up of individuals but of roles; i.e., a family consists of the roles of mother and father, husband and wife, sibling and sibling, and the like. The family is only one set of interacting roles for a group of individuals who also may have extra-familial roles, and hence be involved in other social systems. In the same sense, a political system consists of the roles of nationals, subjects, voters, interacting— as the case may be—with legislators, bureaucrats, judges, and the like. The same individuals who perform roles in the political system perform roles in other social systems, such as the economy, religious community, family, and voluntary associations. As individuals expose themselves to political communication, vote, demonstrate, they shift from nonpolitical to political roles. One might say that on election day as citizens leave their farms, plants, and offices to go to the polling places, they are crossing the boundary from the economy to the polity. It is cros-

sing the boundary in both an objective and a subjective sense. In the objective sense, a man leaves his assembly line, where he is performing a role in a manufacturing process, to enter the polling booth, where he is performing a role in a political process. In a psychological sense, some shift of norms, values, expectations, and cognitions takes place as well.

The concept of boundary as we apply it to social and political systems is, of course, an analogy. What we really mean by this analogy can be specified only if we examine empirically the actual exchanges which take place between one system and another. Thus, when we speak of the interaction of personalities and the political system, we are thinking of the impulses, attitudes, and values entering into the performance of political roles by the individuals who make up the political system. At some point in this interactive process, properties which we associate with personality, such as hostility and rigidity, get converted into attitudes toward or choices of particular foreign or defense policies or candidates for public office. In other words, there are boundaries here between general affective and value tendencies, and political attitudes and choices.

There is a boundary between the polity and the economy. For example, an inflation may reduce the real income of certain groups in the population. When these changes in the economic situations of particular groups get converted into demands for public policy or changes in political personnel, there is an interaction between the economy and the polity. What really happens in the empirical sense is that certain psychic states resulting from changes in the economic capabilities of groups are converted into demands on the political system, demands on trade union or other pressure group leaders that they lobby for particular actions by the legislative or executive agencies, and the like. Somewhere along the line here a boundary is passed from one system to another, from the economic system to the political system.

That we are using an analogy when we speak of the boundaries of political systems, and a misleadingly simple analogy at that, becomes clear when we consider the variety of phenomena we include under it. We use it in a simple physical sense, as when we speak of the boundaries of nations or of subnational political jurisdictions. We use it in a behavioral sense, as when we refer to the interactions of voters and candidates, governmental officials and citizens, as these are separated from the interactions of these same individuals in their roles as workers and employers, parishioners and clergy. We use it in a psychological sense, as when we refer to attitudes toward politics, politicians, public officials, and public policies, as these are differentiated from the other contents of the psyches of the members of a polity. Whenever we use the term we need to be clear just which one, or which combination, of these phenomena we have in mind.

Another way of thinking about the interaction of political systems with their environments is to divide the process into three phases, as is usually done in systems theory—input, conversion, output. The inputs and outputs which involve the political system with other social systems are transactions between the system and its environment; the conversion processes are internal to the political system. When we talk about the sources of inputs and how they enter the political system, and how outputs leave the political system and affect other social systems, we shall in effect be talking about the boundaries of the political system.

Three Types of Functions

One further thought before we leave this generic concept of system and turn to political systems, properly speaking. We have talked about the functions of systems and how they give the system its identity. Actually, we need to think of systems as functioning at different *levels*.

One level of functioning involves the unit as a whole in its environment. An animal moves, while plants do not. Some machines process data; others produce power. An economy produces and distributes physical goods and services. Families produce children and socialize them into adult roles and disciplines. Religious systems regulate the relations of their members with authorities and norms to which supernatural qualities are attributed. What we focus on at this level is the behavior of the system as a unit in its relations with other social systems and the environment.

The second kind of functioning is internal to the system. Here we refer to "conversion processes," such as the digestion of food, the elimination of waste, the circulation of the blood, the transmission of impulses through the nervous system. The conversion processes or functions are the ways particular systems transform inputs into outputs. Obviously the two levels of behavior are related. In order for an animal to be able to move, hunt, dig, and the like, energy must be created in the organism and the use of the energy controlled and directed. The level and kind of performance of the system in its environment are tied up with a particular kind of structural-functional performance inside the system.

In talking about politics, we shall speak of the performance of the political system in its environment as the political system's "capabilities." What happens inside the political system we shall refer to as "conversion functions." To illustrate, we shall speak here of the "responsive capability" of political systems, meaning by the term the openness of the political system to demands coming from various groups in the society, or from the international political system. This capacity to respond is associated with the performance inside the political system of such functions as communication, interest articulation, aggregation, and rule-making.

Finally, we shall speak of "system-maintenance and adaptation functions." For an automobile to perform efficiently on the road, parts must be lubricated, repaired, replaced. New parts may perform stiffly; they must be "broken in." In a political system the incumbents of the various roles (diplomats, military officers, tax officials, and the like) must be recruited to these roles and learn how to perform them. New roles are created and new personnel "broken in." These functions (in machines, maintenance and replacement of parts; in politics, *recruitment* and *socialization*) do not directly enter into the conversion processes of the system; they affect the internal efficiency and operations of the system, and hence condition its performance.

When we compare classes of political systems with each other, or individual political systems with each other, we need to make these comparisons in terms of *capabilities, conversion functions,* and *system-maintenance and adaptation functions,* and the interrelations among these three kinds of functions. And when we talk about political development, it will also be in terms of the interrelations of these three kinds of political functions. A change in capability will be associated with changes in the performance of the conversion functions, and these changes in turn will be related to changes in political socialization and recruitment.

While the individual categories that we use may, on empirical test, turn out to be inappropriate, this threefold classification of functions is important for political analysis, and we believe it will hold up under testing and examination.[7] The

theory of the political system will consist of the discovery of the relations among these different levels of functioning—capabilities, conversion functions, and system-maintenance and adaptation functions—and of the interrelations of the functions at each level. The theory of political change deals with those transactions between the political system and its environment that affect changes in general system performance, or capabilities that in turn are associated with changes in the performance of the system-adaptation functions and the conversion functions.

The Political System: Inputs and Outputs

This discussion of the concept of system has been useful, but we shall be open to the criticism of being carried away by an analogy if we fail to bring these analytical tools into the world of politics. What is the political system? What gives it its special identity? Much has been written on this subject, and it is difficult to get agreement among political theorists on the precise language of their definitions. Common to most of these definitions is the association of the political system with the use of legitimate physical coercion in societies. Easton speaks of *authoritative allocation of values,* Lasswell and Kaplan of *severe deprivations,* Dahl of *power, rule, and authority.*[8] Common to all of these definitions is their association of politics with legitimate heavy sanctions.[9] We have suggested elsewhere that "Legitimate force is the thread that runs through the inputs and outputs of the political system, giving it its special quality and salience and its

[7] This approach to functional requisites analysis is related to earlier work but differs in its explicit differentiation of these three classes of function. For other applications of functional theory to the study of political systems, see in particular David Apter, *The Gold Coast in Transition* (Princeton, 1955), 325 ff.; Apter, "A Comparative Method for the Study of Politics," *American Journal of Sociology,* **64** (November 1958), 221–237; and Apter's contribution to Harry Eckstein and David Apter, eds., *Comparative Politics* (New

York, 1963), 723 ff.; also William C. Mitchell, *The American Polity* (New York, 1962), 7 ff.
[8] David Easton, *The Political System* (New York, 1953), 130 ff.; Harold Lasswell and Abraham Kaplan, *Power and Society* (New Haven, 1950), 176; Robert Dahl, *Modern Political Analysis* (Englewood Cliffs, N.J., 1963), 5 ff.
[9] See Max Weber, "Politics as a Vocation," in Hans Gerth and C. Wright Mills, eds., *From Max Weber* (New York, 1946), 78.

coherence as a system. The inputs into the political system are all in some way related to claims for the employment of legitimate physical compulsion, whether these are demands for war or for recreational facilities. The outputs of the political system are also in some way related to legitimate physical compulsion, however remote the relationship may be. Thus public recreational facilities are usually supported by taxation, and any violation of the regulations governing their use is a legal offense...."[10] When we speak of the political system, we include all of the interactions—inputs as well as outputs—which affect the use or threat of use of physical coercion. "We mean to include not just the structures based on law, like parliaments, executives, bureaucracies, and courts, or just the associational or formally organized units, like parties, interest groups, and media of communication, but *all of the structures in their political aspects*, including undifferentiated structures like kinship and lineage, status and caste groups, as well as anomic phenomena like riots, street demonstrations, and the like."[11]

This is not the same thing as saying that the political system is solely concerned with force, violence, or compulsion, but only that its relation to coercion is its distinctive quality. Political elites may be concerned with peace, social welfare, individual freedom and self-realization, but their concern with these values as politicians is somehow related to compulsory actions such as taxation, lawmaking and law enforcement, foreign and defense policy. The political system is not the only system that makes rules and enforces them, but its rules and enforcements go "all the way" in compelling obedience or performance.

David Easton, who was the first political scientist to write about politics in explicit "system" terms, distinguishes two classes of inputs into the political system—

demands and *supports*.[12] Demand inputs may be subclassified in a variety of ways. We suggest that they may be classified under four headings: (1) demands for goods and services, such as wage and hour laws, educational opportunities, recreational facilities, roads and transportation; (2) demands for the regulation of behavior, such as provision of public safety, control over markets and labor relations, rules pertaining to marriage and the family; (3) demands for participation in the political system, for the right to vote, hold office, petition governmental bodies and officials, organize political associations, and the like; and (4) symbolic inputs, such as demands for the display of the majesty and power of the political system in periods of threat or on ceremonial occasions, or demands for the affirmation of norms, or the communication of policy intent from political elites.

Support inputs may be classified under four headings: (1) material supports, such as the payment of taxes or other levies, and the provision of services, such as labor contributions or military service; (2) obedience to laws and regulations; (3) participation, such as voting, joining organizations, and communicating about politics; and (4) manifestation of deference to public authority, symbols, and ceremonials.

On the output side, we may speak of four classes of transactions initiated by the political system that tend to match up with the supports we have listed above and may or may not be responsive to demands, depending on the kind of political system that is involved. These are: (1) extractions, which may take the form of tribute, booty, taxes, or personal services; (2) regulations of behavior, which may take a variety of forms and affect some subset of the whole gamut of human behavior and relations; (3) allocations or distributions of goods and services, op-

---

[10] Almond and Coleman, eds., *Politics of the Developing Areas*, 7.

[11] *Ibid.*, 8.

[12] "An Approach to the Analysis of Political Systems," *World Politics*, 9 (April 1957), 383–400.

portunities, honors, statuses, and the like; and (4) symbolic outputs, including affirmations of values, displays of political symbols, statements of policies and intents.

When we speak of a stable political system, what we usually have in mind is a particular pattern of flow into and out of the political system, a particular kind of input-output flow. In the political system, properly speaking, the inputs of demands and supports are *converted* into extractive, regulative, distributive, and symbolic outputs. The demands can be handled by the political system; the strains which they impose are bearable without any basic change in structure or culture. The outputs are responsive to the demands in expected or legitimate ways; and the supports are responsive to the outputs again in expected or legitimate ways. When these conditions obtain, the political system may be said to be in a state of equilibrium both internally (in the performance of conversion functions by political structures) and in its relations with its environments.

One last point should be made about the flow of inputs and outputs. This is the question of the source of the inputs. We do not wish to leave the impression that inputs necessarily come only from the society of which the political system is a part, and that the political system must be viewed only in "conversion" terms. It is typical of political systems that inputs are generated internally by political elites— kings, presidents, ministers, legislators, and judges. Similarly, inputs may come from the international system in the form of demands and supports from foreign political systems. The flow of inputs and outputs includes transactions between the political system and the components of its domestic and foreign environments, and inputs may come from any one of these three sources—the domestic society, the political elites, and the international environment.

Something should be said about the relations between demands and supports. Generally speaking, demands stemming from inside or outside of the political system affect the policies or goals of the system, whether they be responsive, distributive, regulative, or the like, while supports of goods and services, obedience, deference, and the like provide the resources available to the political system which enable it to extract, regulate, and distribute—in other words, to carry out these goals.

The Conversion Functions

This brings us to the events which occur in the political system, properly speaking, or to what we have called the conversion functions. In every political system there is a set of political structures which initiates or processes inputs, and converts them into outputs. The demands entering the political system are articulated, aggregated, or combined; converted into policies, rules, regulations; applied, enforced, adjudicated. These kinds of conversion events occur in all political systems; they are incidental to any political process, no matter how simple or undifferentiated it may be. But the kinds of structures, institutions, or roles which perform these functions, and the way they perform them, vary from the intermittent political structure of a primitive band hardly distinguishable from the family, religious, and economic system, to the highly differentiated political systems of modern societies, with their complex interactions between domestic social and international systems, and the internal interaction of electorates, interest groups, political parties, media of communication, parliaments, bureaucracies, and courts. This conceptual language in regard to the political system enables us to discriminate effectively among these systems, to talk intelligently about their performance and prospects.

This list of political conversion functions is not derived from generic system theory, or from concepts in use in sociological theory. Whatever virtue this classification of functions has results from the fact that it is derived from the observation of political systems. In other words, we are not forcing our data into categories that fit system concepts formulated in other disciplines, but developing concepts which can help us codify and classify political events.

The problem of developing categories to compare the conversion processes in different kinds of political systems is not unlike the problem of comparative anatomy and physiology. Surely the anatomical structure of a unicellular organism differs radically from that of a vertebrate, but something like the functions which in the vertebrate are performed by a specialized nervous system, a gastro-intestinal tract, a circulatory system, are performed in the amoeba by intermittent adaptations of its single cell. Hence we may say that the amoeba performs the same physiological functions as does the vertebrate. In addition we use the functional concepts which we derive from the study of more advanced biological forms to compare them with the less differentiated forms. Indeed, it is only by using the categories of physiological functioning derived from the analysis of differentiated organisms that we can compare them with the more simple ones.

In the same sense, if we look at complex political systems, we can observe specialized structures performing distinctive tasks. We observe electorates, media of communication, pressure groups, parties, parliaments, bureaucracies, and courts. By observing these structures and their interactions, we can explicate what distinctive jobs are being done in the process of converting political inputs into outputs. And we can use these functional categories to compare complex political systems with one another, and these with the less differentiated ones.

We suggest a sixfold classification of political conversion functions: (1) the articulation of interests or demands, (2) the aggregation or combination of interests into policy proposals, (3) the conversion of policy proposals into authoritative rules,

(4) the application of general rules to particular cases, (5) the adjudication of rules in individual cases, and (6) the transmission of information about these events within the political system from structure to structure and between the political system and its social and international environments.

The Capabilities of Political Systems

More than four decades ago when Max Weber delivered his lecture on "Politics as a Calling," he discouraged us from thinking of politics in terms of performance. He told us: "... The state cannot be defined in terms of its ends. There is scarcely any task that some political association has not taken in hand, and there is no task that has always been exclusive and peculiar to political associations. ... Ultimately, we can define the modern state only in terms of the specific means peculiar to it ... namely, the use of physical force."[13] Contemporary empirical political theory tends to follow Weber in its stress on power and process, the "who" and the "how" of politics. It emphasizes two questions: (1) Who makes decisions? (2) How are decisions made?[14] The performance of political systems tends to be inferred from structure and process or evaluated according to moral and ideological norms. When we introduce the concept of capabilities, their development and transformation, we explicitly add two more questions to the "who?" and the "how?" The first of these is what impact does the political system have, what does it do, in its domestic and international environments? And the second question is, what impact does the society and the international environment have on the political system?

Parsons comes closer to meeting the needs of the contemporary political theo-

---

[13] Gerth and Mills, eds., *From Max Weber*, 77.
[14] See, for example, Harold D. Lasswell, *Politics: Who Gets What, When and How* (Glencoe, 1959); Dahl, *Modern Political Analysis*.

rist when he speaks of the function of the polity as that of the ". . . mobilization of societal resources and their commitment for the attainment of collective goals, for the formation and implementation of 'public policy.' "[15] Francis Sutton similarly emphasizes the importance of the functions of political systems in their social and international environments, stressing integration for the internal environment and representation for the international.[16] The development of the concept of the capabilities of political systems represents a pursuit of these leads, but we have had to go farther in specifying types of relationships between the political system and its environments, for "goal attainment," "integration," and "representation" must be broken down into their components, and these elements treated as continua, if we are to be able to code the performance of political systems in the environment in a discriminating way.

The concept of capabilities, then, is a way of characterizing the performance of the political system and of changes in performance, and of comparing political systems according to their performance. Our particular classification of capabilities is a coding scheme, derived from a kind of informal pre-testing operation. We have to try it out to determine whether it helps us discriminate among political systems, or handle political development in a meaningful way.

We suggest five categories of capability derived from our classification of inputs and outputs proposed at an earlier point. These are: (1) extractive, (2) regulative, (3) distributive, (4) symbolic, and (5) responsive. These five categories of capability may be viewed as functional requisites; that is, any political system—simple or complex—must in some measure extract resources from, regulate behavior in,

distribute values in, respond to demands from, and communicate with other systems in its environments. There are surely other ways of categorizing the functional requisites of political systems at the system-environment level;[17] but this particular classification is presented as a useful starting point. It is the product of an informal coding of historical and contemporary political systems. A rigorous test of their usefulness can be made only by formal and explicit employment of these categories in coding historical and contemporary data.

But to say that these are functional requisites of any political system is only the beginning, since we are not interested in defining the minimal political system. We are concerned with characterizing real political systems both historical and contemporary, comparing them with one another at the system-environment level, dividing them into meaningful classes, and discovering their developmental properties.

For these purposes, we need to treat capabilities as performance magnitudes, either actual performance or potential performance. We stress that capability refers to performance and has to be separated from the institutions and agencies involved in the performance. To relate the institutions and structures to performance is one of the central problems of political analysis, and we ought not to confuse rates of performance with the means or instruments of performance.

Perhaps capabilities may be best thought of as ranges of particular kinds of performance. An examination of a particular political system may show variation in its rate of resource extraction over time. In war situations, the rate may be high; in normal periods, the rate may be substantially lower. But the problem of ascertaining the range of capability is more complex than examining rates of per-

[15] Talcott Parsons, *Structure and Process in Modern Societies* (Glencoe, 1960), 181.
[16] "Social Theory and Comparative Politics," in Eckstein and Apter, eds., *Comparative Politics*, 77.

[17] See, for example, David Apter, "A Comparative Method for the Study of Politics," in *ibid.*, 82 ff.

formance in normal and crisis situations. We may need to specify the extractive *potential* of a political system. What rate of extraction is this system capable of and under what conditions? This is only partly inferable from past record of performance. To get at this aspect of the range of capability we need to look at the support aspects of capabilities.

It is also necessary to distinguish between capabilities and elite policies and goals. Elite policies and goals may and usually do involve more than one capability. For example, a policy of economic development will require increases in resource extraction, and regulation, perhaps holding the line on distribution, and coping with demand inputs by increasing the symbolic capability. From this point of view capabilities may be viewed as ends intermediate to the policy goals of the elites. Since policies are made up of different doses of the different classes of outputs, capabilities analysis is essential to rigorous comparative policy analysis. It may enable us to distinguish sharply and operationally among different kinds of economic development, welfare, and other kinds of public policies.

It may also be in order to point to the implications of capabilities analysis for normative political theory. The inclusion of the performance or capabilities aspect of political systems may help bridge the gap which has been developing between the scientific and normative study of political systems. Questions regarding the "proper ends" of the state need to be grounded on empirical evidence of the different ways different kinds of political systems interact with individuals and groups in their domestic societies, and with political and social systems in the international environment. Empirical studies of the *performance* of political systems, of the *what* of politics (in addition to the *who* and *how*), should enable us to grapple operationally with what we mean when we speak of good and evil, just and unjust, political systems.

We may turn now to definitions of the five categories of capability. By the *extractive* capability, we mean measures of the range of performance of the political system in drawing material and human resources from the domestic and international environment. We separate this capability out because there have been political systems like the Mongol Empire, the warlords in China, guerrilla chieftains in Mexico, which have had little more than an extractive capability. Thus it makes sense to treat it separately, since it is to be found in all political systems, and is the distinguishing mark of a particular class of political systems. The extractive capability may be estimated quantitatively as a proportion of the national product; and its variations may be estimated quantitatively over time.

The *regulative* capability refers to the flow of control over behavior and of individual and group relations stemming from the political system. It is even more difficult to express it in quantitative terms than is the extractive capability, though aspects of it are measurable, and in a general way its magnitude, its pattern, and changes in its magnitude and pattern can be estimated. Here we have to concern ourselves with the objects of regulation, the frequency and intensity of regulation, and the limits of tolerance of regulation. While formulating indices to measure changes in this capability is a complex problem, the utility of this concept as an approach to political classification and development is evident. With these two capability concepts we can distinguish between primarily extractive political systems such as those referred to above, and extractive-regulative ones such as the historic bureaucratic political systems described by Eisenstadt in his recent book.[18] Furthermore, we can chart the developmental process from the one to the other, as regulative outputs cease being primarily unintended consequences of or instrumental to extraction and acquire

[18] S. N. Eisenstadt, *The Political Systems of Empires* (Glencoe, 1963).

goals of their own, such as some conception of social justice, order, economic advantage, or religious conformity.

The *distributive* capability refers to the allocation of goods, services, honors, statuses, and opportunities of various kinds from the political system to individuals and groups in the society. It is the flow of activity of the political system as dispenser of values or as redistributor of values among individuals and groups. Some aspects of this capability are more readily measurable than others. The structure of taxation may be viewed in its distributive aspects. The magnitude of welfare and educational programs can be expressed quantitatively, as proportions, and in terms of the social strata affected. Thus, while the general impact of public policy on social stratification is difficult to express quantitatively, there are aspects of it which are measurable, and the total pattern may be characterized for comparative and developmental purposes.

What we have said about political capabilities suggests a logic of capability analysis. An extractive capability implies some regulation and distribution, though these consequences may be unintended. A regulative capability implies an extractive capability, if only to gain the resources essential to regulation; and it is difficult to conceive of a regulative capability which would not in some way affect the distribution of values and opportunities. They are not only logically related. They suggest an order of development. Thus political systems which are primarily extractive in character would appear to be the simplest ones of all. They do not require the degree of role differentiation and specialized orientations that extractive-regulative systems or extractive-regulative-distributive ones do. Regulative systems cannot develop without extractive capabilities; thus the development of the one implies the development of the other. Increasing the extractive capability implies an increase in the regulative capability, as when, for example, political systems move from intermittent

collection of tribute or raids to some form of regularized taxation. Similarly, a distributive system implies an extractive capability, and obviously can reach a higher distributive level if it is associated with a regulative capability as well.

At an earlier point we spoke of *symbolic* inputs, referring to demands for symbolic behavior on the part of political elites—displays of the majesty and power of the state in periods of threat or on ceremonial occasions, affirmations of norms, or communication of policy intent from political elites. We referred to symbolic supports, meaning such behavior as showing respect for, pride in, or enthusiasm for political elites, physical symbols of the state such as flags and monuments, and political ceremonials. And we spoke of symbolic outputs, including affirmations of values by elites, displays of physical symbols, displays of incumbents of sacred or honored offices, or statements of policies and intents. Thus we need to deal with the *symbolic capability* of political systems and treat its relations to the other forms of capability. Surely we do not mean by symbolic capability simply the quantitative flow of symbolic events into and out of the political system. If capability is a profile of rates of performance—e.g., rates of extraction, regulation, and distribution —then symbolic capability is a rate of *effective symbol flow*, from the political system into the society and the international environment. The displays of flags, troops, and ships, the conduct of ceremonies on the occasion of anniversaries, or on the birth, marriage, coronation, and death of princes, kings, presidents, and the like, the construction of monuments, visits by royalty or high officials, are symbolic outputs either in response to demands or independently initiated by elites. The effectiveness of symbolic outputs of this kind are difficult to measure, but political elites (and journalists and scholars) often attempt to do so by counting crowds and audiences, recording the decibels and duration of applause, examining reports on the demeanor of audiences, or conducting surveys of attitudes. Similarly, affirmations of values by elites may be effective or ineffective. They may create or mobilize reserves of support, as did Churchill's speeches during World War II. Statements of policies may facilitate other kinds of system capability, increasing the rate of acquiescence in extraction, obedience to regulation, acceptance of distribution, and reducing the input of demands.

Symbolic output is not the same thing as symbolic capability. The output of symbols may cease to be edifying, menacing, stirring, credible, or even observed, listened to, or read. Royalty or high officials may be spat upon, pelted with rotten vegetables, statues thrown down from high places, pamphlets cast aside, television and radio sets turned off. Or, as in the case of new nations, the symbolism may have little if any resonance. Symbolic messages may be transmitted but not received. The symbols of local authority may be the only ones granted legitimacy, while the central symbolic output may have little, if any, meaning or effect.

While extractive, regulative, distributive, and symbolic capabilities are ways of describing the pattern of *outputs* of the political system into the internal and external environments, the *responsive* capability is a relationship between *inputs*, coming from the society or the international political system, and *outputs*. The responsive capability is an estimate of the degree to which outgoing activity is the consequence of demands arising in the environments of the political system. Again, the usefulness of this concept is suggested by the fact that it implies operational measures, i.e., a given quantity of responses to demands over the total of the demands. We are not minimizing the difficulties in translating this concept of responsiveness into specific measurable relationships. Obviously, in reality we shall have to settle for approximations, for measurement of aspects of the relationship between inputs and outputs.

The reader must forgive the crudeness of this provisional formulation of the concept of political capability. It is the logical next step from treating the political system in terms of interaction with its foreign and domestic environments, in input-conversion-output terms. The capabilities of a political system are a particular patterning of input and output, particular performance profiles of political systems. We are more interested in demonstrating the importance of this level of analysis than in making claims for the effectiveness of this particular schema, more concerned with focusing and directing theoretical speculation and research than in presenting what would be a prematurely formalized theory. The truth of the matter is that we shall only arrive at a good capabilities theory through historical and contemporary studies in which we test out these and other coding schemes.

Tentatively we suggest that we may use the same capabilities scheme for the international interaction of political systems. Just as a political system may have an extractive capability in regard to its own society, so also may it have an extractive capability in regard to the international environment. Thus it may draw spoils, booty of war, and tribute from the international environment, or it may conduct or protect trade and investment, receive subsidies or loans. In the same sense a political system may have an international regulative capability, as in the conquest and the assimilation of other territories and peoples, or in limiting the freedom of other political systems in their political, religious, or military arrangements, or through participation in international organizations which affect the conduct of nations. An international distributive capability may be expressed in tariff arrangements, the granting of subsidies, subventions, loans, and technical aid. The international symbolic capability is a set of measures of the impact of symbol output on political systems in the international environment. Revolutionary symbol output may have great impact on the performance and development of other political systems, and increase the impact of other capabilities in the international environment. Symbol output into the international environment in the form of appeals to common culture and tradition may similarly affect the performance and development of other political systems, and initiate feedbacks which benefit the initiating political system. Statements by political elites of foreign policies and intents may have important effects on the other capabilities of the initiating political system, as well as on the capabilities of other political systems. An international responsive or accommodative capability may be expressed as a relation between its extractive, regulative, and distributive capabilities, and demands from the international environment.

Again this concept of capabilities enables us to handle the relations between internal and international capabilities more systematically than has been the case in the past, just as it enables us to handle the relations among capabilities. Thus a political system which has developed only an internal extractive capability is unlikely to develop other forms of capability in the international environment. Only when a political system develops the institutions and orientations necessary for societal regulation is it likely to pursue regulative goals in the international environment. Similarly, a political system which has not developed an internal distributive capability is unlikely to pursue distributive goals in the international environment. Finally, a political system which has a high internal responsive capability will manifest a different kind of international responsiveness than a system in which internal responsiveness is less well developed. What we suggest here is that there are relations between domestic and international capabilities. But beyond this we can only say that the interrelation among domestic and international capabilities is a matter for deductive and empirical method used

together, rather than for simple reliance on logical inference.

Thus the aims of research on political systems must be: (1) to discover and compare capabilities profiles summarizing the flows of inputs and outputs between these political systems and their domestic and international environments; (2) to discover and compare the structures and processes which convert these inputs into outputs; and (3) to discover and compare the recruitment and socialization processes which maintain these systems in equilibrium or enable them to adapt to environmental or self-initiated changes.

We have also to speak of the capabilities of other social systems. Just as the political system has a particular level and range of performance which we can summarize in terms of a capabilities profile, so also do other social systems in the society of which the political system is a part, and the international political system of which it is a member, have capabilities. Such social systems as the economy, the religious community, or family, kinship, and tribal structures also extract resources from the environment, regulate behavior, distribute values, display and transmit symbols, and respond to demands. Similarly, political systems in the international environment have capabilities, and the international political system may have some extractive, regulative, distributive, symbolic, and responsive capability. The flow of inputs into political systems, the kinds of problems they confront, and the pressure on them to develop capabilities will vary with the performance patterns or the capabilities of these other social systems. The distributive capability of an economy will affect the rate and intensity of demands for distribution, regulation, and the like entering into the political system. The need for developing the regulative capability of a political system will vary with the regulative capability of other social systems, including the international political system. When we think of the factors affecting the capabilities of a particular political system, we must see this problem in the context of interacting social systems, of which the political system is only one.

The Support Aspects of Capability

Thus far we have stressed the performance aspect of capability, the rates which may be computed from the volume of particular kinds of output over time. We have already suggested that the range of capability can only partly be inferred from these performance rates, since political systems may operate at "less than capacity," or they may be drawing on reserves which in time will be exhausted. To get at this aspect of capability we need to deal with the question of supports. If we undertook the task of estimating the extractive capability of a political system, we would look for measures of the quantity or value of the money receipts, goods, and services drawn from the society in proportion to the total product of the society. But there are two aspects of political extraction which such a measure of the extractive capability would leave out. The first of these is the relation between the quantities "levied" by the political system, and the quantities delivered. How much tax evasion is there? How much evasion of military service, desertion? Is a day's work given for a day's pay? Do troops stand under fire? We speak of French and Italian *incivisme*, meaning by that a tendency toward nonperformance, evasion, unresponsiveness, desertion. In other words, we need some way of estimating social performance in response to the outputs of the political system. Does the population pay its taxes, obey the laws, accept the reallocation of values, opportunities, and wealth stemming from the political system, respond to symbolic displays and appeals?

Related to this support performance is the idea of "support potential." The tax receipts of a political system, the proportion of taxes paid to taxes levied, will not tell us what the tax potential of a political system is. In the same sense, measures of the output of obedience to regulations will not tell us what the obedience potential of a political system is.

The support aspect of capability has to be measured, therefore, in terms of the resources delivered in relation to the resources levied, the obedience accorded in proportion to the obedience required, the allocations accepted in relation to the allocations imposed, the responsiveness of the population to symbolic outputs in relation to that which is expected. And in addition to these support performance measures, we need to know what rate of extraction, regulation, distribution, and symbol receptivity a society might accept, under varying conditions, from its political system without fundamental structural change in the relations between the political system and the society.

This may appear to be needless conceptual complication, but we are constantly making judgments of this kind about political systems, estimating loyalty, morale, and commitment in relation to the performance and stability of political systems. What we are suggesting is that the support aspect of capability may be measured in two ways, by estimates of support performance—in other words, of behavior— —and by probing the political culture in order to ascertain what the support possibilities are, the depth of the loyalty, the intensity of the commitment, the availability of support for various purposes, and the like. These constitute a kind of political system "reserve," and we need to know something about this reserve in comparing political systems, or in speculating about developmental prospects.

One further point must be made about the support aspect of capability, and particularly about its system reserve aspect. It is a general reserve up to a point. It may be drawn upon in the form of support for the extractive, regulative, distributive, or symbolic outputs of the political system. Political loyalty and commitment, for example, may be drawn upon for support of a higher rate of taxation, a greater extent of regulation, a greater degree of social distribution, a more aggressive international capability. But there may be, and usually are, rigidities in the exchangeability of support for one kind of activity as against another. There may be greater potential support available for extractive measures than for distributive ones, or greater potential support for distributive measures than for regulative ones. And these potential supports will vary in different strata of the population, and under different circumstances. The system reserve component of capability is an aspect of political culture, the "support propensities" which are distributed among the various strata of the population, and the various roles of the political system. We have to estimate the content of this reserve, its magnitude, and its mobility, if we are going to be able to explain and predict political performance.

Dysfunctional Inputs

What we have presented so far is more than a classification of variables and less than a theory of political systems. It is more than a taxonomy, since it suggests interrelations among capabilities, and between capabilities, the structure and culture of the political system, and the performance of the system maintenance and adaptation functions. These relations, derived at least in part deductively, may be formulated as hypotheses for empirical testing against historical data. It is less than a theory, since prior to systematic study it is an open question whether these particular categories of capability and of conversion and maintenance functions will help us to discriminate the variables we need to know about in order to construct a good theory.

They may be viewed as a proposed first step toward constructing a theory of the political system and of the development of political systems. For example, our analysis of capabilities is suggestive of a theory of political growth, obviously not in any simple or unilinear sense. It is clear from the logic of capabilities analysis that there

can be no extractive capability without some regulative capability, no regulative capability without a particular kind and level of extractive capability, no distributive capability without both a regulative and extractive capability, and that these output capabilities will be greatly affected by the development of a responsive capability. In addition, support of political system performance will be affected by the magnitude, content, and interrelations of the other capabilities, and in particular by symbol capability, and in turn will affect them. Finally, the particular pattern of domestic capabilities will significantly limit and affect, and be limited and affected by, the pattern of international capability.

In addition, capabilities theory enables us to relate the performance of the political system in its domestic and international environments to its internal characteristics. We mean that any level or pattern of system-environment performance rests on a set of structural and cultural conditions. An extractive capability, no matter how simple it may be, rests on some structural specialization and role orientations. A regulative capability requires some military, policing, and bureaucratic structure, and "command-obedience" expectations and orientations. A distributive capability requires further specialization of structure (a welfare bureaucracy, an educational system) and the development of distributive, welfare, and egalitarian orientations within the political system. A symbolic capability rests on some political liturgy and iconography, revered and respected offices and officeholders, and the development of attitudes of reverence and respect for these political rites and ceremonials, political roles, political persons. A responsive capability rests on the development of a specialized infrastructure and a political culture of participation, and the adaptation of the rest of the political system to their emergence. Finally, changes in the level and pattern of system performance require system adaptation in the form of role differentiation, changing recruitment patterns, and new forms and contents of political socialization.

What we have presented is less than a theory in still another sense. An analysis of the capabilities of a political system will enable us to characterize the kind of development a political system has attained, but it does not tell us what factors affect political change or development, what produces change in capabilities.

Changes in capability are the consequence of the interaction of *certain kinds* of inputs with the political system. Consider, for a moment, a political system in equilibrium. There are flows of demands and supports from various groupings in the society; flows of demands and supports from the international political system; and inputs from the political elites (within the political system itself). There are flows of output—extractions, regulations, allocations, communications—from the political system into the society and the international political system. Within the political system the demand and support inputs are converted into extractions, regulations, allocations, communications. When all these flows have a particular range of content and level of magnitude, such that the existing structure and culture of the political system can cope with them, we may speak of the political system as being in equilibrium. But suppose there is a change in the content or magnitude of any one or combination of these input flows.

Suppose there is a depression and the unemployed in a political system demand jobs and food from the government, or a war breaks out and a neighboring power threatens its territory. Or suppose a new dynasty in a political system wants to engage in large-scale construction of temples, palaces, and tombs. Or suppose a political elite embarks on a radical departure in taxation; or requires religious conformity of its entire population and suppresses other religions; or embarks on a large-scale program of welfare. Any one of these input flows may be innovative, dysfunctional—i.e., they may require signi-

ficant changes in the magnitude and kind of performance of the political system. These dysfunctional input flows are what "cause" changes in the capabilities of political systems, in the conversion patterns and structures of the political system, and in the performance of the socialization and recruitment functions. What we need to know is how these dysfunctional flows affect political development, what kinds of dysfunctional flows affect what kinds of capability patterns.

To cope with this question operationally we need to lay out the dimensions in which the flow of inputs may vary. We suggest that they may vary (1) quantitatively, (2) in their substance or content, (3) in their intensity, (4) in their source, and (5) in the *number of kinds* of dysfunctional inputs affecting the political system at a given point in time. We also need to keep in mind, in considering the significance of these flows for political development, the reactions of elites to dysfunctional inputs from the domestic and international environments, and the capabilities of systems other than the one we are examining—other social systems in the same society and the international political system—as they affect or are affected by the processes of the political system. We will take these questions up separately.

First, the quantitative dimension. Dysfunctional inputs may be incremental. Thus demands for participation may begin in the middle classes, spread among the urban working classes, and then to the rural workers. In other countries, demands for participation may be for universal suffrage all at once. For lack of better terms, we may speak of this quantitative variable as a continuum with one extreme labeled "incremental" and the other "high magnitude." The quantity of dysfunctional inputs are of importance for political development because this will affect the scale of the cultural and structural adaptations which the political system is called upon to make. An incremental increase in demands for participation may require only a small adjustment in attitude and a limited set of structural adaptations; while a high magnitude increase may require a fundamental cultural reorientation and the establishment of a complex political infrastructure.

Second, dysfunctional inputs pertain to particular subject matter areas, such as the regulation of land-tenure, or of market relations, enfranchisement or eligibility for public office, religious practices, and family relations. The substance or content of the innovative flow will also significantly affect the pattern of political development, for a political system may be able, for example, to tolerate welfare innovations more readily than regulatory or participatory ones. In other words, the dysfunctionality of a particular kind of input will vary with the existing culture and structure of the political system.

Third, dysfunctional inputs may vary in their intensity. Demands by new strata of the population for the right to vote may take the form of orderly petitions or of violent demonstrations. Low-intensity demands will confront the political system with a different problem of adaptation than high-intensity demands. Low-intensity demands may produce no system adaptation, while high-intensity demands may result either in a change in the responsive capability of the political system in the form of enfranchisement of a new stratum of the population, or a change in the regulative capability in the form of a substantial increase in police forces and repressive action.

Fourth, dysfunctional inputs may vary according to their source. It will make a great deal of difference for the adaptation of the political system if the innovative flow comes from the international political system, from the political elite, or from the domestic society. And in the case of the last it will make a great deal of difference as to which stratum or subsystem of the domestic society is the source of the flow of demands. A political system which has been exposed to large-scale wars over a long period of

time will develop a very different capability profile, and political structure and culture, than one which has been relatively protected from threats to its security. Innovation stemming from the political elites may be more immediately translated into changes in political capability than innovations stemming from either the domestic society or the international political system. And dysfunctional demands from the upper classes may involve less of a structural and cultural change in the political system than those emanating from less advantaged strata of the population.

Fifth, it will make a great deal of difference whether the political system is simultaneously confronted by demands for more than one kind of innovation. For example, a political system may be confronted by the threat of war at the same time that it is confronted by a rise in demands for political participation or welfare. It may have to choose among dysfunctional demands, responding to some and suppressing others. The political culture and structure of political systems will be fundamentally affected by such "simultaneous" or cumulative revolutions, just as those which have had the advantage of being able to meet crises one by one will show the marks of such historical experience.

We may also view political development from the vantage point of dysfunctional outputs. Whatever the source of the innovative outputs may be—the domestic society, the political system, the international political system—they may initiate a process of social change which affects inputs into the political system, or which produces capabilities in other social systems that affect the flow of demands and supports into the political system. But the relation of dysfunctional outputs to political development are indirect, through "input feedbacks." Thus the development of a welfare capability may produce changes in social structure and attitudes which will increase the support inputs of some elements of the society and the demand inputs of others. A shift from an aggressive to an accommodative foreign policy may increase the resources available for the development of a welfare capability, and result in innovative welfare inputs by the political elites.

In talking about dysfunctional inputs, we have stressed changes in the quantity, content, intensity, and incidence of different kinds of *demands*. But dysfunctionality can result from fluctuations in the flow of *supports* as well—losses of morale, failures of recruitment campaigns, declines in tax yields, widespread disobedience to regulations. Needless to say, fluctuations in support will be affected by the kinds of demands made by political elites on the society, as well as by the responsiveness of elites to demands stemming from the society.

The extent to which the political system is loaded by dysfunctional flows will vary with the capabilities of other social systems in the domestic society and international system. An economy may develop new capabilities—new systems of production and distribution—and as a consequence the loading of the political system with distributive demands may be significantly reduced, thereby affecting political development. Or a religious system may develop regulative capabilities that reduce the flow of innovative demands on the political system. Or the international political system may develop a regulative or distributive capability that reduces the pressure on the political system. A case in point would be the international military or technical assistance units of the United Nations that reduce the pressure for the development of extractive and regulative capabilities in some of the new nations. Thus the existence of, or the development of, capabilities in other social systems may affect the rate of flow of dysfunctional inputs, keeping the flow at the incremental and low-intensity level, and perhaps help avoid some of the disruptive consequences of multi-issue dysfunctional pressures.

We must never lose sight of innovation and change outside the political system in

trying to account for a particular pattern of political development. But one variable which we must treat in greater detail is the reaction pattern of political elites, the behavior of important role incumbents in the political system as they are exposed to dysfunctional demands or supports. Perhaps the term "reaction" is incorrect, for it may lead us to overlook the originative and creative activities of political elites. Political elites both originate innovative flows and respond to innovative flows which originate elsewhere. When political elites are themselves the source of innovation, when they develop new goals and new capabilities in the pursuit of these goals, then we n.ust examine these changes in capability and follow through the consequences of such developments for the society and the international system, and from these environments back into the political system again.

When political elites are "reacting" to dysfunctional inputs, then we must examine the relation between these reactions and the loading of the political system. The reaction pattern of political elites will often determine whether a flow of innovative demands changes from a low magnitude to a high magnitude, from a low intensity to a high intensity, from a simple to a multi-issue flow, from a single source to many sources. This interaction between dysfunctional pressures and elite reaction is on the same level of importance as is the response patterns of other social systems from the point of view of the development of political system capabilities.

A political elite confronted by dysfunctional flows of demands and supports has available to it three possible modes of reaction or some combination of these reactions. It may react adaptively. For example, if there is a demand for the suffrage among strata in the population, it may yield to these demands and accept the changes in culture, structure, and performance that this requires. An adaptive reaction is an acquiescence to demands in terms of those demands. Thus demands for innovation in welfare programs are met by such innovation, although even such adaptive behavior usually will require some creativity on the part of the elites. The content of a welfare program has to be specifically elaborated, staff recruited and trained, and modes of enforcement devised, tested, perfected.

A second possible mode of elite reaction may be described as rejective. The rejection of demands may take the form of elite indifference ("Let them eat cake"), explicit refusal to accept demands for innovation, or repression of the demands. The mode of rejection will, of course, affect the development of capabilities. Indifference may result in an accumulation of demands, in increases in their number, intensity, and the groups involved in the demands. The rise in pressure for innovation may reach the point where the elite must react either adaptively or repressively. Either reaction will affect the capabilities, culture, and structure of the political system but in different ways. For example, adaptation may result in the swelling of the welfare capability; repression may result in a swelling of the regulative capability.

The third mode of elite response is substitutive. Demands for "bread" may be met with an increased output of "circuses." Demands for the suffrage may be met by a tender of symbolic affirmations of national glory, an aggressive foreign policy, or by welfare measures. The history of elite reactions to dysfunctional demands— particularly for welfare and political participation—is full of examples of substitutive responses of this and other kinds. The ways in which substitutive elite behavior affects the development of the political system are rather complex. The substitutive reaction may "absorb" the dysfunctional demands, as in the case of Germany in the period after the establishment of the Second Reich, when the middle classes tended to "forget" their liberal impulses in their satisfaction with national unity and glory. Or the substitutive reaction may postpone the rendezvous with the

innovative demands. Or it may do some of both. In addition, the substitutive reaction may in itself involve a change in capability—e.g., an expansion of international capability with all that this might entail in the development of bureaucracy, in the relative power of military and civil elites, and in political culture.

System Adaptation, Recruitment, and Socialization

New roles and new attitudes are the essence of system change. New capabilities or levels of capability, new political institutions and processes, call for new elites, changes in elite training and indoctrination, and changes in expectation, commitment, values, and beliefs among the various strata of the population. The socialization and recruitment processes of a political system have a special relation to political change. We need to consider the different ways in which these system adaptation functions can become involved in the process of political change.

One common way in which recruitment and socialization patterns affect political development is through changes occurring in other social systems. Consider, for example, the process of industrialization. The spread of industrial technology and associated phenomena such as urbanization and the spread of mass communication tend to mobilize (in Karl Deutsch's terms) new strata of the population, recruit them into new economic and social roles and attitudes. These changes in activity and attitude may spill over into political orientations and stimulate new demands for participation and welfare. New elites (middle- or working-class demagogues and organizers) may be recruited and constitute the source of demands for structural change in the political system. Adults recruited into the industrial economy will be resocialized; children raised in urban-industrial families will be socialized differently from children in rural-agricultural families. This illustrates a sequence in which industrialization affects general socialization, role differentiation, and recruitment, which affects political socialization and recruitment, which in turn builds up innovative pressure on the political system.

Changes in the religious system may have similar consequences. The Protestant Reformation and the rise of individual sects, such as Methodism, changed the content and form of socialization and recruitment in England. New religious elites—clerical and lay—were recruited and came to constitute a stratum from which political elites were drawn. In the case of Methodism, the early British trade union and labor leaders were in many cases recruited from the Methodist subculture; just as the "radical" middle-class elites of the first part of the nineteenth century were recruited in part from the earlier nonconformist sects.

A second way in which recruitment and socialization may affect political change is through actions originating with the political elites themselves. Thus a political elite may directly manipulate the socialization and recruitment processes. This is dramatically illustrated in the policies of totalitarian countries, where the whole social infrastructure of family, community, church, and school is infiltrated, and where the party sets up an organizational system to indoctrinate and recruit among the younger generations. Resocialization of adults through party and party-controlled organizations and control of the mass media is also a totalitarian tactic. While this pattern is more deliberately manipulative in totalitarian countries, it is common in many others. The introduction of civic training in the schools is a common practice in democratic countries; and in clerico-authoritarian countries the church and its schools are self-consciously used as a device for political socialization.

A third pattern is one in which elite reaction to innovative pressures may affect socialization and recruitment in an indirect way. An adaptive reaction by political elites to demands for participation and welfare will not only produce immediate changes in political culture, structure, and capabilities. It may also have the longer-run consequences of affecting family and community socialization processes, producing young adults committed to the political system, providing it with support in the form of goods, services, and loyalty. Passive or alienated adults may be resocialized by adaptive and responsive behavior among the political elites, changing from alienated to allegiant orientations. Rejective reactions among political elites may have the contrary effect, transforming allegiant to alienative orientations and affecting the flow of support into, and the support potential of, the political system.

The consequences for political socialization and recruitment of aggressive foreign policies and frequent warfare should also be stressed. If successful, an aggressive foreign policy may increase support and introduce a nationalist-militarist content into family, community, and school socialization. If unsuccessful or excessively costly, it may produce a withdrawal of support and alienative tendencies in a population. French and German political history is instructive in these connections. The radicalization and alienative tendencies of French political culture during the life of the Third and Fourth Republics have often been attributed in part to the humiliating defeats and costly victories of the Franco-Prussian War and World Wars I and II. The rapid growth of the French Communist Party has been attributed in part to the strong pacifist currents set in motion by the enormous casualties of World War I. The fall of the Fourth Republic was triggered off by army officers who had experienced military defeat and the collapse of the French colonial empire.

The failure of efforts to democratize Germany has been attributed to the bureaucratization and militarization of Prussian and German society in the course of their aggressive expansion in recent centuries. The German educational system and family life were shaped in this military-authoritarian society and tended to produce obedient subjects lacking in "civil courage." The National Socialist elites recruited heavily among the "irregulars" of World War I, the men who could not adjust to peaceful routines after years of battlefield life.

The sequence here involves a particular pattern of foreign policy which produces a feedback of socialization and recruitment consequences, which in turn affects the flow of demands and supports into the political system. In our efforts to relate political development to dysfunctional interaction among political systems and their social and international environments, we need particularly to illuminate the recruitment and socialization processes as they reflect social change and stimulate political change, as they are the direct instruments of political change, or as they become the instruments of political change through a particular pattern of public policy.

What we have been suggesting here is that the performance of a political system (e.g., its "immobilism" or "mobilism"), its conversion characteristics (e.g., the congruence or incongruence of its structures, the cohesion or fragmentation of its culture), the operations of its recruitment and socialization processes, are explainable in terms of a particular history of interaction between the political system and its social and international environments.

We are not simply making the obvious point that we can learn much about political development from the study of history. What we are proposing is an approach to political development in terms of systematic comparative history. This has to be done with a common coding scheme, a set of categories, and hypotheses about their interrelations. The adaptation of political systems theory proposed here may serve as a starting point. We need to meet both prongs of the critique of recent tendencies in comparative politics at the same time—by formulating a conception of the political system which is developmental, and by testing and elaborating this conception against the richness of knowledge of man's historical experience with politics.

PART II

INDIVIDUALS AND IDEAS IN DEVELOPING POLITIES

INTRODUCTION

Part I indicated the theoretical and empirical concerns of this book and set forth an approach to the analysis of social and political systems and the processes of change. Our interest is in political development, a process closely related to other dimensions of social change but occupying a uniquely central position in it. As aptly phrased by Karl von Vorys, "It is a process which includes social and economic changes, but whose focus is the development of the governmental capacity to direct the course and the rate of social and economic change."[1] Political development, then, depends upon, is associated with, and, most important, may regulate, control, and order other kinds of social change when a society chooses to modernize. Therefore, it is essential for us to understand some of the many social changes which occur when a society modernizes and how these changes relate to political development.

A significant distinction between styles of life in traditional society and modern society is how the individual relates to his environment. In both the actual and the cognitive sense, man in traditional society is dominated by the vicissitudes of nature and feels that he has little control over his environment. He lacks confidence and a sense of power in his ability to manipulate either his physical or social environment, an attitude reinforced by experience. He is likely to be born in a village with an ascribed status that determines his occupation, expectations, and relations with other people. His physical and mental horizon are limited. He will spend his life in or near the village of his birth and, in many instances, he will never travel more than a day's distance from his home. His mental outlook is equally constricted as he remains isolated from new ideas, new technology, and the influences of modernity that may exist but a few hundred miles from his village. The forces of nature which constantly harass him appear overwhelming. Drought, floods, pests, and crop disease are unceasing threats to his farm. Disease, famine, and accidents punish him and his family. With his limited powers these forces are beyond his control and his helplessness breeds a sense of

---

[1] "Toward a Concept of Political Development," *Annals of the American Academy of Political and Social Science*, **358**, 19, March 1965.

impotence; he finds it dangerous to experiment in the face of all these odds.

This sense of impotence and of danger in the environment induces him to rely on other people for decisions—the elders of the family, village leaders, landlords, and others in positions of authority. In turn, he expects the same submissiveness and dependence from those beneath him as he gives to his superiors. Thus, as a parent, elder, or village leader he may be authoritarian. Impotence, dependence, and anxiety at experimenting are bred into each successive generation. This style of life inhibits the formation of a creative or innovative personality so that life goes on the same generation after generation. The social and political structure remains hierarchical, if not authoritarian, methods of production continue unchanged or are modified only slightly, and the level of income and standard of living remain constant.[2]

Traditional man experiences life in communities. A community has a common cultural configuration which knits people together. There is a single set of stable, habitual preferences and priorities in men's behavior, thoughts, and feelings. As a result of learned habits, common memories, operating preferences, symbols, events in history, and personal associations, a people become used to certain food, clothes, taxes, and marriage ceremonies; they have similar ideas about good and bad, what is beautiful and ugly, or what is familiar and strange; and they bring up their children expecting them to behave in similar ways. Karl W. Deutsch defines community as a "collection of living individuals in whose minds and memories the habits and channels of culture are carried."[3]

In a community, habits and preferences are transmitted by a system of communications. Indeed, the "processes of communication are the basis of the coherence of societies, cultures, and even of the personalities of individuals."[4] Thus, a community consists of people who communicate with one another. People are better able to communicate when they have a common language— a condition which is defined as one of assimilation.

In contrast to modern society where communications, technology, mobility, and patterns of interdependence have resulted in what may be called a national community, traditional society finds each village and tribe constituting a small community isolated from other small communities. The people within each village are assimilated but other villages in the same national territory—in many cases in nearby villages—may have significantly different cultural characteristics, including dissimilar language. Deutsch defines a nationality as "an alignment of large numbers of individuals from the middle and lower classes linked to regional centers and leading social groups by channels of social communication and economic intercourse, both indirectly from link to link and directly with the center."[5] Thus, to the extent

[2] See Everett E. Hagen, "A Framework for Analyzing Economic and Political Change," in Robert E. Asher, ed., *Development of the Emerging Countries: An Agenda for Research*, The Brookings Institution, Washington, D.C., 1962, pp.12–15.
[3] *Nationalism and Social Communication: An Inquiry into the Foundations of Nationality*, John Wiley & Sons, Inc., New York, 1953, p. 63.   [4] *Ibid.*, p. 61.
[5] *Ibid.*, p. 75.

that being a member of a nation consists of the ability to communicate effectively on a wide range of subjects with members of one large group, the cohesiveness and semi-isolation of villages in traditional society constitute impediments to the emergence of a nation.

The convulsive impact of modernization on traditional and transitional society is merely suggested by the quantitative and structural indicators employed by social scientists to describe this transformation. Patterns of child rearing begin to change; new personality types challenge and replace the dominant position of traditional personalities; marginal men, creative and innovative personalities appear with greater frequency and assume increasingly major roles in the transitional process. Changes in residence and occupation occur as people move from farm to flat, from field to factory. New social opportunities appear as status and prestige are no longer ascribed. Patterns of group affiliation and conceptions of personal identity undergo change. Daniel Lerner has spoken of these changes in terms of mobility: "Physical mobility released man from his native soil; social mobility freed man from his native status; psychic mobility liberated man from his native self.[6]

The learning of many new habits and unlearning of many old ones is an excruciatingly slow process that may extend over decades or generations. However, some changes in the process of modernization today may be rapid. Urbanization may occur quickly as masses of people decide to move to the city, even though jobs may not be immediately available. The skills and processes of science and technology may be introduced in a relatively short period of time. New, modern transportation and communications systems may be installed relatively quickly and markets may expand rather rapidly. The concentration of people in cities and new work situations force people into new contacts. Economic, social, and technological developments make mass media of communications possible and permit a lightning-like exchange of ideas. The barriers between the little communities begin to fall and regional, and eventually national, communities emerge. Under these circumstances people experience, in Deutsch's term, "social mobilization." This is a process in which "major clusters of old social, economic and psychological commitments are eroded or broken and people become available for new patterns of socialization and behavior." Old habits are uprooted and mobilized persons, participating in intensive communications, are inducted into some relatively stable new patterns of group membership, organization, and commitment.

A mobilized population is a social and political public and nationalism is an inevitable consequence of such a nationally mobilized community. In the developing nations, nationalism itself often becomes the dominant ideological commitment, in turn leading to a higher degree of mobilization. All these changes have a cumulative impact and are reflected in individual and group political behavior—apathy, insularity, and the hold of the "past" are replaced

[6] *The Human Meaning of the Social Sciences*, Meridian Books, Inc., New York, 1959, p. 18.

by political organizations and attitudes more appropriate to the difficulties of coping with modernity. In short, these changes are the makings of "mass politics."

In this part of the book we focus on some of the basic psychological and social changes in developing polities which appear to move men toward modernity. The following part will concentrate on economic changes and other transformations related to economic development that have consequences for political development. Over a long period of time, psychological changes occur in the personality makeup of individuals. New ideas emerge that motivate people to action and influence the course of development. As ideas are communicated between larger and larger groups of people, social mobilization is achieved. How, and by whom, are these changes initiated and promoted? How, and by whom, are they resisted and obstructed?

The search for "first causes" of development started in the more limited field of economic development. Economists sought to explain how development begins. When economic theories of growth and development did not provide complete and satisfactory answers, they began to explore for causes in social, administrative, and political institutions, as did other social scientists. This search produced a spate of literature on social and cultural obstacles to development and the identification of social, political, and other preconditions for economic development. In pushing the exploration ever more deeply, economic historians and sociologists identified a range of beliefs, attitudes, and values which they believed permitted or encouraged the generation of enterprise and entrepreneurship. Max Weber's exposition of the "Protestant ethic hypothesis" was a classic statement of the influence of attitudes and values, and it continues to exert an impressive influence on many authors searching for the causes of economic growth.

The inevitable next step was to push the search into the foundations of human behavior and motivation. Psychologists and psychologically-oriented social scientists are now exploring the dependence of entrepreneurship and economic development on the emergence of innovative personalities or the presence of achievement motivation in individuals.

Everett E. Hagen, an economist, provocatively employs the insights of sociology and psychology to construct a theory of social change which attempts to explain how economic growth begins.[7] He inquires into the forces which disrupt the great stability of traditional society and cause groups to emerge which abandon traditional ways and turn their energies to the tasks of modernization. What influences some groups to alter substantially their needs, values, and cognitions? His answer is formulated in the concept of "withdrawal of status respect." Hagen finds that the innovational and creative personality is a deviant individual who belongs to a rejected group. He is a member of some social group which perceives that its purposes and values in life are not rightfully acknowledged by other groups in society whose respect and esteem they value.

[7] Everett E. Hagen, *On the Theory of Social Change*, Dorsey Press, Homewood, Illinois, 1962, Ch. 4.

Albert O. Hirschman has elsewhere questioned whether the relationship between deviance and the emergence of able and vigorous entrepreneurs is reliable. He asks, "aren't there some deviants, for example, homosexuals or ex-convicts, who have not shown particularly strong entrepreneurial inclinations? Must social scientists perhaps entertain the Toynbee-type hypothesis of 'optimum deviancy,' with all the attendant difficulties of defining the optimal point?"[8] Furthermore, Hirschman suggests that Hagen's deviants may well make for economic development, but development in turn creates an *esprit de corps* among its principal agents and welds them into an identifiable group, with a personality and perhaps an ideology of its own. Thus, looking back it may appear as though the separateness of the group was a cause of development when, in actual fact, it was its result.[9]

In an article summarizing his imaginative and significant study, *The Achieving Society*,[10] David C. McClelland discusses the conditions and personality traits which lead particular individuals and groups in society to become entrepreneurs—to exploit opportunities, to take advantage of favorable trade conditions, and, in general, to shape their own destinies. Explanation is found in changes which occur in the minds of men: a personality characteristic becomes more prevalent in individuals which McClelland designates as a "need for Achievement." Where a high need for Achievement is found, economic development is likely to follow. He does not merely argue that the achieving society possesses large numbers of individuals with a high need for Achievement. McClelland contends, based on systematic empirical investigations along historical lines, that the presence of individuals with a high need for Achievement is *antecedent* to entrepreneurship and economic growth. He also sees need Achievement to be the link between the Protestant ethic and the rise of capitalism.

The critical questions, then, are: What produces the need for Achievement? and, How can need Achievement be stimulated? The need for Achievement is seen as resulting from the way parents bring up young children, the nature of an individual's childhood training, and early socialization. The answer to the second question seems tentative and incomplete. However, while we may be on uncertain grounds as how to stimulate need Achievement McClelland is convincing in the effectiveness by which he identifies this characteristic in individuals. As a consequence, there have been experimental efforts in developing nations to identify individuals with high need Achievement and give them the kinds of training that would best enable them to express their entrepreneurial personalities and contribute to economic growth.

In explaining the origins of development, both Hagen and McClelland concentrate on psychological changes occurring within the individual. At another level, however, ideology may be a force which is equally important in

[8] "Comments on 'A Framework for Analyzing Economic and Political Change,'" In Asher, *op. cit.*, p. 39.
[9] *Ibid.*, pp. 39–40; see also, Hirschman, "The Search for the Primum Mobile," *The Strategy of Economic Development* (New Haven: Yale University Press, 1958), pp.1–7.
[10] D. Van Nostrand Company, Inc., Princeton, New Jersey, 1961.

the multiple dimensions of the modernization process. Rupert Emerson and Mary Matossian discuss the impact of ideology on nation building and modernization. Whereas Emerson's presentation is thoroughly a political analysis of the role of ideology, Matossian undertakes a psychological investigation of the use made of ideology by the new elites in developing countries.

Emerson contends that nationalism is "the most important single force behind the revolutionary drive of the rising peoples of Asia and Africa." Poverty-stricken people in Asia and Africa are willing to pay the price of temporary economic privation to achieve national salvation. Emerson also explains that nationalism has characteristically been the property of the new elites, who are often oriented toward the West and modernization. However, although the Western education of the nationalist elites as well as the aspirations of the people may point them toward democracy, nationalism also contains ingredients which can turn in undemocratic or antidemocratic directions. Thus, Emerson concludes on the disquieting note that even though nationalism is the most important driving force for change, by itself it gives the answer to few of the problems arising from the ubiquitous demand for development.

The nationalist elites who make use of ideology are termed "assaulted" individuals by Matossian because they are caught between the pressures of traditionalism and modernization. The West may be resented, but the intellectuals who construct the ideology are partly Westernized. Their desire is to resolve the conflict resulting from exposure to the West and to create a sense of identity for themselves as individuals and for the nation as a whole. They search for their true selves and endeavor to create a national character.

The ideologies these elites formulate and embrace also attempt to reduce the ambiguity between the newness of the West and the oldness of the indigenous culture. The past is turned to many uses, both negative and positive. It may be employed as an escape, or it may be used to sanction innovation and national self-strengthening.

From the analysis of Matossian it becomes clear why the intelligentsia of developing nations may be sincerely attached to contradictory premises. Their ideologies provide criticism and comfort, stand for class equality and exhort the masses to follow orders and accept unequal rewards, and condemn the peasant for his backwardness while praising him for being a *real* representative of his culture. In these tensions is the hint of an explanation why "all-people's" parties are so common in the developing nations during the initial phases of educating the masses for democracy, a topic to which we will return in Part V.

The article by Malenbaum and Stolper flatly questions the usefulness of political-economic ideology in providing answers to the difficult problems of economic development. The authors are not concerned with the symbolic and nation-building utility of ideology, but confine their analysis to the question of whether economic growth is dependent on any particular ideology. Is there a distinct ideological route that best serves the cause of economic progress? The authors compare the economic ideologies and rates of economic growth of India and Communist China and of West Germany and East Germany, and conclude, on the basis of their investigation, that economic progress is not determined by the ideology to which a nation adheres except to the extent that that ideology happens to coincide with conditions and needs of the nation. The Communist formula did not contain the essential ingredient for more rapid progress in East Germany as contrasted with West Germany, but democracy in a free society did not provide an assurance of rapid economic achievement in India as contrasted with Communist China.

Robert N. Bellah, in the last article of this chapter, distinguishes between religion and ideology and identifies the role of each in the process of modernization. In traditional societies religion is a prescriptive value system containing relatively specific norms which govern social, political, and economic life. In modern society, religious values lay down the basic principles of ethical conduct, but the religious system does not attempt to regulate the details of concrete behavior. It is ideology rather than religion which governs economic, political, and social life, thereby permitting behavioral flexibility.

When Turkey and Japan modernized, "new religions" were introduced to permit greater flexibility rather than scrapping the existing religions. Islam was replaced by Kemalism in Turkey in such a way that it had the legitimacy of religious symbols. In Japan an ideological movement—essentially political in nature, with the objective of modernizing Japan after the Meiji Restoration—was given an openly religious coloration. The central value of loyalty to the emperor was used to legitimize the immense changes that were being made in all spheres of social life and to justify abandoning many of the sacred prescriptions of the traditional orders.

Both cases neatly convey the functional utility of ideology in modernization. However, in both countries the traditional religion has not disappeared —the differentiation between religion and ideology remains to be completed. Traditional religion persists in political life.

The transformation that occurs in modes of communicating ideas and attitudes—from the oral system, involving face-to-face conversation, to the media system using print, film, and radio—is central to the changes in personality, ideology, and modernizing society in general. According to Daniel Lerner, the modernization process begins when people achieve physical mobility. The principal form of physical mobility today is urbanization, the movement of people from scattered hinterlands to urban centers. This movement is also the usual vehicle of social mobility, the gradual change in people's social status. Physical mobility is the first step in the modern expansion of human communication—conditions are provided for, more widespread participation and, furthermore, increases in urbanization tend to be accompanied by increases in the production and availability of communication media. However, once the initial conditions were created for media production, continuing urban growth no longer automatically assures equivalent increases in consumption of communications media.

The next phase is the need for literacy, since literacy provides the basic skill required for operation of a media system. Therefore, as a result of physical mobility, and with the help of literacy and the mass media, people achieve psychic mobility. Psychic mobility, Lerner explains, means that more people now command greater skill in imagining themselves as strange persons in strange situations, places, and times than did people in previous times. He characterizes persons who have achieved psychic mobility as mobile personalities who have a capacity for *empathy*. They have the capacity to see themselves in other persons' situations. This is an indispensable skill for people moving out of traditional settings. The simple villager who moves out of his traditional environment must meet new individuals, recognize new roles, and learn new relationships involving himself. Traditional society had been nonparticipant—people were deployed by kinship into communities isolated from each other and from a center; it developed few needs requiring economic interdependence; people's horizons were limited by their locale; and their decisions involved only other *known* people in *known* situations.[11]

By contrast, not only is modern society industrial, urban, and literate, it is also participant. Modern society is participant in that it functions by consensus—individuals making personal decisions on public issues must concur often enough with other individuals they do not know to make possible a stable common governance.

Thus, psychic mobility is required in modern society, where much individual participation must be vicarious. A high proportion of people are expected to "have opinions" on public matters—and as a corollary there is the expectation that the opinions of these people will matter. It is this subtly complicated structure of reciprocal expectation which sustains widespread empathy. Consequently, the result of higher literacy, media participation, and empathy is the increasing availability and use of facilities for participation in all sectors of the social system. An index of this involvement is political participation, which reaches its most developed expression in government by participation.

In the last article in Part II, Karl W. Deutsch extends his analysis of social mobilization by relating it to political development and by constructing a quantitative model of the process of social mobilization. He sees the process of social mobilization falling into two stages: (1) uprooting or breaking away from old settings, habits, and commitments (as a result of physical, social, and psychic mobility); and (2) inducting the mobilized persons into some relatively stable new patterns of group membership, organization, and commitment (made possible by urbanization, literacy, the mass media, and the emergence of empathic personalities).

Deutsch highlights the implications of the process of social mobilization for

[11] See also Daniel Lerner, *The Passing of Traditional Society* (Glencoe, Illinois: The Free Press, 1958). Ch. 2.

political development. A change in the quality of politics occurs by changing the range of human needs that impinge upon the political process. These new needs for housing, employment, social security, municipal services, and medical care, among others, cannot be met by traditional types of government. The pressures are for an increased scope of government, a greater relative size of the government sector in the economy, and, consequently, an increase in the capabilities of government. Usually, an increase in the numbers and training of governmental personnel, an increase in governmental offices and institutions, and a significant improvement in administrative organization and efficiency are required.

Similar to its impact on government, social mobilization also tends to generate pressures for a general transformation of the political elite. Their numbers are expanded, their functions are broadened and transformed, and their recruitment and communications are changed. The increasing numbers of mobilized population, and the greater scope and urgency of their needs for political decisions and governmental services often result in increased political participation, but with a time lag. There is a tendency toward a higher voting participation of those already enfranchised and an extension of the franchise itself to additional groups of the population. Finally, Deutsch suggests that rapid social mobilization may be expected to promote the consolidation of the states whose peoples already share the same language, culture, and major social institutions, a process to which we will return in the final chapter in this book.

Chapter 4

Personality and Entrepreneurship

HOW ECONOMIC GROWTH BEGINS: A THEORY OF SOCIAL CHANGE

Everett E. Hagen

This paper proposes a theory of how a "traditional" society becomes one in which continuing technical progress (hence continuing rise in per-capita production and income) is occurring. I shall define a traditional state of society in the following section. The hypotheses which I present to explain the change from this state to one of continuing technological progress may be relevant also to the analysis of other types of social change.

The theory does not suggest some one key factor as causing social change independently of other forces. Rather, it presents a general model of society, and deals with interrelationships among elements of the physical environment, social structure, personality, and culture. This does not imply a thesis that almost anything may cause something, so that one must remain eclectic and confused. Rather, certain factors seem of especial importance in initiating change, but their influence can be understood only by tracing inter-

SOURCE. Everett E. Hagen, "How Economic Growth Begins: A Theory of Social Change," *Journal of Social Issues*, **19**, 20–34, January 1963. This manuscript is derived in part from and in a few paragraphs is identical with an article in *Development Research Digest*, Vol. **1**, No. 3, January 1963 (prepared by the National Planning Association, Washington, D.C.).

relationships through the society. It is implied that general system analysis is a fruitful path to advance in societal theory. Since presented in brief compass, the model is necessarily presented rather starkly here.[1]

The purely economic theories of barriers which explain the absence of growth seem inadequate. The assumption that the income of entire populations is too low to make saving easy; that markets in low-income countries are too small to induce investment; that costly lumps of expenditure for transport facilities, power plants, etc., which low-income countries cannot provide, are a requisite to growth—these and related theories are internally consistent but seem without great relevance to reality. Empirical study of low-income societies demonstrates that the supposed conditions and requirements do not in fact exist or are not of great importance.

Neither are the differences among nations with respect to growth explained by differences in the degree of contact with the West. Contact with the technical knowledge of the West is a requisite for growth,

[1] The model is presented at greater length in E. E. Hagen, *On The Theory of Social Change* (Homewood, Illinois: Dorsey Press, 1962). This paper is in essence an abstract of various chapters of that book.

but forces quite independent of the degree of contact determine whether a nation uses that knowledge. The most spectacular example of this fact is that among the four great Asian nations, Indonesia and India had the most contact with the West during the period 1600–1900, China had an intermediate amount, and Japan the least. Moreover, Indonesia and India experienced the most Western investment, China an intermediate amount, and Japan none whatever until her economic growth was already well under way. Yet among the four countries Japan began to develop first, and has developed rapidly; Indonesia is the laggard; and if China solves her agricultural problem here growth will probably be faster than that of India.

These facts suggest some hypotheses which a theory of growth should not emphasize. Certain other facts give more positive indications of the elements with which a plausible theory must deal.

Economic growth has everywhere occurred interwoven with political and social change. Lipset and Coleman have demonstrated the correlation between economic change and the transition from authoritarian to "competitive" politics in Asia, Africa, and Latin America, and the same relationship is found in every country elsewhere that has entered upon economic growth.[2] The timing is such that it is clear that the economic growth does not occur first and cause the political-social change. Rather, the two are mutually dependent. Whatever the forces for change may be, they impinge on every aspect of human behavior. A theory of the transition

to economic growth which does not simultaneously explain political change, or explains it merely as a consequence of the economic change, is thus suspect.

One last consideration will serve to lead up to the exposition of the model. It is this: the concept is rather widely held in the West that the present low-income societies can advance technically simply by imitating the technical methods already developed in the West. That concept is ethnocentric and incorrect. Mere imitation is impossible. A productive enterprise or process in the West depends for its efficiency on its position in a technical complex of facilities for supplies, services, transportation, and communication, and on a complex of economic, legal, and other social institutions. The management methods which work well within the plant and in its relationships to other units, depend on a complex of attitudes toward interpersonal relationships which are not closely paralleled by attitudes elsewhere. When the process is lifted out of its complex, to adapt it so that it will function in an underdeveloped economy requires technical and especially social and cultural creativity of a high order.

Requirements for the transition to economic growth, then, are (1) fairly widespread creativity—problem-solving ability, and a tendency to use it—and (2) attitudes toward manual-technical labor and the physical world such that the creative energies are channeled into innovation in the technology of production rather than in the technology of art, war, philosophy, politics, or other fields. I believe that exploration of these facets of the process of economic growth is a useful approach to a theory of social change.

What is in point is not widespread genius but a high degree of creativity in a few individuals and a moderately high level in a larger number. I shall suggest reasons to believe that the traditional state of a society is associated with a rather low level of creativity among the members of the society. Further, the persons in tradi-

[2] S. Lipset, "Some Social Requisites of Democracy: Economic Development and Political Legitimacy," *American Political Science Review*, Vol. 53 (March 1959); G. A. Almond, J. S. Coleman *et al.*, *The Politics of the Developing Areas* (Princeton: University Press, 1960). Adapting their method slightly, I used it in "A Framework for Analyzing Economic and Political Change," in R. Asher and others, *Development of the Emerging Countries: An Agenda for Research* (Washington, D.C.: Brookings Institution, 1962).

tional society who are in position to innovate are the elite—perhaps the lower elite, but certainly not the peasants and urban menials. It is well known that being concerned with tools, machinery, and in general physical processes seems demeaning to the elite and is repugnant to them. It seems to me that a theory of economic growth must give considerable attention to the forces which change those two aspects of personality.

The Stability of Traditional Society

When I refer to a traditional society I have in mind a traditional agricultural society, for while there have also been traditional hunting and fishing societies and traditional pastoral societies,[3] they can hardly accumulate many artifacts and hence continuing technical progress is hardly possible in them. A traditional agricultural society is of course one in which things are done in traditional ways, but two other characteristics which have been typical of the world's traditional societies and turn out to be essential qualities of the type are also worthy of note here.

First, the social structure is hierarchical and authoritarian in all of its aspects—economic, political, religious. The existence of an authoritarian hierarchy does not refer merely to a large mass who were submissive and to a small class who rule. Rather, every individual in a traditional hierarchy except perhaps for one or a few at the very apex is submissive to authoritarian decisions above him, and in turn exercises authority on persons below him. And this is true even of the lowliest peasant, who as he grows older and becomes a husband, a father, and an elder in his village, becomes increasingly an authority in some aspects of his social relations.

Secondly, one's status in the society is, with little qualification, inherited. One

[3] Industrial societies will probably also become traditional in time, which is to say that technical progress will come to an end, at least for a time.

does not earn it; one is born to it. The families of the politically dominating groups, who usually also are economically powerful landed groups, provide the officers of the armed forces and the professional classes as well as the political leaders. Lesser elites also perpetuate their status, though with somewhat greater mobility.

These characteristics of the society as well as its techniques of production are traditional and change very slowly. While the model of a completely unchanging traditional society is a construct, an ideal type, it is sufficiently relevant to reality to be useful. From the beginning of agriculture in the world until say 1600 the traditional state of society persisted everywhere except that occasionally, here and there, was a bursting out of the traditional mode for a few hundred years, then a lapse back into it, sometimes at the original technical level, sometimes at a higher one. The present-day transition to economic growth is such a bursting out. We must ask, Why has the traditional state of society been so persistent? and then, Why have the bursts of change occurred? Or at least, Why have the modern bursts of change occurred?

One condition sometimes suggested as an answer to the first question is that the instruments of power were in the hands of the elite. The traditional authoritarian hierarchical state persisted, it is suggested, because the elite kept the simple folk in subjection by force. This explanation seems inadequate. It is possible for a small group to keep an unwilling ninety-seven per cent of a society in subjection by force for a decade or two, or perhaps for a generation or two, though if the subjection persists even this long one must ask whether it really was entirely unpleasing. But that the masses were kept in subjection primarily by force for many centuries seems improbable. The authoritarian hierarchical traditional social structure must have persisted because submitting to authority above one, as well as exercising authority, was satisfying, and secondly because the conditions of life recreated personalities, generation after generation, in which it continued to be so.

CREATIVE AND UNCREATIVE PERSONALITY

To suggest probable reasons why authoritarian social structure was satisfying, let me digress to discuss certain aspects of personality.

Many elite individuals in traditional societies are prevented from using their energies effectively in economic development by their repugnance to being concerned with the grubby material aspects of life. The repugnance includes being concerned with the details of running a business effectively, as well as performing manual-technical labor—"getting their hands dirty." Often the repugnance is largely unconscious; the individuals concerned often deny it, because it does not occur to them that any middle- or upper-class person anywhere would have any more favorable attitude toward engaging in such activity than they have. Why does this attitude exist?

It is deep rooted. I would explain it as follows. Every person in any society who holds or gains privileged position in life must justify it to himself, in order to be comfortable. If he has gained it by his abilities, justification is easy. The person who gains it by the accident of birth is forced to feel that it is due him because he is essentially superior to the simple folk. Typically, the elite individual in traditional societies feels that his innate superiority consists in being more refined than the simple folk. One evidence of his greater refinement is that he does not like the grubby attention to the material details of life which is one of their distinguishing characteristics. However this attitude may have developed historically, once it exists the elite child acquires it from infancy on by perceiving the words, the attitudes, the tone of voice of his elders. By the time he is six or eight years old, it is deeply bred into his personality.

This attitude alone would not contribute

to the lack of innovation in social and political fields. Presence of a low level of creativity, however, would help to explain absence of innovation in these fields as well as in techniques of production.

The explanation of a low level of creativity and justification for the assertion that it exists are more complex.

One component of creativity is intelligence, and intelligence is in part due to biological characteristics. However, although individuals differ greatly in inherited intellectual capacity, the best evidence suggests no reason to assume any appreciable average difference in this respect between the individuals of traditional societies and those of other societies. There are varying degrees of innate intelligence in both. Persons in traditional societies are not less creative because they are less intelligent.

A more relevant component is certain attitudes. In formal psychological terms, I would suggest as characteristics central to creativity high need (for) achievement, high need autonomy, high need order (though this needs further definition), and a sense of the phenomena about one as forming a system which is conceptually comprehensible, rather than merely being arbitrary external bundles.

A person who has high need achievement feels a sense of increased pleasure (or quite possibly a lessening of chronic anxiety, which is the same thing) when he faces a problem or notes a new and irregular phenomenon in a field of interest to him; by the pleasure he anticipates in using his capacities he is drawn to use his energies to understand and master the situation. A person with high need autonomy takes for granted that when he has explored a situation in an area of interest to him, his evaluation of it is satisfactory. He does not think he "knows it all"; he seeks ideas; but when he has thus gained a perspective he assumes that his discriminations and evaluations are good; he feels no anxiety about whether the judgments of other persons differ from his.

He does not rebel against the conventional view for the sake of rebelling, but neither does he accept it because it is generally accepted. In Rogers' phrase, the "locus of evaluative judgment is within him."[4]

A person with high need autonomy and also high need order, in the sense in which I use that phrase here, tolerates disorder without discomfort, because sensing that the world is an orderly place, he knows that within the disorder there is complex and satisfying order, and he is willing to tolerate the disorder, and in fact even enjoys it somewhat, until the greater order shall suggest itself to him. Such a person is alert to phenomena which contradict his previous assumptions about the scheme of things, for he assumes that he will be able to perceive the order implicit in them and thus gain an enlarged understanding of the world. In Poincaré's terms, he has a "capacity to be surprised"; in Rogers', "openness to experience."[5]

These characteristics are not fully independent of each other. In technical jargon, they may not be orthogonal. This categorization of personality therefore does not quite go to the roots of things. But it will do for my present purpose.

This personality complex may be contrasted with one which for the moment I shall term merely uncreative. It includes low need achievement and need autonomy, high need dependence, high need submission-dominance, and a sense of the world as consisting of arbitrary forces.

If an individual does not trust his own capacity to analyze problems, then when he faces a problem, anxiety rises in him. He anticipates failure, and avoids problems. He will find comfort in the consensus of a group (not on a majority decision opposed by a minority, for this involves a clash of judgment and the necessity of choosing between the two judgments). He will find it comfortable to rely on authority for guidance—the authority of older men or of the appropriate person in the hierarchy of authority and status which is always found in a traditional society. He will enjoy having a position of authority himself; one reason for this is that if he must make a decision, he can give it the sanction of his authority; persons below him, if they in turn find it comfortable to rely on authority, will not question his decision, and he does not need to feel anxiety lest analysis of it would prove it to have been wrong. It is right because a person with the proper authority made it.

A person with such needs will avoid noting phenomena that do not meet his preconceptions, for their existence presents a problem. In any event, since he senses the world as consisting mainly of arbitrary forces, an unexpected phenomenon provides no clue to him. It is simply a possible source of failure or danger.

I shall suggest below that the experiences in infancy and childhood which give a person this perception of the world inculcate rage and need aggression in him, but also fear of his own need aggression, and therefore anxiety in any situation within his group in which power relationships are not clearly defined and conflict leading to aggressiveness might occur. Hence he likes a clearly defined structure of hierarchical authority, in which it is obviously proper for him to submit to someone above him or give orders to persons below him, without clash of judgment. In addition, his need aggression also causes him to feel pleasure in dominating those below him—his children, his juniors, his social inferiors.

Thus there are dual reasons why the authoritarian hierarchy is satisfying. It is appropriate to give this personality type not merely the negative label "uncreative" but also the positive one "authoritarian."[6]

---

[4] H. H. Anderson, ed., *Creativity and Its Cultivation* (New York: Harper & Bros., 1959), p. 76.

[5] Poincaré's phrase is quoted by Erich Fromm in H. H. Anderson, *op. cit.*, p. 48; Rogers' is at *ibid.*, p. 75.

[6] It is not congruent in all respects with the one portrayed by Adorno and associates in *The Authoritarian Personality*.

While it is evident that these two personality types exist, to this point it is purely an assumption that authoritarian personality is typical in traditional societies. One reason for thinking that this is true is that this hypothesis explains many things about traditional societies which otherwise are puzzling. It explains, for example, why many persons in traditional societies not only follow traditional methods, but seem to cling almost compulsively to them, even though to an outsider trial of a new method seems so clearly to their advantage. It explains why the method of decision of local problems in so many traditional societies is by consensus of the village elders, through a long process of finding a least-common-denominator solution on which all can agree, rather than by majority vote. It explains, too, why authoritarian social and political systems have persisted in such societies for such long periods.

That a hypothesis explains a number of phenomena which are otherwise puzzling is strong reason for accepting it. However, there is also more direct reason for believing that authoritarian personality is unusually prevalent in traditional societies. This reason lies in the existence of some evidence that childhood environment and childhood training in traditional societies are of the kind which tend to produce such personality.

Perhaps the factor which is most important in determining whether childhood environment will be such as to cause the formation of creative personality or such as to cause the formation of authoritarian personality is the opinions of the parents concerning the nature of infants and children. Suppose that the parents take for granted that infants are organisms which, while delicate and in need of protection for a time, have great potentials; organisms which as they unfold will develop capacity for understanding and managing life. A mother who regards this as an axiomatic fact of life will if she is sensible take precautions to keep her child's explorations of the world around him from causing harm or alarm to him, but she will let him explore his world and will watch with interest and pleasure as his muscular capacities develop, his range of activity expands, and he accomplishes in endless succession the hundreds of new achievements which occur during infancy and childhood.

His repeated use of his new physiological capacities, as they unfold, is from his viewpoint problem solving—intensely interesting problem solving. Assume that it is successful because his mother has taken safeguards so that he will not fall out of his crib, cut himself, break the glassware, fall down stairs, etc., and because his mother offers advice and restraint when necessary. Assume, however, that his venturings do not meet repeated restraint, because his mother trusts his developing capacities and does not check his every step. Then he will repeatedly feel joy at his own successful problem solving and pleasure in his mother's pleasure. There will be deeply built into him the pattern that initiative is rewarded, that his judgment is adequate, that solving problems is fun.

If his mother wants him to be self-reliant, presses him to do things as soon as his capacities have developed, usually refuses to let him lapse into babyhood after he has gained capacities, and shows displeasure when he does not do things for himself, then the stimulus of her displeasure when he does not show initiative will be combined with that of her pleasure when he does so. I have mentioned only his mother. During the first year or more of his life, her attitude is the most important one in his life; after that the attitude of his father (and so that of his siblings) toward his behavior will also be important.

Suppose, alternatively, that the child's parents have as a part of their personalities the judgment that children are fragile organisms without much innate potential capacity to understand or manage the world. Then during the first two years or so of life the mother is apt to treat the child over-solicitously, and to shield him somewhat anxiously from harm. In doing so, unintentionally she also keeps the child from using his unfolding initiative. The use of initiative comes to alarm him, because it alarms her. Then, after these first few years of life, when the parents think the child is old enough to be trained, parents with the view that children are without much potential inner capacity train the child by a continual stream of commands and instructions concerning what is good to do and not good to do, the proper relationships to them and to others, and in general how he should live. Exercise of initiative on his part frequently brings alarm and displeasure and hence causes him anxiety. He can avoid anxiety only by passively obeying the instructions of these powerful persons so important in his life. The instructions will often seem arbitrary to him, and the repeated frustration of his initiative will create anger in him. He will repress it, but this does not mean that it disappears.

The practices and attitudes of older siblings and playmates who have been brought up under the same influences will provide models which in various ways will reinforce the same lesson.

The impact of these parental attitudes on the child may be reinforced by certain related attitudes of the parents. The existence of any child restricts the freedom of his parents, and interferes with their relations to each other. Moreover, the child exerts a will independent of theirs, and they are not always sure that they can control him. If the parents, especially the mother, are relaxed confident people, they will not be disturbed by these problems. Suppose, however, that they are somewhat anxious persons who feel that they themselves do not understand the world (as they are apt to feel if their own childhood was like that which I have just described). Then their child may repeatedly make them anxious, and unconsciously they

may hate him for causing them anxiety and also interfering with their freedom. The child is sure to sense their hostility; it will both make him more afraid to venture and increase his pleasure in venting his frustration by controlling someone below him later in life.

Exposure to the one or the other of these parental attitudes will have an impact on the child through infancy and childhood, but for brevity I shall mention specifically only the most conspicuous manifestation, that during the "period of infantile genitality," which usually occupies about the fourth and fifth years of life. At this age a boy knows that he is a male, like his father, and that he will become big, like his father, and he begins to wonder whether he can successfully rival his father. Specifically, he becomes a rival of his father for his mother's attentions. If his father and mother are perceptive and understanding persons, they will accept him into their fellowship and let him gain an adequate degree of the feminine attention he needs. However, without anxiety or arbitrariness, they will teach him that he can postpone his demands when the circumstances require it, and need not feel anxiety at the postponement. He will learn, as before, that one's initiative must be judicious, and he will also reinforce powerfully the earlier lesson that the exercise of his initiative is safe and brings pleasure.

If the father is weak and the mother is not arbitrary and somewhat rejecting, the son may gain his mother's attentions not because his parents understand his needs and meet them but because his father gives up at the boy's aggressive persistence. In this case too the son will learn that initiative is successful, though he will learn it with overtones of anxiety.

Suppose, however, that the parents doubt their own ability to manage problems, and, having no faith in the capacities of children, regard the boy's initiative as a danger rather than a valuable attribute. Then they will be disturbed by the boy's emerging rivalry with his father during the period of infantile sexuality, will resent the boy's encroachment, and will "put the boy in his place." The experience will reinforce the anxiety and alarm that the boy felt earlier at the exercise of initiative. It will also reinforce the anger that the boy felt earlier at his parents' arbitrary restrictions, and since he cannot vent his anger at his parents, there is apt to build up in him an unformed desire to exercise arbitrary authority himself, and lord it over someone under him, later in life—just as the college freshman humiliated by hazing at the hands of sophomores often waits his turn to vent his humiliation on the new freshmen the next year.

The impact of the one or other type of parental personality on girls during this period is not quite parallel to that on boys, because of the different sexual role which girls have already learned. The differences will not be discussed here.

In these ways, creative or authoritarian personality is formed. There are many other aspects to the process, and many other aspects of authoritarian and creative personalities, which cannot be discussed here:[7] This brief discussion will, I hope, give the general flavor of both the personality types and the process which forms them.

I think that the reader may already have realized that the parental attitudes which lend to create authoritarian personality in the children are themselves components of authoritarian personality in the parents. That is, persons in whom authoritarian personality was created by the circumstances of their childhoods are apt to have such a view of life that they will in turn create an environment which will cause authoritarian personalities to appear in their children. The type, like most other personality types, tends to be self-perpetuating.

It is of great importance, then, that the scattered evidence which is available suggests that precisely the sort of childhood environment and training sketched above as conducive to the emergence of authoritarian personality is the sort prevalent in traditional societies. Fairly intensive sketches of childhood environment in Burma by Hazel Histon[8] and in Java by Hildred Geertz,[9] and more fragmentary sketches relating to many Latin societies, indicate that in all of these cases childhood environment is precisely of this type. These sketches refer primarily to the simple folk, but there is some empirical evidence to suggest that they are true of personality and childhood environment among the elite as well.

And there is even more convincing evidence that various of the conspicuous characteristics of authoritarian personality are present in many traditional societies in Latin America and Asia. Though our knowledge concerning African countries is more limited, they are probably present in those countries as well. Hence it seems likely that a low level of creativity is also characteristic of such societies.

Presumably this personality type developed initially because the every day phenomena of the physical world were bewildering to unscientific man. Convinced of his inability to fathom the world, man began to protect his children jealously when they were infants and then train them minutely in the way in which they should behave to be safe. And so authoritarian personality appeared and perpetuated itself. Repugnance to concerning oneself with the humble material matters of life and with manual-technical labor also appeared among the elite, in the way

[7] For example, models are important in personality formation, and it is of interest to ask where the son of a weak father obtains models of successful behavior. There are several possibilities. This and other complexities must be passed over here.

[8] "Family Patterns and Paranoidal Personality Structure in Boston and Burma" (Ph.D. dissertation, Radcliffe College, April 1959).
[9] *The Javanese Family* (New York: Free Press of Glencoe, Inc., 1955) and "The Vocabulary of Emotion: A study of Javanese Socialization Processes," *Psychiatry*, **22**, (August 1959), 225–37.

sketched earlier in this essay, and tended to perpetuate itself.

Social Change

How, then, did social change ever occur? and technological progress and economic development ever begin?

Study of a number of countries in which there has occurred a transition from a traditional state to continuing economic development suggests that an important factor initiating change was some historical shift which caused some group or groups of the lesser elite, who previously had had a respected and valued place in the social hierarchy, to feel that they no longer were respected and valued. This derogation in some societies consisted of explicit indication of contempt for the functions or position of the lesser elite, in others of behavior by a new higher elite which seemed immoral, unmanly, or irreligious to the groups below them, and thus indicated contempt for the moral standards of the lesser elite.

I shall omit the example of England, which is complex and difficult to mention briefly, and shall refer briefly to highlights of three other examples. In the 1650's the Tsar of Russia and Patriarch of Moscow, to attain diplomatic ends by adopting Greek practices, ordered certain changes in the ritual of the Orthodox church which the faithful felt to be heretical and to endanger their souls. There followed conflict and persecution, in waves of varying severity, even down to 1900. The Old Believers, who were the victims of this withdrawal of respect for their status in the society, were prominent in economic development in Russia in the nineteenth century. Concerning the twentieth I have no information.

In Japan the feudal group known as the Tokugawa, who gained national power in 1600, imposed a peace which deprived the samurai of their traditional function; imposed rigid distinctions among social classes which had the effect of relegating the so-called wealthy peasants, descen-

dants of the lesser elite, to the rank of peasant; and to some extent demeaned other feudal groups, the so-called outer clans. It was the lesser samurai and wealthy peasants, apparently especially of the outer clans, who were the innovators in Japan's industrial revolution.

In Colombia, in the 1530's the Spanish settled on a high plateau around Bogotá and in the valleys around Cali and Medellín. Through historical developments I shall not sketch, during the next two centuries the settlers of the other two areas came to look down on those in Antioquia, the valley around Medellín. The social friction continues to the present; and the Antioqueños have been the leaders in economic innovation out of all proportion to their numbers in the population.

I shall call such events "withdrawal of status respect" from the group no longer accorded its old place. It is important to note that the situation is one in which a group of the elite once had full status respect and later lost it. What are the results? Let me speculate concerning them.

I suggest that among the adults of the first generation so affected, the reaction is anger and anxiety. Their children, however, seeing that their parents' role in life causes anxiety, do not find it a fully satisfying model. Alternative roles are in general not open to them, and so they respond by repressing somewhat within themselves their parents' values—by ceasing to have *any* role values with the same clarity and intensity their parents did. The process, I suggest, is cumulative in successive generations, and in the second or third or fourth generation there appears pronounced "normlessness," shiftlessness, anomie, or, in Merton's term, retreatism. It can be observed, for example, in Negroes of the southern United States, American Indians on any reservation, first and second generation immigrants, and colonial subjects.[10]

[10] In groups who are not of the lower elite, but instead are of the "simple folk," the later reaction may be not creative innovation but violent social revolt. For lack of space, that

Historical records suggest that it also characterized the Antioqueños, the samurai, and the Old Believers.

There is reason to suspect that retreatism affects men more than women because of the differences between the normal social roles of the sexes. After several generations, then, there will appear men who are retreatist and weak, but women who are less so. The women will probably feel some pity for their children's lot in life, and will cherish them tenderly. But, reacting to the ineffectiveness of their husbands, the women will have an intense desire that their sons shall be more effective, and will respond with delight to each achievement in infancy and boyhood. During the period of infantile sexuality, the boy will win in the rivalry with his father, both because his initiative pleases his mother and because his father is weak.

Obviously not all home environments in some generation of a group of the lesser elite from whom status respect has been withdrawn will be like this, but it is plausible to believe that some such environment will appear occasionally, or even fairly often. Some combinations and intensities of such maternal attitudes, combined with weakness in the father, provide an almost ideal environment for the formation of an anxious driving type of creativity.

Where a considerable degree of creativity is inculcated, but the anxiety is great, a variant type of individual may appear, one who gives himself security by being traditional and authoritarian in most aspects of his behavior, and then dares to be bold and creative in some other aspect. Henry Ford was such a person, as was J. Pierpont Morgan. And this type has been important in economic development in Japan, the Soviet Union, and Germany.

Thus, I suggest, there gradually emerges a group of individuals, creative, alienated from traditional values, driven by a

[*footnote 10 continued*
branch of the theory cannot be expounded here.

gnawing burning drive to prove themselves (to themselves, as well as to their fellows), seeking for an area in which to do so, preferably an area in which they can gain power, and preferably also one in which in some symbolic way they can vent their rage at the elites who have caused their troubles. Moreover, their (perhaps unconscious) rage at the group disparaging them will cause them to turn against some of the values of the group disparaging them. The fact that the disparaging group, in the cases cited above, was traditional, is one of the reasons why the disparaged group rejected traditional values and turned to innovation.

What they turn to will be determined in part by the models they find during their childhood somewhere in their history or their folklore or the tales their elders tell them of the life around them, and in part by the objective opportunities of the world around them. In the modern world, to few socially rebellious groups of traditional societies will any other road to power, recognition, and proof to oneself of one's ability seem as inviting as economic prowess, and creative individuals in most such groups will become economic innovators. In the cases of England, Japan, and Colombia, which I have examined in some detail, such groups have provided a disproportionate share of the leaders in the transition to economic growth.

A word is in point concerning the complexity of the situation in colonial societies. Here there has been rather harsh withdrawal of status respect, but by invading groups from the West who became colonial conquerors. These groups have not traditional but "modern" values toward manual-technical work. The tendency of disparaged groups to reject the values of the disparaging group may cause them to reject engaging their energies in the occupations of the conquerors. Thus even though they desire to gain symbols of economic power, an additional emotional block is put in the way of the indigenous elite becoming effective industrialists. This fact may explain some of the ambivalence and erratic behavior sometimes manifested.

The theory of some of whose central points have been sketched so briefly above proceeds in broad sweeps, and of course is subject to a corresponding margin of error. It seems plausible to me because it is internally consistent and because it explains many aspects of social, political, and economic behavior in low-income countries for which no other very logical explanation seems available.

If it is correct it does not follow that economic growth will succeed only where certain rather special historical conditions have existed. For the forces of modern history have caused social tensions among the social classes of low-income societies themselves, by virtue of which some degree of withdrawal of status respect has existed among the indigenous social classes of almost all of them, and what values various groups are alienated from or drawn to is confused and uncertain. However, innovational personality is clearly appearing, in varying degree. The drive for security, self-reassurance, and power will surely lead many innovational individuals to technological innovation, though frequently within social forms differing from those of the West.

THE ACHIEVEMENT MOTIVE IN ECONOMIC GROWTH[1]

David C. McClelland

From the beginning of recorded history, men have been fascinated by the fact that civilizations rise and fall. Culture growth, as Kroeber has demonstrated, is episodic, and sometimes occurs in quite different fields.[2] For example, the people living in the Italian peninsula at the time of ancient Rome produced a great civilization of law, politics, and military conquest; and at another time, during the Renaissance, the inhabitants of Italy produced a great civilization of art, music, letters, and science. What can account for such cultural

SOURCE. David C. McClelland, "The Achievement Motive in Economic Growth," in Bert F. Hoselitz and Wilbert E. Moore, eds., *Industrialization and Society* (The Hague: UNESCO and Mouton, 1963, pp. 74–96.

[1] This paper is a summary of the author's book. *The Achieving Society*, published by Van Nostrand Co. in Princeton, N.J., in the fall of 1961.
[2] A. L. Kroeber, *Configurations of Culture Growth* (Berkeley, California, 1944).

flowerings? In our time we have theorists like Huntington, who stresses the importance of climate, or Toynbee, who also feels the right amount of challenge from the environment is crucial though he conceives of the environment as including its psychic effects. Others, like Kroeber, have difficulty imagining any general explanation; they perforce must accept the notion that a particular culture happens to hit on a particularly happy mode of self-expression, which it then pursues until it becomes overspecialized and sterile.

My concern is not with all culture growth, but with economic growth. Some wealth or leisure may be essential to development in other fields—the arts, politics, science, or war—but we need not insist on it. However, the question of why some countries develop rapidly in the economic sphere at certain times and not at others is in itself of great interest, whatever its relation to other types of culture growth. Usually, rapid economic growth has been explained in terms of "external" factors—favorable opportunities for trade, unusual natural resources, or conquests that have opened up new markets or produced internal political stability. But I am interested in the *internal* factors—in the values and motives men have that lead them to exploit opportunities, to take advantage of favorable trade conditions; in short, to shape their own destiny.

This interest is not surprising; I am a psychologist—and, furthermore, a psychologist whose primary research interest is in human motivation, in the *reasons* that people behave as they do. Of course, all people have always, to a certain extent, been interested in human motivation. The difference between their interest and the twentieth-century psychologist's interest is that the latter tries to define his subject matter very precisely and, like all scientists, to measure it. How can human motives be identified, or even measured? Psychologists' favorite techniques for conducting research in this area have always been the interview and the questionnaire. If you want to know what a man's motives are, ask him. Of course, you need not ask him directly; but perhaps, if you talk to him long enough in an interview, or ask him enough in a questionnaire, you can infer what his motives are—more or less the same way that, from a number of clues, a detective would infer who had committed a crime.

Whatever else one thinks of Freud and the other psychoanalysts, they performed one extremely important service for psychology: once and for all, they persuaded us, rightly or wrongly, that what people said about their motives was not a reliable basis for determining what those motives really were. In his analyses of the psychopathology of everyday life and of dreams and neurotic symptoms, Freud demonstrated repeatedly that the "obvious" motives—the motives that the people themselves thought they had or that a reasonable observer would attribute to them—were not, in fact, the real motives

for their often strange behavior. By the same token, Freud also showed the way to a better method of learning what people's motives were. He analyzed dreams and free associations: in short, fantasy or imaginative behavior. Stripped of its air of mystery and the occult, psychoanalysis has taught us that one can learn a great deal about people's motives through observing the things about which they are spontaneously concerned in their dreams and waking fantasies. About ten or twelve years ago, the research group in America with which I was connected decided to take this insight quite seriously and to see what we could learn about human motivation by coding objectively what people spontaneously thought about in their waking fantasies.[3] Our method was to collect such free fantasy, in the form of brief stories written about pictures, and to count the frequency with which certain themes appeared—rather as a medical technician counts the frequency with which red or white corpuscles appear in a blood sample. We were able to demonstrate that the frequency with which certain "inner concerns" appeared in these fantasies varied systematically as a function of specific experimental conditions by which we aroused or induced motivational states in the subjects. Eventually, we were able to isolate several of these inner concerns, or motives, which, if present in great frequency in the fantasies of a particular person, enabled us to know something about how he would behave in many other areas of life.

Chief among these motives was what we termed "the need for Achievement" (*n* Achievement)—a desire to do well, not so much for the sake of social recognition or prestige, but to attain an inner feeling of personal accomplishment. This motive is my particular concern in this paper. Our early laboratory studies showed that people "high" in *n* Achievement tend to work harder at certain tasks; to learn

[3] J. W. Atkinson (ed.), *Motives in Fantasy, Action, and Society* (Princeton, N.J., 1958).

faster; to do their best work when it counts for the record, and not when special incentives, like money prizes, are introduced; to choose experts over friends as working partners; etc. Obviously, we cannot here review the many, many studies in this area. About five years ago, we became especially interested in the problem of what would happen in a society if a large number of people with a high need for achievement should happen to be present in it at a particular time. In other words, we became interested in a social-psychological question: What effect would a concentration of people with high *n* Achievement have on a society?

It might be relevant to describe how we began wondering about this. I had always been greatly impressed by the very perceptive analysis of the connection between Protestantism and the spirit of capitalism made by the great German sociologist, Max Weber.[4] He argues that the distinguishing characteristic of Protestant business entrepreneurs and of workers, particularly from the pietistic sects, was not that they had in any sense invented the institutions of capitalism or good craftsmanship, but that they went about their jobs with a new perfectionist spirit. The Calvinistic doctrine of predestination had forced them to rationalize every aspect of their lives and to strive hard for perfection in the positions in this world to which they had been assigned by God. As I read Weber's description of the behavior of these people, I concluded that they must certainly have had a high level of *n* Achievement. Perhaps the new spirit of capitalism Weber describes was none other than a high need for achievement— if so, then *n* Achievement has been responsible, in part, for the extraordinary economic development of the West. Another factor served to confirm this hypothesis. A careful study by Winterbottom had shown that boys with high *n* Achieve-

ment usually came from families in which the mothers stressed early self-reliance and mastery.[5] The boys whose mothers did *not* encourage their early self-reliance, or did not set such high standards of excellence, tended to develop lower need for achievement. Obviously, one of the key characteristics of the Protestant Reformation was its emphasis on self-reliance. Luther stressed the "priesthood of all believers" and translated the Bible so that every man could have direct access to God and religious thought. Calvin accentuated a rationalized perfection in this life for everyone. Certainly, the character of the Reformation seems to have set the stage, historically, for parents to encourage their children to attain earlier self-reliance and achievement. If the parents did in fact do so, they very possibly unintentionally produced the higher level of *n* Achievement in their children that was, in turn, responsible for the new spirit of capitalism.

This was the hypothesis that initiated our research. It was, of course, only a promising idea; much work was necessary to determine its validity. Very early in our studies, we decided that the events Weber discusses were probably only a special case of a much more general phenomenon —that it was *n* Achievement as such that was connected with economic development, and that the Protestant Reformation was connected only indirectly in the extent to which it had influenced the average *n* Achievement level of its adherents. If this assumption is correct, then a high average level of *n* Achievement should be equally associated with economic development in ancient Greece, in modern Japan, or in a preliterate tribe being studied by anthropologists in the South Pacific. In other words, in its most general form, the hypothesis attempts to isolate one of the key factors in the economic development, at least, of all civilizations. What evidence do

[4] Max Weber, *The Protestant Ethic and the Spirit of Capitalism*, trans. Talcott Parsons (New York, 1930).

[5] M. R. Winterbottom, "The Relation of Need for Achievement to Learning and Experiences in Independence and Mastery," in Atkinson, *op. cit.*, pp. 453–478.

we have that this extremely broad generalization will obtain? By now, a great deal has been collected—far more than I can summarize here; but I shall try to give a few key examples of the different types of evidence.

First, we have made historical studies. To do so, we had to find a way to obtain a measure of *n* Achievement level during time periods other than our own, whose individuals can no longer be tested. We have done this—instead of coding the brief stories written by an individual for a test, we code imaginative literary documents: poetry, drama, funeral orations, letters written by sea captains, epics, etc. Ancient Greece, which we studied first, supplies a good illustration. We are able to find literary documents written during three different historical periods and dealing with similar themes: the period of economic growth, 900 B.C.–475 B.C. (largely Homer and Hesiod); the period of climax, 475 B.C.–362 B.C.; and the period of decline, 362 B.C.–100 B.C. Thus, Hesiod wrote on farm and estate management in the early period;

Xenophon, in the middle period; and Aristotle, in the late period. We have defined the period of "climax" in economic, rather than in cultural, terms, because it would be presumptuous to claim, for example, that Aristotle in any sense represented a "decline" from Plato or Thales. The measure of economic growth was computed from information supplied by Heichelheim in his *Wirtschaftsgeschichte des Altertums.*[6] Heichelheim records in detail the locations throughout Europe where the remains of Greek vases from different centuries have been found. Of course, these vases were the principal instrument of Greek foreign trade, since they were the containers for olive oil and wine, which were the most important Greek exports. Knowing where the vase fragments have been found, we could compute the trade area of Athenian Greece for different time periods. We purposely omitted any consideration of the later

[6] F. Heichelheim, *Wirtschaftsgeschichte des Altertums* (Leiden, 1938).

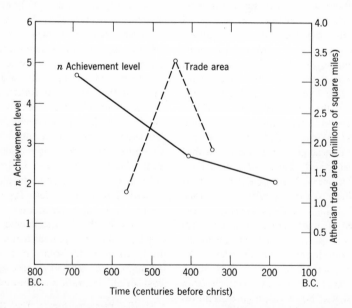

Figure 1. Average *n* Achievement level plotted at midpoints of periods of growth, climax, and decline of Athenian civilization as reflected in the extent of her trade area (measured for the sixth, fifth, and fourth centuries B.C. only).

expansion of Hellenistic Greece, because this represents another civilization; our concern was Athenian Greece.

When all the documents had been coded, they demonstrated—as predicted—that the level of *n* Achievement was highest during the period of growth prior to the climax of economic development in Athenian Greece. (See Figure 1.) In other words, the maximum *n* Achievement level preceded the maximum economic level by at least a century. Furthermore, that high level had fallen off by the time of maximum prosperity, thus foreshadowing subsequent economic decline. A similar methodology was applied, with the same results, to the economic development of Spain in the sixteenth century[7] and to two waves of economic development in the history of England (one in the late sixteenth century and the other at the beginning of the industrial revolution, around 1800).[8] The *n* Achievement level in English history (as determined on the basis of dramas, sea captains' letters, and street ballads) rose, between 1400 and 1800, *twice*, a generation or two before waves of accelerated economic growth (incidentally, at times of Protestant revival). This point is significant because it shows that there is no "necessary" steady decline in a civilization's entrepreneurial energy from its earlier to its later periods. In the Spanish and English cases, as in the Greek, high levels of *n* Achievement preceded economic decline. Unfortunately, space limitations preclude more detailed discussion of these studies here.

We also tested the hypothesis by applying it to preliterate cultures of the sort that anthropologists investigate. At Yale University, an organized effort has been made to collect everything that is known about all the primitive tribes that have been studied and to classify the information systematically for comparative purposes. We utilized this cross-cultural file to obtain the two measures that we needed to test our general hypothesis. For over fifty of these cultures, collections of folk tales existed that Child and others had coded.[9] just as we coded literary documents and individual imaginative stories, for *n* Achievement and other motives. These folk tales have the character of fantasy that we believe to be so essential for getting at "inner concerns." In the meantime, we were searching for a method of classifying the economic development of these cultures, so that we could determine whether those evincing high *n* Achievement in their folk tales had developed further than those showing lower *n* Achievement. The respective modes of gaining a livelihood were naturally very different in these cultures, since they came from every continent in the world and every type of physical habitat; yet we had to find a measure for comparing them. We finally thought of trying to estimate the number of full-time "business entrepreneurs" there were among the adults in each culture. We defined "entrepreneur" as "anyone who exercises control over the means of production and produces more than he can consume in order to sell it for individual or household income." Thus an entrepreneur was anyone who derived at least 75 per cent of his income from such exchange or market practices. The entrepreneurs were mostly traders, independent artisans, or operators of small firms like stores, inns, etc. Nineteen cultures were classified as high in *n* Achievement on the basis of their folk tales; 74 per cent of them contained some entrepreneurs. On the other hand, only 35 per cent of the twenty cultures that were classified as low in *n* Achievement con-

[7] J. B. Cortés, "The Achievement Motive in the Spanish Economy between the Thirteenth and the Eighteenth Centuries," *Economic Development and Cultural Change*, **9** (1960), 144–163.

[8] N. M. Bradburn and D. E. Berlew, "Need for Achievement and English Economic Growth," *Economic Development and Cultural Change*, 1961.

[9] I. L. Child, T. Storm, and J. Veroff, "Achievement Themes in Folk Tales Related to Socialization Practices," in Atkinson, *op. cit.*, pp. 479–492.

tained any entrepreneurs (as we defined it) at all. The difference is highly significant statistically (Chi-square $= 5.97$, $p < .02$). Hence data about primitive tribes seem to confirm the hypothesis that high n Achievement leads to a more advanced type of economic activity.

But what about modern nations? Can we estimate their level of n Achievement and relate it to their economic development? The question is obviously one of the greatest importance, but the technical problems of getting measures of our two variables proved to be really formidable. What type of literary document could we use that would be equally representative of the motivational levels of people in India, Japan, Portugal, Germany, the United States, and Italy? We had discovered in our historical studies that certain types of literature usually contain much more achievement imagery than others. This is not too serious as long as we are dealing with time changes within a given culture; but it is very serious if we want to compare two cultures, each of which may express its achievement motivation in a different literary form. At last, we decided to use children's stories, for several reasons. They exist in standard form in every modern nation, since all modern nations are involved in teaching their children to read and use brief stories for this purpose. Furthermore, the stories are imaginative; and, if selected from those used in the earliest grades, they are not often influenced by temporary political events. (We were most impressed by this when reading the stories that every Russian child reads. In general, they cannot be distinguished, in style and content, from the stories read in all the countries of the West.)

We collected children's readers for the second, third, and fourth grades from every country where they could be found for two time periods, which were roughly centered around 1925 and around 1950. We got some thirteen hundred stories, which were all translated into English. In all, we had twenty-one stories from each of twenty-three countries about 1925, and the same number from each of thirty-nine countries about 1950. Code was used on proper names, so that our scorers would not know the national origins of the stories. The tales were then mixed together, and coded for n Achievement (and certain other motives and values that I shall mention only briefly).

The next task was to find a measure of economic development. Again, the problem was to insure comparability. Some countries have much greater natural resources; some have developed industrially sooner than others; some concentrate in one area of production and some in another. Economists consider national income figures in per-capita terms to be the best measure available; but they are difficult to obtain for all countries, and it is hard to translate them into equal purchasing power. Ultimately, we came to rely chiefly on the measure of electricity produced: the units of measurement are the same all over the world; the figures are available from the 1920's on; and electricity is the *form* of energy (regardless of how it is produced) that is essential to modern economic development. In fact, electricity produced per capita correlates with estimates of income per capita in the 1950's around .90 anyway. To equate for differences in natural resources, such as the amount of water power available, etc., we studied *gains* in kilowatt hours produced per capita between 1925 and 1950. The level of electrical production in 1925 is, as one would expect, highly correlated with the size of the gain between then and 1950. So it was necessary to resort to a regression analysis; that is, to calculate, from the average regression of gain on level for all countries, how much gain a particular country should have shown between 1925 and 1950. The actual gain could then be compared with the expected gain, and the country could be classified as gaining more or less rapidly than would have been expected on the basis of its 1925 performance. The procedure is directly comparable to what we do when we predict, on the basis of some measure of I.Q., what grades a child can be expected to get in school, and then classify him as an "under-" or "over-achiever."

The correlation between the *n* Achievement level in the children's readers in 1925 and the growth in electrical output between 1925 and 1950, as compared with expectation, is a quite substantial .53, which is highly significant statistically. It could hardly have arisen by chance. Furthermore, the correlation is also substantial with a measure of gain over the expected in per-capita income, equated for purchasing power by Colin Clark. To check this result more definitively with the sample of forty countries for which we had reader estimates of *n* Achievement levels in 1950, we computed the equation for gains in electrical output in 1952–1958 as a function of level in 1952. It turned out to be remarkably linear when translated into logarithmic units, as is so often the case with simple growth functions. Table 1 (next page) presents the performance of each of the countries, as compared with predictions from initial level in 1952, in standard score units and classified by high and low *n* Achievement in 1950. Once again we found that *n* Achievement levels predicted significantly (r = .43) the countries which would perform more or less rapidly than expected in terms of the average for all countries. The finding is more striking than the earlier one, because many Communist and underdeveloped countries are included in the sample. Apparently, *n* Achievement is a precursor of economic growth—and not only in the Western style of capitalism based on the small entrepreneur, but also in economies controlled and fostered largely by the state.

For those who believe in economic determinism, it is especially interesting that *n* Achievement level in 1950 is *not* correlated either with *previous* economic growth between 1925 and 1950, or with the level of prosperity in 1950. This strongly suggests that *n* Achievement is a *causative* factor—a change in the minds of men which produces economic growth rather than being produced by it. In a century dominated by economic determinism, in both Communist and Western thought, it is startling to find concrete evidence for psychological determinism, for psychological developments as preceding and presumably causing economic changes.

The many interesting results which our study of children's stories yielded have succeeded in convincing me that we chose the right material to analyze. Apparently, adults unconsciously flavor their stories for young children with the attitudes, the aspirations, the values, and the motives that they hold to be most important.

I want to mention briefly two other findings, one concerned with economic development, the other with totalitarianism. When the more and less rapidly developing economies are compared on all the other variables for which we scored the children's stories, one fact stands out. In stories from those countries which had developed more rapidly in both the earlier and later periods, there was a discernible tendency to emphasize, in 1925 and in 1950, what David Riesman has called "other-directedness"—namely, reliance on the opinion of particular others, rather than on tradition, for guidance in social behavior.[10] *Public opinion* had, in these countries, become a major source of guidance for the individual. Those countries which had developed the mass media further and faster—the press, the radio, the public-address system—were also the ones who were developing more rapidly economically. I think that "other-directedness" helped these countries to develop more rapidly because public opinion is basically more flexible than institutionalized moral or social traditions. Authorities can utilize it to inform people widely about the need for new ways of doing things. However, traditional institutionalized

[10] David Riesman, with the assistance of Nathan Glazer and Reuel Denney, *The Lonely Crowd* (New Haven, Conn., 1950).

TABLE 1.   *Rate of growth in Electrical Output (1952–1958) and National* n *Achievement Levels in 1950*

Deviation from Expected Growth Rate[a] in Standard Score Units

National n Achievement levels (1950)[b]	Above Expectation			Below Expectation
High n Achievement				
3.62 Turkey	+1.38			
2.71 India[c]	+1.12			
2.38 Australia	+ .42			
2.32 Israel	+1.18			
2.33 Spain	+ 0.1			
2.29 Pakistan[d]	+2.75			
2.29 Greece	+1.18	3.38 Argentina	− .56	
2.29 Canada	+ .08	2.71 Lebanon	− .67	
2.24 Bulgaria	+1.37	2.38 France	− .24	
2.24 U.S.A.	+ .47	2.33 U. So. Africa	− .06	
2.14 West Germany	+ .53	2.29 Ireland	− .41	
2.10 U.S.S.R.	+1.61	2.14 Tunisia	−1.87	
2.10 Portugal	+ .76	2.10 Syria	− .25	
Low n Achievement				
1.95 Iraq	+ .29	2.05 New Zealand	− .29	
1.86 Austria	+ .38	1.86 Uruguay	− .75	
1.67 U.K.	+ .17	1.81 Hungary	− .62	
1.57 Mexico	+ .12	1.71 Norway	− .77	
.86 Poland	+1.26	1.62 Sweden	− .64	
		1.52 Finland	− .08	
		1.48 Netherlands	− .15	
		1.33 Italy	− .57	
		1.29 Japan	− .04	
		1.20 Switzerland[e]	−1.92	
		1.19 Chile	−1.81	
Correlation of n Achievement level (1950) × deviations from expected growth rate = .43, p < .01		1.05 Denmark	− .89	
		.57 Algeria	− .83	
		.43 Belgium	−1.65	

[a] The estimates are computed from the monthly average electrical production figures, in millions of Kwh, for 1952 and 1958, from United Nations, *Monthly Bulletin of Statistics* (January 1960), and *World Energy Supplies*, 1951–1954 and 1955–1958 (Statistical Papers, Series J).
The correlation between log level 1952 and log gain 1952–58 is .976.
The regression equation based on these thirty-nine countries, plus four others from the same climatic zone on which data are available (China-Taiwan, Czechoslovakia, Roumania, Yugoslavia), is: log gain (1952–58) = .9229 log level (1952) + .0480.
Standard scores are deviations from mean gain predicted by the regression formula (M = −.01831) divided by the standard deviation of the deviations from mean predicted gain (SD = .159).
[b] Based on twenty-one children's stories from second-, third-, and fourth-grade readers in each country.
[c] Based on six Hindi, seven Telegu, and eight Tamil stories.
[d] Based on twelve Urdu and eleven Bengali stories.
[e] Based on twenty-one German Swiss stories, mean = .91; twenty-one French Swiss stories, mean = 1.71; over-all mean obtained by weighting German mean double to give approximately proportionate representation to the two main ethnic population groups.

values may insist that people go on behaving in ways that are no longer adaptive to a changed social and economic order.

The other finding is not directly relevant to economic development, but it perhaps involves the means of achieving it. Quite unexpectedly, we discovered that every major dictatorial regime which came to power between the 1920's and 1950's (with the possible exception of Portugal's) was foreshadowed by a particular motive pattern in its stories for children: namely, a low need for affiliation (little interest in friendly relationships with people) and a high need for power (great concern over controlling and influencing other people).

The German readers showed this pattern before Hitler; the Japanese readers, before Tojo; the Argentine readers, before Peron; the Spanish readers, before Franco; the South African readers, before the present authoritarian government in South Africa; etc. On the other hand, very few countries which did not have dictatorships manifested this particular motive combination. The difference was highly significant statistically, since there was only one exception in the first instance and very few in the second. Apparently, we stumbled on a psychological index of ruthlessness— i.e., the need to influence other people (*n* Power), unchecked by sufficient concern for their welfare (*n* Affiliation). It is interesting, and a little disturbing, to discover that the German readers of today still evince this particular combination of motives, just as they did in 1925. Let us hope that this is one case where a social science generalization will not be confirmed by the appearance of a totalitarian regime in Germany in the next ten years.

To return to our main theme—let us discuss the precise ways that higher *n* Achievement leads to more rapid economic development, and why it should lead to economic development rather than, for example, to military or artistic development. We must consider in more detail the mechanism by which the concentration

of a particular type of human motive in a population leads to a complex social phenomenon like economic growth. The link between the two social phenomena is, obviously, the business entrepreneur. I am not using the term "entrepreneur" in the sense of "capitalist": in fact, I should like to divorce "entrepreneur" entirely from any connotations of ownership. An entrepreneur is someone who exercises control over production that is not just for his personal consumption. According to my definition, for example, an executive in a steel production unit in Russia is an entrepreneur.

It was Joseph Schumpeter who drew the attention of economists to the importance that the activity of these entrepreneurs had in creating industrialization in the West. Their vigorous endeavors put together firms and created productive units where there had been none before. In the beginning, at least, the entrepreneurs often collected material resources, organized a production unit to combine the resources into a new product, and sold the product. Until recently, nearly all economists— including not only Marx, but also Western classical economists—assumed that these men were moved primarily by the "profit motive." We are all familiar with the Marxian argument that they were so driven by their desire for profits that they exploited the workingman and ultimately forced him to revolt. Recently, economic historians have been studying the actual lives of such entrepreneurs and finding— certainly to the surprise of some of the investigators—that many of them seemingly were not interested in making money as such. In psychological terms, at least, Marx's picture is slightly out of focus. Had these entrepreneurs been above all interested in money, many more of them would have quit working as soon as they had made all the money that they could possibly use. They would not have continued to risk their money in further entrepreneurial ventures. Many of them, in fact, came from pietistic sects, like the

Quakers in England, that prohibited the enjoyment of wealth in any of the ways cultivated so successfully by some members of the European nobility. However, the entrepreneurs often seemed consciously to be greatly concerned with expanding their businesses, with getting a greater share of the market, with "conquering brute nature," or even with altruistic schemes for bettering the lot of mankind or bringing about the kingdom of God on earth more rapidly. Such desires have frequently enough been labeled as hypocritical. However, if we assume that these men were really motivated by a desire for achievement rather than by a desire for money as such, the label no longer fits. This assumption also simplifies further matters considerably. It provides an explanation for the fact that these entrepreneurs were interested in money without wanting it for its own sake, namely, that money served as a ready quantitative index of how well they were doing—e.g., of how much they had achieved by their efforts over the past year. The need to achieve can never be satisfied by money; but estimates of profitability in money terms can supply direct knowledge of how well one is doing one's job.

The brief consideration of the lives of business entrepreneurs of the past suggested that their chief motive may well have been a high n Achievement. What evidence have we found in support of this? We made two approaches to the problem. First, we attempted to determine whether individuals with high n Achievement behave like entrepreneurs; and second, we investigated to learn whether actual entrepreneurs, particularly the more successful ones, in a number of countries, have higher n Achievement than do other people of roughly the same status. Of course, we had to establish what we meant by "behave like entrepreneurs"—what precisely distinguishes the way an entrepreneur behaves from the way other people behave?

The adequate answers to these questions would entail a long discussion of the sociology of occupations, involving the distinction originally made by Max Weber between capitalists and bureaucrats. Since this cannot be done here, a very brief report on our extensive investigations in this area will have to suffice. First, one of the defining characteristics of an entrepreneur is *taking risks* and/or innovating. A person who adds up a column of figures is not an entrepreneur—however carefully, efficiently, or correctly he adds them. He is simply following established rules. However, a man who decides to add a new line to his business *is* an entrepreneur, in that he cannot know in advance whether his decision will be correct. Nevertheless, he does not feel that he is in the position of a gambler who places some money on the turn of a card. Knowledge, judgment, and skill enter into his decision-making; and, if his choice is justified by future developments, he can certainly feel a sense of personal achievement from having made a successful move.

Therefore, if people with high n Achievement are to behave in an entrepreneurial way, they must seek out and perform in situations in which there is some moderate risk of failure—a risk which can, presumably, be reduced by increased effort or skill. They should not work harder than other people at routine tasks, or perform functions which they are certain to do well simply by doing what everyone accepts as the correct traditional thing to do. On the other hand, they should avoid gambling situations, because, even if they win, they can receive no sense of personal achievement, since it was not skill but luck that produced the results. (And, of course, most of the time they would lose, which would be highly unpleasant to them.) The data on this point are very clear cut. We have repeatedly found, for example, that boys with high n Achievement choose to play games of skill that incorporate a moderate risk of failure. Figure 2 represents one study. The game was adapted from one used by the psychologist Kurt Lewin. Each child was given a rope ring and told that he could stand at any distance that he

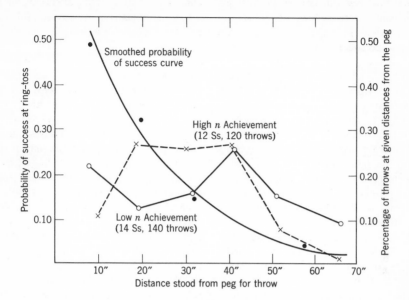

Figure 2. Percentage of throws made by five-year-olds with high and low "doodle" *n* Achievement at different distances from the peg and smoothed curve of probability of success at those distances. 26 *S*s, 10 throws each. Plotted at midpoints of intervals of 11 inches beginning with closest distance stood (4 in. to 14 in., 5 in. to 15 in., etc.).

preferred from the peg, to try to throw the ring over the peg. The children with high *n* Achievement usually stood at middle distances from the peg, where the chances of success or failure were moderate. However, the children with low *n* Achievement evinced no particular preference for any position. They more frequently stood at extremes of distance—either very close to the peg, where they were sure to throw the ring over it, or very far away, where they were almost certain not to. They thus manifested behavior like that of many people in underdeveloped countries who, while they act very traditionally economically, at the same time love to indulge in lotteries—risking a little to make a great deal on a very long shot. In neither of the two last examples do the actors concentrate on the realistic *calculated* risk, as do the subjects with high *n* Achievement.

We have recently concluded a somewhat analogous study, which indicated that boys with high *n* Achievement tend to perform

better and to work harder under conditions of moderate risk—boys not only in the United States, but also in Japan, Brazil, and India. In each of these countries, the boys with high *n* Achievement did not invariably perform a laboratory task better than the boys with low *n* Achievement. They did better only under conditions involving some degree of competition, some risk of doing worse than others or of not getting a sense of personal achievement. There was still another group of boys in the sample from each country. These boys were identified by their optimistic attitude toward life in general, as manifested in their answers to a questionnaire. The members of these groups always had more success than the others, no matter what the competitive or risk situation was. I like to think of these boys as the conscientious ones, who will do their work cheerfully and efficiently under any kind of incentive conditions. They may form the backbone of the civil service, because they can tolerate routine; but they will not be the business entrepreneurs, because the latter constantly seek situations in which they can obtain a sense of personal achievement from having overcome risks or difficulties.

Another quality that the entrepreneur seeks in his work is that his job be a kind that ordinarily provides him with accurate knowledge of the results of his decisions. As a rule, growth in sales, in output, or in profit margins tells him very precisely whether he has made the correct choice under uncertainty or not. Thus, the concern for profit enters in—profit is a measure of success. We have repeatedly found that boys with a high *n* Achievement work more efficiently when they know how well they are doing. Also, they will not work harder for money rewards; but if they are asked, they state that greater money rewards should be awarded for accomplishing more difficult things in games of skill. In the ring-toss game, subjects were asked how much money they thought should be awarded for successful throws from different distances. Subjects with high *n* Achievement and those with low *n* Achievement agreed substantially about the amounts for throws made close to the peg. However, as the distance from the peg increased, the amounts awarded for successful throws by the subjects with high *n* Achievement rose more rapidly than did the rewards by those with low *n* Achievement. Here, as elsewhere, individuals with high *n* Achievement behaved as they must if they are to be the successful entrepreneurs in society. They believed that greater achievement should be recognized by quantitatively larger reward.

We are now investigating to learn whether business executives do, in fact, have higher *n* Achievement. Our analysis of this question is not yet finished; but Figure 3 indicates what, on the whole, we shall probably find. Four conclusions can be drawn from it. (1) Entrepreneurs ("junior executives") have higher *n* Achievement than do a comparable group of nonentrepreneurs ("adjusters"), whose chief job was quasijudicial (tax claim and insurance adjusters). A very careful study in the General Electric Company has confirmed this finding: on the average, production managers have higher *n* Achievement than do staff specialists of comparable education and pay. (2) The more successful junior executives have higher *n* Achievement than the less successful ones. (3) Turkish executives have a lower *average* level of *n* Achievement than American executives. This finding supports the general impression that the "entrepreneurial spirit" is in short supply in such countries. (4) Nevertheless, the more successful Turkish executives have a higher level of *n* Achievement than do the less successful ones. This confirms our prediction that *n* Achievement equips people peculiarly for the business executive role—even in a country like Turkey, where business traditions are quite different from those of the West.

There are two successful, and one unsuccessful, methods by which the business community recruits people with the "entrepreneurial spirit"—with high *n* Achievement. The unsuccessful way is easiest to describe and is still characteristic of many underdeveloped countries. In a study of the occupational likes and dislikes of boys in Japan, Brazil, Germany, India, and the United States, we found that (as Atkinson had predicted on theoretical grounds) the boys with high *n* Achievement usually aspire toward the occupation of highest prestige *which they have a reasonable chance to enter and to succeed.*[11] For example, their ambitions will be centered on the professions, which are the highest prestige occupations in most countries—*if* the boys themselves are from the upper class and thus have the opportunity and backing to enter the professions. In other words, when the business leadership of a country is largely recruited from the élite (as it is in many countries, because only the élite

[11] J. W. Atkinson, "Motivational Determinants of Risk-Taking Behavior," *Psychological Review*, **64** (1957), 359–372.

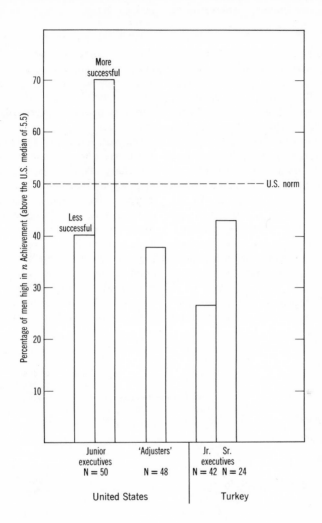

Figure 3. Percentages of different types of executives high in *n* Achievement in the United States and Turkey (after data supplied by N. M. Bradburn).

Has access to capital and to government), it will *not* tend to attract those with high *n* Achievement who are not from the upper class.

Developments in many of the Western democracies were quite different. In the most rapidly advancing countries, business leadership was drawn, at least in the early stages, largely from the middle classes.

A business career was the highest prestige occupation to which a middle-class boy with high *n* Achievement could aspire— especially if he were a member of a disliked minority group, like the Protestants in France or the Jews in many countries, to whom other channels of upward mobility were closed. Thus a constant "natural" flow of entrepreneurial talent from the middle classes provided economic leadership of a high quality.

The other successful method of recruiting entrepreneurial talent is the one that has been adopted, for example, in the U.S.S.R. There, the central government took a severe, achievement-oriented, "pass-or-fail" attitude toward its plant managers, so that only the "fittest" survived. We believe that those "fittest" were the ones with the highest *n* Achievement, although we have no supporting evidence as yet. In the free enterprise system, the recruiting method may be compared to a garden in which all plants are allowed to grow until some crowd the others out. In the Soviet system, it is comparable to a garden in which plants that have not reached a specified height by a certain time are weeded out. In many underdeveloped countries, it is comparable to a garden where only certain plants are permitted to live in the first place, so that the gardener has to take them whatever size they attain.

Of course, no country represents a pure type; but perhaps the analogy, oversimplified though it is, helps to illustrate my point.

What produces high *n* Achievement? Why do some societies produce a large number of people with this motive, while other societies produce so many fewer? We conducted long series of researches into this question. I can present only a few here.

One very important finding is essentially a negative one: *n* Achievement cannot be hereditary. Popular psychology has long maintained that some races are more energetic than others. Our data clearly contradict this in connection with *n* Achievement. The changes in *n* Achievement level within a given population are too rapid to be attributed to heredity. For example, the correlation between respective *n* Achievement levels in the 1925 and 1950 samples of readers is substantially zero. Many of the countries that were high in

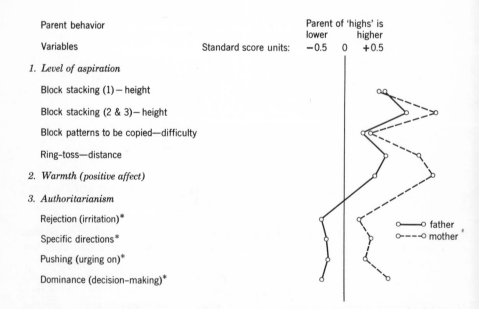

Figure 4. Mean differences in the behavior of parents of sons with low and high *n* Achievement working in task situations (after Rosen and D'Andrade). The asterisk indicates parents of "highs" predicted to be lower, permitting more independence.

n Achievement at one or both times may be low or moderate in *n* Achievement now, and vice versa. Germany was low in 1925 and is high now; and certainly the hereditary makeup of the German nation has not changed in a generation.

However, there is substantiating evidence that *n* Achievement is a motive which a child can acquire quite early in life, say, by the age of eight or ten, as a result of the way his parents have brought him up. Winterbottom's study of the importance of early self-reliance and achievement training has been supplemented by a much more detailed inquiry by Rosen and D'Andrade.[12] They actually entered the homes of boys with high and low *n* Achievement and observed how the boys were treated by their parents while they were engaged in various kinds of work, e.g., stacking blocks blindfolded. The principal results are summarized in Figure 4, which indicates the differences between the parents of the "high *n* Achievement boys" and the parents of boys with low *n* Achievement. In general, the mothers and the fathers of the first group set higher levels of aspiration in a number of tasks for their sons. They were also much warmer, showing positive emotion in reacting to their sons' performances. In the area of authority or dominance, the data are quite interesting. The mothers of the "highs" were more domineering than the mothers of the "lows," but the *fathers* of the "highs" were significantly *less* domineering than the fathers of the "lows." In other words, the fathers of the "highs" set high standards and are warmly interested in their sons' performances, but they do not directly interfere. This gives the boys the chance to develop initiative and self-reliance.

What factors cause parents to behave in this way? Their behavior certainly is involved with their values and, possibly, ultimately with their religion or their

general world view. At present, we cannot be sure that Protestant parents are more likely to behave this way than Catholic parents—there are too many subgroup variations within each religious portion of the community: the Lutheran father is probably as likely to be authoritarian as the Catholic father. However, there does seem to be one crucial variable discernible: the extent to which the religion of the family emphasizes individual, as contrasted with ritual, contact with God. The preliterate tribes that we studied in which the religion was the kind that stressed the individual contact had higher *n* Achievement; and in general, mystical sects in which this kind of religious self-reliance dominates have had higher *n* Achievement.

The extent to which the authoritarian father is away from the home while the boy is growing up may prove to be another crucial variable. If so, then one incidental consequence of prolonged wars may be an increase in *n* Achievement, because the fathers are away too much to interfere with their sons' development of it. And in Turkey, Bradburn found that those boys tended to have higher *n* Achievement who had left home early or whose fathers had died before they were eighteen.[13] Slavery was another factor which played an important role in the past. It probably lowered *n* Achievement—in the slaves, for whom obedience and responsibility, but not achievement, were obvious virtues; and in the slaveowners, because household slaves were often disposed to spoil the owner's children as a means for improving their own positions. This is both a plausible and a probable reason for the drop in *n* Achievement level in ancient Greece that occurred at about the time the middle-class entrepreneur was first able to afford, and obtain by conquest, as many as two slaves for each child. The idea also clarifies the slow economic development of the South in the United States by attributing

[12] B. C. Rosen and R. G. D'Andrade, "The Psychosocial Origins of Achievement Motivation," *Sociometry*, **22** (1959), 185–218.

[13] N. M. Bradburn, "The Managerial Role in Turkey" (unpublished Ph.D. dissertation, Harvard University, 1960).

its dilatoriness to a lack of *n* Achievement in its élite; and it also indicates why lower-class American Negroes, who are closest to the slave tradition, possess very low *n* Achievement.[14]

I have outlined our research findings. Do they indicate ways of accelerating economic development? Increasing the level of *n* Achievement in a country suggests itself as an obvious first possibility. If *n* Achievement is so important, so specifically adapted to the business role, then it certainly should be raised in level, so that more young men have an "entrepreneurial drive." The difficulty in this excellent plan is that our studies of how *n* Achievement originates indicate that the family is the key formative influence; and it is very hard to change on a really large scale. To be sure, major historical events like wars have taken authoritarian fathers out of the home; and religious reform movements have sometimes converted the parents to a new achievement-oriented ideology. However, such matters are not ordinarily within the policy-making province of the agencies charged with speeding economic development.

Such agencies can, perhaps, effect the general acceptance of an achievement-oriented ideology as an absolute *sine qua non* of economic development. Furthermore, this ideology should be diffused not only in business and governmental circles, but throughout the nation, and in ways that will influence the thinking of all parents as they bring up their children. As Rosen and D'Andrade found, parents must, above all, set high standards for their children. The campaign to spread achievement-oriented ideology, if possible, could also incorporate an attack on the extreme authoritarianism in fathers that impedes or prevents the development of self-reliance in their sons. This is, however, a more delicate point, and attacking this, in many countries, would be to threaten

values at the very center of social life. I believe that a more indirect approach would be more successful. One approach would be to take the boys out of the home and to camps. A more significant method would be to promote the rights of women, both legally and socially—one of the ways to undermine the absolute dominance of the male is to strengthen the rights of the female! Another reason for concentrating particularly on women is that they play the leading role in rearing the next generation. Yet, while men in underdeveloped countries come in contact with new achievement-oriented values and standards through their work, women may be left almost untouched by such influences. But if the sons are to have high *n* Achievement, the mothers must first be reached.

It may seem strange that a paper on economic development should discuss the importance of feminism and the way children are reared; but this is precisely where a psychological analysis leads. If the motives of men are the agents that influence the speed with which the economic machine operates, then the speed can be increased only through affécting the factors that create the motives. Furthermore—to state this point less theoretically —I cannot think of evinced substantial, rapid long-term economic development where women have not been somewhat freed from their traditional setting of "Kinder, Küche und Kirche" and allowed to play a more powerful role in society, specifically as part of the working force. This generalization applies not only to the Western democracies like the United States, Sweden, or England, but also to the U.S.S.R., Japan, and now China.

In the present state of our knowledge, we can conceive of trying to raise *n* Achievement levels only in the next generation—although new research findings may soon indicate *n* Achievement in adults can be increased. Most economic planners, while accepting the long-range desirability of raising *n* Achievement in future generations, want to know what

[14] B. C. Rosen, "Race, Ethnicity, and Achievement Syndrome," *American Sociological Review*, **24** (1959), 47–60.

can be done during the next five or ten years. This immediacy inevitably focuses attention on the process or processes by which executives or entrepreneurs are selected. Foreigners with proved entrepreneurial drive can be hired, but at best this is a temporary and unsatisfactory solution. In most underdeveloped countries where government is playing a leading role in promoting economic development, it is clearly necessary for the government to adopt rigid achievement-oriented standards of performance like those in the U.S.S.R.[15] A government manager or, for that matter, a private entrepreneur, should have to produce "or else." Production targets must be set, as they are in most economic plans; and individuals must be held responsible for achieving them, even at the plant level. The philosophy should be one of "no excuses accepted." It is common for government officials or economic theorists in underdeveloped countries to be weighed down by all the difficulties which face the economy and render its rapid development difficult or impossible. They note that there is too rapid population growth, too little capital, too few technically competent people, etc. Such obstacles to growth are prevalent, and in many cases they are immensely hard to overcome; but talking about them can provide merely a comfortable rationalization for mediocre performance. It is difficult to fire an administrator, no matter how poor his performance, if so many objective reasons exist for his doing badly. Even worse, such rationalization permits, in the private sector, the continued employment of incompetent family members as executives. If these private firms were afraid of being penalized for poor performance, they might be impelled to find more able professional managers a little more quickly. I am not an expert in this field, and the mechanisms I am suggesting may be far from appropriate. Still, they may serve to illustrate

my main point: if a country short in entrepreneurial talent wants to advance rapidly, it must find ways and means of insuring that only the most competent retain positions of responsibility. One of the obvious methods of doing so is to judge people in terms of their *performance* —and not according to their family or political connections, their skill in explaining why their unit failed to produce as expected, or their conscientiousness in following the rules. I would suggest the use of psychological tests as a means of selecting people with high *n* Achievement; but, to be perfectly frank, I think this approach is at present somewhat impractical on a large enough scale in most underdeveloped countries.

Finally, there is another approach which I think is promising for recruiting and developing more competent business leadership. It is the one called, in some circles, the "professionalization of management." Harbison and Myers have recently completed a world-wide survey of the efforts made to develop professional schools of high-level management. They have concluded that, in most countries, progress in this direction is slow.[16] Professional management is important for three reasons. (1) It may endow a business career with higher prestige (as a kind of profession), so that business will attract more of the young men with high *n* Achievement from the élite groups in backward countries. (2) It stresses *performance* criteria of excellence in the management area—i.e., what a man can do and not what he is. (3) Advanced management schools can themselves be so achievement-oriented in their instruction that they are able to raise the *n* Achievement of those who attend them.

Applied toward explaining historical events, the results of our researches clearly shift attention away from external factors and to man—in particular, to his motives and values. That about which he thinks and

[15] David Granick, *The Red Executive* (New York, 1960).

[16] Frederick Harbison and Charles A. Myers, *Management in the Industrial World* (New York, 1959).

dreams determines what will happen. The emphasis is quite different from the Darwinian or Marxist view of man as a creature who *adapts* to his environment. It is even different from the Freudian view of civilization as the sublimation of man's primitive urges. Civilization, at least in its economic aspects, in neither adaptation nor sublimation; it is a positive creation by a people made dynamic by a high level of *n* Achievement. Nor can we agree with Toynbee, who recognizes the importance of psychological factors as "the very forces which actually decide the issue when an encounter takes place," when he states that these factors "inherently are impossible to weigh and measure, and therefore to estimate scientifically in advance."[17] It is a measure of the pace at which the behavioral sciences are developing that even within Toynbee's lifetime we can demonstrate that he was mistaken. The psychological factor responsible for a civilization's rising to a challenge is so far from being "inherently impossible to weigh and measure" that it has been weighed and measured and scientifically estimated in advance; and, so far as we can now tell, this factor is the achievement motive.

[17] Arnold J. Toynbee, *A Study of History* (abridgment by D. C. Somervill; Vol. 1, New York, 1947).

Chapter 5

Ideology and Nationalism

NATIONALISM AND POLITICAL DEVELOPMENT

Rupert Emerson

If it were necessary to select the most important single force behind the revolutionary drive of the rising peoples of Asia and Africa, the choice would inevitably go to nationalism. For none of its potential rivals can an effective case be made. Indeed, almost all of them contribute in one fashion or another to the mounting nationalist demand. Arnold Toynbee, profuse with capitals, may denounce Nationalism as a "disastrous corruption," "a perversion of Industrialism and Democracy," or "the monstrous outcome of the impact of our modern Western Democracy upon the Parochial State"; but to the peoples newly asserting their claim to equal status in the world, nationalism is the essence of what they seek.

In the debates in the United Nations on the Covenants on Human Rights the right of self-determination has frequently been considered the foundation on which all other rights rest; self-determination denied, no other right can be secure. It is in this light that peoples around the globe have viewed nationalism, assuming that the remaining goods they seek will flow from its attainment. The usual version of this goal is an acknowledged equality expressed in sovereign independence; more rarely, an adequate substitute may be found in free association with another country as is the case between Puerto Rico and the United States, or between British Togoland and Ghana, or perhaps within the French Community.

The prime rival to nationalism as a driving force is presumed to be the desire for an improved standard of living. From time to time it is asserted that the ordinary poverty-stricken Asian and African is really interested only in seeing an end put to his poverty. This is a highly dubious proposition. The evidence indicates that he regards at least temporary economic privation as an appropriate price to pay for national salvation. It has also been contended that his real demand is for a transition to modernity, as manifested in economic and social development. In some part the pressure for economic development derives from the same root as the desire for an improved standard of living. However, it also has nationalist implications in its drive for equality.

However strong the urge toward better living conditions and economic development, it tends always to take second place to the political claims of nationalism. The individual who protects his economic position by refusing to undertake the sacrifices which patriotism demands reads himself out of the community of right-

SOURCE. Rupert Emerson, "Nationalism and Political Development," *Journal of Politics*, **22**, 3–28, February 1960.

minded, nation-fearing men. As one of the standard phrases of nationalism has it: we would rather be governed like hell by ourselves than well by someone else. Furthermore, the issue between nationalism and material advancement here posed is seen as a quite unreal one since the nationalist creed normally embraces the belief that material improvement will surely follow in the wake of national self-realization. Both well-being and economic development are considered unattainable in the shadow of imperialism. Only when the national destiny is safely entrusted to national and not alien hands is it possible to move confidently ahead on the path which leads to wealth, strength, and modernity. Nationalism opens the way to a new economic era, and the latter in turn lends new power to the nation.

Communism might be put forward as a contemporary threat to nationalism and undoubtedly, in certain cases, individuals and groups have given to the Party a priority which they deny to the nation. More frequently, however, and particularly in the revolt against imperialist domination, Communism is seen as an alternative means of reaching national goals. Although objective reality may contradict them, Asian and African Communists are far more likely to view their Party membership as a positive expression of their nationalism than as a negation of it. Official Communist dogma itself puts self-determination in the forefront of its doctrines (even though the small print always carefully reduces it to an instrument to be used for Party purposes) and distinguishes between the rightful patriotism of the unfree peoples and the proper devotion to proletarian internationalism of those whose national identity is old-established. It has often been contended that the success of the Communists in Asian countries hinges upon their ability to identify themselves with the local nationalist cause.

The priority of nationalism has been vigorously affirmed by both Jawaharlal Nehru and Kwame Nkrumah. In his opening address to the IPR conference at Lucknow in 1950, the Indian Prime Minister described nationalism as a war cry which warms the heart of almost every Asian: "Any other force, any other activity that may seek to function, must define itself in terms of this nationalism. . . . No argument in any country of Asia is going to have weight if it goes counter to the Nationalist spirit of the country, Communism or no Communism." Supporting much the same theme, Ghana's Prime Minister cited the motto of the Convention People's Party, which was his own creation. "We prefer self-government with danger to servitude in tranquillity" and followed it up with what he called the party's policy, "Seek ye first the political kingdom and all things shall be added unto you."[1] It is to the attainment of the political kingdom of the nation that the guiding spirits of the new states and their followers have looked, confident that the nation came first and that the rest would follow after.

It is a great deal easier to assert the priority given nationalism than to lay out with any measure of precision its content. Rarely does nationalism represent a coherent and positive body of doctrine and belief, reaching significantly beyond insistence on the establishment of an

[1] The citation from Nehru is to be found in William L. Holland (ed.), *Asian Nationalism and the West* (New York, 1953), pp. 353–354: Nkrumah's statement appears in his autobiography, *Ghana* (New York, 1957), pp. 162–163. In his opening speech at the Pan-African Conference in Accra on December 8, 1958, Prime Minister Nkrumah repeated this conviction: "My first advice to you who are struggling to be free is to aim for the attainment of the Political Kingdom—that is to say, the complete independence and self-determination of your territories. When you have achieved the Political Kingdom all else will follow. Only with the acquisition of political power—real power through the attainment of sovereign independence—will you be in a position to reshape 'your lives and destiny: only then will you be able to resolve the vexatious problems which harrass our Continent."

independent state. Freedom from partition or alien intrusion is normally a far better defined matter than are the uses to which freedom would be put. In the speech cited above, Nehru commented on the fact that a large element in nationalism is negative. "Nationalism is essentially an anti-feeling," he has written elsewhere, "and it feeds and fattens on hatred and anger against other national groups, and especially against the foreign rulers of a subject country."[2]

The negative or "anti"-character of nationalism in a colonial setting is simple enough to explain, but it is by no means unique to colonialism. Everywhere the national "we" has been to a considerable degree defined by contrast to the alien and opposing "they," and in most instances no operationally significant statement of what the nation stands for can be expected. Indeed, this may be held to be a standard feature of all nationalism until one arrives at what Carlton Hayes called integral nationalism or what might today be called totalitarian nationalism. I take it to be characteristic of liberal nationalism that its particular content remains very largely unspecified, allowing for a multitude of sins as well as virtues. The Fourth of July oration of the past, praising America's blue skies and broad horizons. its heroes and its great achievements, reached an approximately acceptable level of specificity. It roused a glow of pride in being an American and yet did not rule out any significant number of Americans who were heretical on one or another point mentioned by the speaker. Tom Paine, George Washington, Alexander Hamilton, Thomas Jefferson, and Andrew Jackson must all fit within the American heritage; New England, the South, the Middle West and the Far West must find an equal place. If any of them are to be ruled out by authorized fiat we have come to the proto-Fascist phase when some body arrogates to itself the right to determine among Americans what is to be

[2] *Toward Freedom* (New York, 1941), p. 74.

accepted as American. France must embrace the *ancien régime*, the Revolution, Napoleon, and the twists and turnings of the last century and a half. To demand that each nation have a single positive content and program for nationalism is to ask that it select from a diverse history certain strands which alone will constitute its legitimate national heritage. Not far down this road lies the *Gleichschaltung* of the Nazis.

The new states are, however, peculiarly divided within themselves by the gaps which separate different elements in the population. Not only do they have as diverse and internally contradictory a history as do other peoples, but they are also afflicted by an unusual degree of distance between the bulk of the population and the newly arisen leadership. The most notable gap is the one which divides the active, Western-educated urban group from the inert, uneducated, tradition-bound mass mainly composed of the peasantry. It is the first group from which the heirs of empire have been drawn to constitute the new élite, putting its stamp on the states which it has been largely responsible for bringing into being. Here are the makings of a fundamental dilemma. It is arguable that any nation's claim to a distinctive place in the sun must be derived from the past which has shaped it in this peculiar national fashion, yet the entire leadership of the new states tends to be made up of those most removed from the traditional society of their ancestors. Nationalism has characteristically been the property of the constantly expanding but still relatively slight minority most influenced by the West.

The social structure in Asian and African nations, then, is that a newly fashioned élite, oriented toward the West and modernization despite its passionate repudiation of Western imperial control, has taken a predominant lead in societies the bulk of whose members are still close to their ancestral past. In such a circumstance the definition of the national purpose must evidently be a hazardous process. We do not as yet have any accurate evidence or body of precedent by means of which to determine what course the new states are likely to take. We do not know whether the gaps which are now so apparent will be filled with greater or less speed, and whether the mass will tend to move in the Westernizing and modernizing direction of its currently ruling élite (which seems most probable) or the élite move toward reabsorption into the mass and the older patterns of life (which is highly unlikely as a general phenomenon). Against the current trend toward an optimistic view of the prospects for development must be set the general failure of almost all non-Western countries save Japan to swing into the modern stream during the last century. Furthermore, the record shows that many Latin American countries not only relapsed into lethargy but also made little headway in achieving the national integration of different elements of their population. It may be that a similar decline into stagnation on the part of Africa and Asia is precluded by the speed at which the world now moves and the new modes of production, transport, and communication which work to break down old barriers and isolationisms. The precedents of the past have perhaps become irrelevant in the face of such developments as the deep penetration of virtually every society by Western forces and ideas, the inescapable pressure of outside events, and the presence of Communism, ready to exploit every difficulty or failure. Both what has already happened and the widespread expectations for a different kind of future render a return to the old ways impossible. The clear probability is that the West has loosed forces the forward sweep of which can only temporarily be diverted or checked, though no reliable estimate can be made either of the speed of change or of the form it will take. The nationalist movements have themselves been the spearhead of the demand for change.

The existence of great gaps in the society of the new states raises a further question. How real is the solidarity of a nation when it is so profoundly divided within itself? It is evident that no single and all-embracing answer can be given to such a question since the backgrounds and present situations of the different countries vary so greatly. What can be said of Egypt has no necessary bearing for Ghana or the Philippines, and India's prospects may be quite unrelated to those of its neighbors, Pakistan, Burma, Ceylon, and Afghanistan. Precisely the "anti"-character of nationalist movements in colonial or quasi-colonial countries is likely to lend a deceptive sense of national unity. The fact that a people can stage a consolidated anti-imperial movement conveys no assurance that it will be able to maintain political coherence once the imperial enemy has vanished. It is, of course, true that the mere carrying on of an extended and concerted struggle is in itself a significant factor in the creation of national sentiment, but a more basic identity is necessary if the national unity is to endure. The sense of belonging together through the experience of a common history and of facing a common destiny is not something which can be created overnight.

How great importance should be attached to the gap between the Western-oriented élite and the mass is not a matter on which a precise estimate can now be given. When a nationalist movement has gotten into full swing, the people at large are likely to follow the lead of the active nationalist élite though they may have given little prior evidence of political interest. One commentator has remarked that there is no difference between African peoples which is as great as their collective difference from the Europeans who have ruled them. When India was aflame with nationalism in the 1930's, Gandhi and his lieutenants were able to win the support of many whose knowledge of what the struggle involved must have been slight. Similarly, when the euphemistically labelled police actions of the Dutch were carrying colonial warfare to the Indonesians, an unexpectedly broad segment of the population gave its backing to the nationalist forces. And yet the gap remains. The mass has so far demonstrated only meagre interest in taking an active part in day-to-day political life. The leaders, for their part, have often shown an inclination to see themselves as an élite, properly entrusted with the destinies of their untutored countrymen. "Guided democracy," which Sukarno considers suitable to the present state of development in Indonesia, also describes the élite conception of government in many other countries. Nor have the mass of the people up to this point been inclined to challenge the élitist claim of their new leaders, although the military have presented a decisive challenge in several countries. Where democratic institutions survive for an extended time and the people come to feel that political power is actually in their hands, the present relationship between mass and élite may take on a quite different cast.

At this point it is in order to turn to three more specific topics: the role of nationalism in laying the foundations on which all further political development must build; the bearing of nationalism upon particular types of political institutions; and a glance at other roles played by nationalism in political development.

The social contract theorist, in his purer flights of fancy, pictured a world in which distinct atoms of human beings, impelled by reason and other pressures, came together to make a contract which brought state and government into being. In the contemporary scene, the nation-state, as the term indicates, assumes that the state is built upon, or is the institutional embodiment of, a community of men who are already joined by intimate and old-established links. The state is not the product of random particles arbitrarily joined in political cooperation, but the expression of the close prior bonds which has brought this "We" to a sense of difference from the alien "They." Society derives, so to speak, not from a contract but from natural and organic growth.

If political institutions are to be established, a first necessity is that the demographic and geographic limits which define the scope of those institutions should be laid down. In a tribal era they are as extensive as the tribe—which may, of course, be nomadic and thus have no spatial boundaries. When religion is predominant, the religious community sets the standard; at another time the city-state is the accepted unit; and in monarchical days the limits are set by the range of the ruler's jurisdiction. What is important in the latter system is not that a common history has brought the people to a sense of community but that they are all subjects of the appropriate majesty. We are just emerging from the imperial era in which a few of the states of the West, belatedly joined by Japan, extended their political sway to embrace most of the rest of the world.

With the coming of nationalism all these political systems move into the discard or at least make a suitable pretense of adapting themselves to the new demands. Henceforward it is not a king nor a religion nor imperial conquest nor even a contract which legitimizes a state, but the coincidence of state and nation. Where the state fails to be built upon the nation there is every presumption that the structure must be redesigned to approximate the ideal. Where empires embrace more than one nation, they must undergo the surgeon's knife, as has already happened in Europe and in Asia and is now rapidly under way in Africa. Only in the Soviet Union, successor to the empire of the Tsars, does the multinational state survive on the grand scale. Where the state falls short of the nation, as in the partition of Germany, Korea, or Vietnam, and perhaps in the case of the Arab states, it is necessary to work toward reunification in order to satisfy the present criteria of legitimacy. Given the assumptions of the nationalist age, the first prerequisite is the determination of the national units which form the foundation of the state system.

As it is the presumption that the modern state is built upon the nation, so it is also the presumption that the nationalist speaks on behalf of a nation already in existence. Members of the nation may need to be roused to awareness of their national identity, but national unity itself is taken for granted. To question its existence is almost an insult to intelligence, and is certainly an insult to political ambition. The relationships are, however, in some instances reversed. In a great many cases in the past, and not infrequently in the present, it is the state which appears to have been the determining element in the creation of the nation, and at least on some occasions the nationalists have had to play a significant role in bringing into being the nation whose cause they have espoused.

Over and over again, if the origin of a nation is traced, it will be found that there was a state structure, or at least a political system approximating a state, which coincided to a striking degree with the modern nation in terms of the territory and people it embraced. The regularity of this coincidence furnishes good evidence for the thesis that, more often than not, the nation is a deposit which has been left behind by the state—although this evades the query as to whether the original state itself was perhaps the product of prior ethnic unity. Where the state has survived for many generations reasonably intact within an approximation of the same frontiers, as is the case with France, England (though here Great Britain becomes more problematical), Ireland, Spain, Portugal, Egypt, China, Japan, and certain others, the argument is so obvious as to need no elaboration. Poland, Hungary, Bohemia, and Bulgaria can serve as good examples of states which vanished from the historical scene for longer or shorter periods of time but left behind them firmly established national precipitates.

Outside Europe the role of the state as the formative factor in the shaping of nations is at least as great. Certainly in the Americas the state played a crucial role in setting the boundaries within which nations were to appear. In Latin America the boundaries of the states tend to have a high degree of coincidence with the provincial jurisdictions marked out by Spain and other ruling powers; and it is the successor states which have shaped the Latin American nations insofar as national entities have in fact been welded together out of the disparate human materials. In North America the national separation between Canada and the United States can be attributed to a series of historical accidents. Two distinct states came into existence which worked upon their peoples in different fashions and gradually evolved into distinctive national communities. The independent states which the political processes have created in the Americas have operated not only to intensify but even to create the feeling of national separateness and identity.

Nowhere is the significance of the state in its capacity as nation-maker more inescapably evident than in the colonial sphere. In some cases, of course, such as those of the Burmese and Vietnamese, the peoples who have recently claimed nationhood had achieved a vigorous earlier communal identity, despite the presence of minorities, and could look back to long-lived state systems of their own. In other cases, such as those of the Philippines and Indonesia, the lines drawn on the map by the imperial power were the determining element in establishing the boundaries within which peoples have developed a sense of national awareness. Here the common government was a major instrument in pressing ethnic diversity into a common mold.

The role of government in bringing to peoples the experience of a common destiny is obviously immense, but the human material involved sharply limits the effect of the forces set in motion by the achievement of political unification. Integration is possible where peoples have an original similarity and may be totally or virtually excluded where they are divided by large-scale disparities in such basic elements as race, culture, religion, and language. Thus the closely related native communities of the Indonesian Archipelago lent themselves easily to assimilation to a general national pattern when they were brought under a single roof by Dutch rule, although the scattered islands and the divisive nature of the Dutch system made national unity a somewhat tenuous matter. The Chinese in Indonesia, however, presented almost insuperable barriers to any comparable assimilation. Immense difficulties obviously attend the effort to bring about a national consolidation of the Malays, Chinese, and Indians in Malaya, and there is good reason to assume that no government would have been able to merge the Arabs and Jews of Palestine. In such instances the bonds of prior communal attachment were too deeply rooted and the differences between the peoples too profound. Similarly in Africa through the superimposition of a colonial government a group of African tribes may achieve a sense of national identity in which Europeans and Indians living under the same government are highly unlikely to share, despite the brave slogans of partnership. The effectiveness of the state in forging a nation dwindles away to the vanishing point in such a situation as that of South Africa where the *apartheid* doctrine explicitly rejects any conception of building a single national community. The introduction of communalism, as in India and East Africa, also serves as an obstacle.

One case which is peculiarly complex and perennially absorbing is that of India. Here a vast subcontinent, a Europe in itself, characterized by a diversity of languages, religions, and patterns of life, achieved over the millennia some feeling, however loose and ill-defined, that all the diversities had their place in a single whole. This amorphous spiritual identity had found virtually no expression in political

unity: the characteristic political condition was a shifting array of states and principalities, conquests and alliances, lending color to the trite comment that India was only a geographical expression. Whether India would have established itself as a consolidated nation-state or disintegrated into a plurality of states and peoples if the British had not taken over is a speculation in the blue which is entertaining but unanswerable. Certainly it is evident that the effect of British rule—plus modern innovations in transport and communications—in promoting a working sense of Indian unity was of vital importance. The maintenance of law and order, administrative unity, the introduction of a common body of social and political concepts and values, the appearance of English as a *lingua franca*, fiscal and economic integration, all served to link together the disparate elements which made up the Indian society—as did the common national struggle against British rule. At least for the newly rising leaders who created the nationalist movement the fact of a common British background, as well as of a common British enemy, seems almost as important as the common Indian heritage. When India secured independence, the British trained and educated elements dominated the scene—British trained and educated even though many of them had spent much of their lives in British jails—and the Indian Civil Service, one of the most strikingly successful products of the British connection, carried on the administration through the first difficult years.

Despite the generally unifying effect of British rule, the last turn of the wheel brought not unity but partition. This is an irrefutable demonstration, confirmed also by Ireland's partition, that a single political system does not necessarily bring political unification in its train. Whether the cause be assigned to the divide-and-rule Machiavellianism of the British, to the irreconcilable original cleavage between Hindu and Muslim finding new expression under changed conditions, or to more ephemeral and accidental elements such as the character of Gandhi or the role and ambitions of Jinnah, the fact remains that from one British India there emerged two independent states, each endowed with its own variant of nationalism.

For other Asian territories the effect of the era of colonialism was less marked both because the duration of colonial rule was briefer and because the ethnic identity of the peoples had already been well established. Since Korea, for example, had an ancient heritage of independent existence under its own rulers, Japanese domination served less as a unifying force than as a stimulant to national awareness and political action. In Indochina much the same was true for the Vietnamese and Cambodians both of which peoples look back to long centuries of separate, if checkered, existence. In setting up a federal rather than a unitary structure the French colonial régime took these differences explicitly into account. It went beyond them in its tripartite division of Vietnam without succeeding in breaking up the unity of the Vietnamese people, although the latter were destined to undergo a new partition at the end of the French era.

Africa, south of the Sahara, offers a terrain in which a unique opportunity to bring nations into being is given to the nationalist and to the state, the latter appearing usually in the guise of a colonial administration. Elsewhere in the world the determinants of national allegiance can often be traced back to a remote past, and reasonably fixed landmarks of history, culture, and religion separate one nation from another. In Africa such national landmarks are at best much less evident and clearcut, and at worst have as yet not come into visible existence at all. The precolonial history of the continent had its quota of internal wars, conquests, and empires, but their effect in integrating large masses of people into potentially national communities was markedly more limited than in other parts of the world. The clan and the tribe, varying greatly in

size in different parts, have been, and in large measure remain, the typical social and cultural units. If nations are to appear, they are still for the most part in the making. As to what the next decade or two ahead may hold in the way of unification and division of African peoples, I believe that a glance into any one crystal ball is about as good as another.

For the moment, however, Africa is the continent *par excellence* to sustain the thesis that colonial governments, given appropriate circumstances, may be the major instruments in shaping nations. In the first round political demands are directed to the colonial authorities, and the implicit or explicit assumption is likely to be made that since "national self-determination" is what the contemporary world expects, anti-colonial movements assume the title of nationalism and are assumed to be serving as the agents of nations.

On the face of it, the current drift has unquestionably been toward a new territorial nationalism in Africa which takes the existing colonies as setting the frame of political reference. The caveat should, however, immediately be added that the cases on which we can generalize as to the relations between colonies and African nations are still so few in number, so limited in time, and so uncertain in their bearing, as to make any generalization immediately suspect. It is, in fact, nearer the truth to assert that there are as yet no coherent nations in sub-Saharan Africa than to claim that each of the political jurisdictions has shaped a nation within its ethnically arbitrary frontiers. Even among the whites of South Africa the Afrikaner has been by no means prepared to accept absorption into a single South African nation with his British-descended countrymen. As the oldest of the African states, Ethiopia embraces wide ethnic diversity and Liberia remains deeply divided between the Africans of the *hinterland* and the descendants of the settlers from America, even though significant efforts have been made of late to bring the two within a common framework. The Sudan and Ghana, in their different fashions, are likewise made up of heterogeneous elements which only much patience, time, and tactful labor can weld together. Nigeria is notoriously a precarious lumping together of peoples whose separate identity is at least as real a matter as their acceptance of national unity.

The French colonial territories present an even more baffling picture of national ambiguity. The British system, despite its fondness for indirect rule which maintains a particularistic tribal solidarity, tends to produce a measure of identification with the territory concerned. The French system has operated in a much more diffuse fashion. With Paris as its all-absorbing center and with central political institutions in which Africans were represented, the local territorial community and institutions tended to be lost from sight. Furthermore, the vast African holdings of France were divided into the two large federations of West and Equatorial Africa, the former of which had eight and the latter four provincial subdivisions. A substantial number of alternatives presented themselves. Was the unit of ultimate national allegiance to be the total Franco-African community, as some French spokesmen were given to assert, or the whole of French Africa, or each of the two federations, or the individual territories within the federations, or some other grouping of these territories based, perhaps, on still continuing tribal ties? A huge amount of jockeying for position and of more basic community formation obviously lies ahead, in the course of which the kinds of political allegiance which will dominate the future and determine the drawing of the new African frontiers will gradually become clear.

The uncertainties of the present situation can be illustrated on every side. The independence of Guinea, for example, suddenly asserted at the time of the referendum of the de Gaulle constitution, carried no necessary implication that the new state represented a national entity, and the decision to join forces with Ghana in some undesignated fashion again changed the terms of reckoning. At recent African conferences and in the pronouncements of leading spokesmen, much has been heard of the existence of an "African personality" and of pan-Africanism or of some merger of West African territories. The one constant factor in the situation is that Africa is caught up in a ferment of change and political upheaval, whose end is not yet in sight and whose ultimate form is still subject to a great measure of variation. Neither the older tribal units nor the present colonial boundaries are likely to furnish the full blueprint of the future, and it is even more unlikely that any grandiose conception of a consolidated Pan-African union will be created in any foreseeable future. The establishment of a number of separate and independent states, each of which will have its own body of vested interests and distinctive features, will work to make mergers increasingly difficult, but a number of present colonial jurisdictions seem palpably unviable and must seek to join forces with neighboring areas.

In Nigeria and Tanganyika, in the Congo, Guinea, and Equatorial Africa, the European powers have been engaged in a process which has a great bearing on the formation of nations, whether or not nations directly emerge from the colonial régimes which are now one by one vanishing. The work of the colonial administrators is actively supplemented by that of the nationalists who, in Africa even more than elsewhere, may claim the title of nation builders as well as political leaders. Everywhere the nationalists are by definition in the forefront of the national movements and are assumed to have a more acute awareness of its existence than the ordinary man, but it is also assumed that their role is not that of creating the nation but of rousing it to consciousness.

The nation is something which is there as a great historical fact; it requires only the appropriate circumstances and the appeal of the leaders to swing it into political action. The task of the men of mid-nineteenth century Germany, Meiji Japan, or early twentieth-century Egypt was not to forge disparate elements into a hitherto non-existent identity but to give full expression to the deep underlying sense of national community which generations of living together had produced.

In Africa this approach to the national issue is in great part an illusion. It might, indeed, be argued with only slight exaggeration that the nations so far exist only in the persons of the nationalists themselves since they are the only people who have moved beyond the tribal horizons and have come to a broader sense of the society in which they live. The mass of the population in whose name they claim to speak continues to be divided into tribes which are bound together by little, if anything, in the way of language, religion, culture, or shared historical experience. The one common aspect of their lives has been the brief period of subjection to European rule, and this, for the bulk of them, has often meant virtually nothing in the way of a common life. Formally speaking they have been under a common government with its uniform economy and system of law and administration, but in practice they have lingered very largely within the framework of their traditional societies and have perhaps only recently been brought into any significant degree of association with their fellow colonials. As a random sample of what is involved one might cite the comment of James S. Coleman in 1956 that "Until the last five years the overwhelming majority of the peoples of northern Togoland were unaware of the existence of Togoland."[3] In the African setting the nationalists speak for nations yet to be born and themselves have a great responsibility for their emergence.

[3] *Togoland* (*International Conciliation*, September 1956), p. 5, note 1.

Anti-colonialism may serve as a rallying-cry to build up a popular front of resistance, but the constructive work of bringing forth nations out of a motley colonial assemblage of tribes still remains almost wholly a matter for the future even after sovereign independence has been achieved.

The nation establishes the demographic and geographic frontiers of the state. For the survival of the state nationalism furnishes another vital element in that it supplies the emotional cement which holds the members of the state together when disagreements threaten to pull them apart. What the social contract sought to provide by engaging men in formal obligations to each other came to be provided in the contemporary world by the social-historical fact of being born, brought up, and educated within the close-knit and emotion-laden confines of the nation. In the theory of the national era the state exists in order to realize the purposes of the nation, and, short of external attack, it can maintain its unity as long as the "We" of the nation takes priority over all the divergent pulls which might distract and disrupt.

Does nationalism have a clear tendency to produce one or another type of political institution? The answer to this question must be a slightly hesitant "No"; slightly hesitant because nationalism has in it democratic elements which cannot be ignored even where it has turned in ruthlessly authoritarian directions.

In fact, to assign to nationalism any particular political coloration is presumably impossible since it has been associated with almost every conceivable régime and attitude. Even though an impressive case can be made for the proposition that every true nationalism rests on democratic underpinnings of sorts, there are many ardent and unmistakable nationalisms in which democracy as a specific type of political system is either non-existent or is no more than a facade of outward conformity with current political fashions. Where the general constellation of forces has been such as to promote democracy, as most notably in Western Europe and the countries which it has settled overseas, nationalism has maintained a predominantly democratic outlook; where the foundations of democracy have been weak, as in most of the rest of the world, nationalism has betrayed the democratic promise which the nineteenth-century liberal saw in it and has become an instrument of the established ruling groups or of totalitarianism. It is, of course, always the champion of self-government in the sense of national as opposed to alien rule, but it is only accidentally self-government in the sense of rule by the many as opposed to rule by the few. Reduced to its bare bones, nationalism is no more than the assertion that this particular community is arrayed against the rest of mankind. This sense of separate identity can by itself give no clue as to how the community may choose to manage its own affairs.

At a time when nationalism in the West has often drifted in reactionary or militarist directions and when the most dangerous and abhorrent elements in it have so recently been arrogantly paraded by the Fascists and Nazis, it may appear paradoxical, or even outrageous folly to suggest the existence of an essential bond between nationalism and democracy; yet both in idea and in actual historical development there has been such a bond. Hans Kohn has put the matter in the extreme form of saying that "nationalism is inconceivable without the ideas of popular sovereignty preceding—without a complete revision of the position of ruler and ruled, of classes and castes."[4] On the face of the historical record no statement as uncompromisingly sweeping as this can be sustained ... and yet it has more than a germ of fundamental truth.

Once full-fledged nationalism has appeared, a transformation of deep and lasting importance in the relations of people, rulers, and state tends to occur.

[4] *The Idea of Nationalism* (New York, 1941), p. 3.

Even in the Fascist variants the role which the people play is sharply distinguished from their role in the earlier type of dictatorship or monarchy, as witness the efforts of Fuehrer and Duce to carry the masses with them, to give at least the appearance of popular consultation through plebiscitary techniques, and to spread the tentacles of the Party down into every cranny of the society. This, certainly, is not democracy in any acceptable sense, and yet it is equally certainly a perverse offshoot from democratic roots. The Leader and the Party put themselves forward as emanations of the popular will, as a truer distillation of the national *volonté générale* than the people themselves can produce.

To reduce the question to its most basic terms, the argument linking democracy and nationalism would run something as follows. Nationalism is peculiarly a product of or a response to the distinctive forces which have gone into the shaping of the modern world. Those forces are inherently and inevitably "democratic" in the sense that they mobilize submerged elements and classes of society into new social roles, eat away at traditional attachments and relationships, and work toward the building of a new great society into which, in principle, all men are actively drawn. Obviously what is involved here is by no means necessarily a democratic constitutional structure nor even an immediate approximation of a society striving toward egalitarianism, although both of these are likely to be present at least as active aspirations. Far more, it is the general conception, derived from the changing social scene, that the people, the mass of ordinary humans, are of consequence, that they are achieving a sense both of their own worth and of their right and ability to do something about it, and that the leaders must speak in their name. The national era comes to be an era of mass communications and mass production, inescapably headed toward mass politics.

The heart of the argument is the proposition that the rise of nationalism is normally associated with deep-running social ferment and change which disrupt the old order of society and bring about a rise in social consequence and awareness of ever-widening segments and classes of the people at large. On this basis nationalism is seen as one of the major and typical manifestations of what Karl Mannheim has spoken of as "the fundamental democratization of society," the stirring "into action of those classes who formerly played a passive part in political life."[5] As the peoples themselves—or, at least, a significant new element among them—begin to come of age and to a new consciousness of themselves, they demand a new place in a society in process of transformation. One of the characteristic forms which this demand has taken is insistence upon the centrality of the national community and upon the latter's right to make the state the sovereign organ of its identity and will. The people, after all, compose the nation, and it is not beyond the bounds of reason to suggest the revolutionary importance of the fact that the social-political community which has come to occupy the center of the contemporary stage—taking over the state in its own name and establishing a new criterion of legitimacy—should, therefore, be defined in terms of the people. In the new dispensation the state could no longer be seen as made up of the ruler and those who happened to be his subjects, but became in principle the emanation and instrument of the nation. The forward thrust of the bourgeoisie in Europe and later of the masses, had its close overseas parallel in the awakening rebellion of colonial people, in roughly similar circumstances and under similar leadership.

The rise of democracy as a political phenomenon has coincided too closely with the emergence of nations as conscious entities to be explained in terms of random chance. The lines of interconnection between the two are many. The most evident

[5] *Man and Society in an Age of Reconstruction* (London, 1940), p. 44.

is the one which has already been briefly discussed: the fact that nationalism is one of the major manifestations of the modern social ferment which overturns traditional relationships and gives new consequence to formerly submerged elements of society.

A second line of interconnection is the immense prestige which democracy has achieved—even among those who have no serious intent of practicing it. Democracy is taken as an ultimate good to which all peoples must aspire, but which only the advanced peoples can hope to master. The imperial centers—Britain, France, the Low Countries, the United States—which have so largely set the tone for the world as it has evolved in the last century and more, have established the pattern of democratic supremacy, and have, at least until recently, made no effort to conceal their belief that the "lesser breeds of man" could not be trusted to manage a democratic system. The imperial powers themselves, properly democratic at home, must impose a benevolently autocratic rule on the peoples whose tutelage they had undertaken. For the nationalists struggling to win their equality with the imperial masters here was a challenge: democracy was the political system whose realization would serve as a symbol that the bonds of inferiority had been broken.

Nor was the striving for democratic institutions only a matter of prestige. Assuming the nationalist leaders to be in almost every instance the product of Western education at home or abroad, the political philosophy and political history with which they were imbued pointed to democracy as the form of government which represented man's highest achievement and as the form which modern man naturally adopted. If they lived and studied abroad, they were likely to come in contact with democratic institutions, and in dependent countries the imperial authorities grudgingly introduced installments of democracy at which their wards were allowed to try their hand under close supervision. Political education in both a formal and a practical sense had the concepts and institutions of democracy in large part at its center, and other approaches to democracy were made in the new era through the upcoming political parties, trade unions, cooperative organizations, and other such bodies, all of which represented popular adaptation to the new Western forces coming in under the aegis of imperialism.

Furthermore, a swing in the democratic direction was a matter of vital political necessity for the nationalists. Their legitimacy in the eyes of their imperial opponents, and, no doubt, in their own as well, rested in very considerable part on their ability to demonstrate that they had the mass of their people behind them. If it could be established that they spoke for a nation with the blessing of its people, their moral claim to take over approached the irrefutable. To this moral aspect of their struggle must be added the hard political fact that if they were to represent enough of a political force to have a serious impact on the imperial power whose position they contested, they must be able to enlist the masses in battle behind them. Particularly in the colonial areas the effective strength of the nationalists rested upon their ability to have a larger hold on the loyalty of the people than could be exercised by the colonial officials. As the grandest sample of all, when the Indian National Congress under Gandhi's guidance became a mass organization in the 1920's and 1930's the British authorities could no longer maintain the claim that the people at large really preferred alien rule nor could they count on having their orders generally obeyed. Prisons and bayonets still served to keep the system temporarily in operation, but they were an unacceptable substitute for consent.

In these and other fashions nationalism works to promote democracy, but it also contains ingredients which can with the greatest of ease turn in undemocratic or anti-democratic directions. Wherever nationalism is the main driving force, there is the temptation to give priority to the attainment of national unity, strength, and independence. In such circumstances the liberalism of democratic nationalism may yield to the demand for unity put forward in the name of the nation itself. The problem is always present of giving specific content to the national will and singling out those who formulate it. Rousseau's *volonté générale*, itself only precariously identified with the concrete wills of actual human beings, is sublimated by Hegel into a *Volksgeist* which manifests itself in a realm above that of ordinary mortals but must be brought down to earth. The national will speaks with irresistible authority, yet whose voice speaks for it? The national soul may reside in the simple peasant, villager, or worker, but his ignorance and lack of experience of the great world render him, it may be contended, unable to give it true expression. In his stead the élite or the charismatic leader takes over as the emanation of the national will. The nation is sovereign, but the exercise of that sovereignty, so the argument all too fluently runs, should, for the good of the nation itself, be entrusted to those who can use it rightly. By this time the national democracy is well on the way toward transformation into nationalist autocracy; and it was down this road that the Germans were stampeded into the disaster of Nazism.

If the nation is one entity with a single sacred destiny, how can it be allowed to dissipate its energies in internal disaffection and conflict, particularly when it is threatened by external danger and is embarked on basic internal reconstruction? In the actual situation of the new states the attraction of power and the estimate of national need combine to enhance the already strong élitist tendency of Western-oriented leaders who are amply aware of the illiteracy, backwardness, and inexperience of the bulk of their countrymen. And where the civilian élites do not themselves step in to furnish the "guided democracy," the military are likely to be standing by to impose their version of order and of the national will on peoples whose ability to manage the democratic constitutions they have decreed for themselves is minimal. Latin America and the Middle East furnish unhappy models which are already having their imitators elsewhere, often with explicit insistence that the democratic order is being overturned only in order to lay solider foundations for a return to democracy. At the next remove the Communists will gladly furnish their own improved rendering of democracy.

No great confidence can be placed in the general populace as the defender of threatened democratic institutions. Poverty-ridden peoples in a climate of rising expectations are not likely to make their first concern the preservation of political forms and liberties whose meaning is obscure to them and whose promise appears of less significance than other prospects that are held out to them. If democracy fails to produce results with adequate speed and if authoritarian methods seem to hold the remedy, the masses cannot be counted on to rise to the defense of unfamiliar political machineries. In general they lack not only the democratic tradition but also the more basic tradition of standing up to do battle for their rights against the remote and superior authorities who have through the ages pushed them around. Nothing in their experience has brought home to them the belief that they are the possessors of human rights and fundamental freedoms which they are entitled to and able to defend. The present array of democratic institutions has been imposed on them from above almost as much as any of the previous systems; certainly the constitutions have not been adopted in response to a demand from below. All too often it is probable that the people would feel more at home with a government which, in traditional style, tells them what to do.

Whatever their composition, the ruling authorities in this democratic or post-democratic age will seek popular consent or approval to establish the legitimacy of their title to power, but this can be handled through the familiar plebiscitary techniques without disturbing the people by placing alternatives before them.

In the West nationalism is now often denounced as being a divisive and anachronistic force—bad enough at any time and intolerable in the atomic era. From this the moral is drawn, most frequently in France, that the Asian and African peoples should resign themselves to recognition that the world has arrived at a time of interdependence which renders a demand for sovereignty absurd. Of the grievousness of nationalism's faults there can be no doubt. They can exact a high price, yet what is bought at that price is also of great value, particularly, perhaps, for those who are just entering into the modern national phase. The divisiveness of nationalism has a different bearing for the people of the new states than for those who are old established and even outgrowing their nationhood, and the element of anachronism is to be measured not only by the calendar but by the life-span of the particular nationalisms as well.

Even for the Western peoples whose reaping of the fruits of nationalism is of relatively old standing the undermining of the nation by insistence on its shortcomings could create a worse rather than a better situation unless preferable forms of community, acceptable to the people, were ready at hand. The brotherhood of man finds much of its present working expression within the nation, even though its other face is hostility to those outside. Whatever changes in the structure of the global society may lie just around the corner, they are still sufficiently concealed to make it impossible to see the form and nature of the nation's successors. We have, unhappily, no necessary reason to assume that if the nation were to lose its hold the next stage would mark any appreciable advance toward a more desirable world. France presented no pretty picture in the years just before World War II when the idea of the nation had lost its force for both the right and the left, and many in the center as well.

In the newly rising countries nationalism has functions to perform which it has largely exhausted in the West. While in the West the nation has come to represent the actual outer boundaries of communal allegiance for most men or has set limits which are already found too confining, in Asia and Africa it constitutes a great potential widening of the social and political horizons of most of the people. Far from forcing men to live within restricted quarters, it opens new doors and windows. Where men's lives have traditionally been bounded by family, tribe, or caste, by village, market town, or petty state, the emergence of nationalism creates pressures which force men into larger communities, as nationalism is itself a response to similar pressures. That lesser communities can put up strong resistance to full absorption into the nation, or what claims to be the nation, is demonstrated on a small scale by the existence in all countries of isolated pockets of people who have not effectively been drawn into the broader national society. On a larger scale there are any number of evidences of growing pains such as the demands of linguistic communities in India, the revolts in different parts of Indonesia, and Nigeria's troubles with its tribes and regions. In some instances, as in Pakistan's split from India, even the assertion that there is a single nation embracing the peoples concerned may be successfully denied. For many individuals and groups considerable time will surely elapse before their social-political consciousness expands to the new national limits, but the forces of the modern world are on the whole conspiring to make man's age-old parochialism impossible.

For the leaders and organizers of national movements it is obviously a matter of the first importance to wean as many people as possible away from their more local attachments and bring them to active awareness of their national ties. In addition to ethical and religious considerations Gandhi was moved by a simple political calculation in pleading the case for the untouchables: if the latter remained outside the national fold, the Indian nation could bring that much less pressure to bear on the British in its struggle for independence. In taking the national cause to the masses, men like Gandhi, Sukarno, Nasser, and Nkrumah have not only immeasurably strengthened their political position but have also taken a creative part in shaping the nations they represent. All the agitation and propaganda associated with nationalist parties and upheavals dramatize the issues and serve to make the nation a living reality for people who have had no consciousness of its existence. To the extent that the new concept is grasped, the peasant isolated in his village becomes a citizen of a nation which takes its place in the world's councils. The nation is itself still far removed from meeting the needs of an age of jet planes, radio, and intercontinental ballistic missiles, but it is at least an advance in social magnitude over what preceded it.

To the national unity which it brings to the new states nationalism adds another vital ingredient for survival: a revolutionary zeal and a sense of devotion to the nation and the state which is to be its instrument. In the new states and in those which are in process of formation the nation is not something which can be taken casually for granted but an exciting new achievement, worthy of love and sacrifices. Independence has been won as the result of campaigns whose emotional momentum in some part carries over and may be utilized in dealing with the problems of the difficult years ahead. Particularly in colonial areas but also to some extent in any country still living under some variant of the *ancien régime*, the nation and nationalism open the possibility of tapping sources of popular energy and participation which no alien or old-style autocratic ruler could hope to tap. To carry on warfare, to put through major reforms, or to require present sacrifices for future benefits enlists a new dimension of popular support if it can be called for by national leaders as a part of the nation's due.

How long the zeal and devotion will last and how usefully they can be channeled into dealing with the postindependence tasks are questions the answers to which the heirs to imperial power must anxiously seek. Certainly there can be no simple transference. At the extreme the youngster who has carried on years of guerrilla warfare against the Dutch in Indonesia or against the French in Indochina or Algeria is unlikely to be the most suitable candidate for a desk job in the Ministry of Reconstruction and not even perhaps for the routines of a peace-time army. More broadly, the demonstrated ability of the nationalist leadership to perform the political function of rallying the people against imperial domination can give no guarantee of ability to perform another and quite different job. A strong case can be made for the proposition that the sacrifices and basic social changes which development calls for can only be got across to the people by the political leader and not by the expert or bureaucrat, but the nationalist revolutionary who has been victorious in one setting may fumble badly in another. The dramatic and heroic temper of nationalist battle is far from being a wholly suitable mood in which to tackle the problems of managing a stable and progressive polity and a modernized and expanding economy.

Nationalism by itself gives the answer to virtually none of the particular problems arising from the ubiquitous demand for development and, indeed, to very few of the multitude of questions which confront peoples coming to independence.[6]

[6] I have elaborated somewhat on this theme in "The Progress of Nationalism" in Philip W. Thayer (ed.), *Nationalism and Progress in Free Asia* (Baltimore, 1956), pp. 71–82.

Its most vital contribution is in the realms of the intangibles of the spirit: the restoration of self-respect, the building up of morale, and the stimulation of social solidarity. It does not, however, determine the choice between alternative and often conflicting values, each legitimately put forward as embraced within the national destiny; it does not provide all the good things associated with independence; and it does not establish the institutions necessary for further advance. One must look elsewhere than to nationalism to decide even such over-all questions as whether a free enterprise system or Communism, liberal democracy or centralized authoritarianism, is most fitting and the vast majority of lesser decisions must also be taken primarily on other than nationalist grounds. In almost every instance, to hold up the concept of the national interest as the determinant of decision and action is to produce an empty symbol whose content is in dispute between different factions within the nation. Even in the realm of foreign affairs where nationalism most evidently comes into play, it is likely to give no conclusive answer to questions concerning entry into this alliance or that, neutralism or commitment. The danger is also real that nationalism may serve as an actual impediment to advance, as, for instance, in curtailing access to alien goods, skill, and capital, and it can always be paraded as a screen to hide domestic failures or abuses.

The dimensions of the task which lie ahead of the new states are staggering. They cannot rest content with taking their newfound sovereignty and enjoying it, as they might have at some earlier point in history. Both national pride and the imperatives of survival now demand that they move speedily into the modern world, rivalling the achievements of peoples who have long preceded them on the road. Despite illiteracy, inexperience, and tragic shortages of trained manpower, the latest model of the welfare state plus modernized armed forces is to be produced by governments equipped with all the trappings of parliamentary democracy. Economic systems are to be transformed and the remnants of backwardness wiped from the slate. The new national community is to take its place in the organized society of nations, be represented at a multitude of international conferences and meetings, and furnish an appropriate quota of personnel for international secretariats.

In moving toward goals such as these, nationalism can be of immense assistance if it is wisely and skillfully used by those responsible for the guidance of the new states. If it is used merely to inflame and obscure, its contribution can be disastrous.

IDEOLOGIES OF DELAYED INDUSTRIALIZATION

Mary Matossian

History and value are worlds apart, but men are drawn to both, with an emotional commitment to the first and an intellectual commitment to the second; they need to ask the two incompatible questions, and they yearn to be able to answer "Mine" and "True." [1]

J. R. LEVENSON

It is difficult to discern, at first glance, any important common characteristics in ideologies such as Gandhism and Marxism-Leninism, Kemalism, and Shintoism. If they have anything in common, it seems to be a strong infusion of self-contradiction. But on second glance the diverse characteristics and geographic origins of these ideologies fade into the background. In their very self-contradictions one may detect recurrent patterns.

SOURCE. Mary Matossian, "Ideologies of Delayed Industrialization: Some Tensions and Ambiguities," *Economic Development and Cultural Change*, 6, 217–228, April 1958. Reprinted by permission of The University of Chicago Press. Copyright 1958 by The University of Chicago Press.

[1] J. R. Levenson, " 'History' and 'Value': Tensions of Intellectual Choice in Modern China," *Studies in Chinese Thought*, Arthur Wright, ed., Chicago, 1953, p. 150.

The recurrent patterns can, I think, be accounted for by the similarity of context in which these ideologies have emerged. This context is the industrially backward country which has the following characteristics: (1) it has been in contact with the industrial West for at least fifty years; (2) in it there has emerged a native intelligentsia composed of individuals with at least some Western education; and (3) large-scale industrialization is currently being contemplated or has been in progress for no more than twenty-five years. The ideologies which have emerged in such conditions would include Marxism-Leninism, Shintoism, Italian Fascism, Kemalism, Ghandism, the current Egyptian Philosophy of the Revolution, Sun Yat-sen's Three Principles of the People, the Indonesian Pantjasila, and many others. [2]

Industrially backward countries have two common problems; the destruction of traditional institutions and values, sometimes even before the impact of industrialism is felt; and the challenge of the

[2] Perhaps Nazism should be included, even though it emerged on the German scene about sixty years after industrialization began. In any case, Nazism has many characteristics of ideologies of delayed industrialization.

modern West.[3] The "assaulted" individual must reorient himself in at least three directions: (1) in his relationship to the West, (2) in his relationship to his people's past, and (3) in his relationship to the masses of his own people. It is the "assaulted" intellectual, and his relationship to the uneducated masses, which will be considered here in particular: for although everyone has ideas and wishes, only intellectuals devise ideologies.

Ideology may be defined as a pattern of ideas which simultaneously provides for its adherents: (1) a self-definition, (2) a description of the current situation, its background, and what is likely to follow, and (3) various imperatives which are "deduced" from the foregoing. In ideology there is a strong tendency to merge fact and value, to superimpose upon "things as they are" the things that are desired.[4] Sjahrir, the Indonesian socialist, said that the weaker the intellect, the greater the element of wish in the formulation of a man's thought. He has held that

the element of wish is strongest among "backward" persons.[5] Perhaps it would be more accurate to say that the intellectual in an industrially backward country cleaves to contradictory propositions because of the situation in which he finds himself. His experience and his present problems tend to direct his reasoning into certain channels. His ego needs protection which science and logic cannot provide. This seems to be true of all men to some extent. If the intellectual is to lead the masses of an industrially backward country in the undertaking of great endeavors, he must provide them with incitement balanced by comfort, with self-criticism balanced by self-justification.

To seek a "morphology" and "natural history" of ideologies of delayed industrialization seems premature, given the present state of Western knowledge. The following analysis is not intended to provide neat answers to big questions, but to indicate some areas where further probing might be productive.

The impact of the modern industrial West is the initial challenge in the industrially backward country. The various ways in which the West has disrupted traditional societies are beyond the scope of this analysis. The point to note here is that irreversible processes are set in motion. The contemporary scene is littered with fallen idols, desecrated by unsanctioned violence, an uncomfortable place in which to live. Thus, all ideologies of delayed industrialization are essentially revolutionary—in Mannheim's usage, utopian.[6] They direct activity toward changing a social order which is already changing. Even the superficially conservative ideologies turn out to be pseudo-conservative in the sense that they advocate a change in the status quo. Pseudo-conservative or radical, these ideologies advocate the

[3] These are the two important situational factors with which Rupert Emerson accounts for Asian nationalism. See "Paradoxes of Asian Nationalism," *Far Eastern Quarterly* 13 (February 1954), pp. 131–142.
John K. Fairbank has pointed out that as contact with the West increases, the response increases but is less discernible because Western culture has been incorporated in indigenous culture. He says, " 'Westernization' gives way to 'modernization,' the demand for defense is followed by the demand for reform, and by the time when a reform accelerates into a revolution, the entire society has become involved in a process of change which is too cataclysmic and far-reaching, too autonomous, to be called any longer a mere 'response.' " See "China's Response to the West: Problems and Suggestions," *Journal of World History*, 3, pp. 404–405.
[4] In a moment of unusual insight Gamal Abdul Nasser wrote: "Our souls are the vessels in which everything we are is contained; and everything we are, everything placed in this vessel, must take their shape, even truth. I try as much as humanly possible to prevent my soul from altering the shape of truth much, but how far can I succeed? That is the question." *Egypt's Liberation: The Philosophy of the Revolution*, Washington, D.C., 1955, p. 29.

[5] Soetan Sjahrir, *Out of Exile*, New York, 1949, pp. 89–90.
[6] See Karl Mannheim, *Ideology and Utopia*, London, 1936.

manipulation of the disagreeable Present. In this sense, *Les extremes se touchent.*[7]

The first problem of the "assaulted" intellectual is to assume a satisfactory posture *vis-à-vis* the West. The position taken is frequently ambiguous, embracing the polar extremes of xenophobia and xenophilia. The intellectual may resent the West, but since he is already at least partly Westernized, to reject the West completely would be to deny part of himself.

The intellectual is appalled by discrepancies between the standard of living and "culture" of his own country, and those of modern Western nations.[8] He feels that something must be done, and done fast. He is a man on the defensive, searching for new defensive weapons. As Gamal Abdul Nasser wrote to a friend in 1935:

> Allah said, "Oppose them with whatever forces you can muster!" But what are these forces we are supposed to have in readiness for them?[9]

Another characteristic of the "assaulted" intellectual is his uneasy attitude toward himself and his own kind—the intelligentsia and middle classes. Often he scorns his kind (and by implication, himself) as "pseudo," "mongrel," neither truly native nor truly Western. In order to find self-

respect, he goes in search of his "true self"; he tries to "discover India"; he revisits the West. For example, Gandhi wrote in 1908:

> You, English, who have come to India are not good specimens of the English nation, nor can we, almost half-Anglicized Indians, be considered as good specimens of the real Indian nation...[10]

Speaking of the lack of good Indonesian literature, Sjahrir wrote in 1934:

> In reality, our cultural level is still too low for a real renaissance. There is no thought, no form, no sound, and what is worse, there is not yet enough earnestness and integrity among us. There is still only unsavory counterfeit, which is published with great fuss, but which still has little merit.[11]

Nehru, while in prison in 1944, recalled:

> The present for me, and for many others like me, was an odd mixture of medievalism, appalling poverty and misery and a somewhat superficial modernism of the middle classes. I was not an admirer of my own class or kind, and yet inevitably I looked to it for leadership in the struggle for India's salvation; that middle class felt caged and circumscribed and wanted to grow and develop itself.[12]

Nehru leans toward xenophilia, but his close associate Gandhi took an emphatic xenophobic posture. He asserted that Indians, to be successful in dealing with the British, must "consciously believe that Indian civilization is the best and that the European is a nine days' wonder." Of course, Indian civilization has some defects, he admits, such as child marriage and religious prostitution. But, "the tendency of Indian civilization is to elevate the moral being, that of the

---

[7] See Samuel P. Huntington, "Conservatism as an Ideology," *American Political Science Review*, **51**, p. 460. Levenson (*loc. cit.*, p. 149), holds that the very existence of traditionalism belies its ultimate doctrine.

[8] The usage of the word "culture" depends on the extent to which the ideologist is Westernized. It may mean ideals, values, or simply habits. Sun Yat-sen, a trained physician, deplored such Chinese habits as spitting, letting gas loudly, and never brushing the teeth, as "uncultured." He said that foreigners "can see that we are very much lacking in personal culture. Every word and act of a Chinese shows absence of refinement: one contact with the Chinese people is enough to reveal this." *San Min Chu I*, Shanghai, 1927, pp. 135–138.

[9] Nasser, *op. cit.*, p. 27. See also Jawaharlal Nehru, *The Discovery of India*, London, 1946, p. 34.

[10] Mohandas K. Gandhi, *Hind Swaraj*, Ahmedabad, 1946, p. 73.

[11] Soetan Sjahrir, *op. cit.*, p. 5.

[12] Nehru, *op. cit.*, p. 36.

Western civilization is to propagate immorality."[13]

The "assaulted" intellectual works hard to make invidious comparisons between his own nation and the West. He may simply claim that his people are superior, as did Gandhi: "We consider our civilization to be far superior to yours."[14] Or he may hold that his ancestors had already rejected Western culture as inferior.[15] But these assertions can elicit conviction only among a few and for a short while. More often the intellectual says, "We are equal to Westerners", or "You are *no better* than I am." Around this theme lies a wealth of propositions: (1) "In the past you were no better (or worse) than we are now."[16] (2) "We once had your good qualities, but we were corrupted by alien oppressors."[17] (3) "We have high spiritual qualities despite our poverty, but you are soulless materialists."[18] (4) "Everything

worthwhile in your tradition is present or incipient in ours."[19] The slogan, "trade, not aid," when used metaphorically is another variation on this theme. The nationalist claims to seek a blend of the "best" in East and West. But why must both East and West inspire the new culture? Behind this there is perhaps the implicit wish to see the "East" a genuine partner, an equal, of the West.[20]

The foregoing postures *vis-à-vis* the

materialism of the West. I have heard this countless times, but it has never convinced me." *Op. cit.*, pp. 66–67.

[13] Gandhi, *op. cit.*, pp. 45–46 and 74.

[14] *Ibid.*, p. 72.

[15] *Ibid.*, p. 46, and Levenson, *loc cit.*, p. 158.

[16] For example, see Sun Yat-sen, *op. cit.*, p. 140. This is a common assertion of Arab ideologists. Of course, there is truth in it, but how does it serve to solve the problem at hand, except to bolster the ego of the "assaulted"?

[17] Levenson, *loc. cit.*, p. 167, reports that the Chinese used the Manchus as their scapegoat. The Arabs blame the later Ottoman sultans, and the Russians blame the Mongols. There is some truth in these assertions—but it remains to be seen why the native subject peoples failed to get rid of their "alien oppressors."

[18] For example, "European superiority to China is not in political philosophy, but altogether in the field of material civilization." Sun Yat-sen, *op. cit.*, p. 98. See Herman Finer, *Mussolini's Italy*, New York, 1935, p. 170 for the Fascist case. See Masaki Kosaka, "Modern Japanese Thought," *Journal of World History*, 3, p. 610, for the Japanese case. The Indonesian socialist, Sjahrir, however, rejects the notion:

"Here there has been no spiritual or cultural life, and no intellectual progress for centuries... Most of us search unconsciously for a synthesis that will leave us internally tranquil. We want to have both Western science and Eastern philosophy, the Eastern 'spirit' in the culture. But what is this Eastern spirit? It is, they say, the sense of the higher, of spirituality, of the eternal and religious, as opposed to the

[19] See Levenson, *loc. cit.*, pp. 160–161, for a Chinese case; or Mohammed Naguib, *op. cit.*, p. 134: "There is nothing in the Koran that calls for theocratic government; on the contrary, the Prophet was in favor of parliamentary rule."

[20] Levenson, *loc. cit.*, p. 174. The "assaulted" intellectual is sometimes comforted by the thought that Westerners have borrowed some element from his own culture. K. M. Panikkar, in *Asia and Western Dominance*, London, 1953, devotes two chapters to the subject of the impact of Asia on the West. However, the element that Westerners borrow may be one which the native intellectual has already rejected as "backward." For example, Americans in Arab countries who adopt the bedouin headdress on occasion are a source of amusement or irritation to the educated city Arab. He looks down on the bedouin, and he does not want the American to identify Arabs with bedouins. Speaking of such British adventurers as Doughty, Lawrence, and Glubb, an Egyptian intellectual remarked: "We're sick to death of Britishers who can recite the Koran." (As quoted by Roland Pucetti, "Three British Bedouins," *Middle East Forum*, 33, p. 34.)

Sjahrir thinks that Westerners who are seeking "Light from Asia" are wasting their time. He says: "I know only too well what the Eastern attributes, so admired by the Westerner, really are. I know that those attributes are molded and nourished only by the hierarchical relationship of a feudal society—a society in which a small group possess all the material and intellectual wealth, and the vast majority live in squalor, and are made acquiescent by religion and philosophy in place of sufficient food.

"That longing of Westerners for the East, in effect, amounts to the same thing as longing for the lost land of the Middle Ages, and the greater goodness and universality that presumably characterized it." *Op. cit.*, p. 160.

West may be comforting to the intellectual, but they will not stimulate action unless certain imperatives are "deduced" from them. For example, "We must purge our national culture of alien corruptions and realize our true character which has been lying dormant within us." But doses of self-criticism are equally important incentives to action, because they make it impossible to relax in complacency. In 1931, Joseph Stalin, leader of one of the most spectacular cultural transformations in human history, told Soviet industrial managers,

> One feature of the history of old Russia was the continual beatings she suffered for falling behind, for her backwardness. She was beaten by the Mongol khans. She was beaten by the Turkish beys. She was beaten by the Swedish feudal lords. She was beaten by the Polish and Lithuanian gentry. She was beaten by the Japanese barons. All beat her—for her backwardness: for military backwardness, for cultural backwardness, for political backwardness, for industrial backwardness, for agricultural backwardness. She was beaten because to do so was profitable and could be done with impunity. . . .
>
> That is why we must no longer lag behind. . . . We are fifty or a hundred years behind the advanced countries. We must make good this distance in ten years. Either we do it, or they crush us.[21]

Another man who administered blunt criticism was Mustafa Kemal Ataturk, who told the Turkish Grand National Assembly in 1920,

> We have accepted the principle that we do not, and will not, give up our national independence. Although we always respect this basic condition, when we take into consideration the level of prosperity of the country, the wealth of the nation, and the general mental

level, and when we compare it with the progress of the world in general, we must admit that we are not a little, but very backward.[22]

Ataturk praised the Turkish nation, however, for high moral qualities and great past achievements. Although he was probably a xenophile by conviction, he succeeded to a remarkable degree in overcoming the xenophobia of his people by means of his ideological rhetoric. When it was suggested that to borrow from the West "all that Turkey needs" might conflict with the national ideal, Ataturk retorted that the national principle itself had become *internationally* accepted; and also,

> Countries are many, but civilization is one and for the progress of a nation it is necessary to participate in this one civilization.[23]

Ataturk justified the importation of specific alien inventions, such as terms from non-Turkish languages, with the assertion that the so-called import was actually indigenous: according to the Sun Language Theory, Turkish was the mother of all the languages of the world, so that "borrowed" words were actually prodigal sons come home.[24] This technique of encouraging an import by calling it indigenous was complemented by the technique of eradicating the indigenous by calling it imported. For example, Ataturk pointed out that the fez was a headgear imported from Europe a hundred years before.

When the intellectual in an industrially backward country surveys modern Western civilization, he is confronted with five hundred years of scientific, artistic, social, economic, political, and religious developments. He sees a flood of heterogeneous Western cultural elements, from jazz to steel mills, pouring into his country. Then,

[21] J. S. Stalin, *Problems of Leninism*, Moscow, 1947, p. 356.

[22] Mustafa Kemal Ataturk, *Atatürk'ün Söylev ve Demeçleri*, I, Istanbul, 1945, p. 29.
[23] Ataturk, *op. cit.*, 3, Ankara, 1954, pp. 67–68 and 87.
[24] Uriel Heyd, *Language Reform in Modern Turkey*, Jerusalem, 1954, pp. 33–34.

fearing that he will be "swamped" by the deluge, and lose his own identity, he tries to control cultural imports. In order to do this, he must find a standard to determine exactly what should be borrowed. The standard used by the nationalist is that the element to be imported should be in "conformity" with his own national culture and should serve to strengthen his nation. This formula is very elastic, and can be used to justify the borrowing or rejection of practically anything. But the Marxist-Leninist holds that the element to be imported should be one that is "progressive" in terms of the Marxist-Leninist pattern of social evolution. According to this pattern, the "bourgeois" West is decaying; it is the "toilers" of both East and West who ride the wave of the future.[25] Imperialism is the highest and the last stage of capitalism. However, Western industrialism and science are the great hope for the non-Western peoples; and the Soviet Union is represented as a model of rapid industrialization and scientific development. If the industrially backward nation borrows from the West only what is most "progressive," it can skip a part, or a stage, of the long and difficult social development of the West. Then, as the West decays, the former backward nations will surpass the best that the West has ever achieved.

The tension between archaism and futurism is another ambiguity in ideologies of delayed industrialization. It is closely related to the xenophobia–xenophilia tension, because the West is "the new" and the native culture is "the old" at the onset of contact.

Archaism is an attempt to resurrect a supposed "golden age," or some part of it. This "golden age" is usually not in the disagreeable recent past, but in a more

remote period, and it can only be recovered by historical research and interpretation. For example, Mussolini gloried in imperial Rome and the medieval "corporate state"; the Slavophiles glorified the peasant *mir* and the indigenous Christian Orthodox practices in Russia; the Shintoists revived an ancient mythology that defied the Emperor; Sun Yat-sen and Chiang Kai-shek exhorted the Chinese to revive Confucian ethics; Gandhi urged that India return to the age of "Rama Raj"; and Ataturk exulted in the barbaric virtues of the Osmanli nomads. According to Gandhi,

> It was not that we did not know how to invent machinery, but our forefathers knew that, if we set our hearts after such things, we would become slaves and lose our moral fibre. They, therefore, after due deliberation, decided that we should only do what we could with our hands and feet. They further reasoned that large cities were a snare and a useless encumbrance and that people would not be happy in them, that there would be gangs of thieves and robbers, prostitution and vice flourishing in them, and that poor men would be robbed by rich men. They were, therefore, satisfied with small villages.[26]

[25] Marxism-Leninism is of course not the only ideology that contains this proposition. Western ideologists who talk of "the Decline of the West" and "the Awakening of the East" have contributed to, and reinforced, such sentiments.

[26] *Hind Swaraj*, p. 46. Gandhi's archaism went to incredible lengths. In the same work (pp. 42–43) he indicted Western medicine:
"I have indulged in vice, I contract a disease, a doctor cures me, the odds are that I shall repeat the vice. Had the doctor not intervened, nature would have done its work and I would have acquired mastery over myself, would have been freed from vice and would have been happy.
"Hospitals are institutions for propagating sin. Men take less care of their bodies and immorality increases."
These opinions might be dismissed as unimportant since they were expressed so early in Gandhi's career. However, in a preface to a new edition of *Hind Swaraj* which Gandhi wrote in 1938, he said:
"The booklet is a severe condemnation of 'modern civilization.' It was written in 1908. My conviction is deeper today than ever. I feel that, if India will discard 'modern civilization,' she can only gain by doing so." p. 11.

According to Mussolini,

> Rome is our point of departure and of reference; it is our symbol, or if you like, it is our Myth. We dream of a Roman Italy, that is to say wise and strong, disciplined and imperial. Much of that which was the immortal spirit of Rome resurges in Fascism.[27]

According to Sun Yat-sen,

> So, coming to the root of the matter, if we want to restore our race's standing, besides uniting all into a great national-body, we must first recover our ancient morality—then, and only then can we plan how to attain again to the national position we once held.[28]

But Nehru condemns archaism:

> We have to come to grips with the present, this life, this world, this nature which surrounds us with its infinite variety. Some Hindus talk of going back to the Vedas; some Moslems dream of an Islamic theocracy. Idle fancies, for there is no going back, there is no turning back even if this was thought desirable. There is only one-way traffic in Time.[29]

Archaism may slip into a futuristic ideology, such as Marxism, and create an ambiguity. Adam Ulam has suggested that Marxism has its greatest appeal for semiproletarianized or uprooted peasants who are nostalgic for the "good old days" when their actions were governed by nature, the village elders, the family patriarch, and the religious authorities—instead of the less congenial factory boss and the state. To the uprooted peasant Marxism offers a comforting strain of archaism: that is, it envisions a utopia in which state and factory, as coercive institutions, have "withered away."[30]

Whenever a resurrection of the past is contemplated, the question arises, "What part of the past?" or "Which age was our golden age, and why?" Sometimes the age selected is an imperial age, when the people in question enjoyed their greatest authority over others. Sometimes a period of "pristine simplicity" is admired. But new imperial conquests are incompatible with the weak political and economic position of industrially backward countries, and a return to the "simple life" is incompatible with industrialization. In such cases archaism is not a solution to the problem at hand, but an escape from it.

However, there are more constructive uses of the past. The intellectual may discover that in the remote past his people possessed the very virtues which are supposed to make a modern nation great. For example, the Kemalists glorify their ancestors as brave, tolerant, realistic, generous, peaceful, and respectful of women; in short, "spiritual" exemplars of the well-bred Western European gentleman. These "genuine" Turks were temporarily "corrupted" by Arab-Persian-Byzantine culture, but they are now due to take their rightful place among "civilized" nations.[31] The manifest content of such an ideological position may be archaistic, but its latent content is futuristic.

The Communists also use the past in this way. But they have characteristic standards for determining what elements of the past are desirable. The Chinese Communists have cultivated peasant literature and art because they are "progressive," being products of a "progressive" class; whereas gentry culture is rejected as "feudal."[32] In the Soviet Union the pre-revolutionary leaders most cherished by the Communist regime are those it considers "progressive" for their time (such as Peter the Great), whereas "reactionaries" (such as Dostoyevsky, until recently) have been under a cloud.

---

[27] As quoted by Finer, *op. cit.*, p. 191.
[28] Sun Yat-sen, *op. cit.*, pp. 125–126.
[29] Nehru, *op. cit.*, p. 447.
[30] Adam Ulam, "The Historical Role of Marxism and the Soviet System," *World Politics*, **8**, pp. 20–45.
[31] See Halide Edib Adivar, *Turkey Faces West*, New Haven, 1930, pp. 1–9.
[32] Levenson, *loc. cit.*, p. 184.

Nationalists, when selecting elements from their past, ask, "What will tend to strengthen the nation?" But tradition has lost its natural charm, and traditionalism is something the nationalist must "work at." He uses the shared traditions of his people as raw material with which to build national morale; but tradition is a means, existing only for the sake of national strength, and not as an axiomatic, self-justified good.[33] For example, Sun Yat-sen said in 1924:

> Our position now is extremely perilous; if we do not earnestly promote nationalism and weld together our four hundred millions into a strong nation, we face a tragedy—the loss of our country and the destruction of our race. To ward off this danger, we must espouse nationalism and employ the national spirit to save the country.[34]

There are other uses of the past besides escapism, the sanctioning of innovations, the glorification of "progressive" individuals and groups, and national self-strengthening. The past may be used to eradicate what the intellectual feels to be undesirable in the present and for the future. By publicizing the results of historical research, showing that a supposedly indigenous cultural element (like the fez) is of foreign origin, he may thereby stigmatize it. He may use other grounds to stigmatize the Ottoman and Chinese literary languages; they are the languages of reactionary and oppressive ruling classes who have cared only for their own welfare, rather than the welfare of the people.

The concern of both nationalists and Communists for vernacular languages and peasant arts is closely related to a third problem of the "assaulted" intellectual: his relationship with the uneducated masses. Some intellectuals have a sentimental, patronizing, or contemptuous

attitude toward the masses.[35] Sun Yat-sen said:

> The Ming veterans spread the idea of nationalism through the lower classes; but, on account of their childish understanding, the lower classes did not know how to take advantage of the ideas, but were, on the contrary, made tools of by others.[36]

Mohammed Naguib of Egypt wrote in 1955:

> Given the deplorable conditions in Egyptian villages, however, the distinction between compulsion and co-operation is irrelevant. The average *fellah* has fallen too low to be able to help himself without a great deal of compulsory assistance from the government.[37]

Other intellectuals, like Nehru, wonder if the peasants are the "true" Indians, while they (the intellectuals) are only "pseudos." The Russian Narodniki went "back to the people" to learn from them and to teach them; and so have Turkish intellectuals in our own century. Undeniably, many intellectuals have felt sincere compassion for the sufferings of the peasants and sincere respect for the folk arts. But it is unlikely that the attitude of an intellectual toward the uneducated masses in an industrially backward country (or in any country) is free from ambiguity: he looks up to "the people" and down on "the masses."

However he may feel about the majority of his compatriots, the intellectual must face the practical problems of industrializa-

---

[33] Levenson, *loc. cit.*, pp. 172–173. See also Emerson, *loc. cit.*, pp. 136–142.
[34] Sun Yat-sen, *op. cit.*, p. 12.

[35] See the statement of an Arab, al-Kawakebi, in Hazim Z. Nuseibeh's *The Ideas of Arab Nationalism*, Ithaca, 1956, p. 132. See also D. P. Mukerji, "The Intellectual in India," *Confluence*, **4**, p. 446, and James Mysberg, "The Indonesian Elite," *Far Eastern Survey*, **26**, p. 39.
[36] Sun Yat-sen, *op. cit.*, pp. 61–62.
[37] Naguib, *op. cit.*, p. 149.

tion and modernization. The intellectual knows that a government which really *represents* the thinking of the uneducated masses will not attack these problems boldly and comprehensively. The peasant may long for riches, but he is not eager to give up his traditional ways. To attain its ends, the intelligentsia must arouse the masses to strenuous effort, or, as Alexander Gerschenkron puts it, give them an emotional "New Deal."[38]

The intelligentsia must provide just the right amount of criticism, and just the right amount of comfort necessary to make the masses follow its lead into the "battle" of industrialization. That is why ideologies of delayed industrialization condemn the peasant for his backwardness, and then praise him for being a *real* representative of the indigenous culture. Such ideologies may stand for class equality and simultaneously exhort the masses to follow orders and to accept unequal rewards, both as individuals and as occupational groups. This does not mean that "assaulted" intellectuals are necessarily cynical and manipulative; they may be sincerely attached to contradictory premises.

In most cases, when an ideology of delayed industrialization emerges, the traditional rulers (king, sultan, tsar, etc.) have been overthrown, or are on the verge of being overthrown. But when traditional rulers remain in power, as in Japan, they are supported by new social groups and assume new social functions. They must now mobilize the masses to meet the challenge of the modern industrial West. Whether there has been a massive social revolution or a "circulation of elites," the cultural revolution is inevitable.

Rupert Emerson has suggested that if reform and revolution in industrially backward countries are led by Westernized intellectuals drawn from various social strata rather than by traditional elites, the prevalent ideology tends to include a stronger egalitarian element. The intelligentsia, having no solid power base of its own, is especially in need of mass support. This is particularly true, he believes, in areas which have been longest under Western domination, such as India, where the traditional native elite lost most of its power and indoctrination in Western political values went deep. But in countries like Japan, where the traditional elite took command of social and economic reform, the prevalent ideology tends to put a premium on hierarchical values: loyalty, obedience, respect.[39] This theory may be useful in explaining differences between developments in India and Japan, but its applicability elsewhere is dubious. It is important here to distinguish between symbolic values, which may be egalitarian, and their accompanying operational values, which may be hierarchical. It is also important to define "equality": is it legal, economic, spiritual, or does it refer to the possession of a common culture?

The tension between egalitarian and hierarchical values is sometimes resolved theoretically by the doctrine of "tutelage." According to this doctrine democracy must be introduced into a country in two stages. In the first stage, a single, "all-people's" party of the most "enlightened" and "progressive" elements of the nation takes over the government and acts as a faculty for educating the masses in democratic ways. At some time in the indefinite future the masses will be ready for direct self-government and the "all-people's" party will "wither away." This doctrine, with various modifications, has appeared in Turkey, India, and China; but when the doctrine has been applied, it has led to a variety of unexpected results.

In order to understand an ideology it is important to determine what problems its

[38] Alexander Gerschenkron, "Economic Backwardness in Historical Perspective," in *The Progress of Underdeveloped Areas*, Bert Hoselitz, ed., Chicago, 1952, pp. 22–25.

[39] Emerson, *loc. cit.*, p. 140.

initiators are trying to solve. In the case of intellectuals in industrially backward countries, the three main problems are: (1) What is to be borrowed from the West? (2) What is to be retained from the nation's past? (3) What characteristics, habits, and products of the masses are to be encouraged. It is remarkable that intellectuals in widely separate parts of the world have reacted similarly to these problems.

POLITICAL IDEOLOGY AND ECONOMIC PROGRESS: THE BASIC QUESTION

Wilfred Malenbaum and Wolfgang Stolper

In the underdeveloped countries—where live most of the world's people—the hope for economic progress now flames with great intensity. The new international capital facilities of the postwar period, the new programs for sharing modern science and technology, the new interest of wealthy lands in progress in the poor countries— all these present the latter with an opportunity to be rid of the poverty and squalor of their material existence. Their eyes naturally turn to the more developed countries for capital and technical knowledge, and for ideas.

The United States and the democratic nations of the West took the postwar initiative in international programs of financial and technical assistance. These countries were confident that their own vigorous progress, under the stimulus of market demand in a free society, would provide a helpful model for expanded rates of economic growth in the poorer nations. Since 1953, however, Russia and its satel-

SOURCE. Wilfred Malenbaum and Wolfgang Stolper, "Political Ideology and Economic Progress," *World Politics*, **12**, 413–421, April 1960. This article was written while both authors were staff members of the Center for International Studies, M.I.T. The present form of the paper reflects the major editorial contribution of Richard W. Hatch of the Center. But the authors alone are responsible for the views presented.

lites have also played an active role; they now provide a wide range of development assistance to poorer nations— including important politically uncommitted nations like India. Russia's economic history offers a different model, with programed progress in a totalitarian society. Moreover, the Communist lands, focusing attention on their own rates of economic expansion, proclaim their intention to overtake the nations of the West and thus provide unequivocal evidence to the world of how outmoded are capitalist economic systems.

Since the aspirations of the people in the poor countries as well as the urgings of popular leaders require that these nations pay heed to whatever methods and procedures promise to increase their rate of economic advance, the present competition between democratic and Communist models has inevitably given economic programs for accelerating a nation's growth a significant political dimension. Ideological alternatives are thrust upon the less-developed nations. Even where the ways of totalitarianism are repugnant to leaders and to traditions—as is certainly true in many such lands—domestic political pressures demand an open mind, perhaps an open door.

Leaders in the new and underdeveloped countries are bound to ask: Are totalitarian regimes more adept at initiating a process of continuous economic growth than democratic governments? If the methods of communism do in fact promise a surer or less expensive route to economic well-being, some of these nations, deeply committed as they are to a free society, may also ask: How much more economic progress in five or ten years, say, for how much less freedom? The relevance of these questions is clear. These nations need material progress; they are confronted with alternative roads differentiated on ideological grounds.

These questions may raise no problem for the Soviet policy maker. He has been given a doctrinaire identification of means and ends. Unwittingly, perhaps, the policy maker in the West accepts a similar pattern of thought. Preoccupied with the importance of "democratic means," he tends to identify the ends—progress—with his means—the market economy, the private sector, individual freedom of choice. It is necessary therefore to pose the more basic question: To achieve economic progress, must there be a choice of ideologically distinct routes?

Comparative Performance

History now provides the material for some judgment on the role of ideology in economic progress under today's conditions. In each of two pairs of comparable lands—India and China, West Germany and East Germany—there is available reasonably documented experience of some ten years of effort to achieve more rapid rates of economic growth from essentially the same starting points. India and West Germany chose paths under democracy; in both lands, government places a high premium upon private property and individual privilege. In East Germany and in China, on the other hand, the methods used can be traced directly to the totalitarian experience of the Soviet Union; in the development effort, as in other aspects of the social order, individual rights are completely subordinated to those of the state.

In 1950 both India and China had per-capita incomes of about $50—lower than in any other large nation. The two countries initiated their development operations at about the same time and from the same type of economic structure. In both, at least 80 per cent of the working force was in agriculture and small-scale enterprise. If anything, India gave promise of greater progress in view of its advantages in basic resources per man, in transport facilities and modern industry, and in training and leadership attributes. Thus, India apparently had greater scope for using its surface water potential and for exploiting the intensive margins of agricultural cultivation. With the same relative efforts, therefore, larger returns could be anticipated in India than in China. So, at any rate, did it seem in the pre-Plan period.[1]

Yet by 1959 per capita gross national product in India was only some 12–15 per cent above its 1950 level, while in China it had expanded to about double the earlier figure. Almost half (45 per cent) of this difference in performance can be associated with the proportionately greater investment made in China; the remaining difference measures the extent to which each additional unit of capital in China was associated with larger flows of current income.

With an initial gross investment ratio just below 10 per cent, absolute real investment in China had increased by 1958 to five times the 1950 level; in India it about doubled. Foreign aid did not explain this difference: indeed, China's investment was more nearly financed from its current output than was India's. Communist methods made possible a relatively large (40 per cent) feedback of new output into China's domestic investment. But India's voluntary per-

[1] For an analysis of the comparative pre-Plan status and subsequent performance of the two countries, see Wilfred Malenbaum, "India and China: Development Contrasts," *Journal of Political Economy*, **64** (February 1956), 1–24; and *idem*, "India and China: Contrasts in Development Performance," *American Economic Review*, **49** (June 1959), 284–309.

formance in this respect was impressive also. During favorable harvest years, marginal savings rates in India may well have exceeded those in China.

The Chinese put more effort into expanding physical output as against services; a larger proportion of new capital was allocated to agriculture and small industry; the degree of utilization of resources, and especially of labor, was increased significantly. Over the whole period, government played a much larger role in economic life in China than in India. And of course, compared with India's, China's producers and consumers had limited freedom of choice—in techniques of production, in final goods for consumption. Greater regimentation in China was accompanied by considerable flexibility on the part of government. In response to actual developments in the economy, relative emphasis was shifted away from the initial concentration on heavy industry, for example. By and large, China's economic progress has been steady. In India, government adheres to models of growth which are permissive; comparatively few restraints are imposed on individuals whose usual ways of life did not in the past generate economic expansion. There have been impressive spurts of industrial output in India's essentially private modern industry sector, as well as some record crops in years with favorable monsoons. The total performance has been less even; the degree of plan fulfillment has not increased steadily, for example.

In prewar years, East and West Germany constituted an historical, cultural, and economic whole. Their labor and other factor endowments were quite similar; their industrial and agricultural establishments were comparably modern and efficient. While actual output per man showed a slight margin for the western half of the country, there was probably little difference in the productive potential of the two parts. The west did have a real advantage in its soft coal resources and in the lower cost of water transport and

water power facilities. In order to escape the effects of Allied bombings in the west during the war, industry in the east was favored. Later, while the Marshall Plan was pumping funds into West Germany, Russian reparations and levies were exacting a heavy toll—perhaps one-fourth of industrial production—from current output in East Germany. While Allied troops were basically fed from outside, the Russian occupation lived off the land. Still Russian demands did serve to stimulate output, particularly in coal and potash, in synthetic rubber and gasoline. There is some evidence that East Germany was getting on its feet more rapidly in the years to 1948. Although it still had a significantly lower product per person than West Germany (some 40 per cent lower) in 1950, an objective appraisal suggested that, as of that date, output potential over the next decade, say, could be more rapid than in the west.[2]

West Germany expanded its gross national product about 10 per cent more than did East Germany between 1950 and 1958. In the light of the different roles of the occupying authorities, it is not surprising that West Germany was able to maintain both higher investment and higher consumption levels. More surprising is the fact that the output gain associated with each unit of investment was also greater in the west, despite the opportunities

[2] For an analysis of the comparative status and performance of the two countries, see Wolfgang Stolper, *The Structure of the East German Economy*, to be published by Harvard University Press. Preliminary results have appeared in Wolfgang Stolper, "The Labor Force and Industrial Development in Soviet Germany," *Quarterly Journal of Economics*, **71** (November 1957), 518–545; and *idem*, "The National Product of East Germany," *Kyklos*, **12** (April 12, 1959), 131–166. A German translation of the *Kyklos* article has appeared in *Konjunkturpolitik*, (West) Berlin, 1959, No. 6, together with two extremely interesting critical discussions by Werner Gebauer, "Eine neue Berechnung des mitteldeutschen Sozialprodukts," *ibid.*, pp. 344–353, and by Bruno Cleitze, "Niveauentwicklung und Strukturwandlung des Sozialprodukts Mitteldeutschlands," *ibid.*, pp. 374–382.

which under-utilized facilities offered East Germany in 1950.

In contrast to West Germany, East Germany focused on heavy industry and self-sufficiency. There was a relative neglect of agriculture and consumer-goods output generally. Emphasis on heavy industries, especially from an uneconomic raw materials base, was costly for an area renowned for its skilled labor and the quality of its machinery output (optics, electrical goods, and fine mechanical products). The rigid system of controls imposed by East German authorities encountered heavy resistance, especially in farm areas. Major difficulties arose in meshing the complex components of a modern industrial system. All this stands in great contrast to a West Germany which gave ready scope to its entrepreneurs by maintaining a predominantly free market. The effects of these alternative approaches are most apparent in foreign trade—of basic importance in both countries. With competitive prices and market incentives, West Germany expanded its international role along the lines of its comparative advantage. Controlled prices, allocation schemes borrowed from Russia, and the inefficient bilateralism of a trade in which three-fourths of the total was dominated by Russia and the satellites meant that East Germany could not realize its industrial capabilities.

The advocates of neither democratic nor Communist methods can find in the experiences of India and China, of West and East Germany, evidence of a systematic relationship between ideology and the rate of economic progress. Leaders in the underdeveloped lands—and policy-makers in the wealthier nations—cannot expect dogma to bring the growth they seek. Do the two sets of case histories permit a consistent explanation?

Underlying Factors

By focusing on the technical determinants of economic growth, some light can be thrown upon the apparent paradox.

Let us think of the rate of growth as the product of the rates at which output per unit of capital changes and the capital stock itself expands. By committing itself to the achievement of more rapid economic expansion, a government commits itself to change the nation's savings (or investment) ratios and its capital-output ratios—usually both. There are alternative courses of action to these ends. And it is with respect to the methods, more than to the ends, that a government's action reflects its adherence to democracy or to communism. Totalitarian regimes can squeeze consumption, or can limit the increases in consumption in ways unacceptable to a government dependent on the ballot box. Thus, at some time in East Germany or China, rationing has been carried to extreme levels; family life has been communalized; a large part of crop production has been procured from the peasantry under pressure at low prices for resale at high prices. While such measures permit larger allocation to investment, it may be noted that under Communist control they also permitted large appropriations to the Soviet Union, as in the case of East Germany. On the other hand, in West Germany, where there was a clear opportunity for gain by the investor, voluntary savings increased rapidly. Even in a poor nation like India, consumption habits did permit very large voluntary savings in years when there was rapid growth in income for the mass of the people.

The capital-output ratios depend upon the economic wisdom in new investment allocation as well as the vigor with which the nation's human resources are applied to already existing capital. We know well that, in free societies, individual motivations have resulted in efficient over-all performance, in large returns per unit of capital. On the other hand, the right of freedom of economic choice scarcely assures such results everywhere. Russia and China provide concrete evidence that the much larger range of centralized economic decisions necessary to achieve progress in a controlled system can be made with effective results. However, this has not always been true either; indeed, involuntary transfers of savings have been known to generate apathy and even active noncooperation on the part of the population.

The needed changes in the savings ratios and in input-output relationships can certainly be visualized with democratic as well as Communist methods. These basic parameters have not only economic but psychological and sociological dimensions. Both Communist and democratic regimes will find the new measures more effective if they take cognizance of existing relationships in the society. This is particularly true for democratic nations, which depend much more upon voluntary cooperation and hence upon the existing pattern of motivational forces in the society. Success by Communist methods places upon government the requirement for more action and more perseverance in assuring its fulfillment; success 'under democracy requires action based on greater insight into the structure of the society and the economy.

These observations can be illustrated in the two sets of countries. Both East and West Germany had relatively modern, efficient, and complex industrial and agricultural organizations. The profit incentive—even modified in some measure by restraints of a government seeking social-welfare objectives—was of tremendous importance for economic performance. The situation in India and China was completely different. Their economies were market-oriented to only a limited degree. Custom and tradition were of pervasive importance in economic activity—especially in rural areas, where most of the population, workers, and even output are centered. Attainment of specific objectives required carefully planned governmental programs much more than reliance upon the price and profit mechanism.

The very different economic circumstances prevailing in the two sets of coun-

tries place very different sets of requirements upon governments seeking more rapid economic progress—whether by democratic or by Communist methods. West Germany's faith in the free market made obvious sense; the government's recognition of the need for change permitted it to superimpose a broad and flexible system of fiscal controls, as well as capital allocations, wherever these were necessary to make the nation's resource endowments best serve its economic needs. In this free society, state control increased; about half of all investments were directly or indirectly affected by government.

In contrast, East German planners slavishly copied the Russian model, a pattern prepared for substantially different resource endowments thàn prevailed in East Germany. Steel produced with Ukrainian iron ore and Polish coal was expensive. In Germany it was exceedingly difficult for government to acquire the know-how for establishing and administrating precise controls. Thus, it is hard to substitute, for example, for the consistent price system which competitive forces can mold. With the currency reforms in 1948, West Germany acquired such a system. In East Germany, it has yet to evolve. Ubiquitous government may long incur the costs of an inefficient combination of resources.

China's ties to a Russian model of rapid, large-scale industrialization did not impede early recognition of the emptiness of industrialization without agricultural advancement in a nation where most people will long remain rural; of the complementarities, rather than the competitiveness, of large industry and many types of small enterprises suitable to a heavy endowment of labor. Important deviations from Communist economic lore were soon made in the allocation of large percentages of investment resources to agriculture and the small-scale sector. A form of communal organization was created with continuous and strong guidance and controls to assure the change that the economy on its own could not generate.

The government of India's models of growth are largely derived from the patterns and relationships found in Western capitalist societies; neither the concepts, nor the values, of the multipliers relevant to a market-conscious economy in the throes of expansion are directly applicable in an institutionalized and static society. The major task of rural improvement and growth was placed upon a national community development and extension scheme. While this action recognized the need, especially in the initial years, of injecting into rural India a new force for change, government did not provide the programs with sustained, strong leadership. In modern industry, where the parallels between Western nations and India were greatest, borrowed doctrine was often in conflict with India's own formulation of the needs of a socialist state. India tries to allocate 50–60 per cent of all investment to the government sector while expecting the private sector to produce more than 90 per cent of total product. These contrasting ratios are not necessarily in conflict; but they do demand close scrutiny of day-to-day investment and production developments to assure that the drive to high levels of investment in the public sector does not impede continued performance and expansion in the private sector.

This examination of underlying factors permits an interesting conclusion. The two more successful nations—Communist China and democratic West Germany—operated on the same sets of technical determinants of growth as did India and East Germany. Their relative success was due to the degree to which they geared their development programs to the existing structure of their economies. Cold and objective appraisals were made of the stages necessary to achieve a state of continuing progress from inadequate starting points. Throughout, they demonstrated flexibility in selecting courses of action. Only those were finally adopted in

which practice gave promise of the changes needed in savings rates and in technical input-output coefficients. In democratic India and Communist East Germany, on the other hand, governmental operations on these basic parameters have manifested much less objectivity and flexibility. Indeed, India, where growth under democracy demands a greater interplay of new and old relationships in the society, evidenced less of an experimental and flexible approach to its problem of expansion than did China.

Ideology and Economic Progress

Thus no simple ideologic-economic relationship exists. The West German performance means that the Communist formula does not contain the essential ingredient to more rapid progress; nor has democracy in a free society provided India with a guaranty of rapid economic achievement. Not only is economic progress not determined by the ideology to which a nation adheres; indeed, it can be most costly for a nation to adhere persistently to doctrines which counter indigenous economic and social relationships.

Whenever doctrine and policy are borrowed, whenever the results of foreign experience are applied, actual experience with them must be subjected to constant analysis. Only such study can indicate the changes needed to achieve effective results —whether these changes be in the knowledge or ideas imported, or in indigenous habits or relationships. It is not an ideology or an economic theory that will bring growth; it is more energetic and imaginative responses to the record as revealed by intensive study. This is especially true for democratic nations which rule out change by force; new programs must take root indigenously.

The growth record in the poorer nations over the past decade can scarcely give unmitigated satisfaction either to the leaders in the underdeveloped areas or to the policy-makers in the West. At the least, there is still room for great humility with respect to our know-how about the process of growth. The free market and private enterprise may work—as by and large they have under our conditions—but they may also have but limited relevance in the economic and social circumstances prevailing in the poorer lands. West Germany seems to have worked out a compromise between free enterprise and controls which serves its growth needs. There is undoubtedly some composite path which will provide the centralized direction and coordinated performance needed in India, consistent with its democratic aspirations. The specific actions to be taken can be deduced only from a full reading of the actual record of the decade. Dogma can give way to hypothesis, certainty to experimentation.

It is such a composite path—well within the extremes of permissiveness and compulsion—which nations seeking economic progress under democracy need to pursue. Given the limited growth achievements of these lands in the past decade, capital-exporting countries will inevitably provide greater assistance. It is high time that major research efforts—perhaps on a joint basis in each developing nation—be applied to discovering the actual bottlenecks which have been hindering that nation's economic expansion. A development program tailored to these specific tasks has a chance of both achieving material progress and nurturing democratic political ideals.

RELIGIOUS ASPECTS OF MODERNIZATION IN TURKEY AND JAPAN[1]

Robert N. Bellah

The process of modernization of the "backward" nations such as Turkey and Japan, which will be considered here, involves changes in the value system as well as economic, political, and social changes. In traditional societies the value system tends to be what Howard Becker calls

SOURCE. Robert N. Bellah, "Religious Aspects of Modernization in Turkey and Japan," *American Journal of Sociology*, **64**, 1–5, July 1958. Reprinted by permission of The University of Chicago Press. Copyright 1958 by The University of Chicago Press.

[1] This paper is a fragment of a larger study of the relations between religion and politics in modern Asia and the tentative conclusions put forward here may be altered as a result of the larger study. I am indebted to Niyazi Berkes and Talcott Parsons for reading earlier versions of this paper.

"prescriptive."[2] A prescriptive system is characterized by the comprehensiveness and specificity of its value commitments and by its consequent lack of flexibility. Motivation is frozen, so to speak, through commitment to a vast range of relatively specific norms governing almost every situation in life. Most of these specific norms, usually including those governing social institutions, are thoroughly integrated with a religious system which invokes ultimate sanctions for every infraction. Thus changes in economic or political institutions, not to speak of family and

[2] For a recent definition of "prescriptive" and "principial" see Howard Becker, "Current Sacred-secular Theory and Its Development," in Howard Becker and Alvin Boskoff (eds.), *Modern Sociological Theory in Continuity and Change* (New York: Dryden Press, 1957).

education, in traditional societies tend to have ultimate religious implications. Small changes will involve supernatural sanctions.

Yet such a society, when faced with grave dislocations consequent to Western contact, must make major changes in its institutional structure if it is to survive. What changes must be made in the organization of the value system so that these structural changes may go forward?

We may say that the value system of such a society must change from a prescriptive type to a "principial" type, to borrow again from Becker. Traditional societies, as we have said, tend to have a normative system, in which a comprehensive, but uncodified, set of relatively specific norms governs concrete behavior. But in a modern society an area of flexibility must be gained in economic, political, and social life in which specific norms may be determined in considerable part by short-term exigencies in the situation of action, or by functional requisites of the relevant social subsystems. Ultimate or religious values lay down the basic principles of social action; thus such a normative system is called "principial," but the religious system does not attempt to regulate economic, political, and social life in great detail, as in prescriptive societies. Looking at this process another way, we may say that there must be a differentiation between religion and ideology, between ultimate values and proposed ways in which these values may be put into effect. In traditional prescriptive societies there is no such discrimination. Difference of opinion on social policy is taken to imply difference as to religious commitment. The social innovator necessarily becomes a religious heretic. But in modern society there is a differentiation between the levels of religion and social ideology which makes possible greater flexibility at both levels.

How is the normative system in a traditional society to be changed from prescriptive to principial, and how is the differentiation of the religious and ideological levels

to be effected, especially in the face of the concerted effort of the old system to avoid any changes at all? I would assert that only a new religious initiative, only a new movement which claims religious ultimacy for itself, can successfully challenge the old value system and its religious base. The new movement, which arises from the necessity to make drastic social changes in the light of new conditions, is essentially ideological and political in nature. But, arising as it does in a society in which the ideological level is not yet recognized as having independent legitimacy, the new movement must take on a religious coloration in order to meet the old system on its own terms. Even when such a movement is successful in effecting major structural changes in the society and in freeing motivation formerly frozen in traditional patterns so that considerable flexibility in economic and political life is attained, the problems posed by its own partly religious origin and its relation to the traditional religious system may still be serious indeed.

Let us turn to the example of Turkey.[3]

Ottoman Turkey in the eighteenth century was a traditionalistic society with a prescriptive value system. Virtually all spheres of life were theoretically under the authority of the religious law, the Shari'ah. Indeed, the government was supposed to have an area of freedom within the law. But this freedom had become narrowly restricted. Precedents of governmental procedure were tacitly assimilated to the religious law.

Beginning with Selim III in the late eighteenth century, a series of reforming sultans and statesmen attempted to make major changes in Turkish society in an effort to cope with increasingly desperate internal and external conditions. While some changes were made, especially in areas remote from the central strongholds of the

[3] Throughout the discussion of Turkey I shall rely heavily on lectures and unpublished material of Niyazi Berkes, of the Islamic Institute at McGill University, who is undertaking a pioneering study of Turkish modernization.

religious law, the reforming party was unable to attain any ultimate legitimation in the eyes of the people, and, although Turkish society was shaken to its foundations, periods of reform alternated with periods of blind reaction in which reformers were executed or banished.

The last of these reactionary periods was that of the rule of the despotic Sultan Abdul Hamid II, who was overthrown in 1908 by a coup of young army officers whom we know as the "Young Turks." By this time it had become clear to leading intellectuals that more was needed than another interim of liberal reform. They saw that a basic change in the cultural foundation of Turkish society was demanded if the long-delayed changes in economic, political, and social structure were to be effected. Some felt that a modern purified Islam could provide the new cultural basis, but orthodox Islam was so deeply imbedded in the fabric of traditional society that the Islamic modernists found little response in the religious party. Others looked to Western liberal democracy as a satisfactory foundation. Those sensitive to the mind of the Turkish masses, however, pointed out that the Turkish people would never accept a value system so obviously "made abroad" and which could so easily be condemned by the conservatives with the stigma of unbelief.

It was Ziya Gökalp, a sociologist much influenced by Durkheim, who ardently championed Turkish nationalism as the only satisfactory cultural foundation for the new Turkey.[4] Gökalp found the referent for all symbols of ultimate value in society itself. His answer to the religious conservatives was that the true Islam was that of the Turkish folk, not of the effete religious hierarchy which was largely educated in the Arabic and Persian languages rather than the Turkish language. Here at last was an ideology to which the people could respond with emotion and which could challenge religious conservatism on its own grounds.

[4] A translation by Niyazi Berkes of selected writings of Ziya Gökalp is forthcoming.

But the course of world history did as much as Gökalp's eloquence to decide in favor of the nationalist alternative for Turkey. Not only did World War I shear Turkey of her empire, but the subsequent invasions of Anatolia threatened the very life of the nation itself. Mustafa Kemal, who led the ultimately successful effort of national resistance, partly chose and partly was impelled to make the nation the central symbol in his subsequent drive for modernization. As a result, the highest value and central symbol for the most articulate sections of the Turkish people became not Islam but Turkism, or nationalism, or Kemalism, or, simply, "the Revolution." Having a strong national and personal charismatic legitimacy, Mustafa Kemal, later known as "Ataturk," was able to create a far-reaching cultural revolution in which the place of religion in the society was fundamentally altered. We may note some of the landmarks in this revolution. In 1924 the office of caliph was abolished. In the same year all religious schools were closed or converted into secular schools. The most important change of all took place in 1926: the Muslim Civil Law was abandoned and the Swiss Civil Code adopted almost without change. Finally, in 1928, the phrase in the constitution stating that the religion of Turkey is Islam was deleted, and Turkey was declared a secular state.

That the Turks were deeply conscious of what they were doing is illustrated by the following quotation from Mahmud Essad, the minister of justice under whom the religious law was abandoned:

The purpose of laws is not to maintain the old customs or beliefs which have their source in religion, but rather to assure the economic and social unity of the nation.

When religion has sought to rule human societies, it has been the arbitrary instrument of sovereigns, despots, and strong men. In separating the temporal and the spiritual, modern civilization has saved the world from numerous calamities and has given to religion an imperishable throne in the consciences of believers.[5]

This quotation illustrates well enough the transition from prescriptive to principial society and the differentiation of religion and ideology as two distinct levels. It is clear that the great advances of Turkish society in economic, political, and social life are based on this new cultural foundation. But implicit in Essad's words are some of the yet unsolved problems about that new cultural pattern.

For Essad and other Turkish reformers "the Revolution" was a criterion for everything, even for the place of religion in society, and thus, whether consciously or not, they gave the revolution an ultimate, a religious, significance. The six principles upon which the constitution is based—republicanism, nationalism, populism, étatism, secularism, and revolution—are taken as self-subsisting ultimates. Thus the religious implications of the political ideology remain relatively unchecked. These express themselves in party claims to ultimate legitimacy and in an inability on the part of the party in power to accept the validity of an opposition, which are not in accord with the flexibility appropriate in a modern principial society.

On the other hand, Islam in Turkey has not on the whole been able to redefine its own self-image and face the theological issues involved in becoming a religion primarily, in Essad's words, "enthroned in men's consciences." Nor has it been able to provide a deeper religious dimension of both legitimation and judgment of the six principles which are the basis of the new social life. It remains, on the whole, in a conservative frame of mind in which the ideological claims are considerable, thus still posing a threat, possibly a great one, to return the society to a less differentiated level of social organization. Considering the trend of the last forty years, however, we seem to be observing a differentiation

in the process of becoming, but it is too soon to say that it has been entirely accomplished.

Japan, while illustrating the same general processes as Turkey, does so with marked differences in important details.[6] Premodern Japan was a traditionalistic society with a prescriptive normative system closely integrated with a religious system composed of a peculiar Japanese amalgam of Shinto, Confucianism, and Buddhism. In the immediate premodern period, however, a conjuncture of the Confucian stress on loyalty and a revived interest in Shinto began to have explosive consequences. The actual rule at this time was in the hands of a military dictator, or Shogun, hereditary in the Tokugawa family. The emperor was relegated to purely ceremonial functions in the palace at Kyoto, But, as economic and social conditions deteriorated under Tokugawa rule, important elements in the population became alienated from the political status quo. They proved extremely receptive to the religious message of the revival Shintoists and legitimist Confucians, who insisted that the true sovereign was the emperor and that the Shogun was a usurper. According to their conception, the emperor is divine, descended from the sun-goddess, and his direct rule of the Japanese people could be expected to bring in a virtually messianic age.

This movement was already vigorous when Perry's ships moved into Tokyo Bay in 1853. The inability of the Tokugawa government to keep foreigners from desecrating the sacred soil of Japan added the last fuel to the flames of resentment, and, with the slogan "Revere the Emperor; expel the barbarians," a successful military coup overthrew the Tokugawa and restored the emperor to direct rule.

I would suggest that Japan was at this point, in 1868, virtually at the beginning of serious Western influence, in a position

---

[5] Quoted in Henry E. Allen, *The Turkish Transformation* (Chicago: University of Chicago Press, 1935), p. 34.

[6] For a more extensive treatment of the Japanese case, especially the premodern background see my *Tokugawa Religion* (Glencoe, Ill.: Free Press, 1957).

that Turkey reached only in the early 1920's under Mustafa Kemal. But she reached it in quite a different way. Unlike Turkey, one of the very foundations of the old traditional order in Japan, the divine emperor, provided the main leverage for the radical reorganization of that order. The young samurai who put through the Meiji Restoration used the central value of loyalty to the emperor to legitimize the immense changes they were making in all spheres of social life and to justify the abandoning of many apparently sacred prescriptions of the traditional order. No other sacredness could challenge the sacredness inherent in the emperor's person.

Here we see an ideological movement, essentially political in nature, whose aim was the strengthening and thus the modernizing of Japan, taking a much more openly religious coloration than was the case in Turkey. There was in the early Meiji period an attempt to make Shinto into the national religion and a determined effort to root out all rival religions. Christianity was sharply discouraged, but it was on Buddhism, the chief native religious tradition with little relation to the imperial claims to divinity, that the ax fell. The Buddhist church was disestablished, and all syncretism with Shinto prohibited. In the words of D. C. Holtom:

Members of the royal family were debarred from continuing in Buddhist orders; Buddhist ceremonials in the imperial palace were prohibited; Buddhist temples all over the land were attacked and destroyed. A blind fury of misplaced patriotic zeal committed precious Buddhist writings, fine sculptures, bronzes, woodcarvings, and paintings to the flames, broke them in pieces, cast them away, or sold them for a pittance to whosoever would buy. Buddhist priests were prohibited from participating in Shinto ceremonies. They were subjected to beatings and threatened with military force. Monks and nuns in large numbers were obliged to take up secular callings.[7]

Grave foreign protests on the subject of Christianity plus serious unrest among the masses devoted to Buddhism forced the abandoning of the policy of religious persecution. Liberal elements within the country agitated for the complete separation of church and state, and the Meiji leaders were brought to understand that religious freedom was a principle of the modern society they were trying to establish. Consequently, the government included in the constitution of 1889 a clause guaranteeing freedom of religion. At the same time it continued its support of the state Shinto cult, whose main aim was the veneration of the emperor. It solved this seeming contradiction by declaring that state Shinto was not a religion but merely an expression of patriotism. Nevertheless, the existence of the national cult imposed a real limitation on the independence and effectiveness of the private religious bodies. Though in the 1920's there was a strong tendency to differentiate religion and ideology, in times of stress such as the late 1930's and early 1940's religion was completely subordinated to and fused with a monolithic ideology, an ideology which had demonic consequences both for Japan and for the rest of the world. The new, 1946, constitution, by disestablishing Shinto and deriving sovereignty from the people rather than from the sacred and inviolable emperor, theoretically completed the process of secularization.

But, in fact, serious religious problems remain. All religious groups with the exception of the Christians were compromised by their connection with the nationalistic orgy. In the absence of any really vigorous religious life, except for the popular faith-healing cults and the small Christian community, the religious impulses of the Japanese people find expression for

[7] D. C. Holtom, *Modern Japan and Shinto Nationalism* (Chicago: University of Chicago Press, 1947), p. 127.

the more radical in the symbol of socialism, for the conservatives in a longing for a new and more innocent version of state Shinto. Here, as in Turkey, the differentiation between religion and ideology remains to be completed.

Other examples of the processes we have been discussing come readily to mind. Communism is an example of a secular political ideology which successfully came to power in the prescriptive, religiously based societies of Russia and China. But Communism itself makes an ultimate religious claim, and here, as in the case of Japan, a secular ideology claiming religious ultimacy has embarked on courses of action which hinder, rather than further, the transition to modern principial society. It is perhaps safe to say that alongside the serious political and economic problems which Communism faces today is the perhaps even more serious cultural problem, the problem of the differentiation of the religious and ideological levels.

In conclusion, it seems worthwhile to stress that the process of secularization, which is in part what the transition from prescriptive to principial society is, does not mean that religion disappears. The function of religion in a principial society is different from that in a prescriptive society, but it is not necessarily less important. Moreover, in the very process of transition religion may reappear in many new guises. Perhaps what makes the situation so unclear is its very fluidity. Even in highly differentiated societies, such as our own, traditional religion, so deeply associated with the prescriptive past, is still in the process of finding its place in modern principial society.

Chapter 6

Communications and Social Mobilization

COMMUNICATION SYSTEMS AND SOCIAL SYSTEMS—A STATISTICAL EXPLORATION IN HISTORY AND POLICY[1]

Daniel Lerner

People who live together in a common polity develop patterned ways of distributing information, as of distributing other commodities. These patterns of information flow interact at many points with the patterns of power, wealth, status, and other values to form a *system*, i.e., institutional variation in one is accompanied by regular and determinate variations in the others. This paper aims to determine the degree of systemic relationship between communication and other institutions in most of the societies around the world.

We have identified two main types of public communication systems—media and

oral. These are differentiated according to the paradigmatic question of communication research: who says what, how, to whom? On these four variables the differences are as follows:

	MEDIA SYSTEMS	ORAL SYSTEMS
Channel	Media (broadcast)	Oral (point-to point)
Audience	Mass (heterogeneous)	Primary (homogeneous)
Source	Professional (skill)	Hierarchical (status)
Content	[Descriptive][2]	[Prescriptive][2]

Media systems have been described in detail by communication specialists. The main flow of public information is activated

SOURCE. Daniel Lerner, "Communication Systems and Social Systems. A Statistical Exploration in History and Policy," *Behavioral Science*, **2**, 266–275, October 1957. A later, shorter version of this article appeared as "The System of Modernity" in Lerner's *The Passing of Traditional Society* (New York: The Free Press of Glencoe, 1958), 54–65.

---

[1] I wish to thank R. S. Eckhaus, E. E. Hagen, B. F. Hoselitz, and H. D. Lasswell for suggestions which have been incorporated in this paper. Case studies of the theoretical structure here outlined are reported in the author's book entitled *The Passing of Traditional Society*.

[2] These are bracketed because the only systematic evidence of content variation between the two types available to me is confined to a study made in the Middle East several years ago. I suspect, but cannot demonstrate, that there is regularity in this variation around the world.

by a professional corps of communicators, skilled in producing descriptive messages ("news") for transmission through impersonal "media" (print, film, radio) to relatively undifferentiated mass audiences.

Oral systems we know mainly from the reports of anthropologists. Since preliterate networks are considerably more diverse than media systems (which have an "homogenizing" effect on behavioral styles) their public institutions exhibit much variation. In some oral systems, for example, power is not rigidly hierarchized. In the modal type, however, messages usually emanate from sources authorized to speak by their place in the social hierarchy, i.e., by status rather than skill criteria. These messages typically appear to be prescriptive rather than descriptive, i.e. announcing the regulations that are to govern audience behavior toward imminent events of community-wide interest, such as tax collections and military drafts. They are transmitted through oral channels to highly differentiated audiences, i.e., the "natural" primary groups of kinship, worship, work, or play. Each of these groups completes the diffusion pattern of an oral network by acting as a relay channel of mouth-to-ear communication within and between groups.[3]

If we accept this terse formulation as satisfactorily differentiating the characteristics of two general models of communication systems, we come next to the problem of describing their occurrence with sufficient accuracy to discriminate consistently

[3] Comment by H. D. Lasswell: "One interesting variant is the role of drumming and similar media channels in predominantly oral systems. Such modes of communication are simply telegraphic devices more like conventionalized signposts than expressive or prescriptive statement-making. The sign-symbol ratio is high, by which I mean the physical events that serve as channel are rather extensive. A visual system seems essential to cut down the sign-symbol ratio and approach the 'pure' sign. Such visual systems may be 'manufactured' when they appear and copyists arise. The demand must be great—as at a dominant capital or at another urban locus."

between media and oral systems in the observable world. Here we run into trouble, for there are few societies that give a perfect fit to either of these idealized sets of paired comparisons. For example, in Britain, where public communication approximates most closely the model of a media system, people still talk to each other about public issues. Conversely, in Saudi Arabia, which corresponds to the oral system, there is a radio station. In most societies, as we move from the ideal types into empirical data, various elements in the patterns begin to shift. Most societies in the world appear to be in some stage of transition from one pattern to the other.

We notice, however, two general features that appear to be common to all societies. First, the *direction* of change is always from oral to media system (no known case exhibits change in the reverse direction).[4] Second, the *degree* of change in communication behavior appears to correlate significantly with other behavioral changes in the social system. These observations indicate that we are dealing with a secular trend in communication systems, a long-term process of historical change that is unilateral in direction. Moreover, this trend appears to be systemic, since it occurs interdependently with a variety of non-communication factors. From this we derive the proposition that a communication system is both index and agent of change in a total social system. Leaving aside the genetic question of causality (on the view that once the process is started, chicken and egg in fact "cause" each other), the hypothesis may be formulated in a suitable manner for testing as a correlation matrix, viz:

[4] This discussion excludes the new totalitarian systems, which have revived the ancient importance of the Agitator, using oral modes of communication. This special case appears to fill a "communication gap" created by the excessive development of capacity to produce messages through the media (especially print) over the capacity to consume mediated messages (e.g., by reason of illiteracy or lack of equipment).

	TYPE I	TYPE II
Communica-tion	Media	Oṛal
Socioeconomic	Urban	Rural
Political	Representa-tive	Nonrepre-sentative
Cultural	Literate	Illiterate

Associated with each communication system is a "profile" of economic, political, and cultural attributes. To sharpen the differences, they are stated above in dichotomous fashion. The dogmatic character of such a formulation need trouble no one, however, for empirically we treat them as continuous variables, on which differences are calibrated. Just as there is no perfect media system, so there is no perfectly urban or perfectly representative or perfectly literate society. Our model is probabilistic, our measures are distributive, and our test of fit is correlational.

The procedure was to determine the actual degree of correlation among these indices, for all societies of the world which supplied data. These indices were defined in such fashion as to permit maximum use of the statistical data reported by UNESCO and other U.N. agencies. As the number of countries reporting varies from one index to another, our correlations apply to groups of nations ranging from 54 to 73 in number.[5]

[5] The statistics were used as reported by UNESCO [7]. This was checked wherever possible against other UNESCO sources (for typographical errors) and against the U.N. *Statistical Yearbook* [10] and *Demographic Yearbook* [11] (for errors of information and computation). Wherever significant differences appeared which could not be reconciled, the case was excluded from our analysis. Otherwise all "self-governing territories" are included. The writer is unable to offer any definitive evaluation of these U.N. data, which are assembled from reports prepared separately by each nation. There are national differences in definition of indices and accuracy of reporting. Whereas magnitudes of "error" cannot be

Each index is considered a reliable guide to the state of public participation in its "sector" as a whole. Thus the literacy index, by specifying the proportion of population which can read in one language, is considered to give a fair picture of national participation in the whole cultural sector. Also, the proportion of population actually voting in national elections indexes participation in the whole political sector. Similarly, urbanization, computed as the proportion of population living in cities over 50,000, is taken as an index of participation in the whole economic sector. While urbanization is usually taken more narrowly, as a measure only of occupational distribution, a broader interpretation can be based on previous studies showing high intercorrelations between occupational distribution, per-capita income, and literacy.[6]

These indices express degree of participation within four sectors which, in this discussion, can be taken to represent the whole social system. What they differentiate is the participant style of modern democratic societies from the nonparticipant ways of traditional hierarchic societies. By "participant style" we mean here the *frequency*, not the quality, of participation by individuals. The point is simply that *more* individuals receive and use the opportunity to participate, regardless of the "value" of their participation. Accordingly, the items selected to form the communication index also focus on frequency of participation by the general population. These items are: (*a*) circulation of daily newspapers; (*b*) number of radio receivers; (*c*) seating capacity of cinemas.

checked systematically, the direction of error, in those cases I have checked, always tend toward overstating one's progress in modernization—i.e., underdeveloped countries are likely to report larger rather than smaller estimates of urbanization, literacy, voting, etc.

[6] Literacy around the world correlated at .84 with per-capita income, at .87 with industrialization measured by proportion of gainfully employed males in nonagricultural occupations. See Refs. [2], [9].

Each of these items was first correlated separately with the other indices. After their separate coefficients had been determined, the three items were handled jointly as a single index. (In all cases they were expressed, for comparability between items and countries, as proportion per 1000 population.)

Testing the Communication Items

Each of the three communication items was correlated with the cultural index of literacy.[7] The coefficients, for a group of 73 self-governing countries, were as follows:

ITEM	CORRELATION WITH LITERACY
Daily newspaper circulation	.75
Number of radio receivers	.74
Cinema seating capacity	.61

It is obvious that newspaper circulation should correlate better with literacy than does movie attendance, the enjoyment of which does not require literacy. The high correlation of radio receivers leads, for explanation, in another direction. Whereas building cinemas (in which *imported* feature films are shown) requires no advanced technology, the mass production of radio receivers does require a fair rate of industrialization on a high technological level.

The differential rate of industrialization is subsumed, up to a certain determinate point, under our index of urbanization. Having established that a high correlation exists between literacy and media, we now seek to establish that urbanization is interdependent with both. Rising production and distribution of the media usually occur only where and when there is the minimal urbanization required for modern industrial processes. By the same token, urbanization requires rising literacy for industrial participation. At a certain point, when urbanization has done its work, literacy becomes the independent variable in the process of growth and a new phase of modernization begins. But the growth of literacy itself, in this phase, soon becomes closely associated with the growth of media. The media teach literacy, and growing literacy develops the market which consumes the media product. The high coefficients correlating literacy with each of the media suggest that these may be considered as reciprocal causes and effects in a communication market whose locus can only be, at least in its historical inception, urban.[8]

The role of cities becomes clearer if we consider the further suggestion that sheer density of population, without countervailing urbanization, tends to operate as an antiliteracy force in most societies. This appears to be so despite the fact that education is cheaper when pupils live close together and hence, other things being equal, density should be associated with greater literacy. But, in the absence of significant urbanization, other things are *not* equal— i.e., the production, distribution, and consumption of wealth are much lower. This has a direct depressing effect on all public services, notably free public education. In dense nonurban societies, where national

---

[7] Literacy is reported by UNESCO in five categories, each covering a range of 20 percentage points. All other items were handled as ungrouped data. The standard deviation for the literacy distribution is high (31.4).

[8] Comment by B. F. Hoselitz: "I tend to believe that literacy is the independent variable, at least in some cases, since the general experience in South Asia seems to be that the proportion of literates among migrants to cities is greater than among the rural population whence they came. In other words, people with a higher degree of empathy engage in migration to towns. On the other hand, the urban development, partly because of the availability of better schooling facilities, tends to produce a higher degree of literacy. One would, therefore, have to make a distinction between literacy rates of those who were born, or at least lived, in the urban environment since they were of school age, and those who migrated to the city as grownups."

income is relatively small, few schools are maintained by public funds; also, since per-capita income is lower and less widely distributed, fewer individuals can afford to attend school [5]. Hence, the more people there are in a given area, the smaller is the proportion being educated and the harder it is to get a rising proportion of literates among them—until they begin to be re-deployed into cities. In sparsely settled lands the influence of urbanization is less marked and literacy rates will probably respond directly to rises in per-capita national income. But in populous societies urbanization is the intervening variable and is crucial for the "take-off" toward increasing literacy. It appears that only when dense populations show a significant rate of urbanization do literacy rates begin to rise. The rise of literacy levels off, however, after a certain degree of urbanization is present in the society. This means that the continued growth of literacy—say, after the society has become half-literate—depends upon some factor other than the continued growth of cities.

The counter-literacy force of sheer population density is evident in the populous Asian societies, such as India and Indonesia, where significant rates of urbanization have not yet occurred. The suggested interplay of density and urbanism as factors conditioning literacy may be represented as follows:

	Urbanism	
	HIGH	LOW
HIGH	High (literacy)	Low (literacy)
Density		
LOW	High (literacy)	High/Low (literacy)

To facilitate testing of these relationships between density, urbanization, and literacy, we formulated three distinct hypotheses:

(*a*) that literacy and population density, in areas of low urbanization, vary inversely and exhibit a negative correlation; (*b*) that the rate of literacy increases positively as the degree of urbanization increases (whether density is low or high); (*c*) that when urbanization exceeds a determinate figure then literacy will be high, regardless of population density, but will no longer be raised simply by rising urbanization. (No hypothesis is offered under the fourth set of conditions, where *both* urbanization and density are *low*, the impact of rising urbanization upon literacy being indeterminate in this case.)

A more complex formulation would take these three hypotheses together and would seek to determine the triadic conditions under which monotone relations actually obtain between urbanization, density, and literacy. Here we take the simpler course of testing the pairwise relationships by correlation. Our main interest here being to establish the crucial role of urbanization in the early phase of modernizing a social system, we suggest its differential functioning under conditions of low and high density only as a lead for future investigation. In computing these correlations, population density was defined as the number of persons per square kilometer of territory, and urbanization was defined as the proportion of total population living in cities over 50,000. Correlation of literacy with population density gave us a negative coefficient of −.60. Inspection of the two sets of figures showed that this inverse relationship was due to the massive nonurban societies—China, India, Indonesia, Egypt, etc. (cf. [8]). This may be regarded as confirmation of the first hypothesis that sheer density of population, in areas of low urbanization, is a counter-literacy factor—as density rates increase, literacy rates tend to decrease.

Confirmation of the second hypothesis, that literacy *increases* as urbanization increases, was also clear from the coefficient of correlation between these variables: +.64. (It should be noted that inaccuracies in the raw statistical data tend to bias the results against this hypothesis. Density is computed by formal territorial jurisdiction rather than effective area of habitation; since the densest countries tend to have the largest "waste" areas this minimizes their actual density. Also the cutting point of 50,000 excludes many cases of genuine urbanization in the less dense and populous countries, where cities of smaller size represent a significant degree of urbanization. Hence, making the raw data more accurate would tend to raise all coefficients in the direction hypothesized.)

Our third hypothesis, that after a certain point in urbanization has been passed literacy is high regardless of other demographic variables, was made more plausible (though not completely confirmed) when we ranked all 73 countries with respect to literacy and urbanization.

NUMBER OF COUNTRIES	LITERACY	URBANIZATION (MEAN)
22	Over 80%	28.0%
4	61–80	29.2
12	41–60	25.0
13	21–40	17.0
22	Under 20	7.4

Clearly, urbanization is an important factor up to the point at which one-fourth of the population lives in cities over 50,000. The direct and monotonic relationship between literacy and urbanization (the surplus of 1.2 per cent in the second row, which contains only four countries, is insignificant) is clearest from the time urbanization reaches 10 per cent until it passes 25 per cent. Beyond this point urbanization levels off, while literacy continues to rise "independently" (in countries of extremely high *and* extremely low population density).

If we take 10 per cent and 25 per cent as approximate cutting points in the scale of

urbanization, we are able to classify societies into three categories which also discriminate quite consistently the degree of literacy and media participation in each society. Let us designate these three categories as Modern, Transitional, Traditional, to mean the following:

	LITERACY	URBANIZATION	COMMUNICATION SYSTEM
Modern	Over 61%	Over 25%	Media
Transitional	21–60	10–25	Media-Oral
Traditional	Under 20	Under 10	Oral

These cutting points are somewhat arbitrary, of course, in the sense that their outcome is partly determined by the statistical input. (Had urbanization been indexed by cities over 20,000 rather than 50,000 population, for example, the upper cutting point on this continuum might well be located at 20 per cent rather than 25 per cent).

The results do enable us, however, to specify two main phases in the process of secular change toward a participant social system. The first phase, speaking summarily, is urbanization. It is the transfer of population from scattered hinterlands to urban centers that provides minimum conditions needed for "take-off" toward widespread participation. Only cities have developed the industrial complex of machines and skills which produces, among other things, newspapers and radio networks and motion pictures. In this first phase, accordingly, increases in urbanization tend in every society to be accompanied by increases in the production and availability of communication media. Once the basic industrial plant is in operation, however, the development of a participant society passes into a subsequent phase. Increasing urbanization, once having provided the initial conditions of production, no longer automatically assures equivalent increases in consumption. The need now shifts to increasing the conditions which govern consumption.

Of this next phase, literacy is both the index and agent, since literacy provides the basic skill required for operation of a media system. Only the literate produce the media contents which, as our literacy-media correlations showed, mainly the literate consume. Hence, in societies which are about 25 per cent urbanized, the highest correlation of media consumption is with literacy. We shall soon explain more clearly why literacy is the pivotal agent in the transition to a fully participant modern society. Here we wish to stress, in summary fashion, that by the time this modern phase gets well under way, a different social system is in operation than that which governed behavior in a society that was under 10 per cent urbanized and under 40–60 per cent (roughly, less than half) literate. With higher literacy and media participation comes also increasing availability and use of facilities for participation in all sectors of the social system. An index of this is political participation, which reaches its most developed expression in governance by representation. We refer here to representation that reflects popular choice between real alternatives made through an electoral mechanism that gives one equal vote to every person defined as adult ("universal suffrage").[9]

The Systemic Tests

To test the hypothesized relationships set forth above, a four-index correlation matrix was used. To the three indices of urbanization, literacy, and communication (media participation) as already defined, a fourth index of political participation was added. This consisted of the proportion of *actual* voters to total population, from the

most recent election back through a maximum of five elections. The figure for each country is the average of the voting figures in all elections recorded.

In addition to simple correlations between each pair of indices, multiple correlations were computed using each index in turn as the "dependent" variable for the whole matrix. For the latter operation, only those countries could be included which reported comparable data on all four variables. This reduced the total number of countries, in the multiple correlations, to 54. As this eliminated the countries with the least adequate statistical records, which tend also to be the "least developed" countries, this skewed all distributions involving urbanization—since urbanization is an important factor only during the phase when a society is developing its communication media, but not before nor particularly after this phase. Thus, with $N = 73$ the coefficient of correlation between urbanization and media participation was .47; with $N = 54$ the coefficient jumped to .58. This is a significant increase, as we would expect, because the developed nations have achieved "optimum" relations between urbanization and literacy, while the developing nations exhibit variant growth patterns (deviations from the regression lines)—some more urban than literate, others the reverse.

The high pairs of simple correlations for $N = 54$, again as hypothesized, were those involving literacy. With voting, literacy correlated at 80. With media, literacy correlated at .82.[10] Between these two variables, at all levels, there is a systemic interaction affecting the distribution of information in a manner akin to the production-consumption reciprocal of any commodity in an expanding distribution system.

The essential demonstration of our hypothesis is in the results obtained by

[9] Accordingly, plebiscite-type elections of the sort staged in totalitarian systems are not included in the computations reported below.

[10] A noteworthy feature of these literacy correlations is their stability regardless of sample size: e.g., with $N = 73$, literacy and media correlated at .84.

multiple correlation. This procedure enabled us to rotate each of the four factors in the matrix as the "dependent variable," thereby obtaining the simultaneous degree of relationship of each to all the others. The coefficients of multiple correlation, reported in turn for each dependent variable, were as follows:

DEPENDENT VARIABLE	MULTIPLE- CORRELATION COEFFICIENT	STANDARD ERROR
Urbanization	.61	.09
Media participation	.84	.04
Literacy	.91	.03
Political participation	.82	.05

Both the size of these coefficients and their ascending order are relevant. Their consistent significance demonstrates that the relationship between these four series of independent events is *systemic*—that rates of growth in these four sectors of the participant society have in fact "gone together" in most extant societies. Their ascending order supports the historical phasing that was sketched in the preceding pages.

Urbanization constitutes the initial phase of modernization. Our calculus indicates that at least 10 per cent of the population must be urbanized before the "take-off" toward self-sustaining growth occurs in the other sectors. Thereafter, throughout the period we call the first phase, they tend to grow together. But after a certain degree of urbanization exists, and the society has taken off, then the further growth of cities no longer affects growth of other factors in the same degree. In our computation (based on cities over 50,000) this upper limit was 25 per cent. Urbanization ceases to play a determinant role after this critical level has been reached. As our sample includes many countries which passed this 25 per cent limit long ago, the urbanization correlations naturally yield the lowest coefficient.

Media participation, which indexes the adaptation of advanced technology to communication needs in the second phase of a modernizing society, obtains a considerably higher coefficient. The production and consumption of media products remain functional for growth long after urbanization has passed its dynamic limits. This was the phase in which the West developed, among other things, the "penny press" (cf. [4]). This is the phase in which, as its characteristic functions mature, production of radio sets becomes a useful index of growth in the total industrial production [1].

The diffusion of literacy, which increases rapidly in the posturbanization phase, produces an extremely high correlation coefficient. Literacy continues to be functional for growth at every step in the modernization process. For, with literacy, people acquire more than the simple skill of reading. They gain access, in the very act of achieving distance and control over a formal language, to the world of vicarious experience and the complicated mechanism of empathy which is needed to cope with it. (Throughout the Middle East, illiterate respondents often said of their literate compatriots words to the effect that "They live in another world.") This is why media consumption, in every country we have studied, exhibits a centripetal tendency. Those who read newspapers also tend to be the heaviest consumers of movies, broadcasts, and all other media products.

Thus literacy becomes the sociological pivot in the activation of psychic mobility, which is a modal personality attribute of participant society. Psychic mobility (i.e., a high capacity for empathy) is required in modern society, where much individual "participation" occurs in a universe of vicarious experience. The empathic capacity to relate oneself to a large variety of secondary symbols and public issues is a skill aught by the mass media. This is the psychocultural tie which binds together the diversified activities of modern man's daily round into a homogeneous "participant lifestyle." It explains why the literate urbanite has tended to be not only the main media consumer but also the cash customer and the voter. It explains why, historically, our variables have grown so closely together [3].

We come, then, to the diminished coefficient of .82 obtained by political participation, which requires explanation. Political democracy comes late, historically, and typically appears as a crowning institution of the participant society. That the voting coefficient is lower than the literary coefficient indicates either that the historic link of voting has become everywhere somewhat less intimate than we have supposed, or that some recent "stochastic factor" is at work in some parts of the world. Such a factor appears to be the new global fashion to install some voting mechanism as a symbol of modern desires rather than as a functional agency of modern governance. Democracy has become a world fad, spread across national lines by diffusion, rather than an institutional fulfilment of needs developed internally by an increasingly participant society.

But policy cannot emulate Humpty Dumpty and make events mean just exactly what it wishes. The deliberate policy decision by many underdeveloped countries to induce certain traits of modernity willy-nilly, rather than to await their evolution in the historical sequence, produces "ahistorical" results. Some of these countries show inordinately high voting rates. Indeed, whereas high correlation of voting with the other variables occurs among the modern countries in our sample, the sharp deviations are largely accounted for by the figures reported from India and Southeast Asia, Turkey and the Middle East, South America. These are the great "underdeveloped areas," which have in common the poverty of their current

resources relative to the soaring heights of their current aspirations. They are underurbanized, undertechnologized, underliterate, relative to their urge rapidly to move into the common practices of modern participant society. Thus, India in 1952 and again in 1957 offered universal suffrage in national elections to a population which is predominantly remote from the urban centers, outside the reach of mass media, and illiterate. So Egypt, in 1956, ordered its impoverished rural masses to "vote" in a single-option plebiscite, which gave Abdul Nasser the 97 per cent endorsement common in such performances. Such "ahistoricity" raises questions.

History and Policy

If we take the present findings as reasonable evidence that historically, say over the past two centuries, there has been a systemic relationship between the rates of urbanization, literacy, voting, and media participation, what inferences seem appropriate for those interested in development programs for the retarded areas of the world? First, these findings cannot simply be disregarded; in the absence of *other factors* it is likely that radical departures from these historic relationships will lead to serious imbalances and possible breakdowns in the social systems which attempt these departures. India's rank order is very much higher on the indices of political and media participation (the latter reflecting its extraordinarily high film output) than could be "justified" by its urbanization and literacy rates. *If* "other factors" were equal, one might expect a severe relapse (or even collapse) of India's electoral system and film industry on the basis of these deviations from the historical regularities.

However, and this is the second inference to be drawn, there is no necessity for other factors to be equal. Our aim is not prophecy, but the formulation of an essential question: Since the stability of modern societies has been associated over past centuries with the whole "system" of participant behavior gradually evolved, how can these new societies-in-a-hurry hope to achieve stability while acquiring mobility? The question is not rhetorical; the writer does not believe that he knows "the" answer. History is a matter of secular trends, not eternal laws, and the persistence of a certain pattern of social change in the past does not mean that things must always be so. On the contrary, the very act of describing past trends, and clarifying the conditions of their occurrence, may provide the enlightenment needed to redirect the course of history by the pressure of wise policy. The historical "other factors" can be varied, within limits, to suit new policy goals. One new sort of "other factor" is the set of innovations used to orient the huge electorate in the Indian election—i.e., the use of symbolic devices and other techniques not needed in cases where literacy and the franchise have gone together.

The widespread *planning* of economic development for India is another sort of new "other factor," which was not present in the societies whose historical evolution has been studied here. This could have the effect of raising per-capita income rapidly among illiterate villagers, thereby enabling them to become participants in the newer media (radio, film, television) without moving to a city or going to school. This would produce a participant population radically different, on key attributes, from the historical population of participants. New institutions of social consensus and social control would be brought into being by such a rearrangement of the historic factors. The task of policy planners is to study the new deviations and foresee appropriate institutions—those which will enable them to change the historic patterns successfully.

In planning the future, it is likely that they will have to give special attention to the accelerated shift of many underdeveloped societies from oral to media systems of public communication. It is a distinctive innovation of twentieth century social change that, in much of the underdeveloped world, people are acquiring psychic mobility before they have acquired social mobility. When the modern West took shape, in the eighteenth century, the reverse condition obtained. Thomas Jefferson expressed a basic operating principle of democratic governance when he asserted that the franchise should be exercised by those with a stake in public policy (i.e., property) and with a capacity for forming opinions about policy decisions (i.e., education). Out of this conviction grew such democratic institutions for qualifying voters as the literacy test and the poll tax.[11]

Nowadays, the theory of public participation is changing—largely under the impact of the mass media. Atatürk was perhaps the century's shining model of how to stimulate take-off toward modernization in a traditional society by means of a "communication revolution." Many are following this path. How well they will succeed in working out new relationships for the participant society of the future remains to be seen. That they mean to try is clear from their conviction that the old relationships no longer apply. A clear declaration of independence from the historic regularities that governed relations between communication systems and social systems over the past two centuries was expressed, on January 7, 1957, by President Gamal Abdul Nasser:

It is true that most of our people are still illiterate. But politically that counts for far less than it did 20 years ago.

Literacy and intelligence are not the same thing. Radio has changed everything. Once the villagers had no knowledge of what was happening in the capital. Government was run by small coteries of people who did not need to

[11] The next phase of this inquiry will be to determine the historic regularities and current deviations, in the relationships between our matrix and a direct economic measure such as per-capita income.

take account of the reactions of the people, who never saw a newspaper or could not read it if they did.

Today people in the most remote villages hear of what is happening everywhere and form their opinions. Leaders cannot govern as they once did. We live in a new world. [6].

REFERENCES

[1] Bergson, A. (ed.) *Soviet economic growth.* Evanston, Ill.: Row, Peterson, 1953.

[2] Golden, H. H. Literacy and social change in underdeveloped countries. *Rural Social.,* 1955, **20**, 1–7.

[3] Lerner, D., & Riesman, D. Self and society. Reflections on some Turks in transition. *Explorations,* 1955, **20**, 67–80.

[4] Lowenthal, L., & Fiske, M. Reaction to mass media growth in 18th-century England. *Jour. Quart.,* 1956, **33**, 442–455.

[5] Matthews, R. D., & Akrawi, M. *Education in the Arab countries of the Near East.* Washington, D.C.: American Council on Education, 1949.

[6] Thompson, D. Nasser talks nonsense. *Boston Daily Globe,* January 7, 1957.

[7] United Nations Educational, Scientific and Cultural Organization. *World communication, press, radio, film, television.* (Paris, 2nd ed., 1951). Publication 942.

[8] United Nations Educational, Scientific and Cultural Organization. *Progress of literacy in various countries.* (Paris, 1st ed., 1953). No. 6 of a series, Monographs on Fundamental Education.

[9] United Nations Statistical Office. *National and per capital income in 70 countries (1949).* ST/STAT/Ser E–1. No. 8, Sales Publication **17**, 1952.

[10] United Nations Statistical Office. *Statistical Yearbook.* Published annually. New York: Columbia University Press.

[11] United Nations Statistical Office. *Demographic Yearbook.* Published annually. New York: Columbia University Press.

SOCIAL MOBILIZATION AND POLITICAL DEVELOPMENT

Karl W. Deutsch[1]

Social mobilization is a name given to an overall process of change, which happens to substantial parts of the population in

SOURCE. Excerpted from Karl W. Deutsch, "Social Mobilization and Political Development," *American Political Science Review,* **55**, 493–514, September 1961; using only pp. 493–511. A draft version of this paper was presented at the meeting of the Committee on Comparative Politics, of the Social Science Research Council, Gould House, Dobbs Ferry, June 10, 1959. An earlier version of this text is appearing in *Zeitschrift für Politik* (Köln, Germany).

[1] Further work on this paper was supported in part by the Carnegie Corporation, and I am indebted for assistance in statistical applications to Charles L. Taylor and Alex Weilenmann.

countries which are moving from traditional to modern ways of life. It denotes a concept which brackets together a number of more specific processes of change, such as changes of residence, of occupation, of social setting, of face-to-face associates, of institutions, roles, and ways of acting, of experiences and expectations, and finally of personal memories, habits and needs, including the need for new patterns of group affiliation and new images of personal identity. Singly, and even more in their cumulative impact, these changes tend to influence and sometimes to transform political behavior.

The concept of social mobilization is not merely a short way of referring to the collection of changes just listed, including any extensions of this list. It implies that these processes tend to go together in certain historical situations and stages of economic development; that these situations are identifiable and recurrent, in their essentials, from one country to another; and that they are relevant for politics. Each of these points will be taken up in the course of this paper.

Social mobilization, let us repeat, is something that happens to large numbers of people in areas which undergo modernization, i.e., where advanced, nontraditional practices in culture, technology and economic life are introduced and accepted on a considerable scale. It is not identical, therefore, with this process of modernization as a whole,[2] but it deals with one of its major aspects, or better, with a recurrent cluster among its consequences. These consequences, once they occur on a substantial scale, influence in turn the further process of modernization. Thus, what can be treated for a short time span as a consequence of the modernization process, appears over a longer period as one of its

[2] For broader discussions of the modernization process, see Rupert Emerson, *From Empire to Nation* (Cambridge, Harvard University Press, 1960); Harold D. Lasswell, *The World Revolution of Our Time* (Stanford University Press, 1951); and Gabriel A. Almond and James S. Coleman, eds., *The Politics of the Developing Areas* (Princeton, Princeton University Press, 1960). Cf. also Daniel Lerner, *The Passing of Traditional Society* (Glencoe, 1958), and Lerner, "Communication Systems and Social Systems: A Statistical Exploration in History and Policy," *Behavioral Science*, 2 (October 1957), 266–275; Fred Riggs, "Bureaucracy in Traditional Societies: Politics, Economic Development and Administration," American Political Science Association Annual Meeting, September 1959, multigraphed; Dankwart Rustow *Politics and Westernization in the Near East* (Center of International Studies, Princeton University, 1956); and Lyle Shannon, "Is Level of Development Related to Capacity for Self-Government?" *The American Journal of Economics and Sociology*, 17 (July 1958), 367–381, and Shannon, "Socio-Economic Development and Political Status," *Social Problems*, 7 (Fall 1959), 157–169.

continuing aspects and as a significant cause, in the well known pattern of feedback or circular causation.

Viewed over a longer time perspective, such as several decades, the concept of social mobilization suggests that several of the changes subsumed under it will tend to go together in terms of recurrent association, well above anything to be expected from mere chance. Thus, any one of the forms of social mobilization, such as the entry into market relations and a money economy (and hence away from subsistence farming and barter) should be expected to be accompanied or followed by a significant rise in the frequency of impersonal contacts, or in exposure to mass media of communication, or in changes of residence, or in political or quasi-political participation. The implication of the concept is thus to assert an empirical fact—that of significantly frequent association—and this assertion can be empirically tested.

This notion of social mobilization was perceived early in intuitive terms, as a historical recollection or a poetic image. It was based on the historical experiences of the French *levée en masse* in 1793 and of the German "total mobilization" of 1914–18, described dramatically in terms of its social and emotional impact by many German writers, including notably Ernest Jünger. A somewhat related image was that of the long-term and world-wide process of "fundamental democratization," discussed in some of the writings of Karl Mannheim.[3] All these images suggest a breaking away from old commitments to traditional ways of living, and a moving into new situations, where new patterns of behavior are relevant and needed, and where new commitments may have to be made.

Social mobilization can be defined, therefore, as the process in which major clusters of old social, economic and psychological commitments are eroded or broken and

[3] Karl Mannheim, *Man and Society in an Age of Reconstruction* (New York, 1940).

people become available for new patterns of socialization and behavior. As Edward Shils has rightly pointed out,[4] the original images of "mobilization" and of Mannheim's "fundamental democratization" imply two distinct stages of the process: (1) the stage of uprooting or breaking away from old settings, habits and commitments; and (2) the induction of the mobilized persons into some relatively stable new patterns of group membership, organization and commitment. In this fashion, soldiers are mobilized *from* their homes and families and mobilized *into* the army in which they then serve. Similarly, Mannheim suggests an image of large numbers of people moving away *from* a life of local isolation, traditionalism and political apathy, and moving *into* a different life or broader and deeper involvement in the vast complexities of modern life, including potential and actual involvement in mass politics.

It is a task of political theory to make this image more specific; to bring it into a form in which it can be verified by evidence; and to develop the problem to a point where the question "how?" can be supplemented usefully by the question "how much". In its intuitive form, the concept of social mobilization already carried with it some images of growing numbers and rising curves. In so far as the constituent processes of social mobilization can be measured and described quantitatively in terms of such curves, it may be interesting to learn how fast the curves rise, whether they show any turning points, or whether they cross any thresholds beyond which the processes they depict have different side effects from those that went before. Notable among these side effects are any that bear on the performance of political systems and upon the stability and capabilities of governments.[5]

An Analytical Formulation

Let M stand for the generalized process of social mobilization, and let us think of it as representing the general propensity or availability of persons for recommitment. In this sense, M could be measured by the average probability that any person, say between fifteen and sixty-five years old, would have undergone, or could be expected to undergo during his lifetime, a substantial change from old ways of living to new ones.

In order to define this change more precisely, it is necessary to make three assumptions: (1) there are different forms of social recommitment relevant for politics; (2) these forms tend to be associated with each other; and (3) these forms tend to reinforce each other in their effects. Two further points may be noted for investigation: (4) each of these forms may have a threshold at which some of its effects may change substantially; and (5) some or all of these thresholds, though not identical in quantitative terms, may be significantly related to each other.

For these constituent processes of social mobilization we may then choose the symbols $m_1, m_2, m_3, \ldots, m_n$. Thus we may call m_1 the exposure to aspects of modern life through demonstrations of machinery, buildings, installations, consumer goods, show windows, rumor, governmental, medical or military practices, as well as through mass media of communication. Then m_2 may stand for a narrower concept, exposure to these mass media alone. And m_3 may stand for change of residence; m_4 for urbanization; m_5 for change from agricultural occupations; m_6 for literacy; m_7 for per-capita income; and so on.

Our m_1 could then stand for the percentage of the population that had been exposed in any substantial way to significant aspects of modern life; m_2 for the

[4] Edward Shils, at the Social Science Research Council Conference on Comparative Politics.
[5] For a broader discussion of quantitative indicators, bearing on problems of this kind, see Karl W. Deutsch, "Toward an Inventory of Basic Trends and Patterns in Comparative and International Politics," *The American Political Science Review*, **54** (March 1960), 34.

percentage of those exposed to mass media, i.e., the mass media audience; m_3 for the percentage of the inhabitants who have changed their locality of residence (or their district, province or state); m_4 for the percentage of the total population living in towns; m_5 for the percentage of those in nonagricultural occupations among the total of those gainfully occupied; m_6 for the percentage of literates; m_7 could be measured simply by net national product, or alternatively by gross national product in dollars per capita. At this stage in the compilation of evidence the exact choice of indicators and definitions must be considerably influenced by the availability of statistical data. In many cases it may be most satisfactory to use the data and definitions published by the United Nations, in such volumes as the *United Nations Demographic Year Book*, the *United Nations World Social Survey*, the *United Nations Statistical Year Book*, and a host of more specialized UN publications.[6]

In a modern, highly developed and fully mobilized country m_7 should be above $600 gross national product per capita; m_1, m_2, and m_6 should all be well above 90 per cent; m_4 and m_5 should be above 50 per cent, even in countries producing large agricultural surpluses beyond their domestic consumption; and even m_3, the change of residence, seems to be higher than 50 per cent in such a country as the United States. In an extremely underdeveloped country, such as Ethiopia, m_7 is well below $100 and the remaining

[6] Cf. the pamphlets issued by the Statistical Office of the United Nations, Statistical Papers, Series K, No. 1, "Survey of Social Statistics," (Sales No.: 1954. **17**, 8), New York, 1954, and Statistical Papers, Series M, No. 11, Rev. 1, "List of Statistical Series collected by International Organizations," (Sales No.: 1955. **17**, 6), New York, 1955. For somewhat earlier data, see also W. S. Woytinsky and E. S. Woytinsky, *World Commerce and Governments: Trends and Outlook* (New York, The Twentieth Century Fund, 1955), and *World Population and Production: Trends and Outlook* (New York, The Twentieth Century Fund, 1953).

indicators may be near 5 per cent or even lower.

In the course of economic development, as countries are becoming somewhat less like Ethiopia and somewhat more like the United States, all these indicators tend to change in the same direction, even though they do not change at the same rate. They exhibit therefore to some extent a characteristic which Paul Lazarsfeld has termed the "interchangeability of indicators"; if one (or even several) of these indicators should be missing it could be replaced in many cases by the remaining ones, or by other indicators similarly chosen, and the general level and direction of the underlying social process would still remain clear.[7] This characteristic holds, however, only as a first approximation. The lags and discrepancies between the different indicators can reveal much of interest to the student of politics, and some of these discrepancies will be discussed below.

The first and main thing about social mobilization is, however, that it does assume a single underlying process of which particular indicators represent only particular aspects; that these indicators are correlated and to a limited extent interchangeable; and that this complex of processes of social change is significantly correlated with major changes in politics.

The overall index of social mobilization, M, is a second order index; it measures the correlation between the first order indices $m_1 \ldots m_n$. It should express, furthermore, the probability that the $(n+1)$th index will be similarly correlated with its predecessors, regardless of how large a number n might be provided, only that the index itself was appropriately chosen. Differently put, to assert that social mobilization is a "real" process, at certain times and in certain countries, is to assert that there exists for these cases a large and

[7] See Hortense Horwitz and Elias Smith, "The Interchangeability of Socio-Economic Indices," in Paul F. Lazarsfeld and Morris Rosenberg, *The Language of Social Research* (Glencoe, 1955), 73–77.

potentially unlimited number of possible measurements and indicators, all correlated with each other and testifying by their number and by the strength of their correlation to the reality of the underlying phenomenon.

In practice, of course, the range of available measurements and indicators is likely to be limited, and ordinarily there should be no need to compile for any particular time and country even all those data that could be found. On the contrary, one's usual aim will be economy: to get the greatest amount of useful information from the smallest body of data. The seven indicators of social mobilization listed above as m_1 to m_7 should quite suffice, in most cases, to give a fairly good first picture of the situation. They were chosen in part on grounds of availability and convenience, but also because they are less closely correlated, and hence less completely interchangeable, than some other indices might be.

Each of the seven processes chosen could itself be measured by several different indicators, but in each case these sub-indicators are apt to be very closely correlated and almost completely interchangeable. Literacy, for instance, can be measured as a percentage of the population above fifteen or above ten, or above seven years of age; it could be defined as the ability to recognize a few words, or to read consecutively, or to write. Each of these particular definitions would yield a different numerical answer, but so long as the same definition was used for each country, or for each period within the same country, each of these yardsticks would reveal much the same state of affairs. If applied to Morocco between 1920 and 1950, e.g., each of these tests would have shown how the number of literate Moroccans began to outgrow the number of literate Frenchmen in that country, with obvious implications for its political future.

Similarly, urbanization could be measured in terms of the population of all localities of more than 2000 or more than 5000, or more than 20,000 or 50,000 inhabitants; or it could be measured, less satisfactorily, in terms of the population of all those localities that had a charter or a city form of government. Each of these criteria of measurement would have revealed the same process of large-scale urban growth in Finland between 1870 and 1920, for instance, or in India between 1900 and 1940, which had such far-reaching effects on political life in these countries. A recent unpublished study by Frederick E. Tibbetts 3rd suggests once again the close interchangeability of different indicators of urban growth in Canada, as they bear upon the problems of assimilation and differentiation among the French-speaking and English-speaking population of that country. Urbanization, Tibbetts finds, has outstripped in recent decades the learning of English among French-Canadians; he finds among urban residents, and generally in nonagricultural occupations, a growing number of persons who speak no other language but French. The political significance of this development, which was largely concentrated in the province of Quebec, is highlighted by his observation that in 1951 Quebec (omitting Montreal), with 21 per cent of the total population of Canada, had only 4 and 7 per cent, respectively, of the veterans of World Wars I and II.[8]

Among the seven major indicators of social mobilization proposed in this paper, the correlations between economic development and literacy are less complete and the discrepancies more revealing. Ethiopia and Burma both have per-capita gross national products of about $50, but Ethiopia has less than 5 per cent literates and is politically stable; Burma reports

---

[8] Frederick E. Tibbetts 3rd, "The Cycles of Canadian Nationalism," Yale University, typescript, 1959, pp. 24, 26–31. For details of the Finnish and Indian cases referred to above, see K. W. Deutsch, *Nationalism and Social Communication* (New York, 1953), pp. 102–111, 170–182, 197–204.

over 45 per cent literates and is not.[9] Of the states of India, Kerala, with one of the highest rates of literacy, elected a Communist government in the late 1950's.

It may thus be useful to seek answers to two kinds of questions: (1) how good is the correlation between the seven main indicators and (2) how interesting are the variant cases? As regards the first question, it has already been pointed out that the numerical values of the seven main indicators will not be identical. However if we think of each of these indicators as forming a separate scale, on which each country could rank anywhere from, say, the top fifth to the bottom fifth, then we could measure the extent to which the rankings of a country on each of these indicator scales are correlated. From general impressions of the data, I should surmise that these rank order correlations should have coefficients of correlation of about 0.6 to 0.8, accounting on the average for perhaps one-half of the observed variation. As regards the second question, each of the cases showing substantial discrepancies between some of the main indicators will have to be studied separately, but the examples of Burma and Kerala, just mentioned, suggest that such cases may well repay investigation, and that the comparison of indicators may serve political scientists as a crude but perhaps useful research device.

For a somewhat more refined study the notion of two thresholds may be introduced. The first of these is the threshold of significance, S, that is, the numerical value below which no significant departure from the customary workings of a traditional society can be detected and no significant disturbance appears to be created in its unchanged functioning. For each of the particular indicators, m_1 through m_7, we should expect to find a corresponding particular threshold of signi-

ficance, s_1 through s_7; and our concept of social mobilization should imply that once several major indicators move to or beyond this threshold of significance, the remaining indicators should also be at or above their respective levels of significance. The probability that this will be in fact the case should indicate once again what degree of reality, if any, may be inherent in the concept of social mobilization as an overall process.

The second threshold would be that of criticality for significant changes in the side effects, actual or apparent, of the process of social mobilization. At what level of each of the indicators we listed above do such changes in social or political side effects appear?

The indicator of literacy may serve as an example. It has often been remarked that even a considerable advance in literacy, say from 10 per cent to 60 per cent of the population above fifteen years of age, does not seem to be correlated with any significant change in the birthrate, if one compares literacy and birthrate levels of a large number of countries in the 1950's. At the level of 80 per cent literacy, however, there appears a conspicuous change: for the same collection of countries, not one with a literacy rate above 80 per cent has a birthrate above 3 per cent a year.[10] As a provisional hypothesis for further testing, one might conjecture that a literacy rate of more than 80 per cent might indicate such an advanced and thoroughgoing stage of social mobilization and modernization as to influence even those intimate patterns of family life that find their expression in the birthrate of a country. Obviously such a hypothesis would require other evidence for confirmation, but even in its quite tentative stage it may illustrate our point. If it were true, then the 80 per cent level would be a threshold of criticality on the particular

---

[9] Note however, the comment on Burmese literacy, in the Appendix to this article, below.

[10] Rosemary Klineberg, "Correlation of Literacy Rates with 1956 Birth Rates," Fletcher School of Law and Diplomacy, 1959, unpublished.

scale of literacy as an indicator of social mobilization.

Since we called the indicator of literacy m_6, we might write c_6 for the particular threshold of criticality on that scale and put it as equal to 80 per cent. It would then be a matter for further investigation to find out whether other critical changes also occur near the passing of the 80 per cent literacy level. If so, c_6 might turn out to be the main threshold of criticality for this indicator. If important side effects should show critical changes at different literacy levels, we might have to assume several thresholds of criticality, which we might write c_6', c_6'', and so on.

Other indicators might well have their own thresholds of criticality at other percentage points on their particular scales. It might turn out, for instance, that most of the countries with more than 80 per cent literacy were also more than, say, 40 per cent urban, and that the apparent side effects observable above the 80 per cent literacy mark were also observable above the 40 per cent level on the urbanization scale. If such different but correlated thresholds of criticality could be found for all of our seven indicators, then the concept of social mobilization could be expressed as a probability that, if for some country n different indicators should show values equal to or greater than their respective critical levels, then any relevant $(n+1)$th indicator also would turn out to be at or above its own critical threshold.

Much of what has been said thus far may be summarized in concise notation. If we write P as the conventional symbol for probability, M_S as the symbol for the overall process of social mobilization in regard to the thresholds of significance, and M_C as the symbol for the same process in regard to the thresholds of criticality, then we may write the general concept of social mobilization briefly as follows:

1. $M_S = P$ (if $m_n \leqslant s_n$, then $m_{n+1} \leqslant s_{n+1}$) or briefly,
$$M_S = P \ (m_n \leqslant s_n)$$

and

2. $M_C = P$ (if $m_n \leqslant c_n$, then $m_{n+1} \leqslant c_{n+1}$) or briefly,
$$M_C = (m_n \leqslant c_n)$$
and perhaps also

3. $M = P \ (M_S = M_C)$

None of these shorthand formulas should require further comment here. They merely summarize what has been said at greater length in the preceding pages. Readers who find such formulations uncongenial may skip them, therefore, without loss, so long as they have followed the verbal argument.

Some Implications for the Politics of Development

In whatever country it occurs, social mobilization brings with it an expansion of the politically relevant strata of the population. These politically relevant strata are a broader group than the elite: they include all those persons who must be taken into account in politics. Dock workers and trade union members in Ghana, Nigeria, or the United States, for instance, are not necessarily members of the elites of these countries, but they are quite likely to count for something in their political life. In the developing countries of Asia, Africa, and parts of Latin America, the political process usually does not include the mass of isolated, subsistence-farming, tradition-bound and politically apathetic villagers, but it does include increasingly the growing numbers of city dwellers, market farmers, users of money, wage earners, radio listeners and literates in town and country. The growth in the numbers of these people produces mounting pressures for the transformation of political practices and institutions, and since this future growth can be estimated at least to some extent on the basis of trends and data from the recent past, some of the expectable growth in political pressures—we may call it the potential level of political tensions—can likewise be estimated.

Social mobilization also brings about a change in the quality of politics, by changing the range of human needs that impinge upon the political process. As people are uprooted from their physical and intellectual isolation in their immediate localities, from their old habits and traditions, and often from their old patterns of occupation and places of residence, they experience drastic changes in their needs. They may now come to need provisions for housing and employment, for social security against illness and old age, for medical care against the health hazards of their crowded new dwellings and places of work and the risk of accidents with unfamiliar machinery. They may need succor against the risks of cyclical or seasonal unemployment, against oppressive charges of rent or interest, and against sharp fluctuations in the prices of the main commodities which they must sell or buy. They need instruction for themselves and education for their children. They need, in short, a wide range and large amounts of new government services.

These needs ordinarily cannot be met by traditional types of government, inherited from a precommercial and preindustrial age. Maharajahs, sultans, sheikhs, and chieftains all are quite unlikely to cope with these new problems, and traditional rule by land-owning oligarchies or long-established religious bodies most often is apt to prove equally disappointing in the face of the new needs. Most of the attempts to change the characteristics of the traditional ruling families—perhaps by supplying them with foreign advisers or by having their children study in some foreign country—are likely to remain superficial in their effects, overshadowed by mounting pressures for more thoroughgoing changes.

In developing countries of today, however, the increasingly ineffective and unpopular traditional authorities cannot be replaced successfully by their historic successors in the Western world, the classic institutions of eighteenth and nineteenth-century liberalism and *laissez-faire*. For the uprooted, impoverished and disoriented masses produced by social mobilization, it is surely untrue that that government is best that governs least. They are far more likely to need a direct transition from traditional government to the essentials of a modern welfare state. The developing countries of Asia, Africa and parts of Latin America may have to accomplish, therefore, within a few decades a process of political change which in the history of Western Europe and North America took at least as many generations; and they may have to accomplish this accelerated change almost in the manner of a jump, omitting as impractical some of the historic stages of transition through a period of near *laissez-faire* that occurred in the West.

The growing need for new and old government services usually implies persistent political pressures for an increased scope of government and a greater relative size of the government sector in the national economy. In the mid-1950's, the total government budget—national, regional and local—tended to amount to roughly 10 per cent of the gross national product in the very poor and poorly mobilized countries with annual per-capita gross national products at or below $100. For highly developed and highly mobilized countries, such as those with per-capita gross national products at or above $900, the corresponding proportion of the total government sector was about 30 per cent. If one drew only the crudest and most provisional inference from these figures, one might expect something like a 2.5 per cent shift of national income into the government sector for every $100 gain in per-capita gross national product in the course of economic development. It might be more plausible, however, to expect a somewhat more rapid expansion of the government sector during the earlier stages of economic development, but the elucidation of this entire problem—with all its obvious political implications—would require and reward a great deal more research.

The relationship between the total process of social mobilization and the growth of the national income, it should be recalled here, is by no means symmetrical. Sustained income growth is very unlikely without social mobilization, but a good deal of social mobilization may be going on even in the absence of per-capita income growth, such as occurs in countries with poor resources or investment policies, and with rapid population growth. In such cases, social mobilization still would generate pressures for an expansion of government services and hence of the government sector, even in a relatively stagnant or conceivably retrograde economy. Stopping or reversing in such cases the expansion of government or the process of social mobilization behind it—even if this could be done—hardly would make matters much better. The more attractive course for such countries might rather be to use the capabilities of their expanding governments so as to bring about improvements in their resources and investment policies, and an eventual resumption of economic growth. To what extent this has been, or could be, brought about in cases of this kind, would make another fascinating topic for study.

The figures just given apply, of course, only to non-Communist countries; the inclusion of Communist states would make the average in each class of government sectors higher. It would be interesting to investigate, however, whether and to what extent the tendency toward the relative expansion of the government sector in the course of social mobilization applies also, *mutatis mutandis*, to the Communist countries.

A greater scope of governmental services and functions requires ordinarily an increase in the capabilities of government. Usually it requires an increase in the numbers and training of governmental personnel, an increase in governmental offices and institutions, and a significant improvement in administrative organization and efficiency. A rapid process of social mobilization thus tends to generate major pressures for political and administrative reform. Such reforms may include notably both a quantitative expansion of the bureaucracy and its qualitative improvement in the direction of a competent civil service—even though these two objectives at times may clash.

Similar to its impact on this specific area of government, social mobilization tends to generate also pressures for a more general transformation of the political elite. It tends to generate pressures for a broadening and partial transformation of elite functions, of elite recruitment, and of elite communications. On all these counts, the old elites of traditional chiefs, village headmen, and local notables are likely to prove ever more inadequate; and political leadership may tend to shift to the new political elite of party or quasiparty organizations, formal or informal, legal or illegal, but always led by the new "marginal men" who have been exposed more or less thoroughly to the impact of modern education and urban life.

Something similar applies to elite communications. The more broadly recruited elites must communicate among themselves, and they must do so more impersonally and over greater distances. They must resort more often to writing and to paper work. At the same time they must direct a greater part of their communications output at the new political strata; this puts a premium on oratory and journalism, and on skill in the use of all mass media of communication. At the same time rapid social mobilization causes a critical problem in the communications intake of elites. It confronts them with the ever present risk of losing touch with the newly mobilized social strata which until recently still did not count in politics. Prime Minister Nehru's reluctance to take into account the strength and intensity of Mahratti sentiment in the language conflict of Bombay in the 1950's and his general tendency since the mid-1930's to underestimate the strength of communal and linguistic sentiment in India suggest the seriousness of this problem even for major democratic leaders.

The increasing numbers of the mobilized population, and the greater scope and urgency of their needs for political decisions and governmental services, tend to translate themselves, albeit with a time lag, into increased political participation. This may express itself informally through greater numbers of people taking part in crowds and riots, in meetings and demonstrations, in strikes and uprisings, or, less dramatically, as members of a growing audience for political communications, written or by radio, or finally as members of a growing host of organizations. While many of these organizations are ostensibly nonpolitical, such as improvement societies, study circles, singing clubs, gymnastic societies, agricultural and commercial associations, fraternal orders, workmen's benefit societies, and the like, they nevertheless tend to acquire a political tinge, particularly in countries where more open outlets for political activities are not available. But even where there are established political parties and elections, a network of seemingly nonpolitical or marginally political organizations serves an important political function by providing a dependable social setting for the individuals who have been partly or wholly uprooted or alienated from their traditional communities. Such organizations may serve at the same time as marshalling grounds for the entry of these persons into political life.

Where people have the right to vote, the effects of social mobilization are likely to be reflected in the electoral statistics. This process finds its expression both through a tendency towards a higher voting participation of those already enfranchised and through an extension of the franchise itself to additional groups of the population. Often the increase in participation amongst those who already have the right to vote precedes the enfranchisement of new classes of voters, particularly in countries where the broadening of the franchise is occurring gradually. Thus in Norway between 1830 and 1860, voting participation remained near the level of about 10 per cent of the adult male population; in the 1870's and 1880's this participation rose rapidly among the enfranchised voters, followed by extensions of the franchise, until by the year 1900, 40 per cent of the Norwegian men were actually voting. This process was accompanied by a transformation of Norwegian politics, the rise to power of the radical peasant party *Venstre*, and a shift from the earlier acceptance of the existing Swedish-Norwegian Union to rising demands for full Norwegian independence.[11] These political changes had been preceded or accompanied by a rise in several of the usual indicators of social mobilization among the Norwegian people.

Another aspect of the process of social mobilization is the shift of emphasis away from the parochialism and internationalism of many traditional cultures to a preoccupation with the supralocal but far less than worldwide unit of the territorial, and eventually national, state.

An as yet unpublished study of American communications before the American Revolution, which has been carried on by Richard Merritt, shows how during the years 1735–75 in the colonial newspapers the percentage of American or all-colonial symbols rose from about 10 to about 40 per cent, at the cost, in the main, of a decline in the share of symbols referring to places or events in the world outside the colonies and Britain, while Britain's share in American news attention remained relatively unchanged. Within the group of American symbols, the main increase occurred among those which referred to America or to the colonies as a whole, rather than among those referring to particular colonies or sections.[12]

[11] See Raymond Lindgren, *Norway-Sweden: Union, Disunion, Reunion* (Princeton, Princeton University Press, 1959); and K. W. Deutsch, *et al.*, *Political Community and the North Atlantic Area* (Princeton University Press, 1957).

[12] Richard Merritt's monograph, "Symbols of American Nationalism, 1735–1775," which is

More recent experiences in some of the "development countries" also suggest a more rapid rise of attention devoted to national topics than of that given to world affairs, on the one hand, and to purely local matters, on the other. This, however, is at present largely an impression. The nature and extent of attention shifts in mass media, as well as in popular attitudes, in the course of social mobilization is a matter for research that should be as promising as it is needed.[13]

Some data on the flow of domestic and foreign mails point in a similar direction. Of five development countries for which data are readily available the ratio of domestic to foreign mail rose substantially in four—Egypt, Iran, Nigeria, and Turkey —from 1913 to 1946–51; the fifth, Indonesia, was an exception but was the scene of internal unrest and protracted warfare against the Dutch during much of the latter period. The trend for Egypt, Iran, Nigeria, and Turkey is confirmed in each case by data for the intermediate period 1928–34, which are also intermediate, in each case, between the low domestic-foreign mail ratio for 1913 and the high ratios for 1946–51. Many additional development countries—including the Gold Coast (now Ghana), the Belgian Congo, Malaya, French Morocco, Kenya-Uganda, Tanganyika, Mozambique, and Malaya— for which data were found only for the 1928–34 to 1946–51 comparison, show upward trends in their ratios of domestic to foreign mail.[14] Here again, a relatively moderate investment in the further collec-

tion and study of data might lead to interesting results.

According to some data from another recent study, a further side effect of social mobilization and economic development might possibly be first a substantial expansion, and then a lesser but significant reduction, of the share of the international trade sector in the national economy. Thus, in the course of British development, the proportion of total foreign trade (including trade to British overseas possessions) rose from an average of 20 per cent in 1830– 40 to a peak of 60 per cent in 1870–79, remained close to that level until 1913, but declined subsequently and stood at less than 40 per cent in 1959. Similarly, the proportion of foreign trade to national income rose in Germany from about 28 per cent in 1802–30 to a peak of 45 per cent in 1870–79, declined to 35 per cent in 1900–09, and by 1957 had recovered, for the much smaller German Federal Republic, to only 42 per cent. In Japan, the early proportion of foreign trade to national income was 15 per cent in 1885–89, rising to peaks of 41 per cent in 1915–19 and 40 per cent in 1925–29; but by 1957 it stood at only 31 per cent. Data for Denmark, Norway, France, and Argentina give a similar picture, while the same foreign-trade-to-national-income ratio in the United States fell, with minor fluctuations, from 23 per cent in 1799 to less than 9 per cent in 1958.[15] Here again the evidence is incomplete and partly contradictory, and the tentative interpretation, indicated at the beginning of this paragraph, still stands in need of confirmation and perhaps modification through additional research.

to cover eventually one or more newspapers from Massachusetts, New York, Pennsylvania, and Virginia, respectively, will be published in due course.

[13] For examples of pioneering contributions of this kind, see the series of Hoover Institute Studies by Harold Lasswell, Ithiel Pool, Daniel Lerner, and others, and particularly Pool, *The Prestige Papers* (Stanford, Stanford University Press, 1951).

[14] See charts 1, 3, and 4 in Karl W. Deutsch, "Shifts in the Balance of Communication Flows: A Problem of Measurement in International Relations," *Public Opinion Quarterly*,

20 (Spring 1956), 152–155, based on data of the Universal Postal Union.

[15] See Karl W. Deutsch and Alexander Eckstein, "National Industrialization and the Declining Share of the International Economic Sector, 1890–1957," *World Politics*, **13** (January 1961), 267–299. See also Simon Kuznets, *Six Lectures on Economic Growth* (Glencoe, 1959), esp. the section on "The Problem of Size" and "Trends in Foreign Trade Ratios," 89–107.

The problem of the ratio of the sector of internationally oriented economic activities relative to total national income—and thus indirectly the problem of the political power potential of internationally exposed or involved interest groups vis-à-vis the rest of the community—leads us to the problem of the size of states and of the scale of effective political communities. As we have seen, the process of social mobilization generates strong pressures towards increasing the capabilities of government, by increasing the volume and range of demands made upon the government and administration, and by widening the scope of politics and the membership of the politically relevant strata. The same process increases the frequency and the critical importance of direct communications between government and governed. It thus necessarily increases the importance of the language, the media, and the channels through which these communications are carried on.

Other things assumed equal, the stage of rapid social mobilization may be expected, therefore, to promote the consolidation of states whose peoples already share the same language, culture, and major social institutions; while the same process may tend to strain or destroy the unity of states whose population is already divided into several groups with different languages or cultures or basic ways of life. By the same token, social mobilization may tend to promote the merging of several smaller states, or political units such as cantons, principalities, sultanates, or tribal areas, whose populations already share substantially the same language, culture, and social system; and it may tend to inhibit, or at least to make more difficult, the merging of states or political units whose populations or ruling personnel differ substantially in regard to any of these matters. Social mobilization may thus assist to some extent in the consolidation of the United Arab Republic, but raise increasing problems for the politics and administration of multilingual India—problems which the

federal government of India may have to meet or overcome by a series of creative adjustments.[16]

In the last analysis, however, the problem of the scale of states goes beyond the effects of language, culture, or institutions, important as all these are. In the period of rapid social mobilization, the acceptable scale of a political unit will tend to depend eventually upon its performance. If a government fails to meet the increasing burdens put upon it by the process of social mobilization, a growing proportion of the population is likely to become alienated and disaffected from the state, even if the same language, culture, and basic social institutions were shared originally throughout the entire state territory by rulers and ruled alike. The secession of the United States and of Ireland from the British Empire, and of the Netherlands and of Switzerland from the German Empire may serve in part as examples. At bottom, the popular acceptance of a government in a period of social mobilization is most of all a matter of its capabilities and the manner in which they are used—that is, essentially a matter of its responsiveness to the felt needs of its population. If it proves persistently incapable or unresponsive, some or many of its subjects will cease to identify themselves with it psychologically; it will be reduced to ruling by force where it can no longer rule by display, example, and persuasion; and if political alternatives to it appear, it will be replaced eventually by other political units, larger or smaller in extent, which at least promise to respond more effectively to the needs and expectations of their peoples.

[16] For more detailed arguments, see Deutsch, *Nationalism and Social Communication*, and Deutsch, *et al.*, *Political Community and the North Atlantic Area;* see also the discussions in Ernst B. Haas, "Regionalism, Functionalism and Universal Organization," *World Politics*, **8** (January 1956), and "The Challenge of Regionalism," *International Organization*, **12** (1958), 440–458; and in Stanley Hoffmann, *Contemporary Theory in International Relations* (Englewood Cliffs, N.J., Prentice-Hall, 1960), 223–240.

In practice the results of social mobilization often have tended to increase the size of the state, well beyond the old tribal areas, petty principalities, or similar districts of the traditional era, while increasing the direct contact between government and governed far beyond the levels of the sociologically superficial and often half-shadowy empire of the past.

This growth in the size of modern states, capable of coping with the results of social mobilization, is counteracted and eventually inhibited, however, as their size increases, by their tendency to increasing preoccupation with their own internal affairs. There is considerable evidence for this trend toward a self-limitation in the growth of states through a decline in the attention, resources, and responsiveness available for coping with the implicit needs and explicit messages of the next marginal unit of population and territory on the verge of being included in the expanding state.[17]

The remarks in this section may have sufficed to illustrate, though by no means to exhaust, the significance of the process of social mobilization in the economic and political development of countries. The main usefulness of the concept, however, should lie in the possibility of quantitative study which it offers. How much social mobilization, as measured by our seven indicators, has been occurring in some country per year or per decade during some period of its history, or during recent times? And what is the meaning of the differences between the rates at which some of the constituent subprocesses of social mobilization may have been going on? Although specific data will have to be found separately for each country, it should be possible to sketch a general quantitative model to show some of the interrelations and their possible significance.

[17] Cf. Karl W. Deutsch, "The Propensity to International Transactions," *Political Studies*, **8** (June 1960), 147–155.

A Quantitative Model of the Social Mobilization Process

For a quantitative description, it is convenient to express our first six indicators not in terms of the total percentage of the population which is literate, or exposed to modern life, etc., but in terms only of that average annual percentage of the total population which has been added to, or subtracted from, the total share of the population in that category. If for some country our indicator showed, say, 40 per cent exposed to significant aspects of modern life in 1940, and 60 per cent so exposed in 1950, the average annual percentage shift, dm_1 would be 2 per cent. The seventh indicator, per-capita increase, may be broken up into two elements and written as the annual percentage of the total income added, dm_7 and the annual percentage of population growth, p.

Adopting these conventions, we may use in this model, for purposes of illustration, crudely estimated magnitudes from various collections of data. If we add indicators for the increase in voting participation, and in linguistic, cultural or political assimilation, we may write for a case of fairly rapid social mobilization a small table of the sort shown in Table 1. The case represented by this table is an imaginary one, but the different rates of subprocesses of social mobilization are not necessarily unrealistic, and neither are the consequences suggested by this model, for the stability of the government in any country to which these or similar assumptions would apply.

Before discussing these consequences more explicitly, it should be made clear that the annual rates of change are likely to be realistic, at most, only for countries during the rapid middle stages of the process of social mobilization and economic development—say, for a range of between 10 and 80 per cent literacy and for analogous ranges of other indicators of economic development. In the earliest stages, the annual percentages of the population shifting into a more mobilized

TABLE 1. *A Hypothetical Example of a Country Undergoing Rapid Social Mobilization: Rates of Changes*

SYMBOL OF INDICATOR	DESCRIPTION	AVERAGE ANNUAL % OF TOTAL POPULATION OR INCOME ADDED TO CATEGORY	
		RANGE	MEDIAN
Group I: dm_1	Shift into any substantial exposure to modernity, incl. rumors, demonstrations of machinery or merchandise, etc.	2.0 to 4.0	3.0
dm_2	Shift into mass media audience (radio, movies, posters, press)	1.5 to 4.0	2.75
dm_8	Increase in voting participation	0.2 to 4.0	2.1
dm_6	Increase in literacy	1.0 to 1.4	1.2
dm_3	Change of locality of residence	1.0 to 1.5	1.25
p	Population growth	(1.9 to 3.3)	(2.6)
Group II: dm_5	Occupational shift out of agriculture	0.4 to 1.0	0.7
dm_4	Change from rural to urban residence	0.1 to 1.2	0.5
a	Linguistic, cultural or political assimilation	−0.5 to 1.0	0.25
dy	Income growth	(2.0 to 8.0)	(5.0)
dm_7	Income growth per capita	—	(2.3)

Note. Figures in parentheses refer to percentage increases against the previous year, and thus are not strictly comparable to percentage shifts among sub-categories of the total population. A shift of 1.2 per cent of all adults into the category of literates, for instance, would refer to the total adult population, including the part just added by population aging; etc.

state are apt to be much smaller, and in the late stages of the process something like a "ceiling effect" may be expected to appear—once 80 or 90 per cent of the population have become literate, any further annual gains in the percentage of literates in the population are likely to be small.

Within the middle stages of development, however, which are appropriate to the assumptions of the model, a cumulative strain on political stability may be expected. All the rates of change in group I tend to make for increased demands or burdens upon the government, and all of them have median values above 1 per cent per year. The rates of change in group II are related to the capabilities of the

government for coping with these burdens, but the median values of all these rates, with only one exception, are well below 1 per cent. If it were not for this exception—the assumed 5 per cent annual increase in national income—one would have to predict from the model an annual shift of perhaps 1 per cent or more of the population into the category of at least partly socially mobilized but largely unassimilated and dissatisfied people.

If one assumes, in accordance with this model, an annual entry of 2.75 per cent of the population into the mass media audience and a shift of only 0.6 per cent into nonagricultural employment, then the expectable increase in the numbers of not adequately reemployed new members of the mass media audience might be as high as 2.15 per cent of the population per year, or more than one-fifth of the population within a decade. This might be the proportion of people newly participating in their imagination in the new opportunities and attractions of modern life, while still being denied most or all of these new opportunities in fact—something which should be a fairly effective prescription for accumulating political trouble. The spread of more effective methods of production and perhaps of improved patterns of land tenure, rural credit, and other betterments within the agricultural sector could do something to counteract this tendency; but short of major and sustained efforts at such agricultural improvements the dangerous gap between the fast-growing mass media audience and the slow-growing circle of more adequately employed and equipped persons is likely to remain and to increase.

If linguistic, cultural or political assimilation—that is, the more or less permanent change of stable habits of language, culture, legitimacy, and loyalty—is also a relevant problem in the country concerned, then the lag of the slow assimilation rate, put at only 0.25 per cent per year in our model, behind the far more rapid mobilization rates of 0.5 to 3.0 per cent for the various subprocesses in our model, might be even larger for some of them, and potentially more serious.

Table 2 shows some of the implications of our model for a hypothetical country of 10 million population, $100 per-capita income, a principal language spoken by 35 per cent of its inhabitants, and a relatively low degree of social mobilization in 1950. Conditions somewhat similar to these can in fact be found in several countries in Africa and Asia. Table 2 then shows the expectable state of affairs for our imaginary country in 1960 and 1970, if

TABLE 2. *A Hypothetical Example of a Country Undergoing Rapid Social Mobilization: Assumed Levels for 1950 and Expectable Levels for 1960 and 1970*

SYMBOL OF INDICATOR	DESCRIPTION	PER CENT OF TOTAL POPULATION		
		1950	1960	1970
Group I: m_1	Population exposed to modernity	35	65	95
m_2	Mass media audience	20	47.5	75
m_8	Actual voting participation	20	41	62
m_6	Literates	15	27	39
m_3	Persons who changed locality of residence since birth	10	22.5	35
P	Total population (millions)	(10)	(12.9)	(16.7)
Group II: m_5	Population in non-agricultural occupations	18	25	32
m_4	Urban population	15	20	25
A	Linguistically assimilated population	35	35.5	40
Y	Total income (million $)	(1000)	(1629)	(2653)
m_7	Per capita income ($)	(100)	(126)	(159)

Note. Figures in parentheses refer to absolute numbers, not percentages. Because of rounding, calculations are approximate.

we assume the rates of change given in our model, as set forth in Table 1, and their persistence over twenty years. As can be seen from Table 2, the cumulative effects of these changes from 1950 to 1960 will appear still moderate, but by 1970 these effects will have become so great that many of the political institutions and practices of 1950 might be no longer applicable to the new conditions.

As Table 2 shows, a major transformation of the underlying political and social structure of a country could occur—and could pose a potential threat to the stability of any insufficiently reform-minded government there—even during a period of substantially rising per-capita income.

To be sure, many of these political and social difficulties could be assuaged with the help of the benefits potentially available through the 5 per cent increase in total national income, which was assumed for our model. Such a 5 per cent growth rate of total income is not necessarily unrealistic. It is close to the average of 5.3 per cent, found by Paul Studenski in a recent survey of data from a large number of non-Communist countries.[18] Since the rate of population growth, assumed for the model, was 2.6 per cent—which is well above the world average in recent years— the average per-capita income might be expected to rise by slightly more than 2 per cent per year.[19] These additional amounts of available income might well go at least some part of the way to meet the new popular needs and expectations aroused by the mobilization process, if the income can be devoted to consumption and price levels remain stable. But any incre-

[18] Cf. Paul Studenski, *The Income of Nations* (New York, New York University Press, 1958), p. 249; cf. also pp. 244–250.
[19] Cf. United Nations, Department of Social and Economic Affairs, Population Studies No. 28, "The Future Growth of World Population" (New York, 1958), and United Nations, Bureau of Social Affairs, *Report of the World Social Situation* (Sales No.: 1957, **4**, 3) (New York, 1957), p. 5.

ments of income will also be needed for savings (in addition to loans and grants from abroad) to permit a high rate of investment and an adequate rate of expansion of opportunities for education, employment, and consumption for the growing numbers of the mobilized population.

These beneficial consequences could only be expected, however, if we assume that an adequate share of the increase in income would go directly or indirectly to the newly mobilized groups and strata of the population. Unfortunately, no assumption of this kind would be realistic for many of the developing countries of Asia and Africa.

It would be far more realistic to assume that in most of these countries the top 10 per cent of income receivers are getting about 50 per cent of the total national income, if not more. If we assume further, as seems not implausible, that in the absence of specific social reforms the increase in income will be distributed among the various strata of the population roughly in proportion to the present share of each group in the total national income, then we may expect that the richest 10 per cent of the people will get about 50 per cent of the additional income produced by income growth. At the same time, since these richest 10 per cent are not likely to be much more fertile than the rest of the population, they are likely to get only 10 per cent of the population increase; and they will, therefore, on the average not only get richer in absolute terms, but they will also retain the full extent of their relative lead over the rest of the population; and so they will increase in absolute terms the gap in income that separates them from the mass of their countrymen. Under the same assumptions, however, we should expect that the poorest nine-tenths of the population will get only one-tenth of total income gain, but that they will get up to nine-tenths of the entire population growth; and that on the average these poorest 90 per cent of the people will remain in relative terms as far below the level of the rich one-tenth as ever. The fact that the poorer majority will have become slightly richer in absolute terms may then in the main increase their awareness of the wide gap between their living standards and those of their rulers; and it might at the same time increase their ability to take political action.

Differently put, if for the entire country the *average* per-capita income was assumed to rise, we must now add that under the assumptions stated, the "social gap"— the gap between the incomes of the poorest 90 per cent and those of the top 10 per cent—may well be expected to increase. Political stability, however, may well be more affected by changes in the income gap than by changes in the average which in this respect might be little more than a statistical abstraction. Our model would lead us to expect, therefore, on the whole the danger of a significant deterioration of political stability in any development country to which its assumptions might apply. Since these assumptions were chosen with an eye to making them parallel, as far as possible, to the more rapid among the actual rates found in countries of this type, the expectations of rising political tensions in countries undergoing rapid social mobilization may not be unrealistic.

To rely upon automatic developments in economic and political life in those countries of the Free World to which the assumptions of our model apply, would be to court mounting instability, the overthrow of existing governments and their replacement by no less unstable successors, or else their eventual absorption into the Communist bloc. Deliberate political and economic intervention into the social mobilization process, on the other hand, might open up some more hopeful perspectives. Such intervention should not aim at retarding economic and social development, in the manner of the policies of the regime of Prince Metternich in Austria during much of the first half of the nineteenth century. Those policies of

slowing down social mobilization and economic development in the main only diminished the capabilities of the government, paved the way to domestic failures and international defeats and were followed over the course of three generations by the persistent backwardness and ultimate destruction of the state. A more promising policy might have to be, on the contrary, one of active intervention in favor of more rapid and more balanced growth; a somewhat more even distribution of income, related more closely to rewards for productive contributions rather than for status and inheritance; the more productive investment of available resources; and a sustained growth in the political and administrative capabilities of government and of ever wider strata of the population.

The crude model outlined above may have some modest usefulness in surveying and presenting in quantitative terms some of the magnitudes and rates of change that would be relevant for understanding the basic problems of such a more constructive policy in developing countries.[20] Somewhat as the economic models of the late Lord Keynes drew attention to the need of keeping the national rates of spending and investment in a country in balance with the national propensity to save, so it may become possible some day for political scientists to suggest in what areas, in what respects, and to what extent the efforts of government will have to be kept abreast of the burdens generated by the processes of social mobilization. The first steps toward this distant goal might be taken through

[20] For other highly relevant approaches to these problems, see Almond and Coleman, eds., *The Politics of the Developing Areas*, esp. the discussion by Almond on pp. 58–64. The problem of rates of change and their acceleration is discussed explicitly by Coleman, *ibid.*, pp. 536–558. While this work presented extensive data on levels of development, it did not take the further step of using explicit quantitative rates of change, which would be needed for the type of dynamic and probabilistic models that seem implicit in the long-range predictions of the authors, as set forth on pp. 58–64, 535–544.

research which would replace the hypothetical figures of the model by actual data from specific countries, so that the model could be tested, revised, and advanced nearer toward application.

Any cooperation which social scientists and other students of cultural, political, and economic development and change could extend to this effort—by improving the design of the model or by suggesting more precise or refined definitions of some of its categories, or by furnishing specific data—would be very much appreciated.

APPENDIX

A GLANCE AT ACTUAL CASES: PARTIAL DATA FOR 19 COUNTRIES

(with the assistance of Charles L. Taylor and Alex Weilenmann)

The following data, presented in Tables 3 to 5, have been compiled or computed, respectively, in order to illustrate the possibility, in principle, of the kind of analysis proposed in the main body of this paper, and to demonstrate the availability

TABLE 3-A. *Selected Indices of Social Mobilization for Nineteen Countries: Aggregate Levels*

COUNTRY	(1) GNP PER CAPITA (1955) US $	(2) GNP (1955) MILLION US $	(3) POPULATION (1953, 1958) 1,000	(4) RADIO AUDIENCE %	(5) NEWSPAPER READERS %	(6) LITERATES %	(7) WORK FORCE IN NON-AGRIC. OCCUPATIONS %	(8) URBAN POPULATION %
Venezuela	762	4,400	5,440 6,320	12.8 ('48) 48.9 ('57)	— 30.6 ('56)	43.5 ('41) 51.0 ('50)	50 ('41) 59 ('50)	39 ('41) 50 ('50)
Argentina	374	7,150	18,400 20,248	51.2 ('50) 65.0 ('59)	— 54.0 ('58)	69.4 ('14) 86.7 ('47)	75 ('47) 77 ('55)	53 ('14) 63 ('47)
Cuba	361	2,180	5,829 6,466	42.7 ('49) 59.3 ('59)	— 38.7 ('56)	71.8 ('31) 76.4 ('53)	59 ('43) 58 ('53)	50 ('43) 57 ('53)
Colombia	330	4,180	12,111 13,522	17.6 ('50) 24.7 ('56)	— 17.7 ('58)	55.8 ('38) 61.5 ('51)	28 ('38) 46 ('51)	29 ('38) 36 ('51)
Turkey	276	6,463	22,850 25,932	4.8 ('48) 17.6 ('59)	— 9.6 ('52)	20.9 ('35) 34.3 ('50)	18 ('35) 23.('55)	24 ('40) 25 ('50)
Brazil	262	15,315	55,772 65,725	19.2 ('50) 25.5 ('58)	— 18.9 ('57)	43.3 ('40) 48.4 ('50)	33 ('40) 42 ('50)	31 ('40) 37 ('50)
Philippines	201	4,400	21,211 24,010	1.6 ('49) 5.2 ('57)	— 5.7 ('56)	48.8 ('39) 61.3 ('48)	27 ('39) 43 ('58)	23 ('39) 24 ('48)
Mexico	187	5,548	28,056 32,348	11.4 ('48) 34.6 ('58)	— 14.4 ('52)	48.4 ('40)[a] 56.8 ('50)[a]	35 ('40) 42 ('58)	35 ('40) 43 ('50)
Chile	180	1,220	6,437 7,298	36.9 ('49) 38.4 ('58)	— 22.2 ('52)	71.8 ('40) 80.6 ('52)	65 ('40) 70 ('52)	52 ('40)[b] 60 ('52)[b]
Guatemala	179	580	3,058 3,546	2.8 ('50) 4.6 ('54)	— 6.6 ('58)	34.6 ('40)[a] 29.7 ('50)[a]	29 ('40) 32 ('50)	27 ('21) 32 ('50)
Honduras	137	228	1,556 1,828	5.9 ('48) 7.2 ('57)	— 7.5 ('57)	32.6 ('35)[a] 35.2 ('50)[a]	17 ('50) 16 ('56)	29 ('45) 31 ('50)
Ghana	135	624	4,478 4,836	0.8 ('48) 8.9 ('59)	— 11.4 ('58)	20–25 ('50) 	— —	— —
Egypt	133	3,065	22,003 24,781	4.8 ('49) 13.2 ('57)	— 7.5 ('52)	14.8 ('37) 22.1 ('47)	29 ('37) 36 ('47)	25 ('37) 30 ('47)
Thailand	100	2,050	19,556 21,474	0.5 ('50) 1.6 ('58)	— 1.2 ('52)	52.0 ('47) 64.0 ('56)	11 ('37) 12 ('54)	 10 ('47)
Republic of the Congo (Leopoldville)	98	1,639	12,154 13,559	0.2 ('48) 1.0 ('59)	— 0.9 ('57)	35–40 ('50) 	— 15 ('55)	 16 ('47)
India	72	27,400	372,623 397,390	0.3 ('48) 1.6 ('59)	— 2.7 ('58)	9.1 ('31)[c] 15.1 ('41)[c] 19.9 ('51)	29 ('51) 30 ('55)	11 ('31)[c] 13 ('41)[c] 17 ('51)
Nigeria	70	2,250	30,104 33,052	0.2 ('48) 1.0 ('58)	— 2.4 ('58)	11.5 ('52/3) —	26 ('31) —	4 ('31) 5 ('52)
Pakistan	56	4,560	80,039 85,635	0.3 ('50) 1.2 ('58)	— 2.7 ('54)	9.1 ('31)[c] 15.1 ('41)[c] 13.5 ('51)[a]	24 ('51) 35 ('54/6)	11 ('31)[c] 13 ('41)[c] 11 ('51)
Burma	52	1,012	19,272 20,255	0.2 ('48) 0.5 ('56)	— 2.4 ('52)	40.2 ('31) 57.3 ('54)	32 ('31) 30 ('55)	10 ('31)

[a] Unequal age groups.
[b] Variation of definition of "urban."
[c] Applies to prepartition India, i.e., to India and Pakistan together.

TABLE 3-B. *Selected Indices of Social Mobilization for Nineteen Countries: Aggregate Levels: Projected for 1945 and 1955*

COUNTRY		(4) RADIO AUDIENCE %	(6) LITERATES %	(7) WORK FORCE IN NON-AGRIC. OCCUPATIONS %	(8) URBAN POPULATION %	(9) EXPOSURE TO MODERNITY %
Venezuela	'45	1	47	54	44	63
	'55	41	55	64	56	75
Argentina	'45	44	85	74	62	>95
	'55	59	92	77	65	>95
Cuba	'45	36	75	59	51	83
	'55	52	77	58	58	84
Colombia	'45	12	59	38	33	60
	'55	22	63	52	38	72
Turkey	'45	1	30	21	24	34
	'55	13	39	23	26	40
Brazil	'45	15	46	37	34	52
	'55	23	51	46	40	61
Philippines	'45	0	57	32	24	56
	'55	4	71	41	25	70
Mexico	'45	4	52	37	39	57
	'55	28	61	41	37	64
Chile	'45	36	75	67	56	89
	'55	38	83	71	62	>95
Guatemala	'45	1	32	31	31	40
	'55	5	27	34	33	42
Honduras	'45	6	35	18	29	40
	'55	7	36	16	33	43
Ghana	'45	0	—	—	—	—
	'55	6	—	—	—	21[b] (1950/58)
Egypt	'45	1	20	35	29	40
	'55	11	28	42	34	47
Thailand	'45	0	49	12	—	38
	'55	1	63	12	—	47
Republic of the Congo (Leopoldville)	'45	0	—	—	—	—
	'55	1	—	—	—	33[b] (1947/50)
India	'45	0	18[a]	27	14[a]	28[c]
	'55	1	24[a]	30	16[a]	34[c]
Nigeria	'45	0	—	—	5	—
	'55	1	—	—	5	23[b] (1931/53)
Pakistan	'45	0	18[a]	7	14[a]	20[c]
	'55	1	24[a]	35	16[a]	37[c]
Burma	'45	0	50	31	—	50
	'55	0	58	30	—	55

Data in Columns 4, 6, 7, 8 based on corresponding data in Tables 3-A and 4-A.

Data in Column 9 are 125 per cent of means of the two highest figures in each of the other columns.

[a] Prepartition India.

[b] Based on the two highest data for country in Table 3-A.

[c] No distinction made between prepartition India and India and Pakistan respectively.

TABLE 4-A. *Selected Indices of Social Mobilization for Nineteen Countries: Shifts and Rates of Growth*

COUNTRY	LEVEL (1) PER-CAPITA GNP (1955) US $	AVERAGE ANNUAL RATES OF GROWTH (2) TOTAL GDP (1954–58) %	(3) POPULATION (1953–58) %	(4) PER-CAPITA GDP (1954–58) %	AVERAGE ANNUAL SHIFTS (5) RADIO AUDIENCE %	(6) LITERATE POPULATION %	(7) WORK FORCE IN NON-AGRIC. OCCUPATIONS %	(8) URBAN POPULATION %	(9)* POPULATION EXPOSED TO MODERNITY %
Venezuela	762	(8.8)	(3.0)	(7.5)	4.0 (1948–57)	0.8 (1941–50)	1.0 (1941–50)	1.2 (1941–50)	1.2 / 3.2 / 2.2
Argentina	374	(2.4)	(1.9)	(0.5)	1.5 (1950–59)	0.7 (1914–47)	0.3 (1947–55)	0.3 (1914–47)	0.0 / 1.4 / 0.7
Cuba	361	(3)a (1957–60)	(1.9)	(1.1)c (1957–60)	1.7 (1957–60)	0.2 (1949–59)	−0.1 (1931–53)	0.7 (1943–53)	0.1 / 1.5 / 0.8
Colombia	330	(3.1)	(2.2)	(0.8)	1.2 (1950–56)	0.4 (1938–51)	1.4 (1938–51)	0.6 (1938–51)	1.2 / 1.6 / 1.4
Turkey	276	(8.1)	(2.7)	(5.2)	1.2 (1948–59)	0.9 (1935–50)	0.3 (1935–55)	0.1 (1945–50)	0.6 / 1.3 / 1.0
Brazil	262	(6.4)	(2.4)	(4.0)	0.8	0.5 (1950–58)	0.8 (1940–50)	0.5 (1940–50)	0.9 / 1.0 / 1.0
Philippines	201	(4.8)	(2.5)	(2.2)	0.5 (1949–57)	1.4 (1939–48)	0.8 (1939–58)	0.1 (1939–48)	1.4 / 1.4 / 1.4
Mexico	187	(4)a (1957–60)	(2.9)	(1.1)c (1957–60)	2.3 (1948–58)	0.8e (1940–50)	0.4 (1940–58)	0.8 (1940–50)	0.7 / 1.9 / 1.3
Chile	180	(2.0)	(2.5)	(−0.6)	0.2 (1949–58)	0.7 (1940–52)	0.4 (1940–52)	0.7f (1940–52)	0.6 / 0.9 / 0.8
Guatemala	179	(8.3)	(3.0)	(5.2)	0.4 (1950–54)	−0.5e (1940–50)	0.3 (1940–50)	0.2 (1921–50)	0.2 / 0.4 / 0.3
Honduras	137	(6.6) (1954–57)	(3.3)	(3.2) (1954–57)	0.1 (1948–57)	0.2c (1935–50)	−0.2 (1950–56)	0.4 (1945–50)	0.3 / 0.4 / 0.4
Ghana	135	(3)a (1957–60)	(1.6)	(1.4)c (1957–60)	0.7 (1948–59)	—	—	—	— / 0.9
Egypt	133	(2.1) (1954–56)	(2.4)	(−0.3) (1954–56)	1.0 (1949–57)	0.7 (1937–47)	0.7 (1937–47)	0.5 (1937–47)	0.7 / 1.0 / 0.8
Thailand	100	(3.1)b (1950–54)	(1.9)	(1.2)d (1950–54)	0.1 (1950–58)	1.3 (1947–56)	0.1 (1937–54)	—	0.9 / 0.9 / 0.9
Rep. of the Congo (Leopoldville)	98	(1.7)	(2.2)	(−0.8)	0.1 (1948–59)	—	—	—	— / 0.1
India	72	(3.3)	(1.3)	(1.9)	0.1 (1948–59)	0.6g (1931–41)	0.3 (1951–55)	0.2g (1931–41)	0.6h / 0.6h / 0.6
Nigeria	70	(4)a (1957–60)	(1.9)	(2.1)c (1957–60)	0.1 (1948–58)	—	—	(1931–52)	— / 0.1
Pakistan	56	(1.8)b (1950–54)	(1.4)	(0.4)d (1950–54)	0.1 (1950–58)	0.6g (1931–41)	2.8 (1951–54/6)	0.2g (1931–41)	1.7h / 2.1h / 1.9
Burma	52	(3.8)	(1.0)	(2.8)	0.0 (1948–56)	0.7 (1931–54)	−0.1 (1931–55)	—	0.5 / 0.4 / 0.4

* In each box of Column 9, the first figure is based on the levels in Table 3-B, Column 9; the second figure is based on the two largest shifts for country (Columns 5–8, this table), and the third figure is the average of the two preceding figures in the box.
ª Growth in GNP.
ᵇ Growth in national income.
ᶜ Growth in per-capita income.
ᵉ Based on unequal age groups.
ᶠ Variation in definition of "urban."
ᵍ Applied to prepartition India, i.e. to India and Pakistan together.
ʰ No distinction made between prepartition India and India and Pakistan respectively.

TABLE 4-B. *Selected Indices of Social Mobilization for Nineteen Countries: Averages in Shifts and Rates of Growth*

	LEVEL	AVERAGE ANNUAL RATES OF GROWTH			AVERAGE ANNUAL SHIFTS				
	(1)	(2)	(3)	(4)	(5)	(6)	(7) POPULA-TION EN-GAGED IN NON-AGRI-CULTURAL OCCUPA-TIONS %	(9)	(9)[a]
RANGE (ACC'D. TO PER-CAPITA GNP) US $	PER-CAPITA (1955) US $	TOTAL GDP[b] %	TOTAL POPULA-TION %	GDP PER CAPITA %	RADIO AUDIENCE %	LITERATE POPULA-TION %		URBAN POPULA-TION %	POPULA-TION EX-POSED TO MODERN-ITY %
400+ (N = 1)	762	(8.8)	(3.0)	(7.5)	4.0	0.8	1.0	1.2	1.2 3.2 2.2
300–399 (N = 3)	355	(2.8)	(2.0)	(0.8)	1.5	0.4	0.5	0.5	0.4 1.5 1.0
200–299 (N = 3)	246	(6.4)	(2.5)	(3.8)	0.8	0.9	0.6	0.2	1.0 1.2 1.1
100–199 (N = 7)	150	(4.1)	(2.5)	(1.6)	0.7	0.5 (N = 6)	0.3 (N = 6)	0.5 (N = 5)	0.6 (N = 6) 0.9 0 8
50–99 (N = 5)	70	(2.9)	(1.6)	(1.3)	0.1	0.6[c] (N = 2)	1.0 (N = 3)	0.1[c] (N = 2)	0.9 (N = 3) 0.7 0.8
Total 50–750 (N = 19)	209	(4.2)	(2.2)	(2.0)	0.8	0.6[c] (N = 15)	0.6 (N = 16)	0.4 (N = 14)	0.7 (N = 16) 1.1 0.9

These averages are entirely based on data of Table 4-A.
[a] In Column 9, in each box, the first figure is the average of shifts based on highest levels, the second figure is the average of shifts based on largest shifts, and the third figure is the average of the first two.
[b] GDP = gross domestic product.
[c] Data for prepartition India were used only once in calculating the average.

TABLE 5. *Selected Indices of Social Mobilization for Nineteen Countries: Projected Minimum Levels in 1960, 1970*

	(1) RADIO AUDIENCE %		(2) LITERATES %		(3) PERCENTAGE OF ECONOMICALLY ACTIVE POPULA-TION IN NON-AGRICULTURAL OCCUPATIONS %		(4) URBAN POPULATION %		(5) EXPOSURE TO MODERNITY %	
COUNTRY	1960	1970	1960	1970	1960	1970	1960	1970	1960	1970
Venezuela	61	>95	59	67	69	79	62	74	86	95
Argentina	67	82	>95	>95	79	82	67	70	95	95
Cuba	61	78	78	80	57	56	60	65	87	93
Colombia	30	42	65	69	59	73	41	47	79	93
Turkey	19	31	43	52	24	27	26	27	45	55
Brazil	27	35	53	58	50	58	42	47	66	76
Philippines	7	12	78	92	45	53	25	26	77	91
Mexico	39	62	65	73	43	47	51	59	70	83
Chile	39	41	86	93	73	77	66	73	95	95
Guatemala	7	11	25	20	35	38	34	36	44	47
Honduras	8	9	37	39	15	13	35	39	45	49
Ghana	10	17	—	—	—	—	—	—	—	—
Egypt	16	26	31	38	45	52	37	42	51	59
Thailand	2	3	69	82	13	14	—	—	52	61
Rep. of the Congo (Leopoldville)	1	2	—	—	—	—	—	—	—	—
India	2	3	26[a]	32[a]	32	35	17[a]	19[a]	37	43
Nigeria	1	2	—	—	—	—	5	6	—	—
Pakistan	1	2	26[a]	32[a]	49	77	17[a]	19[a]	46	65
Burma	1	1	62	69	30	29	—	—	57	61

[a] On basis of prepartition India.

of enough actual data to get such work at least started.

For certain categories—such as voting participation, immigration and internal migration, linguistic and cultural assimilation, and the inequality of income distribution—not enough data were readily available to permit even the simple type of tabulation presented here. Even for the data that we have collected, the gaps in such countries as Ghana, Nigeria, and Congo illustrate the need for more research.

Moreover, the data being presented on the basis of the figures that appear in United Nations publications and similar sources make no attempt to estimate the margins of error to which they may be subject, or the differences in significance which a particular indicator of social mobilization may have in the cultural context of certain countries, in contrast with its significance in others. The high literacy rates reported for Burma and Thailand, e.g., include a substantial pro-portion of literates trained through traditional monastic institutions. These rates show only a weak correlation to other indicators of modernity for those same countries, while the high literacy rates for Chile by contrast, refer to the effect of a more modern type of school system and are far better correlated to other indicators.

We have tried to take some account of these matters by basing estimates of overall exposure to modernity not on the highest single indicator but on the average of the two highest indicators for each country, so as to discount to some extent the effects of any single indicator that seems too far out of line with the rest. Despite these precautions, the figures in projection offered here represent at best a crude beginning intended to stimulate far more thorough and critical statistical work, and its critical evaluation by experts on each of the countries and areas concerned.

[The Notes which discuss the specific data and sources have been deleted.]

PART III

THE CONCOMITANTS OF POLITICAL DEVELOPMENT

INTRODUCTION

The impact of personality changes, ideology, and nationalism on the general process of modernization was examined in Part II. Urbanization, literacy, and media participation were identified as aspects of modernization which make possible social mobilization and, eventually, political participation.

Diamant noted in Part I that during the process of modernization the political system undergoes transformation, both in its structure and its functions. In this transformation the relations between the political system and society are both autonomous and interdependent. Political development is partly independent of economic, social, or other forms of change. But also, it influences and is influenced by social and economic developments including industrialization and urbanization. The political system in modernizing society comes to deal with an ever wider range of problems; it becomes, as was pointed out, the generalized problem solver for the entire society. For example, the political system comes to occupy a dominant role in economic development. However, since political development is a process by which a political system acquires an increased capacity to sustain successfully and continuously new types of goals and demands and the creation of new types of organization, political development may depend, in turn, upon basic changes in society and the economy.

In this part we are concerned with changes in the environment within which political development occurs, namely, economic development, social changes relative to economic development, industrialization, and urbanization. These concomitants of political development have sometimes been viewed as the preconditions of political development and at other times as the consequences of political development. Moreover, political development may take place relatively independently of these changes. At the same time it must be noted that these interrelationships are both positive and negative. That is, the relationship may be one of stimulation and inducement; it may also be one of hampering and preventing.

The analysis by W. W. Rostow is a provocative theoretical statement on the changes that occur prior to and at the time of "take-off" into economic development. His hypothesis, supported by historical data, is that economic development proceeds in several distinguishable stages: the preconditions for "take-off," the "take-off," and sustained economic progress.[1]

In brief, the sequence of economic development consists of a long period (up to a century or, conceivably, more) when the preconditions for take-off are established. The take-off is the brief interval of two or three decades during which the economy and the society of which it is a part transform themselves in such ways that economic development is, subsequently, more or less automatic. This is followed by a long period during which economic growth becomes relatively self-sustaining and regularized.

J. J. Spengler focuses his discussion precisely on the political preconditions of economic development and then shows their interrelations by extending his analysis to the political consequences of economic development. In other words, he identifies what he regards as the minimum political preconditions of economic development and proceeds to show the changes that take place in these preconditions as economic development moves ahead.

The *precondition approach* to economic development is viewed by Albert Hirschman as a "council of perfection." His sharp critique, although not included in this volume, is introduced below and should be considered when reading Rostow and Spengler. According to Hirschman, theories which postulate a specific precondition for development are empirically vulnerable as development has occurred somewhere without benefit of that prerequisite. Moreover, he argues, different theories neutralize one another. For instance, it seems difficult to insist at one and the same time that the general climate of opinion must be favorable to industrial progress and that a strategic factor of particular importance is the presence of minority groups or of individuals with deviant, i.e., socially disapproved, behavior. "One rather suspects that when economic opportunity arises it will be perceived and exploited primarily by native entrepreneurs or by deviant minorities, depending on whether or not the traditional values of the society are favorable to change."[2]

Continuing his discussion of the search for the *primum mobile*, Hirschman writes: "While we were at first discouraged by the long list of resources and circumstances whose presence has been shown to be needed for economic development, we now find that these resources and circumstances are not so scarce or so difficult to realize, *provided, however, that economic development itself first raises its head*. This is of course only a positive way of stating the well-known proposition that economic development is held back by a series of 'interlocking vicious circles.' Before it starts, economic development is hard to visualize, not only because so many different conditions must be fulfilled

---

[1] Subsequently, Rostow elaborated this analysis by adding the stage of traditional society before the preconditions stage and dividing the period of sustained economic progress into the drive to maturity and the age of high mass consumption. See "The Stages of Economic Growth," *The Economic History Review*, **12**, 1–16, August 1959. The older article appears here because of the more detailed treatment given to the precondition and the take-off stages, which are more crucial to an understanding of the process of modernization.

[2] Albert O. Hirschman, *The Strategy of Economic Development* (New Haven: Yale University Press, 1958), p. 4.

simultaneously but above all because of the vicious circles: generally the realization of these conditions depends in turn on economic development. But this means also that once development has started, the circle is likely to become an upward spiral as all the prerequisites and conditions for development are brought into being."[3]

Hirschman concludes that "This approach permits us to focus on a characteristic of the process of economic development that is fundamental for both analysis and strategy: development depends not so much on finding optimal combinations for given resources and factors of production as on calling forth and enlisting for development purposes resources and abilities that are hidden, scattered, or badly utilized."[4]

Spengler's discussion of the "political preconditions" also includes a consideration of when state intervention is indicated to achieve economic development. The need for government action and its shortcomings are examined. Alexander Eckstein in the following article suggests a potential correlation between individualism and economic development. "The extent to which this potential is translated into reality will depend upon the role played by individual choice and initiative in resource allocation, regardless of whether the choices and decisions are in fact arrived at primarily within the confines of the economic or political process."

Eckstein sees economic growth as a broadening of the range of alternatives open to society. In traditional society there is little scope for the exercise of choice, individual or social. In modern society there is a much greater scope for individual choice and decentralized decision-making in the economic sphere. This condition is an important aspect of individualism.

In summing up his discussion of the role of the state and the categories of state action in the process of economic development, Eckstein suggests that it may be useful to attempt to work with the concept of an "optimum level and pattern of state intervention." This optimum would have to be defined in relation to two broad sets of objectives: (1) striving for rising standards of living combined with an increase, and/or (2) preservation of the scope for the exercise of individual choice and initiative.

The relationship of the political system to economic growth is only one aspect of societal interdependence. Bert F. Hoselitz points out that economic development is a process which affects the entire social, political, and cultural fabric of a society. When the rapidly "explosive" take-off occurred, Hoselitz observes, social institutions had been created which allowed capital formation and made available a number of highly skilled and specialized services. The creation of these social institutions and the institutionalization of entrepreneurship (defined as "an innovating uncertainty-bearing activity") required the establishment of a social framework within which these developments could take place. Hoselitz, like Hagen in Chapter 4, sees such a social framework being created as a result of the appearance of behavioral deviance, i.e.,

---

[3] *Ibid.*, p. 5.   [4] *Ibid.*

the emergence of cultural or social marginality, and the process of redefinition of societal objectives by an elite.

Manning Nash is also concerned with the relation of economic development to its antecedent and subsequent social and cultural changes, but he broadens his analysis to include more than social institutions. He feels that generalizations about the process of economic development in terms of pattern variables are not very useful because shifts in pattern variables are never specified in amount or degree. On the other hand, the more empirical literature presents no systematic or consistent interpretation of the way in which different social and cultural arrangements affect development.

Therefore, Nash proceeds to build an intermediate diagnostic scheme based on the proposition that economic development is a process of social and cultural change. Social and cultural change is viewed as a function of the alternatives generated by a given social system and, since different groups or individuals are differentially situated in the social structure, there exists in any society a variety of realistic impulses to change. Nash identifies three cultural features which may affect social decisions to undertake economic development: (1) the pattern of stratification in society and the amount of social mobility possible, (2) the system of social values which justify, explain, and define social position and the means of attaining it, and (3) the organization of the economic and political subsystems for self-sustained development. These categories of analysis are used to compare and contrast the potential for development in Burma and Cambodia. In conclusion, a scheme is offered as a preliminary way of gauging the social and cultural factors which are most intimately associated with economic development so that a society's potential for economic development may be assessed.

Industrialization is not identical with or a necessary cause of modernization, even though it appears to be widely desired by developing nations. In the West, modernization did occur as a result of the twin processes of industrialization and commercialization, but in many non-Western areas modernization has been a result of commercialization and bureaucracy, rather than industrialization.[5] Some of the values appropriate to industrial countries have been spread by enterprising men, sometimes in the context of politics and trade, sometimes in the context of religion and education. Thus, modernization should be viewed as a separate and distinct process from industrialization—caused by it in the West but causing it in other areas.

Many developing nations are attempting to industrialize, sometimes too soon or too rapidly. The analysis by George A. Theodorson of the consequences of industrialization for the social patterns of non-Western nations is a vivid portrayal of the concomitants of political development. He argues that industrialization will lead to new societal patterns and "These patterns will resemble, in time, certain dominant patterns of western industrialized society, which *may not be rejected by any people who accept the machines of the West.*"

[5] David E. Apter, *The Politics of Modernization* (Chicago: The University of Chicago Press, 1965), pp. 43–44.

These changes are presented within the framework of systems analysis, using Parsons' pattern variables, which were introduced in Chapter 1.

The changes result in a creation of new roles, new facilities, and new rewards, and in recognition of previously unimportant resources and skills. As a result, new individuals are placed in positions of power. This new power structure challenges the old and creates one of the many pressures for political development. Like the "assaulted" individuals Matossian describes, these leaders are men of two cultures—they are emotionally tied to the old system, but at the same time they are anxious to reap the benefits of a system which promises to relieve some of their economic problems. If they endeavor to stop the inevitable social change which Theodorson insists will accompany industrialization, they will increase social disorganization. Less productivity and a serious delay in the achievement of the desired basic economic goals will result. On the other hand, if only those elements of the old culture are retained which do not conflict with the new human relationships that inevitably accompany a machine society, modernization may proceed without serious disruption. Devising such a strategy poses a real test of the social and political acumen of the new leaders.

Urbanization is sometimes, but not always, a consequence of industrialization. Shantri Tangri asserts that urbanization is neither a necessary nor sufficient condition for economic development. It can be a desirable condition for development, but under certain conditions it can be a factor which slows it down. Reminiscent of the sociologists of previous generations, he contends that the role of urbanization cannot be determined without estimating the costs or benefits of such urban phenomena as *anomie*, political and ideological ferment, and transformation of cultural and social values.

As discussed in Part II, there is an ideology of economic development which may dictate a number of costly investments in modern factories, transportation systems, and the attendant social institutions which the people today demand when industrialization and urbanization occur. India, for example, has tried to become a welfare state before creating the basic economy required to sustain it. The ideology of the elites and the political leaders of developing nations tends to outrun technological and economic capabilities.

As a result, economic and other frustrations soon ensue with serious political consequences. Urban unemployment is often high. From the swelling ranks of the colleges and universities emerge the intelligentsia, who provide the leadership for political action—often mob action. Physical densities, media communications, and other facilities in cities make political organization easier. Political action may substitute for traditional social patterns. The political party in India, for example, is described as an alternative social structure to the traditional family. The purposelessness of life in the city may be transformed into a cause. Fanaticism and an ethos of dedication are used to maintain political unity around charismatic leaders. The consequences are dangerous for democracy.

Tangri poses an alternative to leaders faced with these political problems.

He urges a return to the village. Appropriate allocations and actions for the development of the countryside are necessary, supplemented by an ideological campaign. He feels that the village still has a romantic, emotional, political, or philosophical attraction for many. By exporting the problems of unemployment and poverty to cities, political instability is increased, but, Tangri maintains, there is a greater level of tolerance for these old and familiar problems in the village. Is this a strategy of despair, romantic idealism, or sound political advice for the leaders of the developing nations?

Chapter 7

Economic Development

THE TAKE-OFF INTO SELF-SUSTAINED GROWTH[1]

W. W. Rostow

The purpose of this article is to explore the following hypothesis: that the process of economic growth can usefully be regarded as centering on a relatively brief time interval of two or three decades when the economy and the society of which it is a part transform themselves in such ways that economic growth is, subsequently, more or less automatic. This decisive transformation is here called the take-off.[2]

The take-off is defined as the interval during which the rate of investment increases in such a way that real output per capita rises and this initial increase carries with it radical changes in production techniques and the disposition of income flows which perpetuate the new scale of investment and perpetuate thereby the rising trend in per-capita output. Initial

SOURCE. W. W. Rostow, "The Take-Off into Self-Sustained Growth," *The Economic Journal*, **66**, 25–48, March 1956.

[1] I wish to acknowledge with thanks the helpful criticisms of an earlier draft by G. Baldwin, F. Bator, K. Berrill, A. Enthoven, E. E. Hagen, C. P. Kindleberger, L. Lefeber, W. Malenbaum, E. S. Mason, and M. F. Millikan.
[2] This argument is a development from the line of thought presented in *The Process of Economic Growth* (New York, 1952), Ch. 4, especially pp. 102–105. The concept of three stages in the growth process centering on the take-off is defined and used for prescriptive purposes in *An American Policy in Asia* (New York, 1955), Ch. 7.

changes in method require that some group in the society have the will and the authority to install and diffuse new production techniques;[3] and a perpetuation of the growth process requires that such a leading group expand in authority and that the society as a whole respond to the impulses set up by the initial changes, including the potentialities for external economies. Initial changes in the scale and direction of finance flows are likely to imply a command over income flows by new groups or institutions; and a perpetuation of growth requires that a high proportion of the increment to real income during the take-off period be

[3] We shall set aside in this article the question of how new production techniques are generated from pure science and invention, a procedure which is legitimate, since we are examining the growth process in national (or regional) economies over relatively short periods. We shall largely set aside also the question of population pressure and the size and quality of the working force, again because of the short period under examination; although, evidently, even over short periods, the rate of population increase will help determine the level of investment required to yield rising output per capita (see below, p. 28, note 2). By and large, this article is concerned with capital formation at a particular stage of economic growth; and of the array of propensities defined in *The Process of Economic Growth* it deals only with the propensity to accept innovations and the propensity to seek material advance, the latter in relation to the supply of finance only.

returned to productive investment. The take-off requires, therefore, a society prepared to respond actively to new possibilities for productive enterprise; and it is likely to require political, social, and institutional changes which will both perpetuate an initial increase in the scale of investment and result in the regular acceptance and absorption of innovations.

In short, this article is an effort to clarify the economics of industrial revolution when an industrial revolution is conceived of narrowly with respect to time and broadly with respect to changes in production functions.

Three Stages in the Growth Process

The historian examining the story of a particular national economy is inevitably impressed by the long-period continuity of events. Like other forms of history, economic history is a seamless web. The cotton-textile developments in Britain of the 1780's and 1790's have a history stretching back for a half century at least; the United States of the 1840's and 1850's had been preparing itself for industrialization since the 1790's, at the latest; Russia's remarkable development during the two pre-1914 decades goes back to 1861 for its foundations, if not to the Napoleonic Wars or to Peter the Great; the remarkable economic spurt of Meiji Japan is incomprehensible outside the context of economic developments in the latter half of the Tokugawa era; and so on. It is wholly legitimate that the historian's influence should be to extend the story of the British industrial revolution back into the seventeenth century and forward far into the nineteenth century; and that Heckscher should embrace Sweden's transition in a chapter entitled, "The Great Transformation (1815–1914)."[4] From the perspective of the economic historian the isolation of a take-off period is, then, a distinctly arbitrary process. It is to be judged, like such other arbitrary exercises

as the isolation of business cycles and secular trends, on whether it illuminates more of the economic process than it conceals; and it should be used, if accepted, as a way of giving a rough framework of order to the inordinately complicated biological problem of growth rather than as an exact model of reality.

There is difficulty in this set of conceptions for the statistical analyst of economic development as well as for the historian. At first sight the data mobilized, for example, by Clark, Kuznets, Buchanan and Ellis exhibit a continuum of degrees of development both within countries over time and as among countries at a given period of time, with no *prima facie* case for a clearly marked watershed in the growth process.[5] In part this statistical result arises from the fact that historical data on national product and its components are only rarely available for an economy until after it has passed into a stage of more or less regular growth; that is, after the take-off. In part it arises from the fact that, by and large, these authors are more concerned with different levels of per-capita output (or welfare)—and the structural characteristics that accompany them—than with the growth process itself. The data they mobilize do not come to grips with the inner determinants of growth. The question raised here is not how or why levels of output per capita have differed but rather how it has come about that particular economies have moved from stagnation—to slow, piece-meal advance— to a situation where growth was the normal economic condition. Our criterion

[4] E. F. Heckscher, *An Economic History of Sweden*, Tr. G. Ohlin (Cambridge, Massachusetts, 1954), Ch. 6.

[5] Colin Clark, *The Conditions of Economic Progress* (London, 1951, second edition); Simon Kuznets, "International Differences in Capital Formation and Financing" (mimeographed; Conference on Capital Formation and Economic Growth, November 1953) (National Bureau of Economic Research, New York, 1953); Norman Buchanan and Howard Ellis, *Approaches to Economic Development* (Twentieth Century Fund, New York, 1955). See also the United Nations data presented as a frontispiece to H. F. Williamson and John A. Buttrick, *Economic Development* (New York, 1954).

here is not the absolute level of output per capita but its rate of change.

In this argument the sequence of economic development is taken to consist of three periods: a long period (up to a century, or conceivably, more) when the preconditions for take-off are established; the take-off itself, defined within two or three decades; and a long period when growth becomes normal and relatively automatic. These three divisions would, of course, not exclude the possibility of growth giving way to secular stagnation or decline in the long term. It would exclude from the concept of a growing economy, however, one which experiences a brief spurt of expansion which is not subsequently sustained; for example, the United States industrial boom of the War of 1812 or the ill-fated spurts of certain Latin American economies in the early stages of their modern history.

Take-offs have occurred in two quite different types of societies; and, therefore, the process of establishing preconditions for take-off has varied. In the first and most general case the achievement of preconditions for take-off required major change in political and social structure and, even, in effective cultural values. In the vocabulary of *The Process of Economic Growth*, important changes in the propensities preceded the take-off. In the second case take-off was delayed not by political, social, and cultural obstacles but by the high (and even expanding) levels of welfare that could be achieved by exploiting land and natural resources. In this second case take-off was initiated by a more narrowly economic process, as, for example, in the northern United States, Australia and, perhaps, Sweden. In the vocabulary of *The Process of Economic Growth*, the take-off was initiated primarily by a change in the yields; although subsequent growth brought with it changes in the propensities as well. As one would expect in the essentially biological field of economic growth, history offers mixed as well as pure cases.

In the first case the process of establishing preconditions for take-off might be generalized in impressionistic terms as follows:

We start with a reasonably stable and traditional society containing an economy mainly agricultural, using more or less unchanging production methods, saving and investing productively little more than is required to meet depreciation. Usually from outside the society, but sometimes out of its own dynamics, comes the idea that economic progress is possible; and this idea spreads within the established *élite* or, more usually, in some disadvantaged group whose lack of status does not prevent the exercise of some economic initiative. More often than not the economic motives for seeking economic progress converge with some non-economic motive, such as the desire for increased social power and prestige, national pride, political ambition and so on. Education, for some at least, broadens and changes to suit the needs of modern economic activity. New enterprising men come forward willing to mobilize savings and to take risks in pursuit of profit, notably in commerce. The commercial markets for agricultural products, domestic handicrafts, and consumption-goods imports widen. Institutions for mobilizing capital appear; or they expand from primitive levels in the scale, surety and time horizon for loans. Basic capital is expanded, notably in transport and communications, often to bring to market raw materials in which other nations have an economic interest, often financed by foreign capital. And, here and there, modern manufacturing enterprise appears, usually in substitution for imports.

Since public-health measures are enormously productive in their early stages of application and, as innovations go, meet relatively low resistance in most cultures, the death rate may fall and the population begin to rise, putting pressure on the food supply and the institutional structure of agriculture, creating thereby an economic depressant or stimulus (or both in turn), depending on the society's response.[6]

The rate of productive investment may rise up to 5 per cent of national income;[7] but this is unlikely to do much more than keep ahead of the population increase. And, in general, all this activity proceeds on a limited basis, within an economy and a society still mainly characterized by traditional low-productivity techniques and by old values and institutions which developed in conjunction with them. The rural proportion of the population is likely to stand at 75 per cent or over.

In the second case, of naturally wealthy nations, with a highly favorable balance between population and natural resources and with a population deriving by emigration from reasonably acquisitive cultures, the story of establishing the preconditions differs mainly in that there is no major problem of overcoming traditional values inappropriate to economic growth and the inert or resistant institutions which incorporate them; there is less difficulty in developing an *élite* effective in the investment process; and there is no population problem.[8] Technically, much the

same slow-moving process of change occurs at high (and, perhaps, even expanding) levels of per-capita output, and with an extensive growth of population and output still based on rich land and other natural resources. Take-off fails to occur mainly because the comparative advantage of exploiting productive land and other natural resources delays the time when self-reinforcing industrial growth can profitably get under way.[9]

The beginning of take-off can usually be traced to a particular sharp stimulus. The stimulus may take the form of a political revolution which affects directly the balance of social power and effective values, the character of economic institutions, the distribution of income, the pattern of investment outlays and the proportion of potential innovations actually applied; that is, it operates through the propensities. It may come about through a technological (including transport) innovation, which sets in motion a chain of secondary expansion in modern sectors and has powerful potential external economy effects which the society exploits. It may take the form of a newly

[6] Historically, disruptive population pressure has been generated in pretake-off societies not only by the easy spread of highly productive measures of public health but also by the easy acceptance of high-yield new crops, permitting a fragmentation of land holdings, earlier marriage and a rise in the birth rate; e.g., Ireland and China.

[7] The relation of the investment rate to growth depends, of course, on the rate of population rise. With stagnant population or slow rise a 5 per cent investment rate could yield substantial growth in real output per capita, as indeed it did in pre-1914 France. On the other hand, as noted on page 242 investment rates much higher than 5 per cent can persist in primitive economies which lack the preconditions for growth, based on capital imports, without initiating sustained growth. For some useful arithmetic on the scale and composition of capital requirements in a growing economy with a 1 per cent population increase see A. K. Cairncross, *Home and Foreign Investment* (Cambridge, 1953), Ch. 1.

[8] Even in these cases there have often been significant political and social restraints which

had to be reduced or eliminated before take-off could occur; for example, in Canada, the Argentine and the American South.

[9] Theoretically, such fortunate societies could continue to grow in per-capita output until diminishing returns damped down their progress. Theoretically, they might even go on as growing nonindustrial societies, absorbing agricultural innovations which successfully countered diminishing returns. Something like this process might describe, for example, the rich agricultural regions of the United States. But, in general, it seems to be the case that the conditions required to sustain a progressive increase in agricultural productivity will also lead on to self-reinforcing industrial growth. This result emerges not merely from the fact that many agricultural improvements are labor-saving, and that industrial employment can be stimulated by the availability of surplus labor and is required to draw it off; it also derives from the fact that the production and use of materials and devices which raise agricultural productivity in themselves stimulate the growth of a self-sustaining industrial sector.

favorable international environment, such as the opening of British and French markets to Swedish timber in the 1860's or a sharp relative rise in export prices and/or large new capital imports, as in the case of the United States from the late 1840's, Canada and Russia from the mid-1890's; but it may also come as a challenge posed by an unfavorable shift in the international environment, such as a sharp fall in terms of trade (or a wartime blockage of foreign trade) requiring the rapid development of manufactured import substitutes, as in the case of the Argentine and Australia in the 1930's and during the Second World War.[10] All these latter cases raise sharply the profitability of certain lines of enterprise and can be regarded as changes in the yields.

What is essential here, however, is not the form of stimulus but the fact that the prior development of the society and its economy result in a positive sustained, and self-reinforcing, response to it: the result is not a once-over change in production functions or in the volume of investment, but a higher proportion of potential innovations accepted in a more or less regular flow, and a higher rate of investment.

In short, the forces which have yielded marginal bursts of activity now expand and become quantitatively significant as rapid-moving trends. New industries expand at high rates, yielding profits which are substantially reinvested in new capacity; and their expansion induces a more general expansion of the modern sectors of the economy where a high rate of plough-back prevails. The institutions for mobilizing savings (including the fiscal and sometimes the capital-levy activities of govern-

ment) increase in scope and efficiency. New techniques spread in agriculture as well as in industry, as increasing numbers of persons are prepared to accept them and the deep changes they bring to ways of life. A new class of business-men (usually private, sometimes public servants) emerges and acquires control over the key decisions determining the use of savings. New possibilities for export develop and are exploited; new import requirements emerge. The economy exploits hitherto unused backlogs in technique and natural resources. Although there are a few notable exceptions, all this momentum historically attracted substantial foreign capital.

The use of aggregative national-income terms evidently reveals little of the process which is occurring. It is nevertheless useful to regard as a necessary but not sufficient condition for the take-off the fact that the proportion of net investment to national income (or net national product) rises from (say) 5 per cent to over 10 per cent, definitely outstripping the likely population pressure (since under the assumed take-off circumstances the capital–output ratio is low),[11] and yielding a distinct rise

---

[10] Historically, the imposition of tariffs has played an important role in take-offs, e.g., the American Tariffs of 1828 (cotton textiles) and 1841–42 (rail iron); the Russian tariffs of the 1890's, etc. Although these actions undoubtedly served to assist take-off in leading sectors, they usually reflected an energy and purpose among key entrepreneurial groups which would, in any case, probably have done the trick.

[11] The author is aware of the substantial ambiguities which overhang the concept of the capital–output ratio and, especially, of the dangers of applying an overall aggregate measure. But since the arithmetic of economic growth requires some such concept, implicitly or explicitly, we had better refine the tool rather than abandon it. In the early stages of economic development two contrary forces operate on the capital–output ratio. On the one hand there is a vast requirement of basic overhead capital in transport, power, education, etc. Here, due mainly to the long period over which such investment yields its return, the apparent (short-run) capital–output ratio is high. On the other hand, there are generally large unexploited backlogs of known techniques and available natural resources to be put to work; and these backlogs make for a low capital–output ratio. We can assume formally a low capital–output ratio for the take-off period because we are assuming that the preconditions have been created, including a good deal of social overhead capital. In fact, the aggregate marginal capital–output ratio is likely to be kept up during the take-off by the requirement

in real output per capita. Whether real consumption per capita rises depends on the pattern of income distribution and population pressure, as well as on the magnitude, character, and productivity of investment itself.

As indicated in Table 1, I believe it possible to identify at least tentatively such take-off periods for a number of countries which have passed into the stage of growth.

The third stage is, of course, the long, fluctuating story of sustained economic progress. Overall capital per head increases as the economy matures. The structure of the economy changes increasingly. The initial key industries, which sparked the take-off, decelerate as diminishing returns operate on the original set of industrial tricks and the original band of pioneering entrepreneurs give way to less single-minded industrial leaders in those sectors; but the average rate of growth is maintained by a succession of new, rapidly growing sectors, with a new set of pioneering leaders. The proportion of the population in rural pursuits declines. The economy finds its (changing) place in the international economy. The society makes such terms as it will with the requirements for maxi-mizing modern and efficient production, balancing off, as it will, the new values against those retarding values which persist with deeper roots, or adapting the latter in such ways as to support rather than retard the growth process. This sociological calculus interweaves with basic resource endowments to determine the pace of deceleration.

It is with the problems and vicissitudes of such growing economies of the third stage (and especially with cyclical fluctua-tions and the threat of chronic unemploy-ment) that the bulk of modern theoretical economics is concerned, including much

[*footnote 11 continued*
of continuing large outlays for overhead items which yield their return only over long periods. Nevertheless, a ratio of 3–1 or 3.5–1 on average seems realistic as a rough bench-mark until we have learned more about capital–output ratios on a sectoral basis.

recent work on the formal properties of growth models. The student of history and of contemporary underdeveloped areas[12] is more likely to be concerned with the economics of the first two stages; that is, the economics of the preconditions and the take-off. If we are to have a serious theory of economic growth or (more likely) some useful theories about economic growth, they must obviously seek to embrace these two early stages—and notably the economics of the take-off. The balance of this article is designed to mobilize tentatively and in a preliminary way what an economic historian can contribute to the economics of take-off.

The Take-off Defined and Isolated

There are several problems of choice involved in defining the take-off with pre-cision. We might begin with one arbitrary

[12] A number of so-called underdeveloped areas may have, in fact, either passed through the take-off process or are in the midst of it, e.g., Mexico, Brazil, Turkey, the Argentine, and India. I would commend for consideration —certainly no more until the concept of take-off is disproved or verified—the dropping of the concept of "underdeveloped areas" and the substitution for it of a quadripartite distinc-tion among economies: traditional; pre-take-off; take-off; and growing. Against the background of this set of distinctions we might then consider systematically two separable questions now often confused. First, the stage of growth, as among growing economies. It is legitimate to regard Mexico and the United States, Great Britain and Australia, France, and Japan, as growing economies, although they stand at very different points along their national growth curves, where the degree of progress might be measured by some kind of index of output (or capital) per head. Second, the foreseeable long-run potential of growing economies. Over the long pull, even after they are "fully developed," the per-capita output levels that different economies are likely to achieve will undoubtedly vary greatly, depend-ing notably on resource endowments in relation to population. The arraying of levels of output per capita for different economies, now con-ventional, fails to distinguish these three ele-ments; that is, the current rate of growth; the stage of growth; and the foreseeable hori-zon for growth.

TABLE 1. *Some Tentative, Approximate Take-off Dates*

COUNTRY	TAKE-OFF	COUNTRY	TAKE-OFF
Great Britain	1783–1802	Russia	1890–1914
France	1830–1860	Canada	1896–1914
Belgium	1833–1860	Argentine[c]	1935–
United States[a]	1843–1860	Turkey[d]	1937–
Germany	1850–1873	India[e]	1952–
Sweden	1868–1890	China[e]	1952–
Japan[b]	1878–1900		

[a] The American take-off is here viewed as the upshot of two different periods of expansion: the first, that of the 1840's, marked by railway and manufacturing development, mainly confined to the East—this occurred while the West and South digested the extensive agricultural expansion of the previous decade; the second the great railway push into the Middle West during the 1850's marked by a heavy inflow of foreign capital. By the opening of the Civil War the American economy of North and West, with real momentum in its heavy-industry sector, is judged to have taken off.

[b] Lacking adequate data, there is some question about the timing of the Japanese take-off. Some part of the post-1868 period was certainly, by the present set of definitions, devoted to firming up the preconditions for take-off. By 1914 the Japanese economy had certainly taken off. The question is whether the period from about 1878 to the Sino-Japanese War in the mid-1890's is to be regarded as the completion of the preconditions or as take-off. On present evidence, I incline to the latter view.

[c] In one sense the Argentine economy began its take-off during the First World War. But by and large, down to the pit of the post-1929 depression, the growth of its modern sector, stimulated during the war, tended to slacken; and like a good part of the Western World, the Argentine sought during the 1920's to return to a pre-1914 normalcy. It was not until the mid-1930's that a sustained take-off was inaugurated, which by and large can now be judged to have been successful despite the structural vicissitudes of that economy.

[d] Against the background of industrialization measures inaugurated in the mid-1930's the Turkish economy has exhibited remarkable momentum in the past five years founded in the increase in agricultural income and productivity. It still remains to be seen whether these two surges, conducted under quite different national policies, will constitute a transition to self-sustaining growth, and whether Turkey can overcome its current structural problems.

[e] As noted in the text it is still too soon (for quite different reasons) to judge either the Indian or Chinese Communist take-off efforts successful.

definition and consider briefly the two major alternatives.

For the present purposes the take-off is defined as requiring all three of the following related conditions:

1. a rise in the rate of productive investment from (say) 5 per cent or less to over 10 per cent of national income (or net national product);

2. the development of one or more substantial manufacturing[13] sectors, with a high rate of growth;

[13] In this context "manufacturing" is taken to include the processing of agricultural products or raw materials by modern methods; e.g., timber in Sweden; meat in Australia; dairy products in Denmark. The dual requirement of a "manufacturing" sector is that its processes set in motion a chain of further modern sector

3. the existence or quick emergence of a political, social and institutional framework which exploits the impulses to expansion in the modern sector and the potential external economy effects of the take-off and gives to growth an on-going character.

The third condition implies a considerable capability to mobilize capital from domestic sources. Some take-offs have occurred with virtually no capital imports; e.g., Britain and Japan. Some take-offs have had a high component of foreign capital; e.g., the United States, Russia, and Canada. But some countries have imported large quantities of foreign capital for long periods, which undoubtedly contributed to creating the preconditions of take-off, without actually initiating take-off; e.g., the Argentine before 1914, Venezuela down to recent years, the Belgian Congo currently. In short, whatever the role of capital imports, the preconditions for take-off include an initial ability to mobilize domestic savings productively, as well as a structure which subsequently permits a high marginal rate of savings.

This definition is designed to isolate the early stage when industrialization takes hold rather than the later stage when industrialization becomes a more massive and statistically more impressive phenomenon. In Britain, for example, there is no doubt that it was between 1815 and 1850 that industrialization fully took hold. If the criterion chosen for take-off was the period of most rapid overall industrial growth, or the period when large-scale industry matured, all our take-off dates would have to be set forward; Britain, for example, to 1819–48; the United States to 1868–93; Sweden to 1890–1920; Japan to 1900–20; Russia to 1928–40. The earlier dating is chosen here because it is believed, on present (often inadequate) evidence, that the decisive transformations

[*footnote 13 continued*
requirements and that its expansion provides the potentiality of external economy effects.

(including a decisive shift in the investment rate) occur in the first industrial phases; and later industrial maturity can be directly traced back to foundations laid in these first phases.

This definition is also designed to rule out from the take-off the quite substantial economic progress which can occur in an economy before a truly self-reinforcing growth process gets under way. British economic expansion between (say) 1750 and 1783, Russian economic expansion between (say) 1861 and 1890, Canadian economic expansion between 1867 and the mid-1890's—such periods—for which there is an equivalent in the economic history of almost every growing economy—were marked by extremely important, even decisive, developments. The transport network expanded, and with it both internal and external commerce; new institutions for mobilizing savings were developed; a class of commercial and even industrial entrepreneurs began to emerge; industrial enterprise on a limited scale (or in limited sectors) grew. And yet, however essential these pretake-off periods were for later development, their scale and momentum were insufficient to transform the economy radically or, in some cases, to outstrip population growth and to yield an increase in per-capita output.

With a sense of the considerable violence done to economic history, I am here seeking to isolate a period when the scale of productive economic activity reaches a critical level and produces changes which lead to a massive and progressive structural transformation in economies and the societies of which they are a part, better viewed as changes in kind than merely in degree.

Evidence on Investment Rates in the Take-off

The case for the concept of take-off hinges, in part, on quantitative evidence on the scale and productivity of investment in relation to population growth. Here, as noted earlier, we face a difficult problem; investment data are not now available historically for early stages in economic history. Following is such case as there is for regarding the shift from a productive investment rate of about 5 per cent of NNP to 10 per cent or more as central to the process.[14]

A PRIMA FACIE CASE

If we take the aggregate marginal capital–output ratio for an economy in its early stage of economic development at 3.5–1 and if we assume, as is not abnormal, a population rise of 1–1.5 per cent per annum it is clear that something between 3.5 and 5.25 per cent of NNP must be regularly invested if NNP per capita is to be sustained. An increase of 2 per cent per annum in NNP per capita requires, under these assumptions, that something between 10.5 and 12.5 per cent of NNP be regularly invested. By definition and assumption, then, a transition from relatively stagnant to substantial, regular rise in NNP per capita, under typical population conditions, requires that the proportion of national product productively invested move from

[14] In his important article, "Economic Development with Unlimited Supplies of Labour," *Manchester School*, May 1954, W. Arthur Lewis indicates a similar spread as defining the transition to economic growth:

> The central problem in the theory of economic development is to understand the process by which a community which was previously saving and investing 4 or 5 per cent of its national income or less, converts itself into an economy where voluntary saving is running at about 12–15 per cent of national income or more. This is the central problem because the central fact of economic development is rapid capital accumulation (including knowledge and skills with capital). We cannot explain any "industrial" revolution (as the economic historians pretend to do) until we can explain why saving increased relatively to national income.

Presumably Mr. Lewis based this range on empirical observation of contemporary "underdeveloped" areas on which some data are presented below. As in footnote 7, page 236, it should be emphasized that the choice of investment proportions to symbolize the transition to growth hinges on the assumptions made about the rate of population increase.

somewhere in the vicinity of 5 per cent to something in the vicinity of 10 per cent.

THE SWEDISH CASE

In the appendix to his paper on international differences in capital formation, cited above, Kuznets gives gross and net capital formation figures in relation to gross and net national product for a substantial group of countries where reasonably good statistical data exist. Excepting Sweden, these data do not go back clearly to pretake-off stages.[15] The

[15] The Danish data are on the margin. They begin with the decade 1870–79, probably the first decade of take-off itself. They show net and gross domestic capital formation rates well over 10 per cent. In view of the sketch of the Danish economy presented in Kjeld Bjerke's "Preliminary Estimates of the Danish National Product from 1870–1950" (Preliminary paper mimeographed for 1953 Conference of the International Association for Research on Income and Wealth), pp. 32–34, it seems likely that further research would identify the years 1830–70 as a period when the preconditions were actively established, 1870–1900 as a period of take-off. This view is supported by scattered and highly approximate estimates of Danish National Wealth which exhibit a remarkable surge in capital formation between 1864 and 1884.

Estimates of National Wealth in Denmark

	1000 millions of kroner.	Source
1864	3.5	Falbe-Hansen, *Danmarks statistik*, 1885.
1884	6.5	Falbe-Hansen, *Danmarks statisik*, 1885.
1899	7.2	Tax-commission of 1903.
1909	10.0	Jens Warming, *Danmarks statistik*, 1913.
1927	24.0	Jens Warming, *Danmarks erhvervs- or samfundsliv*, 1930.
1939	28.8	Economic expert committee of 1943, *Økonomiske efterkigrsproblemer*, 1945.
1950	54.5	N. Banke, N. P. Jacobsen og Vedel-Petersen, *Danske erhvervsliv*, 1951.

(Furnished in correspondence by Einar Cohn

Swedish data begin in the decade 1861–70; and the Swedish take-off is to be dated from the latter years of the decade. Kuznets' calculations for Sweden are shown in Table 2.

THE CANADIAN CASE

The data developed by O. J. Firestone[16] for Canada indicate a similar transition for net capital formation in its take-off (say, 1896–1914); but the gross investment proportion in the period from Confederation to the mid-nineties was higher than appears to have marked other periods when the preconditions were established, possibly due to investment in the railway net, abnormally large for a nation of Canada's population, and to relatively heavy foreign investment, even before the great capital import boom of the pre-1914 decade (Table 3).

THE PATTERN OF CONTEMPORARY EVIDENCE IN GENERAL[17]

In the years after 1945 the number of countries for which reasonably respectable national income (or product) data exist has grown; and with such data there have

[footnote 15 continued
and Kjeld Bjerke.) It should again be emphasized, however, that we are dealing with a hypothesis whose empirical foundations are still fragmentary.
[16] O. J. Firestone, Canada's Economic Development, 1867–1952, with Special Reference to Changes in the Country's National Product and National Wealth, paper prepared for the International Association for Research in Income and Wealth, 1953, to which Mr. Firestone has kindly furnished me certain revisions, shortly to be published. By 1900 Canada already had about 18,000 miles of railway line; but the territory served had been developed to a limited degree only. By 1900 Canada already had a net balance of foreign indebtedness over $1 billion. Although this figure was almost quadrupled in the next two decades, capital imports represented an important increment to domestic capital sources from the period of Confederation down to the pre-1914 Canadian boom, which begins in the mid-1890's.
[17] I am indebted to Mr. Everett Hagen for mobilizing the statistical data in this section, except where otherwise indicated.

developed some tolerable savings and investment estimates for countries at different stages of the growth process. Within the category of nations usually grouped as "underdeveloped" one can distinguish four types.[18]

1. *Pretake-off economies*, where the apparent savings and investment rates, including limited net capital imports, probably come to under 5 per cent of net national product. In general, data for such countries are not satisfactory, and one's judgment that capital formation is low must rest on fragmentary data and partially subjective judgment. Examples are Ethiopia, Kenya, Thailand, Cambodia, Afghanistan, and perhaps Indonesia.[19]

2. *Economies attempting take-off*, where the apparent savings and investment rates, including limited net capital imports, have risen over 5 per cent of net national product.[20] For example, Mexico (1950)

[18] The percentages given are of net capital formation to net domestic product. The latter is the product net of depreciation of the geographic area. It includes the value of output produced in the area, regardless of whether the income flows abroad. Since indirect business taxes are not deducted, it tends to be larger than national income; hence the percentages are lower than if national income was used as the denominator in computing them.
[19] The Office of Intelligence Research of the Department of State, Washington, D.C., gives the following estimated ratios of investment (presumably gross) to GNP in its Report No. 6672 of August 25, 1954, p. 3, based on latest data available to that point, for countries which would probably fall in the pretake-off category:

	Per cent		Per cent
Afghanistan	5	Pakistan	6
Ceylon	5	Indonesia	5

[20] The Department of State estimates (*ibid.*) for economies which are either attempting take-off or which have, perhaps, passed into a stage of regular growth include:

	Per cent		Per cent
The Argentine	13	Colombia	14
Brazil	14	Philippines	8
Chile	11	Venezuela	23

Venezuela has been for some time an "enclave

TABLE 2[a]

DECADE	DOMESTIC GCF GNP (%)	DOMESTIC NCF NNP (%)	DEPRECIATION TO DGCF (%)
1. 1861–70	5.8	3.5–	(42)
2. 1871–80	8.8	5.3	(42)
3. 1881–90	10.8	6.6	(42)
4. 1891–1900 . . .	13.7	8.1	43.9
5. 1901–10	18.0	11.6	40.0
6. 1911–20	20.2	13.5	38.3
7. 1921–30	19.0	11.4	45.2

[a] (Kuznets). Based on estimates in Eric Lindahl, Einan Dahlgren and Karin Kock, *National Income of Sweden, 1861–1930* (London: P. J. Kingston, 1937), Parts One and Two, particularly the details in Part Two.

These underlying totals of capital formation exclude changes in inventories.

While gross totals are directly from the volumes referred to above, depreciation for the first three decades was not given. We assumed that it formed 42 per cent of gross domestic capital formation.

TABLE 3. *Canada: Gross and Net Investment in Durable Physical Assets as Percentage of Gross and Net National Expenditure (for Selected Years)*

	GCF GNP	NCF NNP	CAPITAL CONSUMPTION AS PERCENTAGE OF GROSS INVESTMENT
1870	15.0	7.1	56.2
1900	13.1	4.0	72.5
1920	16.6	10.6	41.3
1929	23.0	12.1	53.3
1952	16.8	9.3	49.7

NCF/NDP 7.2 per cent; Chile (1950) NCF/NDP 9.5 per cent; Panama (1950) NCF/NDP 7.5 per cent; Philippines (1952) NCF/NDP 6.4 per cent; Puerto Rico economy," with a high investment rate concentrated in a modern export sector whose growth did not generate general economic momentum in the Venezuelan economy; but in the past few years Venezuela may have moved over into the category of economies experiencing an authentic take-off.

(1952) NCF (Private)/NDP 7.6 per cent; India (1953) NCF/NDP, perhaps about 7 per cent. Whether the take-off period will, in fact, be successful remains in most of these cases still to be seen.

3. *Growing economies*, where the apparent savings and investment rates, including limited net capital imports, have reached 10 per cent or over; for example, Colombia (1950) NCF/NDP, 16.3 per cent.

4. *Enclave economies* (1) cases where the apparent savings and investment rates, including substantial net capital imports, have reached 10 per cent or over, but the domestic preconditions for sustained growth have not been achieved. These economies, associated with major export industries, lack the third condition for take-off suggested above (p. 32). They include the Belgian Congo (1951) NCF/NDP 21.7 per cent; Southern Rhodesia (1950) GCF/GDP 45.5 per cent, (1952) GCF/GDP 45.4 per cent. (2) Cases where net capital exports are large. For example, Burma (1938) NCF/NDP, 7.1 per cent; net capital exports/NDP, 11.5 per cent; Nigeria (1950–51) NCF/NDP 5.1 per cent; net capital exports/NDP, 5.6 per cent.

THE CASES OF INDIA AND COMMUNIST CHINA

The two outstanding contemporary cases of economies attempting purposefully to take-off are India and Communist China, both operating under national plans. The Indian First Five Year Plan projects the growth process envisaged under assumptions similar to those in paragraph 1, page 241. The Indian Planning Commission estimated investment as 5 per cent of NNP in the initial year of the plan, 1950–51.[21] Using a 3/1 marginal capital–output ratio, they envisaged a marginal savings rate of 20 per cent for the First Five Year Plan, a 50 per cent rate thereafter, down to 1968–69, when the average proportion of income invested would level off at 20 per cent of NNP. As one would expect, the sectoral composition of this process is not fully worked out in the initial plan; but the Indian effort may well be remembered in economic history as the first take-off defined *ex ante* in national product terms.

We know less of the Chinese Communist First Five Year Plan than we do of the concurrent Indian effort, despite the

[21] Government of India, Planning Commission, *The First Five Year Plan*, 1952, Vol. **1**, Ch. 1.

recent publication of production goals for some of the major sectors of the Chinese economy.[22] Roundly, it would appear that, from a (probably) negative investment rate in 1949, the Chinese Communist regime had succeeded by 1952 in achieving a gross rate of about 12 per cent; a net rate of about 7 per cent.

On arbitrary assumptions, which have a distinct upward bias, these figures can be projected forward for a decade yielding rates of about 20 per cent gross, 17 per cent net by 1962.

So far as the aggregates are concerned, what we can say is that the Indian planned figures fall well within the range of prima facie hypothesis and historical experience, if India in fact fulfils the full requirements for take-off, notably the achievement of industrial momentum. The Chinese Communist figures reflect accurately an attempt to force the pace of history, evident throughout Peking's domestic policy, whose viability is still to be demonstrated. In particular, Peking's agricultural policy may fail to produce the minimum structural balance required for a successful take-off, requiring radical revision of investment allocations and policy objectives at a later stage.

We have, evidently, much still to learn about the quantitative aspects of this problem; and, especially, much further quantitative research and imaginative manipulation of historical evidence will be required before the hypothesis tentatively advanced here can be regarded as proved or disproved. What we can say is that prima facie thought and a scattering of historical and contemporary evidence suggests that it is not unreasonable to consider the take-off as including as a necessary but not sufficient condition a quantitative transition in the proportion of income

[22] These comments are based on the work of Alexander Eckstein and the author in *The Prospects for Communist China* (New York and London, 1954), Part V, pp. 222 ff. The statistical calculations are the work of Mr. Eckstein.

productively invested of the kind indicated here.

The Inner Structure of the Take-off

Whatever the importance and virtue of viewing the take-off in aggregative terms—embracing national output, the proportion of output invested, and an aggregate marginal capital–output ratio—that approach tells us relatively little of what actually happens and of the causal processes at work in a take-off; nor is the investment-rate criterion conclusive.

Following the definition of take-off (pp. 238–240 above), we must consider not merely how a rise in the investment rate is brought about, from both supply and demand perspectives, but how rapidly growing manufacturing sectors emerged and imparted their primary and secondary growth impulses to the economy.

Perhaps the most important thing to be said about the behavior of these variables in historical cases of take-off is that they have assumed many different forms. There is no single pattern. The rate and productivity of investment can rise, and the consequences of this rise can be diffused into a self-reinforcing general growth process by many different technical and economic routes, under the ægis of many different political, social and cultural settings, driven along by a wide variety of human motivations.

The purpose of the following paragraphs is to suggest briefly, and by way of illustration only, certain elements of both uniformity and variety in the variables whose movement has determined the inner structure of the take-off.

THE SUPPLY OF LOANABLE FUNDS

By and large, the loanable funds required to finance the take-off have come from two types of sources: from shifts in the control over income flows, including income-distribution changes and capital imports;[23]

and from the plough-back of profits in rapidly expanding particular sectors.

The notion of economic development occurring as the result of income shifts from those who will spend (hoard[24] or lend) less productively to those who will spend (or lend) more productively is one of the oldest and most fundamental notions in economics. It is basic to the *Wealth of Nations*,[25] and it is applied by W. Arthur Lewis in his recent elaboration of the classical model.[26] Lewis builds his model in part on an expansion of the capitalist sector, with the bulk of additional savings arising from an enlarging pool of capitalist profits.

Historically, income shifts conducive to economic development have assumed many forms. In Meiji Japan and also in Czarist Russia the substitution of government bonds for the great landholders' claim on the flow of rent payments led to a highly Smithian redistribution of income into the hands of those with higher propensities to seek material advance and to accept innovations. In both cases the real value of the government bonds exchanged for land depreciated; and, in general, the feudal landlords emerged with a less attractive arrangement than had first appeared to be offered. Aside from the confiscation effect, two positive impulses arose from

horizons open up, rather than merely from a shift of income to groups with a higher (but static) propensity to save. He may well be right. This is, evidently, a matter for further investigation.

[24] Hoarding can, of course, be helpful to the growth process by depressing consumption and freeing resources for investment if, in fact, nonhoarding persons or institutions acquire the resources and possess the will to expand productive investment. A direct transfer of income is, evidently, not required.

[25] See, especially, Smith's observations on the "perversion" of wealth by "prodigality"—that is, unproductive consumption expenditures—and on the virtues of "parsimony" which transfers income to those who will increase "the fund which is destined for the maintenance of productive hands." Routledge edition, London, 1890, pp. 259–260.

[26] *Op. cit.*, especially pp. 156–159.

[23] Mr. Everett Hagen has pointed out that the increase in savings may well arise from a shift in the propensity to save, as new and exciting

land reform: the state itself used the flow of payments from peasants, now diverted from landlords' hands, for activity which encouraged economic development; and a certain number of the more enterprising former landlords directly invested in commerce and industry. In contemporary India and China we can observe quite different degrees of income transfer by this route. India is relying to only a very limited extent on the elimination of large incomes unproductively spent by large landlords; although this element figures in a small way in its program. Communist China has systematically transferred all nongovernmental pools of capital into the hands of the State, in a series of undisguised or barely disguised capital levies; and it is drawing heavily for capital resources on the mass of middle and poor peasants who remain.[27]

In addition to confiscatory and taxation devices, which can operate effectively when the State is spending more productively than the taxed individuals, inflation has been important to several take-offs. In Britain of the late 1790's, the United States of the 1850's, Japan of the 1870's there is no doubt that capital formation was aided by price inflation, which shifted resources away from consumption to profits.

The shift of income flows into more productive hands has, of course, been aided historically not only by government fiscal measures but also by banks and capital markets. Virtually without exception, the take-off periods have been marked by the extension of banking institutions which expanded the supply of working capital; and in most cases also by an expansion in the range of long-range financing done by a central, formally organized, capital market.

Although these familiar capital-supply functions of the State and private institutions have been important to the take-off, it is likely to prove the case, on close examination, that a necessary condition for take-off was the existence of one or more

[27] *Prospects for Communist China*, Part IV.

rapidly growing sectors whose entrepreneurs (private or public) ploughed back into new capacity a very high proportion of profits. Put another way, the demand side of the investment process, rather than the supply of loanable funds, may be the decisive element in the take-off, as opposed to the period of creating the preconditions, or of sustaining growth once it is under way. The distinction is, historically, sometimes difficult to make, notably when the State simultaneously acts both to mobilize supplies of finance and to undertake major entrepreneurial acts. There are, nevertheless, periods in economic history when quite substantial improvements in the machinery of capital supply do not, in themselves, initiate a take-off, but fall within the period when the preconditions are created: e.g., British banking developments in the century before 1783; Russian banking developments before 1890, etc.

One extremely important version of the plough-back process has taken place through foreign trade. Developing economies have created from their natural resources major export industries; and the rapid expansion in exports has been used to finance the import of capital equipment and to service the foreign debt during the take-off. United States, Russian, and Canadian grain fulfilled this function, Swedish timber and pulp, Japanese silk, etc. Currently Chinese exports to the Communist Bloc, wrung at great administrative and human cost from the agricultural sector, play this decisive role. It should be noted that the development of such export sectors has not in itself guaranteed accelerated capital formation. Enlarged foreign-exchange proceeds have been used in many familiar cases to finance hoards (as in the famous case of Indian bullion imports) or unproductive consumption outlays.

It should be noted that one possible mechanism for inducing a high rate of plough-back into productive investment is a rapid expansion in the effective demand for domestically manufactured consumers' goods, which would direct into the hands of vigorous entrepreneurs an increasing proportion of income flows under circumstances which would lead them to expand their own capacity and to increase their requirements for industrial raw materials, semi-manufactured products and manufactured compounds.

A final element in the supply of loanable funds is, of course, capital imports. Foreign capital has played a major role in the take-off stage of many economies: e.g., the United States, Russia, Sweden, Canada. The cases of Britain and Japan indicate, however, that it cannot be regarded as an essential condition. Foreign capital was notably useful when the construction of railways or other large overhead capital items with a long period of gestation, played an important role in the take-off. After all, whatever its strategic role, the proportion of investment required for growth which goes into industry is relatively small compared to that required for utilities, transport and the housing of enlarged urban populations. And foreign capital can be mightily useful in helping carry the burden of these overhead items either directly or indirectly.

What can we say, in general, then, about the supply of finance during the take-off period? First, as a precondition, it appears necessary that the community's surplus above the mass-consumption level does not flow into the hands of those who will sterilize it by hoarding, luxury consumption, or low-productivity investment outlays. Second, as a precondition, it appears necessary that institutions be developed which provide cheap and adequate working capital. Third, as a necessary condition, it appears that one or more sectors of the economy must grow rapidly, inducing a more general industrialization process; and that the entrepreneurs in such sectors plough back a substantial proportion of their profits in further productive investment, one possible and recurrent version of the plough-back process

being the investment of proceeds from a rapidly growing export sector.

The devices, confiscatory and fiscal, for ensuring the first and second preconditions have been historically various. And, as indicated below, the types of leading manufacturing sectors which have served to initiate the take-off have varied greatly. Finally, foreign capital flows have, in significant cases, proved extremely important to the take-off, notably when lumpy overhead capital construction of long gestation period was required; but take-offs have also occurred based almost wholly on domestic sources of finance.

THE SOURCES OF ENTREPRENEURSHIP

It is evident that the take-off requires the existence and the successful activity of some group in the society which accepts borrowers' risk, when such risk is so defined as to include the propensity to accept innovations. As noted above, the problem of entrepreneurship in the take-off has not been profound in a limited group of wealthy agricultural nations whose populations derived by emigration mainly from north-western Europe. There the problem of take-off was primarily economic; and when economic incentives for industrialization emerged commercial and banking groups moved over easily into industrial entrepreneurship. In many other countries, however, the development of adequate entrepreneurship was a more searching social process.

Under some human motivation or other, a group must come to perceive it to be both possible and good to undertake acts of capital investment; and, for their efforts to be tolerably successful, they must act with approximate rationality in selecting the directions toward which their enterprise is directed. They must not only produce growth but tolerably balanced growth. We cannot quite say that it is necessary for them to act as if they were trying to maximize profit; for the criteria for private profit maximization do not necessarily converge with the criteria for an optimum rate and pattern of growth in various sectors.[28] But in a growing economy, over periods longer than the business cycle, economic history is reasonably tolerant of deviations from rationality, in the sense that excess capacity is finally put to productive use. Leaving aside the question of ultimate human motivation, and assuming that the major overhead items are generated, if necessary, by some form of state initiative (including subsidy), we can say as a first approximation that some group must successfully emerge which behaves as if it were moved by the profit motive, in a dynamic economy with changing production functions; although risk being the slippery variable, it is under such assumptions Keynes' dictum should be borne in mind: "If human nature felt no temptation to take a chance, no satisfaction (profit apart) in constructing a factory, a railway, a mine or a farm, there might not be much investment merely as a result of cold calculation."[29]

In this connection it is increasingly conventional for economists to pay their respects to the Protestant ethic.[30] The historian should not be ungrateful for this light on the grey horizon of formal growth models. But the known cases of economic growth which theory must seek to explain take us beyond the orbit of Protestantism. In a world where Samurai, Parsees, Jews, North Italians, Turkish, Russian, and Chinese Civil Servants (as well as Huguenots, Scotsmen and British North-country-

men) have played the role of a leading *élite* in economic growth John Calvin should not be made to bear quite this weight. More fundamentally, allusion to a positive scale of religious or other values conducive to profit-maximizing activities is an insufficient sociological basis for this important phenomenon. What appears to be required for the emergence of such *élites* is not merely an appropriate value system but two further conditions: first, the new *élite* must feel itself denied the conventional routes to prestige and power by the traditional less acquisitive society of which it is a part; second, the traditional society must be sufficiently flexible (or weak) to permit its members to seek material advance (or political power) as a route upwards alternative to conformity.

Although an *élite* entrepreneurial class appears to be required for take-off, with significant power over aggregate income flows and industrial investment decisions, most take-offs have been preceded or accompanied by radical change in agricultural techniques and market organization. By and large the agricultural entrepreneur has been the individual land-owning farmer. A requirement for take-off is, therefore, a class of farmers willing and able to respond to the possibilities opened up for them by new techniques, landholding arrangements, transport facilities, and forms of market and credit organization. A small purposeful *élite* can go a long way in initiating economic growth; but, especially in agriculture (and to some extent in the industrial working force), a wider-based revolution in outlook must come about.[31]

---

[28] For a brief discussion of this point see the author's "Trends in the Allocation of Resources in Secular Growth," Ch. 15, *Economic Progress*, ed. Leon H. Dupriez, with the assistance of Douglas C. Hague (Louvain, 1955), pp. 378–379. For a more complete discussion see W. Fellner, "Individual Investment Projects in Growing Economics" (mimeographed), paper presented to the Center for International Studies Social Science Research Council Conference on Economic Growth, October 1954, Cambridge, Massachusetts.

[29] *General Theory*, p. 150.

[30] See, for example, N. Kaldor, "Economic Growth and Cyclical Fluctuations," *Economic Journal*, March 1954, p. 67.

[31] Like the population question, agriculture is mainly excluded from this analysis, which considers the take-off rather than the whole development process. Nevertheless, it should be noted that, as a matter of history, agricultural revolutions have generally preceded or accompanied the take-off. In theory we can envisage a take-off which did not require a radical improvement in agricultural productivity: if, for example, the growth and productivity of the industrial sector permitted a

Whatever further empirical research may reveal about the motives which have led men to undertake the constructive entrepreneurial acts of the take-off period, this much appears sure: these motives have varied greatly, from one society to another; and they have rarely, if ever, been motives of an unmixed material character.

LEADING SECTORS IN THE TAKE-OFF

The author has presented elsewhere the notion that the overall rate of growth of an economy must be regarded in the first instance as the consequence of differing growth rates in particular sectors of the economy, such sectoral growth rates being in part derived from certain overall demand parameters (e.g., population, consumers' income, tastes, etc.), in part from the primary and secondary effects of changing supply factors, when these are effectively exploited.[32]

On this view the sectors of an economy may be grouped in three categories:

1. *Primary growth sectors*, where possibilities for innovation or for the exploitation of newly profitable or hitherto unexplored resources yield a high growth rate and set in motion expansionary forces elsewhere in the economy.

2. *Supplementary growth sectors*, where rapid advance occurs in direct response to —or as a requirement of—advance in the primary growth sectors; e.g., coal, iron, and engineering in relation to railroads.

withering away of traditional agriculture and a substitution for it of imports. In fact, agricultural revolutions have been required to permit rapidly growing (and urbanizing) populations to be fed without exhausting foreign exchange resources in food imports or creating excessive hunger in the rural sector; and as noted at several points in this argument, agricultural revolutions have in fact played an essential and positive role, not merely by both releasing workers to the cities, and feeding them, but also by earning foreign exchange for general capital-formation purposes.

[32] *Process of Economic Growth*, Ch. 4, especially pp. 97–102; and, in greater detail, "Trends in the Allocation of Resources in Secular Growth," see page 248, footnote 28.

These sectors may have to be tracked many stages back into the economy, as the Leontief input–output models would suggest.

3. *Derived growth sectors*, where advance occurs in some fairly steady relation to the growth of total real income, population, industrial production or some other overall, modestly increasing parameter. Food output in relation to population, housing in relation to family formation are classic derived relations of this order.

Very roughly speaking, primary and supplementary growth sectors derive their high momentum essentially from the introduction and diffusion of changes in the cost–supply environment (in turn, of course, partially influenced by demand changes); while the derived-growth sectors are linked essentially to changes in demand (while subject also to continuing changes in production functions of a less dramatic character).

At any period of time it appears to be true even in a mature and growing economy that forward momentum is maintained as the result of rapid expansion in a limited number of primary sectors, whose expansion has significant external economy and other secondary effects. From this perspective the behavior of sectors during the take-off is merely a special version of the growth process in general; or, put another way, growth proceeds by repeating endlessly, in different patterns, with different leadings sectors, the experience of the take-off. Like the take-off, long-term growth requires that the society not only generate vast quantities of capital for depreciation and maintenance, for housing and for a balanced complement of utilities and other overheads, but also a sequence of highly productive primary sectors, growing rapidly, based on new production functions. Only thus has the aggregate marginal capital–output ratio been kept low.

Once again history is full of variety: a considerable array of sectors appears to have played this key role in the take-off process.

The development of a cotton-textile industry sufficient to meet domestic requirements has not generally imparted a sufficient impulse in itself to launch a self-sustaining growth process. The development of modern cotton-textile industries in substitution for imports has, more typically, marked the pretake-off period, as for example in India, China, and Mexico.

There is, however, the famous exception of Britain's industrial revolution. Baines' table on raw-cotton imports and his comment on it are worth quoting, covering as they do the original leading sector in the first take-off.[33]

Why did the development of a modern factory system in cotton textiles lead on in Britain to a self-sustaining growth process, whereas it failed to do so in other cases? Part of the answer lies in the fact that, by the late eighteenth century, the preconditions for take-off in Britain were very fully developed. Progress in textiles, coal, iron

[33] E. Baines, *History of the Cotton Manufacture* (London, 1835), p. 348.

and even steam power had been considerable through the eighteenth century; and the social and institutional environment was propitious. But two further technical elements helped determine the upshot. First, the British cotton-textile industry was large in relation to the total size of the economy. From its modern beginnings, but notably from the 1780's forward, a very high proportion of total cotton-textile output was directed abroad, reaching 60 per cent by the 1820's.[34] The evolution of this industry was a more massive fact, with wider secondary repercussions, than if it were simply supplying the domestic market. Industrial enterprise on this scale had secondary reactions on the development of urban areas, the demand for coal, iron and machinery, the demand for working capital and ultimately the demand for cheap transport, which powerfully stimu-

[34] The volume (official value) of British cotton goods exports rose from £355,060 in 1780 to £7,624,505 in 1802 (Baines, *op. cit.*, p. 350). See also the calculation of R. C. O. Matthews, *A Study in Trade Cycle History* (Cambridge, 1954), pp. 127–129.

TABLE 4. *Rate of Increase in the Import of Cotton-wool, in Periods of Ten Years From 1741–1831.*[a]

	PER CENT		PER CENT
1741–1751	81	1791–1801	67½
1751–1761	21½	1801–1811	39½
1761–1771	25½	1811–1821	93
1771–1781	75¾	1821–1831	85
1781–1791	319½		

[a] From 1697 to 1741, the increase was trifling: between 1741 and 1751 the manufacture, though still insignificant in extent, made a considerable spring: during the next twenty years, the increase was moderate: from 1771 to 1781, owing to the invention of the jenny and the water-frame, a rapid increase took place: in the ten years from 1781 to 1791, being those which immediately followed the invention of the mule and the expiration of Arkwrights's patent, the rate of advancement was prodigiously accelerated, being nearly 320 per cent: and from that time to the present, and especially since the close of the war, the increase, though considerably moderated, has been rapid and steady far beyond all precedent in any other manufacture.

lated industrial development in other directions.[35]

Second, a source of effective demand for rapid expansion in British cotton textiles was supplied, in the first instance, by the sharp reduction in real costs and prices which accompanied the technological developments in manufacture and the cheapening real cost of raw cotton induced by the cotton gin. In this Britain had an advantage not enjoyed by those who came later; for they merely substituted domestic for foreign-manufactured cotton textiles. The substitution undoubtedly had important secondary effects by introducing a modern industrial sector and releasing in net a pool of foreign exchange for other purposes; but there was no sharp fall in the real cost of acquiring cotton textiles and no equivalent lift in real income.

The introduction of the railroad has been historically the most powerful single initiator of take-offs.[36] It was decisive in the United States, Germany and Russia; it has played an extremely important part in the Swedish, Japanese, and other cases. The railroad has had three major kinds of impact on economic growth during the take-off period. First, it has lowered internal transport costs, brought new areas and products into commercial markets and, in general, performed the Smithian function of widening the market. Second, it has been a prerequisite in many cases to the development of a major new and rapidly enlarging export sector which, in turn, has served to generate capital for internal development; as, for example, the American railroads of the 1850's, the Russian and Canadian railways before 1914. Third, and perhaps most important for the take-off itself, the development of railways has led on to the development of modern coal, iron, and engineering industries. In many countries the growth of modern basic industrial sectors can be traced in the most direct way to the requirements for building and, especially, for maintaining substantial railway systems. When a society has developed deeper institutional, social and political prerequisites for take-off, the rapid growth of a railway system with these powerful triple effects has often served to lift it into self-sustaining growth. Where the prerequisites have not existed, however, very substantial railway building has failed to initiate a take-off, as, for example, in India, China, pre-1895 Canada, pre-1914 Argentine, etc.

It is clear that an enlargement and modernization of Armed Forces could play the role of a leading sector in take-off. It was a factor in the Russian, Japanese, and German take-offs; and it figures heavily in current Chinese Communist plans. But historically the role of modern armaments has been ancillary rather than central to the take-off.

Quite aside from their role in supplying foreign exchange for general capital-formation purposes, raw materials and foodstuffs can play the role of leading sectors in the take-off if they involve the application of modern processing techniques. The timber industry, built on the steam saw, fulfilled this function in the first phase of Sweden's take-off, to be followed shortly by the pulp industry. Similarly, the shift of Denmark to meat and dairy products, after 1873, appears to have reinforced the development of a manufacturing sector in the economy, as well as providing a major source of foreign exchange. And as Lockwood notes, even the export of Japanese silk thread had important secondary effects which developed modern production techniques.[37]

[35] If we are prepared to treat New England of the first half of the nineteenth century as a separable economy, its take-off into sustained growth can be allocated to the period, roughly, 1820–50 and, again, a disproportionately large cotton-textile industry based substantially on exports (that is, from New England to the rest of the United States) is the regional foundation for sustained growth.

[36] For a detailed analysis of the routes of impact of the railroad on economic development see Paul H. Cootner, *Transport Innovation and Economic Development: The Case of the U.S. Steam Railroads*, 1953, unpublished doctoral thesis, M.I.T.

[37] W. W. Lockwood, *The Economic Development of Japan* (Princeton, 1954), pp. 338–339.

To satisfy the demands of American weaving and hosiery mills for uniform, high-grade yarn, however, it was necessary to improve the quality of the product, from the silkworm egg on through to the bale of silk. In sericulture this meant the introduction of scientific methods of breeding and disease control; in reeling it stimulated the shift to large filatures equipped with machinery; in marketing it led to large-scale organization in the collection and sale of cocoons and raw silk ... it exerted steady pressure in favor of the application of science, machinery, and modern business enterprise.

The role of leading sector has been assumed, finally, by the accelerated development of domestic manufacture of consumption goods over a wide range in substitution for imports, as, for example, in Australia, the Argentine, and perhaps in contemporary Turkey.

What can we say, then, in general about these leading sectors? Historically, they have ranged from cotton textiles, through heavy-industry complexes based on railroads and military end products, to timber, pulp, dairy products, and finally a wide variety of consumers' goods. There is, clearly, no one sectoral sequence for take-off, no single sector which constitutes the magic key. There is no need for a growing society to recapitulate the structural sequence and pattern of Britain, the United States or Russia. Four basic factors must be present:

1. There must be enlarged effective demand for the product or products of sectors which yield a foundation for a rapid rate of growth in output. Historically this has been brought about initially by the transfer of income from consumption or hoarding to productive investment; by capital imports; by a sharp increase in the productivity of current investment inputs, yielding an increase in consumers' real income expended on domestic manufactures; or by a combination of these routes.

2. There must be an introduction into these sectors of new production functions as well as an expansion of capacity.

3. The society must be capable of generating capital initially required to detonate the take-off in these key sectors; and especially, there must be a high rate of plough-back by the (private or state) entrepreneurs controlling capacity and technique in these sectors and in the supplementary growth sectors they stimulated to expand.

4. Finally, the leading sector or sectors must be such that their expansion and technical transformation induce a chain of Leontief input–output requirements for increased capacity and the potentiality for new production functions in other sectors, to which the society, in fact, progressively responds.

Conclusion

This hypothesis is, then, a return to a rather old-fashioned way of looking at economic development. The take-off is defined as an industrial revolution, tied directly to radical changes in methods of production, having their decisive consequence over a relatively short period of time.

This view would not deny the role of longer, slower changes in the whole process of economic growth. On the contrary, take-off requires a massive set of preconditions going to the heart of a society's economic organization and its effective scale of values. Moreover, for the take-off to be successful, it must lead on progressively to sustained growth; and this implies further deep and often slow-moving changes in the economy and the society as a whole.

What this argument does assert is that the rapid growth of one or more new manufacturing sectors is a powerful and essential engine of economic transformation. Its power derives from the multiplicity of its forms of impact, when a society is prepared to respond positively to this impact. Growth in such sectors, with new production functions of high productivity, in itself tends to raise output per head; it places incomes in the hands of men who will not merely save a high proportion of an expanding income but who will plough it into highly productive investment; it sets up a chain of effective demand for other manufactured products; it sets up a requirement for enlarged urban areas, whose capital costs may be high, but whose population and market organization help to make industrialization an on-going process; and, finally, it opens up a range of external economy effects which, in the end, help to produce new leading sectors when the initial impulse of the take-off's leading sectors begins to wane.

We can observe in history and in the contemporary world important changes in production functions in non-manufacturing sectors which have powerful effects on whole societies. If natural resources are rich enough or the new agricultural tricks are productive enough such changes can even outstrip population growth and yield a rise in real output per head. Moreover, they may be a necessary prior condition for take-off or a necessary concomitant for take-off. Nothing in this analysis should be read as deprecating the importance of productivity changes in agriculture to the whole process of economic growth. But in the end take-off requires that a society find a way to apply effectively to its own peculiar resources what D. H. Robertson once called the tricks of manufacture; and continued growth requires that it so organize itself as to continue to apply them in an unending flow, of changing composition. Only thus, as we have all been correctly taught, can that old demon, diminishing returns, be held at bay.

ECONOMIC DEVELOPMENT: POLITICAL PRECONDITIONS AND POLITICAL CONSEQUENCES

J. J. Spengler

For good or ill, life under the conditions imposed by the modern industrial system ... is in the longrun incompatible with the prepossessions of mediaevalism.

THORSTEIN VEBLEN, IN "THE OPPORTUNITY OF JAPAN".

This paper has to do with the political preconditions and the political consequences of economic development. It relates principally to the underdeveloped world, a

SOURCE. J. J. Spengler, "Economic Development: Political Preconditions and Political Consequences," *Journal of Politics*, 22, 387–416, August 1960; Using only pp. 387–389, 392–393, 395–416. This is a revised version of a paper prepared for the Social Science Research Council Committee on Comparative Politics.

term which embraces Asia (with the exception of Soviet Asia, Japan, and Israel), almost all of Africa, much of Latin America and portions of Southern and Eastern Europe. Around 1950, according to Shannon, 147 of the world's 195 political entities, embracing about 54 per cent of the world's landed area, were classifiable as underdeveloped. Within areas variously described as underdeveloped live between 60 and 75 per cent of the world's population.[1]

[1] See L. W. Shannon, *Underdeveloped Areas* (New York, 1957), pp. 6–12, 478–479. See also P. T. Bauer and B. S. Yamey, *The Economics of Underdeveloped Countries* (London, 1957), Ch. 1; N. S. Buchanan and H. S. Ellis, *Approaches To Economic Development* (New York, 1955), Ch. 1; G. M. Meier and R. R. Baldwin, *Economic Development* (New York, 1957), Ch. 1 and pp. 478–479; Eugene Staley, *The*

After passing in review some of the characteristics of the underdeveloped world and touching upon the determinants of economic development, I shall examine, in order, the growth-oriented role of government in general, the specific roles or functions of government affecting economic development, the minimum political preconditions of economic development, and the changes that take place in some of these preconditions as economic development proceeds.

Concomitants or Indicators of Underdevelopment

Of the concomitants or indicators of economic development, the cultural and the political are most significant for the present discussion, though the economic, the technological, and the demographic are most important from the immediately economic point of view. Here it is necessary only to note that, in the underdeveloped world, per-capita income, capital equipment, and capital formation are very low; inferior technologies predominate; enterprise is lacking; accessible natural resources are badly exploited; natality and (usually) natural increase are relatively high, in part because so much of the population is rural and agricultural; and the age composition of the population is unfavorable to productivity and the education of youth.[2]

Economic backwardness is associated with various cultural circumstances unfavorable to economic growth. Society is tradition-bound, stable and disposed to preserve stability. The family often is of the extended sort. Land may be communally owned and operated. Educational attainment, together with literacy, is low. Much economic activity may remain un-

[*footnote 1 continued*
Future of Underdeveloped Countries (New York, 1954), Ch. 1.
[2] E.g., see Harvey Leibenstein, *Economic Backwardness and Economic Growth* (New York, 1957), Chs. 4–5; Benjamin Higgins, *Economic Development* (New York, 1959), Part I.

monetized and free of the regulative influence of markets. The "middle class" is unimportant, and the socio-legal system in effect usually unduly restricts enterprise. The values stressed may not encourage economic development, and incentives favorable to work and enterprise may be weak. And so on. Of course, as a country progresses economically, its cultural environment becomes more favorable to economic progress, within limits. It is usually assumed, however, that the rapidity with which a nation's cultural environment becomes favorable to economic development may be increased through appropriate governmental action, particularly when there are at hand successful working models. It is also taken for granted that persistent economic growth is most likely to get under way *after* suitable institutional arrangements have been established in respect of law, family, education, motivation, reward systems, and the like.

Developed countries resemble each other more closely in economic than in political respects, since the prerequisites to economic development are more specific and exacting than those essential to political development and self-government. Underdeveloped countries resemble one another in some but not in all respects, in part because a given political condition may be favorable to economic development under some circumstances, but not under others. For example, while sometimes absolutist régimes have effectively promoted economic development (e.g., in the Soviet Union), at other times they have retarded it by establishing sanctions against deviant persons who might initiate development.[3] Similarly, parliamentary régimes

[3] See B. F. Hoselitz, "Noneconomic Factors in Economic Growth," *American Economic Review*, **47** (May 1957), 39; also Talcott Parsons, *Structure and Process in Modern Societies* (Glencoe, 1960), pp. 101–102, 106. In the eighteenth and early nineteenth centuries, states often indirectly fostered economic growth by allowing freedom of action to private individuals whose enterprise gave rise to economic development.

have sometimes fostered and sometimes retarded economic growth. Self-government, though typically a concomitant of economic development, has not always brought it about. The pseudo-biblical precept engraved on Premier K. Nkrumah's statue in Accra ("Seek ye first the political kingdom and all other things shall be added unto you") has yet to acquire the status of a political axiom. For while only nine negligibly populated non-self-governing political units out of a total of 106 units-so describable were economically developed around 1950, but 39 of the 89 self-governing political entities were so classifiable. Moreover, the 50 self-governing underdeveloped entities included 55 per cent of the world's population, whereas the 97 non-self-governing underdeveloped units included only 8 per cent.[4] Of the political characteristics common to all underdeveloped countries, the most important is a dearth of administrative personnel possessed of technical competence and other requisite attributes. . . .

Determinants of Economic Development

The determinants of economic development have been variously classified. One may, with Lewis, group them under three principal heads: (1) wide-ranging efforts to economize in the sense of minimizing input per unit of output, or of maximizing output per unit of input; (2) "the increase of knowledge and its application," particularly to production; (3) "increasing the amount of capital or other resources per head."[5] But such a grouping, even though

it allows adequate weight to the role of the entrepreneur, tends to understate the roles of cultural, political, and other non-economic factors. It may also overlook social-structural and related obstacles to the formation and the effective investment of capital. There is merit, therefore, in lists of determinants such as the one Rostow has proposed. He suggests that growth depends upon certain propensities which reflect a society's underlying value system and summarize its response to its environment: (1) the propensity to develop fundamental physical and social science; (2) "the propensity to apply science to economic ends"; (3) "the propensity to accept innovations"; (4) "the propensity to seek material advance"; (5) the propensity to consume, by which saving also is conditioned; (6) "the propensity to have children." The propensities are related, on the one hand, to the more immediate economic causes of economic growth, and, on the other, to determinants or circumstances underlying the propensities in question.[6]

Typological studies suggest that growth-favoring factors, being intercorrelated, tend to cluster even as do growth-retarding factors. Facilitation of a society's economic development therefore initially entails the introduction and the strengthening of enough favorable factors. In proportion as these variables are loosely instead of tightly interconnected, initial growth-favoring changes must be large if they are to be propagated through the system of inter-related variables and bring about new, intervariable equilibria that remain sufficiently unstable to make for continuing growth. . . .[7]

[4] Shannon, *op. cit.*, p. 27, also pp. 468ff.; *idem*, "Is Level of Development Related to Capacity for Self-Government?" *American Journal of Economics and Sociology*, **47** (July 1958), 367–381, and "A Re-examination of the Concept 'Capacity for Self-Government'," *Journal of Negro Education*, **26** (Spring 1957), 135–144. See also W. S. and E. S. Woytinsky, *World Commerce and Governments* (New York, 1955), pp. 563–567, 582–583, 586.

[5] William Arthur Lewis, *The Theory of Economic Growth* (London, 1955), p. 11.

[6] See Rostow, *The Process of Economic Growth* (New York, 1952), Chs. 1–3. For yet another list of factors which directly or indirectly affect economic development, see J. J. Spengler, "Economic Factors in the Development of Densely Populated Areas," *Proceedings of the American Philosophical Society*, **95** (1951), 21–24.

[7] See Parsons, *op. cit.*, Chs. 3–4, and *The Social System* (Glencoe, 1951), Ch. 5; Leibenstein,

The Role of Government in General

The role of government with reference to economic development may be described in various ways. It may, for example, be described simply as one of increasing the magnitude and the effectiveness of the immediate determinants of economic growth, or it may be analyzed in terms of function, or of economy-oriented tasks associated with government.

The rate of economic growth is dependent upon the functions performed in a society, upon the skill with which they are performed and upon the relative importance attached to some functions as compared with others. Through time each of these conditions may change. The total number of functions performed in a society may change, both because new ones are introduced and because the relative importance of old ones becomes negligible. These two types of change are most likely to be correlated immediately with changes in a people's individual and collective aspirations and objectives, though they may also be correlated with changes in methods of production. The skill with which functions are performed is affected by (among other things) the manner in which responsibility for their performance is distributed among the institutions that might assume such responsibility—some institutions are comparatively better suited than others to provide for the performance of particular functions. At any one time, however, the manner in which these functions are distributed may be quite stable and relatively unmodifiable. This is likely to be the case if much of the existing distribution has won the sanction of history and has acquired, therefore, the support of various groups. Under such circumstances it may be difficult to introduce a more efficient distribution. Witness the difficulties attendant upon introducing into Country B economic arrangements found effective in Country A when their introduction into B entails changes in arrangements which, even though making for inefficiency, enjoy widespread support in B.[8]

Functions or operations which are essentially economic in character have been variously distributed among institutions, in time and in space. Similarly, the manner in which these functions, together with the institutions responsible for them, have been coordinated in societies has differed from time to time and from country to country. We may turn to the theory of the firm for a partial analogy. Within limits, some functions or operations carried on by business firms require smaller inputs per unit of output as the total volume of output rises. Other functions are performed with maximum efficiency—i.e., input per unit of output is minimized—at relatively low levels of output. Accordingly, allowing for the extent to which particular functions are interrelated, some distributions of functions among firms are more efficient, from the standpoint of the economy as a whole, than are other distributions; and firms tend to vary greatly in size, with their magnitudes affected by the kinds of functions or operations performed. Furthermore, whereas the activities carried on within any firm will be coordinated by its management, the activities of all firms viewed as firms will be coordinated by a mechanism existing outside firms and providing indicators in the light of which they adjust their activities. This mechanism usually is the "market," or if not, a set of coordinating arrangements that functions in a manner analogous to that of the "market."

[*footnote 7 continued*
op. cit., Chs. 9, 12; W. E. Moore, "Problems of Timing, Balance and Priorities in Development Measures," *Economic Development and Cultural Change*, 2 (January 1954), 239–248; G. A. Theodorson, "Acceptance of Industrialization and Its Attendant Consequences for the Social Patterns of Non-western Societies," *American Sociological Review*, **18** (October 1953), 477–484.

[8] E.g., see James Baster, "Development and the Free Economy: Some Typical Dilemmas," *Kyklos*, 7 (Fasc. 1, 1954), 10–11.

It is commonly supposed that, in an economy which is competitive, or which behaves in accordance with rules suited to maximize efficiency when demand patterns are given, functions tend to become optimally distributed among firms and the activities of firms tend to be efficiently coordinated. In reality, of course, economic functions do not always get so appropriately distributed among firms, or among the institutions that might perform them; and this is particularly true of societies in which the economy is neither highly differentiated within itself, nor quite sharply differentiated from other subsystems or sets of specialized institutions. Accordingly, from the fact that, in space and time, economic functions have been variously distributed among institutions,[9] it is not to be inferred that the resulting distribution was necessarily the "best" attainable, or the one most favorable to economic development. It is only to be inferred that functions have been variously distributed and coordinated, and that the resulting distributions often were unfavorable to economic developments. It is also to be inferred that societies and economies have been relatively inflexible and resistant to economic change when economic functions have become intermixed with noneconomic functions in the same institutional context (e.g., in the family, in the village community or in essentially religious or political institutions). It is to be inferred, finally, that it is difficult to transfer, with little or no modification, to Country B from Country A, the particular cluster of economic (or of economic and noneconomic) functions that

have gotten assembled and coordinated in A.

As has been noted, the economically oriented role of government varies in intensity over time. Why this is so has been dealt with by Talcott Parsons and N. J. Smelser. They note that a society tends to become differentiated into four analytically distinguishable subsystems (or social structures), each of which becomes specialized in the performance of one of the four primary functions (or sets of functions) whereon depends satisfaction of a society's "needs," and hence its continuity. The first, the economy, performs the adaptive function. It is primarily responsible for the production of income, of generalized facilities which may be put to an indefinite number of uses, and which support the performance of the other three functions. A second subsystem has to do with social control, with maintaining "solidarity," with so relating the prevalent cultural value-patterns to the motivational structures of individuals that "undue internal conflict" can be avoided and that society, as a totality, can continue to function. This subsystem focuses upon *inter*unit relationships, which integrate various social units and subsystems into a society. A third subsystem performs a somewhat similar function at the *intra*unit level; it institutionalizes and maintains values and behavior patterns in the face of change and copes with the tensions that originate in the strains to which the system is subject. This subsystem insures that individuals fulfill the roles assigned to them.

The fourth subsystem, or polity, has to do with the attainment of essentially collective goals, with the mobilization of wealth or output to accomplish a society's overall or system goals. It embodies a "generalized capacity to mobilize the resources of the society including wealth, 'political responsibility,' etc., to attain particular and more or less immediate collective goals of the system." Its function is carried out by government in that "political goals and values tend to have primacy over other

[9] Concerning the manner in which various functions have been redistributed among institutions, or sets of interrelated institutions, see P. A. Sorokin, *Social and Cultural Dynamics* (New York, 1937), **3**, Part I, esp. Ch. 7. On the functions of the firm, see G. J. Stigler, "The Division of Labor Is Limited by the Extent of the Market," *Journal of Political Economy*, **59** (June 1951), 185–193; R. H. Coase, "The Nature of the Firm," *Economica*, **4** (November 1937), 386–405.

in an organ of government."[10] The polity is concerned to maximize a society's capacity to realize collective goals. It may make capital (i.e., generalized purchasing power) available and encourage productive enterprise, subject to the condition that it retains the right to intervene and select the uses to which facilities are put.[11] The polity may also affect the economy indirectly through the medium of either of the integrating subsystems, each of which conditions the functioning of the economy. The polity's potential role is greatest in a modern society. In a relatively undifferentiated society, economic and noneconomic functions tend to be fused; in a modern totalitarian society, on the contrary, the economy is dominated by the polity.[12]

Because it is the function of the economy to supply output to the other subsystems, its behavior is not always and solely dominated by the satisfaction of individual wants.

The goal of the economy is not simply the production of income for the utility of an aggregate of individuals. It is the maximization of production relative to the whole complex of institutionalized value-systems and functions of the society and its sub-systems. . . . Utility . . . is the *economic value* of physical, social or cultural objects in accord with their *significance as facilities* for solving the adaptive problems of social system.[13]

Accordingly, and because individual motivation is "conceived as a process of the internalization of social norms," neither

economic nor social welfare is completely reducible to terms of individual welfare functions. This argument, insofar as it is valid, weakens that supporting consumer sovereignty, even as do arguments suggested by modern welfare economics.[14]

The significance of economic and political values varies. In Western societies, "economic values occupy a high position in the hierarchy [of values];" yet even here a significant part of the individual's "economic" motivation is independent of the rewards to be had.[15] It is to be inferred that, as societies undergo economic development, the relative importance of economic values increases, at least until they are weakened by growing affluence, and that the rationality of economic behavior—i.e., its adaptability as a means to given ends—increases. Even so, the importance of the role of the state (or governmental organs) tends to fluctuate considerably. When collective or system goals command little effective attention, the use to which resources are put will be determined largely within the economic subsystem where consumer desires play a major role. When, however, collective or system goals become ascendant, the demands of the polity upon the economy greatly increase, and much more of the available supply of economic facilities is directed to the satisfaction of these goals.[16] Econo-

[10] Parsons and Smelser, *Economy and Society* (Glencoe, 1956), pp. 48–49; also pp. 14ff. Non-governmental agencies frequently are affected with public interest, and governmental organs may be intermixed with private. See *ibid.*, pp. 60, 82–85.
[11] E.g., see *ibid.*, pp. 56–78, 98–99.
[12] *Ibid.*, pp. 79–83.
[13] *Ibid.*, p. 22; author's italics. The goal of the economy may be viewed as "defined strictly by socially structured goals." *Loc. cit.*

[14] *Ibid.*, p. 32. The argument supporting consumer freedom respecting the use of disposable income is weakened only slightly. For other criticisms of consumer freedom, see R. A. Dahl and C. E. Lindblom, *Politics, Economics, and Welfare* (New York, 1953), pp. 164ff., 394ff., 414–430; F. D. Holzman, "Consumer Sovereignty and the Rate of Economic Development," reprinted from *Economia Internazionale*, 11 (May 1958), 1–20. See also J. de V. Graaf, *Theoretical Welfare Economics* (Cambridge, 1957); J. E. Meade, *Trade and Welfare* (London, 1955).
[15] Parsons and Smelser, *op. cit.*, pp. 175–184. The system of rewards prevailing in society tends to encompass too much inequality in some ranges and too little in others.
[16] See B. F. Hoselitz's paper in Hugh G. J. Aitken (ed.), *The State and Economic Growth* (New York, 1959).

mic development itself is a system goal (or a set of system goals), especially in countries bent upon economic development. Since economic and noneconomic obstacles to economic development are numerous, it is widely held that economic development requires a great deal of governmental intervention and activity.

When is State Intervention Indicated?

The upsurge of interest in "forced" economic development and in the capacity of "welfare economics" to furnish policy-guiding norms has been accompanied by much questioning of the liberal democratic theory of the relationship of government to economic activity. This theory has held that, under free competition, optimal marginal equivalences tend to be approximated in the overwhelmingly predominant private sector, and that most, though not all, economically warrantable goals tend to be realized. It has also held that, when private enterprise is unable to achieve a specified goal, the state may intervene, either by assisting private enterprise or by itself undertaking to transform inputs into the desired output. It has generally been held that, so long as the social benefit supposedly consequent upon a course of action exceeds its cost (appropriately defined), the action should be undertaken. It should be undertaken under state auspices if private enterprisers are no longer able, at the relevant conduct-determining margin, to derive enough gross income from the undertaking to cover the costs entailed.[17] The state may intervene, either indirectly through recourse to penalties (e.g., taxes) and grants-in-aid (e.g., subsidies) designed to induce entrepreneurs to shunt resources into the sector

indicated for further expansion, or directly through recourse to governmental entrepreneurship or joint governmental participation with private enterprisers.

The liberal theory outlined has contemplated principally actions whose benefits are indiscriminate, in that recipients thereof cannot be made to pay sufficiently for the services benefitting them (e.g., the services of public-health or public-education facilities). At issue in any given situation, therefore, is whether the action in question is truly indiscriminate, whether it has significantly beneficial side effects for which the responsible entrepreneur is unable to obtain adequate remuneration from the beneficiaries of these effects.[18] Underlying the assessment of a contemplated action is the supposition that great weight must be given to consumer sovereignty and freedom of choice, and the inference that, with few exceptions, the changes sought are relatively small, and hence quite easy to evaluate in terms of current individual preferences.

Economic development, especially when "forced," is likely to require considerable sacrifice of consumer freedom and sovereignty, and to be accompanied by effects which, being large and only imperfectly foreseeable, are not unarbitrarily assessable. (1) Decision may consist in determining whether to undertake a heavy investment that is likely to produce a notable but not wholly anticipatable change in an economy's structure. If an economy is stagnant and requires transformation, the domestic market may offer little guidance; in fact, even in underdeveloped but developing countries the guidance to be had from the domestic market may be quite limited. Under the circumstances, it is unlikely that actual and prospective yields directly realizable from the investment in question would cause it to be undertaken by private entrepreneurs, even though careful judgment suggested that it should be undertaken; hence state intervention would be indicated. (2) Setting developmental pro-

---

[17] The underlying problem has been treated extensively. E.g., see A. Lerner, *Economics of Control* (New York, 1944); W. J. Baumol, *Welfare Economics and the Theory of the State* (Cambridge, 1952); J. de V. Graaf, *Theoretical Welfare Economics*. I ignore the companion case in which social costs exceed social benefits even though private gain remains in excess of private cost at the relevant margin.

[18] Bauer and Yamey, *op. cit.*, p. 164.

cesses in motion may call for considerable capital-intensive investment (even though analysis based on essentially static premises suggests that, in capital-short and labor-long economies, capital-intensive investment should not be emphasized). Such heavy initial investment, much of it capital-intensive, may be recommended on the ground that it breaks the fetters of the past; or that it opens up "new product horizons;"[19] or that it is highly conducive to economic growth in the long run, in that it checks population growth, stimulates investment in skills and physical assets and permits escape from a low-income subsistence equilibrium. In the event that enough private investment is not forthcoming to meet these various requirements, state intervention or support becomes necessary. (3) It may also be contended that, since the expansion of any particular kind of output depends upon the commensurate expansion of both the demand for it and the supply of those particular inputs from which it is made, growth in general presupposes a more or less parallel expansion of all the relevant sectors of an economy. Such balanced expansion is attainable, it is sometimes argued, only if the state intervenes.[20]

[19] See A. O. Hirschman, "Investment Policies and 'Dualism' in Underdeveloped Countries," *American Economic Review*, **47** (1957), 561–569. Hirschman is concerned also with the interregional spread of development.

[20] The issues raised in this paragraph are treated by Higgins, *op. cit.*, by A. O. Hirschman, *The Strategy of Economic Development* (New Haven, 1958); by Leibenstein, *op. cit.*; and by A. Gerschenkron in B. F. Hoselitz (ed.), *The Progress of Underdeveloped Areas* (Chicago, 1952), pp. 3–29. On balanced growth, see also R. Nurkse, *Problems of Capital Formation in Underdeveloped Countries* (New York, 1953), pp. 11ff.; Bauer and Yamey, *op. cit.*, pp. 247–250; M. Fleming, "External Economies and the Doctrine of Balanced Growth," *Economic Journal*, **65** (June 1955), 241–256. Leibenstein (*op. cit.*, Ch. 15) points out that urban-industrial investment is more conducive to the growth of per-capita productive power than is rural investment. The former gives rise to an environment more

Two sets of difficulties attend attempts to make state policies contribute to economic growth compatibly with the principles of "welfare economics," even though distributive effects are ignored. (1) Application of these principles is encumbered when an economy is imperfectly competitive and (therefore) a number of adjustments may be indicated; or when a large, future-oriented structural change is contemplated, for which adequate, nonarbitrary guidance is not to be found in the present.[21] (2) Even though welfare is defined in a sufficiently arbitrary manner to evade some difficulties of the latter sort, there remains the need to ascertain if a policy is performing up to expectations, and to respond appropriately. Agencies of the state tend to be less able than private entrepreneurs to determine whether undertakings are proceeding successfully, and they are commonly less disposed to make such determination. It is usually essential, therefore, to establish competent and informed independent bodies charged with the critical assessment of governmental undertakings affecting economic development.[22] Private entrepreneurs, being interested primarily in profits, continually assess ventures in terms of their actual or prospective profits, and tend to take suitable corrective action. There is not, in respect of many ventures undertaken by the state, so sensitive an indicator of per-

favorable to the development of an entrepreneurial class, of knowledge and new skills and techniques, of an essentially intellectual and innovational climate, and of fertility control. Leibenstein's argument is partly based upon the premise that the relevant variables are loosely connected, with the result that relatively heavy stimuli are required to modify the socioeconomic and demographic equilibrium existing in underdeveloped countries.

[21] E.g., see J. E. Meade, *Trade and Welfare*, Chs. 4–8; J. de V. Graaf, *op. cit.*, Chs. 6, 12.

[22] See E. A. Shils, "The Intellectuals, Public Opinion, and Economic Development," *Economic Development and Cultural Change*, **6** (1951), 55–62; also my forthcoming essay, "Public Economic Policy in a Dynamic Society."

formance as a profits index. Furthermore, both politicians and civil servants, together with the interest groups they represent, may be reluctant to discover failure, let alone rectify it. For these and other reasons, one encounters fewer and less effective corrective mechanisms in the public sector than in the private. This lack may be accentuated, furthermore, if the rate at which the future is discounted in the public sector is too low and too much emphasis is placed upon the distant future and long-term policies (e.g., in the formulation of conservation policies). It may be accentuated also insofar as the positive and presumably beneficial effects of governmental ventures prove easier of observation than do the associated negative and presumably detrimental effects.

Specific Roles or Functions of Government

The state, of course, may contribute, positively or negatively, to economic development by pursuing courses which indirectly or directly affect economic growth. It may contribute indirectly through actions suited to strengthen the private sector, and directly by carrying on appropriate activities in the public sector. An economy is not always reducible, of course, to terms of a private sector and a public sector. The two sectors may overlap and become intermixed, inasmuch as many of the choices available lie on a continuum running from one extreme to the other.[23]

The negative actions of government include failure to maintain law and order; corruption in public administration, together with plundering of commercial and other enterprising classes; exploitation of submerged classes, together with denial to them of access to superior occupations; abuse or exclusion of foreigners possessing requisite skills, enterprise, capital, new tastes, etc.; nonmaintenance of essential public services; failure to provide critical assistance and stimuli to economic sectors in which development may be triggered off; unduly restrictive regulation of economic activities; diversion of an excessive fraction of the community's surplus above consumption into unproductive forms of public capital; imposition of taxes which are arbitrary, uncertain and of a sort to blunt incentive; waste of resources in war; premature development of effective trade unions, together with "welfare-state" legislation; denial of adequate returns on private investments in public utilities, etc.; and diversion of resources from economic to uneconomic activities.

Economic activity can be carried on in the private sector, with some prospect of eventuating in continuing economic development only if certain functions are satisfactorily performed by the government. These include: (1) the maintenance of law and order and security against aggression; (2) sufficient support of education and public health; (3) adequate support of basic research, of the introduction of scientific findings from abroad and of the diffusion of applied scientific knowledge through agricultural extension and similar services; (4) provision, insofar as economically indicated and possible, of certain basic forms of overhead capital. Just as, through (2) and (3), the state may foster the development of a more effective labor force, so through (1) it may augment the capacity of the society to withstand the tensions that accompany economic development.

Satisfying the money requirements of economic development presupposes performance of at least two sets of functions: (5) control of the issue and supply of paper money and bank credit, through an effective central banking system and in a manner capable of preventing marked inflation; (6)

[23] In this section, I draw heavily upon Lewis, *op. cit.*, Ch. 7. See also Parsons, *Structure and Process* . . . , Chs. 3–4; R. A. Dahl and C. E. Lindblom, *Politics, Economics and Welfare*, pp. 6–8; and, on the limitations to which governmental development efforts are subject, Bauer and Yamey, *op. cit.*, and Buchanan and Ellis, *op. cit.*,

making provision, insofar as practicable and necessary, for action on the part of the central banking system and cognate agencies to prevent undue deflation. It does not seem advisable for an underdeveloped country to pursue monetary policies designed to maintain full employment. Its situation, together with the nature of its unemployment (much of it in agriculture and of long standing), differs from that encountered in developed countries; moreover, factor immobility is too great and bottlenecks are too many to permit such policies to work. (7) Provision needs to be made for the establishment, under public or public-private auspices, of financial institutions suited to assemble small savings (e.g., savings banks), to supply short-term and intermediate credit, to channel long-term capital from its sources to securities markets and to facilitate the inflow of foreign capital. (8) The government may contribute notably to the formation of attitudes favorable to economic development. (9) It may influence the uses to which resources are put (e.g., through conservation policies, zoning regulations, etc.), the manner in which industry is dispersed in space (so as to prevent excessive concentration, depressed areas, etc.), the degree of specialization (e.g., to prevent monoculture, etc.). (10) Should the government undertake to influence income distribution, it must proceed warily lest capital formation, the acquisition of skill, the suitable distribution of the labor force, etc., be checked. (11) The system of taxes employed should be so constituted as to diminish private capital formation and economic incentive very little. (12) to meet the many needs of a developing economy, a well-tested, stable, appropriately oriented, and explicit legal and administrative structure is required, together with effective administrative and judicial personnel. Among the needs that must be met are: provision for the establishment and operation of required types of business organization (e.g., partnership, private corporation, cooperative, public

and quasi-public corporations, trade union) and for the associated forms of decision-making power; rules facilitating the holding and the conveyance of property; guarantees of mobility and of freedom of entry on the part of labor and other factors of production into employments for which they are technically qualified; suitable definitions and regulations relating to contractual content, sanctions, limitations, etc.; rules insofar as required to avert retardation of growth by quasi-monopolistic and related arrangements; and so on. (13) A government may facilitate economic development by institutionalizing public as well as private initiative, since both are likely to be required, and by drawing on the relevant experience of countries which have achieved high levels of development.

More positive action may be undertaken by a government. It may undertake reform of the system of land tenure. It may attempt to step up capital formation and investment through facilitation of foreign loans, higher taxation and limited inflation, or through the use of unemployed and under-employed manpower to construct economic overhead capital (e.g., highways, railways). The success of such measures turns largely on whether resources are diverted from consumption or from the formation of private capital (which, frequently, is put to more productive use than public capital), and on whether increases in money-income restore to non-savers (e.g., wage-earners) what inflation and increased taxes have taken away from them. The state may draw up a plan to put resources to particular uses and attempt to implement it by giving to entrepreneurs acting in conformity therewith greater access to resources in short supply (e.g., capital, foreign exchange, skilled labor). It may attempt to affect the course of development directly, by setting up a development corporation to which it channels public revenue, by utilizing public revenue to finance the construction of economic and social overhead capital, by establishing specific agencies to perform entrepreneurial functions, and so on.

Minimal Political Conditions for Economic Development

While it is not possible always to distinguish sharply between political and economic factors, it is possible to identify a number of essentially political conditions,[24] most of which are prerequisite to economic development in the present-day underdeveloped world. The kind of society envisaged is noncommunist (in the contemporary empirical sense); it may be democratic in the American or British sense, or "dictatorial" in the Latin American sense. The minimal requirements may be grouped under four main heads: minimal public services; growth-supporting and growth-stimulating arrangements; personnel; and political instruments.

Minimal Public Services. If the state does not make provision for certain minimal services, not much economic activity can be carried on, and little impetus can be given to economic growth. It is, of course, a matter of judgment how large at the minimum the supply of any of these services must be. Here it is noted only that this minimum must be met and that as it is increased economic growth tends (within limits) to be stimulated, though not necessarily in proportion to the increase in services. Having already discussed these services, I shall merely list what the state needs to do:

1. Maintain law, order, and security.
2. Support education and public health.
3. Provide for the issue and suitably controlled supply of paper money and bank credit.
4. Provide for the creation of banks to

assemble savings, to supply short-term and intermediate credit and to afford access to domestic and foreign long-term capital.

5. Provide as much of a legal and administrative structure as is required to permit various types of business organization to function, to maintain private and public property and to prevent excessive monopolization of important activities.

6. Treat foreign personnel and capital so that as much is attracted as is warranted by the desire to get economic development under way.

Growth-Supporting and Growth-Stimulating Arrangements. Only the last-mentioned of the services just enumerated actually gives impetus to economic development. Impetus is supplied by entrepreneurs, private or public, but it can be provided only if they have access to capital, to land and natural resources, and to technology that reduces input requirements and creates new goods. Accordingly, the state must pursue positive policies calculated to give support to entrepreneurs while minimizing the impact of policies that are unwelcome to enterprise.

1. Tax revenue needs to be raised through taxes that diminish very little both incentive to economic activity and propensity to form capital.

2. Governmental expenditure should, insofar as possible, assume forms essential or relatively conducive to economic growth.

3. Inasmuch as effective highly centralized planning under government auspices is quite out of the question in most, if not all, underdeveloped countries, reliance must be placed largely upon decentralized, private economic decision-making which provides entrepreneurs and others with ample incentive to uncover and test potential opportunities. Hence the state must support a climate of opinion in which entrepreneurial decisions can be made freely and effectively.

4. The state must support basic research, together with the adaptation and diffusion of applied technological knowledge.

[24] For analysis of political science research on such conditions, see Ralph Braibanti, "The Relevance of Political Science to the Analysis of Underdeveloped Areas," in Braibanti and J. J. Spengler (eds.), *Tradition, Values and Socio-Economic Development* (Durham, 1960).

5. The state must facilitate the provision of economic and social overhead capital where need for it is indicated, even though the prospective current return on such capital is insufficient to attract private investment.

6. It is desirable, on a number of grounds, among them national prestige, that something like a five-year plan be kept in effect, and that there be established a development corporation, perhaps to help administer such plan and perform various other functions now normally carried on by such corporations. It is desirable that such a plan be subject to revision from year to year as the relative importance of different objects of investment changes. Such a plan, together with changes in it, needs to be made in consultation with the private sector; for, since much of the investment undertaken should serve to increase the productivity of private facilities, or to assist newly developing private enterprise, it should be directed into channels where it gives greatest stimulus to long-run growth. Given such a plan, public capital expenditures are more likely to be made in light of their comparative capacity to stimulate economic growth, and if a public development corporation has been established, better direction tends to be given to expenditures included under (4) and (5). The existence of such a plan may even facilitate foreign borrowing. It is always essential, however, whether such a plan be in existence or not, that attention be directed to estimating whether public or private investment expenditure would be the more productive. It is essential also to recognize that the effectiveness with which a development corporation can function turns on its position in the governmental hierarchy and, therefore, varies as this position changes.

7. It is possible, given the arrangements described under (6), that the ever present tendency to inflation can be better kept under control. For then budgetary practice can be more nearly arranged to keep governmental income and outgo in balance,

unless imbalance in the private sector indicates some need for an offsetting imbalance in the public sector.

8. It has already been noted that the effectiveness of governmental economic policy is much less subject to critical assessment and rectification than is private economic policy. Furthermore, in many underdeveloped countries there do not exist competent private agencies (e.g., universities, research bureaus) which are both free and able to evaluate governmental economic policies. Hence, governmental expenditure tends to be less conducive to development than it might be. It is essential, therefore, that such competent and free critical agencies be developed and that they have access to the information requisite for periodical assessments of governmental economic policies.[25]

Personnel. Under this head we consider personnel in the employ of agencies of the state. In any economy with both a public and a private sector, between which personnel are free to migrate, it is not possible to specify the number of employees in the public sector, or their quality, since migration may modify both number and quality. From the standpoint of a country's development, of course, migration of relatively skilled personnel from one sector to the other necessarily weakens the capacity of the personnel-losing sector to contribute to economic development. Respecting governmental personnel, at least two conditions may be laid down as essential to economic development.

1. *Quantity and quality of governmental personnel.* The available information indicates that, as yet, in all of the underdeveloped countries, the supply of suitable personnel available to fill governmental posts, particularly those having to do with economic development, is insufficient for getting economic growth under way. Furthermore, much of this personnel is short of technical knowledge, probity and

[25] On this problem see Shils, *op. cit.*, pp. 56–62.

other qualities essential to effective performance. The defects noted—in quantity and quality—are similar to those characteristics of personnel in the private sector. It is generally true that personnel improve in quality at about the same rate in both the public and the private sector, and it is probable that the degree of shortage of qualified personnel is no more pronounced in the public than in the private sector.[26] The shortage of qualified governmental personnel is particularly serious in many underdeveloped countries in which the government is being counted upon to perform much of the innovating and pioneering role largely performed by the private entrepreneur in the West.[27]

The stock of qualified personnel at the disposal of a government thus sets an upper limit to the developmental functions that it can undertake. While a government may draw personnel from the private sector in order to raise this limit, it does not follow that development will thereby be made greater. The outcome depends upon

where the personnel in question could make the greater contribution to economic development, in the private or in the public sector. It is essential, therefore, that the stock of qualified personnel be increased in both the private and the public sector, through investment in appropriate education, and so on.

2. *Disposition of governmental personnel.* Because of the shortage of qualified personnel that can perform functions which the state may need but not undertake, it is particularly important that use of governmental personnel be carefully economized. Governmental personnel should be employed only in undertakings in which the input of personnel per unit of output is relatively low, with high priority being given to the performance of the "minimal public services" discussed above. Such personnel should not be engaged in the performance of tasks which non-governmental personnel can do quite (if not more) effectively, in part because *technically qualified* personnel tend to be more scarce in the public than in the private sector. For, under civil-service regulations, the attributes specified as being requisite in those who would perform given sets of tasks tend to be greater than is required in reality or in the private sector. For example, one may need to possess, if he would perform a set of tasks S efficiently, only attributes $abcd$; and yet he may be required by civil-service regulations to possess, at a minimum, attributes $abcdef$ to qualify for the occupational post to which responsibility for the performance of S is assigned. In this instance, attributes ef are nonessential; moreover, in the private sector, they tend to be treated as nonessential, with the result that in this sector under *ceteris paribus* conditions the potential supply of performers of S is relatively greater than in the public sector. It is largely because civil-service rules so frequently are inimical to the economical use of manpower, skilled and otherwise, that efforts have been made, though not with much success, to exempt public corporations and com-

[26] We may turn to several sources for indications of shortages of governmental personnel sufficiently qualified to fill the posts to which they are assigned. Each year, in its Annual Report, the Consultative Committee on the Colombo Plan discusses the shortage of technical personnel and the role of technical assistance under the plan in somewhat alleviating this shortage. Similarly, in the reports of Missions of the International Bank for Reconstruction and Development, the development-retarding effects of shortages of technical personnel, together with qualitative defects in the technical attainments of such personnel, are noted. See also J. J. Spengler, "Public Bureaucracy, Resource Structure, and Economic Development: A Note," *Kyklos*, **11** (Fasc. 4, 1958), 459–486; F. W. Riggs, "Public Administration: A Neglected Factor in Economic Development," *Annals of the American Academy of Political and Social Science*, **305** (May 1956), 70–80; P. Franck, "Economic Planners in Afghanistan," *Economic Development and Cultural Change*, **1** (February 1953), 323–340.

[27] On how this shortage retards development, see e.g., H. W. Singer, "Obstacles to Economic Development," *Social Research*, **20** (Spring 1953), 19–31; also Shils, *op. cit.*, pp. 55–56.

panies from the incidence of these rules.[28] Economical use of a nation's more skilled manpower virtually requires, therefore, that the bulk of the business of transforming inputs into outputs, be these indicated by the market or by agencies of the state, be confined to the private sector.[29]

Political Instruments. Under this head are considered the roles of two instruments, here labelled "political," namely, party structure and welfare state.

1. *Party structure.* As has been indicated, the economic and social costs of economic development are bound to be heavy; there is scope for much controversy regarding priorities; and there are many individuals whose situation will be affected adversely, at least for some time, by economic development. The resulting burden will vary with country, of course, being much greater in heavily populated, low-income countries (e.g., in Asia) than in those where population pressure is less marked and the capacity to increase per-capita income is greater (e.g., in much of Latin America and parts of Africa). In many of these countries (especially in those situated in Asia), economic development is much more likely to be realized, given one dominant political party (e.g., the Congress Party in India), or a pair of parties,[30]

each strongly committed to economic development, than given a multiplicity of parties (as in pre-1940 France).[31] Only a well-entrenched party, or a pair of parties strongly committed to economic development, is likely to be able to keep the ideology of development effectively alive, to impose the necessary costs of development on the population, and yet to remain in office long enough to get economic growth effectively under

calculated to appeal to a majority of the voters, and each will arrive at much the same estimate regarding the content of this position (again making allowance for certain differences in "party" appeal). This is the kind of situation found in the United States. If attitudes are not distributed fairly evenly along a continuum, or if there are more than two parties, the party (or parties) temporarily in power will not have a sufficiently strong and persisting mandate from the voters to carry out a development program. This line of argument is based upon H. Hotelling's "Stability in Competition," *Economic Journal*, **39** (March 1929), 41–57, esp. Part II.

[31] The above argument must make allowance for a country's stage of development and for its social structure at or near the time its growth is getting effectively under way. In nineteenth-century Germany and Japan, the social structure, together with cognate conditions, was favorable. Capital formation could continue at high levels and labor remained content with the share going to it. This seems to have been true also in Britain and France in that the trade-union movement was not strong at the time economic development was getting under way. In general, the underlying population did not resist bearing the costs of development, any more than did the post-1945 German population; hence the presence of two or more parties did not prove inimical to development. A similar situation is not so likely to be found in present-day underdeveloped countries. E.g., see Karl de Schweinitz, "Industrialization, Labor Controls, and Democracy," *Economic Development and Cultural Change*, **7** (July 1959), 385–404, and comments on this article by Robert Freedman, together with de Schweinitz's reply, in *ibid.*, **8** (January 1960), 192–198. Of course, union pressure may operate, in a quite imperfectly competitive society, to compel entrepreneurs to improve methods of production, etc. See A. Sturmthal, "Unions and Economic Development," *ibid.*, pp. 204–205.

[28] E.g., see A. H. Hanson, *Public Enterprise and Economic Development* (London, 1959), pp. 459–464.
[29] See *ibid.*, Ch. 15, also Chs. 5, 11–14; also Spengler, "Public Bureaucracy . . . ," *loc. cit.* The discussion above relates to mixed economies. Weaknesses inherent in bureaucratic undertakings in mixed economies are present also in centralized economies, but their output-depressing effects may be swamped by very high rates of capital formation. E.g., see Janos Kornai, *Overcentralization in Economic Administration* (London, 1959); also M. Polanyi, *The Logic of Liberty* (London, 1951), Chs. 8–10.
[30] Normally, in a two-party country with attitudes distributed rather regularly along a continuum, the platforms of the two parties will tend to be quite similar (given allowance for ambiguities), since each will take a position

way.[32] A dictatorship might find itself in a somewhat similar position, given that it sought to promote economic growth and had fairly widespread support.[33]

2. *Welfare state.* This term is used to denote a state which diverts a considerable fraction of the national income to the support of so-called welfare objectives (various forms of social security, highly subsidized housing) and which sanctions legislation (e.g., minimum-wage legislation) and institutions (e.g., a strong trade-union movement) which exercise heavy upward pressure on real wage rates. While it may be granted that some provision for state-administered social-welfare objectives is essential (particularly since the security-providing extended family and clan and village organizations will probably be undergoing dissolution), and while it may be admitted that some increase in real

wages is necessary (to sustain faith in the gradual advent of a better economic world), it is not compatible with capital formation and economic development for these two objectives to be given strong support. Nor need they be, inasmuch as a rising per-capita income is compatible with an increasing rate of capital formation so long as both output per head and the marginal propensity to save are rising. It may be concluded, therefore, that, for the present and for some years to come, no more than a quite limited welfare state is compatible with a high rate of economic growth in presently underdeveloped lands. For this reason a multi-party system is not compatible with economic growth; it is too likely to give in to ever present demands for "liberal" welfare-state provisions.

Economic Development and Changing Political Conditions

As economic development proceeds, growth-affecting political conditions and requirements change. Per-capita expenditure for education and health tends to increase significantly. Institutional provisions respecting "money" become more complex. There is greater emphasis upon preventing deflation; monetary policy is increasingly directed to narrowing economic fluctuations and fostering fuller employment; less attention is given to cushioning fluctuations in the prices of primary goods. Moreover, as an economy progresses, its banking system becomes more differentiated, and its ratio of paper to physical assets rises. The legal structure also becomes more complex and differentiated as does the public and the private organizational structure for which legal institutions must design appropiate rules.[34] Foreign economic relations tend to become subject to greater regulation, much of it restrictive, especially after external trade has begun to lag behind national income.

As an economy advances, it may toler-

[32] As was noted earlier, even when there is not initially a single party, the processes associated with carrying out a development program tend to channel power into the hands of a single party. See Brzezinski, *op. cit.*, pp. 62–64. The fact that economic development in the West was accomplished under predominantly private entrepreneurial leadership, democratic auspices, and the political leadership of two or more parties has little influence today in underdeveloped countries (see *ibid.*, pp. 58–59; Shils, *op. cit.*, pp. 55–56). Furthermore, the examples of Russia and China are at hand, and the Communist Party is now representing itself as the political instrument through which industrialization is to be achieved. See Kautsky, *op. cit.* Presumably, in countries where durable political parties have been lacking, development is likely to be retarded. If this be true, and if D. A. Rustow is correct in remarking the absence of durable political parties from a number of underdeveloped countries, lack of effective party organization may be a political deterrent to growth. See Rustow, "New Horizons for Comparative Politics," *World Politics*, **9** (July 1957), 541–542.

[33] The above analysis suggests that, if there are but two parties, a parliamentary system may be better suited to foster economic growth than a federal system of the sort found in the United States. Under the latter, power is more widely dispersed, with the result that, except in times of crisis, it is very difficult to focus attention, effort, and resources upon as costly an undertaking as economic development.

[34] E.g., see E. V. Rostow's account of the newly acquired rules of public law, in *Planning for Freedom* (New Haven, 1959).

ate larger amounts of growth-checking taxation and public expenditure, since the economic system itself becomes more autonomous and more able and willing to supply growth-capital. While emphasis upon governmental intervention and centralized economic planning may for a time increase as an economy progresses, it eventually tends to decline insofar as the need for economic and social overhead capital and for state aid to newly developing industries falls off. This outcome is quite likely. Such increase in emphasis upon the public sector may, for a time, make conditions worse in the private sector, though this is not a necessary outcome. Development corporations are not likely to be continued after an economy has become autonomous and characterized by self-sustaining growth. Budgetary policy becomes of greater importance as the economy progresses, particularly if, as some believe, the advent of "affluence" makes greater freedom increasingly necessary, together with the supply of "cultural" and "collective" goods and services, the production and/or distribution of which are not considered well suited to private enterprise. Economic progress is attended also by a great increase in the competence of private criticism of governmental economic policies, though not necessarily in its effectiveness.

While highly skilled personnel are always in short supply, governmental personnel tend to improve in quantity and quality as an economy improves, thereby permitting the government to undertake more of those economic tasks of which it is empirically capable, given adequacy of personnel. Rising income is associated with the increase of skilled personnel, income and personnel interacting through time to augment each other.

In general, as has been implied, economic development tends eventually to be accompanied by both political and economic decentralization. It is accompanied by decentralization of both legal norm-making power and use-determining, economic decision-making power, with both forms becoming more widely distributed in

space and among households and/or corporate groups. The disposition of economic power in space and among groups and individuals tends to be rather closely associated with that of political power. Political decentralization entails the distribution of norm-making power among a plurality of groups or organs, together with the subjection of centralized norm-making to restraints imposed by dispersed, norm-affecting groups whose initially heterogeneous aspirations enter into such consensus as comes to underlie norms held valid for all members of a society.[35] Economic decentralization requires that the mechanisms employed to discover what final goods and services should be produced reflect an ever widening range of consumer preferences, be these mechanisms "free markets" in which price and effective economic demand rule, or political devices designed to register such non-economic indicators as votes. Such decentralization results because, as an economy becomes more consumer-oriented, centralized determination of what is to be produced becomes increasingly difficult.

Among the concomitants of decentralization are the decline of one-party rule and the rise of the welfare state. An effective one-party system, though often favorable to economic growth, appears to be incompatible with a complex economy in which consumer goods, together with a high level of education, have come to play a paramount role. Similarly, the welfare state, though initially incompatible with the effective development of economically retarded lands, eventually becomes a part of the set of arrangements whereby, in high-income economies, collective goods and services are supplied and expenditure is kept abreast of "full-employment" output in pacific times.

[35] See Hans Kelsen, "Centralization and Decentralization," in Harvard Tercentenary Conference, *Authority and the Individual* (Cambridge, 1937), pp. 210–239, esp. 212–213, 216–217, 223, 227–229; also 231–232 on struggles for local autonomy, and 233–234 on federalism as a form of decentralization.

INDIVIDUALISM AND THE ROLE OF
THE STATE IN ECONOMIC GROWTH

Alexander Eckstein

I

Economic growth can be viewed as a broadening of the range of alternatives open to society. Clearly, technological and resource constraints are likely to be so compelling and overriding in primitive or underdeveloped economies as to leave comparatively little scope for the exercise of choice—either individual or social. On the other hand, the situation is quite different—at least in degree—at more advanced stages of economic development. At these stages, one of the principal manifestations of this broadening in the range of alternatives is precisely the greater opportunity to exercise choice over the form in which choices in the economy become institutionalized. This, in turn, requires a delineation of the spheres of public vs. private choice and a determination of the relative weight of each sphere.

One of the aspects of individualism, and possibly the one most relevant for our purposes, is the scope for individual choice and decentralized decision-making in the economic sphere. In a preponderantly free enterprise market economy the institutionalization of these ingredients of individualism is more or less automatically assured. This does not, however, mean that this system necessarily assures equal scope for the exercise of choice on the part of all individuals in the economic system, or that it provides a greater scope for individual

SOURCE. Alexander Eckstein, "Individualism and the Role of the State in Economic Growth," *Economic Development and Cultural Change*, **6**, 81–87, January 1958. Reprinted by permission of The University of Chicago Press. Copyright 1958 by The University of Chicago Press. Read at the January 1957 meeting of the American Council of Learned Societies, Panel II on Economic Growth and the Individual.

choice than an alternative system might. In contrast to preponderantly free enterprise market systems, in economies in which the public sector looms quite large, the scope for individual choice and decision making may be more a function of the political rather than the economic system. Thus the mechanism through which economic policy is formulated and the role of the ballot box in economic policy formulation become major conditioning factors.

In essence, what this suggests is that there is a potentially positive correlation between individualism and economic development. The extent to which this potential is translated into reality will depend upon the role played by individual choice and initiative in resource allocation, regardless of whether the choices and decisions are in fact arrived at primarily within the confines of the economic or political process. With this context in mind, let us attempt to spell out some of the factors and variables that are likely to condition the role the state may be expected or forced to play in the process of economic growth and its impact upon the position of the individual.

II

In analyzing the role of the state in the process of economic growth, the following elements may be considered as essential:

1. *The hierarchy of objectives, goals, and ends of economic development.* This necessarily involves an examination of both the qualitative and quantitative aspects, that is, the character, range, and variety of the ends sought as well as the level to be attained. The interplay of these dimensions of content, range, and level will be one of the principal factors defining the ambitiousness of the particular economic develop-

ment program. In respect to content, several broad categories of objectives or motivations may be cited, for instance, those revolving around nationalism and those related to a striving for rising standards of living. In a sense, these might be considered as ultimate ends which need to be, and are in fact, broken down into a series of derived and possibly more concrete goals. Thus, at the stage when these objectives are disaggregated and sorted out as to the ranges and levels involved, they inevitably tend to become competitive rather than complementary entities in the sense that under *ceteris paribus* assumptions, the wider the range, the lower will have to be the level, and vice versa.

2. *The time horizon in economic development.* This entails a definition of the rate at which the goals are to be attained. In a sense, it is but another aspect of the hierarchy of objects, since rapid or leisurely growth may be an explicitly stated end in and of itself.

3. *The means available* for attaining—at the desired rate—the content, range, and level of ends explicitly or implicitly formulated. Here one would have to consider such variables as resource and factor endowments and the state of the arts prevailing in the particular economy.

4. *The structure and character of institutions: social, economic, and political.* This is possibly the most complex of all the categories listed here. The considerations most relevant for our purposes revolve around the rigidity of the institutional framework, its capacity to generate, absorb, and adapt itself to economic change and to the disruptive forces of industrialization. This would mean investigating factors such as the prevailing value system, class structure, social mobility, contractual and legal arrangements, degree and character of urbanization, land tenure system, degree of commercialization and monetization, character and structure of state organization, structure of political power, etc. However, analysis of these variables is greatly complicated by virtue of the fact that some of them are rather intangible, while their particular chemical max—that is, the nature of combinations and interaction between the different institutional factors—and the reaction produced may be quite unpredictable. In effect, it is much easier to provide *ex post facto* rationalizations or explanations as to why and in what ways certain types of institutional structure were more conducive to industrialization than others, than to assess *ex ante* the height and the tensile strength of institutional barriers and their resistance to economic development.

5. *The relative backwardness of the economy.* From an economic point of view, relative backwardness—and the emphasis should be on relative—involves certain advantages and disadvantages. The disadvantages lie principally in the field of foreign trade, while the so called "advantages of backwardness" may be found in the realm of technology. Thus industrially advanced countries enjoy certain competitive advantages in world markets, and particularly in the markets of the underdeveloped areas themselves. This in and of itself can under certain conditions become a major handicap in the industrialization of backward countries. On the other hand, as Professor Gerschenkron has pointed out, one of the essential ingredients of relative backwardness is a gap in the levels of technology used and applied. Therefore the backward country can reap large potential gains by importing advanced technology from abroad and thus, in effect, make a technological leap from comparatively primitive to highly advanced levels.

At this point another aspect of relative backwardness may be usefully introduced, namely the gap in material welfare or standards of living, and the gap in national power produced by differences in levels of industrialization. All three of these gaps—in consumption, technology, and power—could be viewed as different aspects of a "demonstration effect" through which the gulf between a potential and actual state is forcefully brought home. Characteristically, it is in this shape that the pressure for industrialization of backward countries is manifested. Once the disequilibrating and innovating forces of modernization, industrialization, and urbanization have been introduced on an appreciable scale,[1] one could say that, *ceteris paribus*, the greater the relative backwardness, the more acute will tend to be the "tension" arising from this chasm between the potential and the actual, and thus the greater will be the pressure for industrialization.

Given the five categories of elements and variables considered above, we are now in a position to state our hypothesis concerning the conditions under which the state will tend to play a greater or lesser role in the process of economic growth. On this basis then one could say that:

a. The greater the range of ends and the higher the level of attainment sought;

b. The shorter the time horizon within which the ends are to be attained, that is the more rapid the rate of economic growth desired;

c. The more unfavorable the factor and resource endowments;

d. The greater the institutional barriers to economic change and industrialization;

e. The more backward the economy in relative terms the greater will tend to be the urge, push, and pressure for massive state intervention and initiative in the process of industrialization, and at the same time, the greater will be the need for such intervention if a breakthrough, rather than a breakdown, is to be attained.

III

Assuming that the state is compelled to make a major commitment on behalf of industrialization, what types of measures may the state be expected to adopt and what effect may these have upon the position of the individual, or more specifically, upon the individual choice and decentralized decision-making in the economic sphere? From this point of view, a sharp distinction needs to be made between the elements and the degree of state power applied in the process of economic growth.

In analyzing the qualitative aspects of state intervention affecting the economic sphere, one could perhaps distinguish between five categories of action: provision of social overhead, provision of economic overhead, application of direct and indirect levers and controls, government operation of enterprises extending beyond the overhead sectors, and central planning.

Provision of social overhead might entail maintenance of law and order in the society, provision and enforcement of legal and contractual obligations, supply of educational, health, and social welfare facilities, assumption of military and defense functions, etc. In effect, these are categories of action which to the extent that they are provided at all, are usually furnished by public rather than private agencies.

Provision of economic overhead may involve the institution of central banking and of monetary and fiscal facilities, the development of a highway and railroad network and of other public utilities.

Application of direct or indirect levers and controls may be based on a wide variety of measures, such as introduction of tariffs, railroad rate discrimination, tax privileges and other types of subsidies, rationing of goods and of credit, price controls, etc.

Government operation of enterprises extending beyond the overhead sectors may range from management of some industries, or a few firms in different industries, to public ownership of all means of production.

Central planning may involve more or less total concentration of economic decision-making in the hands of a national planning board.

Admittedly, this fivefold classification is arbitrary, and the line of demarcation

---

[1] This scale effect is, of course, both crucial and indeterminate, in the sense that what will be the operationally significant range will inevitably vary from country to country, depending upon size, institutional framework, etc.

between the different categories is quite blurred. Yet, in terms of their effect upon the exercise of individual choice and initiative, they present qualitatively rather significant differences. Thus, most of the items in the first two categories belong to what, in industrializing societies at least, are usually considered as the minimal and essential functions of a state. In contrast, centralized and comprehensive planning combined with total government operation of the economy may be regarded as maximum functions. One of the key questions that needs to be posed in this context is which one, or which combination, of categories will the state use to promote economic development? Whichever means it uses, how massively, to what degree, and with what intensity will it apply its power to the provision of these different categories? Moreover, how will particular kinds and degrees of state intervention affect factor supply, particularly the supply of capital and entrepreneurship?

It may turn out that the more massively and rapidly the state provides what can be considered its minimum functions, the less may be the pressure or the need for it to provide the maximum functions. Therefore, the reliance upon maxima may in effect be a function of past and current failure to provide the minima. In these terms, then, one could say that a necessary precondition for the broadening of opportunities for the exercise of individual choice, individual initiative, and the growth of individual values in underdeveloped countries, launched on a development program, is a high degree and rapid application of state power for the supply of social and economic overhead, combined with partial controls and planning as circumstances may demand them.

Theoretically one could, of course, visualize a system in which amidst public ownership of the means of production, national planning, and resource allocation was—within wide limits—based upon the operation of free consumer choice and consumer autonomy. Realistically, how-ever, it would be extremely difficult to build sufficient checks and balances into such a Lange-like model to prevent it from slipping into a totalitarian mold. On the other hand, this is much less true in the case of partial planning and partial government operation of enterprises, which in many situations is needed to reinforce the provision of social and economic overheads, if comprehensive government planning and management is to be avoided.

The failure of the state in the minimum fields tends to be more or less directly reflected in capital formation and the growth of entrepreneurship. Thus, in many traditional societies, accumulations of merchant and other forms of capital tend to be dissipated because of: (1) the absence of adequate and contractual arrangements to protect these holdings from the more or less arbitrary ravages of officialdom, and (2) the failure of the state to institute a social security system, so that old age assistance, poor relief, and similar functions must be privately assumed through the family and kinship system. At the same time, condition (1) tends to reinforce the economic risks of various types of business and industrial investments. Moreover, the same condition further encourages the flow of capital into land investment, which in an environment of acute population pressure and agrarian value orientation, represents one of the safest and most profitable forms of holding. However, from the standpoint of the economy, this is merely a transfer payment, ultimately representing a leakage of investment into consumption. In effect, then, this is a milieu in which the state—through sins of commission and omission—tends to undercut actual and potential sources of capital accumulation, while at the same time making its contribution to the narrowing of business opportunities. Under these conditions the scarcities of entrepreneurial and technical talent tend to be further intensified through the neglect of education facilities. Moreover, to the extent that some education is provided, its orientation is frequently inhospitable to the growth of scientific and technical knowledge.

Viewed in these terms, perhaps one of the most important contributions the pre-industrial European city made to the industrialization of the continent was that it provided a legally and more or less militarily protected haven for the accumulation and conservation of capital, and for its investment in fields that were eminently productive from a point of view of economic development.

Amidst such circumstances, the formidable barriers to modernization and industrialization are likely to be perpetuated, while economic, social, and political tensions mount under the impact of innovating influences ushered in—as a rule—through foreign contact. Unless some means are found for alleviating these tensions through a process of change and adaptation, the potentially explosive forces in society may be expected to burst forth, sweeping away the older order, capturing the state, and using it as a total and far-reaching instrument for mounting an industrial revolution.

On this basis, one could argue that if India, for instance, wishes to avoid a totalitarian path to industrialization, her current plans and efforts do not provide for enough, rather than for too much, state intervention. Thus the large gap in the financial resources available for the implementation of the Second Five Year Plan may be a symptom of the inability and the reluctance of the Indian state to mobilize the means adequate for the implementation of the ends sought. But, even more fundamentally, perhaps, the inadequacy of the government efforts to spread adult education—both basic and technical education—rapidly, may be an important factor in inhibiting the attainment of certain economic objectives, while at the same time it serves to reinforce the great gulf between the small elite and the rural masses—a factor representing marked potential dangers in the political realm.

To sum up this phase of my argument,

it may perhaps be useful to attempt to work with the concept of an "optimum level and pattern of state intervention" paralleling other optima—e.g. the optimum propensity to consume—incorporated in different types of economic and social science models. For our present purposes, this optimum would have to be defined in relation to two broad sets of objectives, i.e., striving for rising standards of living combined with an increase and/or preservation of the scope for the exercise of individual choice and initiative. The definition would also have to take account of the specific circumstances in each case, particularly in relation to the qualitative and quantitative aspects of state intervention, and to the variables listed in Section II above.

IV

We have discussed thus far the role the state may need to play in the process of economic growth without any reference to the character of the state and its capacity to perform the tasks required of it. Historically, however, particularly in the underdeveloped countries, the state—and the social structure on which it was based—was one of the very agencies hampering economic development. The same conditions that create the need for massive state intervention in one form or another, also tend to breed a type of state which is singularly unequipped to intervene effectively on behalf of economic development. That is economic backwardness is usually associated with political and other forms of backwardness.

Thus in China, for instance, the state has played a passive to actively negative role vis à vis the economy. The very concept of economic change and economic dynamism was alien to such a society with the nexus between economic growth and national power and/or welfare only very dimly understood, if perceived at all. The function of the economy was a largely static one, being charged with the primary task of supporting the ruling elite. Therefore, the state assumed very few responsibilities in the economy, beyond assuring that it would provide a stable, continuing, and adequate source of revenue for the imperial household and the gentry-bureaucracy.

The continuing failure of the traditional Chinese state to respond to the challenge of modernization, the institutional rigidities permeating the traditional social structure, the incapacity and unwillingness of the ruling classes to come to terms with change, their inability to understand the character of the innovating influences and to follow a policy of enlightened self-interest, have all served to retard the process of industrialization for so long that cumulative tensions of such explosive proportions were generated that they could no longer be contained, while at the same time perhaps nothing short of such an explosive force could have broken the shackles of the old order and swept away the barriers to economic growth. The violent eruption of the Chinese economy into what seems to bear the earmarks of an industrial revolution under totalitarian control can thus be viewed as an illustration of a resort to maximum solutions in the face of repeated and continued failure of the old state to perform and furnish the minimal functions referred to in the preceding section.

This course of development contrasts sharply with that experienced in Japan, where the breakdown of the old order accelerated by innovating influences produced a realignment of elites. The new elite, which bore some continuity with the old, then set out very deliberately to use the state as an instrument for modernization and industrialization. In doing this, the state from the outset paid major attention to developing rapidly the social and economic overhead sectors and to provide a general framework within which all types of enterprises, private and public, large and small, would grow. The state in effect conceived its role as initiator and promoter of the development process, leaving much of the execution to private enterprise.

While this is not intended to suggest that the Japanese experience can necessarily be duplicated in other countries, and in different circumstances, it is worthwhile to note that the state was able to perform this kind of a role amidst conditions which *ex ante* would have seemed exceptionally unfavorable. Not only were factor and resource endowments poor—in many respects poorer, perhaps not only absolutely but relatively, than those of some major underdeveloped areas today—but institutional barriers were formidable too.

However, an analysis of the conditions under which the state would or would not be *capable* of performing the functions required of it would be beyond the scope of this paper. Rather, I have tried to confine myself more specifically to a spelling out of the conditions under which and the ways in which the state may be *required* to assume a large role in initiating and promoting economic development without jeopardizing the growth of opportunities for the exercise of individual choice and initiative in the economic sphere.

Chapter 8

Social Aspects of Economic Development

ECONOMIC GROWTH AND DEVELOPMENT: NONECONOMIC FACTORS IN ECONOMIC DEVELOPMENT

Bert F. Hoselitz

An adequate treatment of the varied ways in which economic and noneconomic factors interact in a process of economic growth or development would require an entire book. In order to remain within the short space at my disposal, I shall therefore discuss a special problem and hope that this discussion will convey in a rough way the general flavor of the manner in which we might proceed with a consideration of noneconomic factors in economic development. I should like to select the question of the change which occurs in an economy as it leaves a state of relatively slow growth or stagnation and starts a process of rapid growth. This apparently discontinuous break with the past, which is usually associated with rapid industrialization, has often been described. Students of the different industrial revolutions have pointed to the rapid pace with which an economy broke out of a previous condition of relative immobility and attained within one or at most two generations a level of performance on which self-

sustained growth was possible. Much of this evidence has recently been collected in an interesting paper by W. W. Rostow on "The Take-off into Self-Sustained Growth" (*Economic Journal*, 1956). Apart from a detailed discussion of the take-off period, Rostow's essay also contains a discussion of three stages with the take-off as center. The first stage or period is one of preparation in which the preconditions of the take-off are established. This period may last a century or more. The second stage is the take-off itself, and the third period is the stage of self-sustained growth, when the further development of the economy occurs as a more or less normal and self-generating process.[1]

If we view the development process as following roughly such a tripartite schema,

[1] Rostow was, of course, not the first to have discovered the sudden incidence of industrial revolutions, nor to have stipulated a tripartite periodization. A similar scheme was presented by G. Célestine, "Dynamique des niveaux de production et de productivité," *Économie et Humanisme*, July–August 1952, pp. 60–67; and in one of my articles, "Algunos aspectos de las relaciones entre el cambio social y el desarollo económico," *De Economía*, July–August 1954, pp. 611–624. Further references to this process are cited in that article.

SOURCE. Bert F. Hoselitz, "Economic Growth and Development: Noneconomic Factors in Economic Development," *American Economic Review*, **47**, 28–41, May 1957.

we are confronted with the problem of how to account for this explosive change which has so aptly been called an industrial revolution. Its inception is, as has often been observed, rather striking and sudden, and it usually ends almost as suddenly as it began. It has been accompanied in most cases by a concomitant population "explosion" which has obscured somewhat the rapidity and suddenness of economic growth during the discontinuous take-off period if measured in terms of per-capita income. What is perhaps most important about the structural changes taking place during the take-off period is the adaptation of previously existing institutions for new ends, especially for capital formation. In fact, Rostow makes the difference in the rate of investment (i.e., the ratio of net capital formation to net national product) the criterion of whether an economy is in a pre-take-off stage or is entering the phase of industrial revolution. Now why should an economy suddenly be capable of saving and investing a larger proportion of its net income, especially if it has apparently been unable to alter the rate of net investment for a very long period previous to the take-off? The answer may be found if we ask whether or not general environmental conditions have been created in the pre-take-off phase which make an increase in net capital formation attractive and achievable.

These "environmental conditions" must be sought chiefly in noneconomic aspects of the society. In other words, apart from the build-up of economic overhead capital, such as a communications and transport system and investment in harbor facilities, some warehouses, and similar installations favoring especially foreign trade, most of the innovations introduced during the preparatory period are based upon changes in the institutional arrangements in the legal, educational, familial, or motivational orders. Once these new institutions have been created, they operate as "gifts from the past," contributing freely to the vigorous spurt of economic activity in the period of take-off. We may then consider

that from the point of view of providing an explanation of the process of economic growth, the main functions of the preparatory stage are the changes in the institutional order, especially in areas other than economic activity, which transform the society from one in which capital formation and the introduction of modern economic organization is difficult or impossible, to one in which the accumulation of capital and the introduction of new production processes appear as "natural" concomitants of general social progress.

Let us examine a few cases more in detail in order to see what role some noneconomic institutions have played in bringing about the explosive situation of an industrial revolution and in particular how they have affected the supply of productive factors. For although it has often been asserted that the chief bottleneck experienced by underdeveloped countries is the shortage of capital, there are other factors which are relatively scarce—above all, certain types of skilled labor (including the services of entrepreneurial personnel). For this reason there is special interest in institutional changes during the preparatory period which tend to affect the supply of capital or of such services as administrative and entrepreneurial activity and technical and scientific skills.

The need for capital on a relatively large scale requires the availability of institutions through which savings can be collected and channeled into projects employing productive capital. Hence a banking system or its equivalent in the form of a state agency collecting revenue and spending it on developmental projects is required. What is also required in a society in which investment decisions are made by private individuals is a legal institution, such as the corporation, which allows the combination of capitals of various individuals in order to support enterprises which, for technological reasons, can be undertaken economically only on a large scale. In Britain all these institutions were in existence at the time its industrial revolution began. It is granted that joint stock companies required a special charter for their formation, and up to the early nineteenth century such charters were granted only for overseas commercial enterprises or for large-scale transportation enterprises. But as capital requirements in industry increased, the corporate form of enterprise came to be more and more widely applied to industry also. By the third decade of the nineteenth century, corporate charters for industrial firms were not uncommon and within the next fifteen years they became the rule in all but small enterprises.

It is also true that bank credit did not play an overwhelming role in the early phases of the industrial revolution in Britain. In fact, in contrast to France and Germany, a relatively large amount of capital employed in the early cotton and iron industry was supplied by merchants and even landowners. But here again, as the requirements of capital supply grew in dimension, the banks began to play a more and more important role.

Institutions providing for the collective use of capital also had been established in other European countries long before they entered the take-off phase. In France, the Napoleonic codes provided for joint-stock companies of two kinds (*sociétés en actions* and *sociétés en commandite*), and both these types of corporate enterprise were adopted by other European countries. The German legal reform lagged behind that of France, but it is significant that a Prussian commercial code, embodying much of the French type of company legislation, was introduced at a very early stage in the industrial upsurge of Germany, whereas the general civil code did not become law until the turn of the twentieth century.

In Japan, because of the absence of traditions of corporate bodies similar to the medieval European company and because of the strong governmentally induced impetus to industrialization in its early phase, the supply of capital had to be channeled through institutions which dif-

fered from those of the West. Although Japan adopted in due course the institution of the Western corporation, the immediate post-restoration process of capital formation relied upon governmental capital creation and, more importantly, upon a change in the structure and hierarchy of Japanese society. In the new social order inaugurated with the Meiji restoration there developed an association of *samurai* and large-scale capitalist merchants and farmers. This association, which later also aided in the development of the monopolistic *zaibatsu*, had antecedents which reach far back into the pre-Meiji period. All through the nineteenth century, the economic basis of Tokugawa society had begun to crumble. Although political power remained officially in the hands of the *shogun*, it began slowly to pass into the hands of some of the more powerful clans; at the same time the economic basis of a predominantly agrarian quasi-feudal society had ceased to function. There were masses of impoverished *samurai* who, in order to make a livelihood, were forced into a life of business or farm administration. Moreover, there was a simultaneously rising class of merchants and large farmers and farmer-money-lenders, whose presence disturbed the officially imposed rough equality among the members of the nonnoble classes. The gradual acquisition of power by these elements and their association with disgruntled *samurai* was a phenomenon whose beginning must be looked for in the period when, on the surface, the rule of the *shogun* appeared unimpaired. But this association was an important factor leading to a reinterpretation on the part of Japan's political elite of the over-all systemic objectives of the society. Whereas before the Japanese government had been concerned only with power, it was not clearly recognized that within this concern the development of the economy was an important, and perhaps the most important, feature. In this way an institutional framework, supported by an ideology, was created which became an efficient and powerful support of capital formation.

It is within a framework of this kind that a comparative institutional analysis of patterns of capital formation in economic development might be undertaken. Given the social and political forces at play, one could appraise by means of such an analysis the role which might be played by development corporations and investment banks or fiscal bodies in the collection of savings and the channeling of these savings into productive investment. One could appraise in this latter case the alternative function of a policy of forced savings either by inflation or by taxation and could relate the potential efficacy of each of these alternative policies to existing social and political institutions.

At the same time, one would find that the lack of suitable institutions or the presence of institutions which may lead to dissipation of accumulated savings will tend to prevent a society from arriving at a stage in which a take-off is likely or even possible. For example, nineteenth-century China had a series of institutional arrangements which facilitated the accumulation of capital. One was the institution of licensed merchants, such as the *hong* merchants at Canton who were supported by the government in their monopolistic control of foreign trade; another was the institution of imperially licensed salt merchants who enjoyed regional monopolies in the production and sale of salt. There were other groups of privileged traders, and even a large number of not specially privileged ones, who achieved considerable success in the amassing of large fortunes. But within the Chinese system the merchants operated upon the sufferance and with the support of the bureaucracy, and thus any profits made in trade or industry had to be shared with officials. The officials invested their share in land or spent it on luxury consumption, with the result that large accumulations of liquid funds tended to become sporadically dissipated rather than channeled into productive investment.

Moreover, even in the few instances in which, with the aid and support of officials, capital was invested in productive enterprises, profits, instead of being reinvested, were distributed among a large number of claimants among the officialdom; the demands on trading, shipping, or industrial firms for the distribution of earnings among officials on all levels of the administrative scale were so strong that it was often difficult to maintain the initial capital intact. Thus the institutional tie-up between the merchant class and officialdom in China, superimposed upon the heavy tax system, contributed in Ch'ing China to the unavailability of capital accumulations of sufficient magnitude to form a foundation for rapid industrial development.

Let us now turn to the second problem of supply: the availability of skilled labor of various kinds, chiefly entrepreneurial services and the services of skilled administrators, engineers, scientists, and managerial personnel. These rather than manual skills are the types of labor normally in short supply in nonindustrialized countries, and it is the overcoming of bottlenecks in the supply of these kinds of services that a major developmental effort usually needs to be made. Since entrepreneurship and administrative talent on the one hand and scientific and engineering services on the other usually are associated with different institutions, it will be convenient to separate the discussion of the institutions within which these skills and inclinations to the pursuit of these occupations are fashioned. We shall first turn to the problem of the diffusion of science and technology.

As in the case of institutions designed to aid in the accumulation of capital, technological and scientific investigations had become institutionalized in Western Europe long before the countries which experienced a period of take-off actually entered the phase of industrialization on a rapid scale. For Britain this fact is well documented and has often been noted. The Royal Society was officially formed in

1662, although by 1645 there had been already in existence a small club of "divers worthy persons, inquisitive into natural philosophy, and particularly of what was called the New Philosophy, or Experimental Philosophy." Although its early extensive interest in technology was not fully maintained throughout the early eighteenth century,. it was revived by the middle of the century and strengthened by the establishment in 1754 of the Society for the Encouragement of Arts, Manufactures, and Commerce. It is superfluous to describe in this place the institutionalization of scientific and technical progress in Britain during the seventeenth and eighteenth centuries more specifically, since a perusal of Robert K. Merton's *Science, Technology and Society in Seventeenth Century England* (Bruges, 1938) and G. N. Clark's *Science and Social Welfare in the Age of Newton* (Oxford, 1937) will yield exhaustive descriptions of this process. By the onset of the industrial revolution, technological research was widespread and had spilled over from being practiced in the laboratories of "experimental philosophers" to being carried on also in workshops, mines, and manufactories. In France and also in Germany, academies similar to the Royal Society were established in imitation of this organization, soon after it had started to operate, and in France especially technological training was given a tremendous impetus by the foundation of the École Polytechnique in 1794. This school became the pet of Napoleon, and it was through its influence more than any other that by the beginning of the nineteenth century France was in the forefront of scientific achievement. By 1825, Justus Liebig, who had studied under Gay-Lussac in Paris and had there convinced himself of the superiority of the French method, introduced laboratory science into Germany, and from that time on experimental and applied research in mechanics, chemistry, metallurgy, and other fields became common in German universities and technological institutes.

Thus in the various European countries there existed firmly entrenched institutions for scientific and technological research and training well before the onset of rapid industrialization. Similarly in Japan there had been considerable interest in "Dutch studies" under the Tokugawa. Many Japanese were engaged in learning Dutch and by means of this language became acquainted with Western science and technology. Schools for Dutch studies were established, not only by the *shogun* himself, but also by some of the more important clans, notably the Saga in whose territory Nagasaki was located. These schools taught not only languages but also such subjects as Western mathematics, astronomy, geography, physics, and metallurgy. The result was that before Perry's arrival there had been founded a number of iron smelting plants and foundries built by native engineers on the Western model, and by 1853 the Saga foundry cast the first satisfactory iron gun. In the same year a reverberatory furnace was built by Japanese engineers of the Satsuma clan, and shortly thereafter two more furnaces and supporting fabricating works by the Satsuma clan and the Mito clan.[2] It would be false to exaggerate the influence of these institutions and technical attainments. They are symptoms rather than results of a change in institutional arrangements affecting scientific research and technological achievement in Japan. But the practice of Dutch studies and the adoption of Western techniques before the fall of the *shogunate* set a stage which made possible the rapid adoption of Western educational and research facilities in science and technology once the new order had set in.

Again the picture was different in nineteenth-century China. Rather than enter into a lengthy elaboration of the role of Western science and technology in Ch'ing China, I should like to cite a passage from

[2] Cf. Thomas C. Smith, *Political Change and Industrial Development in Japan: Government Enterprise, 1868–1880* (Stanford, 1955), pp. 4–7.

Hsiao-Tung Fei, who is an accurate and imaginative interpreter of Chinese "traditional" society. Fei says:

> In Chinese traditional society the intelligentsia have been a class without technical knowledge. They monopolized authority based on the wisdom of the past, spent time on literature, and tried to express themselves through art. Chinese literary language is very inapt to express scientific or technical knowledge. This indicates that, in the traditional scheme, the vested interests had no wish to improve production but thought only of privilege. Their main task was the perpetuation of established norms in order to set up a guide for conventional behavior. A man who sees the world only through human relations is inclined to be conservative, because in human relations the end is always mutual adjustment. And an adjusted equilibrium can only be founded on a stable and unchanging relation between man and nature. On the other hand, from the purely technical point of view, there are hardly any limits to man's control of nature. In emphasizing technical progress, one plunges into a struggle in which man's control over nature becomes ever changing, ever more efficient. Yet these technical changes may lead to conflict between man and man. The Chinese intelligentsia viewed the world humanistically. Lacking technical knowledge, they could not appreciate technical progress. And they saw no reason to wish to change man's relation to man.[3]

If we turn to institutions regulating the supply of entrepreneurial or managerial services, the picture is similar. But with reference to entrepreneurship in particular, there appears also to be involved not only an institutional but above all a motivational factor. Accumulation of capital and technical or scientific knowledge can be

[3] Hsiao-Tung Fei, *China's Gentry* (1953), p. 74.

explained by pointing to the institutions through which practices of behavior leading to investment or the acquisition of technical knowledge may be furthered. Entrepreneurship is a more evasive thing. It is not so much a particular set of institutions through which it is brought to bear, but its presence or absence; its vigor or debility depends rather upon a whole series of environmental conditions and appropriate personal motivations. It has been shown—in my opinion successfully—that entrepreneurship is associated with a personality pattern in which achievement motivation is strong. But the presence of strong achievement motivation in a group of individuals does not necessarily produce an abundance of entrepreneurs unless certain other general conditions of social structure and culture strongly favor achievement-oriented individuals to enter economic pursuits. High achievement motivation has also been found among military leaders and may be found among scholars, priests, and bureaucrats. It is not too difficult to show that in a society in which the acquisition of wealth is regarded as a good thing in itself, persons with the appropriate motivational disposition will tend to enter an entrepreneurial career. But what about societies in which the accumulation of wealth in itself is frowned upon, or where it is considered to be a worthy object only if performed under certain restrictive conditions? What about a society in which the warrior, the priest, or the government official is rated vastly above the merchant or the industrialist?

Thus when we discuss the factor of entrepreneurship we must go beyond the mere analysis of social institutions in a limited sense and must include in our purview the entire social fabric in which this type of social behavior becomes predominant. But if we put the question in this form, we are immediately confronted with the further question of whether the same type of social constellation which provides a fruitful field for the development and exercise of entrepreneurial activity does not simultaneously further institutions designed to facilitate capital formation and scientific and technical progress. I believe, on the basis of my reading of the social and economic history of those peoples which have shown the capacity for rapid economic advance and those which have so far failed in this capacity, that the overall social framework which favors entrepreneurship also favors scientific and technical progress and the development of institutions fostering the formation of capital.

In support of this proposition, one could show that the countries of Western Europe and Japan which have developed viable institutions for the accumulation of capital and its channeling in large lumps into productive investment and institutions enhancing the supply of persons capable of tackling the scientific and technological problems required for efficient production, also have developed vigorous entrepreneurial personalities, and that China, which in the nineteenth and early twentieth century has failed to produce these institutions, also has had a paucity of able entrepreneurs. The fact that Chinese emigrants in South Asia have, on the whole, succeeded in commerce and, at any rate, appear to have outdistanced in business acumen and entrepreneurial spirit members of their host peoples is rather a confirmation of this proposition. For I do not mean to argue that the Chinese have less inherent capacity for business leadership than other nations. The social fabric of imperial China was such that whenever potential motivations for entrepreneurial activity developed in aspiring young men, they were deflected into other career lines; and the men who in Western Europe or Japan would have taken on a business career tended to become officials or scholars in China. And once they had attained such positions their preoccupation was, as Professor Fei has argued, directed upon preservation of existing human relations rather than on innovations either in technology or in business enterprise.

Let me summarize the argument presented so far in a few sentences, in order to outline the conclusions at which we might arrive. Economic growth is a process which affects not only purely economic relations but the entire social, political, and cultural fabric of a society. The predominant problem of economic growth in our day is the overcoming of economic stagnation, which normally takes place through a process of industrialization. In most recorded cases in which industrialization took place and led to a level of self-sustaining growth, this phase of economic development was initiated by a rapidly "explosive" period which, in concordance with Rostow, we may call the take-off. The rapid structural and organizational changes affecting the productivity of a society which take place during the take-off phase are made possible because in a previous phase social institutions were created which allow the successful overcoming of supply bottlenecks, chiefly in the field of capital formation and the availability of a number of highly skilled and specialized services. The creation of these social institutions in turn, especially the "institutionalization" of entrepreneurship, i.e., an innovating uncertainty-bearing activity, requires the establishment of a social framework within which these new institutions can exist and expand. In the last resort, we may thus have to answer the question of how such a social framework develops or is brought about by conscious design.

The answer to this question must be based on a general theoretical understanding of the nature of social and cultural change and, so far as I am aware, no general theory of social change which is universally accepted by sociologists exists as yet. It is clearly impossible for a non-specialist to develop such a theory, but from the existing literature some general hints of what are some of the main points in this process of theorizing may be gleaned. Among these pieces of a theory of change, three concepts and their implications appear to be most significant for our problem. These are the appearance of behavioral deviance, the emergence of cultural or social marginality, and the process of redefinition of societal objectives by an elite. I have discussed these processes more extensively in another place and shall confine myself here, therefore, to presenting merely a sketch.[4]

Let us first turn to a brief consideration of social deviance. Although it may occur in many fields of social action, we are concerned here primarily with those forms of deviant behavior which are relevant for economic activity and organization. Now if the concept of deviance is to have operational meaning, it cannot be interpreted as signifying simply behavior which is new, but it must imply that this set of innovating acts is opposed in some way to existing social norms or approved forms of behavior. In other words, a deviant always engages in behavior which constitutes a breach of the existing order and which is either contrary to, or at least not positively weighted in, the hierarchy of existing social values. If we apply this concept to the behavior displayed by businessmen and merchants in the course of the economic development of Western Europe, we find that we can speak of genuine deviance in those periods and societies in which entrepreneurial behavior did not belong in the category of social actions which were considered as constituting the "good life." As late as the fifteenth century this was true of financial entrepreneurship, which was always tainted by the official opposition against usury. And later, when financial entrepreneurship became fully respectable, industrial entrepreneurship came to be regarded with some disdain because it dirtied one's hands. These sentiments toward business or financial activity as not

[4] Cf. my article "Sociological Approach to Economic Development," in Centro Nazionale di Prevenzione e Difesa Sociale, *Atti del Congresso Internazionale di Studio sul Problema delle Aree Arretrate* (Milan, 1955), pp. 755–778.

quite proper for a gentleman to carry on are familiar in many underdeveloped countries today. For this reason, deviant behavior is often exercised by persons who, in some sense, are marginal to society. In medieval Europe the earliest moneylenders were often foreigners. In Italy at the time of Gothic and Langobard rule, they were Syrians, Jews, and Byzantines. Later when Italians turned to financial entrepreneurship on a large scale, the Genoese and Pisans, Sienese and Florentines, who were all lumped together under the name of "Lombards," became the financial entrepreneurs north of the Alps.

The role of marginal individuals in various economic pursuits in many underdeveloped countries is eminently manifest today. One could cite the Chinese in various South Asian countries, the Indians in East Africa, and the widely scattered Lebanese who make their appearance as businessmen in West Africa, Latin America, and elsewhere in less advanced countries. We also should count a considerable number of American and other voluntary Western expatriates among this class of marginal individuals. Some who attempt to find an escape from their marginal position in the arts have tended to congregate on the Seine or the Arno, but those who find business more congenial are to be found all over Latin America and more recently also in many parts of Asia and Africa.

What is the mechanism which allows marginal individuals to perform the roles they apparently have so widely accepted? As Robert E. Park, the inventor of the concept and of the significance of social marginality, has stressed, marginal men are—precisely because of their ambiguous position from a cultural, ethnic, or social standpoint—very strongly motivated to make creative adjustments in situations of change, and, in the course of this adjustment process, to develop genuine innovations in social behavior. Although many of Park's very general propositions about marginality have been considerably refined by subsequent researchers, the theory of social marginality has not advanced enough to supply sufficiently convincing evidence for the role it may play in the explanation of episodes of social deviance wherever they occur. Even if it is admitted that marginal individuals tend to make creative adjustments more often than to relapse into new or old orthodoxies, the record is not at all clear, and there are some students who warn us that marginal individuals are more prone than others to experience *anomie* and thus to become carriers of trends leading towards social disorganization rather than to innovations of a creative type.

In circumstances in which a certain amount of deviant behavior has been displayed, the establishment of a new social institution is invaluable. E. H. Carr, writing in a different context, expressed the opinion that "the ideal, once it is embodied in an institution, ceases to be an ideal and becomes the expression of a selfish interest, which must be destroyed in the name of a new ideal."[5] Carr here expresses succinctly the interaction between social deviance and the growth of institutions. Once a form of deviant behavior can find the shelter of an institution, it becomes routinized, it ceases to be deviant, and it tends to become an accepted mode of social action. But the institution in which it is "laid down" forms an advance post, so to speak, from which further deviance is possible. Thus the institutions which arose in Western Europe before the industrial revolution and in Japan before the Meiji restoration were already the end products of a process of social change; but they, in turn, made possible, by their very existence, further social and economic change.

Whether or not deviant social behavior will lead to new social institutions and the routinization of new forms of behavior depends upon a number of factors which we cannot discuss here in detail. However, it is clear that one of the most important

[5] Edward Hallet Carr, *The Twenty Years Crisis* (London, 1940), p. 92.

determinants of the relative success of deviance will be the system of sanctions which exist in a society. Such sanctions may be internalized, i.e., they may reside ultimately in the values and beliefs of people; or they may be external sanctions, i.e., they may be imposed by individuals in power, by the elite, against actual or would-be deviants. In imperial China, it appears that both types of sanctions were very strong. In pre-Meiji Japan, internal sanctions had broken down in some areas and the power of the *shogun* had decreased sufficiently so that many external sanctions were not adequate to prevent the formation of new institutions, or at least of their rudiments.

But it is clear from what has been said that the over-all strength and multiplicity of sanctions is an important determinant of the forms of deviance which are possible and successful, the kinds of persons (marginal or nonmarginal individuals) who may engage in deviant action, and the speed with which deviance will result in new social institutions. Moreover, we should remember that sanctions rest with a different force upon different individuals in a society and that often the position in the social scale which a person occupies determines the degree to which he is subject to internal or external sanctions. We may then distinguish two cases in which change is slow because sanctions against deviance are strong. One is the case of an authoritarian regime in which external sanctions are strong and in which deviant behavior is often reserved for outsiders or marginal persons. The autocratic empires of antiquity and the medieval period roughly conformed to this picture, although in all these instances the force of external sanctions was buttressed by a vigorous system of widely accepted social values which constituted supporting internal sanctions.

The other case—which is of greater importance for us—is the country in which internal sanctions against social change among the masses of the people are quite strong and in which the members of the elite wish to employ this for whatever societal objects they favor. As long as an elite is interested primarily in maintaining its own position of power and privilege, this may mean that the masses are degraded, that economic progress is slow, and that general poverty prevails. But in a few cases the members of the elite have reinterpreted the social objectives to lie in the direction of economic progress. This, I believe, was one of the main changes in Japan after the Meiji restoration, and it appears to be paramount in many underdeveloped countries of today.

In general, the outward aspects of social transformation occurring under the impact of deviance, as against one taking place through a reorientation of social objectives on the part of an existing elite, will vary. The second type of social change may be more "orderly"; rather than developing entirely new institutions, new meaning may be given to existing old ones; and whereas in the former process industrialization will be preceded normally by a substantial alteration in relations between social classes, this will not take place, or only to a smaller extent, in the second case. For example, the basic social relations in Japan have changed singularly little from the time it was a quasifeudal empire based primarily upon agriculture to the present when it is a predominantly industrial nation. Similarly, in some underdeveloped countries, where the development effort is spearheaded by the governmental elite, rigorous controls are often exercised to prevent social disorganization of various forms from setting in or taking on major proportions.

Since the development of new institutions by means of deviance has usually been outside the control and often even in opposition to the aims of the elite, it has been designated as an autonomous process.

It also has involved conflict, and in Marxian theory it was described as a dialectic process called forth by the intrinsic historical forces of the class struggle. The alterations of social institutions by the elite, on the other hand, may be designated as a process of induced or planned change and, depending upon the distribution of power within a society, may proceed at a controlled rate. Moreover, in a system of induced change, some influence may be exerted on the timing with which new social institutions are created or old ones imbued with new meanings. Thus the clear distinction between a preparatory period for a take-off which could be relatively easily identified for countries with autonomous patterns of social and economic change becomes blurred in a country with induced change. Nevertheless, it appears that even in conditions in which social and economic change is controlled very tightly, the function of new institutions to influence changes in social behavior must not be overlooked with impunity. This seems to indicate that ultimately a theoretical system may have to be evolved in which the interrelations between the various processes determining institutions embodying social change are elucidated. We have more precise knowledge on the manner in which deviance leads to the establishment of new social institutions than on the process of how this is attained by methods of induced social change, because the former can be studied on the example of the social and economic history of Western countries. There, numerous sources exist, and the process has been going on for centuries. It would be an important step forward in our understanding of the noneconomic aspects of economic development if we could develop more certain knowledge of these processes as they occur presently in situations of induced economic growth.

SOME SOCIAL AND CULTURAL ASPECTS
OF ECONOMIC DEVELOPMENT

Manning Nash

The aim of this paper is to replace the omnibus category of an "undeveloped country or region" with a set of concepts which discriminates among the existing varieties. The diagnostic scheme is based on social and cultural features of low percapita income populations. Three assumptions underlie the rationale of procedure:[1]

1. Long stagnant or slow-growing economies require structural change to develop rapidly, and structural change is a form of social and cultural transformation.

2. Undeveloped regions differ in their susceptibility and resistance to the process of social transformation from a state of relatively slow growth to a state of self-sustained growth.

3. A specification of social and cultural variables indicates differential strategies for different kinds of undeveloped societies.

To decide which social and cultural aspects of a society are relevant for the diagnosis of its particular condition of poverty requires steering between two

SOURCE. Manning Nash, "Some Social and Cultural Aspects of Economic Development," *Economic Development and Cultural Change*, 7: 137–150, January, 1959. Reprinted by permission of The University of Chicago Press. Copyright 1959 by The University of Chicago Press.

[1] I take as given the resource base, the physical environment, and other technical-economic factors. The two sets of data—techno-economic and socio-cultural—of course must always be combined in a single model, if sense is to be made of any case. The matter of relative vs. absolute growth, as well as ways of relating the techno-economic to the socio-cultural, is discussed by C. P. Kindleberger, *Process of Economic Development*, New York, 1958, Chs. 1–3.

poles of analysis. On the one hand is the anthropological empiricism of building up culture areas by the mapping or plotting of discrete cultural traits, complexes, or patterns; on the other is the *Ideal typenstellung* which divides the world into the polarities of "modern" versus "traditional." Both procedures yield analytically useful classifications. Certainly at one level of analysis, the anthropological contention that social life is some kind of organized whole and that no part of a people's life may be ignored in analysis is relevant for the study of social change. Similarly, the ideal type provides a few clear-cut themes by which the empirical diversity may be ordered and held in the mind, while the significant questions about interdependence of parts may be posed.

I seek to balance between empirical complexity and analytical simplification by developing a notion of the areas of social and cultural life most intimately related to and strategic for social change in the direction of increased wealth and income. My procedure is to describe a series of cultural patterns and social structures at a level of abstraction which permits their identification in more than one society or one culture. The notion or model I offer is diagnostic, i.e., it is a provision for organizing concepts which can discriminate between existing varieties of underdevelopment, but which is still close enough to reality to encompass a wide variety of data. The cultural and social features of relevance to this scheme are of two kinds: (1) those which current theory indicates are most pertinent and relevant for the understanding of social change, and (2) those commonly taken to be intimately connected with the structure and dynamics of the economic subsystem of a society. I shall use, illustratively, material from Burma and Cambodia, so that a categorization on the basis of the concepts can be inspected.

A relatively voluminous body of literature, both analytic and descriptive, is concerned with the relation of economic development to its antecedent and subsequent cultural change. There are statements that the general nature of the social transformation involved in economic development is contingent upon changes in social structure. These structural shifts are from functionally particular allocation of economic roles, functional diffuseness in carrying out such roles, ascription criteria in the attainment of the roles, to the polar opposite set, i.e., universalistic, specificity, achievement, and collectivity features. Levy has, for example, applied this schema to China and Japan and finds that variations in the development of the two nations are related to these variables.[2] Hoselitz has modified Levy's ideas and generalized about the process of economic growth in terms of these aspects of social structure.[3] But such a schema will not perform the task set in this paper, for as Hagen notes, shifts in the "pattern variables" are never specified in amount or degree and perhaps cannot be empirically stipulated.[4]

If we move from the most general statements, as exemplified above and manifested

in various other general theories,[5] to the literature which takes a more empirical bent by listing factors of society and culture thought to be related to economic development, we find no systematic or consistent interpretation of the way in which different social and cultural arrangements affect development. Kindleberger makes a careful survey of a good part of the anthropological and sociological literature on the inhibiting or facilitating role in economic development of one or another social feature, but arrives at no determinate system of grading the variables.[6] Another attempt to survey some of the literature treating specific social and cultural factors in economic development is found in Shannon.[7] This work is a reflection of the vast amount of information, partial theory, and speculation which has grown up about the attempts to relate the technical-economic variables in economic growth to the social-cultural aspects of the process.

Drawing on this literature and asserting without further documentation the consensual areas of knowledge about the social and cultural factors involved in economic development, I shall build my intermediate diagnostic scheme.

Economic development is a discontinuous process which, following Rostow, Hoselitz, and others, has been divided into three stages. The central period is a stage of "take-off," the break with the relatively stagnant or slow-growing economic past. Prior to the "take-off" period is a time of building resources and skills, while subsequent to the take-off is a state of self-sustained growth.[8]

---

[2] Marion J. Levy, Jr., "Some Sources of the Vulnerability of the Structures of Relatively Non-Industrialized Societies to Those of Highly Industrialized Societies," in Bert F. Hoselitz, ed., *The Progress of Underdeveloped Areas*, Chicago, 1952, pp. 113–125; and "Contrasting Factors in the Modernization of China and Japan," in Simon Kuznets, W. E. Moore, and J. J. Spengler, eds., *Economic Growth: Brazil, India, Japan*, Durham, N.C., 1956, pp. 496–536.

[3] Bert F. Hoselitz, "Social Structure and Economic Growth," *Economia Internazionale*, 6, 3 (August 1953), 52–72.

[4] Everett E. Hagen, "The Process of Economic Development," *Economic Development and Cultural Change*, 5, 3 (April 1957), 193–215.

[5] W. A. Lewis, *The Theory of Economic Growth*, Homewood, Ill., 1955; and W. W. Rostow, *The Process of Economic Growth*, New York, 1952.

[6] Kindleberger, *op. cit., passim.*

[7] Lyle W. Shannon, *Underdeveloped Areas*, New York, 1957.

[8] W. W. Rostow, "The Take-Off into Self Sustained Growth," *Economic Journal*, 66, 261 (March 1956), 25–48; and Bert F. Hoselitz, "Noneconomic Factors in Economic Development," *American Economic Review*, 47, 2 (May 1957), 28–41.

It is generally conceded that the "take-off" is led by a particular segment of society, either an elite, as in Japan,[9] or a class blocked in social or economic mobility, as in the rise of the bourgeoisie in Western Europe. The success of the dissident social segment and elitist reorientation of goals is closely tied to the group's administrative abilities and to their skills in enlisting the energies and sentiments of a good part of the population in a program of development (or, less likely, their ability to distribute or allocate rewards and benefits which will serve as self-evident attractions for new economic activity). If we accept the widely held and frequently repeated generalization that economic development involves some industrialization and some use of new technology, then part of the process is dependent upon the relations of the developing region to the developed countries, in which the technology, industry, and skill for mechanization is to be found and from whom they must, at least initially, borrow heavily.

Taking the above as true, or at least as highly probable, it is possible to consider economic development as a process of social and cultural change. The process of economic development is analytically composed of three linked kinds of social action: (1) the choice to institute changes and to seek greater wealth and income; (2) the bringing together of the means and facilities to implement the choice; and (3) the organization of social and cultural life so that growth is a built-in feature of the social system. This conceptualization of the process defines the social and cultural features connected with development: what in a people's life is likely to lead to a choice for social change in the direction of development? How are human and nonhuman resources aggregated or developed? What mode of social integration is possible as an emergent for self-sustained growth?

Since social and cultural change is a function of the alternatives generated by a given social system, and different groups or individuals are differentially situated in the social structure, there exists in any society a variety of realistic impulses to change.[10] The first cultural feature to be considered in terms of a social decision to undertake development is the pattern of stratification. If the wealth, power, and prestige of a society is strongly polarized between two groups with relatively little mobility between them, it appears that social change on the structural level is unlikely and that new economic opportunities will not be a chief concern of the dominant group and hardly even a perception of the subordinate group. There is, of course, the instance of the dominant group of a society becoming the subordinate group in relations between societies, but the proposition still holds that if the width of the gap is great, the perception of new economic opportunity is not likely. To make this concrete, consider Burma.[11] In Burma, the elite is based in urban locales and characterized by an incipient class system on Western lines. This group is dominant over a rural peasantry of some 16 millions. But there are channels of social mobility between classes in the cities, and from countryside to town. Educational institutions, both religious and secular, offer means of moving up the hierarchy, and there exists a fairly defined mode of social mobility. Burma, then, is a society with some social mobility, incomplete polarization of wealth, power, and prestige, and therefore has the social environment to induce some group to seek social and cultural change. Cambodia,[12] as another example from the same

[9] W. W. Lockwood, *The Economic Development of Japan*, Princeton, 1954.

[10] Manning Nash, "The Multiple Society in Economic Development: Mexico and Guatemala," *American Anthropologist*, **59**, 5 (October 1957), 825–833.

[11] The information on Burma is taken from Frank N. Trager *et al.*, *Burma*, New Haven, 1956, 3 vols.

[12] The material on Cambodia comes from David J. Steinberg, *Cambodia: Its People, Its Society, Its Culture* (Country Survey Series), New Haven, 1957.

area, exhibits a pattern of stratification like Burma's but with the added complication of an inherited nobility, in some conflict with the urban segments seeking development. Burma's path on structural grounds should be easier than Cambodia's, though the resistance to change in Cambodia is not likely to be extreme.

Apart from the gradation of stratification, though intertwined with it, is the system of social values which justify, explain, and define social position and the means of attaining it. Value systems are hierarchies of related propositions tied directly to, but not determined by, the experiential world of the members of a society. Value hierarchies change over time in the relative importance of given values and in the emergence of new values and the loss or modification of old ones. The repetitiveness over time of patterns of social action is in part a condition for the stability of the value aspect of the social system. Since both Burma and Cambodia have been under foreign domination and both have recently won independence, we may expect, and in fact find, that given this value hierarchy, the elite is able to emphasize goals of economic development and to incorporate new aspirations. The indices of values conducive to development (here combined with the stratification aspect) are these:

1. Conflicting religious systems, philosophies, and world views in a society indicate the malleability of the value complex and the fact that experience may be variably determined.

2. If the prevailing distribution of wealth, power, and prestige is in some contradiction to the value pattern, then social change and new economic patterns are likely to find sanction among a sizeable segment.

Both Burma and Cambodia are Theravada Buddhist countries, and the overwhelming majority of the population is Buddhist. Buddhism's other-worldliness is not in conflict with success in this world, and the twelve-fold path has many roads which may lead to development. In addition to the religious ideology is the presence of Western beliefs in material progress, combined with socialist and nationalist ideologies resulting from the wars for independence. In Burma, there is a social group in the cities aiming to bring about an economically abundant "welfare state." In Cambodia, too, there exists the range of values which would permit accumulation of wealth. A French-trained civil service and middle class aspires to greater income and more industry. In both countries, then, there are "spearhead" groups for economic development. It must be remembered that the "spearhead" group confronts or is in relation to social segments only partially sharing its values or viewing the desirability of social change from the same perspective. Therefore, a further stipulation on the nature of social and normative cleavage is necessary to assess the potential for change and economic growth. A social segment whose conditions of mobility involve others in the society rising in the social scale (either by recruitment, as in the European experience, or by abolition of inherited obstacles to mobility, as India is doing, in part) stands a better chance of perceiving and acting upon new economic opportunity simply because the social risk is less. In this connection, a nationalist ideology, or drives to nationalist integration and incorporation of diverse cultural traditions, provides a potent impulse toward change and development as a course of action; however, it may inhibit the successful organization of growth.

In Burma, the elite group interested in development is in a position to symbolize the aspirations of the whole nation. The organization of the elite group, with its close ties between secular and religious offices, effectively communicates the nationalist, development ideology to the rural peasantry. Buddhism is the vehicle of symbolic identification between the mass of peasants and the development-oriented urban elite. In Cambodia, the elite group is less well organized, and the effective development and transmission of development ideologies is less.

In forging a national consciousness oriented toward development goals, Burma appears slightly more advanced than Cambodia. The economically powerful Chinese minorities are more closely integrated into the economic and administrative structure of Burma than they are in Cambodia. Efforts are being made (in the directions of expulsion and xenophobia) in Cambodia to lessen the dependence of the rural peasantry on the Chinese commercial segment, but so far, the native elite is not well enough organized, socially or ideologically, to modify the structure greatly. The social and cultural pluralism of Cambodian society is greater than that of Burman society, and the national identification of Cambodians is apparently less than in Burma. Consequently, the spatial spread of development drives is more restricted in Cambodia, as is the extent of the market.

It must be repeated that *no* particular cluster of stratification or value patterns is, per se, inhibiting to social change or economic development—all societies change over time, and most social changes have repercussions in the levels of living. What is here maintained is that societies need differing magnitudes of economic opportunity and social rewards before some members are willing or able to emphasize an aspect of their value system leading to development. Burma has a slight edge over Cambodia, though both societies would fall in the same general class.

Given the social decision to undertake social change and development, how can the segment which is the leading group get sufficient means to significantly alter the level of living? This is usually phrased as the problem of capital formation in underdeveloped areas. There are really three problems subsumed in the notion of capital formation: (1) amount of savings, (2) form of savings, and (3) channelling savings into productive investments. The amount of savings is firstly a function of the absolute level of wealth of a society, and secondly of the values and institutions of a culture in relation to patterns of consumption, time perspective, and agencies of accumulation. A poor country produces relatively little which is available for uses other than direct personal consumption: its time perspective of investment is likely to be short and the agencies of aggregation rudimentary. Small peasant farmers, if they make up the bulk of the economically active population, as they do in Burma and Cambodia, do not as individual family or economic units have a large enough level of wealth to permit significant savings. To the extent that a farming family is heavily weighted on the subsistence side of production, as against the exchange side, its savings, whatever the level, do not come in the form which is useful or available for reinvestment in technical progress.

Given the size, number, and kind of economic units operating in Burma and Cambodia, we must weight farm families on a subsistence-exchange ratio. Non-farm economic units must also be weighted by the attractions for them in investment in productive channels.[13]

It is plain that a great deal of saving does in fact go on in any society of national size. But the problem is that savings come in such relatively small doses that they do not usually provide the basis for important reinvestment which would significantly alter the share of the national product reinvested.

The desire to save—the so-called ethic of abstemious living, or puritanical expenditure pattern—is part of a society's value system. No group in the recorded cultures of man saves for the act of saving. Saving is a function of the ends-in-view of the receivers of income. In both Burma

[13] But see the ingenious use of such an index for a Nigerian community by Michael G. Smith, *The Economy of Hausa Communities of Zaria* (Colonial Research Studies No. 16), London, 1955, *passim*, but especially pp. 139 ff.

and Cambodia, farm familes are anchored in small communities. In these rural communities, income is subjected to communal claims in the form of forced loans, feasts, and status maintenance activities. These claims on production are more important, I believe, in reducing the savings available for non-consumption investment, than is the miscalled "extended family." The emphasis on the dilution of incentive to save because individuals are involved in wider networks of kinsmen than they are in our society is a product of armchair anthropology, rather than the result of research. For example, Belshaw indicates that extended families may be important in the initial aggregation of capital and also in the channelling of investment.[14] To put it as generally as possible, in view of the fragmentary empirical data, much of the rural farming section of Burma and Cambodia does not now accumulate capital because: (1) low absolute level of production; and consequently (2) low savings; and those savings made are (3) claimed by communal expenditure or status obligations; (4) so that capital form is of a kind not easily alienated from the economic unit, or oriented toward technical and economic progress.

In the nonrural, nonfarming sectors, rates of saving are higher, but the size of the economic units makes the absolute level of any given firm rather small, thereby inhibiting its ability to bear risk or to promote long-range investment. The agencies for accumulating capital— the joint stock company, the limited liability form of ownership, the stock and securities market, the central banking system—are not well developed or widespread in either Burma or Cambodia. Significant lumps of capital are hard to come by, relative to the amount of savings which the gross national product might indicate. The more developed are the

[14] C. S. Belshaw, *In Search of Wealth*, Memoir No. 80 of the *American Anthropologist*, Menasha, Wis., 1955.

institutions for aggregating large amounts of capital, the closer is a society to the take-off period. Burma's development corporation, part of the national administrative apparatus, is more highly organized than Cambodia's and serves as a more efficient agency of planning and capital aggregation.

Obviously, the government of underdeveloped countries provides one of the chief agencies for the aggregation of capital and for the provision of the legal basis for the emergence of forms of organization capable of forming capital. The government has recourse to development corporations, banking systems, monetary control, taxation, and confiscation.

The abilities of governments to carry out any of the possible measures open to them depends, in large part, on the degree and kind of national integration. Therefore, the extent to which the territory under consideration is in fact welded into a society by a set of conventional understandings is crucial. The greater the social cleavages in terms of cultural definitions as to the ends to be sought, the more difficult it is for a government to perform the aggregating functions of capital formation, and the more difficult it is for a governing group to provide the legal and institutional basis for the private formation of capital.

In societies like Burma and Cambodia, the government has the problem of initiating and sustaining drives to national integration. The task is one of creating a national culture and forming a national society from a plurality of cultural traditions and semi-locally organized societies. The large Chinese and Indian minorities, the rural peasants, the hill tribes, and the urban elites occupy the same territory, but they do not form yet a single society. Burma is a better integrated national entity than is Cambodia, but still the ability to levy on the production of the peasantry is not well developed. Consequently, the government invests money in activities and organizations only tangentially related to economic development, but symbolically or politically important in developing a national consciousness. Investment by government in the means of coercion—armies, police, bureaucracies—in order to maintain power over cultural and social diversity, or to carry out programs of taxation or confiscation, is often a severe drain on limited resources. The closer ties in Burma between the religious agencies and development agencies, as compared to Cambodia, indicates greater possibilities for making palatable to the run of Burmans the sacrifices in immediate consumption for development ends.

The rate of savings, then, the form of savings, and whether or not it goes into productive channels is intimately tied to the social and cultural aspects of a nation, but there is no easy rule for the *ex ante* identification of the institutional locus for promoting or inhibiting savings, for their form, and for their allocation, to ends conducive to further growth. But to date, the urban elite of Burma appears to be in a better position vis-à-vis their cultural diversity than is that of Cambodia.

The third category of social action in economic development is the organization of economic activity for self-sustained growth. The relevant dimensions are of two kinds: (1) the development of persons and organizations who will either invent or adapt new technology and new economic organization; and (2) the spread of the market and the increase of scale of productive enterprise. In these two categories are a host of variables—from schools, books, research institutes, literacy, public health, managerial skills, and labor force commitment; to the provision of roads, uniform currency, weights, and measures, and the reduction of the use of fraud and coercion in business transactions.

The motivational order of self-sustained economic growth is not stressed here, since it is assumed that if levels of living are raised, there will be commitment to the higher level. What the organization of economic development means is the creation of the environment in which continu-

ally improved inputs, human and non-human, are applied to the productive process as a matter of course. The social structures and cultural patterns which foster this are extremely variable theoretically and probably empirically exhibit a wide range.

In Burma, there exists the tradition of learning, of literacy, and of scholarship. The government is stressing literacy oriented toward some of the literature of daily life and work, rather than the esoteric and religious materials which formerly made up the content of Burmese literacy. In Cambodia, the literacy rate is less and the tradition not as widespread. Emphasis on secular learning is something almost exclusively tied to the urban areas.

The government organization involved in providing this social organization of development must prevent the rise of internal monopoly which restricts the market size and creates a larger zone of technological indifference. The royal-client organization of the Cambodian government seems a less promising instrument for these tasks than does the rudimentary parliamentary system of Burma. The danger in both countries is one of bureaucratic commitment to the maintenance of non-economic but state-run or sponsored industry.

The argument has now come full circle—from the conditions under which development is likely to become a goal, to the circumstances which make it self-sustaining. I should like to restate the argument and provide a graphic profile of Burma and Cambodia. Several caveats must be entered, lest serious misunderstanding ensue. There is small probability of a theory of economic development and cultural change which can be stated at a level relevant for action. Given the nature of social causation as "cumulative," the particular constellation of social and cultural features in a given society is the relevant dimension of analysis, rather than the general order of social integration.

This scheme is a way of picking from the welter of social facts those most intimately associated with economic development and cultural change. It offers a first approximation to ordering social and cultural features in a manner consistent with interpreting the major sources of stability and lability in a society.

To assess a society's potential for economic development in terms of meaningful alternatives, these are the diagnostic social and cultural features:

1. The Pattern of Social Stratification

(a) The more extreme the polarization of wealth, power, and prestige between classes or social segments, the less likely is new economic opportunity to be perceived or acted upon.

(b) The more restricted the channels of social mobility between the top group and the segment jus under it, the greater the possibility of the latter group seeking new means of mobility.

(c) The greater the gap between the legitimate sanctioned means of attaining wealth and the actual ways in which current holders of wealth have attained it, the greater likelihood of accepting structural change.

(d) The more frequent the recruitment of lower class members into upper class strata by merit or achievement, the larger the opportunity for seeking development.

2. The Value System

(a) The more there are competing ideologies and philosophies, the easier it is to win commitment to development.

(b) The greater the stress on nationalism, the more probable it is that development can be made one of the national goals.

(c) The greater the value agreement between different segments of the elite, the easier it is to transmit development values.

(d) The more varied the definition of the same general complex, from social segment to social segment, the less the social risk for an elite group in emphasizing the manipulative or material gain aspects of the value complex conducive to development.

3. The Economic Subsystem

(a) The more economic units are weighted on the subsistence side of production and the more they are anchored in local, communal organizations, the more difficult it is for them to save or for savings to take a form useful for rapid development.

(b) The lower the level of absolute wealth, the shorter the time perspective of investment, the more difficult it is to secure capital for long-run projects.

(c) The more developed and varied the agencies of accumulation (joint stock companies, securities markets, central bank, etc.), the more likely that significant amounts of capital can be productively channelled.

(d) The less the market or segments of it are monopolized, the greater the possibility of new investment.

(e) The more the holders of wealth are actually involved in the business of production, the more likely they are to respond to new economic opportunities.

4. The Political Subsystem

(a) The greater the sovereignty of the government over its territory without the use of coercive instruments, the easier is a program of development.

(b) The more organized the group holding political power, the easier it is to embark on development programs.

(c) The greater the allegiance of persons in the territory to ideas of nation and central government, the more likely that development can be undertaken.

(d) The greater the width of recruitment into political office, the more likely that development can be organized.

(e) The less the ideological cleavage in the elite, the greater the possibility of bureaucratic or noneconomic goals (too great a cleavage results in civil war and, of course, no development).

These rubrics are offered as a preliminary way of gauging the social and cultural aspects relevant to economic development and cultural change. Charting or interpreting a given social system according to this scheme is a subtle, unstandardized, and as yet not very reliable operation. The difficulty of stating the range of alternatives to action in a social system is enormous: and this difficulty is increased, rather than lessened, because social scientists cannot assess alternatives without getting into complex action and application programs which involve value and political choices extraneous to research as it is now conceived. Lastly, the notion of "economic development" is not a self-justifying one, and the various social and cultural costs people are willing to pay for material improvement is an open question, since no one is able to specify what sacrifices are involved in one or another course.

The accompanying diagrams are a first approximation to making a cultural and social profile of a given society in terms of the variables enumerated above.[15] Burma and Cambodia, according to the

[15] See figures.

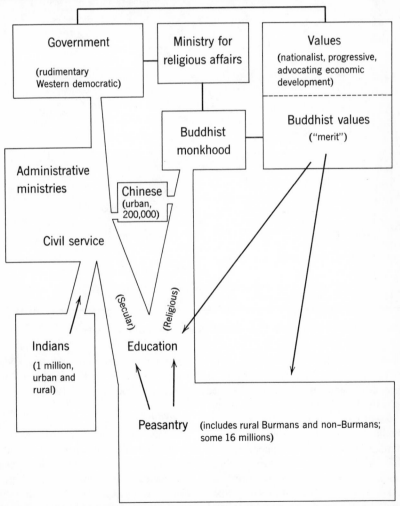

Figure 1. Generalized social profile of Burma.

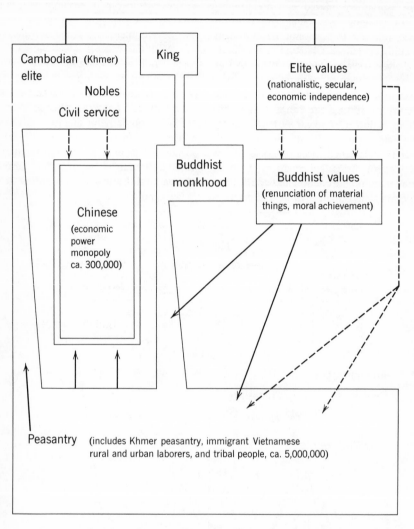

Figure 2. Generalized social profile of Cambodia.

profile, belong to the same "species" as far as economic development potential is concerned. Nonetheless, for reasons stated in the text, Burma's path appears to be less precarious than Cambodia's.

Whether or not this categorization is more than a function of theory and is worthy of the further expansion and elaboration it so obviously requires can only be resolved by empirical work, oriented to the end of examining and specifying alternatives generated by dif-

ferent societies and cultures. Such a research task is on the agenda of anthropology, and perhaps of history.

Appendix

Across the top of the diagrams, it is shown how the elites are divided into two organizations—the political and religious. Connected to these are their corresponding values. Emanating from the elite's structural blocks are the channels of mobility, which depict the hierarchical ladder connecting these sectors to the base of the population—the peasantry.

It should be noted that there is a wide difference between the social structure of the rural peasant communities and that of the urban populations. In both countries, the social organization of the rural villages is primarily based upon traditional age-sex and ascriptive statuses dependent upon kinship and residential criteria, while in the cities an incipient class structure is found which is similar to that found in Western societies. In both the rural and urban settings, however, educational achievement plays probably the most important role as the vehicle for mobility—the rural people beginning in the religious educational institutions and the urban workers in the secular institutions. Criteria of wealth are more important for urban-setting mobility. Thus, for simplicity, the diagrams depict the educational aspect of mobility into the political and religious spheres wherein reside the society's definitions of power and prestige.)

The integration into the social structure of the economically important minority populations in both nations is shown by their direct connections (or cleavages) with other segments and/or mobility among segments. Solid arrows from the value blocks[16] depict their effective trans-

mission to the peasantry, and broken arrows from the value blocks show that attempts are made to instill the more development-oriented values but are hindered by traditional ones.

Organizational contrasts in mobility via educational institutions are evident. The Burman pattern is more closely articulated than the Cambodian, indicating that Burman values are potentially in less conflict with rapid development. The more highly organized governmental agencies for economic development are found in Burma. The block for administration ministries and civil service has the possibility of being more task-oriented than the royal-client form of political organization obtaining in Cambodia. The economically important minority populations are incorporated into the administrative apparatus in Burma, while in Cambodia the economically powerful Chinese are isolated by strong social and cultural barriers from the rest of Cambodian society. The broken arrows from the Cambodian political elite to the Chinese signify that concerted efforts are being made to curtail the economic power of the Chinese, but to date the structure is not much modified. The solid arrows from the Cambodian peasantry to the Chinese minority show the real economic dependence of the peasantry on the Chinese for credit and commercial outlets.

[16] The idea of "value blocks" is a shorthand way of stressing the dominant canons of a complex world view.

Chapter 9

Industrialization and Urbanization

ACCEPTANCE OF INDUSTRIALIZATION AND ITS ATTENDANT CONSEQUENCES FOR THE SOCIAL PATTERNS OF NON-WESTERN SOCIETIES

George A. Theodorson

It is the main thesis of this paper that the industrialization of nonmachine societies will eventually lead to the development of new societal patterns.[1] These patterns will resemble, in time, certain dominant patterns of Western industrialized society, which *may not be rejected by any people who accept the machines of the West.*

The view that only very limited aspects of Western culture can be imported into the nonmachine societies while certain other "less desirable" aspects can be excluded is naive, unless it is based on an understanding of those aspects of culture which are independent of the industrial economic institution, and those which are inextricably tied up with it.

This discussion is pertinent today when many non-industrial societies are anxious to industrialize. A growing industrial plant is

SOURCE. George A. Theodorson, "Acceptance of Industrialization and Its Attendant Consequences for the Social Patterns of Non-Western Societies," *American Sociological Review*, **18**, 477–484, October 1953. Reprinted by permission of The American Sociological Association.

[1] The special case of the mechanization of agriculture will not be discussed here.

seen as security from economic want, economic imperialism, and military threats. In the short run national pride may encourage deliberate policies to perpetuate old customs and beliefs side by side with the new importations. Some of these short range compromises with the old social system may run against the long range interests of the national leaders.

Knowing what must accompany industrialization would save time, money, and effort, and prevent confusion. Any attempt by planners to stop an inevitable social change accompanying industrialization at the same time that industrialization is being encouraged, will increase disorganization and make it impossible for them to achieve their goals. On the other hand, knowledge of what need not change may be used to soften the impact of industrialization, appease vested interests to some extent, and intelligently blend the new with the old. This paper will contribute only indirectly to the solution of the latter problem.

The first half of the discussion will deal with the disorganizing effects of the change in social relationships engendered by the participation of members of a non-industrial society in activity oriented to modern

297

machines. The second half of the paper will deal with the new patterns of social relationships which will develop in relation to the demands imposed by the machine.

Disintegration of Certain Aspects of the Old Order

"Every society is an organized entity. . . . New technological practices are disruptive to such entities. . . ."[2] Thus social disorganization is a short range result of the decline of the old system.

One important change which will occur in a society with the introduction of industrialization will be the creation of new roles. These new roles are predominantly economic in nature—thus introducing an entirely new pattern of behavior into a society. Previously there had been no predominantly economic roles. Economic behavior was performed in roles which integrally combined other institutions with the economic. In non-industrialized and especially non-literate societies economic ". . . forms which we differentiate quite sharply are not only indistinguishable, but in many instances are so intimately linked with the non-economic institutions that we can only discern them at all by giving the closest attention to their economic role."[3]

This separation of the economic functions from a totally integrated system, would throw the entire system into a state of disequilibrium. All role behavior in an integrated system of human interaction tends to maintain and support other aspects of the system. The indigenous power structure is weakened through its loss of control over the economic sanctions. "Schapera describes the influence of money economy

upon the family system of the Kgatla, a Bantu people of Bechuanaland. Here . . . the marriage was arranged by the elders. But with urban employment the sons were released from economic dependence upon the fathers, they were given physical separation from the cultural system, and their marriages were perforce delayed. All three factors combined to make the youth act independently in seeking a marriage partner, to undermine the authority of the parental generation, and to lessen materially the unity of the family as system of interdependence."[4]

Another factor which further disrupts the old system is the decline of certain old roles, such as skilled craftsmen and magicians. This development would incur the opposition of those individuals whose positions are challenged. This was true in the case of the Kgatla cited above.[5]

It may be hypothesized that the conservatism encountered in the form of opposition to industrialization is to a considerable degree resistance on the part of those who expect to lose most from the changes, and not alone due to the resistance of deep seated values. This interpretation may be implied from Wilbert E. Moore's discussion of the problems involved in recruiting indigenous labor for the factory.[6] The fears of the threatened members of the non-industrialized society are based on sound fact, and are not simply an irrational reaction to change. Not only are their skills declining in importance, but new facilities have been created which give their possessors new sources of instrumental power. The people who have gained the new facilities (monetary gains for the factory workers)[7] become economically independent of the old order.

The creation of new facilities leads to the development of new rewards. The

[2] Walter R. Goldschmidt, "The Interrelations Between Cultural Factors and the Acquisition of New Technical Skills," in Bert F. Hoselitz (ed.), *The Progress of Underdeveloped Areas*, Chicago: The University of Chicago Press, 1952, p. 139.
[3] Melville J. Herskovits, *Economic Anthropology*, New York: Alfred A. Knopf, 1952, p. 155.
[4] Goldschmidt, *op. cit.*, pp. 140–141.
[5] *Ibid.*, p. 141.
[6] Wilbert E. Moore, *Industrialization and Labor*, Ithaca: Cornell University Press, 1951, Ch. 2.
[7] It is assumed that there is no question of the fact that the use of money accompanies industrialization.

facilities themselves as signs of instrumental power become rewards to some extent.[8] For example, in the United States money, which is in reality a facility for instrumental activity, has come to be regarded as a reward and a source of direct gratification. In the newly industrializing society the new facilities of the factory workers consist primarily of skills, tools, and money. These facilities, having become rewards, place prestige and higher social status in the hands of new individuals in the society. It is not that these factory workers are supplanting the old elite, but they are rising above agricultural and craftsmen classes to which they were previously inferior, assuming that the poorest and lowliest people are the ones first attracted to the factory.[9] An individual making a choice will always seek to optimize his gratifications. Apparently the persons receiving the least gratifications under the old system will be the first to be attracted to the new possibilities.

Thus far we have discussed those facilities which have been introduced into the society for the first time by industrialization. However, there are elements in the old social system which had not been important previously, such as certain skills and resources, which now become significant. These skills and resources become more important as new symbols of prestige, at the same time that older symbols in the society are losing their former prominence. Thus certain aspects of the old system are discouraged by the introduction of the industrial system, while other aspects become more important. The industrial system tends to respect people who work with their hands, while ". . . in all the unmechanized civilizations the trader and the mechanic rank far down in the social scale."[10] The industrial system values even

more highly certain other skills such as executive and scientific abilities, but these mental skills are quite different from those possessed by the old elite.

The creation of new roles, new facilities, and new rewards, and the prominence of previously unimportant resources and skills, all tend to place new individuals in positions of power. The new power structure challenges the old, and later tends to produce a new elite. Even the common factory workers may come to have more power and influence than certain previously higher classes who remained in agricultural pursuits. This gain of power and influence is even more pronounced in the case of the entrepreneurs, especially when they rise from within the society, and are not merely foreign investors and managers.

Even if the new elite merely consists of members of the old elite this does not affect the analysis. The fact that they are the same individuals makes no difference, for they will have to have new attitudes, behavior, expectations, and values, in order to perform their new roles successfully. Thus from the point of view of the social system there is an entirely new elite. On the other hand, if the new elite consists of individuals who have risen from below and who seek to incorporate themselves into the old elite, they necessarily will modify the old elite in the process. They must maintain role behavior and orientations, compatible with their positions in the industrial system, which will not be the same as the traditional orientations and expectations of the old elite. In either case the analysis holds and the power structure of the society is modified.

A further development which is disruptive of the old order stems from the fact that industrialization always leads to the production of large quantities of cheap goods. Even in a country where a low wage policy prevails, the people will have enough money to buy at least some of the products of industrialization. The mass production of large quantities of cheap goods will make

[8] Talcott Parsons, *The Social System*, Glencoe, Illinois: The Free Press, 1951, p. 513.
[9] Moore, *op. cit.*, p. 304.
[10] Ralph Linton, "Cultural and Personality Factors Affecting Economic Growth," in Hoselitz, *op. cit.*, p. 85.

available to them material products which they never before dreamed of possessing. This will be true not only of the factory workers but also of those who have remained in agriculture, for the growing cities will provide an opportunity to sell surplus produce at a profit. This is an incentive to produce more, and the new agricultural techniques and implements make possible the additional production. This will extend to every village within the circle of the new industrialization. Thus some degree of improvement of the common people's standard of living will occur. However, in countries where a small group wishes, and is able, to keep most of the benefits of industrialization to itself, this improvement will not be very great. Low wages, systems of land ownership, and systems of taxation may keep the majority of the people poor. This situation of only slight improvement for the majority cannot last forever because industrialization eventually provides a greatly improved standard of living for everyone. It may, however, last for some time, long enough to create an explosive situation in the short run.

When people have for centuries held a fatalistic attitude, bad conditions are accepted, and this helps to maintain the stability of the social system. "In a society in which people regularly expect to be hungry annually, and in which traditions and proverbs accustom them to expect such a period of privation, their whole attitude toward economic effort is affected. . . . Among the Bamba scarcity is within the ordinary run of experience, and accepted as such."[11] Some degree of amelioration may open their thinking to the possibilities of even greater improvements, and, ironically, lead to impatience and general dissatisfaction. Thus the people of the areas we are trying to protect from Communism may become more receptive to the seemingly quick and easy solutions offered by the Communists. There should be a sensitivity to the potential dangers of a slow process

[11] Herskovits, *op. cit.*, pp. 293–294, quoted from Audrey J. Richards.

of aid to "underdeveloped areas" by those in charge of these programs.

In the section above the causes of the disintegration of the old order have been discussed. There are, however, certain forces tending to delay this disintegration, thus prolonging the period of disorganization. Among the most important of these is the continued emotional dependence of the workers on the old community. This emotional dependence will cause them to conform to some degree to the normative patterns of the community. This brings them under the influence of the embattled conservative leadership. Thus the emotional dependence provokes modes of orientation which slow down the adjustment of the native factory worker to the new industrial element in his environment. It must be emphasized that the advent of industrialization introduces only instrumental activities, and does not constitute a total functioning social system. When the native recruit is unhappy and discontented in the new factory situation it is not simply that he is nostalgic for the traditional atmosphere of his youth. Although there is this longing for the old way of life, a much more important and more elusive point is that man gains most of his satisfactions and feelings of security from a well rounded and integrated pattern of interaction. This means that he needs an orderly life based on mutual patterns of expectations that cover all phases of his activities within and without the immediate factory situation. The old patterns of interaction and patterns of expectations are inadequate in a system which involves an entirely different economic orientation. Thus social relationships are disrupted. There is a great deal of insecurity, and the morale and efficiency of the factory worker are greatly reduced.

A new social system is needed in the industrial community, a system which would integrate the new economic system with those aspects of the old culture which can be adjusted to industrialization. It should provide reasonably integrated patterns of action and expectations covering all interaction among individuals, no matter how close or how distant. Where the native population has no such integrated system of expectations, the period of adjustment will be longer than where one exists.

An interesting problem is posed here for those who wish to increase the efficiency of native labor, hasten their adjustment to the nonvillage life in the growing factory areas, and to increase the number of workers who come and stay at their new factory positions. The above analysis would imply that some ambitious planner should try to encourage the development of new patterns of expectations in the various institutions of the newly developing social system. This would demand first of all some knowledge of the form the institutions will have to take so that no patterns of expectations will be introduced or encouraged that would later interfere with the projected goals of industrialization envisaged by the national leaders of the "underdeveloped" countries. It is not within the scope of this paper to suggest methods of hastening the development of new patterns of expectations, but the general direction of this development will be discussed in the following section.

So far, the discussion has been concerned with the decline of the old order through the creation of new roles, new facilities, new rewards, and new sources of prestige and power. The resultant general picture of social disorganization presented above is not likely to remain permanently. There is a tendency to restore a relative equilibrium in any ongoing process of interaction.[12] Further changes will develop which will provide the basis for this new integration.

Reorganization of the Social System

The reorganization of the society can be analyzed in terms of four of Talcott Parsons' five pattern variables.[13] The thesis

[12] Parsons, *op. cit.*, pp. 481–482.
[13] Briefly the four pattern variables may be defined as follows: (1) *Specificity*—concern with only one aspect of a person; *diffuseness*—concern with the total person. (2) *Particularism*

advanced here is that an increase in universalism, achievement, suppression of immediate emotional release (affective-neutrality), and specificity all accompany industrialization in the long run. The remainder of this paper will be concerned with the dynamics of this development.

Industrialization means the introduction of machinery, and many leaders of nonindustrial societies have expressed the view that machines, and *only* machines are what they want from the industrial world. This is certainly an oversimplification of what industrialization means. Because machines are very expensive they necessarily must be used economically. In the early stages of industrialization labor is far less scarce than machinery. This means that there is a strong constraint on the part of those related to the industrial process to adjust labor to the machines. It is very difficult to tolerate inefficient use of the machines, insofar as this can be avoided. The necessity of teaching and enforcing these modes of adjustment demands a certain type of social organization. This social organization centered about the need to adjust to the machines in the factory system engenders certain unique social relationships. The native's first major change in the patterning of his relations to others is experienced in the factory situation.

—orientation to a person on the basis of some special relationship to him based on membership in a certain collectivity (e.g. a kinship grouping); *universalism*—orientation based on the possession of a certain attribute or attributes (achieved or ascribed) regardless of the particular person who possesses it. (3) *Achievement*—emphasis on actual performances of an individual; *ascription*—emphasis on certain qualities of an individual, either given at birth or automatically conferred later, regardless of performances. (4) *Affectivity*—giving open expression to immediate desires either to do or not to do something (immediate emotional release); *affective-neutrality*—suppressing immediate desires for a long range interest (suppression of emotional release).

The pattern variable of self-orientation vs. collectivity-orientation is not included in this paper. For a fuller discussion of the pattern variables see: Parsons, *op. cit.*, pp. 58–67.

The Necessity to Adjust to Machinery and its Effects on Social Organization[14]

The first adjustment a man has to make to machines is the long hours he has to spend away from his home community. The extent to which he is away from his old ties determines the degree to which his relationship toward them will change. A long period of the day goes by in a new social situation without the supervision of the old normative system. Furthermore, his relationship to his family changes from the old pattern of responsibilities and expectations which depended on his being with them a good deal of the day. Spending less time in his home community also means that the close relationships formerly possible cannot be the same. Since the immediate family is in the end the most intimate and most psychologically satisfying human group, the worker, with less time, will choose to spend proportionately more of that time with his immediate family, and less time with his extended family[15] and the others in the community. Devoting more of his waking hours to machines, then, means less time with his family, less time with his home community, and proportionately more time with his close family than with his neighbors. Because his constant close relations with his neighbors decrease substantially, his relations to them change. His relations are less dif-

fuse, because he has less time to know them thoroughly. They are less particularistic because there are fewer groups in which he and his neighbors are integrated. Because he is dealing with relatively unfamiliar people on a specific-universalistic basis, his relations with them will be less emotionally involved.

Secondly, because the machines are expensive and complicated the individuals working with them must be selected on the basis of achievement.[16] Thus, in the factory situation achievement becomes dominant over ascription. The ability to run the machines is a specific demand, and diffuse standards become irrelevant. Thus the pattern variable of specificity is further strengthened. Furthermore, it is difficult to combine particularism and achievement as a general pattern. A person's cousin may not be as qualified as someone unrelated to him. It is impossible in the long run for the extended family to comprise the factory unit because the criteria for the old status system of the family will not fit the criteria of the factory (physical strength, dexterity, and the like). Achievement-universalism will be fostered not only by the demand for efficient labor for the expensive machines, but also by the demands imposed on the factory unit by competition from domestic or foreign competitors. The Japanese attempt to integrate the new industrial system with the old familial organization shows unmistakable signs of disintegration.[17]

Third, while in the non-industrialized

[14] In terms of M. J. Levy Jr.'s conceptual scheme as developed in *The Structure of Society*, this is an analysis of the functional requisites of the industrial system and the structural requisites (particularly of relationship structures) that logically and necessarily follow therefrom. This paper will particularly emphasize the derivation of the structural requisites from the functional requisites. Marion J. Levy, Jr., *The Structure of Society*, Princeton: Princeton University Press, 1952.

[15] Some writers have noted the disintegrating effect of industrialization on the extended family. Ralph Linton comments, "Modernization of the unmechanized culture, . . . cannot fail to weaken or even destroy joint family patterns." From Linton, *op. cit.*, p. 84. Talcott Parsons expresses the same view on pages 178 and 510 of *The Social System*.

[16] "Advanced degrees of industrialization greatly accentuate the importance of differences in ability on the part of individuals. . . . Slight differences in skill may be reflected in enormous differences in output under such circumstances. . . . The difference in damage that can be done by the relatively less skilled in highly industrialized situations as opposed to relatively non-industrialized ones is also enormous." Marion J. Levy, "Some Sources of the Vulnerability of the Structures of Relatively Non-Industrialized Societies to Those of Highly Industrialized Societies," in Hoselitz, *op. cit.*, pp. 120–121.

[17] Moore, *op. cit.*, pp. 30–31.

societies discipline is self-imposed, that of the industrial operative is imposed from outside. This routine is imposed on the worker because he is no longer self-employed, because the great expense of the machinery and fuel demands constant operation, and because of the demands for coordination imposed by the greater division of labor. One of the most serious problems facing the new factory in the underdeveloped area is that of absenteeism and labor turnover due to the reluctance of the workers to accept the new factory discipline.[18] The worker must do his work regardless of his private desires of the moment. Gratification must be postponed.

This continuous attention demanded by the machine and the restrictions thus imposed on the worker, in turn, led to a new kind of relationship between him and his superiors, and between him and his fellow workers. Before the introduction of the machine the relation of the individual member of the working group to those who possessed authority was diffuse. In the factory situation the relation of the individual toward his superiors becomes very specific. The superiors are only interested in those aspects of the individual which are relevant to the efficient use of the machines. This is one of the important changes in the relations of the worker which initiates the process of separating the economic from the other institutions in the social system.

In the factory situation the relations of the individual worker to his equals can no longer be based on the diffuse relations which existed when each member of a working group knew every other member as a total individual because of constant contact. The laborers in the factory spend a good deal of their time there, and the main contact they have with the majority of their fellow workers is in this context. All they know of the majority of their fellow workers is their achievements, skills, and personalities as production workers. Evaluations and adjustments are in terms of the factory system. Thus specificity is

[18] Moore, *op. cit.*, Ch. 5.

necessarily dominant. In Japan the attempt to maintain diffuse relationships in the factory system was possible only in the short run.[19] Strains were produced in the Japanese attempt to adapt the machine to their premachine society. These strains eventually led to the breakdown of the system of diffuse factory relations, and to an adjustment more consistent with a machine society which demands the separation of the economic from the other institutions.

Since the economic system has become separated from the other systems, economic considerations become of prime importance in judging individuals and allocating roles within the economic system. With further specialization of the industrial system only one particular skill becomes relevant. Thus, in selecting an electrician, only that skill is significant, and literary and artistic talents, religious and political beliefs, and sociability are not considered. Since instrumental activity is the only kind of performance demanded by these roles, diffuse and particularistic considerations are of no relevance to the individual's ability to perform the role satisfactorily. Although this specificity is not always complete in all situations in an industrial economy, still it is the dominant pattern and the accepted value.

A fourth effect of industrialization is a further growth of specificity due to a new orientation to a larger community. Mass production produces a huge quantity of goods which must be sold to a large and far flung number of people. It would be impossible to know all these people thoroughly—which would be necessary if diffuse standards were to apply. The modern market by its nature demands specific orientations. At the same time the scope of political power grows with industrialization and the authorities of a large nation cannot possibly deal with all citizens on the basis of diffuse standards. In addition, the vastness of the new economic and political relationships are as disruptive of particularism as they are of diffuseness. Time considerations alone

[19] Moore, *op. cit.*, pp. 30–31.

demand a universalistic orientation in the large modern market or nation.

Another impetus to the specificity-universalistic complex is the impersonality of the modern factory. This impersonality is due to the large size of the modern productive enterprise and also to the need for large amounts of capital, which in turn leads to the corporate system with its absentee stockholder owners. In the factory the managers and workers are for the most part strangers to each other, and this is certainly true of the owners and workers, who often never meet. The only kind of standards which can be used for allocation of roles in such a situation must be specific and universalistic.

Since the economic system is very important and generally the dominant system in an industrial society, its values tend to dominate the other systems. Levy writes, "... it is impossible to confine these patterns rigidly to the economic aspect of action.... Highly universalistic relations in the economic aspects of action are functionally incompatible with highly particularistic ones in the political (i.e. allocation of power and responsibility) aspects of action. It is because of such functional interrelationships among different spheres and aspects of action that these clusters of patterns seem on the whole to appear widely diffused in social systems rather than narrowly confined."[20]

The kinship system is an exception to the above analysis for by its nature it is diffuse, emotional, particularistic, and predominantly ascriptive.[21]

Conclusion

There may well be strong attempts on the part of the leaders of some of the industrializing countries to integrate some of the old patterns of human relationships into the newly developing industrial society. It is the opinion of the writer that some of the leaders of these non-industrial societies are in a sense marginal men, or men of two cultural systems. They are emotionally tied to the old system, but at the same time they are anxious to reap the benefits of a system which promises to relieve some of their economic problems. This conscious attempt on the part of many non-industrialized countries to integrate the old culture with a complex technology quite foreign to them can be successful only insofar as the old cultural elements do not, in the long run, conflict with certain patterns of human relationships basic to a machine society. This integration could provide cultural continuity which would most certainly ease the transitional period, make it more productive, and hasten the process of industrialization. However, insofar as old cultural elements are preserved in the face of the demands of the new and promising factory system, there will be additional strains that will have to be overcome in the long run, such as less productivity, and a serious delay in the achievement of the desired basic economic goals. Another interesting question, not within the province of this paper, is the question of what kinds of intermediate adjustments could be made which would tend to support old social relationships, but in which provision is made for their slow dissolution. This writer thinks, however, that this approach would be unrealistic, despite its short run advantages.

While this paper has discussed some of the long run consequences of industrialization for underdeveloped areas, it does not imply that there cannot be any cultural continuity, or cultural forms which are peculiar to the society in question. A good deal of variation in industrialized societies is possible. There is no evidence, for example, that any of the following have to change: music, art, religious beliefs about the nonempirical world, and many folkways.

It must be reiterated that there is no implication that any non-industrial society must accept the pattern of development outlined in this paper. However, insofar as a society does accept the value of industrialization and seeks to bring it about, then the development discussed above is to be expected.

[20] Levy, *op. cit.*, pp. 122–123.
[21] Parsons, *op. cit.*, p. 186.

URBANIZATION, POLITICAL STABILITY, AND ECONOMIC GROWTH

Shanti Tangri

Sociologists and economists have in general tended to agree about the mutually beneficent influence of urbanization and economic development. The argument runs in terms of economies of population aggregation and value transformations conducive to economizing, enterprising, and innovative behavior. Generalizations in this field are based largely on the historical experience of Western developed economies.[1]

I have argued elsewhere that urbanization is neither a necessary nor a sufficient condition for economic growth.[2] Under certain conditions, however, and up to a point, it can be a desirable condition for growth, while under other conditions, or beyond a certain point, it can be a factor in slowing down growth. In contemporary India the process of urbanization, in both magnitude and nature, seems to be a factor retarding rather than accelerating growth.

Here I do not propose to review the highly important but well-discussed issues of social overhead capital, economies of scale for industrial plants and cities as a whole, external economies, consumer densities, pools of labor, skills, and knowledge, centers of communication and innovation, etc.[3] My contention is rather that we cannot determine the role of urbanization without estimating the economic costs or benefits of such urban phenomena as *anomie*, political and ideological ferment, and transformation of cultural and social values. For drawing policy conclusions we need also to know comparable costs and benefits associated with social change among rural populations. I have been unable to find comparative studies of this nature. Reviewing the literature on social and economic change leads me to believe, however, that the socioeconomic costs of tradition-oriented rural attitudes, though never measured, are usually assumed to be prohibitive enough to make growth extremely slow, if not impossible, while similar costs of urbanization are seldom considered to be high enough to prevent or retard change. Indeed, this is what the historical experience of Western societies seems to indicate.[4] That perhaps is not and will not be the case in India and some other underdeveloped countries. As the benefits of urbanization have been discussed extensively in the literature, I will discuss primarily the other side of the case. In this context a few words about the relative rural-urban potential for economic development are in order.

SOURCE. Shanti Tangri, "Urbanization, Political Stability, and Economic Growth," in Roy Turner, ed., *India's Urban Future* (Berkeley: University of California Press, 1962), pp. 192–212.

[1] For a brief (and unsympathetic) review of non-Weberian theories of the city see Don Martindale and Gertrude Neuwirth's Prefatory Remarks (pp. 9–62) in their translation of *The City*, by Max Weber (Glencoe, Ill.: Free Press, 1958). For a more limited and relevant discussion see William L. Kolb, "The Social Structure and Functions of Cities," *Economic Development and Cultural Change*, **3**, 1 (October 1954), 30–46.

[2] "Patterns of Investment and Rates of Growth, with Special Reference to India" (Doctoral dissertation, University of California, Berkeley, 1960). For a historical criticism of the "industrialization through urbanization" thesis see Carl Bridenbaugh, *Cities in the Wilderness* (New York: Ronald Press, 1938), and *Cities in Revolt* (New York: Knopf, 1955).

[3] See, for example, Eric Lampard, "The History of Cities in Economically Advanced Areas," *Economic Development and Cultural Change*, **3**, 1 (October 1954), 81–136.

[4] *Ibid.*, p. 132.

The Rural-Urban Potential for Asset Formation

In the cities, the savings of entrepreneurial and managerial classes tend to be high, and those of middle and lower classes to be low or negative, because of low incomes and/or higher consumption standards and lower earner-dependent ratios in families. Thus, while the proportion invested out of industrial incomes tends to be relatively high, compared to investments out of agricultural income,[5] it is not clear how the total urban savings-income ratio compares on a per-capita basis with the rural savings-income ratio. Lack of empirical information precludes judgment on the relative rural-urban potential for asset formation out of internal savings.

However, the possibilities of asset creation without prior or concomitant savings are quite extensive and impressive in rural areas[6] and insignificant in urban areas. In the villages people often cooperate to help each other in building houses or fences, or in other acts requiring group effort; not so in the cities, where exchange of labor is monetized and thus involves problems of financing. Again, in the villages there are unused resources—such as common village lands, forests, tanks, wells, ponds, labor, and skills which can be used for asset creation given an appropriate program of mobilization. A villager repairs his own home more readily than a city dweller. Also there is a lesser expectation, on the part of an idle villager, as compared to an urbanite, of finding alternative sources of income, whether the relative expectations of the urbanite and villager are justified or not by the realities of job markets.[7] Thus, lower opportunity costs of the villager make it easier for him to donate his labor to his neighbor or to his community. Finally, many materials and assets which the villager has use for are not desired by the urbanite. The villager can dig up clay and lime and bring palm leaves from the outskirts of the village and husks from his fields, to thatch his roof or plaster his walls or add a room to his house. The urbanite will live in a crowded brick hovel rather than in a thatched mud house. He may not be able to afford a new brick house, but a mud house is not an asset in his eyes—and if it were, the municipal authorities would probably not tolerate, much less encourage, its construction.

The deepening, cleaning, and lining of village tanks and wells as sources of water supply for humans and animals and for irrigation and the construction of warehouses

[5] P. N. Rosenstein-Rodan thinks the former ratio is often as high as 35 per cent and the latter between 10 and 15 per cent. (This and other references to him are based on personal conversations and a seminar he gave at the Massachusetts Institute of Technology in the spring of 1959.) Wilfred Malenbaum derives the figure 10 per cent for the latter ratio from sample data on India; cf. *The Non-Monetized Sector of Rural India* (Cambridge, Mass.: Center for International Studies, M.I.T., 1956), p. 11. He thinks the figure may be a slight overestimate. Some economists think the figure is much lower. For an argument that most estimates of rural capital formation are downward biased see Basil S. Yamey and Peter T. Bauer, *Economics of Underdeveloped Countries* (Chicago: University of Chicago Press, 1957), pp. 16–31.

[6] Yamey and Bauer, *op. cit.* A detailed analysis of the rural-urban potential for capital formation in the underdeveloped countries is given in my "Patterns of Investment and Rates of Growth ... "

[7] Whether people are pushed or pulled to towns, one can argue that economic opportunities in towns must be better than in villages, that potential migrants must believe them to be so, and that in the long run their perception must be validated by experience, otherwise the flow of population would cease or reverse itself. If this reasoning is correct, differentials in reality and perceptions of reality by villagers about relative opportunities become irrelevant for long-run population flows. This reasoning assumes that migration can be based on "irrational" considerations only in the short run. In fact, only a small minority of the migrants need realize their expectations in order for the myth to survive that opportunities in the city are greater than in the country—in other words, people's irrational behavior in regard to spatial mobility can persist even in the long run.

for storing agricultural produce—a vital step for stabilizing agricultural prices and increasing output, for preventing significant losses in food supplies, and for freeing the cultivator from the usurious controls of moneylenders—involve the use of local labor, materials, skills, and organization. Constructing schools, clinics, and community centers, digging ditches and canals and building roads, terracing, bunding, and hedging fields, planting suitable trees on fallow land, controling soil and wind erosion, and developing village ponds as sources of fish supplies: these also are dependent on similar uses of labor and skills.

In addition, the potentialities of increased agricultural output resulting from better practices and marketing, and the consolidation of holdings, net of expenses of innovation, seem impressive.[8] Addition of new facilities, such as brickkilns, multiplies this potential several times, brickmaking being one of the simplest and least expensive operations, ideally suited for local production, distribution, and use in most communities.[9]

In ten years of planned development India has not come anywhere near to exploiting this potential fully, and this in spite of the demonstration by Communist China of its powerful role in the initial phases of development.[10]

[8] See, for example, Albert Mayer, McKim Marriott, and Richard L. Park, *Pilot Project, India: The Story of Rural Development at Etawah, Uttar Pradesh* (Berkeley and Los Angeles: University of California Press, 1958), pp. 233–287.
[9] *Kurukshretra: A Symposium on Community Development in India, 1952–1955* (New Delhi: Community Projects Administration, 1955), pp. 298–308. The facts reported here are also cited in Mayer *et al.*, *Pilot Project, India*, pp. 272–278.
[10] Wilfred Malenbaum, "India and China: Contrasts in Development Performance," *American Economic Review*, **46**, 3 (June 1959), esp. pp. 305–307. See also Tillman Durdin, "Red China Plans Vast Irrigation," New York *Times*, November 3, 1958, and other similar reports in the *Times*.

The Cost of Theologies and Ideologies

Around the theory of indivisibilities, ably propounded by Professors Rosentein-Rodan, Nurkse, and others, has grown an almost mystical complex of belief with many variations.[11] Crudely put, it amounts to this: in underdeveloped countries you have got to have a "big push" if you want to generate self-sustaining growth (enough to outstrip population growth). The big push is then related to big projects and the most up-to-date technology.

All of these ideas have some validity. But political beliefs and historical associations have taken this discussion partly from the realm of theory and reality into that of dogma. Many Marxists are for this way of thinking because it fits the Russian model. Some ardent nationalists are for it because other theories seem to stress rural and agricultural development, a thing which the British rulers used to stress.

Rightly or wrongly, to many this British attitude was an indication of Britain's desire to keep India a nonindustrial, raw-material-supplying colony. To some, like Pandit Nehru, the big dams are "temples of a new faith" in India.[12] To others, steel mills are the crux of economic development. To yet others, steel mills and shipyards are the symbols of national power and autonomy. Psychological symbols and national power may legitimately compete with economic goals. Steel mills, unlike shipyards, are perhaps economically justified in India. The point, however, is this: if economic criteria indicate that a network of rural feeder roads is more productive for the economy than an airline, or fertilizer factories are more remunerative than steel mills, it needs to be explicitly stated that the choosing of steel mills and airlines involves the adop-

[11] For a brief review of these theories see Benjamin H. Higgins, *Economic Development, Principles, Problems and Policies* (New York: Norton, 1959), pp. 384–408.
[12] Takashi Oka, "Dam in India Looms as 'Temple of Faith'," *Christian Science Monitor*, January 28, 1958.

tion of other criteria. Indeed, the commitment of the bulk of the nation's resources to construction of dams and irrigation systems with long gestation periods is not easy to justify on economic grounds, when the urgent problems of food, shelter, and clothing can be solved much more quickly with simple technologies, less capital, and more labor.[13]

The example of big dams illustrates that gigantomania is not always biased toward urbanization. However, due to the correlations between economic development, industrialization, and urbanization which most people carry in their minds, it tends to favor urbanization and industrialization, particularly capital-using industrialization at the cost of labor-using, agricultural, and industrial development. It results in inefficient use of resources for the "short run" (which may extend to fifteen or twenty or more years) in exchange for added but more uncertainly anticipated benefits in the "long run." In an economy like that of India, when high interest rates of 40 or 50 per cent per annum,[14] reflecting the scarcity of capital (and not the

artificially controlled low rates of interest, such as 3 or 4 per cent in the imperfect capital market), are used to discount the flow of future outputs, it is not at all clear that such long-run investments are always more productive, even in the long run, than a series of short-run, quick-maturing, and quickly depreciating investments.

I am not aware of any published information which attempts to justify long-run projects in India on such economic grounds. When people are so wedded to their theories that they apply them without even trying to test them, wasteful allocation of resources is likely to occur—and the theories take on the character of theologies. Thus, very often the zeal for setting up the most modern factories and transportation systems increases the real costs of industrialization and urbanization.

Another important reason for the increased expensiveness of urbanization in India is the modern and egalitarian ideology of public welfare. England in the eighteenth and nineteenth centuries could ignore the social costs of slums, unsanitary conditions, and fire hazards to a greater extent than can India in the twentieth century.

Because of bad sanitation, Josiah Strong believed, there were 156,660 "unnecessary" deaths in U.S. cities in 1890.[15] Today, public health measures are introduced first in the cities. The resulting population growth, with overcrowding of housing, schools, hospitals, and transport systems, and shortages of food and other necessities, is a well-known story. Thus are being built the pressures, the strains, and the tensions which may lead to political turmoil or to an authoritarian regime. And hence, as Rostow has stated, the responsibility of the "non-Communist literate elites in . . . transitional societies [to] ensure that the humane decision to save lives does not lead to an inhumane society."[16]

---

[13] If it is assumed that both the production of more consumers' goods and the labor-intensive mode of production for consumers' as well as capital goods will only stimulate population expansion and not raise per-capita incomes, and that population growth cannot be checked otherwise, then a "capital-intensive" investment program may be the only economically feasible program for development. Cf. Walter Galenson and Harvey Liebenstein, "Investment Criteria, Productivity and Economic Development," *Quarterly Journal of Economics*, **69**, 3 (August 1955), 343–370. As I have argued elsewhere (see note 2), such a program is not politically feasible in a democracy. It amounts to controlling population growth by starving a section of the people (the unemployed) or spreading consumption goods more thinly over an expanding population, thus keeping general mortality rates high. Even in Communist Poland such a program was overthrown by the people, and only terror and purges enabled Stalin to carry it through in the Soviet Union.

[14] Rates of interest as high as 5 or 6 per cent per month have been reported to the author by several people in villages and traditional sections of old cities.

[15] *The Twentieth Century City* (New York: Baker and Taylor, 1898), p. 58.

[16] W. W. Rostow, *The Stages of Economic Growth: A Non-Communist Manifesto* (Cambridge: Cambridge University Press, 1960), p. 144.

This welfare philosophy is affecting villages also. Describing wastages of cement and steel in one Indian village, René Dumont wrote, "Even European villages do not yet possess all these amenities. India has tried to become a welfare state before creating the basic economy required to sustain it. Comfort has been given priority over production."[17] But this priority of comfort over production becomes operative first in the cities and then radiates out.

Most experts expect housing conditions to get worse in the urban areas of the underdeveloped areas in the coming decade or two.[18] This certainly appears to be the prospect in India.[19] As congestion and slums grow, the need to spend more on urban areas to provide for public health services and social amenities will also increase. The amenities are more expensive because of higher standards expected by urbanites. And if, in addition, a city has already exceeded the population mark of 400,000–500,000, which Rosenstein-Rodan considers optimal from the point of view of social overhead capital, per unit costs of social services may rise rapidly. The number of cities in excess of this size is likely to increase very rapidly in the coming decades in India, thus making urbanization an increasingly expensive process.

If many of the economic, social, and political troubles of the developed economies flow from the fact that ideology lags behind technology, the troubles of the underdeveloped areas become more acute because ideology outruns technology.

Economic Frustrations: Unemployment, Underemployment, and Misemployment

In spite of all the deficiencies in the available employment statistics,[20] it is evident that the trend of growing unemployment in India is not likely to reverse itself in the near future. Urban unemployment accounts for perhaps half of the total. In the larger cities, Malenbaum points out, of all the employed 51.8 per cent were literate and only 3 per cent had any college education, while of the unemployed 78.4 per cent were literate and 5.1 per cent had college education. Some 46 per cent of all the educated unemployed are concentrated in the four major cities of India.[21]

The interval between completion of education and first employment is often quite long. "Thus, while some 50 per cent of the illiterate unemployed have been out of work for at least a year, 75 per cent of the matriculates and intermediates are in this category."[22] Majumdar's study of a large sample of alumni of Lucknow University holding Master's degrees indicates that the more highly educated are unemployed longer. Of the unemployed in this sample, 44 per cent had been unemployed for over two years, 18 per cent for a year and a half, and 27 per cent for a year. A somewhat similar pattern emerges from a sample survey conducted by the Delhi Employment Exchange.[23]

---

[17] "Agricultural Defeat in India," *New Statesman and Nation*, **58**, 1501 (December 19, 1959), 871.
[18] See, for example, Burnham Kelley (ed.), *Housing and Economic Development* (Cambridge, Mass.: Massachusetts Institute of Technology, 1955).
[19] Pitambar Pant's confident optimism about the housing situation is based on minimal average-cost estimates for the Third and Fourth Plans, far below those actually achieved in the first two Plans.

[20] For a review of these see K. N. Raj, "Employment and Unemployment in the Indian Economy: Problems of Classification, Measurement and Policy," *Economic Development and Cultural Change*, **7**, 3, Part I (April 1959), 258–278.
[21] Wilfred Malenbaum, "Urban Unemployment in India," *Pacific Affairs*, **30**, 2 (June 1957), 138–150.
[22] *Ibid.*, p. 146.
[23] For the Lucknow sample see D. N. Majumdar, *Unemployment Among the University Educated: A Pilot Inquiry in India* (Cambridge, Mass.: Center for International Studies, Massachusetts Institute of Technology, 1957). For the Delhi survey see Motilal Gupta, "Problems of Unemployment in India" (Doctoral dissertation, Netherlands School of

Corresponding to underemployment and seasonal or disguised unemployment in the villages, there is considerable disguised unemployment and/or misemployment in the cities, as reflected in the rapid growth of the low-productivity service sector in which unskilled, uneducated workers, and especially the transients, seek means to subsist. Among the educated in the Majumdar sample, "about three-quarters of those who sought service in a firm and a substantial majority of those who sought service in government or sought a profession of their own failed to achieve it." Economic frustration can only be high in such situations. None of the 237 who answered Majumdar's question as to the factors responsible for difficulty in getting a job blamed it on their own shortcomings. While only about 12 per cent blamed it on bad luck, the rest blamed society in one way or another, to wit: "government," 48 per cent; "society," 13 per cent; "lack of proper and systematic training," 26 per cent—which usually meant lack of opportunities for these.

If the educated unemployed provide leadership, these transients, whom Hoselitz calls the *lumpen proletariat*, provide the raw material for mobs. Political parties, trade unions, business and religious groups, displaced landlords, and princes willing to provide ideological, financial, and organizational resources for making effective use of these two groups are not scarce in the cities.

Rapidly increasing enrollments in colleges and schools, and demographic and economic trends, are likely to swell the ranks of both of these groups in the coming decade. This *lumpen intelligentsia*, as Lewis Feuer calls it, with little skill, opportunity, or capital for entrepreneurship in economic activity, turns to political entrepreneurship where, with less capital, training, and skills, a man can manage to exist, if not get ahead. Moreover, oppor-

tunity costs in economic enterprise are higher than in political enterprise. Social values, historical associations, and ideological fashions make economic enterprise a less and political a more desired activity as a means to status and power.

Physical densities, communication, and other facilities make political organization relatively easier in cities. Groups with resources and tightly knit organizations, like the Communists or the Rashtriya Swayam-Sewak Sangh (R.S.S.) are at a relative advantage in such situations. Part of the success of Communists in Kerala and Bengal, two of the most densely populated areas in India, may be due to this reason.[24] The R.S.S. similarly is, by and large, an urban lower-middle-class movement. Psychological densities—intense interchange of ideas, rumors, and stimulations in crowded situations—are conducive to demagoguery and crowd formations. Speakers and audiences tend to stimulate each other into states of irresponsibility and frenzy in situations of crowding and anonymity which are more easily obtained in cities than in villages. Extremist groups with less scruples and more resources stand to gain from situations in which crowds can be turned into mobs.

Noneconomic Frustrations: Sex, Sports, Recreation, and the Arts

Education, urban environment, increasing interregional and international contacts, and foreign and native motion-pictures are either widening the gap between the old and new generations, or promoting a double standard of morality among many. Students and some illiterates watch Hollywood movies—the former partly and the latter mainly—for their sex appeal. And these very people often turn around to criticize American society, as depicted in these movies, as lewd, materialistic, and corrupt, while describing their frustrating cultural framework as spiritualistic and

[*footnote 23 continued*
Economics, Rotterdam, privately published, 1955), p. 43.

[24] Benjamin Higgins explains the success of the Communist party in the crowded sections of Indonesia partly on the same grounds.

pure. There is less segregation of the sexes in big cities, particularly among students. But economic insecurity and intellectual fashion, by preventing early marriages, are choking off the traditionally accepted avenues for sex gratification, while extramarital sex gratification is severely limited because of strong social mores, joint family living, overcrowded housing and the consequent lack of privacy, and relative immobility of most people (due to the lack of money, motorcars, "metros," and motels). Strong cultural sanctions also operate against prostitution among the educated middle classes. Sexual frustration in this group is, thus, quite high. In addition, there are neither sufficient opportunities to participate in sports nor to attend sports spectacles where, on weekends, like their American counterparts, they may work off their steam by yelling some team to victory. There are few opportunities for youth to develop and display its talents in the theater, literature, or other forms of creative life—the market for art being limited. Rowdy politics becomes a channel for youth's repressed exuberance. For many it is an inexpensive substitute activity, and for some an attractive avenue to social climbing and psychic satisfaction. The dictatorships of Russia, Nazi Germany, and Latin America have well demonstrated their understanding of the role of sports and stadia in politics. Even in an affluent democracy like America, one wonders to what extent the political apathy of college students may be attributable to the existence of vast opportunities for economic, artistic, romantic, and extracurricular satisfactions. In the contemporary Indian urban context, political apathy is conducive and activism is detrimental to political stability. Unless there is a change in the nature of this activism, or in economic trends, the politics of irresponsibility are likely to increase in the cities.

Sources and Patterns of Extremism

Cities either give birth to political and other leaders or draw them there. A major consequence of Western education has been the growth of nationalist and culturally revivalist, as well as socialist and Communist, ideologies.[25] A conservative-liberal coalition is in power in India, but liberalism has as yet not taken deep roots there. It is from the villages that the ruling Congress party derives its support. In the cities it has been losing steadily. Calcutta, though not quite typical of other cities, may yet turn out to be the model of political sickness likely to spread in other cities.

Revolutions, Brinton has remarked, leave behind both a uniting tradition and a memory of successful revolt.[26] The process of winning independence developed self-confidence in the common man and it trained cadres of politically active workers. Students participated more heavily than perhaps any other group in the revolutionary struggles. Theirs were the highest aspirations—theirs also the deepest disappointments—and theirs the strongest and most emotive reactions. Education, youth, and unemployment produce explosive mixtures.

A political party in India, Weiner has pointed out, is often an alternative social structure *vis-à-vis* the traditional family.[27] Some bolt from the discipline, frustration, and pettiness of the joint family wedded to the past to take sanctuary in the discipline, dedication, and intrigues of the political party devoted to the future. Purposelessness of life is transformed into a cause and an overriding loyalty that makes many young persons sacrifice health,

[25] For the Indian case see Bruce T. McCully, *English Education and the Origins of Indian Nationalism* (New York: Columbia University Press, 1940).
[26] Crane Brinton, *The Anatomy of Revolution* (New York: Vintage Books, 1957), pp. 262–264.
[27] Myron Weiner, *Party Politics in India: The Development of a Multi-Party System* (Princeton, N.J.: Princeton University Press, 1957), p. 8. He treats this theme at length in "Politics of Westernization in India" (Institute of East Asiatic Studies, University of California, Berkeley, April 1957). [Mimeographed.]

money, and other careers. The more demanding the discipline of a party, the greater the dedication of its members. Again, in India, dedication and self-sacrifice, per se, as Singer has noted, are time-honored traditions.[28] Thus, the same person will often respect and admire a liberal humanist like Nehru, a conservative reformer like Gandhi, a fascist like Subhash Bose, and a rightist revolutionist like Savarkar. This ethos of dedication, though quite useful for maintaining political unity around charismatic symbols like Nehru and Gandhi, is dangerous for democracy. Fanaticism can grow more easily and nondemocratic charismatic symbols can replace the present ones, in this psychological climate. The tradition has not lost ground in the cities. If anything, it has been intensified by two puritanic movements—Gandhism and Marxism. The saving grace of the villager is his belief in many gods—often warring gods. Through the centuries he has learned to pray to them and yet live without them. Divergences of professed and practiced faith do not generate serious anxieties. But the urbanite is a monotheist, and a true believer. His rationalism leads him to a passion for consistency, and in the context of limited knowledge, poor education, poverty and insecurity, and an atmosphere of superstition, this often leads to intolerance. Educated, urban middle classes provide most of the political leadership, including that of the Communist party.[29] The strongholds of Muslim fanaticism before the creation of Pakistan were in educational centers like Aligarh, Dacca, Lahore, Calcutta, Karachi, Peshawar, and Rawalpindi. Hindu conservatives and reactionaries have derived large numbers of their leaders and workers from Delhi, Nagpur, Poona,

Lahore, and Benares. The chances are that in India, if dictatorship comes, it will be of the Left. Left radicalism appeals more to the science worshiping mind of youth. It also offers a more complete and intellectually satisfying credo. It has international support as well as internationalist ideology. The first yields tremendous organizational advantages, while the second appeals to urban cosmopolitanism.

The ruling party has a reservoir of material resources in its business supporters, but it lacks youthful manpower. The socialists have manpower, but lack material resources. The rightists get their financial backing from feudal social classes which are on the way out. Only the Communists have access to both youthful manpower and finances in ample and increasing quantities. The budget of the Communist party in one state alone is reported to be larger than that of the Praja Socialist party for the entire country. Moreover, the Communist credo has "worked" elsewhere. Communist countries are developing rapidly. To the man in a hurry to change the world, communism seems the wave to ride.

Few young men seek political activity in the ranks of the party in power. To defend the *status quo* is not heroic, especially when there are unemployment, poverty, crime, waste, inequalities, and corruption all around. Besides, the party in power has a fairly well-established hierarchy with large numbers of older people, wherein social climbing is more difficult, while opposition groups have use for any man —trained or untrained. There is more room for expansion of the party machinery —hence more opportunities for status or power within the party structure, and, if one has faith enough in the rightness of one's cause, in society at a later date. Communists, in general, are in a better position to absorb newcomers. Well integrated, well financed, with a ready-made ideology tailored to all levels of comprehension, they have a well-designed program for action, so that each new entrant finds plenty

[28] Milton Singer, "Cultural Values in India's Economic Development," *The Annals of the American Academy of Political and Social Science*, 305 (May 1956), 81–91.
[29] Gene D. Overstreet, and Marshall Windmiller, *Communism in India* (Berkeley and Los Angeles: University of California Press, 1959), pp. 357–364.

to be busy with. The newcomers work like missionaries for a cause and a judgment day. Their internal and external supporters give finances in a big and religious way. Living in a democracy, they are free to organize and operate. When their irresponsible actions are repressed, they acquire a halo of martyrdom. This adds another dimension of romance and adventure to oppositional politics, which thrives in an atmosphere where jailgoing has acquired social prestige.

Whether urban educated youth goes Right or Left,[30] it is not likely to be the standard-bearer of liberal democracy if social and economic conditions continue to worsen. It is perhaps the lower middle class in the cities, unskilled and semi-educated, culturally conservative or confused, and politically adrift, whose politics are the most volatile. This floating population in the political arena makes it easier for opportunistic (as well as idealistic) politicians to resign from and reënter political parties, and to reshuffle political alliances with a staggering and confusing frequency. A kind of unrestrained *laissez-faire* politics prevails. Individuals as well as parties seek to maximize their political gain with little regard to rules and principles essential for the maintenance and growth of a responsible representative political system.[31]

Cities also reveal patterns of mutative extremism. After the death of S. P. Mukerji, the leader of the Rightist Jana Sangha, his parliamentary seat was captured by a Communist. Aligarh University, which was a hotbed of Rightist Muslim politics, became a center of Communist activity after the creation of Pakistan.[32] Egalitarian, populist, and welfare-state ideas are shared by most, if not all, political parties. Emotive issues, like language or corruption, unite radicals of the Right and the Left against all moderates. All kinds of opportunistic alliances between all kinds of political groups take place all the time, but the spiritual and psychological affinity of what Hoffer calls the "True Believers"[33] —the fanatics of all faiths, political and otherwise—makes the actual or potential union of Right and Left radicals more dangerous. As the power of the ruling party declines and as youth becomes increasingly disillusioned with the *status quo*, the liberals and moderates are likely to lose. It may be that the old administrative, religious, and cultural cities like Delhi, Banaras, and Ajmer will move to the Right and industrial-commercial cities like Calcutta, Madras, and Bombay to the Left. Where responsible and strong trade-

---

[30] For the view that the collapse of democracy would lead, initially, to the emergence of a Rightist or military rather than a Communist dictatorship in India see M. F. Millikan and W. W. Rostow, "Foreign Aid: Next Phase," *Foreign Affairs*, April 1958, pp. 418–436. For the opposite view see Taya Zinkin, "India and Military Dictatorship," *Pacific Affairs*, **30,** 1 (March 1959), 89–91.

[31] For a description of such politics see S. L. Polai (ed.), *National Politics and 1957 Elections in India* (New Delhi: Metropolitan Book Company, 1957), esp. pp. 12–15; also, Margaret W. Fisher and Joan V. Bondurant, *The Indian Experience with Democratic Elections* (Indian Press Digest, No. 3 [Berkeley: University of California, December, 1956]), pp. 69ff. For Pakistan see K. S. Newman, "Pakistan's Preventive Autocracy and Its Causes," *Pacific Affairs*, **32,** 1 (March 1959), 18–33.

[32] For the Calcutta by-election see Polai (ed.), *op. cit.*, p. 157. The social, historical, and political causes for this political mutation of Leftist into Rightist extremism, and vice versa, differ from situation to situation. For the Italian case see, for example, "Party-Ocracy versus Democracy: An Exchange Between Ignazio Silone and J. K. Galbraith," *Radical Humanist*, **22,** 45 (November 9, 1958), 527–528 and 531.
The psychological factors that make this mutation possible are, however, fairly constant. See Eric Hoffer, *The True Believer: Thoughts on the Nature of Mass Movements* (New York: Harper, 1951) and *The Passionate State of Mind* (New York: Harper, 1955), and Brinton, *op. cit.*, also, T. W. Adorno *et al.*, *The Authoritarian Personality* (New York: Harper, 1950), and A. H. Maslow, "The Authoritarian Character Structure," *Journal of Social Psychology*, **18,** 2nd half (November 1943), 401–411.

[33] In his book of that title, previously cited.

unions take root, as in Bombay, socialists rather than Communists may gain by this shift. But if unemployment and living conditions continue to worsen, the greatest gains will ultimately be for the extremists.

In such conditions even the villages are likely to go over to extremist politics—but perhaps with a time lag. The swastika may appeal to the peasant and the hammer and sickle to the intellectual, but their transmutation or alliance is not inconceivable—and if it comes it will, like plague and cholera, come from the cities.

Intellectuals and Slums

Growing slums, worsening sanitary conditions, lowering living standards, and unemployment concentrate misery visibly, not in inaccessible villages, but in areas which are the habitat of writers, social reformers, artists, poets, teachers, religious preachers, humane societies, dreamers, city planners, sociologists, journalists, and economists. They arouse the concern and the ire of these and other socially sensitive and articulate individuals and groups. Some of their protest—especially when it comes from professional groups—helps rectify some evils, such as graft, inefficiency, and waste. But, by and large, it merely adds to feelings of dissatisfaction with the *status quo*. Believing that they are bystanders, not participants, in processes of social change, many intellectuals become angry men—young and old. Their anger, in turn, leads only to callousness on the part of authorities, who dismiss their criticism as "destructive." A vicious circle of irresponsible and angry criticisms on both sides is thus initiated.

A society in a perpetual state of anger is not a stable society.

Transients and Anomie

Because of housing shortages, low incomes, transportation costs, and other factors, immigrants from rural areas are primarily males. In the four biggest cities, 60 per cent of the population is male as compared to 51.4 per cent for India as a whole.[34]

This ratio is even higher among working classes and migrants. Gambling, racing, dope peddling, prostitution, and cult religiosity tend to spread in rapidly growing cities. The result is a demoralized, unhealthy, pitiful mass which, unlike an industrial reserve army, Hoselitz asserts, is not easy to convert into a disciplined factory work-force.[35] It is true, as Knowles points out, that these people can be converted into an effective labor force if fed and trained properly.[36] But it is easier to turn them into a riotous mob; it needs less training and discipline, and the demand for this alternative is fairly high and frequent in the cities.

Opportunity costs of political rioting are very low for these marginal people. Crowded housing or, more commonly, lack of any housing whatsoever (one quarter of Bombay's population sleeps on the streets) makes physical access to them very easy. They are eager to talk about their troubles. Political workers find the uprooted urban "rice-roots" receptive to their ideas and leadership. The Communists often have the most convincing explanations for all the troubles of these unfortunates, even though at times, as among the refugees from Pakistan, the rightists manage to get a foothold.

There are no estimates of the total economic costs of social disorganization that arise in such contexts. Juvenile delinquency, drunkenness, murder, theft, and robbery involve increased costs, including those for police and justice administra-

---

[34] Malenbaum, "Urban Unemployment in India." The number of women per thousand men is as follows: Calcutta, 602; Bombay, 569; Ahmedabad, 764; Kanpur, 699. See also Bert F. Hoselitz, "The City, the Factory, and Economic Growth," *American Economic Review*, **45**, 2 (May 1955), 178–179.

[35] *Ibid.*

[36] William H. Knowles, "Discussion on 'Urbanization and Industrialization of the Labor Force in a Developing Economy,'" *American Economic Review*, **45**, 2 (May 1955), 188–190.

tions and for institutions for the detention, reform, and rehabilitation of convicts. Some sketchy information available for three rural-urban districts in Bombay State indicates that over-all crime rates and their economic costs are much higher in the cities.[37]

Besides, political demonstrations and rioting dislocate traffic, trade, and production and result in loss of property and sometimes even of life. No cost estimates for these are available. The greater frequency and magnitude of these in the cities suggests that these costs are higher there.

Workers and Entrepreneurs

Per-capita output and income are generally higher in cities than in villages. This is, however, largely a result of the higher per-capita investment and the associated modern technology in cities. Effects of urban environment, per se, as distinct from those of more investment or superior technology, on labor morale, productivity per man-hour, hours of work, quality of work, and mobility of the labor force need to be ascertained. It is not inconceivable that the proportion of time lost due to strikes (many for noneconomic reasons) increases while the pace of work slows down—at least in the very big cities where relatively more workers are unionized. Unions in India, being largely controlled by political workers from outside

their ranks, can and often do use labor for organizing strikes, protest marches, and demonstrations for furthering their political ends. Language riots in Bombay are a case in point.[38] Husain's study of industrial location in East Pakistan indicates that social disorganization is minimal and workers' morale is maximal where workers are not torn away from their rural habitat.[39] In this respect trade unions can play an important role in reducing rather than aggravating costs of urbanization. By providing a new sense of community and a web of social relationships and activities, they can integrate immigrants into new meaningful and satisfying life-patterns and help build their morale. The responsibility of the unions is high, because in Indian cities there are few secondary social organizations or religious institutions which can create a sense of belongingness corresponding to that provided by the growth of sects like Methodism and Presbyterianism during the Industrial Revolution in England.[40] There are no such significant movements for creating a new social mileu for immigrants in place of the one they left behind. The operation of caste panchayats in cities to some extent prevents the alienation of the worker from his traditional society. In the years to come, however, the strength of this institution is likely to diminish.[41] And to the extent it does

---

[37] See, for example, *Annual Police Administration Report of the State of Bombay, Including Railways for the Year 1957* (Bombay: Government of Bombay, Police Department, 1959), pp. 96–101, 160–171.

Several limitations of the data, as published, do not permit a more definite conclusion, or an exact statement of comparative costs. Available data for 1925 indicate that drunkenness is increasing and social maladjustment is more rife in industrial cities. See B. S. Haikerwal, *Economic and Social Aspects of Crime in India* (London: Allen & Unwin, 1934), p. 46. Haikerwal, however, is inconsistent about his feelings regarding the relative incidence of crime in cities and villages; see, e.g., pp. 12, 48.

[38] For the crucial role of unions in precipitating such disturbances in the autumn of 1956 see Marshall Windmiller, "The Politics of States Reorganization in India: The Case of Bombay," *Far Eastern Survey*, **25,** 9 (September 1956), 129–144.

[39] A. F. A. Husain, *Human and Social Impact of Technological Change in Pakistan* (Dacca: Oxford University Press, 1956). This study contradicts the contrary view expressed by Hoselitz, *op. cit.*, pp. 181–184.

[40] On the role of religion in both resisting and aiding social change, and that of Protestant sects in reintegrating communities disrupted by rapid industrialization and urbanization see W. Arthur Lewis, *The Theory of Economic Growth* (Homewood, Ill.: Richard D. Irwin, Inc., 1955), pp. 101–107.

[41] The role of caste in economic development is the subject matter of much writing which is

not diminish, city society will merely duplicate village society on a large scale. Cities then become collections of villages. The argument for urbanization as a vehicle for value transformations conducive to industrialization then disappears.

Cities, by concentrating the labor force in relatively small areas, and by making possible the organization of labor, are creating conditions in which the clash of labor and entrepreneurial interests becomes more well-defined. Unions are already exercising an influence on governmental policies much greater than is warranted by the size of their membership. The consequent upward pressure on wages and consumption may not be a bar to increased investment, if such wage increases result in equal or larger productivity increases. The relation of wages to productivity in India, however, has not been empirically explored. Again, if entrepreneurial consumption can be kept in check, it will be somewhat easier to restrain workers' consumption. In practice, it has not been easy to restrain the consumption of either group.

Successful measures to keep both wages and profits—or strictly, the share of wages and profits that goes into consumption—from rising would necessitate greater regulation of both groups by government, entailing more political, economic, and social controls, more administrative personnel, and increased costs. It would also necessitate a greater capacity for public agencies to fulfill roles of entrepreneurship if private enterprise should become discouraged as a result of such measures. How far the new educated groups, pouring out of colleges and universities with largely

[*footnote 41 continued*
excellently reviewed by Morris David Morris in "Caste and the Evolution of the Industrial Workforce in India," *Proceedings of the American Philosophical Society*, **104**, 2 (April 1960), 124–133; also, see his "The Recruitment of an Industrial Labor Force in India, with British and American Comparisons," *Comparative Studies in Society and History*, **2**, 3 (April 1960), 305–328.

a nontechnical and half-baked education and with a tradition of averseness to economic enterprise and initiative, will make better managers, directors, and planners of enterprises under public rather than private control is yet an open question.

Exposure Effects: Sociological, Economic, and Political

Cities are being integrated into a growing network in and outside the country more rapidly than villages. With rapidly increasing contacts between different groups, tensions are mounting. Patterns of in-migration tend to heighten the tensions associated with regionalism in India.

Increased intergroup contacts are raising the levels of aspiration, without increasing levels of achievement. Consequently, the sense of *absolute deprivation* is increasing among urbanites. Closer contact with upper classes and their modes of living increases the sense of *relative deprivation*. At the same time, urban political and social ideologies are sensitizing the norms whereby people evaluate "social injustice," thus increasing the intensity of resentment and hostility. English commoners may derive satisfactions from the luxuries that their Queen enjoys—as Samuelson suggests[42]—but commoners in India are becoming averse to such "vicarious consumption" in proportion to the degree of their urbanization. Indian motion-pictures and literature, platforms of political parties and political speeches, and the sermons of preachers and social reformers often reflect as well as stimulate this emergent social ethos. The darshana-seeking villager loses his sense of awe and respect for political and other heroes and elites as he observes them from closer quarters and imbibes urban egalitarian ideas. As the erstwhile demigods look more human to him, their actions appear more inhuman.

[42] Paul A. Samuelson, "The Dilemmas of Housing," in Kelley (ed.), *Housing and Economic Development*, p. 35.

Both the numbers of malcontents and the intensity of discontent increase.

Patterns and levels of consumption also change as a result of exposure or demonstration effects. Lower expenditures on food within some income groups, and a substitution of refined-processed foods and sugar for more nutritious foods, have implications for the health and productivity of urbanites. But the changed pattern, particularly among middle- and upper-income groups, also involves more use of luxuries and foreign goods. Thus, there is the flow of scarce resources away from socially useful expenditure into the manufacturing of luxuries, and also a drain on foreign exchange. Levels of consumption also tend to rise, affecting the volume of internal savings available for capital formation.

Successful revolts in some countries raise the morale of revolutionists in others. The revolution of communications transmits knowledge as well as social unrest across oceans.

Slowing Down the Dynamo

W. Arthur Lewis has said,

Towns tend to be prominent in organizing most political movements, whether their aim is greater freedom or less, if only because government is usually done from cities to which the politically ambitious are attracted. . . . Town is the home of the mob, and mobs are as prone to sweep tyrants into power, who reduce the opportunities for economic freedom, as they are to take part in liberating movements. The town is also the home of monopolists—the traders' associations, the guilds, the workers' combinations—whose aim is to restrict opportunities and to keep out new men. The town takes the lead in movements for reducing the amount of work done, and for working sullenly or resentfully. . . . If therefore a case can be made for saying that towns lead out of stagnation into growth, as good a case can be made

for saying they lead out of growth into stagnation.[43]

In India, towns are not likely to lead into stagnation, but they can lead into slower economic growth and political instability, because of the diversion of resources from more to less productive investments. Urban populations have more access to, and influence on, political processes. As conditions worsen, towns are likely to demand and get progressively larger proportions of the national pie at the cost of the countryside.

As the international economy developed, disparities of income grew between the rich and the poor nations, in the past century or so. Now, as the Indian economy develops, disparities are likely to grow between the village and the city. But what worked politically in the nineteenth-century world of colonial powers is hardly likely to work in the egalitarian twentieth century. This trend can be reversed by appropriate allocations and actions for development of the countryside. There is little reason to believe that the rural exodus would continue if economic and social opportunities for advancement were expanding rapidly enough in the villages. In the Majumdar study, out of 327 respondents, 35 per cent were rural in origin. Of these, 35 per cent were willing to return to their villages after the completion of their studies. The other 65 per cent, who were unwilling to do so, were largely motivated by economic considerations. When the entire group of former students from rural areas was asked whether they were willing to return to villages if given a job similar to the one they held, 60 per cent said yes. Of the rest, 63 per cent again gave an economic reason for their answer— they expected chances for their economic advancement to be better in the cities.[44] If a majority of these highly educated (they all had Master's degrees), "westernized,"

[43] *Op. cit.*, pp. 150–151.
[44] Majumdar, *op. cit.*, pp. 33–34.

urbanized Indians of rural origin were willing to return to the villages, given proper opportunities there, it is not unreasonable to assume that unskilled and tradition-oriented migrants can be persuaded to return with as much, if not greater, ease under similar conditions. And it should certainly be easier for those who are still in the villages to keep on living there.

Economic measures for correcting the pace and nature of urbanization can be supplemented by an ideological campaign, especially, because the village still has a romantic, emotional, political, or philosophical attraction for many, even among the intelligentsia and other groups of urban origins. There is no reason to believe that many idealistic and educated men will not choose to work in villages if they are assured that it is not the end of the road for their careers.

Conclusion

There are more opportunities for making a person a participant in economic planning and development in rural than in urban areas. This, by itself, reduces political disaffection. Also, in villages there is a greater level of tolerance for the old and familiar problems of unemployment and poverty. By exporting these problems to cities, political instability is increased. There are many avenues for significant increases in agricultural and rural industrial output. There are greater opportunities for capital formation with the use of idle labor and other resources in villages. The levels and patterns of consumption unfavorable to economic growth can be prevented from emerging with less difficulty in rural than in urban areas.

Higher direct and indirect costs of social disorganization, welfare ideologies, and overhead capital in cities are reducing the flow of output obtainable from investment of available resources—some of which, like labor, are going to waste partly because of a pattern of development which is urban-oriented. If these trends continue,

political discontent will grow in the cities, and if public discontent fails to change governmental policies peacefully, streets may become the arbiters of political destiny. But the problem cannot be solved by expanding employment only or largely in urban areas. The employment elasticity or urbanization may be greater than one— every new job in the city is likely to attract more than one person from the country, thus worsening the problems and tensions in cities.

Increased sports, circuses, sex, spectacles, festivals, cultural shows, and demonstrations of military prowess can provide some substitute satisfactions and distractions to discontented youth. But the real effective solvent of tensions is rapidly expanding social and economic opportunity for advancement through orderly processes, in rural as well as in urban areas. The former have progressively lost their human and material capital to the latter. This flow can and needs to be reversed for the benefit of both. Communist China is doing it by coercive measures.[45] India has to do it by economic inducement and persuasion.

Meanwhile the great march of men from the backwoods to the metropolises continues at an ever accelerating pace. The new frontier—albeit a dangerous one— is not the wilderness with its promise of freedom, gold, or virgin lands, but the skyscraper with its promise of food and shelter.

Unlike the promise of the wilderness, the promise of this frontier may turn out to be an illusion. Like the countless who fell by the wayside or collapsed after reaching the streets of Calcutta in the Bengal famine of 1942, many more are likely to discover that escaping from the stagnation of the village does not necessarily mean salvation in the city slum.

Development patterns which cannot slow down this explosive and skewed

[45] Gordon Walker, "Old Chinese Socialism Tested," *Christian Science Monitor*, February 8, 1958.

growth of cities (big ones growing faster than the others) will involve a great wastage of human resources. "A social order is stable," Hoffer has said, "so long as it can give scope to talent and youth. Youth itself is a talent—a perishable talent."[46] This is one resource which if not utilized for development is likely to become political lava in a country where the social fabric of democracy is still very inflammable.

[46] *The Passionate State of Mind*, p. 20.

PART IV

THE "MODERNIZERS"

INTRODUCTION

In the discussion of individuals and ideas in Part II, we made frequent reference to the role played by elites in modernizing nations. Similarly, in Part III the discussion of the concomitants of political development pointed up some of the ways elites function to bring about social and economic development. The articles in this part focus specifically on certain significant groups of elites—the intellectuals, the "symbol wielders," the military and the bureaucrats. These groups may be, and usually are, the modernizers in the processes of social transformation, but they also may be forces which lead the resistance to change. Therefore, when we title this Part "The 'Modernizers,'" we are stating a fact and expressing some doubt about the modernizing role played by these elites.

In the process of modernization, social relations change, old norms no longer obtain, the traditions of the past cease to provide guidance for decisions and actions, the old leaders may no longer have status, nor are they always able to wield the social and political power they once held, and sharp discrepancies may be created between those who represent modernity and the masses. These transformations are often stimulated, initiated, or guided by relatively small groups of people whom we have come to call "elites." Elites, according to Harold Lasswell, are those with the most power in a group or a society. They are able to get the most of what there is to get within the system where they wield power. A political elite is the top power group in a political system; they are people who are able to wield power so that they can achieve objectives.

The new elites usually include different individuals from those who constituted the traditional elites. They are the urbanized assaulted individuals; the educated from the universities, the military officers who are entering a middle class, and achievement-oriented bureaucrats who find the destiny of their newly independent nation thrust upon them. These elite also sometimes include in their numbers members of the old elites who are capable of assuming the new roles demanded by the systems-transforming process of modernization. If any of these groups are not in positions of power for the moment, they often are able to wield power in the opposition, which is a force that is assuming greater importance in many developing countries.

These elites must create new social and political institutions that will mobilize the nation, link all the people together into a national communications network, provide the symbols of national integration, and assure a tolerant, if not wholesome, environment for the entrepreneur. The unfortunate reality of many developing nations is that there may be a crippling shortage of professional modernizing politicians, skilled military leaders, risk-taking businessmen, and efficient administrators. Where do the social and political leaders who make modernization possible come from? How do the elites emerge—how are they recruited?

Lester G. Seligman addresses himself to these questions. He sees elite recruitment as both reflecting and affecting the social system. On one hand, it reflects the value system of society, the degree and the type of representativeness of the system, the basis of social stratification and its articulation with the political system, and the structure and change in political roles. On the other hand, elite recruitment patterns determine avenues for political participation and status, influence the kind of policies that will be enacted, accelerate or retard changes, affect the distribution of status and prestige, and influence the stability of the system. Furthermore, as an indicator of development and change, elite recruitment illuminates various changes in the social system: economic changes, as seen in the shifts from agriculture to industry and from rural to urban concentration; in the political system, as seen in new parties, associations, and interest groups; and in the level of politicization, as seen in the new kinds and increasing amounts of participation of the people.

Seligman's discussion of the legitimation of elites builds on a recognition of the dualistic character of transitional society, as identified by Sjoberg, Hauser, Nash, and others of our preceding authors. In pointing to political parties as the principal agencies for selecting and representing political elites, Seligman provides a useful typology of political parties and anticipates the more extensive treatment in Chapter 15 on "Transitional Politics and Party Systems."

The intellectuals are a particularly important elite in the new states of Asia and Africa. Edward Shils, in a pioneering study of the role of elites, maintains that the "gestation, birth, and continuing life" of these states is in large measure the work of intellectuals. They have created the political life of the underdeveloped nations; they have been "its instigators, its leaders, and its executants." By contrast, in the past new states were founded by other groups for distinctly different reasons and using different techniques. In the West politics have never been a preserve of the intellectuals.

Shils characterizes what he means by "intellectuals," explains why intellectuals provide the ideas and political drive in developing countries, and sketches the political outlook of the intellectuals. Using India as his major example, he then outlines three stages in the politics of the intellectuals: constitutional liberalism, politicized nationalism, and assumption of power in a sovereign state ruled by indigenous elites. When the third stage is reached, a schism occurs among the intellectual-politicians—some are in and others are out. The "outs" attract other intellectuals and they become the voice of opposition, persisting in the same types of criticisms of government and the bureaucracy as they made before independence during the period of politicized nationalism. The one new feature which characterized this opposition is disillusionment, which becomes a source of despondent inaction, on one hand, or a rigid form of activist extremism.

In any case, the intellectuals can be expected to play major roles in the political life of the new states for some time in the future. The emerging professional politician and the military elites may not originate among the intellectuals as much as they did, but the opposition parties, the civil service, and higher education will continue to call for intellectuals.

Herbert Feith describes another kind of elite—the symbol wielders in Indonesia. Although his discussion is drawn out of Indonesian experience, he presents his hypotheses within a general political framework which may be applicable to the analysis of similar phenomena in other states. Without using the terminology of Marion J. Levy, Jr. he describes a functional requisite of the Indonesian political system—that is, he portrays symbolic activities as necessary conditions for the maintenance of the political system in the face of serious social cleavages.

This elite in Indonesia wields political symbols that are designed to create and maintain attitudes and states of mind which will help keep the present Indonesian government in power. Since 1958 the Indonesian government has devoted immense resources to symbolic activity, often in ways that detract greatly from the effectiveness of its administrative and economic performance.

Feith describes the various ways in which symbolic activities serve to help the government maintain itself in power, but his more revealing analysis is of the reasons why these means, rather than other available means, are used to buttress the government's power and why the government is willing to incur the costs that symbolic activities involve, particularly the costs in terms of a reduced level of performance in the solving of economic and administrative problems. The first part of his explanation is that Sukarno is using symbolic activity to achieve integration, especially in the face of several serious cleavages which exist within the country and which make more extreme forms of political controls dangerous.

The other part of the answer relates to the competition which exists between skill groups within the government structure. This competition is between the symbol-wielders and army officers on one hand, and economic and administrative specialists on the other, i.e., between those who claim power chiefly on the basis of their revolutionary record and those who claim it chiefly on the grounds of their qualifications for the technical tasks assigned to a particular government department or government firm. This leader-technician conflict is pervasive in government. Thus, the government's intensive concern with symbolic activity is a response to intra-elite politics as well as a recognition of the need for power maintenance and is another way of assuring political integration. (We will return to a discussion of the ways developing nations go about achieving political integration in Chapter 16.)

Although the military leaders may be among the intelligentsia by virtue of education and outlook, the importance of the military in political development does not result from the intellectual capacity of the officer corps but derives from the kinds of skills and resources available to most contemporary armies. Military establishments *everywhere* fare well in competing for resources. The emerging nations, irrespective of national income or resources, appear determined to maintain military establishments patterned after the armies of the wealthier and more industrialized nations. The impetus for such resource allocation may be fear of external aggression or internal insurgency, but it also reflects the psychological needs of newly independent people who may be overly conscious of the differences between themselves and the industrial nations. Modern armies have become a symbolic expression of a commitment to modernization and development. External assistance programs often have encouraged military expenditures but the developing nations have also shown a willingness to invest their own scarce resources in military organizations.

Do these military expenditures constitute nothing more than a means of providing for national defense, thereby draining national budgets that already lack sufficient funds for education, agricultural development, and industrial growth? Or can military expenditures also be justified because they contribute to national development? This question is being asked by serious students of the development process who, although they may feel uncertain about the precise way development takes place, have come to think that there is no single route to development and modernization and that one should not overlook the possibility that the military may stimulate or accelerate modernization. The conviction that the incentives, drives, and stimuli for development may originate in numerous and even unanticipated sectors of society and that diverse structures may play a prominent role in modernization has led to a growing interest in the military as a potential innovator in the development process.

Those who maintain that the military should not be treated as a "necessary evil" only to be used for purposes of national defense argue that there is historical justification for thinking of the military as a system capable of contributing to the development process. This argument is buttressed by citing the "developmental" contribution of the Army Corps of Engineers in the United States which built roads, cleared rivers, and assisted in the construction of railroads in the earlier stages of American development—and still performs some of these functions today. The Turkish and Israeli armies are examples of a military with a high sense of national dedication utilizing their men, machines, materials, and organizational skills in the cause of national development. Because the military is usually a prime beneficiary of internal resources and external aid, the anomalous result in many developing nations is that the military, "the managers of the instruments of violence," possesses more of the skills and resources needed for modernization than almost any other sector, and these skills are only distantly related to the command of violence.

Therefore, a full and realistic analysis of the role of the military must consider (1) the military as a socializing agent, (2) the military as a "modernizing" agent, and (3) the military as an active participant in the national political system. There is historical evidence that the military, under the right conditions, is an effective socializing agent. In Turkey, peasant youths acquired a sense of belonging to the Turkish nation and a feeling for the responsibilities of citizenship as a result of military service. The Israeli and Iranian armies have shown that they can be "modernizing" agents by teaching literacy to soldiers and by building and operating schools in the remote frontier villages. The armies of Latin America have been used to construct transportation arteries and have even been active in various community development projects. However, the activities of building a road, constructing a hospital, teaching the unlettered to read and write, and even disseminating a spirit of citizenship do not add up to the ability to govern.

Furthermore, a professional army committed to modernization may be reluctantly "forced" to intervene in politics when social and political breakdowns occur. Lucian Pye acknowledges that there is validity to this explanation, but points out that it does not adequately account for interventionist behavior by the military. He stresses that the internal organization of the army and its authority relationships convey an overly simplified view that complex problems which baffle political and intellectual elites can be successfully resolved by the "right orders," and the right orders are a possession of the military. Pye's analysis is in general agreement with a penetrating study of the political interventionist military by Morris Janowitz, which concludes that the military intervenes in politics not simply in response to disruptions in the political and social system but, in part, as a consequence of the skill structures and organizational composition of the army in a transitional society. However, Janowitz asserts in that study, "Those organizational and professional qualities which make it possible for the military of a new nation to accumulate political power, and even to take over political power, are the same as those which limit its ability to rule effectively."[1]

Military seizures of political power have occurred with greater frequency in the Middle East than in any other area of the world. Dankwart Rustow examines the history of political intervention by Middle Eastern armies. He combines a scheme for classifying military seizures of power with a series of hypotheses to account for them. Rustow reviews the historical antecedents of military intervention and arrives at a number of observations that indicate that intervention may be as much a result of military disorganization as a consequence of the structure of military organizations. He further notes that the expressed purposes and style of language of the coup leadership invariably reveals a verbal dedication to noble ideals. However, Rustow cautions us that performance is a better indicator of behavior than are words and that we ought to judge the reformist or revolutionary commitments of military leaders by what they do after assuming power rather than what they say. Other writers

[1] *The Military in the Political Development of New Nations: An Essay in Comparative Analysis* (Chicago: The University of Chicago Press, 1964), p. 1.

who have noted the interventionist character of Middle Eastern armies have
suggested that there is some element in Islam which may account for this
behavior. Rustow makes only passing reference to this interpretation, but
he does conclude that the neat distinction often drawn between civilian and
military politics is somewhat artificial in the Middle Eastern context.

Although the nations of Latin America are in no sense "new states,"
they are nevertheless transitional societies experiencing the internal dis-
harmonies so frequently attendant upon that phase of social change. Gino
Germani and Kalman Silvert consider the problem of military intervention in
Latin America and its relationship to politics within individual states. As
was pointed out in the article by Neal Smelser in Part I, a primary cause of
social disturbance in developing nations is the discontinuities between
"differentiation and integration." Germani and Silvert essentially concur,
and treat military intervention into political life as a form of social disturbance resulting from the inability of other institutional arrangements to
accommodate to the demands made on these social systems.

Germani and Silvert formulate a typology of the social structure of the
Latin American states and relate this formulation to the kinds of civil-
military relations found in each country. Although there is a tentative and
qualified tone to the findings of the authors, they are attempting to account
in an orderly way for the relevant variables that may yield a more fundamental
and general understanding of military intervention into politics. While it has
not been our intention to select authors representing any particular viewpoint,
it is clear that all three essays in this chapter arrive, by different methodological routes, at a common conclusion explaining a major cause of military
intervention. Even in the absence of direct intervention, the power position
of the army in transitional societies creates a situation in which the military
leaders must be recognized as elites who may significantly affect political
decisions, and the military may at times be the critical variable in political
development.

The bureaucrats are the final group of "modernizers" to be considered.
S. C. Dube notes that the bureaucracy "forms an important element of the
modernizing elite in many of the economically less developed countries which
have attained national independence during the last two decades." It should
be understood that Dube writes out of a background in India where one
of the most developed forms of colonial bureaucracy in the world evolved and
where a well-prepared, highly skilled cadre of civil officers stood ready
to take over the reins of administration. Non-British colonies did not have as
well trained and organized bureaucracies, nor did other British colonies
outside the subcontinent of India. The assertion that the bureaucracy in their
respective countries was "the first large and organized group to enter the
transitional phase between tradition and modernity . . . that they were among
the pioneers who sought to break away from the traditionally affective and
emotion-based communal society and to set in motion the forces that were
to contribute towards the emergence of a different type of society—a society

characterized by affective neutrality and based on rational ends-means calculations for individual goals" is probably an overstatement. However, his analysis of the major characteristics of bureaucracy in transitional societies and its problems in the context of the culture of politics, the emerging ethos, and the expanding sphere of state activity and new institutional arrangements has a sufficiently generalized quality to be of value in thinking about the role of bureaucracy in many developing societies. It should be noted that Dube uses some of the elements of systems analysis and certain of the pattern variables in his presentation.

Dube contends that as societies undergo the transformation toward modernity, "the supremacy of administration was replaced largely by the sovereignty of politics." In many countries "the bureaucracy was trained well enough to accept political direction, and only in a few exceptional cases did it try to gain the upper hand." At the same time he acknowledges that in several respects "the hard core of bureaucratic culture has been unyielding, and has offered great resistance to innovation."

Fred W. Riggs argues that bureaucratic interests can actually obstruct political development. His general thesis is that "premature or too rapid expansion of the bureaucracy when the political system lags behind tends to inhibit the development of effective politics. A corollary thesis holds that separate political institutions have a better chance to grow if bureaucratic institutions are relatively weak." In support of this proposition he discusses the relation of bureaucracy to the party system, the electorate, interest groups and the legislature. A controversial, and much debated, assertion of Riggs is that the merit system cuts at the root of one of the strongest props of a developing party system, namely spoils. When politics are deprived of spoils, party machines may lose much of their vigor. Political development, by implication, requires vigorous political parties. Therefore, an efficient, career bureaucracy may be able to resist the politician's attempts to assert effective control.

Thus, in considering the role of bureaucracy in the process of political development, we are confronted with one of the numerous dilemmas of modernization. An efficient bureaucracy is required for social and economic development. But a merit bureaucracy may impede the evolution of a functioning party system with the result that political development may be hindered.

Chapter 10
The Role of Elites

ELITE RECRUITMENT AND POLITICAL DEVELOPMENT

Lester G. Seligman

In any political system, political roles must be defined, filled, and vacated. Elite recruitment refers to the process whereby such "staffing" takes place. "The political recruitment function takes up where the general political socialization function leaves off. It recruits members of the particular subcultures—religious communities, statuses, classes, ethnic communities and the like, and inducts them into the specialized roles of the political system."[1] For the actors themselves, recruitment embraces two processes: (1) the transformation from nonpolitical roles to eligibility for influential political roles, and (2) the assignment and selection of people for *specific* political roles. Recruitment includes both *eligibility* for elite status and *selection* or *assignment* to specific

elite positions.[2] Recruitment is therefore a central function of any political system, and the processes of recruitment are a good indicator of the values and distribution of political influence.

The elite recruitment pattern both reflects and affects the society. As a dependent variable it expresses the value system of the society and its degree of consistency and contradictions, the degree and the type of representativeness of the system, the basis of social stratification and its articulation with the political system, and the structure and change in political roles. As a factor which affects change, or as an independent variable, elite recruitment patterns determine avenues for political participation and status, influence the kind of policies that will be enacted, accelerate or retard changes, effect the distribution of status and prestige, and influence the stability of the system.

As an indicator of development and change, elite recruitment is useful because it illuminates several change components. It reflects economic changes in the shifts from

SOURCE. Lester G. Seligman, "Elite Recruitment and Political Development," *Journal of Politics,* **26,** 612–626, August 1964.

---

[1] Almond, G. and Coleman, J., *The Politics of the Developing Areas* (Princeton), p. 31; Lasswell, H. D., Lerner, D., and Rothwell, E., *The Comparative Study of Elites* (Stanford, 1952); Apter, D., "Nationalism, Government and Economic Growth," *Economic Development and Cultural Change,* **7,** 2 (January 1959), 117–136.

[2] Seligman, L., "Political Recruitment and Party Structure," *APSR,* **55,** 1 (March 1961), 77; "Recruitment in Politics," *PROD,* **1** (1958), 14–17.

329

agrarian emphasis to industry and from rural to urban concentration; shifts in the political infrastructure—the organizations, associations, and interest groups; and the level of politicization and the kind and degree of participation of the people. In this way, the various elements of development, which move at an uneven rate, can be apprehended and measured through the analysis of recruitment.

In the following pages several facets of elite recruitment will be discussed comparatively with reference to the new nations. They are as follows: (1) elite legitimation, (2) paths of power, (3) elite representativeness and (4) the relationship between elite recruitment and political change.

Whether a new state can maintain both stability and development hinges, to a large extent, on the integration of its political elites. They stand in the strategic center of development possibilities. Development requires the assimilation of new values, yet development will be self-defeating if it threatens the fabric of society itself or if it inculcates values and behavior incompatible with durable growth. Planned development demands the organization and rationalization of resource allocation consistent with goals of growth and higher levels of income. Development, therefore, disrupts traditional values of status, prestige, and income.[3]

Development entails an uneven distribution of its gains. Vested interests—occupational, religious, linguistic—may be dislocated and deprived, while newer groups receive new opportunities. Older stratifications are disrupted and new social escalators emerge. The balance of deprivation and advantage will be accepted by various elements only if the substantive justifications of the decisions are accepted. Acceptance will also depend upon whether those who gain *and* those who lose retain consensual political identifications. This may be accomplished not only through the products of policies but

[3] Lerner, Daniel, *The Passing of Traditional Society* (Glencoe: Free Press, 1958), pp. 46–50.

through the processes as well. Thus, the management of the tensions depends on the degree to which there is agreement on decision-making methods. This agreement among decision-makers and acceptance of them will depend upon the *integration among the elites.* As Raymond Aron has stated: "The composition of the governing elite may be progressively altered, the relative importance of the various groups in the elite may be changed, but a society can only survive and prosper if there is true collaboration between those groups. In one way or another, there must be unity of opinion and action on essential points in the elite."[4]

The Legitimation of Elite Recruitment

The Central Values. In general, political elites are legitimated by their embodiment and/or evocation of sacred values of the system. In a new state, the goal of development is interwoven with the goals of nationalism. The political oligarchy which led the movement for independence heads the new state. Thus both nationalism and modernization are primary in the legitimation of the governing elites. There are also complementary goals: self-identifications, international prestige, cultural renaissance.

With the gaining of independence, formal democratization is introduced. A parliament, a judicial system, universal suffrage, an electoral system, and a progressive written constitution are introduced. These are, perhaps, among the easiest changes made. But the gaps in the social structure, the loose articulation of various parts of the society make effective democracy remote. The absence of a democratic tradition makes the new democratic constitution only a superficial graft.[5]

This formal democratization manifestly fulfills the goal of popular consent. But

[4] [Italics mine] "Social Structure and Ruling Class," *Br. J. of Soc.* **1** (1950), 10; Nadel, S. F., "The Concept of Social Elites," *Int. Soc. Sci., Bull.* **7**, 3 (1956), p. 420.

[5] Chief H. O. Davis, "The New African Profile," *Foreign Affairs,* **40**, 2 (January, 1962), 293–302 for a perceptive report on this point.

it is also a means toward the solution of a more egregious problem—the weakening of the traditional pluralism and the creation through participation of common identification with the new state and its values. Among the new states, the government is the vehicle for the transition from the vested traditional pluralism to a pluralism more characteristic of modern societies.

Dualistic Legitimations. The nationalistic ideology attempts to cover the traditionalistic cleavages with a patina of solidarity. Citizenship in the new state is upheld as superordinate to the loyalties to tribal, regional, ethnic, linguistic groups. Nonetheless, legitimations remain dualistic. The groups and institutions of the traditional pluralism are deeply rooted and capable of great resistance. Traditional values cannot be totally rejected without threatening solidarity. Paradoxically, the new nationalism itself stimulates the older parochial loyalties. In some respects traditional groups become more sensitive about their identity and status, rather than less so.[6]

The new elite cadres also reflect this dualism. Though they are selected for their achievements in behalf of nationalism, they are products or "ejected groups" of traditional backgrounds.[7] They incorporate the old virtues of family background and respected status plus the newer one of education, skill, and heroic achievement in behalf of national liberation. The ruling are emancipated children of the traditional social structure. While rejecting the old, they cannot help but embody it.

In older democratic systems elites are legitimated by conflicting values. Despite the differentiation of the political sphere, there are ambivalent norms. There are dualistic expectations regarding the ethical norms that invest political roles and expectations of political effectiveness. Alongside legitimations based upon public consent, there are vestigial expectations derived from the mixed Western heritage (monarchy, aristocracy) about political leadership.

Charismatic Leadership as Legitimation. Charismatic leaders[8] are highly functional in the new states, because the Nehrus, Nassers, Sukarnos and Ben Gurions stand above the traditional cleavages in the society. As venerated leaders of a heroic past, they are symbols of the unified nation to all segments of the population. By inviting identification with themselves they foster a broader identification with the nation. These leaders are usually "heroes of renunciation," who gave up much of their lives for the sake of the cause and earned their right to power in this way. They epitomize in their lives the sacrifice and struggle against colonial rule. These leaders play other roles. They are the architects and spokesmen of the drive for economic development.[9] They are also the "central figures"[10] within the national movement that can balance the contending interests. They enjoy international prestige because they are respected in the political world of the West. This recognition nourishes the pride of the citizenry. Thus, charismatic leaders personify and integrate many conflicting needs within emerging nations.[11]

---

[6] Emerson, R., *From Empire to Nation* (Cambridge: Harvard, 1960), p. 329.

[7] The "marginality" explanation of new elites is stressed by E. Hagen, "A Framework for Analyzing Economic and Political Change" in R. E. Asher, ed., *Development of the Emerging Countries* (Washington: Brookings, 1962), pp. 23, 24, and B. Hoselitz, *Sociological Aspects of Economic Growth* (Glencoe: Free Press, 1960) especially Chapter 3.

[8] The ambiguity in Weber's definition of the concept of charisma has been perceptively criticized by Shils, Parsons, Friedrich, Blau, and others.

[9] Rustow, D., *Politics and Westernization in the Near East* (Princeton, 1956), p. 29. Kahin, G. McT., Pauker, Guy J., and Pye, Lucian W., "Comparative Politics in Non-Western Countries," *American Political Science Review*, **49** (1955), 1025.

[10] Seligman, L., "The Study of Political Leadership," *American Political Science Review*, **44** (1950), 904–915, reprinted in *Political Behavior*, ed. H. Eulau (Glencoe: Free Press, 1956), pp. 177–183.

[11] Emerson *op. cit.*, p. 281.

These strong personalities give strident voice to both the hated and loved symbols of the new nationalism. Nasser, Sekou Toure, or Ho Chi Minh invoke a militant anti colonialism almost constantly. Exaggerated national pride compensates for past humiliations and alleged humiliations. Not all charismatic figures fit this pattern. Some, like Houphouet-Boigny of the Ivory Coast, are more moderate and less flamboyant in their appeals. These latter seem more intent on affirmative elaboration of the national goals, rather than the attack on national scapegoats.

Charismatic leaders have not only a mass following, they also have an elite recruitment function. They draw around them a corps of younger "new intellectuals"[12] who serve as acolytes to the master, as catalysts, and shock troops in the march toward modernization. Linked to the charismatic leaders' multiple functions these circles of intellectuals, technicians, and managers also elaborate the ideology of leadership and translate it into action.

The Bases of Eligibility and Selection

Eligibility and the Dominant Values. The recruitment process itself reflects, and thereby reinforces, the dominant values. In highly traditional systems, like Yemen and Saudi Arabia, such ascriptive factors as kinship determine eligibility to rule, and family succession legitimates role selection. In sharp contrast are more modern democratic systems, where popular election is associated with wide eligibility for elite selection. It is the degree of exclusivity of recruitment eligibility which discriminates one political system from another. Systems that confer broad eligibility for elite status and roles tend to be democratic and modern. Those which restrict elite eligibility are more traditional and authoritarian.

There appears to be a high correlation between political prestige and the degree of exclusivity. While political positions enjoy high prestige in both systems, the prestige is higher in the newer states. In general, where political power is concentrated,[13] a political career enjoys high status and is much sought after. Political offices are prized for their prestige, emoluments, and power. The political sphere more exclusively embodies and expresses the sacred values of the society and thereby substitutes for the crumbling traditional values. Deference toward political leaders substitutes for the deference formerly shown tribal leaders and religious leaders and therefore fits the traditional hierarchical patterns.

Political roles enjoy lower prestige in the older democratic political systems. In older, Western systems politics is differentiated and somewhat distinct from religious and economic spheres. It must compete with business and the professions for prestige. There is also a relationship between prestige of political elite roles and the roles which involve the greatest knowledge and responsibility. If the skill involved is considerable, i.e., the exercise of political authority, then the position will be highly valued.

Representation. In Western systems, a basic criterion of eligibility is representativeness. Political careers are launched and impelled by some significant group that chooses a candidate as its agent, spokesman, or symbolic trustee. The group may be a geographic area, occupational group, an ethnic group or circle of party leaders. Representation is achieved by articulating a group interest. Political parties can be differentiated according to whether they are congruent with one type of group or represent a plurality of groups.[14] Parties always legitimate such representativeness.

In the new states as modernization and development take place, new differentia-

---

[12] Benda, Harry J., "Non-Western Intelligentsias as Political Elites," *Political Change in Underdeveloped Countries*, ed. J. H. Kautsky (New York: Wiley, 1962), p. 238 *passim*.

[13] Shils, E., "The Concentration of Charisma," *World Politics*, 11 (1958–59), 2.
[14] Duverger, M., *Political Parties* (New York: Wiley, 1954), Ch. 2.

tions in the society emerge—occupational groups, working-class organizations, professionals, managers, and so on. Society becomes more cross-hatched along functional lines.[15] These new interests seek self-protection through political representation.[16] They are attracted to the dominant party because the policies of this party favor modernization and development, and because this party is the government capable of granting and withholding the supports necessary for development.

A significant shift in legitimations takes place with modernizing advance. Elected and appointed officials become legitimated by their representation of specific groups. Leaders are chosen because they speak for occupational groups or specific geographic areas. This shift may be called a transfer by public officials in the focus of representation. The focus of representation[17] refers to the group of people represented. In other words, the scope of representation changes. Groups may be sectarian, single-interest groups. When the basis of group formation and cohesion may be a broad outlook or *Weltanschauung*, a sectarian group may become a political party. Proportional representation favors such sectarian groups becoming political parties.

Parties and Groups—A Typology

Political parties are the principal agencies for accomplishing the selection and representation of political elites. Parties may be classified on this basis: *Populist parties*, *Sectarian parties*, and *Pluralist parties*.

1. *Populist Parties.* These parties make claim to the broadest representation of the

people as a whole. They may be large or small in size, but they claim to total representation of the people. Such parties espouse an overriding nationalism, that is superordinate to any lesser identification such as class, region, or language.

2. *Sectarian Parties.* These parties are restricted in their representation. They make a specific appeal to a specific group, e.g., religious or ethnic or regional group. They do not aspire to mass membership. Sectarian parties are usually more concerned with maintaining their ideological purity than with winning votes.

3. *Pluralistic Parties.* These are the parties with large memberships, and aggregations of a variety of interests. These are the parties that Duverger calls mass parties. The membership embraces a variety of interests, unified by broadly defined ideology. The party tries to be inclusive rather than exclusive.

In most emerging states, one party, the party of national liberation, dominates the political scene. These are parties born of the nationalist movement, which aggregate a mixture of traditional and modernizing support. (Examples of these are the PRI in Mexico, the Congress Party in India, Mapai in Israel, CPP in Ghana).

In older democratic systems, the competition among political parties for electoral support makes necessary the cooptation of new leadership aspirants. Parties must attempt to represent new segments of the population if they are to maintain their competitive position. The competition for the support of the voters is regularly furthered by a "slate" that reflects a cross section of a highly differentiated population. Parties must also be representative, because expectations of governing effectiveness are associated with it.

Political Skill. Another basis of eligibility and selection is *skill*. In the new states, oratorical ability is a valued and necessary talent for a political leader, because the ability to arouse the public by direct methods is essential for political success. High value

[15] Weiner, M., *The Politics of Scarcity* (University of Chicago Press, 1962).
[16] The converse is not uncommon. A group in the political elites directly fosters the development of an economic interest group.
[17] Eulau, H., Wahlke, J., Buchanan, W., Ferguson, L., "The Role of the Representatives: Some Empirical Observations on the Theory of Edmund Burke," *American Political Science Review*, **53**, 3 (September 1959), 744–745.

is placed upon rhetorical skill in evoking the sacred symbols of the past and present. Ranking after this ability, comes organizational capacity and education. In general, politicians are generalists and amateurs who approach political problems ideologically, rather than in a problem-solving way. In the new states, the recognition comes tardily that technicians and experts are necessary in the political elites. The usefulness of economists, public administrators and sociologists is disputed because they threaten to de-ideologize politics. The men with older scientific skills, e.g., chemistry, physics, pose less threat. The recruitment of the elites by the newer social technical skills is one of the cutting edges of change.

In Western states, politicians play a more differentiated role.[18] Political elites include many specialists in a variety of skills—entrepreneurship, bargaining, organization, propaganda, which are differentiated by their specificity and levels. They tend to resemble the structure of all occupations—callings, trades, professions, etc. They are professionalized, in the sense that the veterans are oriented more toward the techniques rather than goals.[19] Among politicians the mastery of these techniques creates a "community of skills" that transcends partisanship. Negotiating, bargaining, and administrative skills are highly valued. Politicians tend to be pragmatic rather than ideological, and oratory declines in importance.

Associated with skill are criteria about its exercise. In Western systems a public ethics exists which demands moral probity and efficiency among both politicians and administrators. In the new states, this ethics is lacking, both on the professional level and in public norms.

Selection. Selection, the process whereby those eligible for political roles are assigned

roles, takes several forms. Selection may be made by the ruling oligarchy of a party, or by units of the party. The former method results in choosing among deserving veterans on the basis of their loyalty and length of service. A kind of bureaucratic succession to political office occurs. Members anticipate nomination to the highest political positions only at the end of their political careers. The larger and more heterogeneous a party (pluralistic party) the more selection devolves to the component groups. Groups, conversely, will focus their efforts on the nomination and selection of candidates. A primary objective then becomes a party list representative of the constituent groups.

Career Paths and Mobility

In every society there are more or less definable grooves to political power.[20] In highly traditional societies, the route to power is through kinship succession. The politically "eligible" are the aristocrats, and then kinship or family preferments determine the pattern of elite roles. Age is a significant factor in assignment to positions. Seniority weighs heavily in determining level and status.

In modern Western societies, however, the legislative bodies have been the principal training ground for the political elite. Distinction must be drawn between the "pure" politician, who uses the political escalator exclusively, and politicians who enter politics by way of other occupational routes. The "pure" politician is often the party official, who earns his livelihood from political activity and moves into elective office. The mixed type usually enters politics from another occupation, or for whom politics is a part-time activity. To the extent to which political career paths are various, prestige and influence are diffused. An increase in the diversity of the paths to power is a mark of the pluralism of the system.

The rate and kind of political mobility

[18] Pye, L., "The Non-Western Political Process," *Journal of Politics*, **20** (August 1958), 468–486.

[19] Seligman, L., "The Professionalization of Political Elites" (mimeo).

[20] The determinateness of the routes themselves distinguishes one political system from another.

is a significant factor. "It can be shown that many events and developments of history were shaped, in part at least, by whether the actors involved were improving, declining, or remaining stationary in their social and political positions."[21] In general, in normal periods the rate of political ascent tends toward bureaucratic step-by-step escalation. Elite circulation then follows a more or less regular pattern of political attrition, where issues at the focus of attention prevent the entry of some and allow the entry of others.

This doesn't bar another pattern of more rapid entrepreneurial ascent. This is more characteristic during periods of crisis and/or rapid change when men of new skills, status, and personality are much in demand. Just as the rates of upward mobility are significant so are the rates of declining mobility and political mortality significant in elite behavior. From the casualties of the ambitious come the politically dissident. The spurned and defeated are fertile recruiting grounds for the disaffected. Political mobility is therefore an indicator of change and stability in a system.

Elite Representativeness

The security of an elite rests in large part on the degree of its representativeness. An elite must be both *symbolically* and functionally representative. Various segments of the society must have formal opportunity for decision-making and also appear to share in the prestige of political elite status. On the one hand, if the elite becomes too oligarchical it jeopardizes the broad public participation and support it needs to further development goals. On the other hand, if in its desire to be representative it becomes too diffuse, some of its effectiveness may be lost.

The maintenance of representation is difficult and critical. Change gives rise to new elements in the population that seek political recognition. A perennial problem

[21] Marsh, E., *The Mandarins* (Glencoe: Free Press, 1961), p. 11.

for any political elite is how much of new elements it will allow to enter, without threatening its status and power. How many newcomers can an elite accept without jeopardizing its prestige and influence? By the same token, how can "obsolete" elite members be retired, without threatening revolt and dissension? This is part and parcel of an ongoing problem in any political system, i.e., the relationship between internal mobility and stability.[22] This can be better understood by examining some of the dislocations created by an imbalance in representation.

A good index of the dysfunction of political representation is the political weight of those excluded and denied opportunities for elite positions and influential access. The following are some of the common pathologies in emerging nations.

1. *Opposition Elements are Denied Legitimate Participation.* Ruling oligarchies refuse to consult with them or give them recognition. Under extreme conditions members of the oppositions are openly suppressed or driven underground.

2. *Acute Generational Cleavages.* The younger elements, with high aspirations for status, are severely restricted in opportunities for appointive or elective public office. General differences are especially acute in countries undergoing change. Young intellectuals are among the most politically volatile elements.[23] Extremist groups—political sects violently rejecting both traditional and modernist values—are often the result.

3. *Excessive Selection by Particularistic Criteria*, i.e., people from the right families and backgrounds are overrepresented. The skilled elements, who wish their merit recognized, are restricted and their "merit" qualifications insufficiently recognized.

4. *Alienated Aspirants.* Societies under-

[22] Lipset, S. M., and Bendix, R., *Social Mobility in Industrial Society* (London: Heinemann, 1959), p. 3.
[23] Weiner, M., *Party Politics in India* (Princeton: Princeton University Press, 1960), p. 10; also Shils, E., "Intellectuals in the New States," *World Politics*, **12**, 3 (April 1960), 339, *passim*.

going rapid change unleash influences which break up traditional patterns before new associations with socially constructive functions are prepared to stand in their place. As a result, a category of displaced persons is created. These are individuals thrust out of old positions of former authority.

When the normal routes to political influence are blocked to such elements, as commonly occurs in overbureaucratized parties, then an anomic recruitment takes place.[24] Such groups may resort to violence or provocative acts in order to receive political recognition. They may form separate political cliques, cabals, or political parties. Under conditions of severe political repression they may become underground revolutionaries. The particular form of expression is affected by the styles of political activity in each culture.

Elite Integration

All the factors discussed hitherto are relevant to political elite integration: The legitimations of political elites, the way they enter, are selected and trained for elite roles, their representativeness, all affect the degree of harmony among the multiple elites. Whether political discussions can be made with deliberation and without schism can ultimately be related to factors in elite recruitment.

Intra-elite accommodations depend upon the kind of differences to be reconciled. Among emerging non-Western political systems, elite political differences tend to be ideological and intransigent.[25] Competition among elites is enacted in a concealed and secretive manner. Opposition tends to be extremist, extravagant, and conspiratorial. Rival elites view each other as subversive and mutually exclusive. Political parties view the acquisition of power as their permanent monopoly.

In older Western systems, the oppositions are included in decision-making in a variety of ways. Moreover, parties operate

on expectations of some alternations in power. The inclusion within a common framework of rules of the game and substantive values reduces differences to conflicts over issues. The interests to be reconciled are specific. Competition among rival elites is open, election contests and politics are open to public scrutiny. Even in systems hitherto notable for their cleavages, like France, there is a general commitment to common values.[26]

Consensus among elites is sustained by the necessity to bargain and compromise if each interest is to gain anything at all. The very multiplicity of interests (a feature of a modern pluralistic society) makes such balance a necessity. Reasonable harmony is maintained by the instrumental rather than affective character of political life. For many citizens and groups, there are "zones of indifference" about which involvement is low.[27] Elite integration is facilitated by the socialization of politicians, and the professionalization of politics.[28] Politicians derive from common cultural and social background. As politics is increasingly the preoccupation of a corps of skilled experts in administration, bargaining, propaganda, and technology, the amateur politician declines in importance. The Western politician increasingly associates with other professionals—scientists, experts, professional journalists, lobbyists, etc. The political milieu is a community of skill, governed by unwritten codes and characterized by devotion to techniques.

Elite consensus in Western systems is fostered by the overlap of affiliations of elite members.[29] Memberships in voluntary

[24] Apter, *op. cit.*, p. 117.
[25] Apter, *ibid.*; Chief H. O. Davis, *op. cit.*

[26] Williams, Philip, "Political Compromise in France and America," *American Scholar*, **26,** 3 (Summer 1957), 273–288.
[27] Berelson, B., Lazarfeld, P., and McPhee, W., *Voting* (Chicago, 1954), Ch. 14.
[28] Guttsman, W. L., "Changes in British Labor Leadership" in Marvick, D., *Political Decision Makers* (Glencoe: Free Press, 1960), p. 132.
[29] Janowitz, M., "Social Stratification and the Comparative Analysis of Elites," *Social Forces*, October 1956, p. 84.

associations of many types create a social affinity and common sharing of interests. Elites are neither monolithic nor insulated from each other. In the occupational, religious, and social spheres, elite members lead similar lives. Political roles are, therefore, a limited and restricted part of their lives.

POLITICAL DEVELOPMENT AND THE DILEMMAS OF ELITE RECRUITMENT

In new states, the modernizing elites are committed to achievement and performance and are legitimated by their success. At the same time, these elites can never be free of traditional legitimations—the utopian visions of the movement, the past of the people.[30] In this sense the elites must always face in two directions.[31]

Maintaining the balance between the impulse to change and the constraints of conservation is contingent on two factors: (1) rate of change and (2) methods of change. If the rate of change is too rapid, then serious splits with traditional values result.[32] Counter-modernization movements result—religious, linguistic groups rebel and demand a return to fundamentalism.[33] If the rate of change is too slow, then expectations generated by the independence movement cannot be fulfilled. Disillusionment is inevitable and new leaders may arise espousing rapid modernization through more drastic methods.

The tensions between the insistent demands of modernization and tradition result in the rise of a new movement and ideology, which may be called the New Nationalists. This ideology may come from the newer ranks of the governmental bureaucracies, and the new men of skill. Underlying their fresh perspective is a political generational cleavage. They are impatient with traditionalists who resist change.

Another dilemma revolves around the rate of change. With economic development come new social differentiations—chiefly occupational groups. These groups seek political representation as an expression of their social status.[34] Where modernization is too rapid high expectations are fostered by the mobility of these groups. This may impel them to become autonomous centers of power. On the other hand, if change is too slow, the traditional elements may be intransigent in their resistance to the new differentiations.[35]

A third dilemma rotates around the exclusiveness or inclusiveness of the political elites. An expansion of elite membership may diminish control and extend the range of conflict; an elite too restricted is denied its representativeness. In any event, elites must channel or coopt the new differentiations, allowing them representation. If individuals from new strata are not permitted entry into elite positions, then efforts at collective mobility may result. If such groups with their extreme antitraditional outlooks are too rapidly absorbed into power positions, much dissension may result.

What has been presented are categories and propositions that may be used for comparative assessments of elite recruitment in the context of political development. Many aspects of this subject have been omitted, which deserve mention.

First, the mechanisms of new elite emergence deserve fuller treatment. As a

[30] Duverger, *op. cit.*, pp. 425, 426, 427; Eckstein, H., *A Theory of Stable Democracy* (Princeton: Center of International Studies, 1961), pp. 16, 17.
[31] Rustow, D., "New Horizons for Comparative Politics," *World Politics*, **9**, 4 (July 1957), 533.
[32] Emerson, R., *op. cit.*, p. 329.
[33] Hoselitz, B. in *Tradition, Values and Socio-Economic Development*, ed. R. Braibanti and J. Spengler (Duke University Commonwealth Studies Center), 1961, pp. 90–113.

[34] Eisenstadt, S., "Sociological Aspects of Political Development in Underdeveloped Countries," in Lipset, M., and Smelser, N. J., *Sociology* (1961), pp. 608–622.
[35] Milikan, M., and Blackmer, D., *The Emerging Nations* (Boston: Little Brown, 1961), p. 19.

country undergoes change, in what sectors and under what stimuli are the budding aspirant elites likely to emerge? At what points are political opportunity and predispositions likely to converge? Questions of this type can be answered not by aggregate analyses but by smaller scale studies.

Second, in making comparative elite recruitment analysis the starting points must be made clearer. The term "traditional" covers a range of starting levels, that need greater precision if causal propositions are to be formulated. Finally, the concept of *elite* needs further refinement. Too often it is used to apply to an aggregate that on further examination is highly differentiated, segmentalized, and overlapping with other leadership groups.

THE INTELLECTUALS IN THE POLITICAL DEVELOPMENT OF THE NEW STATES

Edward Shils

The Political Significance of Intellectuals in Underdeveloped Countries

The gestation, birth, and continuing life of the new states of Asia and Africa, through all their vicissitudes, are in large measure the work of intellectuals. In no state-formations in all of human history have intellectuals played such a role as they have in these events of the present century.

In the past, new states were founded by military conquest, by the secession of ethnic groups led by traditional tribal and warrior chiefs, by the gradual extension of the power of the prince through intermarriage, agreement, and conquest, or by separation through military rebellion. In antiquity, the demand that subjects acknowledge the divinity of the Emperor was no more than a requirement that the legitimacy of the existing order be recognized.[1] The interests of dynasty and

kinship group, the lure of majesty, considerations of power, aspirations for office, and calculations of economic advantage have been the components of political decisions and the grounds for pursuit of power in the state. It is only in modern times in the West that beliefs about man's nature, his past, and his place in the universe, and about the ethical and metaphysical rightness of particular forms of political order—the concerns of intellectuals—have played an important part in public life.

In the West in modern times, however, politics—particularly civil politics—have never been a preserve of the intellectuals. Well-established aristocrats and landed gentry with ample leisure have provided much of the personnel of politics, both oligarchical and democratic; clergymen and high ecclesiastical officials and, above all, businessmen—the former earlier, the

SOURCE. Edward Shils, "The Intellectuals in the Political Development of the New States," *World Politics*, **12**, 329–368, April 1960. This article is a revised version of a paper presented at a conference on political modernization held under the auspices of the Committee on Comparative Politics of the Social Science Research Council at Dobbs Ferry in June 1959.

[1] The maxim of the Peace of Augsburg: *Cuius regio, eius religio*, was the beginning

of the specifically modern view that a political order must be based on articulately affirmed beliefs. It too, however, was more concerned with the protection of dynastic interests and the guarantee of public order. The substance of the religion was less important than its acceptance, and in this way it differed from the more intrinsically ideological orientation toward politics that is characteristic of the modern intellectual.

latter more recently—have likewise added to the pool. Retired army officers, trade unionists and, of course, mere professional politicians of diverse occupational backgrounds have also been among the incumbents of or contenders for political office and the leaders in the agitation surrounding selection and decision. Intellectuals, too—professors and teachers, scientists, journalists, authors, etc.—have had a substantial share in all these activities. Radical, much more than conservative, politics have been their province, but there too they have had to share the territory with politicians and trade unionists who were not intellectuals. Modern revolutionary politics have been a domain very much reserved for intellectuals; even those who were not intellectuals by training or profession have been almost forced into becoming so by the ideological nature of modern revolutionary politics.

The prominence of intellectuals in the politics of the new states of Asia and Africa arises in part from the special affinity which exists between the modern intellectual orientation and the practice of revolutionary or unconstitutional politics, of politics which are uncivil in their nature. But even in the small space allotted to civil politics before the new states' acquisition of sovereignty and in its larger area since then, intellectuals have had a prominent position. They have not had to share their political role to the usual extent with the other participants in the building and ruling of states.

It was the intellectuals on whom, in the first instance, devolved the task of contending for their nations' right to exist, even to the extent of promulgating the very idea of the nation. The erosion of the conscience and self-confidence of the colonial powers was in considerable measure the product of agitational movements under intellectual leadership. The impregnation of their fellow-countrymen with some incipient sense of nationality and of national self-esteem was to a large extent the achievement of intellectuals,

both secular and religious. The intellectuals have created the political life of the underdeveloped countries; they have been its instigators, its leaders, and its executants. Until Gandhi's emergence at the end of the First World War, they were its main followers as well, but this changed when the nationalist movement began to arouse the sentiments of the mass of the population.

One of the reasons for the political preeminence of the intellectuals of the underdeveloped countries is a negative one. There was practically no one else. In so many of the colonial countries, the princely dynasties were in decay, their powers and their capacities withered, even before the foreigners appeared. Chiefs and princes squirmed under foreign rule; they intrigued and schemed, and at times even resorted to arms, but they organized no political movements and they espoused no ideology. They sought only, when they protested, to retain or regain their own prerogatives. There were no great noble families producing, in generation after generation, courtiers and ministers who with the emergence of modern forms of public politics moved over into that sphere as of right, as they did in Great Britain from the seventeenth to the nineteenth century. The traditional intellectuals, the custodians of sacred texts, usually—with a few great exceptions like al-Afghani—and no political concerns. They were interested in keeping their traditional culture alive, and this traditional culture had little political content other than to recommend leaving authority to those who already had it. They were ready to adapt themselves to any ruler, native or foreign, who left them alone to carry on their scriptural studies, their traditional teaching, and their observances.[2]

[2] The religious reform movements like the Brahmo Samaj, Arya Samaj, the Ramakrishna Mission, and the Muslim Brotherhood which contributed so much to national consciousness were primarily movements for the purification of religious life, and for the reform of social institutions. Their political significance was either indirect or an afterthought.

Moreover, there was generally no military force either to fight against the foreign ruler once he was established or to supply the educated personnel for a modern political movement.[3] There was no military officer class except for a few subalterns in the jealously guarded army of the foreign ruler. There were many professional soldiers, but they were non-commissioned officers and other ranks and had no political interest whatsoever. The movement instigated in 1881 by the Egyptian Colonel Ahmed Orabi Pasha[4] had no counterparts until the tremors and tribulations of independence began to be felt. There was no profession of politics which men entered early, usually from some other profession, and remained in until final and crushing defeat or the end of their lives. There were very few merchants and industrialists who out of civic and "material" interest took a part in politics on a full or part-time scale—although many of them contributed substantially to the financial support of the nationalist and even the revolutionary movements. Prudence and the narrowness of their concerns kept businessmen out of politics. The "foreignness" of many business enterprisers in underdeveloped countries has further diminished the significance of this class as a reservoir of political personnel. There was and there still is scarcely any endogenous trade union movement which produces its own leaders from within the laboring class, and there have been practically none of those self-educated workingmen who helped to give an intellectual tone to the European and American socialist and revolutionary movements in their early years. There was no citizenry, no reservoir of civility, to provide not only the audience and follow-

ing of politics but the personnel of middle and higher leadership. In short, if politics were to exist at all in underdeveloped countries under colonial rule, they had to be the politics of the intellectuals.

The intellectuals did not, however, enter into the political sphere merely because other sections of the population forswore or abdicated their responsibilities. They entered because they had a special calling from within, a positive impetus from without.

The Intellectual Class in Underdeveloped Countries

What Is an Intellectual? We deal here with the modern intellectuals of the new states—not with traditional intellectuals. Whom do we regard as modern intellectuals in the new states? The answer, in a first approximation, is: all persons with an *advanced modern education*[5] and the intellectual concerns and skills ordinarily associated with it. For a variety of reasons, the present definition of the intellectuals is a less selective or discriminating one

[3] The practitioners of the guerrilla warfare and terrorism which have been carried on in various parts of Asia and Africa against the European rulers have always included a significant admixture of intellectuals.

[4] It was, in any case, more of a protest against unsatisfactory service conditions than a political movement.

[5] This definition is ceasing to be adequate because the extension of opportunities for higher education is changing the composition and outlook of the group of persons who have availed themselves of these opportunities. Furthermore, the increase of those with an advanced technical or scientific and specialized education is creating a body of persons whose interests are narrower than their predecessors' in their own countries, and whose contact with the humanistic and political tradition of the hitherto prevailing higher education is becoming more attenuated. They themselves will not merely be different from the conventional political intellectuals of the colonial or recently colonial countries, but will also less frequently identify themselves as "intellectuals." This will make a considerable difference. In this respect, the underdeveloped countries will begin to approximate the more advanced countries.

This definition is not intended to deny the existence of a class of traditional intellectuals, largely religious in their concerns. Nor does it seek to obscure the influence of traditional intellectuals in political life (like the Muslim Brotherhood, the Darul Islam, etc.) or of traditional ideas on modern intellectuals.

than we would use to designate the intellectuals in the more advanced countries. This is in no way condescension toward the new states. It is only an acknowledgment of the smaller degree of internal differentiation which has until now prevailed within the educated class in the new states, and the greater disjunction which marks that class off from the other sections of the society. It is also a recognition of a means of identification employed in the new states by the intellectuals themselves and by others.

In the new states, and in colonies which are shortly to achieve independence, the intellectuals are those persons who have become modern not by immersing themselves in the ways of modern commerce or administration, but by being exposed to the set course of modern intellectual culture in a college or university. Passage through this course of study is the qualification for being regarded as an intellectual, just as the possession of the diploma is regarded as a qualification for practicing a profession which is the prerogative of the intellectual. The "diplomatization" of society to which Max Weber referred, although it exists on a smaller scale than in Germany or Great Britain because there are fewer posts available, is as impressive in underdeveloped countries as in the advanced ones. It is not, however, the diploma which makes the intellectual. It is his prolonged contact with modern culture[6] which does so. The diploma is only an emblem, however valuable, of a part of his outlook which he and others regard as vitally important. The possession of a *modern intellectual culture* is vital because it carries with it a partial transformation of the self and a changed relationship to the authority of the dead and the living.

The Occupational Structure of the Intellectuals. The professions of the intellectuals

in underdeveloped countries are civil service, journalism, law, teaching (particularly college and university, but also secondary-school teaching), and medicine. These are the professions in which intellectuals are to be found and which require either intellectual certification or intellectual skill. (There are other professions with similar qualifications of certification and skill, such as engineering and accounting, which have usually been regarded as marginal to the circle within which the intellectuals dwell.)

The occupational structure which intellectuals enter in the underdeveloped countries is notably different from that of the more advanced countries. The occupational distribution of the intellectuals in underdeveloped countries is a function of the level of economic development and of their having only recently been colonial territories. Because they were impoverished countries, they lacked a fully differentiated middle class. They lacked and still lack a stratum of authors who could live from the sale of their literary products.[7] They have only a very meager class of technical intellectuals (electrical engineers, technologists, industrial chemists, statisticians, accountants). They have lacked the higher levels of scientific and humanistic personnel, the physicists, biologists, geneticists, historians, and philosophers who carry on the intellectual work which is the specific manifestation of the modern intellectual outlook.[8]

---

[6] This does not mean that all intellectuals in underdeveloped countries who possess diplomas are intellectually equal, or that all intellectuals possess diplomas. There are a few who do not.

[7] By very rough methods I estimated that there might be as many as one hundred professional literary men in India who are able to maintain themselves by their writings. The Director of the *Sahitya Akademi* thinks that there are only about fifty. Think then of the size of this stratum in Ghana, Nigeria, Egypt, or the Sudan!

[8] India is a very partial exception. It is practically alone in its possession of a large corps of intellectuals, a fair number of whom work at a very high level. This is partly a function of the much longer period that modern intellectual life has existed in India. The British stayed longer in India and exercised greater influence there than any other European power did in its colonial territory, and as a result many more

They lacked nearly all of these latter professions under colonial conditions, and most of the underdeveloped countries still lack most of them today under conditions of independence. In the colonial era, they lacked them because poverty and the absence of a significant development of industry prevented the emergence of demand for technical intellectuals, because illiteracy prevented the emergence of a market for literary products, and because the higher levels of modern intellectual creation and enquiry received no indigenous impulse and were too costly for poor countries to maintain. As a result, persons trained in those subjects found little opportunity for employment in their own country, and few therefore attempted to acquire these skills.[9]

Under colonial conditions, the underdeveloped countries lacked the effective demand which permits a modern intellectual class, in its full variety, to come into existence. Persons who acquired intellectual qualifications had only a few markets for their skills. The higher civil service was by all odds the most attractive of these, but opportunities were restricted because it was small in size and the posts were mainly pre-empted by foreigners. (In India in the last decade of the British Raj, there were only about 1200 such posts in the Indian Civil Service and, of these, a little less than half were filled by Indians. In other countries, the number of posts was smaller and the proportion held by persons of indigenous origin was also much smaller.)

Journalism, as a result of generally widespread illiteracy, was a stunted growth and provided only a few opportunities, which were not at all remunerative. Journalism under colonial conditions was

[footnote 8 continued
modern intellectual institutions came into being.
[9] There are other important reasons, growing out of the culture of these countries, which precluded interest in these fields. We do not deal with them here since our interest lies primarily in the political sphere.

much more of an unprofitable political mission than a commercially attractive investment, and most of it was on rather minuscule scale.

The medical profession was kept small by the costliness of the course of study, the absence of an effective demand for medical services, and the pre-emption of much of the senior level of the medical service by the government and its consequent reservation for foreigners.

Teaching at its lower levels was unattractive to intellectuals because it involved living in villages away from the lights and interests of the larger towns, and because it was extremely unremunerative. Nor were there many opportunities in it. On the secondary and higher levels, opportunities were also meager. Of all the underdeveloped countries, only India had an extensive modern college and university system before 1920; after that date, the additions to the Indian system of higher education came very slowly until the eve of the Second World War and the chaos which accompanied it. Outside of India there were at most only a few thousand posts available in institutions of higher learning in all of colonial Asia and Africa, and some of these were reserved for Europeans (and Americans, in the two American colleges of the Middle East). Thus opportunities for teaching on the upper levels of an extremely lean educational system were few. Where the authorities sought to maintain a high standard, they were very particular about whom they chose to employ. (It should be added that political considerations, at this time of nationalistic, anti-colonialist effervescence, likewise restricted the chances of entry, since many able young men disqualified themselves by the high jinks of adolescent politics during their student days).

The Legal Profession. For these reasons, many of the intellectually gifted and interested who also had to gain their own livelihood entered the course of legal study and then the practice of the profession of the law. Entry to the legal profession was not restricted on ethnic grounds, the course of study was short and inexpensive and could be easily undertaken. There was, moreover, a considerable effective demand for legal services.

The colonial powers were concerned with order and justice and, in their various ways, had attempted to establish the rule of law in the colonial territories. The wealthy landowning classes and the newer wealthy merchants were frequently engaged in litigations in which huge sums were involved and the possibility of lawyers to earn handsome fees gave an éclat to the legal profession which only the higher civil service otherwise possessed.

Furthermore, in countries like India, Egypt, or Nigeria, for example, what else could a university or college graduate do with his qualifications if he did not wish to settle for a clerkship in the government or in a foreign commercial firm? The law schools were therefore able to attract throngs of students. Once the legal qualification had been obtained, the young lawyer went into the nether regions of the bar, where he had much time for other interests. The leisure time of the young lawyer was a fertile field in which much political activity grew.

This existence of a stratum of underemployed young lawyers was made possible by their kinship connections. The aspirants to the intellectual professions in the underdeveloped countries almost always came from the more prosperous sections of society. They were the sons of chiefs, noblemen, and landowners, of ministers and officials of territories in which indirect rule existed, and of civil servants and teachers in countries under direct rule. In some countries, they occasionally came from prosperous mercantile families, though seldom in large numbers.

These social origins, against the background of the diffuse obligations accepted by members of an extended kinship system, meant that even where the income gained from a profession was inadequate to maintain a man and his immediate family,

he could still continue to associate himself with the profession. The deficiencies in his earnings were made up by his kinsmen. Unlike teaching, the civil service, and most journalism, where membership in the profession is defined not merely by qualification and intermittent practice but by actual employment, a person need not earn a living by legal practice in order to be a lawyer. This is why the legal profession in nearly all the underdeveloped countries has been, before and since independence, crowded by a few very successful lawyers and a great number of very unsuccessful ones.

These are also some of the reasons why the legal profession supplied so many of the outstanding leaders of the nationalist movements during colonial times, and why the lawyer-intellectuals form such a vital part of the political elites of the new states.

Students. No consideration of the intellectual class in underdeveloped countries can disregard the university students. In advanced countries, students are not regarded as *ex officio* intellectuals; in underdeveloped countries, they are. Students in modern colleges and universities in underdeveloped countries have been treated as part of the intellectual class— or at least were before independence— and they have regarded themselves as such. Perhaps the mere commencement of an adult form of contact with modern intellectual traditions and the anticipation—however insecure—that acquisition of those traditions would qualify one for the *modern* intellectual professions conferred that status on university and college students and, derivatively, on secondary-school students.

The student enjoyed double favor in the eyes of his fellow-countryman. As one of the tiny minority gaining a modern education, he was becoming qualified for a respected, secure, and well-paid position close to the center of society, as a civil servant, teacher, or lawyer. As a bearer of the spirit of revolt against the foreign ruler, he gained the admiration and confidence of those of his seniors who were imbued with the national idea.

Formally, the student movements in the colonial countries began their careers only in the 1920's, but long before that the secondary schools, colleges, and universities had been a source of personnel for the more ebullient and aggressive nationalistic movements. Since the beginning of the present century, students have been in a state of turbulence. This turbulence flowed more and more into politics, until the students became vital foci of the national independence movements. The secondary schools, colleges, and universities attended by the students of underdeveloped countries became academies of national revolution. It was not the intention of the administrators and teachers that they should become such; rather, the contrary. Nonetheless they did, both in their own countries and in the metropolitan centers of London and Paris, where many of the most important architects of independence were trained, and where they found the intellectual resonance and moral support which sustained them in lean years.

The London School of Economics in particular has probably contributed much more to the excitation of nationalistic sentiment than any other educational institution in the world. At the School of Economics, the late Professor Harold Laski did more than any other single individual to hearten the colonial students and to make them feel that the great weight of liberal Western learning supported their political enthusiasm.

However, it was not only in the universities of London and Paris, but in shabby clubs and cafés, cheap hotels and restaurants, dingy rooming houses and the tiny cluttered offices of their nationalist organizations that the colonial students were educated in nationalism, acquired some degree of national consciousness, and came to feel how retrograde their own countries were and what they might be if only they became their own masters and

modernized themselves. Personalities like Mr. Krishna Menon, Dr. Nkrumah, and Dr. Banda were themselves formed in these milieux, and in turn formed many of those who were to play an active part in the movement in their own countries.

The political propensities of the students have been, in part, products of adolescent rebelliousness. This has been especially pronounced in those who were brought up in a traditionally oppressive environment and were indulged with a spell of freedom from that environment—above all, freedom from the control of their elders and kinsmen. Once, however, the new tradition of rebellion was established among students, it became self-reproducing. Moreover, the vocational prospectlessness of their post-university situation has also stirred the restiveness of the students.

The Unemployed Intellectual. In most underdeveloped countries during the colonial period, the unemployed intellectual was always a worry to the foreign rulers and to constitutional politicians, and a grievance of the leaders of the independence movement. He still remains a problem in the underdeveloped countries which have had a higher educational system for some length of time and which are not rapidly expanding their governmental staffs. In Ghana or Nigeria, there is a shortage of intellectuals and all graduates can find posts; in Pakistan, which inherited only a very small part of the higher educational system of British India, the government has tried to restrict entrance to the universities, especially in "arts" subjects. In India and Egypt, however, despite rapid expansion of opportunities for the employment of intellectuals in government, there has been a more than proportionate expansion in the number of university graduates and the problem remains as acute as ever.

Yet the difficulty is not so much "intellectual unemployment" as under- and mal-employment. Most of the graduates, sooner or later, do find posts of one sort or another, but they are not posts which conform with expectations. They are ill-paid, unsatisfying in status and tenure, and leave their incumbents in the state of restlessness which they experienced as students.

The Political Outlook of the Intellectuals

Intense Politicization. The nature of the political movements which preceded independence and the indigenous traditions of the underdeveloped countries both forced political life into charismatic channels. Charismatic politics demand the utmost from their devotees.

When the intellectuals of the colonial countries were ready to engage in politics at all, they were willing to give everything to them. Politics became the be-all and end-all of their existence. Those who were not restrained by fear of the loss of their posts in government schools and colleges or by the material and psychological advantages of their jobs became highly politicized. Some of the intellectuals who graduated in the years of nationalistic fervor did not even attempt seriously to enter upon a professional career but went directly into agitational and conspiratorial politics. Their middle-class origins and the economy of the extended family system, together with the relatively few needs of charismatically sensitive intellectuals, helped to make possible this consecration to politics. For these reasons and because an autonomous intellectual life in the modern sense had scarcely taken root in any of the underdeveloped colonial countries, politics of a very intense sort had the intellectual field largely to itself.

The high degree of political involvement of the intellectual in underdeveloped countries is a complex phenomenon. It has a threefold root. The primary source is a deep preoccupation with authority. Even though he seeks and seems actually to break away from the authority of the powerful traditions in which he was brought up, the intellectual of underdeveloped countries, still more than his confrere in more advanced countries,

retains the need for incorporation into some self-transcending, authoritative entity. Indeed, the greater his struggle for emancipation from the traditional collectivity, the greater his need for incorporation into a new, alternative collectivity. Intense politicization meets this need. The second source of political involvement is the scarcity of opportunities to acquire an even temporary sense of vocational achievement; there have been few counterattractions to the appeal of charismatic politics. Finally, there has been a deficient tradition of civility in the underdeveloped countries which affects the intellectuals as much as it does the non-intellectuals. Let us consider each of these aspects.

The intellectual everywhere is concerned with his relations to authority. In underdeveloped countries, where authorities have tended on the whole to be more unitary, and where alternative authorities, and the authority of alternative traditions, have not yet emerged because of the small size of the primordial community and its relatively low degree of internal differentiation, the preoccupation of the intellectual with authority is all the greater. It is difficult for him to escape from a sense of its presence and a feeling of dependence on it. Such continuous presence, and the unindulgent attitude of traditional indigenous authority, once childhood has passed, breed resentment and antipathy which are submerged but not dissolved in the obedience required for the continuance of daily existence in the primordial community.

The external air of submission hides a deeper and unceasing enmity. Distant authority which has force at its disposal, which is impersonal, as bureaucratic authority must be, and which is not suffused with any immediately apprehensible charisma, provides an easy target for this enmity.

When one shares in authority, when one "is" authority, as a leading politician of the ruling party or as a civil servant, the antagonism toward authority is curbed by the counterbalancing need to be absorbed into it. For an intellectual in an underdeveloped country, authority is usually something into which he must be absorbed or against which he must be in opposition. It is seldom something about which he can be neutral while he goes about his business. The very structure of the underdeveloped countries, both in their primordial and in their wider aspects, both during the colonial period and during independence, is such that one can never be indifferent about authority. It cannot be overlooked, one's "business" cannot be carried on without regard to it.

Distant authority carries with it none of the compensations and urgencies of immediately present and permeative authority. Distance does not make for indifference among the politicized, among those whose passions are strong and no longer bound down by the weight of primordiality and tradition. The distance of authority renders revolt against it psychologically more practicable. Distant authority is "alien" authority. Even when it is ethnically "identical" with those over whom it rules, this "alienation" exists in those societies which are used to being ruled by visible and proximate authorities. (When distant authority is also ethnically alien, whether it be of the same general racial and cultural stock or as alien in color, cultural tradition, provenience, and physical appearance as the colonial authorities were, the impulse to revolt is all the stronger.)

The revolt against authority cannot, however, be complete and unequivocal. The need, from which no human being can every wholly liberate himself, to be a member of an authoritative, transcendent collectivity remains. The individual, striving to emancipate himself from his primordial collectivity, must feel himself a part of some other more congenial, alternative collectivity. It must, moreover, be an authoritative one, a charismatically authoritative one. Where, in an underdeveloped society, with its relative churchlessness, its

still feeble professional and civil traditions, and in the face of persisting particularistic loyalties, both subjective and objective, can the modern intellectual find such an authoritative collectivity? It is really only the "nation" which is at hand, and that organized body which represents the "nation"—namely, the "party of national independence."

This is one reason why the intellectual immerses himself, at least for a time, in intense political activities; it is why he seeks a "cause," an encompassing ideal. It is also the reason for the oppositional character of the politics of the intellectuals who themselves do not share in the authority. The belief in the efficacy of political action and in the political sources of evil and the remedies of evil also finds some of its explanation here. This is why the relatively unpolitical intellectual, or the intellectual who is indirectly connected with political affairs, the more specialized intellectual who wishes to work within his own professional intellectual tradition and to exercise his influence in the public sphere over the longer run and beyond the immediate disputes of the parties, is regarded as not being a "genuine intellectual" and even as a traitor to the ideals which the intellectual is properly called to serve.

The intense politicization of the intellectual is accentuated by the provision, through politics, of opportunities for individual effectiveness and achievement. In a society where status is traditionally determined by such primordial qualities as kinship connection, age, sex, and rank order within the family, the possibility of achievement, of making a mark on events by one's own actions, is minimal. In the larger society of the underdeveloped countries, although the narrower primordial determinants of status are to some extent transcended, the possibilities of achievement remain small. The opportunities for the satisfactory employment of an educated person under conditions of colonial rule were meager as long as the most authoritative positions in the civil service and in commerce were reserved to foreigners. They remain small under conditions of sovereignty as long as the economy is backward and posts integral to the modern part of the economy are relatively few, and as long as opportunities for specifically intellectual employment or the sale of the products of creative intellectual work are restricted.

The educated person acquires some degree of emancipation from the predominantly primordial tradition of status-determination. The content of this modern education, and its dissolution of the hold of traditional cultural standards and the traditional patterns of life, arouse in him the need to determine his status and his self-esteem by his own achievements. Where can such a person make his mark in a society which gives him little room to do so?

The political movement with its demands and challenges is almost the only arena open to him. A political movement, unlike a business firm or a university or a government department, can absorb as many people as apply to it. It can give him tasks to perform and it can thereby offer him the possibility of seeing the effects of his actions. By shooting, demonstrating, marching, agitating, threatening and bullying, fighting, destroying, obstructing, helping to organize, running errands, distributing handbills, and canvassing, he can see some effects and can believe in the importance of his deeds in thwarting or coercing a distant impersonal bureaucratic authority, or in serving the will of the new charismatic authority to which he gives himself.

Especially during the period of late adolescence and youth, when the impulses of self-assertion and the striving for individuality and creativity are at their height, and before the traditional system of status has reasserted its empire over him, politics seem to be the only field in which he can act with some expectation of satisfying effectiveness.

Once independence has been attained, the need for effectiveness and achievement does not die away. Politics remain a major alternative to apathetic idiocy or regression into the acceptance of the traditional pattern of life. Politics will in fact remain a major alternative open to the intellectuals for achievement and for absorption into a wider, no longer primordial collectivity as long as the underdeveloped societies remain underdeveloped. Only when they have become more differentiated occupationally, and when they have developed a sufficiently large and self-esteeming corps of professional intellectuals, carrying on the specifically intellectual professions with their own corporate traditions and corporate forms of organization, will the passionate sentiment and energy flow into channels other than the political.

Nationalism. The nationalism of the intellectuals usually made its first appearance alone, free from the complications of socialist and populist ideas. Only in those underdeveloped countries where the nationalist movement has come more lately on the scene has it been involved in other ideological currents which are not necessarily integral to it.

The nationalism of the intellectuals of the underdeveloped countries emerged at a time when there was little sense of nationality among the peoples whose nationality the intellectuals were proclaiming. Its first impetus seems to have come from a deepening of the feeling of distance between ruler and ruled, arising from the spatial and ethnic remoteness of the foreign rulers, and the dissolution of the particularistic tie which holds ethnically homogeneous rulers and ruled together. The identification of oneself as a subject of an unloved (however feared and respected) ruler with others who shared that subjection was one phase of the process. The discovery of the glories of the past, of cultural traditions, was usually but not always an action, *ex post facto*, which legitimated the claims asserted on behalf of that newly imagined collectivity.[10]

[10] The stirrings of religious reform and the effort to rehabilitate the dignity of the tradi-

The assimilation of modern culture, which, historically, was a foreign culture, was an essential element in this process. The first generation of constitutional politicians in most underdeveloped countries were relatively highly "Westernized." The usual antagonism toward the older generation made the next, younger generation more antagonistic toward Western culture, and encouraged their rudimentary attachment to the indigenous traditional culture to come forward a little more in their minds. This provided a matrix for the idea of a deeper national culture and, therewith, of the nation which had only to be aroused to self-awareness. It was neither a simple attachment to their indigenous culture nor a concretely experienced love of their fellow-countrymen which made the intellectuals so fervently nationalistic. These would have presupposed a prior sense of affinity, which for many reasons was lacking and often still is. In fact, however, "fellow-countrymen" became so to the modern intellectuals primarily by virtue of their common differentiation from the foreign ruler. Fierce resentment against the powerful, fear-inspiring foreign ruler was probably a much more significant factor than either a sense of affinity or a conscious appreciation of the traditional culture.

The resentment of the modern intellectual grew from several seeds: one of the most important was the derogation implied in the barrier against entry into or advancement in the civil service. The other, closely related to this, was the feeling of injury from insults, experienced or heard about, explicit or implicit, which the foreign rulers and their businessmen fellow-nationals inflicted on the indigenous modern intellectuals. Lord Curzon's derogatory remarks about the educated Bengali in his famous Calcutta University Convocation Address were only among the

more egregious of an infinite multitude of such slights, injuries, and denigrations. The belittlement extended into every sphere of life, cultural, intellectual, religious, economic, political, and personal. A sense of distress and of anticipated insult became part of the indigenous intellectuals' relationship with foreigners for a long time. Even now in independence, the alertness to insult and the readiness to perceive it persist. They were at their height in the early period of nationalism.

The situation was rendered all the more insufferable by the genuine and positive appreciation which the native intellectuals often felt for the foreign culture, and their feeling of the inferiority of their own in comparison with it. Nationalism of an extremely assertive sort was an effort to find self-respect, and to overcome the inferiority of the self in the face of the superiority of the culture and power of the foreign metropolis.

It was therefore logical that prior to independence the politics of the intellectuals, once the movement for constitutional reform had waned, should have been concerned with one end above all others: national independence. It was generally assumed by most politicized intellectuals that any other desiderata would be automatically realized with the attainment of that condition. The actual attainment of independence and of a condition in which the tasks of political life have become as demanding and as diversified as they must inevitably become in a polity where the state takes unto itself so many powers and aspires to so much, has not greatly altered the situation. Nationalism still remains one of the greatest of all motive forces;[11] it underlies many policies to which it is not really germane and serves as a touchstone of nearly every action and policy.

The socialistic and the populistic ele-

[footnote 10 continued
tional religious culture became political only when there was an alliance of religious leaders with a politicized modern intelligentsia.

[11] Although it is by no means the chief reason, this nationalistic concentration is a significant factor in accounting for the poverty and uniformity of intellectual life of the underdeveloped countries.

ments in the politics of the intellectuals of underdeveloped countries are secondary to and derivative from their nationalistic preoccupations and aspirations. Economic policies have their legitimation in their capacity to raise the country on the scale of the nations of the world. The populace is transfigured in order to demonstrate the uniqueness of its "collective personality." The ancient culture is exhumed and renewed in order to demonstrate, especially to those who once denied it, the high value of the nation. Foreign policy is primarily a policy of "public relations" designed not, as in the advanced countries, to sustain the security of the state or enhance its power among other states, but to improve the reputation of the nation, to make others heed its voice, to make them pay attention to it and to respect it. The "world," the "imperialist world," remains very much on the minds of the intellectuals of the new states. It remains the audience and the jury of the accomplishments of the nation which the intellectuals have done so much to create.

Nonetheless, despite the pre-eminence of the nationalistic sensibility, it does not rest upon a *tabula rasa*, cleared of all other attachments. The intellectuals of underdeveloped countries are not as "uprooted," as "detribalized," as they themselves sometimes assert with so much melancholy, or as, with more spite, their foreign and domestic detractors often allege. They have remained attached in many ways to their traditional patterns of social life and culture. These deeper attachments include parochial attachments to their own tribes and ethnic and caste communities, and almost inevitably seek expression in public policies and in domestic political alignments. The presence of these attachments is a supplementary generator of nationalistic sentiment. It is against them, and in an effort to overcome them—within themselves and in their fellow-countrymen—that many intellectuals in underdeveloped countries commit themselves so fervently to intense nationalism.

By a similar process, the extensive use of a foreign language in daily intellectual life also feeds the force of nationalism. The intellectuals' very large amount of reading in French and English and their feeling of continued dependence on these cultures, their continuing and still necessary employment of French or English for their own cultural creations and even for political, administrative, and judicial purposes, and their awareness of the slow and painful course through which their nation must pass before its own language becomes adequate to the requirements of modern life cannot avoid touching their sensibilities. The constant reaffirmation of their nationalistic attachment is an effort to assuage this wound.

Socialism. The socialism of the intellectuals of the underdeveloped countries grows, fundamentally, from their feeling for charismatic authority, from their common humanity, and from the antichrematistic traditions of their indigenous culture. More immediately, it is a product of the conditions and substance of their education, and of their nationalistic sensibility.

The intellectuals of underdeveloped countries are, in general, devotees of authority, even though they may be inflamed against some particular authority. They regard the existing distribution of authority as the source of present economic and social inequities and they seek a new distribution of authority as the instrument to abolish them. Their critical view of the state as it exists at present in their own country is partly a manifestation of their distrust of impersonal authority and of their faith in a more charismatic alternative.[12] They do not believe in the capacities of businessmen to increase the well-being of the nation. They have little sympathy, conscious or unconscious, with the man who is engaged in the pursuit of wealth.

None of the great traditional cultures

[12] *Vide* the Gandhian socialists and the Bhoodan movement in India.

gives a high rank to the merchant; even when they revolt against the traditional culture, or slip away from it unwittingly, the intellectuals usually retain that part of it which allots no high place to the businessman. In their mind, the life of the businessman is unheroic; it is untouched by sacredness and they will have none of it. Intellectuals very seldom seek careers in private business; when necessity forces them into it, they are ill at ease and restless. The intellectual who works for a private business firm lays himself open to the charge of having deserted his calling, even though he has deserted it no more than a civil servant or a lawyer. The notion of an economic system ruled by the decisions of businessmen, out to make a profit for themselves, is repugnant to the intellectuals of underdeveloped countries—even more than it is in advanced countries, where the businessman does not fare very well either at the hands of the intellectuals.

As long as the intellectuals of underdeveloped countries pursued the paths of constitutional reform and confined their attention to administration and representation, these deeper dispositions whose source was the traditional indigenous culture did not enter into their politics. They accepted most of the existing regime. When, however, they began to direct their attention to the society and the nation, when they ceased being politically "superficial" and began to touch on politically "sacred" things, the socialist potentiality of their fundamental orientation became more manifest.

These inner developments within the intelligentsia of underdeveloped countries coincided with the upsurge of socialist thought among the European intellectuals. To these, the intelligentsia of the underdeveloped countries felt drawn. The attractive power of the metropolis was enhanced by the congeniality of intellectual socialism. From the 1920's to the 1940's, the example of the late Professor Harold Laski elicited and fortified the socialistic

disposition of many young intellectuals of the English-speaking underdeveloped countries; Jean-Paul Sartre has played a parallel role among the French-speaking intellectuals from 1945 onward.

The spread of socialistic ideas was aided by the large-scale migration of Asian and African intellectuals to Europe for further study and professional training. The great stream of Asians to European educational centers began in the 1890's; their intensive politicization, in the 1920's. The stream of the African students began in the 1920's and became much wider after 1945. From the end of the First World War and the Russian Revolution, the young Asians and Africans, impelled by events in the world and at home, found themselves in an atmosphere which gave the encouragement of a nearly universal assent to their socialist aspirations.

The association between socialism as a domestic policy and hostility toward an imperialistic foreign policy—a connection which is inherent in the postulates of socialist thought and its Leninist variant, although not all socialists have at all times shared it—made European, and especially British and French, socialism even more acceptable to the Asian and African students who came to the intellectual capitals of the European metropolis.

To these factors which made socialism appear such a bright ideal should be joined the nature of large-scale business enterprise in their own countries. In practically all instances, large-scale business enterprise in the underdeveloped countries was owned and controlled by foreign capitalists. Not just the Europeans, and latterly the Americans, owned large firms in Africa and Asia, but Chinese, Syrians, Lebanese, Parsees, Armenians, Greeks, and Italians, away from their own countries, showed exceptional enterprise. Encountering few indigenous competitors, they built up extensive organizations and ample fortunes in underdeveloped countries. The ethnic diversity and separateness of the peoples, even within large, centrally governed countries, often brought about a situation in which private businessmen who were of the same "nationality" as those in the midst of whom they lived and conducted their affairs, but who were of a different "community," were regarded as outsiders who had no moral claims on the loyalty of the intellectuals. Businessmen, by the nature of their calling, could never be part of the "people"; their ethnic distinctness was further justification for treating them as alien to the "people."

On the other side, a socialistic economic system conducted in accordance with principles which are of intellectual origin, guided by persons who are imbued with these "principles," seems to be the only conceivable alternative to a privately operated economy. The intellectuals who dare to differ from such obvious conclusions constitute a small fraction of the intellectual classes in most of the underdeveloped countries, both colonial and sovereign.

The socialism of the intellectuals of underdeveloped countries, it should also be stressed, is a product of their pained awareness of the poverty of their own countries. The heightening of national sensibility led perforce to the discovery of the "people." Agitational activities brought them into contact with the "people"; the vague doctrine of nationalism, even in its liberal form, brought the idea of the "people" into the consciousness of the intellectuals. Often, too, on return from a period of foreign study where they had encountered socialist ideas and experienced a heightened national consciousness, the sight of their impoverished fellow-countrymen had a traumatic force. Confrontation with the poverty of their country evoked anguish and desperation in many intellectuals. They have been humiliated by their sense of the backwardness of their country. They have learned how gradually the advancement of the Western countries has moved, and they have heard of the speedy progress of the Soviet Union from a backward country to the status of one of the most powerful industrial nations in the world. What could be more harmonious with their present perceptions, their aspirations, and their background than to espouse a socialist solution to their unhappy problem? And if to this is added the fact that their countries have been held in subjection by capitalistic countries and the socialist countries proclaim their hostility to imperialism, the disposition toward socialism receives another impulsion.

Populism. The populism of intellectual politics in underdeveloped countries has a familial affinity to the populism of the intellectuals of more advanced countries during the past century and a half. It is a part of a universal process consequent on the emergence of an incipient and fragmentary world-wide intellectual community. It is a phenomenon of the tension between metropolis and province which arises from the trend toward that world-wide intellectual community.

The populism of the intellectuals is German in origin. It was a critique of the pretensions of a worldly, urban, and urbane authority. It was a critique of the feebleness of the petty elites of the system of *Kleinstaaterei*, alongside the grandeur of the Holy Roman Empire, and of the Germany which could emerge if the regime of the princelings could be abolished and all of Germany unified. It was a critique of the central institutional system, and particularly of the claims of the state, of the universities, and of the ecclesiastical authorities to embody what was essential in their society and of their insistence, on that basis, on their right to rule over it. It was a rejection of the urban bourgeoisie. It was a denial that the "nation" could be found in existing authoritative institutions and an assertion that the root of the future lay in the "folk."

In Russia, populism was a product of a similar situation, aggravated by resentment against a prevailing enchantment by the West, which was more pronounced than the Francophilia of the princely courts against which the first generations of romantic

German populism had been a reaction. In Russia, the intellectuals had carried on a passionate love affair with Western Europe and many had been disappointed and had even come to feel guilty for deserting their "own" for foreign idols. Alienated from their own authorities of state, church, and university, hostile to their own mercantile bourgeoisie, disillusioned with Western European socialism after its failures in the revolutions of 1848, it had nowhere to turn except to the "people," whom it glorified as a repository of wisdom and as the source of Russia's salvation.

American populism was not very different in its general origins. It, too, was the product of a reaction against the Anglophile intellectual elite of the Eastern seaboard and the political and industrial elities who ruled the country from the Eastern cities. In America, too, therefore, it was an effort to find a firm foundation for intellectuals who were alienated from the authorities of their society and from their xenophilic fellow-intellectuals. In America also it was a phase of the struggle of province against metropolis.

In the underdeveloped countries, the process has been essentially the same. Alienated from the indigenous authorities of their own traditional society—chiefs, sultans, princes, landlords, and priests—and from the rulers of their modern society— the foreign rulers and the "Westernized" constitutional politicians (and since independence, politicians of the governing party)—the intellectuals have had only the "people," the "African personality," the "Indian peasant," etc., as supports in the search for the salvation of their own souls and their own society.

The "people" are a model and a standard; contact with them is a good. Esteem and disesteem are meted out on the basis of "closeness to the people" or distance from them. It is a common worry of and an accusation against the intellectuals of the underdeveloped countries that they are "out of touch with the people," uprooted, déraciné, "brown" or "black" (as the case may be) "Englishmen" or "Frenchmen," etc. Many make the accusation against themselves, most make it against their fellow-intellectuals.

Factually it is usually quite untruthful. Most intellectuals in underdeveloped countries are not as "cut off" from their own culture as they and their detractors suggest. They live in the middle of it, their wives and mothers are its constant representatives in their midst, they retain close contact with their families, which are normally steeped in traditional beliefs and practices. The possession of a modern intellectual culture does remove them, to some extent, from the culture of their ancestors, but much of the latter remains and lives on in them.[13]

The experience to which the allegation of being "cut off" from the "people" refers is not to any serious extent a real result of the intellectuals' acceptance of the "foreign," modern culture. It rests rather on their own feeling of distance from the rest of their fellow-nationals, which is a product of the ethnic, tribal, kinship and caste particularism of these underdeveloped societies and of the consequent lack of a true sense of civil affinity with the rest of their fellow-countrymen. It is the resultant of the superimposition of a nationalistic ideology, which demands fellow-feeling, on a narrower particularism, inharmonious with it and psychologically contradictory to it. There is a genuine feeling of strain; all the burden of this strain is put upon the fact that they possess some elements of an exogenous culture.

The frequent reiteration of the charge testifies to an awareness of this tension, and the choice of the foreign culture as its focus is a manifestation of a desire to find

[13] Much of the intellectuals' self-accusation rests on the populistic assumption that the "people," not being distracted or corrupted by modern culture, are the bearers of the traditional culture in its fullness and its glory. This assumption is probably an error; the "people" are quite unlikely to be in more than fragmentary possession of the corpus of traditional culture.

a way out which will conform to the require-ments of ideological nationalism. Because the intellectuals assert it and, to some extent, believe it, they often try to make amends for it by some form of nativism, which extols the traditional ways of the people and juxtaposes them with modern and thus "foreign" ways.

This nativistic reaction accentuates demagogic political tendencies, and fosters a race among contenders for the distinc-tion of being more "for" the "people" or more "akin" to them. It accentuates prejudice against the educated and a hosti-lity against the modern education which the intellectuals of the new states need if they are to perform intellectual functions in a productive way, and without which they would not be intellectuals and their countries would flounder and sink.

Nonetheless, despite this preoccupation with the "people," the populism of the intellectuals of underdeveloped countries does not necessarily bring with it either intimacy with the ordinary people, a concrete attachment to them, or even a democratic attitude. It is compatible with them but it does not require them. It is equally compatible with a dictatorial regime which treats the people as instruments to be employed in the transformation of the social and economic order, and their culture and outlook as a hindrance to progress.

Populism can be the legitimating prin-ciple of oligarchical regimes, as well as of democratic regimes and of all the inter-mediate types. The "people" constitute the prospective good to be served by govern-ment policy, and they serve as the emblem of the traditional culture which is thus glorified even while it is being eroded and its traditional custodians disregarded or disparaged.

Oppositionalism. The populism of the intellectual is a product of opposition to the authorities who rule at home and to the foreign culture which fascinates him and his fellow-intellectuals in his own country. It is one facet of an oppositional syndrome.

The origins of this inclination to oppose constituted authority seem, at first glance, easy to locate. Practically all politics in the colonial period, once the constitutional phase had passed, consisted and still consist of root and branch opposition. Whether they took the form of conspiracy, sabotage, riots, assassination, clandestine or open journalism, public meetings, boy-cotts, demonstrations and processions, civil disobedience or unco-operative parti-cipation in representative institutions, opposition and obstruction of the foreign ruler were the main aims. Where it was impossible to share in the responsible exercise of authority, opposition was in fact the only alternative.

The degree of alienation from the consti-tuted authority varied but it was almost always deeper and more drastic than the opposition which exists in advanced pluralistic societies.[14] It was the opposition of politicians excluded or withdrawn from the constitutional order, who accepted neither the rules nor the ends of the pre-vailing system. It was, therefore, the oppo-sition of politicians who refused in principle to consider the problems of the govern-ment as real tasks needing resolution. It was an opposition which was convinced by situation, temperament, and principle that it would never share authority with the foreign ruler. The only authority to which it aspired was complete and ex-clusive control of the entire machinery of state. Until that point was reached, its only policy was opposition.

The oppositional attitude of the intellec-tuals has another point of origin far removed from the political experience of a colonial situation. In most underdeveloped countries the traditional character of

[14] Its only parallel in the West is the conduct of the Irish members in the House of Commons in the latter part of the last century and of Communistic members of European parlia-ments when they were a small minority and did not seek a popular front. The "Irish members" had considerable resonance in India and their influence still survives, even where its origin has been forgotten.

the culture sustains diffuseness in the exercise of authority. Diffuse authority, omnicompetent in the tasks facing the society, at least according to legendary beliefs, derives its legitimacy in part from its comprehensive effectiveness. Even though the substantive actions performed by such diffuse traditional authorities are no longer respected by intellectuals, the older pattern of expectation persists. Specific, delimited, impersonal, constitutional authority gives the appearance of being a weak authority, an unloving one which possesses no inner relationship with the ruled. The diffuseness of a charismatic authority is desired, and the bureaucratic rule of the foreign power or of its sovereign indigenous successor arouses little enthusiasm or even willing acknowledgment of any deeper legitimacy. The intellectuals of underdeveloped countries, despite their immersion in modern culture and their overt acceptance of modern political principles, are at bottom averse to a relatively weak, self-limiting government, even when that government is their own, bound to them by common ethnic ties, a common culture, and comradeship in the struggle for independence.

This is one of the underlying grounds for the widespread disillusionment which overcomes so many intellectuals in underdeveloped countries after independence. It must be remembered that, whatever has happened since, practically every new state of the postwar world began as a modern constitutional regime of representative institutions and public liberties. They have all had to employ modern bureaucratic methods of administration, even when they lacked the requisite personnel. They have tried to operate the rule of law. They all began as remote impersonal machines, exercising authority without the diffuseness of charisma or tradition. Their equilibrium has depended on a great charismatic personality who, at the peak of the governmental mountain, offset the distaste for bureaucratic-legal rule.

Thus, the establishment of a tradition

of opposition in political life has, as has happened so often in almost every sphere of life in underdeveloped countries, coincided with a fundamental disposition resting on an indigenous cultural tradition.

It would be wrong perhaps to claim a universal validity for a generalization which could be drawn from Max Weber's criticism of Bismarck and the paralyzing influence which his autocracy in the Reichstag exerted on the opposition parties of that body. It was Max Weber's view that the irresponsible opposition which the Bismarckian regime and its Wilhelmine successor evoked would make the opposition parties incapable of responsible, efficient rule when they were given the opportunity to govern. He also asserted—and this is more important for our present discussion—that they would become incapable of conducting themselves as a responsible opposition, working within the rules of the parliamentary game. In certain of the underdeveloped countries, this generalization does not seem to be applicable. In India, for example, certain of the intellectual politicians, and above all the Prime Minister, have shown great adaptability in turning from a condition of complete and irreconcilable opposition to a responsible hard-headed exercise of authority, and some of the socialists and independents conduct their opposition in a most intelligent and responsible manner. The same obtains in varying degrees in Ghana and in Tunisia. Certain intellectual politicians have shown considerable capacity to rule, even though they have not been as democratic or liberal as they once aspired to be or as Mr. Nehru has succeeded in being. Not a few firebrands of the days of the independence movement have turned out to be responsible parliamentarians of the highest order.

Nonetheless, much truth remains in Max Weber's proposition. The intellectuals of the underdeveloped countries since they acquired independence, insofar as they are not in authority, do incline toward an anti-political, oppositional attitude.

They are disgruntled. The form of the constitution does not please them and they are reluctant to play the constitutional game. Many of them desire to obstruct the government or give up the game of politics altogether, retiring into a negative state of mind about all institutional politics or at least about any political regime which does not promise a "clean sweep" of the inherited order.

Incivility. Although the intellectuals of the underdeveloped countries have created the idea of the nation within their own countries, they have not been able to create a nation. They are themselves the victim of that condition, since nationalism does not necessarily become citizenship. Membership in a nation which is sovereign entails a sense of affinity with the other human beings who make up the nation. It entails a sense of "partness" in a whole, a sense of sharing a common substance. This feeling of being part of the whole is the basis of a sense of concern for its well-being, and a sense of responsibility to it and for it. It transcends ineluctable divisions, softening them and rendering them tolerable to civil order, regarding them as less significant than the underlying community of those who form the nation. In political life, these dispositions form the virtue of civility.

Civility has hitherto not been one of the major features of the politicized intelligentsia of the underdeveloped countries. An intense politicization is difficult to bring into harmony with civility. Intense politicization is accompanied by the conviction that only those who share one's principles and positions are wholly legitimate members of the polity and that those who do not share them are separated by a steep barrier. The governing party in many sovereign underdeveloped states, and those intellectuals who make it up or are associated with it, tend to believe that those who are in opposition are separated from them by fundamental and irreconcilable differences. They feel that they *are* the state and the nation, and that those

who do not go along with them are not just political rivals but *total* enemies. The sentiments of the opposition are, *mutatis mutandis,* scarcely different. These are the fruits of intense politicization.

The incivility of the politicized intellectuals has a history which precedes their birth. Traditional societies, based on kinship and hierarchy, are not civil societies. They do not know the phenomenon of citizenship, since rights and obligations are not functions of membership in a polity determined by territorial boundaries. The primordial qualities of traditional societies —kinship, age, sex, locality, etc.—are not qualities which define the citizen. In a pluralistic society they are not by any means incompatible with citizenship. In the more unitary, traditional society, they suffocate incipient civility.

The moral structure of the independence movement has enabled this uncivil tradition to persist. The independence movement conceived of itself as the embodiment of the nation, and after its victory it became and conceived of itself as identical with the state. Given the oppositional dispositions which come to the surface in parliamentary and journalistic circles not attached to the government party, there often appears to be a semblance of justification for the belief of an impatient and hypersensitive government that the opposition is subversive of the state and cannot be reconciled to it.

This does not imply that there are not civil intellectuals in every underdeveloped country, some of them in the government, some of them in opposition, and some in journalism, the universities, and the other liberal professions. They are, however, in a marked minority. The traditions by which they are sustained, although they do exist in some of the states, are frail.

Three Stages in the Politics of the Intellectuals in Underdeveloped Countries

THE FIRST STAGE

(*a*) *Constitutional Liberalism.* The first efflorescence of the modern intellectual in the underdeveloped countries occurred roughly between the years when India was recovering from the trauma of the Mutiny and its repression and the First World War. In the few countries where there was anything of a class with a modern education and a certain amount of political stirring, these were the years of constitutional liberalism, eloquently and courteously argued. This first stage came considerably later to Black Africa and lasted a shorter time than it did in British India and the Middle East. In Southeast Asia, too, the course of development was greatly telescoped. The backwardness of Southeast Asia and Black Africa in the construction of modern cultural and legal institutions, and the smaller numbers of persons who went abroad for higher studies, resulted in a much smaller intellectual class than in India, and a later, briefer, and feebler life of constitutional liberalism. Where the intellectual class scarcely existed, politics could only be embryonic.

This was the stage of the politics of lawyers and journalists. Their politics were the politics of *honoratiores*. They were well-educated men, many of whom had studied in the metropolitan countries; they had absorbed and appreciated something of the metropolitan culture and the liberal constitutional political outlook, which, in the circles in which they moved in the France and Great Britain of that period, appeared to be almost unchallenged.

They were not revolutionaries and they did not always aspire to independence, at least, not in the immediate future. One of their main grievances in this earliest phase was the restriction of the right of entry of their fellow-countrymen into the civil service which ruled their country on behalf of the foreign sovereign. They also desired that legislative institutions should be a little more representative of persons like themselves. These two concerns could be interpreted crudely as a manifestation of a narrow class interest, but they were actually broader and better than that.[15] There were serious grounds, in

[15] Nor were these their only interests. They

their own self-image, for their claim to share in the administration of the country and for a vote in the determination of the budget.

They had been brought up in a hierarchical tradition in which the landowning classes and the learned, in their own view and that of others, were the possessors of a "stake in the country." Insofar as it was a country, they felt it to be "theirs," and "theirs" almost exclusively. Many came from families which had in the past exercised great influence and which, in the countryside, still continued to do so. It was therefore part of their conception of the right order of things that they should share in the ruling of their own country, under a sovereign whom they were not in the main inclined to challenge in principle.

The liberal constitutional ideas which they acquired in the course of their mainly legal studies fitted in with their conceptions. Europe was boiling with democratic agitation—the labor and socialist movements were in process of formation. In the main, however, the very small trickle of Africans and the larger numbers of Asians who before the First World War went to the metropolis for advanced studies did not, on the whole, come into contact with these circles. They wanted a liberal governmental and legal order in the administration of which they could share.

Since they were largely lawyers, they developed the rhetorical skills and the proposed the liberalization of the legal system, greater equity in its administration, and certain liberal social reforms such as the improvement of the legal position of women, the provision of more ample educational facilities, etc.

Obviously, there was some element of "class" and "self-interest" in some of their demands, such as the insistence that imported foreign manufactures should not be allowed to enjoy any advantages over indigenously produced industrial goods. The interest of the whole society, the interest of a class and of an individual might all coincide on particular issues. This is probably the most that can be credited to the charge against the first generation made by the actors who came on the political stage a little later.

self-confidence in dealing with authority which are an indispensable part of the equipment of the modern politician.[16] The structure of legal practice also gave them the time and the resources to absent themselves from their professional activities. As the occasion demanded, they were able, while still continuing to practice their professions, to devote themselves to public agitation, to attend and address meetings, to write books, pamphlets, and articles for the press, to meet representatives of their rulers from time to time in order to argue their claims, and to participate in consultative and representative bodies.

Side by side with this form of lawyers' politics, a daily and periodical press struggled to come into existence, largely in the metropolitan language but also in the indigenous languages. The journalists were not professionals. They were often political lawyers who had either left their profession or practiced it alongside of journalism; there were also among them men who had been teachers, or who had aspired to join the government service, or had actually been in governmental employ. They were usually well-educated men, with the gravity of the Victorian and Continental bourgeois liberals whom they admired. All this gave dignity and decorum to the political life of that stage of political development.

As journalists, they were not following a career in the material sense of the word. They were not trying to become rich. They were not interested in being purveyors of news and diversion. They were not seeking a livelihood in journalism. Where they could not gain their livelihood from journalism or from their auxiliary professions, they unquestioningly relied on the support of their kinsmen and patrons. They were journalists because there was a small literate public which could be

reached and rendered coherent and articulate on behalf of the ideal of constitutional government in which the best-qualified of the ruled would have some hand.

These journalists and lawyer-politicians had few followers other than themselves, i.e., like-minded men in similar stations of life, such as liberal businessmen or princes, chiefs, and landowners. Leaders and followers together constituted no more than a small group. Only in India were the absolute numbers fairly large. In the Middle East they were fewer, and in the rest of Africa and in Southeast Asia their numbers were negligible. Nonetheless they created, by their activity, the foundations of a still surviving tradition of the modern intellectuals in politics.

They did not have the field to themselves, even at the time of their greatest pre-eminence. They were being challenged by a more aggressive group, less complaisant toward their Western rulers and toward Western culture. These new rivals claimed that· constitutional tactics led nowhere. They were the forerunners of the political type which came to the center of the political arena in the second stage. During the first stage, however, there was also another trend of intellectual activity which profoundly affected subsequent political developments, though it was not in itself primarily political or even political at all.

(*b*) *Moral Renewal.* An impassioned effort of religious and moral self-renewal accompanied the development of political life of the underdeveloped countries during their colonial period. It was at first a feature of the countries which possessed conspicuous evidence of great indigenous achievements in the past—i.e., of the countries with a literary and architectural inheritance which in the midst of present degradation could remind contemporaries that their country had once been great. It was therefore also a characteristic of countries with an indigenous traditional intelligentsia made up of the custodians of sacred writings. Thus it was that in India

[16] It seems to me not accidental that even now the highest flights of Indo-Anglian prose have the rhetorical quality of high-grade lawyers addressing a court or a parliamentary body.

and in the Middle East, through much of the nineteenth century, protagonists of the traditional cultures, and particularly of the religions of Hinduism and Islam, sought to purify their inheritance, to restore it to its pristine greatness or to fuse it with modern elements. Both in India and in the Middle East, the aim was to reinstate the dignity of the traditional religious culture, and the society which was based on it, and thereby to establish its worth in the face of the encroachment of Western culture and religion.[17]

This movement to evoke a national self-consciousness, through the renewal of cultural traditions which had been allowed to decay, was not directly political. There was not much contact between the modern men who represented constitutional liberalism, and the energetic, pious traditionalists.[18] The two movements seemed to run almost independently of each other; there was no antagonism between them, often little mutual awareness.

The agents of moral renewal were not secular social reformers. They were not modern intellectuals in the sense of the word used here. They were men of the traditional culture who were sufficiently sensitive to the impact of modern culture to feel the need to reaffirm their own.[19] Their task was the cleansing of the cultural —and this meant largely religious— inheritance of their society from what they claimed were historically accidental accretions which had brought it into disrepute among modern men and allowed their country to sink in the world's esteem and in its own and, particularly, to appear enfeebled and unworthy in comparison with Western achievements. They claimed

that what was essential in their religious traditions could—by restoration and cleansing or by syncretism—be reformulated in an idiom more appropriate to the modern situation, and that if this were done, it would recommend itself to their fellow-countrymen who were needlessly and even perniciously enamored of Western culture. They were not unqualifiedly fanatical enemies of Western culture. They claimed that much of what it had to offer—particularly science, technology, and forms of organization—were necessary for the improvement of their countries and the reestablishment of their greatness among the nations. They insisted, however, that their countrymen must not lose their own souls to the West. They must instead rediscover their own essential being by the acceptance of a new and purer version of their own cultural tradition.

The older generation of modern "Victorian" intellectuals did not pay much heed to these preachments, although they were not hostile. In the next stage of political development, this effort of moral rediscovery and self-renewal had very profound repercussions. When, in the second stage, constitutional liberalism seemed to disappear or to be confined in a very narrow space, the movement of moral and religious reform was taken up and developed into a passionate nationalism. Now, even where the religious element in the traditional culture is passed over, praise of the essence of the traditional culture has become a plank in the platform of every movement for independence and of every new state.

The Second Stage. From constitutional liberalism and religious-moral renewal, the intellectuals of the colonial countries passed to a fervently politicized nationalism. With this shift, there also occurred a shift in the mode of political action and its audience.

India was the first of all the underdeveloped colonial countries to execute this movement; it was the one in which the traditional indigenous culture was richest

[17] Movements to "re-establish" the glory of African civilization are a much later product.

[18] There were of course exceptions like al-Afghani, Mohammed Abdou, and M. G. Ranade.

[19] Their influence made itself felt, however, in both India and the Middle East, primarily among modern intellectuals. They exerted little effect on their fellow traditional intellectuals, who persisted in their torpor.

and most elaborate and in which that culture had developed most systematically and comprehensively. It was also the country where the foreign rulers had been longest established in a thoroughgoing way and where the contact of the indigenous intellectuals with a metropolitan Western culture had given birth to a longer and richer modern tradition than was possessed by any other country of Asia or Africa. It was the country with the largest and most differentiated modern intelligentsia. The first long phase of fascination with the West had already begun, in the India of the 1880's, to produce from within itself a reaction in favor of more purely Indian things.

This was also the time of growing strength in the socialist movement in Europe and of the growth of anarchism. Terrorism was in the ascendancy in Russia and Ireland. Tales of the Russian underground spread in Asia, together with the repute and glory of the deeds of the "Nihilists" in Russia, the Sinn Fein in Ireland, and the Carbonari in Italy. Massini, Stepnyak, and Kropotkin were names well known among the younger generation of Indian intellectuals. Yeats was becoming a figure of weight among the literary intelligentsia and along with this went a feeling for the Irish Renaissance and a belief in the possibilities of a comparable Indian Renaissance. The writings of these *rishis* became known in India, imported from England; some of them appeared in Bengali translations.

The new generation which came to the surface of public life around the turn of the century was no longer content with constitutional agitation, or with such limited goals as more places in the Indian Civil Service and more consultative and deliberative institutions in which Indians would be amply represented. Indian traditional culture was being revived through the Ramakrishna Mission and the Arya Samaj, and a new Indian self-consciousness took hold of young men who, while not deeming themselves religious, were possessed by a

profound resonance toward traditional Indian symbols. The Maharashtrian and Bengali terrorists gave no thought to the kind of social or political order which they wished to see established. They wished only to have India free of foreign rule, free to be itself, in its own Indian way.

Parallel developments a third of a century later could be seen in areas as far apart as the Gold Coast and Egypt. A half-century later, they began to appear in East Africa. The same pattern was visible in more foreshortened form in Syria and Iraq. The proportions and the tone of the movements in these smaller countries, with much smaller intelligentsias, have been roughly what they were in India.

In these smaller countries, too, there was a tendency to regard the older generation of liberal constitutionalists and piecemeal reformers as excessively subservient to the foreign rulers and as excessively bemused by their foreign culture and their foreign forms of government. The later, populistic phase of intellectual politics, which in a variety of forms continues into the present, only intensified and made more complex and luminous an already established pattern. The generally socialistic orientation of the politics of the Asian and African intellectuals, which took form after the First World War and became preponderant after the Second World War, in a similar fashion only elaborated the inherent potentiality of intense nationalism.

The intensification of political concerns was the outgrowth of the earlier political interest, in fusion with the more acute sense of nationality which the heightened awareness of the traditional indigenous culture had helped to arouse. The politics of the "second generation" touched a very much deeper chord than that which the earlier generation had reached; it is a chord which still vibrates. The greater depth of the new political movement meant also that it was more passionate, more in the complete possession of politics.

The fundamental politicization of the intelligentsia of Asia and Africa led to the discrediting of the first liberal generation. The politics of cultured and urbane gentlemen, speaking French or English to perfection, interested in much else besides politics, was not for this generation.

The politics of the second generation received a further powerful impetus from its participation in a cosmopolitan movement, in which *foreign*, Western countries were involved. The intellectuals of the second generation, like those who preceded and those who have followed, were also held by their attachment to Western culture. The extremist nationalist movements in Asia and subsequently in Africa had a Western legitimation for their strivings. They drew inspiration and comfort from abroad, they felt that their actions were one with a mighty surge all over the world, a surge toward a new order of freedom, with possibilities unknown and unregarded.[20] This sense of being a part of the larger world infused into the politics of the second generation the permanently bedeviling tension between province and metropolis, and added, as it always does, the heat which arises from conflicting loyalties.

When the second generation was still in its youth in India, and only in conception in other Asian and African colonial countries, the Russian Revolution took place. Only a little while thereafter M. K.

Gandhi established his ascendancy over the political scene in India.[21] These two events precipitated the populistic consciousness, which had been only latent in the exacerbated nationalism which had preceded them.

The early leaders of the second generation had been deferential to "ancient traditions," in contrast to the liberal, moderate, and progressive attitude of the earlier constitutional politicians, who had not given political significance to indigenous cultural traditions. The "people" had, however, not yet acquired the eminence which was later to be their due in the political outlook of the intellectuals. Now, under the guidance of Gandhi and an attenuated Leninism, they ascended to a central position.

Socialism was no further away than a step of the imagination. The preceding generation had been neither socialist nor anti-socialist. The issue had never arisen, as long as civil-service personnel policies, the extension of representative institutions, and criticism of the "drain" had been the main objects of political debate.[22] Politics now became "total politics" and its claims on those who gave themselves to it became all-embracing. Politics in colonial countries became a vocation, without becoming professionalized. Many came to live "for" politics, but few lived "from" politics in the way in which professional

[20] The role of exiles and expatriates living in the metropolitan centers of Great Britain, France, Germany, and Switzerland helped to maintain a continuous link between the revolutionary and radical tendencies in the metropolis and those in the underdeveloped countries. These exiles and expatriates provided a sort of training school for young Asians and Africans who had gone abroad to study, and they constituted a continuous representation of the interests of their countries before the public opinion of the ruling metropolis.

Like exiles and expatriates everywhere, they also were more "uprooted" than their countrymen who either stayed at home or returned home after a few years. This "uprootedness" did not, however, diminish the intensity of their politics. Rather, the contrary.

[21] And with it, he began his march toward ascendancy over the Western colonialist conscience. A skeptical attitude about the rightfulness of imperialism had already existed in the West for a long time, but it was Gandhi more than anyone else outside the European Socialist and the Communist movements who impressed it on the consciousness of the Western educated classes. As a result, a body of Western Allies was formed and its existence was a reassurance and a stimulus to the politicized intellectuals who continued to stand in need of a sustaining tie with modern "Western" culture.

[22] In Africa after the Second World War, nationalism, intense politics, socialism, and populism came into life almost simultaneously, as if they were inseparably involved with each other.

politicians live from it. The politics of the colonial intelligentsia became in a sense more profound; that is, they came into contact with the deeper layers of the intelligentsia's existence. The politics of the intellectuals became charismatic politics.

As one might expect from charismatic politics, a tremendous pull was exerted on the youth. Leadership still lay with the lawyers and a few who had once served the government as officials and clerks[23] or had been tempted sufficiently to prepare themselves to do so. A large and important part of the following, however, consisted of students—college and university students in countries with colleges and universities and high school students where these were absent. A great deal of the clamor and volatility of the politics of the second generation of the intellectuals came from the students.

The Third Stage. The third stage of intellectual politics sees the intellectuals in power in a sovereign state, ruled by an indigenous elite.

With this stage the intellectuals who have reaped the fruits of the struggle become dissociated from the intellectual class. A schism occurs in the corps of intellectual-politicians. One sector comes into power and takes to it like a fish to water. The exercise of authority—which is not identical with the efficient exercise of authority—seems to be almost as natural as breathing to those intellectuals who are in power. To an increasing extent, they see themselves as different from the intellectuals who do not share their power, and whom they chide as naggers, unreasonable critics, backsliders from the great national cause. The intellectuals in power feel themselves less continuous with the intellectual class than they did during the struggle

for independence. As the burdens and challenges of office preoccupy them, and as they spend so much of their time with party bosses and machine-men who have never been or who long since ceased to be intellectuals, their own image of themselves as intellectuals wanes and they become more sensitive to the anti-political dispositions of their old companions.

This drift toward schism is aggravated by the fact that the opposition becomes the magnet which draws the intellectuals. Although within the political elite, at the peak of government there are many who were once intellectuals by education, vocation, or disposition and who have now become hardened politicians, no longer paying any attention to things of intellectual interest. Those who remain intellectuals in vocation and disposition seem to find their natural habitat on the opposite benches. There—and in common rooms and cafés—gather the intellectuals who in their outlook, in their studies and their self-identification, remain intellectuals.

The transformation of the intellectuals in power discloses the duality of the oppositional mentality. The hatred of authority is often no more than a facet of the fascination and love that it evokes. When they come to power, intellectuals who have hated it quickly allow the identification with it, against which they struggled previously, to come into full bloom. They attach to themselves the regalia of authority and feel that they and the state are now identical. Whereas during the struggle for independence, they felt that they represented the nation and that all who disagreed with them were outside the national community and had allowed their souls to be possessed by the foreigner, now when they are in power, they regard themselves and the state as identical and all those who disagree with them as enemies of the state.[24]

23 Where there were few indigenous lawyers or others with higher education, leadership was exercised by clerks with secondary or elementary education. The educated, the *évolues*—intellectuals—have kept the lead, the highly educated when they have been available, the less well-educated where the former were lacking.

24 Mr. Nehru is something of an exception, although he too regards the opposition as an unavoidable pestilence, as an inconvenient

On the other side of the floor, where it is allowed to exist, the oppositional mentality retains all of its old forms. Bureaucratic administration is criticized as too remote and too impersonal. The government is charged with corruption; it is alleged to be "too distant" from the people, and to be the betrayer of the national idea. It is accused of damaging the reputation of the country in the world, or of turning the country over to a new form of foreign control.

The oppositional mentality of the third stage, however, possesses one feature which the second did not possess—i.e., disillusionment. Whereas the opposition of the second generation imagined an amorphously happy condition once their antagonists were removed, the oppositional mentality of the post-colonial period has no such utopian euphoria to assuage its present melancholy.

Oppositionalism, which was so involved in an intense politicization, tends among some of those who are out of power to shrivel into an anti-political passivity. It is not that politics no longer engages the attention. It still does, but among many intellectuals it has become a source of despondent inaction.

Among others, a quite substantial bloc, it flows into a more rigid form of activistic extremism. In some instances, this extremist alternative to passivity takes on a traditionalistic guise; in others, it assumes a Leninist visage. Both of these foster the intense and total rejection of the muddled, compromising, and often compromised, incumbent government, in the name of a higher ideal.

The Prospects of the Intellectuals in the Political Life of the New States

Practically every new state has begun its career with a commitment to a regime of

representative government and public liberties. Whatever might be the democratic and consultative elements in the indigenous tradition of government, the particular constitution which was actually chosen to give form to self-government is evidence of the role of intellectuals in the establishment of the new states. It was only through the influence of the intellectuals in contact with the modern political ideas which circulated in the larger world that this decision could have been made. This alone would be sufficient to testify to the still living inheritance of the notables who peopled the first stage of modern political life in the then colonial countries.

The fate of the new states, whether they persist and flourish as democracies, or whether they regress into more oligarchical forms of government, is as undeterminable as anything which lies in the future. As long, however, as they do not disintegrate into tribal and local territorial sovereignties, and as long as they at least aspire to be "modern," the intellectuals will go on playing a large role in the fulfillment of whatever possibilities fortune allots to their societies.

In most of the new states, the intellectuals still constitute a notable part of the ruling political elite, although their position is no longer as preponderant as when politics were a charismatic movement. Politics, as the new states were consolidated, became a profession and ceased to be a calling or a mission. The emerging professional politician, military or civilian in origin, is forced to be less of an intellectual in his outlook. The inevitability of the formation of a political machine has meant, and will continue even more to mean, that organizers with little intellectual disposition, interest, or sympathy will move into a more prominent position in the political elite. Back-benchers and party functionaries will include a very considerable proportion of place-holders, and the tasks they will have to perform will not be very attractive to intellectuals, living in the traditions of modern intellectuals.

[*footnote 24 continued*
part of the community which remains, notwithstanding, as much a part of the community as he himself is. At the other extreme is that other intellectual in politics, Dr Nkrumah, who regards any criticism or disagreement as *staatsfeindlich*.

Nonetheless, even on the government benches, if the regime continues to be more or less democratic there will remain some readiness of the professional party leaders to receive and sponsor intellectuals. The prestige of modern education will continue to be high and any political party and government will therefore wish to draw on its beneficiaries. Furthermore, the reservoir of persons available for political leadership will continue to be limited in the foreseeable future; this will force the party leaders to look in the intellectuals' direction, however reluctantly. At the same time, however, the oppositional tendencies of intellectuals and the hypersensitivity to criticism on the part of politicians of any sort—and of the politicians of new states in particular—will add to this reluctance.

Opposition parties, insofar as they are allowed to exist, will certainly draw on intellectuals for their critical ideas concerning the government and for leadership and following. Such parties are their natural home.

If the underdeveloped countries become completely oligarchical and are ruled by a military junta or a one-party state, the role of intellectuals in political life in the narrower sense will certainly decline. The diminution of public political life will tend to narrow the area permitted to intellectuals. Even then, single-party regimes are likely, because of their ideological nature, to find a place for some intellectuals within their leading circles.[25]

[25] The professional army officer in the new states is to a certain extent an intellectual since he, especially in the technical branches, is the recipient of a modern education. In fact, the intrusion of the military into politics in the Middle East, at least, may be partly attributed to their attachment to modern ideas about order, efficiency, and probity in government, ideas which are not part of the indigenous tradition of government and which come to them through their modern training. The military *coups d'états* which have occurred in many of the new states may be interpreted as, at least in part, revolutions of the technological intelligentsia, acting on behalf of modern ideas of efficiency and progress.

Regardless of the fate of democracy in underdeveloped countries, intellectuals will undoubtedly continue to be called upon for the civil service and for higher education. There will be increasing scope for intellectuals as the governments expand the range of their activities and as the demand grows for highly qualified persons for engineering, teaching, publicity and propaganda, health and social services, and research in social and natural sciences.

If the new states avoid the fate of the Latin American countries in the first century of their independence, and progress economically and socially, then indifferently of the political regime which rules them, the intellectual classes will become larger and more differentiated, and more fully incorporated into their own cultural institutional system in a variety of technological, administrative, educational, and therapeutic capacities.

This incorporation of the intellectuals into their own societies will depend to a large extent on the establishment of an equilibrium between the demand for and the supply of intellectuals. If there always is such a surplus of university and college graduates that their salaries are low and many of them have to take posts which they regard as unsuitable, the process of incorporation will be obstructed. Instead the oppositional mentality will go on reproducing itself. Where a public political life is permitted, there they will be a perpetual source of unsettledness.[26]

[26] This, in turn, would increase the demand for an ideological oligarchy, from outside the government, and would also impel the government itself to adopt oligarchical measures.

There is also the opposite danger of a disequilibrium in the relations between the intellectuals and the central institutional system arising from an excessive demand for intellectuals in technological and administrative roles. In countries which entered upon independence with an insufficient supply of qualified intellectuals and a very scanty complement of intellectual institutions, it is definitely possible to draw practically all of the best intellectuals into executive and technological roles, leaving too few for civil

Let us imagine that the economics of the new states develop toward greater productivity and that a measure of liberal political life survives the burdens under which the new states now labor. The intellectual classes will become more diversified than they are at present, as they find employment in applied science and technology, in governmental, industrial, and commercial administration, in scientific and scholarly research, and in the profession of letters. With this diversification, there will be less unity of sentiment, less sense of a common identity among them. The "intellectuals" will become only one part of the educated class and a situation which already exists in the advanced countries will emerge.

There will be more specialization, more philistinism, and a less general cultural sympathy in the new intelligentsia than in the old. The new intelligentsia will also be much less political in its outlook and more practical and professional. Each intellectual profession will, as it has long since done in the advanced countries, nurture its own traditions and ways of working. As in the past, these traditions will draw on the more differentiated and more elaborate intellectual traditions of the advanced countries. Creativity will come to be more appreciated and one necessary condition for its realization will thus be provided. The intellectuals of the underdeveloped countries will cease in the course of this process to be as dependent and provincial as they are now. They will become, as some already are, full citizens, with completely equal status, in the intellectual community of the world.

The opportunities for fruitful and satis-

[*footnote 26 continued*
and intellectual functions. The rapid growth of the public services and the general trend toward the governmental pre-emption of so many diverse functions might well result in too small a proportion of the intellectual classes being left free for independent creative work and for vital activity in that publicistic borderland between the intellectual and the political.

fying employment of the skills of the intellectuals in the various spheres of civil and economic life and the establishment of absorbing and guiding traditions of an autonomous creativity in intellectual life proper will foster an attenuation of ideological dispositions. It can never eradicate them but it can reduce the commonness of their occurrence and mollify their asperity. Many with political interests will no longer feel the urgent obligation to participate directly in day-to-day political life. More of them will be content to play an equally vital but less immediate part in the formation of the life of their countries. They will concern themselves less than they do now with the issues of the here and now, and will deal with problems which are of longer-run significance, more remote from the immediate issues of party politics and of the prospects and favors of the incumbent political elite. The indirect influence on politics which comes from the cultivation of the matrix of opinion, and from the provision of the personnel and the institutional conditions of long-term development, will bring satisfaction to a larger proportion than it now does, and politicians will perhaps learn to appreciate the equal and perhaps even greater value to the community of this kind of activity on the part of intellectuals.

Their direct participation in politics will probably continue to have a radical bent. The traditions of the modern intellectual are too deeply rooted and the tendency is too intrinsic to the exercise of intellectual powers for this to be avoided— even if it were ever desirable. The radicalism of the intellectual's politics need not however be revolutionary or ideological; it can also work within the civil order. In the espousal of this standpoint at the center of political decision, in party councils, in parliaments and in cabinets, the intellectual will continue to have a unique and indispensable role, the abdication of which cannot be compensated by purely intellectual creativity or the efficient performance of executive, technological, and educational functions. In order, however, for this possibility to exist, the political society—the civil order itself—must first come into existence.

This brings us to one of the prototypical paradoxes of political development. For the intellectuals to inherit their true estate, they must live in a political society. But this civil order cannot be achieved unless the intellectuals, who would be among its greatest beneficiaries, help, against the greatest difficulties, to bring it about. Some of these difficulties reside within the intellectuals themselves, within the political and cultural traditions which enter into their constitution. The outcome then depends on whether those intellectuals who speak for civility in a modern society will by their talents, virtue, and good fortune be able to outweigh their own inhibitions, the dense incivility of their fellow-intellectuals, and the rocky obduracy of the traditional order.

INDONESIA'S POLITICAL SYMBOLS AND THEIR WIELDERS*

Herbert Feith

I

A striking feature of politics in Indonesia, as in some other new states, is the great importance of the government's symbolic activity—gestures, ceremonial, and ritual on the one hand, propaganda and indoctrination on the other. The Indonesian government of the post-1958 period allots immense resources to creating and maintaining particular attitudes and states of mind, in ways which often detract greatly from the effectiveness of its administrative and economic performance. This

SOURCE. Herbert Feith, "Indonesia's Political Symbols and Their Wielders," *World Politics*, **16**, 79–97, October 1963.

* The research on which this article is based was done in August–December 1961, when I visited Indonesia as a Research Fellow in Pacific History of the Australian National University. An earlier version was presented at the August 1962 conference of the Australian Political Studies Association in Canberra. Some of its formulations have also been included in my essay, "Dynamics of Guided Democracy," in Ruth T. McVey, ed., *Indonesia* (New Haven, 1963), 309–409.

article describes this symbolic activity and suggests some hypotheses which may help to account for its importance.

The year 1958 was a watershed in Indonesian politics in a number of respects. The middle of that year saw the reduction to guerrilla proportions of the regionalist rebellion which had broken out in February–March 1958. The effective defeat of this Sumatra-Sulawesi rebellion, together with the "takeovers" of the remaining Dutch enterprises in December 1957, served to put an end to a two-year period of turbulent transition, the death-throes period of the party and parliamentary system which had operated between 1949 and 1956.[1]

The five years since 1958, often called the years of Guided Democracy, have brought a variety of changes. There has been sharp economic decline, with only some sections of the economy recovering from the shocks of the earlier years of

[1] I have argued the case for this periodization in Feith, *The Decline of Constitutional Democracy in Indonesia* (Ithaca, N.Y., 1962), 578ff.

political transition, and with overall levels of output remaining markedly lower than before 1956. While food production for domestic use has risen somewhat, export earnings have fallen seriously and the manufacturing sector has been working at levels far below capacity. Prices rose by approximately 25–30 per cent per annum until late 1961 and have been rising at something like 100 per cent per year since then.[2] Partly in consequence of inflation, there has been a serious aggravation of the old administrative maladies of corruption, overregulation, overstaffing and ineffectiveness of legal controls. At the same time government power has grown, in weight and particularly in scope, and politics has lost more and more of its earlier openness.

But top power has remained in the same hands as in mid-1958, being shared between President Soekarno and the leadership of the army. The position of these two in relation to one another has fluctuated a great deal in the course of the five years. Moreover a major change has taken place since early 1962, with President Soekarno using the last stages of the West Irian campaign to reduce the power of the more vigorously anti-Soekarno elements in the army, weakening the army's capacity to act as a single political organization and then pushing through the lifting of martial law (on May 1, 1963).[3] Finally, Soekarno–army conflict has become less important in the month-to-month politics of Djakarta because of civilian–military interpenetration, particularly as a result of the new

organizations in which officers work with civilians in civilian tasks and of the schemes in which civilians receive military training. And this has increased the relative importance of the entourage type of politics which has existed alongside Soekarno–army politics throughout the post-1958 period, the rise and fall of rival cliques linked with top individuals in the President's circle. However, the President and the army leaders continue to be the chief determiners of government action; there is still much competition and conflict between them; and there has been no change in the alliances which link each of them with other groups in Indonesian society, Soekarno with the Communists and most radical nationalists, the army with the Moslem parties and anti-Communist elements generally. Thus, it may be useful to consider the five-year period as an entity.

Within the power-sharing arrangement which has developed between Soekarno and the army leaders in this period, symbol-wielding has always been the field of the President. The army has been the preponderant power in regional government, in the running of the old Dutch enterprises, and in much of economic management generally, as well as in the handling of rebellions. Soekarno, on the other hand, has had an overwhelming say in matters of foreign policy. He has had the initiative in most of public politics. And it is he who has dominated symbolic activity. He has led the sustained effort to maintain a mystique and sense of momentum in political affairs. He has exercised a conspicuous initiative in almost all of the government's diverse efforts to heighten national pride. And almost all formulations of government ideology have come from him. The army leaders have done a great deal of speech-making, too. They have played a big part in the agencies established to inculcate the government's ideology. And they have developed and propagated a number of doctrines of their own, justifying the army's exercise of

[2] See Douglas S. Paauw, "From Colonial to Guided Economy," in McVey, ed., 155–243; U.S. Economic Survey Team to Indonesia, *Indonesia: Perspective and Proposals for United States Economic Aid. A Report to the President of the United States* (New Haven, Yale University, Southeast Asia Studies, Special Publication, 1962); D. D. Humphrey, "Indonesia's National Plan for Economic Development," *Asian Survey*, **2** (December 1962), 12–21; Economist Intelligence Unit, *Indonesia* (Annual Supplement; London, May 1963).

[3] See J. D. Legge, "Indonesia After West Irian," *Australian Outlook*, **17** (April 1963), 13–16.

civilian functions—doctrines of territorial warfare and people's defense, of the army's role as leader of the country's "functional groups" (workers, peasants, youth, women, etc.), and of the army's civic mission. But they have not attempted to challenge the President's conspicuous monopoly of leadership in symbolic activity addressed to society as a whole.

The symbolic themes which Soekarno has employed can be considered in five broad categories, solidarity and leadership, radical renewal, the demands of the people, national strength, and national identity. Solidarity, national unity, and leadership were particularly important among the themes by which the overthrow of the parliamentary regime was justified. Thus the President argued for a "Guided Democracy," a "democracy with leadership," and a "democracy of all heaving together" to replace the existing "liberal democracy" and "50 per cent plus one democracy." Subsequently he placed great stress on "overall planning," on the "Guided Economy," and "Socialism *à la* Indonesia." The nominated parliament established in 1960 is called a Gotong Rojong (Mutual Aid) Parliament, and party life is said to be established on the principle of NASAKOM (the unity of Nationalists, Religious People, and Communists).

Equally important are the themes of radical and revolutionary renewal. Soekarno had made frequent calls in the years after 1949, what is now officially called the "liberal period," for a "return to the rails of the Revolution," a return to the "spirit of 1945," and this was further intensified in 1959 when he decreed the reintroduction of the 1945 constitution. Since then he has placed particular stress on the doctrine that "Our National Revolution is still unfinished," that "this is still a period of Revolution." From this basis he has gone on to call for initiative, enthusiasm, confidence, dynamism, and momentum, denouncing conservatism, reformism, compromise, hesitancy, routine,

formalism, and legalism. Soekarno appears to reject the present, seeing it as largely a product of the colonial and liberal (1949–59) past, and as redeemed only to the extent that there is movement toward the "just and prosperous society" of the future. Hence he constantly stresses the need for reordering, reshaping, and "retooling." One of his speeches given particularly great prominence in the government indoctrination program is entitled "Building the World Anew."

The demands of the people, national strength, and national personality or identity are lesser but still important themes. The Indonesian Revolution is a People's Revolution, the President insists, and the Mandate of the People's Suffering must be carried into effect. An end must be put to "*l'exploitation de l'homme par l'homme*," he says, and quickly, for "the stomach does not wait." In addition he stresses the need to do battle with imperialism, colonialism and, more recently, neo-colonialism. This is to be done partly by military might, but above all by developing the power potential of the Indonesian masses. Finally Soekarno exhorts his people to be true to their national identity. This means that they should shun rock-and-roll and cha-cha-cha on the one hand, and liberalism, individualism, and intellectualism on the other. The positive content of national identity is left largely unspecified, though there is some idealization of such traditional village practices as *musjawarah* (consultation), *mufakat* (deciding issues according to a felt "sense of the meeting"), and *gotong rojong* (mutual assistance).

These various themes are expounded with the greatest vigor on all public occasions. The President leads, making a great number of speeches every week and constantly rearranging his symbols in new clusters: the Five Principles of the Political Manifesto; the Message of the People's Suffering; Revolution, Socialism, and Leadership; the Threefold Command of the People, and so on. And every other public figure takes his cues from him, exhorting, instructing, and rallying his listeners in these same terms, whether they be soldiers, civil servants, businessmen, journalists, artists, workers, or peasants.

Speech-making is accompanied by gestures, ceremonial, and ritual. Thus special days abound, from National Awakening Day to Electricity and Gas Day, and each and every one is an occasion for ceremonies. Badges and medals are conferred with increasing frequency. First stones are laid and first hoes swung. New and more "national" and "revolutionary" names are given to streets, business houses and shops, movie theaters and groups of musical entertainers, mountains, and the Indian (Indonesian) Ocean. New beginnings in a variety of prosaic activities are ceremonially made under the aegis of dramatic and urgent-sounding phrases; thus a "Prosperity Command" was created to increase rice production and students are "mobilized" to cope with teacher shortages in outlying parts of the country. And there are ceremonial endings, too, as when a large province is declared free from illiteracy.

Perhaps the most striking instance of ritual being infused into economic activity is the Eight-Year Overall Development Plan. This plan was drawn up by a 70-man board headed by a prominent lawyer, poet, ideologue, and non-economist, and finally presented in the form of 17 volumes, 8 parts, and 1945 clauses, these numerals spelling out the date of Indonesia's proclamation of independence. President Soekarno praised the plan as "rich in fantasy" and that it certainly is.[4] On January 1, 1961, the plan was ceremonially inaugurated, with the President swinging a hoe. And on August 17 (Independence Day), 1961, the President opened an exhibition picturing the tasks to be accomplished through it. But for all the radical changes for which its highly ambitious

[4] See Humphrey, "Indonesia's National Plan" and Guy J. Pauker, "Indonesia's Eight-Year Development Plan," *Pacific Affairs*, **34** (Summer 1961), 115–130.

targets would seem to call, the plan has so far had very little effect on the actual functioning of the economy.

The passion for symbols is seen further in the great importance accorded to the insignia of national prestige and power. Thus Indonesia has recently acquired an atomic reactor and begun to build a steel mill in West Java. Immense resources were devoted for over two years to building stadia, hotels, and highway projects in preparation for the Asian Games held in Djakarta in August 1962. Since then preparations have been made for a further large international sports festival, the first "Games of the New Emerging Forces," to be held in Djakarta in November 1963. Work is now near completion on a high National Monument in the center of the capital and a West Irian Struggle Monument nearby. Next in line is a fourteen-story department store in Djakarta and after that comes a Freedom Mosque, to be the largest mosque in the world. Among the most highly prized of recently acquired insignia of prestige are the military ones: a Sverdlovsk-class cruiser, destroyers and "W"-class submarines, MIG-21 fighters, TU-16 long-range bombers, and various types of missiles.

The same period has seen a great increase in the emphasis placed on the personal authority of the President. Soekarno has become more Sultan-like in the externals of his behavior, and in May 1963 he was named President for life. Similarly he has acquired a number of new titles, such as Great Leader of the Revolution, Commander of Mental Operations, and Great Son of West Irian. Since mid-1958 he has made seven overseas trips of between two and ten weeks' duration, usually to a large number of countries and usually with an entourage of from thirty to fifty men, including many of the top government leaders on whom important decisions must wait. In the same period, at least nine foreign heads of state have visited Indonesia and seven heads of government, as well as vice-presidents, crown princes, numerous foreign ministers and ministers of defense, generals, admirals, and cosmonauts. Each of these visitors has received bountiful hospitality, the attentions of numerous government leaders, and often cheering crowds—workers given paid days off by government order.

Finally, a great deal of government effort has gone into the elaboration and inculcation of an explicit national ideology. The tenets of the creed were set down in the President's speech of August 17 (Independence Day), 1959, and then annotated and systematized by the Supreme Advisory Council. Thus there is now an authoritative exposition of the Basis, Aims, and Duties of the Indonesian Revolution, the Social Forces of the Indonesian Revolution, its Nature, Future, and Enemies, and its General Program, covering the political, economic, social, mental, and cultural fields, and the field of security.[5] Several months after the celebrated speech had been given, its central message was said to consist of five ideas—the 1945 Constitution, Socialism *à la* Indonesia, Guided Democracy, Guided Economy, and Indonesian Personality—and the first letters of these five phrases were put together to make the acronym USDEK. With the "Political Manifesto" becoming "Manipol," the new creed became known as "Manipol-USDEK."

Since that time officials, newspaper editors, and political parties have been obliged to take repeated vows affirming their belief in Manipol-USDEK. In addition Indoctrination Committees have been set to work in the schools and universities, among soldiers, civil servants, and employees of government firms, and to a much smaller extent in the population at large, in an effort to see that the doctrines of Manipol-USDEK are enthusiastically accepted.

II

The great prominence of political symbolism in Indonesia is sometimes explained in historical and psycho-cultural terms, with references to the religious character of kingship in pre-colonial days, to the country's long history of messianic movements, or to the continuing importance of status and ceremony in Indonesian society generally.[6] Alternatively (or complementarily) it is said that the government's concentration of attention on symbolic activities results directly from the experience of social and political change. Where economic life is rapidly becoming more market-oriented, cities and towns are growing fast, and more and more men are acquiring modern education, and particularly where old patterns of social relations have been destroyed by war or revolution, many individuals are confronted by the challenge of new values and cognitive patterns and consequently thrown into psychological disarray. Such men, it is argued, can often most easily resolve the conflicts within themselves by accepting a schematic ideology and participating in an expressive (non-instrumental) form of politics, a politics of heroes and villains, of "the movement" and "the enemy," of utopias and betrayals (compromise being a form of betrayal) and of multifarious sacred emblems.

Each of these two types of explanation contains elements of validity, but it would be gross oversimplification to use either of them, or both together, to supply an overall explanation of the prominence of symbolic activity in Indonesian government practice. To do this would be to assume a one-way, "reflective" relationship between government actions and the

[5] Both the speech and the catechism based on it are reproduced in Sukarno, *Towards Freedom and the Dignity of Man* (Djakarta, Department of Foreign Affairs, Republic of Indonesia, 1961). See also *Manipol-USDEK in Question and Answer* (Djakarta: Department of Information, Republic of Indonesia, 1961).

[6] See, e.g., J. M. van der Kroef, "Javanese Messianic Expectations: Their Origin and Cultural Context," *Comparative Studies in Society and History*, 1 (June 1959), 299–323; and Selo Soemardjan, "Some Social and Cultural Implications of Indonesia's Planned and Unplanned Development," *Review of Politics*, 25 (January 1963), 64–90.

attitudes and expectations prevailing in society. The Indonesian government is certainly limited in its choices of action by prevailing attitudes, perspectives, and demands in Indonesian society, and by the psychological needs of key groups of that society. But it also plays a major part in creating these attitudes and needs. Hence historical, psycho-cultural, and sociological explanations are of great importance in accounting for the *limiting conditions* within which the government wields political symbols. But they can be of only second-instance relevance to our central question of why the government devotes such great resources to symbol-wielding activity.

The purpose of this article is to propose a general framework of explanation for this phenomenon, a framework which is fundamentally political in that it rests on a concern with how the Indonesian government keeps itself in power, but which nevertheless leaves room for the historical, psycho-cultural, and sociological explanations given of political orientations in Indonesian society (and in the governing group itself).

How then does its intensive use of symbols help the Indonesian government to maintain its power? There is some evidence that it helps the government to solve economic and administrative problems. Exhortation in terms of nationalist ideals often helps to induce men to work in remote areas of the archipelago. And the ritual of special days often stimulates the performance of humdrum tasks by providing what Hirschman has called "pacing devices."[7] Against this, however, must be set the far stronger evidence that symbol-wielding as currently practiced by the Indonesian government results in lowered administrative and economic effectiveness. What is important here is not the time that civil servants spend at ceremonies or workers at mass rallies or at airport roads when foreign dignitaries arrive. It is rather the creation of an atmosphere or

[7] Albert O. Hirschman, *The Strategy of Economic Development* (New Haven, 1961), 24–28.

climate of opinion which is thoroughly unfavorable to the solving of practical problems. This is an atmosphere in which economic tasks are seen as of secondary importance, ideological truth and political enthusiasm being seen as the highest needs of state. It is an atmosphere in which economic realism is suspect as indicative of hesitancy and irresolution. And it is an atmosphere in which an administrator's concern with rules, precedent, and the specific definition of tasks is readily denounced as the product of a colonial and unrevolutionary mentality.

But if the net effect of symbol manipulation for economic and administrative problem-solving is negative, there is no doubt that it has positive effects as far as direct political control is concerned. Thus government propaganda can be seen as part of a process which operates also through press control, the restriction of free association in groups, and the (sporadic) censorship of mails. Vows and demands for a narrowly focused loyalty are aids to the strengthening of political controls over the bureaucracy, along with the "retooling" of government employees—that is, the pensioning off of political undesirables and their removal from line posts to staff posts. Moreover the government's demand that one should repeatedly reaffirm one's support for its ideological formulations is an important check on the flow of political information, for it forces men to withhold or disguise the expression of their political feelings in many situations. In this way it contributes to an atmosphere of hypocrisy, mistrust, and confusion. This in turn helps to paralyze men's political energies and to lower their effective expectations, leading many to conclude that "Things are bad, but what can we do?" and then often that "Well, come to think of it, it could all be a lot worse."

But perhaps as important as the function of political control is that of making the government legitimate in the eyes of some parts of the population. Some symbolic actions help to do this because they are in effect promises of future achievement; the ceremony to inaugurate the Eight-Year Plan is an example. Others constitute achievements in themselves, achievements which are secured at relatively low cost and are readily visible. Here the frequent response is "Prices are terribly high and there is an awful lot of corruption, but at least the rest of the world has to take notice of Indonesia these days. If you listen to our air force planes breaking the sound barrier or watch the way we are getting the key positions in one Asian-African organization after another, you can't say that we are not getting anywhere."

In addition, a great deal of symbolism serves to create a favorable image of what the government *is*. Thus the President's trips, and especially the visits of powerful overseas leaders to Indonesia, heighten his prestige as a world leader. By speaking frequently of the suffering of the people, he establishes an image of himself as deeply concerned with the fate of the poor and the downtrodden. And by interpreting the tasks and duties of the times, he meets the traditional expectation that kings should link the present with the past and future and give human life its appropriate place in the cosmic order.

Moreover, the themes of the government's ideology are morally appealing to many Indonesians, and so repeated reference to them helps the government to elicit a voluntary acceptance of its authority by these persons. This may well be true in some measure for people at all levels of society, but on this there is little or no evidence. Hence the argument here is confined to responses in what may be called the political public, a group roughly coterminous with the two million or so Indonesians, mostly city and town dwellers and wearers of white collars, who regularly read newspapers.[8]

The anti-Western themes of Manipol-USDEK undoubtedly draw strong positive responses within this public. Many of the members of the Indonesian political public have had humiliating and hurtful experiences at the hands of the white West, and others are ready to blame the West (or "imperialism") for their sense of discomfort about alien influences of various kinds. "Modernity is good, Westernness is bad" is a common way of resolving a common and acute ambivalence. But indeed there is no need to refer to psychological mechanisms to explain why the politically aware sections of the Indonesian community should support a posture of radical protest at the international distribution of wealth, prestige, and power.

In addition, Manipol-USDEK helps many members of the political public to a voluntary acceptance of government authority because of its very ambiguity. Members of different groups in this public read mutually contradictory meanings into its formulations, and so members of each of these groups are provided with acceptable moral grounds for political obedience. Thus numerous Communists are persuaded that Manipol-USDEK is a progressive creed and a powerful weapon against the imperialists. On the other hand, many anti-Communists are convinced that the creed is essentially anti-Communist, and indeed the most subtly effective of ideological means for thwarting Communists.[9]

(and a great deal of convenience) in the working hypothesis that the Indonesian government's effective accountability is limited to the members of this public. I have employed this political public concept for the 1949–57 period in *Decline of Constitutional Democracy in Indonesia* (see especially pp. 108–113), but would add that the usefulness of the concept is more restricted when applied to the more authoritarian situation of the post-1958 period.

[9] This emphasis on the government's use of the Manipol-USDEK ideology should not obscure the fact that the various (legal) parties and groups also use it for their own purposes. Manipol-USDEK having become the language of all public political discourse, particular parties have seized on particular formulations

[8] This concept of the political public is derived largely from the theory of mobilization presented in Karl W. Deutsch, *Nationalism and Social Communication* (New York, 1953), 100–104, 240. There is some initial plausibility

Similarly the ideology has appeal for men whose political outlook reflects traditional ideas, for others whose principal concern is to see Indonesia become a modern nation, and for others again who want release from the confusions of a turbulent period of transition. Many of the more traditionally oriented members of the political public are attracted to Manipol-USDEK by its emphasis on all pulling together, on national interests being placed above the selfish interests of individuals and groups. Many of the same persons are convinced that the President is right in saying that what Indonesia needs above all is men with the right state of mind, the right spirit, the true patriotic dedication. "Returning to our National Personality" is attractive to some who want to withdraw from the challenges of modernity, and also to others who want to believe in the current political leadership but see it as failing in the central tasks of modernization. And for traditionally oriented members of some Indonesian communities—notably, for many Javanese of no strong Islamic conviction—there is real meaning in the various complex schemes which the President presents in elaboration of Manipol-USDEK, schemes explaining the meaning of the current stage of history in relation to others.

For those within the political public who want to see rapid modernization the government's ideology offers an emphasis on socialism and planning. President Soekarno often speaks in praise of science and occasionally of the need for agricultural mechanization. And modernists are often willing to read their own ideas into the government's repeated denunciations of the "old order" and the "old established forces."

Perhaps most important of all, Manipol-

[*footnote 9 continued*
of the ideology and made them their own. Thus repeated references to the Pantja Sila (Five Principles, including The One Deity) now characterize a group as being anti-Communist, whereas accusations of "pseudo-Manipolism" are typically made by Communists.

USDEK has appeal to men for whom the world has become increasingly unintelligible as a result of disruptive social change. To these men it promises to give a *pegangan* —literally, something to which to hold fast. It is not so much what this *pegangan* is that is attractive, and indeed that question leads all too easily back to the deplored disagreements and sense of confusion. It is simply that the President declares that he is offering a *pegangan* and that this is widely felt to be needed. Values and cognitive patterns being in flux and in conflict with one another, many are looking for dogmatic and schematic formulations of the political good. Thus one common response to Manipol-USDEK is "It may not be a very good or complete ideology, but an ideology is certainly what we need."

After all this has been said, it must be added that Manipol-USDEK is actively resented by many in the political public, including, prominently, a large group of modernist Moslems, supporters of the banned Masjumi party. Whereas the government's creed can perhaps be described as representing a highest common factor of political orientations between traditionalists and (one variety of) modernists, it is certainly not a compromise between the nationalist ideology of President Soekarno's Pantja Sila or Five Principles and the political ideology of Islam. Thus references to the legitimizing power of the official creed should not be taken to suggest that it has created a broad consensus. Its importance lies rather in the fact that it has helped to organize voluntary support in one section of society, and within the government's own apparatus, for coercive action against a smaller recalcitrant section.

Finally, political symbols have a function which is not easily classified as either coercive or legitimizing, but in fact falls between them, in the middle range of the continuum between direct compulsion and voluntary obedience. Symbolic activities play a major part in the process of manipulation, the structuring of political situations in such a way that attention is focused on interests and values which are shared by the government and the governed. Thus ceremonies recalling the heroism of the nationalist movement and the Revolution make it possible for the government to maintain a conspicuous initiative in the country's affairs, and to do so as a "leader" rather than a "ruler." Similar effects flow from all foreign policy actions which give rise to a feeling of national pride. They flowed from most of what was done under the banner of the liberation of West Irian—from the government's actions in abrogating diplomatic relations with Holland in August 1960 and subsequently denying Great Britain the right to be Holland's diplomatic representative, from the purchase of arms specifically designated as being for the territory's liberation, from air-raid training and from the military drilling of students and others in the streets of the cities. More recently they have flowed from government and government-encouraged actions carried out in support of the Azahari revolt of December 1962 in Brunei and as part of the "confrontation" of Malaysia. And they flow from the encouragement given by some parts of the government—notably, the more strongly anti-Soekarno and anti-Communist sections of the army—to sentiment against the locally domiciled Chinese; for instance, the statements of army commanders, blaming commodity shortages on "foreigners who are still in control of our economy."

In all of these ways the government highlights conflict between Indonesians and outsiders, and by the same token averts conflict between rulers and ruled inside the community of Indonesians. The government's involvement in these kinds of activities is largely continuous. But their importance is particularly great when disaffection becomes immediately threatening to some of the key groups in power, as it has on a number of occasions in our five-year period; for in these crisis situations, channeling of political emo-

tions is a principal means of inducing catharsis.[10]

Manipol-USDEK as a creed has a similar function, also creating a manipulated but still quasi-voluntary acceptance of authority. In effect it enables the government to build on the genuine appeal which the nationalism of 1945 still has within the political public. Most members of this public are unwilling to accept the whole of the government's interpretation of the existing situation, the view that the nation is moving determinedly toward progress and greatness, restrained in this only by the continuing need to struggle against imperialism, liberalism, and individualism. But many of these men are equally unprepared to reject this view entirely. Outright rejection of the government's claim is possible for a small group of fully trained Communists and well-schooled members of the now-banned modernist Moslem party, Masjumi, men who have clear and firmly held alternative systems of belief and interpretation; and it is possible for a small group of sophisticated intellectuals, particularly persons who have lived overseas long enough to see nationalism from the outside. But members of the political public who are not schooled in any such alternative way of looking at the world are almost obliged to take the view that "There is something in what the government says" or that "Manipol-USDEK is basically the right idea; it is only its execution which is bad." Such men may see their own situation and the country's as bad, disappointing, and shameful, but they have no coherent set of ideas about why this is so, who is to blame, or how improvements might be brought about. Hence they are content to be inactive; they can see no cause worth fighting for. In general government propaganda has so structured the mental worlds of members of the political public that they cannot reject particular ideological formulations on which the govern-

[10] See Harold D. Lasswell and Abraham Kaplan, *Power and Society* (New Haven, 1950), 9ff., 244ff.

ment insists unless they are prepared to break with nationalism itself.

III

But to point to these various ways in which symbolic activities serve to help the government maintain itself in power is not sufficient to explain why these activities are so important. Two related questions remain unanswered: why are these means used so intensively to buttress the government's power, rather than other available means? And why is the government willing to incur the costs which symbolic activities involve, particularly the costs in terms of a reduced level of performance in the solving of economic and administrative problems?

If it is asked what alternative means could conceivably be used to maintain the government's position, one answer is more direct political control. While the last five years have seen a great increase in government restrictions on political activity, considerable freedom remains. The large modernist Moslem party, Masjumi, has been banned, as has the small but influential Socialist Party, but ten other parties continue to have a legal existence, with their own youth, student, labor, and peasant organizations and their own newspapers. The number of political prisoners is still small and there is little fear of secret police. Press censorship is generally stringent, but banned books and overseas magazines are easily available and overseas radio programs are listened to freely. In fact, little effort is made to isolate citizens from the outside world.

Why then has the government chosen to concentrate on symbol manipulation, when it might have been possible for it to achieve a comparable strengthening of its position by further doses of political repression? The answer is probably threefold. In the first place, this is a government which finds it most difficult to impose its will where doing so means inflicting serious deprivations. A great number of its decrees are ignored, sidestepped, or transformed

by those who are charged with their implementation;[11] and this is particularly common where a decree is designed to have a marked deprivational effect. This can be attributed in part to the ineffectiveness of the government's administrative machinery. But, more important, it should be seen as resulting from the weakness of the political elite's cohesion, the heavy dependence of this elite on the bureaucracy as a social class, and the great importance of intra-bureaucratic politics as a force for immobilization of the government.[12] Lacking cohesion and machinery for the effective settlement of conflicts, the government must bargain with those whom it professes to command.

This leads immediately to a second point, that the cleavages within the political elite can be turned into a distinct asset for purposes of power maintenance while political repression remains mild. Thus the army succeeded in the 1958–61 period in imposing severe restrictions on the Communist Party, at the same time as Soekarno was giving it enough status rewards and public acclaim to prevent it from switching to a strategy of rebellion.[13] Similarly the army succeeded in 1961 in winding up the regionalist rebellion which had broken out in 1958. One major ingredient of success here was the willingness of the army leaders to offer the rebels an amnesty under favorable terms. It would certainly be difficult for the regime to maintain this capacity to incorporate or neutralize its potential challengers if it itself became much more repressive.

[11] For some startling admissions of this, see *A Year of Triumph*, Address by the President of the Republic of Indonesia on August 17, 1962 (Canberra, Embassy of the Republic of Indonesia, 1962), 39–41.
[12] Cf. Fred W. Riggs, *The Ecology of Public Administration* (Bombay 1961), 104ff. and passim; also Riggs, "Prismatic Society and Financial Administration," *Administrative Science Quarterly*, **5** (June 1960), 1–46.
[13] See Donald Hindley, "President Soekarno and the Communists: The Politics of Domestication," *American Political Science Review*, **56** (December 1962), 915–926.

Thirdly, there is resistance from President Soekarno to several of the possible further extensions of political control. Thus the President is opposed to a dissolution of the remaining parties and to the proposal that they be merged into the now weak National Front to make this into a strong state party or movement. Measures of this kind would accord with much in the President's proclaimed political creed, but they would probably weaken him *vis-à-vis* the army, for he relies heavily on the political parties (and especially on the large and still organizationally autonomous Communist Party) for support in his intra-coalition tussles with the army. Certain other forms of direct political control which could conceivably be introduced—for instance, a large expansion in the number of men under political arrest—would justify further increases in the military budget, and to that extent they too would work against the President's interests. Conversely the President has a positive interest in the manipulation of symbols because this is the aspect of power maintenance in which his own role is dominant. The present proportion of symbolism to more directly coercive activities is thus in part a reflection of the political balance which exists inside the government between President Soekarno on the one hand, and the army leaders on the other.

But is there not another, quite different, alternative to intensive symbolic activity? Could the government not buttress its position as effectively, or more so, if it devoted a much larger share of its efforts to the solving of economic and administrative problems, and thereby increased the volume of goods and services available for distribution?

A large part of the answer to this question can be given only on the basis of economic and administrative analysis. It is impossible here to describe the economic and administrative vicious circles which would have to be broken for any attempt to reverse the trend of economic decline

to be successful.[14] However, it is possible to advance a general political argument which throws light on the government's reluctance to make a resolute attempt to break these vicious circles. This argument relates to the competition which exists between skill groups within the government structure.[15]

While much of contemporary politics can be explained in terms of the tussles between President Soekarno and the army, there is also much which is intelligible only as one adds a second axis. This is the axis which runs between symbol wielders and army officers on the one hand, and economic and administrative specialists on the other. More precisely it is an axis between those who claim power chiefly on the basis of their revolutionary record, their capacity for "leadership," or their possession of the "spirit of 1945," and others who claim it chiefly on the grounds of their qualifications for the technical tasks for which a particular government department or government firm is responsible.

The conflict on this leader-technician axis is less readily visible than that on the axis between President Soekarno and the army, because much of it is intra-bureaucratic and because the technicians rarely speak in public. But it comes out clearly in the private complaints of older army officers against the recent recruits of the military academies, the "men who have read all the books but don't know what the Revolution meant and have no respect for the sacrifices we made for it." It came out very clearly indeed in President Soekarno's Independence Day speech of 1962 when he attacked those who "have always bleated about ... so-called 'solutions of

[14] The economic vicious circles are analyzed in Paauw, "From Colonial to Guided Economy," and Humphrey, "Indonesia's National Plan." I have described some of the administrative ones in "Dynamics of Guided Democracy."
[15] On skill groups, see Harold D. Lasswell, *Politics: Who Gets What, When, How* (New York, 1958), 97 ff.

problems' according to outworn and conventional formulas . . . which they took from Western textbooks."[16] In this case the President's attack was directed partly against such opposition politicians as Hatta, the former Vice-President, and Sjahrir, a one-time Prime Minister and long-time chairman of the now-banned Socialist Party. But it was directed also against men of pragmatic, technical, and professional orientation in the government's own ranks and in its administration.

Conflict between the leadership men and the technicians is in fact pervasive within the government. It arises at the highest level whenever First Minister Djuanda, an engineer and economist, argues with President Soekarno against the allocation of funds for sports stadia or monuments, or with General Nasution against the dispatch of a new arms-purchasing mission. It arises whenever an economist advances pragmatic arguments for a measure of decontrol and has these denounced as liberal. At lower levels it arises again and again throughout the administration and the state-controlled economy, over a particular appointment or a particular budget allocation. The basic issue is always the same: is power to be with those who want to gear society to the maximization of production, or is it to be with those, both symbol wielders and military men, who can best sustain the mood of "the Revolution goes on"?

Here then is one important explanation of the government's reluctance to take the difficult steps which a resolute concern with economic and administrative problems would require. This is a Soekarno–army government; Djuanda is a junior partner at best. And it is a Soekarno–army administration as well, or largely so, for the lines of functional division which once separated politics from administration have been heavily blurred in the last five years. This means that a great number of officials and other government employees are holding positions for which they lack the

[16] *A Year of Triumph*, 35.

prescribed technical skills, and feel themselves threatened by the availability of other men who do have these skills.

Many of these incumbents are civilian politicians, men who owe their position to the power of their party or group or to the favor of the President. Others are army officers (or ex-officers who are careful to maintain their links with the army), men who have come to have power over civilian affairs since martial law was proclaimed in March 1957, or since the Dutch estates and trading and industrial enterprises were taken over in December of that year. If the government were to speak less of the need to complete the Revolution and instead to declare economic stabilization and development as the principal challenge of the present period, describing development as a slow and difficult task, then men in both of these categories, whether they were section chiefs, district officers, or estate managers, would soon have their positions contested in the name of the government's ideology by others who could claim greater technical competence for them. And such others exist. They include not only people who had influential posts before 1958 and have now lost them, but also a large group of younger men, newly trained engineers, agricultural scientists, economists, and others, who actively resent the obstacles placed in their career paths by what they frequently call the "older generation."

We may conclude then that the government's intensive concern with symbolic activity is a reflection of intra-elite politics as well as of power maintenance. Symbolic activity furthers the interests, in the first instance, of specialists in the wielding of symbols. In addition, all such activity which underscores the doctrine of the unfinished Revolution justifies the retention of power by a larger group of politician-administrators (including some prominent army officers), who have political qualifications for the positions they hold but no technical ones.

Thirdly, symbolic activity serves the interests of a skill group of "fixers," men who can operate effectively in a situation of organizational ambiguity, in which regulations are repeatedly changed and jurisdictional spheres overlap, in which "retooling" is frequent and career expectations unstable.[17] Fixers and symbol wielders are sometimes the same individuals. But in any event the interests of the two groups are closely parallel. Each stands for the ascendancy of informal qualifications over formal ones; and the organizational ambiguities in which the fixers have a vested interest are important in sustaining demand for the ideological medicine which the symbol wielders can dispense.

IV

Finally, brief mention must be made of the dynamic or developmental aspects of symbolic activity. It is clear that the 1958–63 period has seen an overall trend toward intensification of the government's symbol-wielding activity, a growing shrillness of tone, more and more stress on the transcendent qualities of President Soekarno, and a shift of emphasis from the proclamation of goals and the ceremonial demonstration of determination to achieve these goals to the inculcation of beliefs and the channeling of aggression against enemies.

It is not easy to establish the precise connection between this trend and such other overall tendencies of the five-year period as falling production, rapidly rising prices, the diminishing effectiveness of legality and formal rules and controls in the pattern of administration, and the increasing and more arbitrary use of coercion by the government. But in general one can speak of an inverse relationship between symbolic activity and coercion, and of a positive relationship between symbolic activity and economic decline. Symbolic activity has helped to make the government more legitimate and so served to lessen the amount of coercion it has needed to employ.

On the other hand, concentration on symbolic activity has contributed to the process of economic and administrative decline. And closer investigation would almost certainly show that the causal relationship has worked in the opposite direction as well, that the economic and administrative decline of the five-year period has resulted in deprivations which have weakened belief in the government's moral claims, and that the government has consequently had to intensify its indoctrinating and aggression-channeling activities in order to sustain belief in its right to rule.

It would seem, therefore, that a vicious circle exists between economic and administrative decline on the one hand, and increasing concentration on symbol-wielding and coercion on the other. Will this vicious interaction continue until the political order is recast in some radical way? That is at least a major possibility.

On the other hand, it could be that the thoroughly unsatisfactory state of almost all the economic and administrative indicators in 1962–63 is alarming the government sufficiently for it to overcome its reluctance to take radical action in the fields of economics and administration. This possibility is suggested by the persistent emphasis of government statements since mid-1962 (when the last major rebel-bandit movement was defeated and agreement reached for the transfer of West Irian to Indonesia by May 1, 1963) on "Now we shall tackle the problems of the economy." It is suggested by the remarkably realistic tone of an Economic Declaration promulgated by President Soekarno on March 29, 1963. And it is suggested most strongly by a series of measures announced on May 26, 1963, particularly measures to liberalize foreign trade, increase competition between government firms, raise civil service salaries, and remove large subsidies on rail and air fares and postage. But it is too early at the time of writing to judge the effectiveness of these measures or assess the significance of the new departure they represent.

[17] On fixers, see Harold D. Lasswell and Renzo Sereno, "The Changing Italian Elite," in Harold D. Lasswell, ed., *The Analysis of Political Behavior* (London 1947), 158 ff.

Chapter 11

The Military

ARMIES IN THE PROCESS OF
POLITICAL MODERNIZATION

Lucian W. Pye

Only a few years ago it was generally assumed that the future of the newly emergent states would be determined largely by the activities of their Westernized intellectuals, their socialistically inclined bureaucrats, their nationalist ruling parties, and possibly their menacing Communist parties. It occurred to few students of the underdeveloped regions that the military might become the critical group in shaping the course of nation-building. Now that the military has become the key decision-making element in at least eight of the Afro-Asian countries, we are confronted with the awkward fact that there has been almost no scholarly research on the role of the military in the political development of the new states.

An underlying assumption behind much of Western political thought is that political institutions are above all else the products of the dynamic forces peculiar to a particular society and thus reflect the distinctive values and the styles of action common to that society. It is acknowledged, of course, that once institutions are established they tend to become dynamic and hence in-

SOURCE. Lucian W. Pye, "Armies in the Process of Political Modernization," *Archives Européennes de Sociologie*, **2**, 82–92, 1961. Reprinted by permission.

fluence the values and the expectations of the population. There is thus an assumption of a circularity of relationships or a state of equilibrium. The fundamental view, however, is still that the dynamics of the system lie within the society as a whole and that it is the institutions which must be responsive. Government institutions can display initiative, but fundamental change originates within the society.

When we turn to the newly emergent countries this model no longer seems appropriate. For in these societies the historical pattern has been the introduction of institutions from outside, with a minimum concession to the values and behavior of the people. These fundamentally authoritative structures have thus tended to be shaped according to foreign standards. Rather than responding to indigenous values they have often proved to be the dominant factor in stimulating further changes throughout the society.

These considerations suggest that it might be useful to organize our analysis of the political role of the army, first, with respect to the political implications of the army as a modern institution that has been somewhat artificially introduced into disorganized transitional societies: and second, with respect to the role that such an army can play in shaping attitudes toward modernity in other spheres of society. By such an approach we may hope to locate some of the critical factors for explaining why it is that the military has been a vigorous champion of progress and development in some countries and a retarding influence in others. We may also hope to gain a basis for judging the probable effectiveness of armies in promoting national development and eventually democratic practices.

The Army as a Modern Organization

In large measure the story of the underdeveloped countries is one of countless efforts to create organizations by which resources can be effectively mobilized for achieving new objectives. This is the problem of establishing organizations that, as rationalized structures, are capable of relating means to ends. The history of much of the Western impact on traditional societies fits comfortably within this theme, for the businessman, planter, and miner, the colonial administrator, the missionary, and the educator each in his own way strives to fit modern organizations into tradition-bound societies. Similarly, the story of the nationalists and of the other Westernized leaders can be treated on essentially identical terms, for they too try to change the habits of their people by creating modern organizations.

Needless to say, there are not many bright spots in this history, and it is open to question as to who has been the more tragically heroic or comically futile: the Westerners struggling to establish their organizations in traditional societies, or the nationalist politician and the indigenous administrator endeavoring to create a semblance of order out of chaos. On balance the attempts to establish military organizations seem to have been noticeably the most successful.

It would be wrong to underestimate the patient care that has gone into developing and training colonial armies, and in the newly independent countries the military have been treated relatively generously in the allocation of scarce resources. But in comparison to the efforts that have been expended in developing, say, civil administration and political parties, it still seems that modern armies are somewhat easier to create in transitional societies than most other forms of modern social structures. The significant fact for our consideration is that the armies created by colonial administration and by the newly emergent countries have been consistently among the most modernized institutions in their societies. Viewed historically, some of these armies have been distinguished: the Indian Army, the Malay Regiments, the Philippine Scouts, the Arab Legion, the Gurkha Regiments and the King's Own African Rifles, to mention only the more celebrated ones.

It would take us too far afield to explore the relative advantages military leaders have in seeking to establish armies in transitional societies. We need only note that there is a paradoxical relationship between ritualized and rationalized modes of behavior that may account for the ease with which people still close to a traditional order adapt themselves to military life. Viewed from one perspective, a military establishment comes as close as any human organization can to the ideal type for an industrialized and secularized enterprise. Yet from another point of view, the great stress on professionalism and the extremely explicit standards for individual behavior make the military appear to be a more sacred than secular institution. If discipline is needed to minimize random and unpredictable behavior, it is also consonant with all the demands that custom and ritual make in the most tradition-bound organization.

For these reasons, and for others related to the hierarchic nature of the organization, the division between traditional and rationally oriented behavior is not very great within armies.[1] Indeed, in

[1] It is significant that the most common weaknesses of civil bureaucracies in the new

any army there is always a struggle going on between tradition and reason. Historically, during periods of little change in the state of military technology the tendency has been for the non-rational characteristics to become dominant.[2] Given this inherent conflict in any military organization the question arises as to why the forces of custom and ritual do not readily dominate the armies of the newly emergent countries, and so cause them to oppose the forces of change. In societies where traditional habits of mind are still strong one might expect the military to be strongly conservative. Such was largely the case in the West during the pre-industrial period. By contrast, in most of the newly emergent countries armies have tended to emphasize a rational outlook and to champion responsible change and national development.

This state of affairs is largely explained by the extent to which the armies in these countries have been influenced by contemporary Western military technology. In particular nearly all of the new countries have taken the World War II type of army as their model.[3] In so doing they have undertaken to create a

countries—like exaggerating the importance of procedure to the point of ritualizing the routine, and the lack of initiative and of pragmatic and experimental outlook—are not as serious drawbacks to smooth functioning of military establishments. On the contrary, the very qualities that have hobbled civil administration in these countries have given strength and rigidity to their military establishments.

[2] The classic discussion of the spirit of militarism as contrasted with the rational military mind is Alfred Vagts, *A History of Militarism: Romance and Realities of a Profession* (New York, W. W. Norton, 1937).

[3] World War II was in itself a decisive event in the birth of many of these countries and, of course, the availability of large quantities of surplus equipment and arms made it realistic to aspire to a modernized army. American military aid has contributed to making the military the most modernized element not only in recipient countries, but also in neighboring countries which have felt the need to keep up with technological advances.

form of organization that is typical of and peculiar to the most highly industrialized civilization yet known. Indeed, modern armies are essentially industrial-type entities. Thus the armies of the new countries are instinct with the spirit of rapid technological development.

The fact that these new armies in pre-industrial societies are modelled after industrial-based organizations has many implications for their political roles. One of their characteristics is particularly significant: the specialization that modern armies demand in skills and functions is only distantly related to the command of violence. There has generally been a tremendous increase in the number of officers assigned to staff functions as contrasted with line commands. As the armies have striven to approximate their ideal models they have had to establish all manner of specialized organizations and departments that require skills that are either in short supply or non-existent in their societies. The Burmese army, for example, in addition to its engineer and signal corps has special sections on chemical warfare, psychological warfare, and even a historical and archeological section. All the new armies have attempted to introduce specialized training schools and advanced techniques of personnel management and procurement. Consequently, numbers of the more intelligent and ambitious officers have had to be trained in industrial skills more advanced than those common to the civilian economy.

The high proportion of officers assigned to staff functions means that large numbers of officers are forced to look outside their society for their models. The fact that army leaders, particularly the younger and more ambitious, generally come from those trained in staff positions means that they are extremely sensitive to the needs of modernization and technological advancement. This kind of sensitivity bears little relationship to the command of physical violence and tests of human endurance—in short, to the martial spirit as we customarily think of it. In consequence the officers often find that they are spiritually in tune with the intellectuals and students, and those other elements in society most anxious to become a part of the modern world. They may have little in common with the vast majority of the men they must command. In this respect the gap between the officer class and the troops, once largely a matter of social and economic class (as it still is to some degree), has now been widened by differences in the degree of acculturation to modern life.

It should be noted that these revolutionary changes in military life have significantly influenced the status of the military profession in different societies and hence have had an interesting effect on relative national power. Cultures that looked down on the military at an earlier stage of technology now accord high prestige to the same profession as it has raised its technology. For example, when armies depended entirely on human energy and animal power the Chinese placed the soldier near the bottom of the social hierarchy; with present levels of advanced military technology the soldier is now near the top of the social scale in both Communist and non-Communist China. The change has been more in the nature of the military profession than in basic Chinese cultural values. Conversely, peoples once considered "martial" may now show little interest in, or aptitude for, the new kind of soldiering.

Above all else, however, the revolution in military technology has caused the army leaders of the newly emergent countries to be extremely sensitive to the extent to which their countries are economically and technologically underdeveloped. Called upon to perform roles basic to advanced societies, the more politically conscious officers can hardly avoid being aware of the need for substantial changes in their own societies.

It might seem that those occupying positions in other modern-type organizations in underdeveloped societies would also feel much the same need for change. To whatever extent this may be so, three distinctive features of armies seem to make them somewhat more dynamic in demanding changes.

First of all, armies by nature are rival institutions in the sense that their ultimate function is the test of one against the other. All other organizations operate within the context of their own society; although their initial inspiration may have come from abroad, their primary focus is on internal developments. The civil bureaucracy, for example, can, and indeed has to, deal with its domestic problems with little regard for what other bureaucracies in other countries are doing. The soldier, however, is constantly called upon to look abroad and to compare his organization with foreign ones. He thus has a greater awareness of international standards and a greater sensitivity to weaknesses in his own society.

Second, armies for all their concern with rationality and becoming highly efficient machines are relatively immune to pragmatic tests of efficiency on a day-to-day basis. Armies are created for future contingencies, and in many underdeveloped countries these contingencies have never had to be faced. Even in countries where the army is forced to deal with internal security problems, such as Burma and Indonesia, the effects have been mainly to increase the resources available for building up the army according to the ideal model, with remarkably few concessions being made to practical needs. Other modernized organizations in underdeveloped societies have to cope with more immediate and day-to-day problems; hence they must constantly adjust themselves to local conditions. They cannot adhere as rigidly as armies can to their Western prototypes. Just as Western armies have often existed in a dream world of planning for types of wars that never occur, so armies of underdeveloped countries can devote themselves to becoming modernized and more "efficient" with little regard to immediate reality. Members of other modern-type organizations may desire to see social change in their society, but they are likely to be more conscious of the need to accommodate their ambitions to existing conditions.

Finally, armies always stand at some distance from their civilian societies and are even expected to have ways of their own, including attitudes and judgments, that are remote if not completely apart from those of civilian life. Thus again armies of the newly emergent countries can feel somewhat divorced from the realities of a transitional society and focus more on the standards common to the more industrialized world. In consequence they are often unaware of the difficulties inherent in modernizing other segments of their society. Within their tradition all problems can be overcome if the right orders are given.

Armies as Modernizing Agents

So much for the army as one of the more modernized of the authoritative agencies of government in transitional societies. When we consider it as a modernizing force for the whole of society, we move into a less clearly defined area where the number of relevant considerations becomes much greater and where we are likely to find greater differences from country to country. Indeed, we shall be able to deal only generally with the social and political aspects of military service and some of the more indirect influences of armies on civilian attitudes.

In all societies it is recognized that armies must make those who enter them into the image of the good soldier. The underdeveloped society adds a new dimension: the good soldier is also to some degree a modernized man. Thus it is that the armies in the newly emergent countries come to play key roles in the process by which traditional ways give way to more Westernized ideas and practices. The very fact that the recruit must break his ties and associations with civilian life and adjust to the more impersonal world of the army tends to emphasize the fundamental nature of this process, which involves the movement out of the particularistic relationships of traditional life and into the more impersonal and universalistic relationships of an industrialized society.

Army training is thus consistent with the direction taken by the basic process of acculturation in traditional societies. Within the army, however, the rate of acculturation is greatly accelerated. This fact contributes to the tendency of army officers to underestimate the difficulties of changing the civilian society.

Probably the most significant feature of the acculturation process as it takes place under the auspices of the army is that it provides a relatively high degree of psychological security. The experience of breaking from the known and relatively sheltered world of tradition and moving into the more unknown modern world is generally an extremely traumatic one. In contrast to the villager who is caught up in the process of being urbanized, the young army recruit from the village has the more sheltered, the more gradual introduction into the modern world. It is hardly necessary to point out the disturbing fact that the urbanization process as it has taken place in most Asian, African, and Latin American societies has generally tended to produce a highly restless, insecure population. Those who have been forced off the land or attracted to the cities often find themselves in a psychologically threatening situation. These are the people who tend to turn to extremist politics and to look for some form of social and personal security in political movements that demand their total commitment. In contrast, those who are exposed to a more technologically advanced way of life in the army find that they must make major adjustments, but that these adjustments are all treated explicitly and openly. In the army one can see what is likely to happen in terms of one's training and one's future. This is not the case in the city.

It should also be noted that the accultu-rative process in the army often tends to be more thorough and of a broader scope than the urbanization process. In all the main Asian cities there are those who still follow many of the habits and practices of the village. They may live still within the orbit of their family and have only limited outside associations and contacts. These people have made some adjustment to the modern world, but they are likely to be faced with even more in the future, and thus they remain potential sources of political tension.

It should also be noted that the accul-turative process in the army tends to be focused on acquiring technical skills that are of particular value for economic development. Just as the army represents an industrialized organization, so must those who have been trained within it learn skills and habits of mind which would be of value in other industrial organizations. In the West, armies have played a very important role in providing technical training and even direct services in the process of industrial development. The German army trained large numbers of non-commissioned officers who performed important functions as foremen in the German steel mills and in other industries. In the United States the Corps of Engineers, of course, played a central role in the whole development of the West; and after the Civil War army veterans provided con-siderable amounts of the skill and know-ledge which, when combined with the influx of immigrants, provided a basis for much of our industrial development. In Latin America the Brazilian Army has played an important part in opening the interior, in promoting the natural sciences, and in protecting the Indian population. In Asia, too, we can see much the same story being enacted now. Before the war the compulsory training in the Japanese Army provided the whole society with increasing reservoirs of man power which contributed directly to the development of an industrial society. Army veterans in India have played an important role not only in lower-level industrial jobs, but also in managerial positions. In Malaya and the Philippines the army has been the main instrument for training people in operating and maintaining motor vehicles and other forms of machinery.

Politically the most significant feature of the process of acculturation within the army is that it usually provides some form of training in citizenship. Recruits with traditional backgrounds must learn about a new world in which they are identified with a larger political self. They learn that they stand in some definite relationship to a national community. In this sense the army experience tends to be a politicizing ex-perience. Even if recruits are not given explicit training in political matters, they are likely to learn that events in their society are determined by human decisions and not just by chance and fate. Within the army the peasant may come to realize that much in life can be changed and that commands and wishes have conse-quences. Thus even aside from any formal training in patriotism the recruit is likely to achieve some awareness of the political dimensions of his society. It is therefore not surprising that in many of the newly emergent countries veterans have had appreciable political influence even after only limited military experience.

Armies in the newly emergent countries can thus provide a sense of citizenship and an appreciation of political action. In some cases this can lead to a more responsible nationalism. Indeed, the recruit may be impressed with the fact that he must make sacrifices to achieve the goals of national-ism and that the process of nation-building involves more than just the shouting of slogans. At the same time there is always the potential danger that the armies will become the center of hyper-nationalistic movements, as in the case of prewar Japan.

Because the army represents one of the most effective channels for upward social mobility, military-inspired nationalism often encompasses a host of personalized emotions and sentiments about civilian society. Invariably the men, and sometimes even the officers, come from extremely humble circumstances, and it is only within the army that they are first introduced to the possibility of systematically advancing themselves. In transitional societies, where people's station in life is still largely determined by birth, and by chance opportunities, powerful reactions usually follow from placing people in a position where they can recognize a definite and predictable relationship between effort and reward. The practice of giving advancement on merit can encourage people, first, to see the army as a just organization deserving of their loyalties, and then possibly, to demand that the same form of justice reign throughout their society.

Those who do move up to positions of greater respect and power through the army may often carry with them hostilities toward those with greater advantages and authority in civilian society. The tendency of the military to question whether the civilian elite achieved their station by merit adds another conflict to civil-military relations in most underdeveloped countries. More often than not the military show these feelings by seeking to make national loyalty and personal sacrifice the crucial test of national leadership.

The relationship between armies and civilian leaders varies, of course, according to the circumstances of historic development. Broadly speaking, however, it is helpful to distinguish three different general categories of such relationships.

There are first those patterns of development in which the military stand out because in a disrupted society they represent the only effectively organized element capable of competing for political power and formulating public policy. This situation is most likely to exist when the traditional political order, but not necessarily the traditional social order, has been violently disrupted and it becomes necessary to set up representative institutions before any of the other modern-type political organizations have been firmly established. The outstanding example of this pattern of development is modern China from the fall of the Manchu dynasty in 1911 to the victory of the Communists. Indeed, it is possible to think of this period as one dominated by a constant struggle to escape from the grim circumstances that obtained when only military organizations survived the fall of the traditional systems. Hence the military became the only effective political entity. Thereafter nothing could be done without them, and yet the military could do little without effective civilian institutions. Comparable situations seem to exist at present in some Middle Eastern countries where Western influence brought a commitment to republican institutions but left the army as the only effective modern political structure in the entire society.

A second category includes those countries where the military, while formally espousing the development of democracy, actually monopolizes the political arena and forces any emerging civilian elite to concentrate on economic and social activities. In many ways this arrangement is reminiscent of the Belgian variety of colonialism. At present, the most outstanding example of this form of rule is Thailand.

A third major category, which is probably the largest, consists of those countries in which the organization and structures essential to democratic government exist but have not been able to function effectively. The process of modernization has been retarded to such a point that the army, as the most modernized organization in the society, has assumed an administrative role and taken over control. In these cases there is a sense of failure in the country, and the military are viewed as possible saviors.[4]

---

[4] Johnson, John J., ed., *The Role of the Military in Underdeveloped Countries*, Princeton University Press, Princeton 1962.

THE MILITARY IN MIDDLE EASTERN SOCIETY AND POLITICS

Dankwart A. Rustow

There are few major regions of the world where the military have played as prominent or profound a political role as in the Middle East. No international wars have been fought in the Middle East since the end of World War II, except for the Palestine War of 1948–49 and the abortive Sinai-Suez campaign of 1956. Yet the intervention of the armed forces and their officers in the domestic political process has been frequent, drastic, and profound.[1] The Egyptian revolution of 1952 replaced King Faruq and the Wafd party with a military regime. Two years later, General Nagib was ousted by Colonel Nasir. In 1958, Syria joined Egypt in the United Arab Republic after a prolonged crisis in which the army played a leading role; and in September 1961, as a result of another military revolt, Syria dissolved the three-year-old union. In Iran, the Shah was restored to his throne in 1953 by action of the armed forces under General Zahidi. The year 1958 set an all-time record for political intervention by the military: the Iraqi revolution installed the regime of General Qasim; in Lebanon, a brief civil war was terminated by the intervention of U.S. marines and the inauguration of General Shihab as President of the Republic; in Jordan, the Arab Legion, with a brief assist from British

forces, secured the continued rule of King Husayn; and the army in Pakistan, under General Ayub, and in the Sudan, under General Abbud, displayed parliamentary government. Finally, in May 1960, the Turkish armed forces terminated the oppressive regime of Premier Menderes, making way a year later for a second parliamentary republic headed by ex-General Gürsel as President and ex-General Inönü as Prime Minister. All in all, at the beginning of 1962, nine of the thirteen countries of the region had political regimes installed or dominated by the armed forces and their officer corps.

Before turning to a more detailed examination of the contemporary role of the military in individual countries, it will be appropriate to take a comprehensive look at the region as a whole and at the historical, cultural, and social factors that have propelled the military so dramatically and ubiquitously upon the Middle Eastern political scene.

Clubs are Trumps

Politics, Thomas Hobbes once suggested, is like a game of cards: the players must agree which card is to be trump. With this difference, he adds, that in politics, whenever no other card is agreed upon, clubs are trumps.[2] Here is one important explanation of the army's role in Middle Eastern politics and one to which there will be occasion to return in later contexts. Lack of agreement on basic constitutional principles, inexperience with government by discussion, weakness of civilian bureaucracies, atrophy of political parties, and diffuseness of economic interest groups— all of these contribute to an atmosphere where violence becomes not only the ultima

SOURCE. Dankwart A. Rustow, "The Military in Middle Eastern Society and Politics," in Sydney Nettleton Fisher, ed., *The Military in the Middle East: Problems in Society and Government* ("Publications of the Graduate Institute for World Affairs of the Ohio State University," No. 1), published by the Mershon Center for Education in National Security of the Ohio State University, 1963. Copyright 1963 by the Ohio State University Press. ʾnted by permission of the publisher.

ratio, but all too often the prima ratio of politics. It is no coincidence that the four countries of the area which have had no military coups or revolutions in the last decade lie at the two extremes, tradition and modernity, of the cultural spectrum. They include the three remaining patriarchal monarchies of the region—Yemen, Afghanistan, and Saudi Arabia—where petroleum and competitive foreign aid have only just begun to revolutionize agricultural or nomadic subsistence economies. And they include Israel, where the population, composed at first largely of European immigrants, has created a parliamentary system of government based on tightly organized, pluralistic parties and interest groups. It is in the middle ranges of the spectrum that the military becomes a factor to reckon with—in countries caught in the profound and unsettling process of transition from traditional Islam to modern secularism, from feudal or subsistence agriculture to urbanism and industry, from an ascriptive class structure to social mobility, from semi-colonial rule toward national self-government.

Yet, even in this middle spectrum, Hobbes' aphorism explains only part of the story. The military in the Middle East not only fill the contemporary vacuum left by lack of agreement on the political rules of the game; there are also positive historical factors to account for their prominence. Or, to use a simile recently popularized by Gamal Abd al-Nasir, the military not only have responded to the challenge of a political "role in search of a hero,"[3] they have also played an important historical role (if perhaps not always a heroic one) in their own right.

Islamic and Ottoman Antecedents

Because of its focal geographic position at the juncture of three continents and two oceans, the Middle East has been, throughout recorded history, the most frequently invaded region of the globe. Alexander of Macedon and Pompey of Rome came from the west, the early Islamic armies from the Arabian peninsula, Hulagu the Mongol and Timur the Turk from the north, and the Ottomans from Anatolia. More recently, the French, since the days of Napoleon, and the British, since the days of Nelson and Kitchener, have vied for power in the region; and since the end of World War II, the Middle East has become the stage for conflicting Russian and American military interests.

Out of the kaleidoscopic array of conquests and invasions, three forces may be singled out whose historical influence is felt to this day: the advent of Islam, the rise and fall of the Ottoman Empire, and the impact of the modern West.

Islam arose in the seventh century A.D. as a conquering faith which unified, within a century after the Prophet's death, a vast region from the Pyrenees to the Pamirs and imposed on most of it a religious and cultural stamp which thirteen centuries have not deleted. Compared with other world religions, Islam in its theology and jurisprudence accords a high degree of legitimacy to warfare. The doctrine of *jihad*, or Holy War, for example, asserts that the true faith can be spread by conquest as well as by conversion; Muslim international law rests on a basic distinction between the Abode of War and the Abode of Islam; *amir al-mu'minin*, or Commander of the Faithful, is one of the most frequently used titles of the Caliph . . .

and Muslim political philosophers have generally held effective exercise of power to be the chief or sole criterion of governmental legitimacy.

Within the early Islamic domain, the Ottoman state . . . emerged as one of the many principalities founded by frontier warriors along the northern marches. The Ottoman victory over Byzantium (1453) initiated a century of spectacular conquest which carried Ottoman rule as far as Algeria, Hungary, the Ukraine, Iraq, and Yemen. Throughout Ottoman history the army, along with the Sultan's palace establishment, remained the largest, most elaborate, and most expensive part of the Empire's "ruling institution"; and the decline of Ottoman military fortunes in the protracted contest with the Habsburg and Romanov Empires only served to reinforce the military's central position. The impact of modern Europe on the Ottoman Empire was felt most acutely as a military impact—from the breaking of the second siege of Vienna (1683) to Bonaparte's invasion of Egypt (1798) and down to the Great War of 1914–1918. The Ottomans' natural reaction was to try to borrow, first and foremost, the "cutting edge" of Western civilization. With the importation of European military instructors, which began in the late eighteenth century, and the substitution of a newly organized army for the dissolute Janissary corps (1826), the army officers became one of the most Westernized elements in the Empire. The officer corps had always had a wide base of social and geographic recruitment, as a result of the nineteenth-century reforms, it also became one of the most conspicuous channels for merit advancement within the Empire's social structure.[4]

The Ottoman Empire during the reign of Mahmud II and in the days of the *Tanzimat*, and Egypt under Muhammad Ali and his successors, provide two classic illustrations of European military threats as a stimulus for cultural change and of the armed forces as the spearhead of modernization in politics, economics, and society. In both countries administrative and fiscal systems were overhauled to pay for the more expensive modernized army; public works were undertaken to accommodate its strategic requirements; industry fostered to serve its needs of procurement; and higher education instituted to fill its command positions. Mathematics and science, medicine and European languages were introduced first into the military curriculum and only later in separate civilian schools.

Within the rising Westernized elite, military cadets and officers were among the first converts to liberal European ideas of constitutionalism and nationalism. In 1881, Egyptian officers under Colonel 'Urābi attempted the first modern military coup in the Middle East, aimed primarily at subjecting the spendthrift Khedive to the financial control of a representative assembly. A few years later, students at the Ottoman army medical college founded the Society of Union and Progress—the nucleus of the conspiracy which, in the 1908 revolution, overthrew the despotism of Sultan Abdülhamid. The facile tendency of the triumphant Union and Progress officers to equate Ottomanism with Turkish nationalism led to the formation of secret societies among Ottoman Arab officers, who in turn became the first nationalist leaders in the countries of the Fertile Crescent. After the Ottoman defeat of 1918, the ranking generals on active duty, such as Mustafa Kemal (Atatürk), Kâzim Karabekir, and Ali Fuad [Cebesoy], co-operated with local civilian leaders in organizing the Defense of Rights movement in Anatolia, which won the Turkish War of Independence and created the Republican People's party and the First Turkish Republic.

Western Impact

The modernization program of the nineteenth century and the role of army officers in nationalist movements of the twentieth were part of the Middle Eastern response to European military expansionism. But the imperialist challenge itself set important precedents for the crucial role of military action in contemporary Middle Eastern politics. The 'Urābi revolt led, in 1882, to the so-called temporary occupation of Egypt by British forces—an occupation which, in one form or another, was to last fully seventy-four years. Throughout this period, British intervention in Egyptian politics was backed repeatedly by military action or military threat—most notably in 1919, 1924, and 1942. In the Fertile Crescent, British and French mandates were established in the wake of World War I. But the benevolent educational theories of the mandates were quickly belied by the coercive measures required to instal and maintain the new regimes. In Damascus, where Faysal had been proclaimed King of Greater Syria in 1919, French troops surrounded and occupied the city despite Faysal's acceptance of their peremptory ultimatum. The revolt of the nomadic tribes in the Middle Euphrates region of Iraq, in 1921, and in the Druze Mountains of Syria, in 1925, prompted massive military action by the British and the French. In Transjordan the British set up a client government, whose mainstays were an annual subsidy from the British treasury and the British-officered, bedouin-recruited Arab Legion. In Palestine the mandatory government's self-contradictory policy exacerbated the sharp contrast between Arab and Jewish aspirations and at length resulted in a three-cornered civil war.

In World War II, the Middle East was not involved in any of the military operations, except along the Libyan front. Yet the area's pivotal strategic location prompted the Allies to take no chances on an interruption of their lines of communication or on a gradual drift of individual countries into the Axis camp. Again and again, military intervention to change domestic political regimes was the last resort: in the spring of 1941, the suppression of the pro-Axis Rashid Ali government in Iraq by British and Transjordanian forces; a few weeks later, the ejection of Vichy forces from Syria and Lebanon by British and De Gaullist troops; that same summer, the unceremonious occupation of Iran by British and Russian contingents, followed by the deposition and exile of Shah Riza; and early in 1942, British tanks surrounding King Faruq's palace

in Cairo to force replacement of a pro-Italian with a pro-British cabinet.

Not only was Western power throughout the Middle East installed and maintained by force, but the relinquishment of these same power positions came generally in response to the assertion of equal or superior force. The Egyptian nationalist uprising of 1919 brought to the scene the Milner commission, which recommended, for the first time, direct dealings with the exiled nationalist leaders. The precarious reassertion of British control over Iraq in 1941 was followed at once by a shift of British policy toward cautious support of Pan-Arab aspirations. In 1945–46, it took the threat of British military intervention to force French evacuation from Syria in pursuance of a joint Anglo-French wartime undertaking. And in 1956, blunt warnings from the United States—as well as from the Soviet Union—forced the abandonment of the concerted Israeli-French-British attack on Egypt.

This is not to deny that some of the Western policies just reviewed, particularly those during World War II, may have been amply justified by overriding moral considerations. Still the fact remains that the Middle East's experience with Western imperialism has greatly reinforced indigenous tendencies toward coercive politics. Looking at the situation from their viewpoint, one can hardly blame Middle Eastern leaders for suspecting that Western doctrines of self-determination and constitutionalism were intended for domestic consumption and for concluding that, in the Middle East at least, military force alone could be counted upon for decisive results.

What, then, in brief is the legacy of Middle Eastern history as it bears on the present role of the military in society and politics? The Middle East, more than any comparable world region, has been subject to military invasions throughout history. Most states of the region, down to the present, have been established by conquest; most of the recent changes of regime have been effected by military action. The region's traditional culture rests upon a religion that accords great prestige and legitimacy to the military. And the direct and indirect impact of modernity upon the traditional culture further tended to enhance the leading role of the armed forces and their officer corps. Against this background, it is clear that the prominent and decisive role of the military on the current Middle Eastern scene is not a momentary lapse from normal constitutional practice but conforms to ample historical precedent. Conversely, it is the occasional spells of peaceful constitutional government by civilians—as in Turkey from 1922 to 1960, in Lebanon from 1945 to 1958, in Israel since 1948—which must be seen as the exceptional situations.

The Common Pattern of Middle Eastern Coups

The preceding historical survey has provided the necessary background for an examination of the more immediate circumstances in which Middle Eastern armies have wrested power from civilian governments or forced the replacement of one civilian government by another. Although the experiences of each country and each individual military coup offer a great many variations of detail, there are indeed some strikingly common features and patterns. . . . These similarities can be summed up under several headings and some hypotheses suggested to account for them.

There is a remarkable parallel in the timing of the initial military coups in Iraq, Syria, and Egypt. Iraq was released from mandate status in 1932; in 1936, General Bakr Sidqi performed his military coup, which, in the next five years, was to be followed by six others. In Syria, French occupation was withdrawn in mid-1945; in 1949, there were three successive military coups under Colonels Za'im, Hinnawi, and Shishakli. In 1947, the British discontinued their wartime occupation of Egypt proper, concentrating their remaining troops in the Canal Zone; in 1952,

the Free Officers seized power under General Nagib and Colonel Nasir. It is obvious that a military seizure of power by indigenous officers will not occur during foreign occupation; a colonial regime may expect army mutinies, as in India in 1857, but not coups d'état. The Middle Eastern evidence would seem to suggest that it takes four to five years after de facto independence for civilian institutions to be sufficiently discredited and the army officers sufficiently self-confident to set the stage for the first coup.

Armies commonly seize power on the domestic scene after defeat on the battlefield, not after victory. On this point, it may be argued that the historical evidence offers too few examples to support firm generalizations; but it is surely no coincidence that Turkish victory in the War of Independence of 1919–22 was followed by thirty-eight years of military subordination to orderly civilian rule, or that Israel, the one Middle Eastern country to win any battlefield victories in recent decades, is also the only country that has not had a single military coup. Instances on the converse side are equally striking: the Ottoman Empire's defeat in the First Balkan War was followed by the so-called Sublime Porte Incident of January 1913, in which Enver, at the head of a gang of trigger-happy lieutenants, stormed the government offices in Istanbul, shot the war minister, forced the aging Grand Vezir Kâmil Pasha to write out his resignation at pistol point, and established the dictatorship of the famous Young Turk triumvirate of Enver, Cemal, and Talât. In 1919, the defeated Ottoman army under Mustafa Kemal organized nationalist resistance in Anatolia in open defiance of the Sultan and his collaborationist ministers. Finally, the Syrian coups of 1949 and the Egyptian revolution of 1952 were in large part a response to the humiliation of defeat in the Palestine War.

Several convergent explanations may be suggested. The most disciplined and professionalized armies are likely to make the best showing in wartime and are also the likeliest to submit to civilian control. On the other hand, an army that is too weak to beat a foreign enemy still has ample strength to cow its unarmed domestic antagonists. Defeat in war, moreover, is likely to undermine popular confidence in the existing government. The army itself—partly as a result of the psychological law that links frustration to aggression—is tempted to clear its tarnished record by finding a civilian scapegoat. Thus, Enver and his associates reproached Kâmil Pasha with lack of determination to recapture the former capital of Edirne; and Gamal Abd al-Nasir and his fellow conspirators blamed their defeat in Palestine on the inferior equipment supplied by Faruq's corrupt entourage. (It should be noted in passing that the Kemalist revolution does not fully fit this pattern, for here the target of military action was not, primarily, the Sultan but rather the invading Greek, Armenian, and French forces.)

Military coups follow upon a period of internal unrest in which civilian authorities have come increasingly to rely on armed forces to maintain themselves in power. On this point examples abound: The formative experience of the Young Turk conspirators of 1908 was the running and losing fight which Abdülhamid's government was carrying on against rebellious Christian elements in the Balkans and against defiant Arab vassals, such as the Imam of Yemen. Riza Khan, before his 1921 coup in Iran, had distinguished himself by suppressing the secessionist Gilan Soviet Republic. General Bakr Sidqi became a popular hero by his ruthless suppression of the Assyrian uprising in 1933 before seizing power in Baghdad three years later. The Egyptian revolution of 1952 was preceded by four years of near civil war. And the military revolutions in Iraq in 1958 and in Turkey in 1960 were preceded by several years of forcible suppression of political opposition; the Turkish upheaval, in particular, reflected

the army's refusal to let itself be used any further as a tool of Menderes' repressive policies. In short, military seizure of power comes not as a sudden isolated departure but, more commonly, as the climax of a continuously growing military involvement upon the domestic scene—an involvement that adds to the army's skills in domestic coercion and which makes the civilian government more dependent on the army and hence a more vulnerable and tempting target once the army decides on its *volte-face*. Where survival of a civilian government depends on armed power, a coup in which the army switches sides must, *ex hypothesi*, succeed. Prolonged defeat in internal war, as in the Ottoman Empire before 1908 (or in French Algeria in the 1950's), will heighten the army's frustration and hence speed its revolt.

Armed coups d'état occur when mounting popular dissatisfaction can find no peaceful means of forcing a change in government. This is in part a restatement of the previous theorem. It is also the situation that best fits Hobbes' dictum about clubs · being trumps in politics whenever no other card is agreed upon. It is not entirely accurate to think of the army as filling a vacuum; rather it moves in to break a stalemate. An army coup, to succeed, needs civilian support, and the civilians will not lend such support until simpler and less risky avenues have been blocked. Hence the military coup is the standard antidote to traditional despotisms and modern dictatorships—including dictatorships established by previous military coups—as well as to entrenched oligarchies which have thwarted the parliamentary and electoral procedures prescribed in the constitutions.

The precise form of military-civilian co-operation varies. There may be a formal alliance, initiated by either side, between the military and civilian conspirators—as within the Ottoman Union and Progress Society in 1908–13, between Riza Khan and Ziaeddin Tabatabai in Iran in 1921, or between Bakr Sidqi and the Iraqi Ikha party in 1936. There may be a looser ideological or organizational connection as between the Egyptian Officers and the Muslim Brethren in 1952. Or officers may act without any prior understanding but with confident assurance that their action will be welcomed by important segments of the public—such as the universities and the Republican People's party in Turkey in 1960.

There is an equally wide variety of actual techniques for a coup d'état—and it would be interesting to correlate these with the typology that abundant evidence has suggested to Latin American observers. The Young Turk Revolution of 1908, for example, seems to correspond to the bloodless variety known in Peru as a *telegráfico*. Its only two victims were a young officer whom the conspirators suspected of being a stool pigeon (he was kidnapped and murdered with the active participation of his brother-in-law Enver) and one of Abdülhamid's generals shot in broad daylight in the market square of Monastir. The constitutional revolution itself was accomplished by a flood of telegrams that rained upon the Sultan's palace from army commanders, political committees, and provincial governors throughout Macedonia. Only a year later did the Macedonian army march upon the capital to quell a counterrevolutionary mutiny among the Istanbul garrison. A uniquely painless way of accomplishing a military coup was devised in Iraq in 1938: a discreet ultimatum whispered into the premier's ear at a social gathering resulted in the cabinet's resignation only hours later.[5] This last incident, however, reflected a situation where the army for some time had called the tune for the habitual musical-chair game of cabinet formation within the Iraqi oligarchy.

At other times, a determined show of force by the army is required to overthrow a government. Bakr Sidqi's coup in 1936 involved five airplanes dropping quantities of leaflets over Baghdad—as well as four bombs that took a total of seven casualties.

More commonly, army units occupy key communications points around the capital —road junctions, the radio station, the royal or presidential palace, and the government offices. This, with some variation, was the story of the revolutions in Cairo in 1952, in Baghdad in 1958, and in Turkey in 1960. The decisive military phases of the coup are likely to involve little cost of lives: only fools will barehandedly oppose machine guns, tanks, or bombers. The bloodier phases of a military revolution are likely to be the result of deliberate subsequent action, as Bakr Sidqi's murder of the previous war minister and the death sentences imposed on Menderes and a few associates after a year-long trial, or else of an enraged civilian mob tolerated by the army, as in the ferocious massacre in Baghdad in 1958.

The military leaders of most coups solemnly announce that they will not take power for themselves or will return it to civilian hands quickly; yet few live up to that initial promise. Here again the record shows a variety of patterns. A refusal by the military conspirators to take office creates an unstable situation where power is divorced from responsibility, and further coups are the logical sequel. The seven Iraqi coups of the 1936–41 period consisted in as many changes in civilian cabinets enforced by military threats. The very fact that the first such army coup had succeeded in bringing one faction to power created a temptation, or even compulsion, for its opponents to use the same tactics. A chain reaction of coups was the result; and, while it lasted, cabinets were in effect responsible neither to the monarch nor the parliament, let alone the electorate, but rather to informal combinations of key generals and colonels. (In February 1940, one cabinet was ousted as a result of a vote of five to three at one such gathering.) In Syria in 1949, and again from 1954 to 1957, one might be tempted to speak of a Gresham's law of military intervention. Any army coup, unless carried out by the chief of staff himself, will disrupt the discipline and cohesiveness of the officer corps. Once a few generals and colonels have succeeded in seizing power, any aspiring major or captain will soon nurse similar ambitions.

In the recent Egyptian and Turkish revolutions, the military rulers proclaimed their hopes of quickly remedying the evils of the previous regime and of re-establishing an era of civilian normalcy. In each case the sequel exposed the fallacy of this one-shot intervention theory, whether or not sincerely espoused. Nagib and Nasir replaced Faruq with a regency council for his infant son and invited the Egyptian parties to purge themselves of corrupt elements. After some months, they concluded that corruption had been more than skin-deep and that no trained, clean cadres stood ready to take over. With Nasir's victory over Nagib, the initial promise of early elections was dropped altogether.[6] In Turkey, General Gürsel at first thought his task accomplished upon the arrest of the president, premier, and cabinet of the *ancien régime* and the appointment of a commission of law professors to draft a new constitution. The professors pointed out to him that Menderes' dictatorial regime had had the solid support of parliament and the Democratic party, and insisted that the parliamentarians be arrested and the party suppressed. And the learned jurists proved utterly unable to deliver on their overconfident promise of a new constitution within a month. In the end, it took well over a year to get a new constitution adopted, a new parliament elected, and a civilian cabinet formed. The more ambitious tasks envisaged by the National Unity Committee—such as the restoration of the economy, the currency, and public morality—still remain on the agenda of their successors. There were indications, moreover, that continued army pressure was required to bring about the incongruous coalition of pro- and anti-Menderes forces that took office in November 1961; and the abortive coup of March 1962,

again revealed that the political involvement of the military was not yet at an end. The future alone can tell whether the army can henceforth safely withdraw from the political arena.

Finally, *there are often widening rifts within the military junta installed by a coup.* The Egyptian, Iraqi, and Turkish juntas all consisted of officers with the rank of colonel or below, who planned the actual conspiracy, and were supplemented by older generals who were co-opted as respected figureheads or leader figures. The general in each case turned out to be more conservative than his juniors—Nagib insisted on early party elections while Nasir wished to perpetuate the Revolutionary Command Council; Qasim resisted Arif's plans for union with the U.A.R.; Gürsel opposed Türkes' vague ideas of radical social reform under authoritarian military aegis. These three examples also show that the dispute may be resolved either way: in Egypt, the younger radicals won out; in Iraq and Turkey, they lost, at least in the initial round.

The Effects of Military Intervention

Having surveyed the cultural and natural history of Middle Eastern military coups, it remains to survey briefly their effects. The authors of a study of Latin American politics hold that "the armed forces are probably the single most serious impediment to the development of democracy."[7] Another political scientist has argued with equal confidence that, in the Southeast Asia of the 1960's, military dictatorships represent the best hope for the survival and development of free representative institutions.[8] There may be special conditions that make these sweeping judgments more nearly applicable to the regions for which they first were formulated. For the Middle East, at least, any such monistic interpretations should be firmly rejected. There are armies and armies, and there are military coups and military coups. The one thing all military regimes have in common is that, by their very definition, they have a certain amount of coercive power at their disposal—and even in this respect there are important differences in degree. How they will apply that power and what fruits they will reap depend on their own character and the setting in which they operate.

One obvious and fundamental distinction is that between armies based on universal military training—as in Israel, Turkey, Egypt, Syria, and more recently Iraq— and those based on volunteers—as in Iran, Jordan, Saudi Arabia, and Yemen. The conscript armies can serve as an important factor in economic and social development —through training in literacy as in Turkey, or in the national language as in Israel, or through the communication of mechanical, industrial, or even agricultural skills. In these same countries, the officer corps generally is selected upon an egalitarian basis, given professionalized training, and promoted by merit. Where an army with such an officer corps takes power, it is likely to pursue goals of political reform, social modernization, and economic development. How well it will succeed is quite a different matter. Colonel Nasir, for example, must try to reverse a steady decline in Egyptian living standards due to limited resources and a heavy rate of population increase—a problem that would tax the ingenuity of any government, military or civil. General Gürsel's Committee of National Unity was handicapped by the astounding political naïveté of an officer corps long insulated from participation in the civilian political process. On the other hand, the armies of the surviving monarchies of the Middle East clearly serve as props to traditional autocratic or oligarchic regimes. The Iranian army, in particular, which boasts the highest ratio of officers to enlisted men of any Middle Eastern country,[9] has long been known for endemic corruption and favoritism. Unless such an army is itself drastically reformed, it would be idle to expect it to serve as the spearhead of social progress.

It should be noted at this point that the distinction between military coups and military revolutions must properly rest not upon any difference in the technique by which power is seized but rather upon the scope and success of the reform program which is subsequently enacted. All military revolutions begin as coups: the seizure of power out of civilian hands must follow certain rules determined by the prevailing technology of the political and military organizations. In turn, the proclamations that accompany the coup tend to reflect the political philosophy popular at the time and place. In the mid-twentieth century, any serious claimant to power, regardless of his antecedents, associations, or intentions, will justify his claim by professing profound concern for national independence, for popular aspirations, for social justice, and for economic development. Once power is attained, some coups evolve into revolutions. The difference is not in the promise but in the performance.

The most decisive factor is the relationship of the military to the civilian segment of the political process. That a great variety of configurations here is possible within the same over-all setting and period is illustrated by the final years of the Ottoman Empire. The revolutionaries of 1908 were content to see Abdülhamid reproclaim the constitution he had blithely disregarded in three decades of despotic rule and replace the most obnoxious of his ministers with bureaucrats of a moral liberal tinge. In 1909, the same revolutionary group insisted on Abdülhamid's deposition, a revision of the monarchic constitution along parliamentary lines, and the appointment of cabinets subservient to the Union and Progress party. Enver's raid on the Sublime Porte in 1913 brought to power the youthful Unionist hotheads who made a mockery of the electoral process and plunged the country into disastrous defeat in World War I, but who at the same time undertook a series of courageous administrative, legal, fiscal, and educational changes that laid the groundwork for the reform program of the following decades. Finally, Mustafa Kemal's Defense of

Rights movement combined the local civilian organizations left behind by the Unionists with a military apex, won an impressive military and diplomatic victory, created a party and a state in which the military could once again withdraw from politics, and undertook his sweeping legal, social, and cultural transformation.

The Turkish experience under Kemal suggests specifically that after a period of profound military involvement in politics, a conscious decision by the leading general-turned-politician may be the most effective way of re-establishing the separation of civilian and military affairs. Any soldiers who are disinclined to return to their barracks from conviction are more likely to do so from habitual obedience to a prestigious commander.[10]

In conclusion it may be well to point out that the neat distinction drawn throughout this essay between civilian and military politics is somewhat artificial. Until the eighteenth century, there had been no such systematic differentiation in the Middle East or, for that matter, in continental Europe. The sultans of the classical period led their armies into the field in person. The *ulama* (or learned men in Islamic law and theology) had always formed a clearly distinct class; but the empire's civil and military servants— governors, army commanders, judges, ministers—had received the same initial training in the sultan's palace school, and shifts among these careers were common. In most periods of recorded history, the maintenance of armed forces has constituted the irreducible minimum of government. Other public functions such as taxation, education, public works, and social services began either as subsidiary activities or were added as subsequent luxuries. In new countries or at times of internal and external crisis, the lines again become blurred in various ways. In Kemalist Turkey, army officers were barred from sitting in—and even voting for—parliament. Yet former officers filled many of the key positions in the government and in the Republican People's party; the chief of staff held a position independent of ministerial control; generals on active duty continued to double up as provincial governors; and during prolonged periods of siege (in the Kurdish provinces in the 1920's and in Istanbul throughout World War II), civil authority was subordinated to military command. In the early mandate days of Iraq and Syria, centralized administration had to be established by military force. In Israel, defense considerations tend to dominate economic and social planning, and there have been complaints that Prime Minister Ben-Gurion's long tenure as minister of defense has shielded the armed forces from effective civilian control.

Nevertheless, the very complexity of modern government tends toward a reassertion of the distinction between military and civilian affairs. This is seen both in coups, which consist in a mere change of top political leadership, and in military revolutions, which result in more profound political and social transformations. One of the greatest assets of the military in a coup is their reputation for honesty, decisiveness, and efficiency, which, in the eyes of a discontented populace, contrasts favorably with the corruption and inefficiency of the ousted civilian government. But, the officers were efficient while serving the single, simple purpose of national defense. Moving into the unfamiliar political scene, which is by definition an arena of conflicting purposes, and dealing with complex subjects of financial, industrial, or agricultural planning for which they are entirely untrained, the officers may quickly lose their good reputation. In fact, the more extravagant the initial popular enthusiasm, the keener and quicker the disappointment. At this point the stage is set for another military coup (on the facile assumption that the military are indeed uncorrupt and efficient, but the leaders of the first coup happened to be the exception that proves the rule) or, at length, for a return to civilian government (once the military reputation is thoroughly tarnished).

In a military revolution, the officers stay in power longer but the very magnitude of a reform program forces them to sever their active connection with the army. Mustafa Kemal, throughout most of the Turkish War of Independence, relinquished active command at the front in order to preside over the deliberations of the truculent and fractious National Assembly at Ankara. Similarly the colonels and majors in Nasir's Revolutionary Command Council and Gürsel's Committee of National Unity could not continue in command of their regiments or battalions while taking charge of ministries, directorates-general, and provincial governorships. It therefore becomes largely a matter of conceptual definition whether Egypt, a decade after the 1952 revolution, is said to be governed by the military or by a group of civilian ex-officers initially propelled into power by armed force. The shift from military to civilian control is apparent in the fact that Kemal, after the formation of the First Republic, based his support on the Republican People's party—the first Middle Eastern political movement with a farflung constituency organization. Nasir's National Union is an attempt in the same direction.

Only the future can tell whether Nasir in Egypt or Qasim in Iraq will be able to match Kemal's achievement of re-establishing civilian supremacy. In any case, the ultimate success of a military regime depends on its skill in allowing or promoting the rise of effective civilian institutions that will render future military intervention superfluous—in short, in fostering a set of political rules whereby clubs no longer will be trumps.

NOTES

[1] Samuel P. Huntington, surveying the military scene since 1945, observes aptly, "The inhibition of direct intergovernmental violence contrasted with the frequency and variety of violence in the domestic politics of colonial territories and independent states of Latin America, Africa, the Middle East, and southern Asia. These were the principal military arenas in world politics." *Changing Patterns of Military Politics* ("International Yearbook of Political Behavior Research," No. 3 [Glencoe, Ill., 1962]), p. 18.

[2] Thomas Hobbes, *English Works*, ed. Molesworth, **6**, 122. The above was written before the September 1962 military coup in Yemen.

[3] Gamal Abdul Nasser, *Egypt's Liberation: Philosophy of the Revolution* (Washington D.C., 1955), p. 81.

[4] The above two paragraphs are taken from my article, "The Army and the Founding of the Turkish Republic," *World Politics*, **11**, 4 (July 1959), 514 f. The phrase "ruling institution" is that of Albert Lybyer, *"The Government of the Ottoman Empire* (Cambridge, Mass., 1913); the metaphor of the "cutting edge" that of Lewis V. Thomas, in L. V. Thomas and R. N. Frye, *The United States and Turkey and Iran* (Cambridge, Mass., 1951), p. 51.

[5] See Majid Khadduri, *Independent Iraq 1932–1958* (2nd ed.; London, 1960), p. 133.

[6] On the gradual transformation of the Egyptian regime, see the informative study by P. J. Vatikiotis, *The Egyptian Army in Politics* (Bloomington, Ind., 1961), especially pp. 71-96.

[7] Charles O. Porter and Robert J. Alexander, *The Struggle for Democracy in Latin America* (New York, 1961), p. 46.

[8] Guy J. Pauker, "Southeast Asia as a Problem Area in the Next Decade," *World Politics*, **11**, 3 (July 1959), pp. 325–345.

[9] One to fourteen against one to twenty in Pakistan and Jordan and one to forty-eight in Tunisia. See Manfred Halpern's chapter in John J. Johnson (ed.), *The Political Role of the Army in Underdeveloped Areas* (Princeton, N.J., 1962), pp. 292–295, which contains a convenient table giving details of size, recruitment, and training of Middle Eastern armies and their officers.

[10] For details of the relative disengagement of the army from the politics of the First Turkish Republic, see my article cited *supra, note 4*, especially pp. 543–551.

POLITICS AND MILITARY
INTERVENTION IN LATIN AMERICA

Gino Germani and Kalman Silvert

The recent politico-military events of Turkey, Pakistan, Egypt, and even France demonstrate that the application of unabashed armed might to the solution of civic problems is not peculiar to Latin America, nor indeed a phenomenon to be correlated only with economic underdevelopment. Public violence and political instability in Latin America have all too often been treated either as merely comic or else a manifestation of "spirit," "temperament," or "Latin blood." Riots in the streets of Buenos Aires are no less tragic than riots in the streets of Algiers—and no less related to the basic facts of social disorganization as they may be reflected in crises of political legitimacy and consensus.

Military intromission in the political power structure always indicates, of course, at least a relative inability of other social institutions to marshal their power effectively, and at most an advanced state of institutional decomposition. This is to say, if the armed forces are viewed as having a limited and specialized set of functions having only to do with internal order and external defense, then a widening of castrensic activities into other social domains implies a generally weakened and sick social system, no matter the country or even the special cultural conditions concerned. This premise suggests several ways of constructing typologies of civil-military relations: one possibility is to order the types of social pathology to be found, and

then to relate them to the historical facts of politico-military action; another is to order types of public violence, and once again to relate these to the real types of military interventions; and still a third alternative suggests itself in the direct listing of the institutional arrangements between the military establishment and the political institution treated as a variable dependent upon other social factors. This article will employ the latter procedure as being of the most immediate analytical utility, even though direct correlations between military action and the general state of social and economic development are at best vague.

Most Latin American countries have reached their first century and half of independent existence. However, their social development into national states lagged behind formal independence and it is only now that a few of them are reaching a stage of full nationhood. While in some countries the breakdown of the traditional structure began in the last quarter of the nineteenth century, in many others a similar process of structural change did not start until the last two or three decades of the present century. Furthermore, one must remember that nowhere, not even in the most "advanced" Latin American nations, may it be said that the transition is complete.

Let us formulate now a typology of institutional civil-military relations and relate them to the different particular situations of the Latin American countries.[1]

SOURCE. Excerpted from Gino Germani and Kalman Silvert, "Politics, Social Structure and Military Intervention in Latin America," *Archives Européennes de Sociologie*, 2, 62–81, 1961; using only 62–63, 76–81. Reprinted by permission.

[1] For a narrower version of this typology and other suggested categorizations of Latin American politics, see K. H. Silvert, "Political Change in Latin America," in Herbert Matthews, ed., *The United States and Latin America* (New York, The American Assembly, 1959).

1. *The classical military garrison state.* This form develops typically in response to real or imagined external factors. No example of such Spartan organization is to be found in Latin America, where cases of truly serious and devastating wars of sufficient duration to work fundamental institutional change are extremely scarce. The major exception is the Paraguayan War of the last century, but social conditions in that country were insufficiently advanced to permit of the establishment of a truly centralized garrison state, despite the devastating nature of the armed conflict itself.

2. *The modern totalitarian garrison state.* This phenomenon is still, fortunately, an evil dream of imaginative writers, for no historical examples are to be found anywhere. The low state of the technological arts everywhere in Latin America makes this development at present impossible for these republics.

3. *The totalitarian politico-military relations.* This pattern of relationships inextricably intertwines political and military functions within a monolithic public organization, as in Nazi Germany. Once again the insufficiencies of Latin America's technological state have to date prevented the formation of modern, totalitarian states, although such a country as Argentina is beginning to approach at least the material ability to include such a solution within its array of social possibilities. The "national-popular" revolutions have not attained so far this politico-military structure and one reason may be the technical underdevelopment of their bureaucratic organization. On the other hand, the rapid extension of radio, television, and other media of mass communication heightens this possibility as the unilateral dependence on weapons alone

for social control in extreme cases thus becomes less necessary.

4. *The military as institutionalized governors.* This kind of authoritarianism is very common in Latin America, and is a persistent form from the earliest days of independence to the present day. The existence of the armed forces as an organized and ostensibly efficacious group in administrative affairs has tempted to the simple transposition of personnel from military to governmental functions and to subsequent rule as *de facto* and eventually *de jure* governors. Given the long-standing tradition of military privileges (from the colonial period) and military participation (from independence wars) in Latin America, such a pattern is likely to appear whenever the political instability reaches a point at which the social legitimacy of a regime or a government is no longer accepted by the major relevant groups within the society. Such a situation may happen, as we noted earlier, at every level of the transitional process. It is obvious why it would predominate during the early days of independence and the years of confusion and anarchy which followed the failure in establishing modern states in the liberated colonial territories. And it still predominates in the more retarded countries such as the Dominican Republic, Honduras, Haiti and Nicaragua, in all of which the structure of traditional society has changed very little. But it is small wonder that relatively more advanced countries such as Argentina from the early thirties and, in very recent years, Colombia and Venezuela have experienced the same phenomenon. Here the instability must be related, as we indicated before, to a different underlying situation. The crucial common ground of all these cases is an irreconcilable division among the various politically relevant groups, and the lack of shared norms regarding political activity. The military, clearly and loyally, has usually worked in conjunction with important civilian elements, serving as an arm for the maintenance of group interest.

[footnote 1 continued
Also refer to the March 1961 issue of *The Annals of the American Academy of Political and Social Science*, entitled *Latin America's Nationalist Revolutions*, for other pertinent and recent information.

History belies the simplistic belief that such alliances have always been between the most conservative groups and the military. On many important occasions organized military might has been brought to bear to promote the interests of new industrial agglomerations against the pretensions of landed Conservatives and sometimes even the Church. During certain periods of Mexico's growth, for example, the military in combination with civilians contributed heavily to the social experimentation characterizing that country from 1917 until 1940 at least. This important category of events needs, thus, to be subdivided in accordance with the civilian allegiances and ideological orientations of the military, and the resultant effects on the total socio-economic and political structures.

5. *The military as trustee governors.* As naked military intervention becomes increasingly viewed as shameful, this phenomenon has increased in incidence. There are two notable recent cases, that of the Provisional Government of General Pedro Eugenio Aramburu in Argentina (1955–58), and that of Admiral Wolfgang Larrazabal in Venezuela (1958–59). Both governments arose after the fall of dictators, both of whom had risen out of the ranks of the military and subsequently were deposed by the military in combination with civilian groups. Aramburu and Larrazabal committed themselves to "cushion" governments, *interregna* permitting the formation of parties, the holding of legal elections, and the installation of civilian authorities.

6. *The military as orienters of national policy.* This very subtle manifestation involves the exercise of power not on the immediately visible scene but rather in the fashion of a grey eminence. The military in this situation attempt to establish the broad policy limits within which civilian activity may express itself, the sanction for disobedience obviously being deposition of the legally constituted authorities. The significant Mexican developments mentioned above are, in all their real complexity, a combination of this category with the two immediately preceding. Whether or not the Mexican armed forces still effectively limit the freedom of the Mexican Government is a matter of some debate, especially given the strength of the single official party of Mexico and the very wide distribution of the civilian sectors supporting this party system and the incumbent governors.[2] Perhaps the clearest, most evident case of tutelary military behavior can be seen now in Argentina, where the military overtly acts to contain the policies of the Government, openly threatens coups, publicly debates political policies, and on occasion even moves troops to back its demands on the civilian governors. Military budgets are holy, and officers of the armed forces in a limited retirement occupy many important administrative positions in the civil service.

7. *The military as pressure group with veto power.* This rather standard manifestation of military power in many developed countries is still little seen in Latin America, except possibly in the case of Chile. In this situation the military institution has the power to prevent antagonistic civilian action undertaken against it, but cannot initiate independent action or policy in fields outside of its range of professional interest.

[2] Oscar Lewis, in his "Mexico Since Cardenas," *in* Lyman Bryson, ed., *Social Change in Latin America Today* (New York, Harper, 1960), pp. 301–302, writes:

"A comparison of the allocations of federal funds to the various departments over the four presidential administrations from Cardenas to Ruiz Cortines reveals [. . .] some highly significant trends. Especially marked is the sharp decrease in the proportion of funds allocated to national defense, reflecting the demise of *caudillismo* as a serious factor in Mexican life. Adolfo Ruiz Cortines was the first president since the 1920's who did not depend heavily on either the national or a private army to maintain his control."

Professor Lewis then points out that between 1935 and 1940 defense expenditures absorbed 17.3 per cent of the national budget, dropping to 8.1 per cent in the period 1953–56.

8. *The military as simple pressure group.* This stage, the last before the military fades away into complete subordination to the civil authorities, is probably the status of the armed forces of Uruguay alone among the Latin American republics. The very special circumstances of Uruguay's past offer some apparently reasonable explanations of this phenomenon. A buffer state lying between two relatively powerful neighbors, Brazil and Argentina, Uruguay has never been able realistically to dream of armed exploits. Further, the country is politically a city-state, a fact which has contributed to the early development of what can truly be called a "bourgeois" society (in the primitive sense of the term). Moreover, a high degree of political involvement of the citizenry has created areas of civil power not conducive to military adventures.

9. *The military as simple police force in complete subordination to the government.* Costa Rica prides itself on having this kind of civil-military pattern, and is even wont to deny the existence of an army altogether, stating that the civil force is in truth merely a police agency. If the situation is not really such a pure subordination of the armed forces to the civil authorities, still the case offers a reasonable approximation. Once more circumstances unique for Latin America have brought about this situation. Costa Rica was unattractive to early Spanish colonizers, for it had a small indigenous population and no readily available minerals. As a result the Costa Rican central valley was an area of slow and secondary settlement, peopled by persons who had to work the land themselves. This emergence of a landed peasantry permitted the development of a type of "bourgeoisie" (in the figurative sense of the word) which, as in the case of Uruguay, has had long experience in the organization and application of its power to the detriment of armed pretenders.

10. *The military as political arm of the state.* This pattern, obviously closely related to the idealized versions of the functions of the Red Army of the USSR and of the various "People's Armies" invariably tends to emerge from revolutionary situations of the left. The Arevalo-Arbenz Governments of Guatemala (1945–54) and the present Governments of Cuba and Bolivia are the only three cases in Latin America of frankly leftist politics, albeit of different colors. In the Guatemalan case no serious attempts were made to turn the military into an active arm of the government; instead, especially during the interrupted term of President (and Lt. Col.) Jacovo Arbenz Guzman, the design was to keep the army small and the officer corps highly contented. According to available report, the Castro Government has broken the professional army by investing civilian militias with greater power and by politicizing the officer corps of the regular forces. This procedure was also used in Bolivia with the establishment some eight years ago of an armed civilian militia whose primary function was to counterbalance the regular army.

Military intervention in civilian affairs, as is suggested by this typology, clearly does not occur either in an ideational vacuum or in the absence of a sometimes very wide range of interests and pressures. Military politics inevitably and invariably involve identification with wider social interests and ideologies. The patterning of these identifications depends in important measure on the social origins of the officer corps and the social mobility functions which the military institution may serve. Unfortunately there are almost no reliable data available on these questions. From subjective evaluations and informal observation, however, one may suspect a considerable variation in the social origins of officer groups from country to country, and a consequent variation in the political identification of the military. It is also entirely evident that there must be great variation in the opportunities for upward social mobility offered by different armed forces. Wide differences in budgets and in the sizes of the military establishments must affect mobility, of course, as do generalized social attitudes concerning the prestige of the military.[3]

A relatively safe generalization is that throughout Latin America the sons of middle class families are more attracted to the military than are the sons of the upper groups. The result often has been to split the ideological unity of the military, to create inter-service rivalries as well as intra-service discord. This growing fragmentation must be projected against the increasing complexity of Latin American society itself, affected as it is by economic development, changing world ideological currents, and rapidly growing industrial urbanization. Because nowhere in Latin America—even in famed Uruguay and Costa Rica—are the institutional patterns of secular and impersonal representative democracy fully established, many civilian groups are innately revolutionary in their attitudes and predisposed to the use of force as an inherent and thus desirable part

[3] *The Statistical Abstract of Latin America 1960* (Center of Latin American Studies, University of California in Los Angeles), p. 32, offers some partial and tentative figures on the percentage of Latin American budgets devoted to defense expenditures. The data are incomplete for all countries.

COUNTRY	PERCENTAGE OF NATIONAL BUDGET	YEAR
Mexico	11.3	1958
Costa Rica	3.8	1958
El Salvador	10.2	1958
Guatemala	8.8	1958
Honduras	11.7	1957
Haiti	19.1	1957
Argentina	21.1	1958
Brazil	27.6	1958
Chile	21.9	1958
Colombia	5.7	1958
Ecuador	21.6	1957
Peru	23.2	1958
Venezuela	9.5	1959

These figures are admittedly tenuous, and probably err on the low side, of course.

of the social pattern. Both military schisms and military adventures are encouraged by the civilian groups soliciting armed aid for their political ambitions. Even though the following quotation concerns the Spain of the 1930's, it is valid for the Latin American arena as well:

No doubt the generals in 1936 thought they were saving Spain [. . .] The State must be capable of embodying and responding to what Maura called the vital forces of the community. Otherwise, as he warned repeatedly, the army will claim to embody the national will in order to enforce changes which political institutions are impotent to encompass. Above all, no democrat, repeating the follies of the progressive and moderate minorities, can appeal to the sword rather than to conviction, however slow the educative process may be. Though the Republic of 1931 came in on a vote, many Republicans were willing to see it come in through the army. Repeating the tactics of Ruiz Zorrilla, they systematically undermined the loyalty of the army. Some saw the danger. "I would prefer no Republic to a Republic conceived in the womb of the army." Many did not. How could they complain when other forces tampered with the loyalty of the army in 1936?[4]

The military will be reduced to their barracks and their professional functions alone only when Latin American countries develop sufficiently complicated power structures and a society sufficiently flexible and integrated; when social and geographical discontinuities have been greatly lessened and isolated or marginal masses incorporated into the national body; when economic and social conflicts have found institutionalized expression within a common framework of shared norms.

[4] A. R. M. Carr, "Spain," *in* Michael Howard, ed., *Soldiers and Governments: Nine Studies in Civil-Military Relations* (London, Eyre and Spottiswoode, 1957), pp. 145–146.

Chapter 12

The Bureaucracy

BUREAUCRACY AND NATION BUILDING IN TRANSITIONAL SOCIETIES

S. C. Dube

Bureaucracy forms an important element of the modernizing élite in many of the economically less developed countries which have attained national independence during the last two decades. Trained in the colonial tradition, this organized and articulate segment of the native society functioned as a bridge between the dependent indigenous people and the ruling power from the West. Although it had to work under the direction of the imperial power and had largely to carry out its policies, it was not without nationalist sentiments and aspirations. Held suspect during the days of the struggle for freedom, both by politically oriented fellow-countrymen and by the alien rulers, members of this class had, by and large, acquired a progressive orientation and the more sophisticated among them had definite ideas regarding the programmes of economic and social growth to be adopted by their country at the attainment of national independence. In many countries they were the only organized body of natives with considerable training and experience in administration; they naturally found themselves called upon to assume major re-

sponsibilities in the formulation and implementation of national plans for economic development and social change.

The general change in political climate, the assumption of power by the political élite, the changing alignments of power and pressure groups, and the emergence of new institutional and administrative patterns raised in their wake a series of complex problems for the bureaucracy. In consequence, it had to make some significant adjustments in its thought- and work-ways and to adapt itself to the new ethos. On the other hand, in many sensitive areas it found itself either openly resisting or accepting some of the new elements only theoretically. Thus, with or without the overt acceptance of the new patterns, it stood for continuity of some of the established norms. In meeting these intricate problems of adjustment and value-conflict, the character of bureaucracy in transitional societies is undergoing a rapid change. Since it occupies a pivotal position in these societies, and will possibly continue to do so in the foreseeable future, an understanding of the character and culture of bureaucracy is essential for those concerned with the programmes of economic growth and social change in the economically less developed countries.

SOURCE. S. C. Dube, "Bureaucracy and Nation Building in Transitional Societies," *International Social Science Journal*, 16, 229–236, 1964.

Planning for economic growth is an extremely complicated business which involves highly specialized knowledge and developed manipulative skills; the implementation of these plans presupposes deep administrative insights and a keen evaluative perspective. In the context of the programmes of community development, it is common these days to emphasize the ideal of planning by. the people, but the crucial fact that this stage must necessarily be preceded by the stages of planning for the people and planning with the people is not given sufficient emphasis. The acceptance of these three stages means successively diminishing functions for the bureaucracy in matters of local and regional planning and in developmental administration, but it is essential to bear in mind that the gap between the first and the third stage is very considerable and that the transition to the final stage depends largely upon the manner in which the process is initiated and the first two stages are carried out. Both these stages involve considerable direct participation by the bureaucracy; the second stage particularly—which requires the initiation of a process of withdrawal— has critical significance. Optimism, bordering on wishful thinking, cannot alone diminish the importance of bureaucracy; its role in the process of planning and developmental administration is bound to figure prominently for several decades, The problem of the integration of local, regional, and national plans demands knowledge and skills which perhaps only the bureaucracy possesses. Of course, as the process acquires greater complexity the technocrat is drawn into it more deeply, for without the utilization of his specialized knowledge planning for successive stages would become increasingly difficult. Nevertheless, much maligned and distrusted as it is, bureaucracy is not without a vital role to play in the process of planning for economic and social development. Modifications in its structure, values, and work-ways are necessary to adapt it to the idiom of the fast changing situation, but the fact remains that it cannot be done away with. An understanding of its character and the initiation of imaginative plans for changing its structure and values so as to make it a more effective instrument for development must therefore be considered an essential prerequisite to planned change in these countries.

Discriminatingly recruited on the basis of specified criteria and carefully trained according to established and time-tested plans, bureaucracies in most of the former colonies and dependencies became efficient instruments of administration. Although they were oriented more to functions of law and order and the collection of revenues, they were also entrusted from time to time with some nation-building responsibilities. In discharging their responsibilities they showed all the classical characteristics of bureaucracies: they were formally organized with unambiguous demarcation of roles and statuses and were articulated to clearly defined goals; they were efficient and equipped with the required knowledge; they were well-versed in formal rules of procedure and recognized their predominance; and finally they were trained to function in an impersonal manner under conditions of near anonymity.

In addition to the above, bureaucracies in these societies had certain special characteristics. In their respective countries they were perhaps the first large and organized group to enter the transitional phase between tradition and modernity— the twilight zone lying between societal types described variously in continua such as communal-associational, sacred-secular, status-contract, and *gemeinschaft-gesellschaft*. In other words, they were among the pioneers who sought to break away from the traditionally affective and emotion-based communal society and to set in motion the forces that were to contribute towards the emergence of a different type of society—a society characterized by affective neutrality and based on rational ends-means calculations for individual goals. As a distinct subcultural entity within the larger framework of their society, they were at least partly absolved from the traditional obligation of having to share communal attitudes, sentiments, and repressive authority, and were among the first to constitute a group characterized by specialized division of labour, by different but complementary interests and sentiments, and by restrictive authority. It is not suggested here that they could break away completely from tradition to adopt the ideals and values of modernity; in the critical areas of choice-making they had before them a wide zone of fluid values in which were present the elements of both tradition and modernity. The logic and rationale of selectivity in the process of choice-making has not been analysed in depth, but the fact that, gradually and in an increasing measure, bureaucracy adopted several elements of modernity is not without significance.

It might be useful to describe here some special features of these bureaucracies, as they emerged and crystallized during the colonial phase.

1. Bureaucracy constituted a special sub-cultural segment—the high prestige strata of the society. Entrance to it was theoretically not barred to any section of the community, although in actual practice only the traditionally privileged could provide the necessary general background and the expensive education required for success in the stiff tests prescribed for entry into its higher echelons. In limited numbers others also gained entrance into the relatively closed group of higher civil servants. Middle-level and lower positions in it attracted the less privileged. Bureaucracy had a class bias and it tended to have a stratification of its own; its upper crust functioned as a privileged class. On the whole it symbolized achievement rather than ascription. Over time, it came to have distinct vested interests, and was sensitive to all threats to its position and privilege which it guarded jealously against encroachment from any quarter.

2. It existed largely in the twilight zone of cultures. Partly traditional and partly modern, it could and did in fact choose from the elements of both. In several ways it was alienated from the masses and uprooted from the native cultural traditions; significant differences in styles of living and in modes of thought separated the two. The Western rulers, on the other hand, never conceded equality to it. In consequence, bureaucracy maintained dual identification and was characterized by a dual ambivalence.

3. Besides offering security of tenure and relatively higher emoluments, bureaucratic positions carried vast powers which made them additionally attractive and important. The powers vested in a minor functionary gave him prestige, perquisites and privileges far beyond those justified by his emoluments and position in the hierarchy. Formally the role and status of functionaries at different levels were defined, but in actual practice the system of expectation and obligation between them tended to be diffused rather than specific.

4. Within the framework of the over-all policy laid down by the imperial power, in day-to-day administration the bureaucratic machine enjoyed considerable freedom from interference. Thus there were few hindrances to its exercise of power, which was often authoritarian in tone and content. Bureaucracy had, in general, a paternalistic attitude to the masses. The masses, on their part, accepted the position and looked to the administration for a wide variety of small favours.

5. Administration was concerned mainly with collection of land revenue and with maintenance of law and order. The general administrator under these conditions enjoyed supremacy. Subject matter specialists of welfare and nation-building departments were relegated to secondary positions and functioned under the guidance and control of the generalist.

6. Bureaucracy was carefully trained in

formal administrative procedure and routine. Stereotypes in this sphere were well-developed and were scrupulously observed.

7. In the limited framework of its functions and set procedures bureaucracy found a self-contained system. It resented and resisted innovations.

8. Its attitude to the nationalist forces within was most ambivalent. Few within the bureaucracy were devoid of patriotic sentiments and aspirations, but only in rare exceptions could they openly side with the forces of nationalism. Requirements of their official position made them an instrument for the execution of imperialist policies. This naturally aroused in the nationalist leadership feelings of anger and distrust against them. This rejection by the leaders of the nationalist forces as well as by the politically-conscious masses was largely at the root of their ambivalent attitude towards the nationalist forces.

Bureaucracy welcomed the advent of independence as much as any other group in the former colonies and dependencies, but the first years of freedom were for it a period of great stress and strain. It had covertly resented Western domination, but in the first decade of independence it remained under the shadow of suspicion because of its former association and identification with the alien power. While its power and prestige were decreasing, its burdens and responsibilities were increasing. Attacked from several sides simultaneously and with mounting pressures, bureaucracy found itself in a difficult and uncomfortable position.

The more important areas in which it had to work for a redefinition and consequent readjustment of its position and responsibilities were (a) the culture of politics, (b) the emerging ethos, and (c) the expanding sphere of State activity and the new institutional arrangements.

The Culture of Politics

In the new order the supremacy of administration was replaced largely by the sovereignty of politics. Politics became the most important activity and the politician came to occupy a position of unquestionable supremacy in matters of decision making. Within the framework of this culture of politics, there was an unmistakable tendency towards the merging of political roles with personal and social roles; the expectations of the politician from his followers and administrative subordinates were diffused. Politics centred round individuals; informal factions or groups formed around key personalities were thus more meaningful units of political organization than the formal structure of political parties. Personal loyalty to politicians, under these conditions, played an important part in the process of political identification and decision-making. Administration under such leadership could not remain wholly impersonal. The political élite was nurtured more in the politics of agitation than in the politics of nation building, and as a hangover from the past it persisted in its agitational approach. Nucleated around individuals, political processes lacked organic unity; communication was not adequately articulated. In general, political parties represented some kind of a revolutionary world view and philosophy, and on larger international and national issues they stood for an unlimited Utopia. On specific issues, especially of a regional or local character, the position was significantly different; political opinion on them was often narrow, sectarian, and parochial. Thus political thinking regarding issues at different levels lacked cohesion and integration. The attitude of the political élite was characterized by ambivalence. They sought to work for modernization, without giving up their love for tradition; attempts to harmonize, synthesize, and integrate the elements of the two, even on a conceptual level, were neither systematic nor serious.

In many countries the bureaucracy was trained well enough to accept political direction, and only in a few exceptional cases did it try to gain the upper hand.

Adjustment and adaptation to this political culture, however, was not without problems and difficulties. The new order posed a definite threat to bureaucracy's structure, values, and interests. While its formal structure remained intact, the definition of roles and statuses within the hierarchy was disturbed by the emergence of the politician as the focal point of decision-making. The personal nature of political decision-making was another unsettling factor. It not only affected the internal status system of the bureaucracy, but also sometimes bypassed its special knowledge and sidetracked its procedural routine. In many specific contexts administration could not function in an impersonal manner. Interpersonal relations between the politician and the administrator tended to be uneasy. The politician recognized the value and importance of the bureaucracy, but he continued to have a definite antagonism towards it, to exhort and admonish it to change its ways, and to ridicule it for some of its modes of thought and action that were out of tune in the new order. Much of this criticism was valid, but the manner in which it was made was often irritating to the bureaucrats. Many members of the bureaucracy had silently admired the self-sacrificing patriots as heroes, but in close proximity they saw them without the halo that surrounded them during the days of the national struggle. Often, the gap between their profession and their practice particularly annoyed the perceptive members of the bureaucracy. The politician was himself adopting many of the ways which he criticized in the bureaucrat. Some members of the administration were all too willing to adapt, but their over-readiness to do so was viewed by the discerning administrator as a dangerous departure that could in the long run undermine the very character and role of the bureaucracy.

The Emerging Ethos

The emerging ethos also presented bureaucracy with a series of problems. In the new setting it could not maintain its image of power, nor could it continue to exist as a high-prestige class enjoying exceptional privileges. A closer identification with the masses was called for; the paternalistic and authoritarian tone of administration had also inevitably to change. On a theoretical and emotional level the desirability of this basic change was conceded, but a system of rationalization was developed at the same time to justify the maintenance of the *status quo*. Today a great contradiction persists between emotional awareness of the desirable and willingness to accept it in practice.

The Expanding Sphere of State Activity and New Institutional Arrangements

The structure, values, and work-ways of the bureaucracy in almost all former colonies and dependencies were geared to law and order and to revenue administration for which it was efficiently trained. Administration for nation building necessitated a different approach involving a new value attitude orientation and a modified institutional set-up. It is in these spheres that the failures of the bureaucracy are perhaps the most pronounced.

By and large the bureaucracy resists innovations in its structural arrangement. It appears to have a firm faith in the superiority of the pyramidal structure of administration and in the infallibility of the generalist. Efforts to nuclearize the administration for nation building are resented, and there is great resentment if any attempt is made to dislodge the general administrator from his high pedestal. Concepts of inner-democratization, of administrative decentralization, and of delegation of authority and responsibility at best receive only lip service. Coordination becomes difficult because of faulty communication between the general administrator and the technical specialist. Effective utilization of the specialist is blocked by the accepted or assumed supremacy of the general administrator whose self-confidence borders almost on arrogance. The latter perhaps realizes that he is not trained for certain jobs, but he rarely concedes this publicly. Innovations have been made in these spheres, but the marks of bureaucratic resistance are still evident.

Subconsciously the bureaucrat still perhaps believes in the efficacy of the traditional approach to administration. New approaches are discussed and half-heartedly accepted, but only in rare cases do they receive a fair trial. Extension and community development approaches, for instance, have encountered considerable resistance from the bureaucracy. Indeed, many members of the administration would be glad to revert to type, and would willingly reverse the process that has gained partial acceptance for these approaches after years of experimentation and persuasion.

It is generally recognized that the cumbrous administrative routine, good in its time, today practically immobilizes developmental administration. Yet, all attempts to change the rules of procedure result invariably in the formulation of rules that are as complex as those they seek to replace, if not more so.

Efforts at deconcentration of power, such as the experiment of democratic decentralization for development in India, meet with even greater resistance. Doubtless the infant "grass roots democracy" is not without shortcomings, but its threats to the perpetuation of bureaucratic vested interests have alerted the administrator, whose approach to the experiment is extremely guarded, wooden, and unimaginative.

Attempts have been made at reorienting the bureaucracy to the new philosophy of administration, but they have often been viewed as mere short-lived fads and fancies. Indirectly the new approach has made some headway, but there is little evidence to suggest that its utility has been generally accepted.

In the tasks of nation building in transitional societies bureaucracy has a vital role to play. It consists, by and large, of people with progressive motivation, wide administrative experience, and a rich store of pooled knowledge. Far from being written off, it cannot be ignored. It must also be conceded that it has played an important part in the process of economic and social growth and has been willing to go part of the way at least to adjust to the new situation. It has functioned both as a model and as an instrument for modernization. But its effective utilization has been blocked by some of the paradoxes of the new political culture and by the inner contradictions within its own structure and ordering of values. In several respects the hard core of the bureaucratic culture has been unyielding, and has offered great resistance to innovation. The blame does not lie entirely at its own door, but at the same time the present state of uncertainty cannot be allowed to continue indefinitely. Lack of adequate understanding of its culture and values and of a balanced assessment of its past and future roles has been an important factor in the failure to utilize bureaucracy more effectively in programmes of economic growth and planned change.

BUREAUCRATS AND POLITICAL DEVELOPMENT: A PARADOXICAL VIEW[1]

Fred W. Riggs

Introduction

A phenomenon of the utmost significance in transitional societies is the lack of balance between political policy-making institutions and bureaucratic policy-implementing structures. The relative weakness of political organs means that the political function tends to be appropriated, in considerable measure, by bureaucrats. Intra-bureaucratic struggles become a primary form of politics. But when the political arena is shifted to bureaucracies— a shift marked by the growing power of military officers in conflict with civilian officials—the consequences are usually ominous for political stability, economic growth, administrative effectiveness, and democratic values. It seems important, therefore, to give serious attention to the relation between political and administrative development, to the question of how balanced growth takes place.

In this chapter, accordingly, I deal with the way in which bureaucratic interests affect political development; not how the declared political aims of officials impinge on politics, but how the existence and self-interest of bureaucratic institutions affect, directly or indirectly, the growth of political institutions. My theme will be the conditions under which non-bureaucratic power

centers capable of subjecting bureaucrats to political control flourish or decline. I recognize that there are other important respects in which political development can and does occur, but this paper will be limited to this particular aspect of the subject.

In Western countries it has become a habit to think of the bureaucracy as an instrumental apparatus for the execution of policies established through "political," non-bureaucratic institutions. There have, of course, been serious scholars, as well as emotional writers, who have stressed the difficulty of keeping bureaucrats under control or, as the administrative cliché has it, "on tap but not on top."[2]

One consequence of this conventional attitude is that relatively few scholars have devoted themselves to an analysis of the political role of bureaucrats, the part they play in politics or in political development. However, in my opinion bureaucrats probably always have some influence in politics—although the extent of such influence varies from precious little to a great deal. In the developing countries the extent of bureaucratic involvement in politics is exceptionally high. If this opinion is correct, then it is even more important in the study of the developing countries to consider the role of bureaucrats in politics than to examine this topic in the study of more advanced political systems.

In his major work on government,[3] Carl J. Friedrich suggests that constitutionalism can emerge only after a sub-

SOURCE. Excerpted from Fred W. Riggs, "Bureaucrats and Political Development: A Paradoxical View," in Joseph LaPalombara, ed., *Bureaucracy and Political Development* (Princeton: Princeton University Press, 1963), pp. 120–167; using only 120–135, 139–153.

[1] The author is grateful for many useful suggestions made by participants of the Social Science Research Council Conference on Bureaucracy and Political Development, and particularly for the help provided by Professors John T. Dorsey and Edward W. Weidner.

[2] As one example of a serious analysis of the problem of maintaining bureaucratic accountability see Charles S. Hyneman, *Bureaucracy in a Democracy*, New York, Harper, 1950.

[3] *Constitutional Government and Democracy*, rev. ed., Boston, Ginn, 1950, pp. 25–27, 57.

stantial development of the bureaucracy, for without a governmental apparatus to bring under control, the challenge would not be present to bring into being a system designed to impose limitations and rules upon those who exercise administrative authority. I believe the experience of the developing countries is consistent with Friedrich's observation, but it suggests a corollary, namely that the imposition of constitutional control over a bureaucracy is a difficult task, and the more powerful, relatively, the bureaucracy becomes, the more arduous the achievement.

It we make a quick survey of the transitional societies today, we will be impressed by the weakness of their extra-bureaucratic political institutions in contrast with the burgeoning growth of their bureaucracies. In every country a great expansion of governmental agencies and a proliferation of functions has taken place, especially in the new nations that were recently under colonial rule. By contrast, parliamentary bodies have, in the main, proved ineffectual and, even in the countries like India and the Philippines where they have been most vigorous, their role in basic decision making has been questioned.[4]

Elections have often been conducted

[4] For example, Norman Palmer, a careful observer of Indian politics, has written in connection with the operation of the constitutional and parliamentary system, "the main decisions are made to a large degree outside normal channels. This fact calls attention to the great influence of 'nonpolitical' forces in India, to the role of personalities and charismatic leadership. Most of the major policies are in fact determined within the Congress Party and not by the agencies of government; and within the Congress Party they are made by Jawaharlal Nehru and a handful of associates. . . . there is a kind of unreality about the operation of the governmental agencies in India, and any examination of their functioning soon leads to other sources of influence and power." "The Political Heritage of Modern India," in George McT. Kahin, *Major Governments of Asia*, Ithaca, Cornell University Press, 1958, pp. 294–295. This seems like an overstatement—but perhaps it is sufficiently true to support the position taken in this paper.

in such a way as to give but a poor reflection of the popular will; the courts have not generally shown themselves to be bulwarks of the rule of law; and chief executives have more often than not shown themselves to be arbitrary and authoritarian, relying on their charismatic leadership qualities or a party machine rather than on formal political institutions as the basis of power. Under these conditions it is not surprising that bureaucrats themselves have often had to play a crucial part in determining what would, or perhaps *would not*, be done.

In speaking of non-bureaucratic power I have in mind, of course, primarily those institutions through which, in democratic countries, public interests are articulated, aggregated, and communicated to policy makers, there to be translated into decisions which can and are to a large extent subsequently implemented.

However, I do not rule out of the concept those systems in which the representation of popular interests is highly defective, but in which, nevertheless, a non-bureaucratic political system exists which is able to impose its control upon the governmental apparatus. I have in mind those states— whether of the Fascist or Communist type—in which a political party under highly centralized guidance seizes power and uses its party machinery to impose discipline upon the governmental bureaucrats. Because of the close affinity of the party bureaucracy to the formal bureaucracy in such states, some students lump the two groups together as a single bureaucracy. In my opinion this obscures a fundamental political issue, and hence I shall use the term "bureaucracy" to refer only to the formal hierarchy of government officials, speaking of all other bureaucracies, whether of corporations, trade unions, churches, or political parties, as "non-bureaucratic" or as "non-governmental bureaucracies."

Development as Differentiation

The phenomenon of development involves a gradual separation of institutionally distinct spheres, the differentiation of separate structures for the wide variety of functions that must be performed in any society.

It is clear that in very traditional or simple societies such differentiation has taken place to an extremely limited extent. A single set of officials or authorities, as in feudalism, may exercise undifferentiated military, political, administrative, religious, and economic functions.

By contrast, a highly developed political system contains a large number of explicitly administrative structures, each specialized for specific purposes: agricultural, transport, regulatory, defense, budgetary, personnel, public relations, planning, etc. Moreover, a set of political structures—parties, elections, parliaments, chief executives, and cabinets—are designed to formulate the rules and pose the targets which the administrative structures then implement.

Undoubtedly the principle of the separation of politics and administration is as much a target for aspiration as a statement of actual conditions in a real government, like that of the United States; but the extent of realization of this separation is marked indeed if one compares it with what prevailed in any traditional or primitive folk society. Moreover, the separation of politics and administration is only one facet of a differentiated society, since both the political and administrative institutions are themselves differentiated from economic, religious, educational, and social structures of a distinct and separate character in the advanced Western societies.

The process of modernization in the developing countries is marked by the progressive creation of formally distinct social structures, adapted from Western models, to which differentiated political and administrative tasks are assigned. But in this process the older institutional base of a traditional society lingers on. Although eroded and embattled, it struggles to remain alive, to retain positions of influence.

We find, then, in the transitional society, a dualistic situation. Formally superimposed institutions patterned after Western models coexist with earlier, indigenous institutions of a traditional type in a complex pattern of heterogeneous overlapping. The new patterns thrive best at the center and in the higher levels of society; the older patterns persist most vigorously at the periphery, in the rural hinterlands and the lower levels of society; but the mixture is everywhere present and produces new forms characteristic of neither the Western nor the traditional institutional systems.[5]

The relative speed of change in the functional sectors of a transitional society also varies. Those sectors in which technology, the purely instrumental means, predominate are able to change more rapidly than those in which social and personal values are implicated. For this reason it was often in such spheres as military technology, agricultural crops, formal schooling in science, language, and Western learning that innovations were first made in non-Western countries.[6]

[5] Even the most developed societies retain admixtures of traditional elements and are therefore also to some extent "transitional." The differences are not absolute, but in degree and proportions.

[6] This proposition has been elaborately demonstrated with historical examples by Arnold J. Toynbee. By way of summary he writes, in *The World and the West*, New York, Oxford, 1953, p. 68: "When a travelling culture-ray is diffracted into its component strands—technology, religion, politics, art, and so on—by the resistance of a foreign body social upon which it has impinged, its technological strand is apt to penetrate faster and farther than its religious strand ... the penetrative power of a strand of cultural radiation is usually in inverse ratio to this strand's cultural value."

Harold Lasswell and Abraham Kaplan distinguish "techniques" from "technics." The former consist of those parts of a technology which belong to the social order, hedged about by sanctions, mores, values; the latter those which are free of such involvements. "Technicalization" refers to a transformation from technique to technic. (*Power and Society*,

In the governmental sphere, this principle means that development in public administration, bureaucratic change, takes place more readily than counterpart changes in politics: technics change more easily than techniques. The reasons are apparent. The initial demand for Western institutions in many non-Western countries was in the military sphere, for defense against an intrusive imperial power. To develop the means of defense, rulers employed foreign military advisers and sent students to European military academies. The costs of modern arms were high, and so in national finance, in taxation, especially in customs, and state monopolies like salt, in budgeting and accounting, transformations were carried out. Defense needs also created a demand for effective control over outlying areas of a traditional realm, and so led to a reorganization of territorial administration, the creation of a Ministry of Interior, recruitment of a career service of district officers, prefects, governors, and a central secretariat to control their operations.[7]

While this proliferation and expansion of bureaucratic machinery was taking place in most of the non-Western countries, no corresponding development of the non-bureaucratic political system occurred. In the independent countries, political leadership was still provided by traditional rulers—as in Siam, Iran, Ethiopia, Japan—

although in the Japanese case perhaps the greatest success was achieved in establishing new political institutions, a central legislature, political parties, and a cabinet system. This success is, of course, directly relevant to the phenomenal Japanese achievement of industrialization and the greater effectiveness of its governmental institutions as compared to those of other non-Western countries. Even here, however, bureaucratic elements, especially from the armed forces, tended to exercise disproportionate influence in the political structures, notably in the period leading to the Second World War.[8]

In the countries under colonial rule the proposition is even more patently true— at least until recently. Here the colonial administration itself created a bureaucratic apparatus not subject to political control within the dependent territory, so that administrative institutions proliferated while political structures remained embryonic and largely extra-legal, hence unable to relate themselves effectively to control over the bureaucracy. A striking exception was the Philippines under American administration where nationalist opposition groups were quickly given opportunities to share in the conduct of the government. In India, especially after the First World War and the Montagu-Chelmsford reforms, Indian participation in formal politics, notably in provincial government, laid a substantial foundation for the post-independence development of vigorous political institutions. Subsequently in other British dependencies legislative bodies and political parties were permitted, and they began to share in the formation of policy and control over administration. In a somewhat different way, the same has been true, perhaps, in some of the French-controlled territories. Ultimately this legislative ex-

[footnote 6 continued
New Haven, Yale University Press, 1950, p. 51.) In this terminology, the process of modernization has involved technicalization, and change has been more rapid in technics than in techniques.

[7] The general pattern of such transformations is discussed in my article, "Prismatic Society and Financial Administration," *Administrative Science Quarterly*, 5 (June 1960), espec. pp. 9–16. For a detailed case study of one such transformation, see Walter Vella, *The Impact of the West on Government in Thailand*, Berkeley, University of California Press, 1955. See also E. Herbert Norman, *Japan's Emergence as a Modern State*, New York, Institute of Pacific Relations, 1940. The sequence in areas under colonial rule has been different in important respects, but fundamentally similar.

[8] The extent to which postwar, extra-bureaucratic political development in Japan was influenced, directly or indirectly, by the Occupation, will long remain an interesting subject of study.

perience, plus the ordeal of revolutionary opposition, provided the ex-colonial countries with a stronger political foundation than the countries which never felt an imperial yoke.

In the contemporary era of large-scale technical assistance under international and bi-national programs, we see a continued infusion of external pressure and assistance in the expansion and proliferation of bureaucratic organs, with relatively little attention to the growth of strictly political institutions. The reasons are quite evident. Administration is regarded as a technical matter (technics) subject to foreign, "expert" advice, whereas politics is so closely linked with fundamental values and social mores (techniques) that aid would be construed as "intervention."[9]

Moreover, the demand for economic development and modernization impinges directly on agricultural, industrial, public health, and educational spheres in which external assistance is fed directly to segments of the bureaucracy, and only weakly mediated through central political institutions. The foreign experts and advisers, for their part, while competent to deal with technical matters in a variety of program fields, and even the related administrative questions, would scarcely claim any competence to assist in the establishment of new political institutions.

The question naturally arises: what is the relationship between this burgeoning of bureaucratic institutions and the course of political development? The relationship may be examined from two sides: the effect of political weakness on administrative effectiveness,[10] and the consequences of bureaucratic expansion for the political system. In this article

I shall limit myself to an examination of the latter set of relationships.

My general thesis is that premature or too rapid expansion of the bureaucracy when the political system lags behind tends to inhibit the development of effective politics.[11] A corollary thesis holds that separate political institutions have a better chance to grow if bureaucratic institutions are relatively weak.

Some historical evidence for this proposition is suggested by a comparison of the history of feudal societies with those in which traditional government had a more bureaucratic basis. An outstanding example of a traditional bureaucratic system was imperial China.[12] Here the elaborate complexity and pervasiveness

---

[9] Until the last few years it perhaps did not even occur to U.S. policy makers that political development should or could be a goal in overseas programs.

[10] In another paper, "Bureaucracy in Transitional Societies" (mimeo. 1959), I have argued that political weakness has led to administrative ineffectiveness in many of these countries.

[11] A perceptive public administration adviser shrewdly pointed to this problem in the following words: "Efficient administrative machines can be used to prevent as well as to promote development, and much of the effort that it takes to produce the appearance, if not the reality, of improvement in public administration can become, as it has in the Philippines, a means of concealing inability or unwillingness to undertake needed action on other fronts." Malcolm B. Parsons, "Performance Budgeting in the Philippines," *Public Administration Review*, **17**, 3 (Summer 1957), 173–179.

The view taken here is not, of course, that bureaucrats or bureaucracy are essentially evil monsters, and certainly the need for administrative services which can be performed only by public officials argues for an expansion and improvement, not curtailment, of bureaucracy. The argument is presented, however, that effective administration by bureaucrats is contingent upon the simultaneous growth of extra-bureaucratic institutions capable of maintaining effective control over officials, of keeping them responsible to the formal political authorities, and responsive to the public and clientele interests directly affected by their work. Ideally, such responsibility is to the whole population through democratic processes, but even under totalitarian conditions there must be responsiveness to a party control machine with an extra-bureaucratic power base.

[12] Karl A. Wittfogel, *Oriental Despotism*, New Haven, Yale University Press, 1957, is a comprehensive examination of the history and dynamics of bureaucratic systems.

of an ubiquitous bureaucracy may be related to a notable weakness of autonomous political structures. In modern times it was only on the wreck of the bureaucracy, in a period of war-lordism and administrative anarchy, that political parties were finally able to emerge and lay the basis for a powerful one-party structure capable of re-organizing and controlling the bureaucracy. In a sense, the war-lord period represented a feudalization of Chinese society.

Russian history is parallel to Chinese in this respect. The Czarist bureaucracy left little scope for autonomous politics and revolutionary movements could survive only abroad. The war-caused bureaucratic collapse cleared the ground for a short-lived fluorescence of free politics, followed by the triumph of a monocratic party.

In the West, autonomous political institutions developed best in countries with a feudal background, where bureaucratic power was weak and fragmented. This was notably true in England. For different reasons—its frontier character, for example—American bureaucracy was also relatively weak and fragmented. In France, despite a long feudal background, the absolute monarchy consolidated national power through a growing bureaucratic apparatus, and this course of development may be related to the continuingly precarious basis of French political life.

But such historical examples are merely suggestive. Rather than explore them in more detail, it may be more fruitful to investigate the inner workings of the political and bureaucratic systems in contemporary transitional societies to see whether or not we can discover some more specific reasons for the suggested relationships. I will examine, in turn, the relation of bureaucracy to party systems, the electorate, legislatures, courts, and executive leadership.

Bureaucracy and the Party System

Let us consider, first, the basis of recruitment to a bureaucracy and its relation to political development. It has become axiomatic in modern public administration that bureaucrats *ought* to be selected on the basis of universalistic, achievement criteria, best expressed in an examination system; and that employment should be for a career. The pressure of international advisers and the demand for technically qualified personnel to staff the program-oriented services of modern government has meant the proliferation in all the developing countries of civil service and personnel systems rooted in the merit and career concepts. Indeed, so deeply engrained are these ideas that even to question their utility is to risk castigation as a heretic and subversive.

Yet the merit system cuts at the root of one of the strongest props of a nascent political party system, namely spoils. Once political parties are strongly established, once the public is widely mobilized for political action, prepared to give volunteer support, and to contribute financially from a broad base of party membership, it is possible to reduce or perhaps even eliminate spoils as an element of support for party activity.

Certainly, if American history can be taken as suggestive, the spoils system played an important part in galvanizing the parties into action. Even today, although national politics and the federal administration has been substantially purged of spoils, a strong residue of spoils appointments still remains. If local politics, on which our party machines rest, were to be deprived of spoils, they might well lose much of their vigor. Without for a moment denying the evils associated with the spoils system, one cannot escape noting the intimate relation between spoils and the growth of political parties.

It is, of course, no easy matter to organize spoils in such a way as to strengthen political parties. A natural tendency exists to use opportunities for patronage appointments and graft through public contracts to favor relatives and friends of individual politicians rather than to reward those who work for a party as an organization. But without official sanction for at least some degree of spoils in the bureaucracy, it is difficult to institutionalize procedures and rules for the use of spoils to reward bona fide party workers.[13]

A second relation of spoils to political growth ought to be considered. No doubt a career bureaucracy of specialists is administratively more capable than a transitory bureaucracy of spoilsmen. But, by the same token, the career bureaucracy can project greater political power on its own, resist more successfully the politician's attempts to assert effective control. What is lost in administrative efficiency through spoils may be gained in political development, especially if party patronage can also be used as a lever to gain control over administration.

The existence of a career bureaucracy without corresponding strength in the political institutions does not necessarily lead to administrative effectiveness—as I have argued elsewhere.[14] Without firm political guidance, bureaucrats have weak incentives to provide good service, whatever their formal, pre-entry training and professional qualifications. They tend to use their effective control to safeguard their expedient bureaucratic interests—tenure, seniority rights, fringe benefits, toleration of poor performance, the right to violate official norms—rather than to advance the achievement of program goals. Hence the career, merit bureaucracy in a developing country not only fails to accomplish the administrative goals set for it but also stands in the way of political growth.

Not, of course, that one would want to see a wholesale transformation in developing countries of their present career bureaucracies into spoils. However, it might be that, by judicious selection, a range of positions, a "schedule C," could be declared open for political appointment with a counterpart provision that they should be filled only by persons who meet requirements for service to a winning party.[15]

It is characteristic of a one-party state for the dominant group to eliminate all rivals. The loss for freedom is a gain for political and administrative development in the perverse sense that policy direction is sharpened and bureaucratic performance held to a higher level.

But in a polity shaped by bureaucratic dominance, opposition groups tend to be tolerated, and a ruling party takes shape as a coalition of diverse elements. The ruling coalition lacks coherence or unity—although it may well be the inheritor of a revolutionary tradition from an earlier period of common struggle against foreign rule. It would perhaps be too strong to say that the coalition is formed of elements congenial to the bureaucrats, but at least they are typically ambitious men attracted by the crumbs to be gathered off the tables of the elite, rather than by any hope of creating a better political or social order. In a sense they form a sodality of the gentry.[16] Because the distribution of crumbs—"pork," to use the American equivalent—can reach far corners, the coalition, with bureaucratic backing, can usually count on electoral success.

[13] Even the hope of contracts might open sources of finance to opposition parties which would otherwise be doomed to poverty and ineffectiveness.

[14] "Bureaucracy in Transitional Societies," *op. cit.*

[15] Moreover, the needs for technical competence in the twentieth century are undoubtedly greater than they were in the nineteenth. Hence any move to open the door for spoils appointments certainly ought to set minimum standards, and reserve key technical positions for non-partisan recruitment.

[16] The word "gentry" is here used in a technical sense to refer to a "ruling class" whose members base their power primarily on access to bureaucrats or bureaucratic status. Both an aristocracy and a gentry possess wealth (chiefly in land) and power, but an aristocracy's wealth is the source of its power, whereas a gentry's wealth is the fruit of its power. For a perceptive analysis of the most classical instance of a gentry see Chung-li Chang, *The Chinese Gentry*, Seattle, University of Washington Press, 1955.

Without the hope of spoils, and with minimal opportunities for penetrating the career services, the opposition parties can attract only the confirmed idealist, the bitterly disappointed, the fanatic, and the maladjusted: all predominantly drawn from the intelligentsia. Moreover, without real hope of an electoral victory and spoils, there is no strong incentive for these hostile fractions to coalesce, to form a unified opposition, nor is there much reason for them to be loyal to a system of government which offers them no hope of rewards. The hostile political fractions then become cults, sectarian, a total way of life, an absorbing preoccupation for the small minorities attracted to them. Addicted to violence and extremism, to poly-functionalism[17]—since they cater to the religious, social, and economic as well as the political interests of their members— they form cancerous growths in the body politic. They serve, also, as the breeding grounds of a one-party dictatorship since, with an appropriate spin of the wheel of fortune, one of them may someday find itself catapulted into power.[18]

In a working democracy the opposition parties help to keep the party in power politically alert and responsible to public demands. The hostile fractions in a bureaucratic polity, although labeled opposition parties, cannot really have this effect. Instead, they undermine the system, weaken the coherence of the ruling party, and strengthen the relative power of the bureaucracy which may be called on— through police or army—to suppress one or more of the fractions as they resort, in turn, to violence. (In pointing to the role that spoils played in the growth of the party system in the West, I do not mean to suggest that the same course should or will be followed elsewhere— but some functional equivalent must be found if effective party systems are to grow.)

Bureaucracy and the Electorate

It was one of the favorite theses of the colonial regime that political participation ought to begin at the local level. The administration of central government, it was said, ought to be left to the colonial bureaucracy; the development of village, communal, and municipal councils would provide ample opportunity for the political education of the indigenous population. After having mastered the techniques of democratic politics at this level, the population would be prepared to take over a major share in government at the provincial level, ultimately at the national. This theory was also propagated by Sun Yat Sen and the Kuomintang for Nationalist China, and has been tested in recent years in Taiwan.

Strangely enough, nationalist revolutionaries and the intelligentsia of the dependent countries never looked with favor on this thesis. They called it a delaying tactic of imperial rule, and sought to plunge immediately into national politics, bypassing the local level. The same tendency has persisted since independence in the new nations. The dominant elite, having gained control in the center, manipulate the bureaucracy as an instrument of control over local government,

---

[17] "Poly-functionalism" may be defined as a condition intermediate between being functionally "diffuse" and functionally "specific." In other words, it serves fewer ends than a traditional family, but many more than a Western-style "association." Elsewhere I have called such poly-functional groups "clects."

[18] Examples of such tightly knit minority "parties" or fractions are described in many works, but their characteristics are often attributed to racial, ethnic, religious, or other local and cultural features rather than to general functional relationships common to most of the "transitional" societies. See, for a good example, Myron Weiner, *Political Parties in India*, Princeton, Princeton University Press, 1957, especially pp. 223–264. Although Indian political development has been outstanding in comparison with most of the other new states, the inability of sectarian opposition parties to form a stable coalition or unified opposition is a major obstacle to further strengthening of democratic politics in India.

giving little more than lip service to the philosophy of decentralization and local autonomy. One suspects there must be some deep-seated dynamism that moves the ruling groups in a developing country—whether under colonial or native control—to strengthen central bureaucratic administration at the expense of local self-government.

Let us seek clues to this paradox by considering the changes taking place in these countries.

In the former, traditional situation, local affairs were, in fact, largely controlled by local leaders—gentry, notables, petty chiefs, or headmen—and even within the community, the affairs of sub-groupings came under caste, clan, family, and temple control.[19]

The new regimes in developing countries, whether ruled by foreign imperialists or a native intelligentsia, have sought major socio-economic transformations in their societies. In this effort, they uniformly met resistance from traditional leaders and groups at the local levels. Insofar as their modernizing goals were limited, they permitted local affairs to be run in the age-old fashion, but to the extent that they wished to extend the domain and speed of development, they had to seize administrative control and impose change. For a modernizing elite—whether native or

foreign—the value of development always outweighs local autonomy.[20]

As, gradually, local populations became enmeshed in the transformation, some among them began to desire the products of the new order, and so the modernizing central leadership discovered new allies in the small community. It then seemed practical to urge local self-government, with the expectation that rural elites, when exercising local autonomy, would continue and finance the very policies desired by the central authorities—the extension of roads and bridges, building of schools, improved sanitation and health measures, more rational agricultural practices, further expansion of the market system. Interestingly, spokesmen of local interests came, in large measure, to accept these targets, but not their costs. Who would pay for change?

Although central governments always imposed some taxes on the rural population, most of the revenue of the new nations comes from the more productive sectors, located in the major urban areas, and from customs revenues imposed on international trade. Hence the cost of local improvements has been largely financed from the center. Indeed, only this ability to pay for modernization enabled national governments to extend the range of their control as far as they have. If the center had merely demanded change, requiring localities to finance their own development, it is doubtful if the modernization of rural hinterlands would have gone as far as it has—limited as that is.

Proposals for more local self-government, however, have met an impasse, for, while local leaders have been all too willing to manage local improvements, they have been unwilling to finance them. They want the central government to pay for

[19] For an explicit account of this system in village India, see Bernard S. Cohn, "Some Notes on Law and Change in North India," *Economic Development and Cultural Change*, **8** (October 1959), 79–93. An earlier characterization of the same situation in India is provided by Henry Maine in *Lectures on the Early History of Institutions*, London, J. Murray, 1893, p. 380. For an account of Chinese local control in the traditional system see Martin Yang, "Former Rural Control in China" (Unpublished manuscript, no date). Even Karl A. Wittfogel, who argues most strongly for the totally despotic character of the traditional bureaucratic system in China, refers to this characteristic local sphere of autonomy as a "beggars' democracy," *op. cit.* pp. 108–125. In feudalistic societies the extent of autonomy for local ruling groups was, of course, even more marked.

[20] The developmental patterns desired by the elite, of course, are typically one-sided—they serve their own economic, political, or national interests more than the interests of the local populations concerned.

development programs, but not to staff and control them. Naturally, no central regime is willing to turn over its funds for unsupervised use by local authorities. Every bureaucracy insists on maintaining some control over the use of its own money.

By contrast, in the "developed" countries, local self-government, to the extent that it is effective, rests on the ability and willingness of local communities to tax themselves for a substantial part of the services they want. When central funds *are* allocated for use by local authorities, they often involve matching of contributions and, necessarily, some central supervision. Even in developed countries, any programs which are fully financed from the center are typically run by field offices of central government rather than by autonomous local authorities, even where co-opted grass roots organizations participate in making and implementing policies. The measure of local autonomy in a country is certainly related to the ratio of locally financed and controlled programs to local programs which are centrally financed and controlled. In developed countries this ratio is large; in the developing ones, very low.

The weakness of local self-government in transitional societies means, of course, that the bulk of the citizenry are denied meaningful participation in modern-style politics. Of course, traditional forms of self-rule may persist. Even where local elections are held, they tend to be of limited significance. They may, of course, become the focus of great local excitement, and certainly they can have an impact on the local scene.[21] The question is: to what extent do such elections give the population a significant political experience, i.e., one in which meaningful choices are

[21] See Morris Opler, "Factors of Tradition and Change in a Local Election in Rural India," in Richard L. Park and Irene Tinker, eds., *Leadership and Political Institutions in India*, Princeton, Princeton University Press, 1959, pp. 137–150, for a dramatic case study of the impact of elections on a village community.

made. Insofar as effective control of developmental programs are retained—because financed—by field agents of the central bureaucracy, elected local officials lack significant powers of decision making. Their function becomes primarily ceremonial. Electoral contests then determine relative prestige ratings, not program or policy issues. Insofar as any appointments are made by the locally elected officials, purely personal patronage rather than party or program needs are considered. Electoral victory may depend on who can marshal more of the electorate by mobilizing his kinship alliances, rather than on party commitments to specific policy issues. No doubt in all patronage, personal motives are mixed with policy and program goals—but in significant politics there would have to be at least a minimal concern for issues in the contest and resulting patronage.

For local self-government to be significant as a training ground for national politics, I think it must involve electoral choices between alternative programs for which the voters themselves must pay, at least in part. If one party offers an expanded road and school program at the cost of heavier taxation, and the rival party offers a reduced benefit program with lighter taxation, then the community can make a significant choice. Or, the rival parties may offer different packages of public benefits, undertaking to collect the cost by contrasting tax schedules, in which the burden would fall more heavily upon one group or another in the community. Only in this way can both politician and voter learn the meaning of political choice instead of agitation and demagoguery.

These statements should not leave the impression that in the more developed countries local politics always measure up to this idealized account of effective self-government. However, it is argued here that, relatively speaking, local politics and significant choices by local electorates tend to be more meaningful in the industrialized than in developing countries.[22]

The weakness of local government—at its best—in the more developed countries shows how much room for growth still remains in these societies. It should also be noted that in traditional societies, prior to the impact of industrialization, there often existed a substantial measure of local autonomy, though without the formal machinery and ideology of modern self-government.

The most typical situation in the transitional societies, as I see it, weakens political institutions and strengthens bureaucratic. The more local communities have their appetites whetted by the "demonstration effect" for improvements which can be paid for only by the central government, the more unrealistic local politics becomes, and the more extended the central bureaucratic apparatus.

Even the goals of economic development are not necessarily advanced under these conditions. If local schools are built, for example, the most energetic and intelligent young people to graduate leave for higher schools in market centers and universities in the urban areas, where they seek posts in the expanding bureaucracy. The frailty of local politics and development means there is little to hold the most able. Instead of contributing to the vigorous growth of a locality, centrally based development deprives it of its best potential leadership, leaving a residue of partially educated men and women whose level of aspirations has risen more rapidly than their capabilities. Hence the bitterness and frustration of local politics increases without compensating successes in self-realization and achievement.

No doubt similar phenomena can be found in the more developed countries, but there are significant differences of degree. Since the over-all level of educa-

tion is higher in the developed countries, those who remain in rural areas, while less schooled than the urbanites, nevertheless reach a higher level of training than the village folk of transitional societies. Rural families in developed countries, moreover, are typically closer in terms of communication and transportation to secondary urban centers than are the villagers of non-industrialized countries.

The speed of social transformation also means that the gulf between traditional- and modern-minded people—the unschooled and the schooled—is greater in transitional than in industrial societies. This not only reinforces the motivation for those with schooling to leave their uncongenial, rural homes; it also tends to block the application, by those who remain, of skills and values they acquired in school. The level of effective modern education of rural youth does not equal the level of formal schooling they may have enjoyed, and this differential is probably much greater in the newly developing than in the more developed countries.

It may be that political development, at least toward a democratic type of political action, can be attained only at the cost of slower economic and social development. It is often said that authoritarianism can force economic development at a more rapid rate than democracy. Less familiar is the corollary that efforts to speed the rate of economic development may lead toward bureaucratic authoritarianism.

Bureaucracy and Interest Groups

One of the pillars of political action in advanced countries is the "association," through which functionally specific interests are articulated and communicated to decision-making centers. Although interaction between associations and government takes place through bureaucracy as well as through political institutions, the dominant mode tends to be with political party and legislative organs. The importance of interest groups in politics has only recently been recognized, but research on

[22] See, in this connection, A. B. Lewis, "Local Self-Government: a Key to National Economic Advancement and Political Stability," *Philippine Journal of Public Administration*, **2**, 1 (January 1958), 54–57.

the subject has by now produced a substantial literature.

These same associations also play a key role in policy implementation or rule application. The literature of public administration has made this process a subject of study to some extent. Thereby an unfortunate dichotomy has arisen: interest groups as originators of policy proposals, in the "input" process, are regarded as playing a political role, whereas when these same groups participate in policy execution they are regarded as playing an "output" or administrative role. The activities of the groups are thus viewed from two perspectives, but not as a whole. However arbitrary the dichotomy in the context of advanced societies, in the study of developing countries it has a particularly confusing effect.

If by political development we refer primarily to the process of democratization, the growth of popular control over government, then perhaps this distinction is useful. But in another sense political development refers to the process of politicization; increasing participation or involvement of the citizen in state activities, in power calculations, and consequences. In this sense the regimentation of citizens by the rulers is as much politicization as the initiation by citizens of demands upon the rulers. From this point of view, a modern totalitarian regime, with its total political regimentation, is as much politicized as a fully democratic regime. Both differ from the traditional polity in which, to a great extent, the mass of the subject population is little involved in political decisions, largely ignored by the rulers, and hence predominantly indifferent to their actions.

In the process of development the citizenry becomes progressively involved in matters of state, i.e., politicized. The primary vehicle or "transmission belt"—to use Joseph Stalin's colorful phrase—for such politicization is the interest group. However, in view of its dual role as instrument for popular regimentation as well as

for public control, both should be considered in a full analysis of this process. The politicization of a population by its progressive involvement in groups organized by the state as transmission belts for policy implementation is a political matter, even if we label it an administrative development. But the fact that we do label such developments administrative blinds us to their political significance.

In contemporary developing countries, bureaucratic agencies are set up to implement new programs oriented to the concept of the welfare state, intimately affecting much of the population. Ranging from public health, educational, and agricultural services to community development, these programs necessitate a massive coordination of the population. To carry them out, officials must mobilize those affected in many special-interest groups. Educational programs, for example, may require something like the parent-teachers' association to promote family cooperation for the school attendance of children, and to prepare even more ambitious programs of community or fundamental education. Agricultural programs require the creation of farmers' associations to transmit new techniques, improved seeds, fertilizers, and farm equipment. Women's groups and "4-H clubs" carry innovations into the home. Cooperatives handle credit and marketing problems. Community health units facilitate the dissemination of new drugs, police water supplies, enforce immunization drives, and sponsor clean-up campaigns or the installation of privies. Capping all the special interest groups are community development programs which call for the creation of all-purpose councils to plan and implement, under government supervision, a wide range of activities.

Without questioning the utility of these programs, I wish merely to note their political implications. In almost every case, the creation of these interest groups follows a bureaucratic initiative. They are not a spontaneous product of citizen demand in response to felt needs. The groups extend the reach of the bureaucracy, providing it with transmission belts through which total mobilization can, potentially, be achieved. Hence the growth of state-sponsored interest groups augments bureaucratic control, without necessarily strengthening any centers of autonomous political power capable of bringing bureaucratic machines under popular control. In other words, this process leads to political development in the sense of politicization, but not democratization. Quite the reverse, for here we see how accelerated economic and social development contributes to bureaucratic power, and lays the foundation for totalitarianism, weakening the prospects for democratic control over government.

There are many reasons for the weakness of autonomous interest group formation in the developing countries. One is simply the propensity for bureaucrats to be suspicious of autonomous groups outside their control. It is easier to deal with an orderly, unified system, especially if it has been set up to meet their specifications. Hence groups that start to organize on their own, or with external support—from a foreign government, foundation, or religious body—are viewed with hostility and, if not actually suppressed, are at least given little cooperation as compared with officially sponsored groups.

A second reason is financial. In poor countries the cost of voluntary organization can scarcely be obtained from members who barely get enough to meet their own minimum living needs. After collecting dues and contributions, voluntary groups find their resources still hopelessly inadequate. They must succumb to necessity, and either content themselves with a largely ineffective marginal existence or go, hat in hand, to government, begging financial help. The same dynamism that cripples local government weakens voluntary associations that rely on governmental subventions for existence. Inevitably the government takes control as a condition of granting assistance, and so the would-be

private group becomes another transmission belt.

Thirdly, the leadership for modernization comes predominantly from the intelligentsia, an intellectual class schooled in the concepts and aspirations of the "modern" world. This leadership, as I have indicated above, tends to be funneled into the central cities, leaving the hinterland starved of modern leadership. Into this partial vacuum the bureaucracy steps, the local representatives of central government being, by and large, the most modern and best educated persons in their districts. The result, quite naturally, is that in rural areas the bureaucratic leaders of interest groups usually dominate by relative superiority of talent and training the private citizens with whom they deal.[23]

No doubt governmentally sponsored associations sometimes become strong enough to declare their independence of the officials who brought them into being. This might happen in some developing countries. There seems no reason to assume that it would necessarily happen, and under totalitarian conditions mass organizations have remained passive tools of autocracy for a considerable time. Perhaps steps could be taken, as a matter of policy, to offer incentives for the achievement of autonomy by such associations. In any event, the degree of independence of private associations may be determined only by empirical investigation in each case. It is not something which can be assumed a priori.

Urban Interests and Pariah Entrepreneurship

It may be suggested that the situation differs in the urban areas where modern commerce and industry and the nonbureaucratic intelligentsia are concentrated. Here also the example and influence of

[23] For a case study illustrating these and other factors responsible for the weakness of interest groups see my "Interest and Clientele Groups," in Joseph L. Sutton, ed., *Problems of Politics and Administration in Thailand*, Bloomington, Ind., Institute of Training for Public Service, Indiana University, 1962, pp. 153–192.

other countries is strongest. Yet even here powerful factors operate to inhibit the effective political influence of interest groups. Moreover, a new set of factors show up which give a perverse twist to the relation between interest groups, bureaucrats, and politics.

It is at the urban core of government that the processes of development—especially commercial and industrial development—come to focus in the new states. These activities depend for their success upon the enterprise and skill of entrepreneurs who combine the various factors of production and control the process of distribution.

Here is a class which surely has the need, knowledge, and financial capacity to support interest groups—chambers of commerce, trade associations—through which to exercise pressure for the control of government. At least, this has been the history of the democratic developed countries, and an analogy is suggested for the developing areas. However, close inspection suggests risks in this analogy.

All too frequently, the private entrepreneurial class in the new nations suffers from lack of formal access to the political process. Its members are often drawn from a marginal group—racially, ethnically, or religiously—or of alien origin. Discriminatory laws and regulations are imposed against them. In applying these rules, members of the bureaucracy often exploit their power to penalize the entrepreneur unless he rewards them for overlooking infractions of the law.

Hence there develops a symbiotic relationship of "antagonistic cooperation" between government official and private entrepreneur. The official supplements his inadequate official income. In exchange, the businessman is permitted to violate regulations.

Why does such a situation continue? Characteristically in the new nations those who can acquire status, prestige, and power through land or official positions do so in preference to a business career—both because of the low status and

the risks involved. Hence only those who cannot follow the preferred occupations choose entrepreneurship. Thus a self-selecting mechanism restricts the entrepreneurial role to members of marginal or alien communities.

How can the obvious evils of this situation be overcome? Apparently only by imposing the role of law upon bureaucrats, requiring them to enforce the law impartially. At the same time, a legal structure is needed which favors the development of commerce and industry by protecting property and contract rights, imposing non-confiscatory tax rates, opening economic opportunities to all candidates without regard to particularistic criteria, etc. But how can such a regime be established? Clearly a prerequisite is the achievement of sufficient political power by the business community to impose responsibility and favorable laws upon the bureaucrats.

One cannot realistically expect uncontrolled bureaucrats to impose this kind of regime upon themselves when it is clearly against their immediate interests. Moreover, it is in the bureaucratic interest to prevent the creation of any groups in the business community that have a chance of gaining enough power to impose the rule of law upon government. Because entrepreneurs have the greatest potential for group formation, the bureaucrats use their sharpest weapons against them.

A classic bureaucratic weapon designed to meet the threat of entrepreneurial organization is to set up a counter-organization based on would-be entrepreneurs drawn from the dominant community. This counter-organization then seeks policies that discriminate in favor of their members against those of the established entrepreneurial community. Thus political support is mobilized for a continuation of basically anti-entrepreneurial policies, without risking the formation of a strong new entrepreneurial class, since the members of the favored group find it easier to convert their special privileges into cash on the black market than to learn a difficult business and do the hard work required.

Another bureaucratic tactic to counter the threat of growing power in an entrepreneurial community is to establish a public sector, to organize a mixed economy and use public enterprise to set the pace, regulate, or fill the gaps of the private sector. In practice, of course, these governmental undertakings are often run at a loss, requiring subvention from public funds. This enables them to compete with the private entrepreneur, and limit his growth or even force him into bankruptcy. Enterprises which can be readily controlled, especially where the state is the main customer or supplier, are turned into government monopolies, and the private sector eliminated. If a state enterprise is profitable, there may be an irresistible temptation to use official pressure—taxes, regulations, licenses, exchange control— to hamper, perhaps destroy, the competing private enterprises. As a result of these maneuvers, the private entrepreneur is forced to the wall, losing his capacity to organize effective political power. So long as he continues to buy protection from the bureaucracy, he is permitted to survive as a marginal or pariah entrepreneur, but not as a politically influential class.

As to the public sector, it is scarcely possible to expect efficient and honest management of enterprises run by a bureaucracy that is not under political control. Who will prevent officials vested with authority to run public enterprises from dipping into the till, from squeezing the state just as they squeeze the private businessman? If conspicuous peculation is eliminated, more inconspicuous forms abound. Where effective political control over a bureaucracy is lacking, there is no institutional means for preventing bureaucrats from exploiting their power position at the expense of both private entrepreneurs and public enterprise. (Under such conditions, of course, to expect a public

sector to remedy the developmental weakness of the private sector is delusory.)

The condition described is scarcely one of equilibrium. Only a relatively passive bureaucracy, drugged by its own self-indulgence, can perpetuate its own regime indefinitely. With the growing pressure of international opinion and example, and the impact of bi-lateral and multi-lateral aid programs, systems of bureaucratic power are energized and thrown on the defensive. They must create more and more mass organizations as instruments for program administration. But the dissemination of organizational skills is the sowing of dragon's teeth. If the entrepreneurial community could organize power effectively, it might impose a middle class revolution on the government, establish the rule of law, create a favorable environment for economic development and administrative efficiency by means of a democratically controlled bureaucracy. This has been the history of the Western democracies, and to a considerable extent also of Japan. The pre-condition, however, was a relatively weak bureaucracy and a socially entrenched burgher class.

The alternative course of events is, unfortunately, more likely. In the inter-organizational struggle reaped from the Cadmean harvest, victory is more likely to go to a mass-movement led by a political fraction under the leadership of an embittered intelligentsia group of the type described above under political parties. Such a group will build a new Thebes. It may embrace the doctrines of international Communism or, perhaps more likely, it will espouse a national-chauvinistic ideology, fascistic and xenophobic. Among the chief targets of its hatred will be the pariah entrepreneurial community, and so its program will almost surely involve destruction of this group and expansion of state power through nationalization and government monopoly of industrial development.[24] It will, of course,

[24] For an extremely suggestive discussion of the emergence of mass-movement, single

bring the bureaucracy under control. But the price of this kind of political development is social disaster—the loss of individual freedom and the risk of international war.

Bureaucracy and the Legislature

With but few exceptions the history of parliamentarism in the new nations is without lustre. In many, as in Egypt, military regimes have suspended representative institutions altogether, after a period of noisy but ineffective experimentation with legislative bodies and ephemeral constitutions. "Guided democracy" is Sukarno's alternative to parliamentary politics after a period of unsuccessful trial and error. Turkey, Pakistan, Burma, the Sudan, many Latin American states fit this pattern. Since the revolution of 1932, Thailand has tried a variety of parliamentary systems and constitutions, but they have uniformly been pliant tools for the group in power. Since the first republic in 1912 the Chinese have followed parliamentarism as a will-o'-the-wisp.

Notable exceptions have been India and the Philippines. In both instances several decades of vigorous parliamentary experience under colonial rule preceded independence,[25] and the political habits established during dependency have stood these nations in good stead since obtaining their freedom. But even in these exceptional cases, closer scrutiny reveals serious weaknesses in parliamentary power.

The case of Japan is instructive for, with all its weaknesses, the Diet has shown itself, despite black periods and long-term deficiencies, a notably effective legislative body. Perhaps the astonishing success of Japan's industrialization drive and the

[footnote 24 continued
party regimes, see Robert C. Tucker, "Towards a Comparative Politics of Movement-Regimes," American Political Science Review, 55 (June 1961), 281–289. Anti-semitism and the myth of racial superiority were the typical signs of such a path in European political development.
[25] Plus, in the Philippine case, the energetic parliamentarism of the Malolos Constitution during the transition period to American rule.

relative efficiency of its bureaucracy is not unrelated to this fact.

If we ask for an explanation of the miserable record of parliamentary institutions in the new nations, we may look for an answer to the range of parliamentary substructures already examined in this chapter. A parliament or congress is not just an assembly to pass resolutions. As a supreme decision-making body for a polity, it must effectively represent its constituencies and have weapons with which to command the obedience of the governmental apparatus, the bureaucracy.

Among the supports of the legislative body are the electoral system, political parties, and interest groups. Unless the assemblymen have been chosen through an electoral process in which significant choices are registered, they cannot have a meaningful popular mandate. Each or all of the candidates for election may be equally unrepresentative and unresponsive to political demands. If picked up by a ruling clique under plebiscitary conditions, or chosen in a popularity contest or band-wagon-hopping situation where electoral divisions reflect no significant political differences, what and whom do they represent?

As I have suggested above, electoral ineffectiveness largely prevails in the new nations—with some notable exceptions—and the extension of bureaucratic control into local government is one of the reasons for this ineffectiveness. Hence the parliamentary system is undermined at its foundations in most of the new nations, and bureaucratic patterns can be identified as a key element in this weakness.

Unless the political party system is vigorous, assemblies lack an indispensable means of organizing their activities. It is true, I believe, that a strong one-party system can achieve effective control over a bureaucracy. In such a case, however, formally elected parliaments become puppets of the party. If a collegial process does take place in top-level decision making, it is likely to be in a central or political committee of the party rather than in the formal legislature.

One requisite of effective parliamentary life seems to be a vigorous and loyal opposition. But as we have seen, the lack of an effectively organized spoils system in the bureaucracy is one of the reasons why opposition parties are unlikely to be either loyal or unified. Dissident elements take on a sectarian character, and only those driven by fanatical devotion to an alternative political formula are willing, as we have seen, to devote the time and energy needed for the creation of opposition parties or fractions. Such parties undermine the legislative process. They use their positions to disrupt legislation rather than to modify it. Their fanaticism prevents unity as well as loyalty in their opposition. Here again, a fundamental basis of parliamentary vigor is lacking, and one of the contributory factors is the merit and personal patronage system in a bureaucracy oriented to careerism and seniority.

The third pillar of parliamentary vigor is a proliferation of associational interest groups, prepared to speak on behalf of the myriad functional interests of a complex society. Here again, as we have already seen, the weakness of such associations in the new nations, and especially the tendency for bureaucrats to control what associations do exist, deprives legislatures of a major source of independent ideas for policy and for critique of the bureaucracy's performance. In a functioning democracy it is in the bureaucrat's interest to encourage access of interest groups to the legislator—assuming that the bureaucrat's program is already a response, in some degree, to the demands made by the interest groups. In the new nations, by contrast, it is often against the bureaucrat's interest for such a liaison to occur unless the groups are securely under bureaucratic control. Independent interest groups might criticize administrative performance, providing legislators with ammunition for use in establishing legislative supremacy.

But all of these factors are indirect. They involve legislative weaknesses based on non-bureaucratic factors in which bureaucratic factors play an indirect part. In addition, there are reasons for legislative weakness which can be directly attributed to the interaction of bureaucrats with parliamentary bodies. These include matters of *finance* and *policy*.

FINANCE

The traditional basis of parliamentary power in the Western democracies was control over the purse. The need of rulers to seek authorization for new taxes from the representatives of the burghers forced them to limit administrative arbitrariness as a quid pro quo.

In the new nations, under the doctrine that democracy is enhanced by universal suffrage, the vote has been given to a mass public, composed largely of poor peasants and workers who lack any resources for tax purposes. Conversely, those elements of the population which have the most wealth, and hence provide the most promising base for public revenues, are legislatively impotent or disfranchised. The business community in the new states is often composed largely of aliens who, as a matter of constitutional law, are deprived of the vote. Others are drawn from marginal or pariah communities within the state, as we have seen, and lack political power. Even if they can vote, they are swamped in electoral districts where the majority community naturally wins.

Decisions about taxation, therefore, largely involve schedules under which those formally represented in parliament impose taxes upon elements in the population which are not represented.

When those who might pay but are not effectively represented in parliament are called upon to supply the lion's share of the public revenues, it is not surprising that they resist payment—on a principle familiar to all Americans: "no taxation without representation." When revenue officers approach them suggesting that they pay their taxes, they not unexpectedly employ their sharp wits to find ways to evade. One of the most effective ways is to share part of their wealth with the tax collector in order to avoid sharing more of their wealth with the state. Since the bureaucrats are notably underpaid everywhere, and especially in poor countries whose public services expand more rapidly than their national income, they have powerful economic motives for collusion.

To the extent that this situation prevails, bureaucrats even have expedient reasons for encouraging legislatures to impose penalizing taxes and regulations upon the business community. Such measures do not strike at the apparent interests of the majority of the constituents, and they provide a basis for bureaucratic self-enrichment.

A second financial factor has become increasingly important in recent years, namely the extent to which the revenues of many new nations come from external sources. To cite an extreme case, Viet Nam, "more than half of the governmental revenues are directly contributed by American aid, and most of the rest comes from taxes levied on the U.S.-supported commercial import program."[26] While extreme, this situation is typical of many countries, ranging from Korea and Formosa around the Asian rimland to some of the new African countries at the opposite end. The oil-rich lands of the Middle East similarly depend on their royalties.

Insofar as foreign financing prevails, it is apparent that legislatures must again act without effective power. They may adopt budgets expressing a hope for

[26] John D. Montgomery, "Political Dimensions of Foreign Aid," in Ralph Braibanti and J. J. Spengler, eds., Tradition, Values and Socio-Economic Development, Durham, N.C., Duke University Press, 1961, p. 266. Montgomery goes on to note that only 15,000 of the total population of 12.3 million paid income taxes, of whom 12,500 were military and civil bureaucrats paying only a nominal amount.

foreign aid, but are scarcely in a position to make the decisive judgment. Even a country like India, which is more nearly self-supporting than most, has adopted development programs which call for substantial foreign subventions. Success in obtaining these funds depends, in large measure, upon bureaucratic rather than political performance. It is the national planners and the diplomatic representatives of the new nations, the bureau chiefs and counterparts who negotiate with their opposite numbers in the USOMs, international banks, and specialized agency headquarters, who influence the extent and type of foreign aid received. Thus external financing serves, effectively, to reinforce bureaucratic control at the expense of legislative authority.

A third major source of revenue in many developing countries consists of income from state monopolies, lotteries, and other income-producing ventures. Here again, elected representatives have only marginal influence. It is perhaps true that these programs rest upon prior legislative authorization—although even this is not always the case—but, once established, such programs become relatively autonomous bureaucratic empires. The scale of revenue depends upon the economics of the operation, and the skill with which they are managed. Even those which lose money have revenues of their own which can be manipulated to political effect.

If the legislatures are deeply handicapped in their efforts to control public revenues as contrasted with bureaucratic influence in these processes, the same is true of budgetary and expenditures controls. Although data are weak, I do not fear refutation of the statement that in very few of the new nations do the budgetary systems actually used offer legislatures an effective instrument for control over the bureaucracy. Generally old-fashioned types of line-item budget, without much distinction between capital and current expense items, are furnished by the administration. Such budgets may enable the legislators to play bureaucratic politics, supporting their friends in the bureaucracy and punishing their enemies, but they give them no effective weapon for influencing the content and conduct of governmental work. Even where a performance budget has been established, as in the Philippines, it remains largely unimplemented while the legislators cling to the particularistic advantages that the old, line-item budget gives them. The bureaucrats are probably also reluctant to implement the performance budget because in the process they would be compelled to reveal crucial defects in their own performance.

An extreme case, but perhaps illustrative, is that of Bolivia, whose budget office and procedures were created in 1928 in accordance with recommendations of the American Kemmerer mission. A more recent American expert writes of the current state of the Bolivian budget, which includes national and local government expenditures, that it:

"... is prepared by an office that has twelve employees, half of whom have only stenographic and clerical duties. No distinction between capital and current expenses is indicated. Functionally, expenses are broken down by agency into 'Salaries' and 'Other Expenses.' Thus six 'professionals' prepare a budget of better than thirty million dollars . . .

"... only once in the last thirty-one years has the Congress approved the budget prior to the beginning of the fiscal year. Phrased differently, in thirty of the last thirty-one years, the fiscal year has been at least two-thirds over before the Congress has approved the budget."[27]

In the matter of expenditures control, legislatures in developed systems rely upon some form of auditing which enables them to judge the extent to which funds have been spent in accord with the law. Here again, although the documentation is inadequate, I suggest that in most of

[27] Allan R. Richards, *Administration—Bolivia and the United States*, Albuquerque, University of New Mexico, 1961, pp 11–12.

the new nations legislatures lack effective machinery for auditing administrative spending. Even where, under technical assistance, new tools of accounting and auditing have been provided, they have been largely conceived for management purposes, and hence have perhaps strengthened the internal control system of the bureaucracy, the office of president or prime minister, but not the legislature as a political control center.

No doubt these financial powers of legislative bodies are not highly effective in many of the industrially developed countries themselves. It may also be that such procedures as the line-item budget served a useful purpose in helping legislators achieve effective control over bureaucrats, just as the spoils system did. However, these techniques can also be used for personal patronage and favoritism as well as to strengthen party organization. Thus the crucial test is not so much the particular techniques of financial control used—important as they may be—as the way or the purposes for which they are employed.

The position taken here is that, whatever the weaknesses of parliamentary financial controls in developed countries, they have been strong enough to give legislatures substantial leverage in their struggle to impose the rule of law and political policy upon officials. The same cannot be said of most legislative assemblies in the developing countries. But without such controls, how can these bodies hope to formulate enforceable laws?

POLICY

Needless to say, financial control is only one of the supports of legislative effectiveness. Even a good budgetary system—such as may exist in the Philippines, Viet Nam, or India—does not by itself assure parliamentary control over the bureaucracy. If the political party, electoral and associational base is weak, parliaments will still be weak. An effective legislature must also be able to formulate clear and mutually compatible laws. The strange fruit of legislative necrosis is to be found in the realm of policy making.

According to our conventional model, adoption by congress or parliament of a law gives it legitimacy in the popular mind, enforceability through the courts, and a binding authority upon the bureaucracy charged with its implementation. The source of this legitimacy is a political formula, or constitution, on which substantial consensus prevails throughout the population.

Where bureaucrats exercise considerable power, as in most of the new nations, they may themselves take the initiative in seeking legislative authorization for what they wish to do. When such legislation is adopted it does not represent political control over the bureaucracy so much as bureaucratic manipulation of the symbols of legitimacy.

A major source and symptom of weakness for legislatures is even more potent, namely the phenomenon of formalism. Laws on the statute books of the new nations are often not well enforced by the public bureaucracy. The prevalence of corruption in a country is an index of the extent to which bureaucrats are able and willing to violate laws or permit their violation. Bribes may be given to induce officials to perform their duties—as when granting licenses and permits—as well as to overlook non-performance.

Funds and personnel for the enforcement of a law may not be available, so that laws remain dead letters for lack of resources to implement them.

The lack of adequate information—related to the weakness of interest groups—means that legislation is often inherently unenforceable because of technical defects in draftsmanship and unfounded assumptions as well as mutually contradictory norms.

To the extent that formalism prevails in legislation, laws enacted by legislatures cannot be regarded as real decisions. Rather, we have a process of pseudo rule making. It may, of course, be difficult for legislators to tell whether a particular bill or amendment would or would not be enforceable. Moreover, it must be acutely frustrating for a conscientious legislature to learn that hours of work invested in the preparation of a law were of no avail because of non- or mal-administration. Such frustration leads to a variety of responses, including an apathetic disillusionment with the legislative process and hence diversion of interest to other more rewarding types of activity, including direct intervention in administration processes, appointments, contracts, etc. Another response might be to superimpose new, more drastic laws upon the old, unenforced ones, as though a more severe piece of formalistic legislation could correct failures in a milder rule on the same subject. Other legislators, in disgust, become apathetic and turn to private pleasures. The cynicism and hostility of the political fractions toward the whole legislative process is increased.

Here it ought to be acknowledged that one of the forces which aggravates legislative formalism is foreign pressure, precisely because international agencies and aid programs tend to be preoccupied with technical matters of economic development and administration rather than the crucial problem of political development. For example, pressure is applied to the new nations to live up to international standards in a wide variety of fields—health, labor, statistics, legal standards, civil rights, etc. Indeed, model codes are often drafted and adopted by international bodies to provide a guide for developing countries. The governments concerned find that their international status can be improved at relatively little cost merely by putting such laws on their statute books. The prevalence of legal formalism makes it easy to do this since, if laws are widely disregarded, one can virtually adopt any law that will satisfy the foreign critics without having to worry about enforcement. Thus international standards may weaken legislative vigor without securing the hoped-for substantive effects. Such model legislation, indeed, may contribute to administrative corruption and popular disgust with governmental processes. Examples could be cited from laws setting minimum wage standards and regulating labor relations, providing for the control of drugs and food, for sanitary inspection and quarantine of pests.

At a different level, under the impact of technical assistance programs, reorganization plans may be submitted to institutionalize a distinction between line and staff, to decentralize a government agency, establish a position classification scheme, or organize an "O & M" program. Legislation and even formal bureaucratic reorganization to meet these recommendations—including, especially, expansion of the number of governmental units and positions—often follows. But the advisers responsible are subsequently discouraged to find that the anticipated benefits do not result. Indeed, the costs of government may be increased, but not the output of services. The changes have merely rearranged the formalistic surface structures, but not seriously affected the underlying social and power structure which actually determines bureaucratic action.

It is often thought that a constitution provides the major foundation for effective parliamentary rule. However, we might gain a different perspective on this relationship if we tried reversing it, i.e., suggesting that effective legislative performance validates a constitution. When a legislature is unable to make enforceable decisions, public disillusionment and apathy turns against the constitution as well as the assembly. When the constitution itself rests upon a precarious base of support, reflecting the wishes of a small intelligentsia or aristocratic group, it has to legitimate itself by growing success. Without such success, the system is discredited and easily overthrown. Consensus fails to develop.

It would seem that in the transitional societies, with but few exceptions—the Philippines, India, Meiji Japan—parliamentary structures have proved expensive but largely fruitless. They can be given life only by a middle-class revolution capable of imposing the rule of law on the bureaucracy. If a mass-movement regime is installed, they will be totally crushed as a useless decoration. So long as bureaucratic rule predominates, the assembly may be tolerated as an additional crutch to give some color of legitimacy to the administration, but it will not be permitted to exercise the substance of political power.

Parliamentary and constitutional theory in the advanced countries assumes that legislative action provides an effective lever for the control of bureaucratic behavior. My analysis leads me to conclude that this theory works only under special conditions, and that the formal creation of an elected and voting assembly by no means assures its success.

PART V

THE POLITICS OF DEVELOPMENT AND NATION-BUILDING

INTRODUCTION

With the exception of Latin America, most of the transitional societies that we have treated as developing nations have achieved independence in the twentieth century—many in the years since World War II. An unreal optimism and faith accompanied this attainment of independence which found expression in the belief that the cure for "underdevelopment" was national autonomy. Although Western society had relinquished the belief that progress was an inherent quality of life, largely as a result of its own twentieth-century disillusionments, the idea of progress was embraced by the leaders of the developing nations. In spite of the fact that imperialism, to use a Marxian idiom, did appear to contain the "seeds of its own destruction," it simultaneously obscured or silenced many of the tensions and sources of conflict in colonial nations. Colonialism impeded or limited the expression of deeply felt demands that were welling up within the social systems of Asia, Africa, and the Middle East. Thus, the end of imperialism signaled the mobilization of newly independent peoples whose leaders sought "entry" into the twentieth century and the simultaneous release of various social pressures which had been blocked but not relieved under colonialism.

Neither East nor West was prepared for the extraordinary, complex problems which have accompanied independence and for the painful "rites of passage" through transitional society. This state of intellectual, psychological, and even emotional unpreparedness had its origins in an oversimplified understanding of nationalism in the developing nations. It was usually assumed that a single revolution was in progress whereas in reality nationalism was an embracing label for the multiple revolutions which found a point of convergence in it. In addition to the anti-imperialist revolution that culminated in national independence, other forces were operative that one may designate as revolutionary. While acknowledging that nationalism for many was an expressive value, there were significant elements in the new nations who saw it as an instrumental means to rapidly diminish the discrepancies between the industrial nations and their own societies. This approach, of course, assumed accelerated economic growth and industrialization.

A third, and often latent, sentiment of revolutionary proportions was the belief that national independence would also give birth to an internal social revolution eliminating social imbalances and benefiting all elements of society. While only a restricted group of the intelligentsia was committed to egalitarianism, the disadvantaged ethnic, tribal, and religious elements wished to eliminate inequality, specifically those inequalities which were to their disadvantage. Admittedly, these considerations were not present in all of the developing nations; nevertheless, we feel that it is more realistic to conceive of what has transpired and what is still in process in the developing world as part of a multiple revolution rather than a single movement for independence. What is most unfortunate is that these multiple revolutions converged in the time of their appearance rather than having occurred at staggered intervals over a span of decades or even centuries. In the terminology of systems analysis these multiple revolutions created demand overloads on the system.

One may readily grasp the overwhelming character of this problem in developing nations—one which converted the optimism of nationalism into a cynical pessimism among many people—by comparing it with a number of critical events in American history. In a sense the developing nations are confronted at a single point in history with the types of social problems and conflicts inherent in the American Revolution, the framing of the Constitution, the age of Jackson, the Civil War, the Industrial Revolution, the extension of the franchise, the depression of the 1930's, and the "Negro revolt" of today. The issues underlining these historical movements appeared over a period of a hundred and ninety years and have not yet been resolved to the satisfaction of significant segments of American society.

In facing up to these issues—which have increasingly become political issues—the political system of the United States was slowly able to acquire new system capacities and capabilities. At an earlier time in history, for example, the present Negro revolt might have taken place somewhat outside the political system per se. Political development, as Gabriel Almond pointed out in his essay in the first part of the book, implies that more and more issues will be resolved by the political system. The political system in the United States is attacking an increasing number of problems and is acquiring increased capabilities to deal effectively with them. In all probability the American political system will demonstrate a capacity to resolve more or less successfully the issues implicit in the Negro revolt. In the developing nations, comparable issues are being confronted prior to the appearance of political or social mechanisms with the capabilities of resolving them.

The appeal of Marxism to many in the developing nations is based upon an awareness of the complex character of the multiple revolutions for which simple solutions are desired. The development of Western democracy seems remote from the problems experienced on a day-to-day basis by political leaders in the developing nations. Although there has been no marked propensity to embrace Communism, the non-Western intelligentsia seem to sense that the experiences of the Soviet Union and Communist China may be more intimately connected to the transitional state of their own society. Moreover, the West can best explain the problems of developing societies in terms of complexities compounded by other complexities. "Circular causation" has little functional utility for the impatiently discontent. Even the prescriptions for the future offered by the West consist of uncertainties in the form of pragmatism, experimentalism, and the counsel of patience. Marxian ideology, on the other hand, substitutes certainty for uncertainty and provides a causal explanation for the past, a vision of the future, and a direct course of action to achieve this future goal. For millions of people in the developing nations—peasants and intelligentsia alike—the transitional stage signifies the destruction of old beliefs, values, and attitudes without the corresponding emergence of new mental frames and meaningful explanations capable of dealing with change. Traditionalism provided superstitions, myths, and religious explanations for all phenomena—an all-encompassing cosmology. Marxism among contemporary secular ideologies similarly constitutes a *Weltanschauung* appealing to the psychic needs of mass populations.

If there is any validity to the above discussion we may ask: Why has not Communism taken firm hold in the developing nations? There is no satisfactory answer to this problem. We can only speculate that, first, the "game" is not over yet and, second, Communism gained its initial foothold in the developing nations by capitalizing on nationalism and now, in turn, it may become the victim of nationalism. In other words, we are suggesting that somewhere in the development process Communism constitutes a threat to national independence (at least as it is perceived by the political leaders) and begins to loom not as an utopian solution but as a variant of neocolonialism.

There is an attractive, although erroneous, logic in assuming that the developing nations have available to them a number of developmental models in the form of the more advanced or industrialized states and that they have chosen to build their economic and political systems on these models. Despite the manifest accomplishments and general political stability of the more industrialized states, the transitional societies with which we are concerned have in most cases not sought to emulate existing models even though they seek comparable economic development and political stability. Of course, there has been considerable external influence on these transitional systems and the more formal structural arrangements of government sharply resemble those of the more economically advanced societies. Nevertheless, the more pronounced tendency has been to innovate, adapt, fuse, and originate patterns of economic and political development. The developing nations are notably persistent in "going it alone" as they carve out their own styles of political life. We are not implying that they have always been successful in adapting to their own internal needs and aspirations. Rather, we are referring to the empirical evidence which suggests that diversity is the rule, not the exception, and that new forms will probably succeed one another in the political evolution of transitional societies.

The final part of this book deals with the kinds of political systems, governmental arrangements, and adaptive mechanisms employed by the developing nations in the pursuit of political and economic development. Chapter 13 focuses on the political strategies of development and leads to the conclusion, similar to the findings of Stolper and Malenbaum, that there is no one best route to development, either political or economic. The formulas for "success" in one societal setting may spell failure in another.

The initial essay by David Apter examines various political strategies and their relationship and impact on technological change and economic development. Methodologically, Apter demonstrates the utility of structural analysis for comparative research. Based on prior research, mainly, although not exclusively, in Africa, he offers a threefold typology of developmental types, each of which represents a form of regime: (1) the mobilization system, (2) the reconciliation system, and (3) the modernizing autocracy.[1] The crucial point on which he examines each type is whether or not it has the capacity to absorb technological change and to generate new political forms—a criterion of analysis resembling the definition of political development discussed in the first part of this book.

Since the role of government in a country's economic development varies in terms of the goals of development, the level of technology and available resources, and the degree of outside support which the country is both willing and able to enlist, the way that these aspects of economic development are handled depends largely on the nature of the political system in a given country. The development types Apter proposes are different in the ways by which they cope with these facets of economic development. Furthermore, to determine why each type responds in the ways described, a set of variables which can show the process consequences of systems is required. Apter considers four process variables which apply to all three of the developmental types: (1) goals, (2) costs, (3) coercion, and (4) information. As a result of this analysis he indicates the possibilities for development that derive from the given state of available resources and skills and the degree of structural flexibility which a new nation inherits upon independence.

In his article on alternative courses of political development Edward Shils focuses on the political attitudes and aspirations of elites in developing polities and concludes that the predominant political model which they embrace is a regime of *civilian rule* through *representative institutions* in the matrix of *public liberties*. Shils recognizes that these elements of political democracies are not descriptive of the actual regimes evolving in Asia or Africa. They have often veered sharply away from the democratic model in order to push forward with modernization. The deviation of the elites from the democratic model, according to Shils, is not a consequence of desire but a function of necessity.

---

[1] An extended and more elaborate discussion of these types can be found in Apter's recent book, *The Politics of Modernization* (Chicago: The University of Chicago Press, 1965). The neomercantilist society and the military oligarchy are added here as variations, along with the modernizing autocracy, of the same type, namely, the combination of hierarchical authority and instrumental values.

Shils asserts that the political elites retain a preference for the democratic model despite their adoption of nondemocratic political systems. The essential optimism of Shils is tempered by his awareness that over time the alternative adaptive model can come to be viewed as the ideal. Although political ideals are important to the elites and thereby enhance the ultimate prospects of democracy, the quest for "modernity" is the more immediate goal, a quest which may lead to the adoption of authoritarian political styles in order to undermine the deeply rooted forces of traditionalism and to mobilize societal energies in the direction of modernization. Shils' analysis can be questioned on the basis that it may be just as likely that the new oligarchies and authoritarian elites will eventually abandon their modernizing zeal if necessary to perpetuate their elite roles, just as they had earlier adapted political ideals to the exigencies of modernization.

No single nation's experience can provide the definitive answer to the preceding question. The Japanese experience, as described in the article by Robert E. Ward, indicates that authoritarianism may not be destructive of the long-range prospects for democracy. According to Ward's analysis of Japan, authoritarian forms of political organization may be extraordinarily effective in the early stages of modernization and do not preclude the emergence of more democratic forms. A steady and gradual transition from authoritarianism may be essential to the emergence of politics that are both modern and durably democratic.

All societies are stratified—at least for the social analyst—and the developing nations are in the main distinguishable by the sharp cleavages separating strata and the relative lack of mobility among them. In effect, there is a greater likelihood in the developing nations that a person will be born, spend his life, and die in the same social stratum than is likely to be the case in industrialized societies. While there is an economic basis to the systems of social stratification prevalent in preindustrial societies, economic factors are reinforced by and interlaced with traditionalism and ascription. Ultimately, modernization itself involves the substitution of achievement criteria for ascriptive criteria and the emergence of a less rigid system of social stratification.

Until the relatively "closed" stratification systems of the developing nations give way to more "open" systems, social strata will be a far more significant determinant of political behavior than, for example, in Western Europe and the United States, where it is by no means insignificant. This likelihood is enhanced to the extent that a system remains closed and those members of any particular stratum acquire a consciousness of their ranking. Such awareness is what we designate as "class" consciousness and such a consciousness is likely to result in class politics rendering a more strident and combative style to political life. Political instability or authoritarianism are likely consequences of rigid systems of social stratification incapable of adjusting to the impacts of modernization. On the other hand, while social stratification is undoubtedly a source of cleavage, it also performs an integrative function. As Lipset has reminded us, "The organization of working class groups into trade unions or a labor party, for example, both creates a mechanism for the expression of conflict and, perhaps even more important, integrates the workers into the body politic by giving them a legitimate means of obtaining their wants."[2]

We have already been alerted to the importance of social stratification in assessing a society's potential for economic development by Sjoberg's article in Chapter 2. The political implications of some of the patterns of social stratification found in the developing nations are explored in four articles in this volume. Arthur L. Stinchcombe provides an analytical typology of stratification patterns where the dominant economic mode is "agricultural enterprise"—property systems where agricultural production is intended for markets. Unlike stratification in urban areas where occupation is likely to be the significant variable in determining position, rural stratification is conditioned by property arrangements which affect the legal privileges, life styles, distribution of technical knowledge, and the political behavior and organization of rural populations. Inasmuch as the economic base of the developing nations is agriculture and the preponderance of population is rural, Stinchcombe's use of more refined analytical distinctions for understanding class relations and political behavior in rural areas is particularly appropriate for the student of political development.

Despite the numerical and economic importance of rural populations in the developing nations, the reason most students of development have been more concerned with other social sectors is the expectation that the dynamic initiative toward modernization will come from a group which is less tradition-bound and more experienced in the organizational skills of national politics. The next two articles, by Manning Nash and John J. Johnson, conclude that the middle class does not have the political power or the numerical strength to achieve political dominance independently; it will be necessary for the middle class to work out an effective political alliance with other social elements who may find, at least for limited purposes, common cause with the type of modernizing aspirations of the middle class. Nash, who is primarily concerned with Guatemala, suggests that the most likely modernizing coalition will be between the middle class and the rural-based Indian, the same combination that joined forces in Mexico much earlier in this century. Johnson, on the other hand, has based his findings on research in a number of more economically advanced states of Latin America and proposes that in these societies the probable political ally of the middle sectors is the urban working class.

Nash feels that the conventional concepts of culture and society have tended to obscure the presence in the developing nations of at least two distinct cultural traditions that exist simultaneously within the same territorial boundaries. The differences between these two societies in a single country

[2] Seymour Martin Lipset, "Political Sociology," in Robert K. Merton, Leonard Broom, and Leonard S. Cottrell, eds., *Sociology Today* (New York: Basic Books, 1959), p. 111.

are sufficiently great and the points of contact and articulation between them so few that Nash introduces the concept of "the multiple society with plural cultures" as a more useful social type in understanding many of the developing nations. Modern society also demonstrates social and cultural variations; but, Nash would maintain, these are class variations within a basically common culture different in kind and degree from the variations found in "the multiple society."

Johnson, however, discerns that there are strains in the coalition between the middle sectors and urban labor which may induce the middle sectors to look elsewhere for political support. He suggests that the middle sector leadership may attempt to find a source of political support among farm workers by appealing to them through programs of land reform, social reform in rural areas, and improvement of conditions for agricultural labor.

Unlike Latin America where colonial rule was mainly terminated in the nineteenth century, the states of Africa have only recently acquired independence and some are in the process—or struggle—of achieving it. The influence of colonial rule, even after independence, remains a salient factor in understanding African politics and intergroup relations. According to Martin Kilson, colonial rule was the source and beginning of both modernization and political change in Africa. With independence there has been an obvious decline in the influence of the metropolitan state; however, as before, "expatriate interest groups" from the metropolitan state "continue their monopoly of the financial, industrial, technical and strategic ingredients of modernization." While they are, in a sense, vestigial holdovers from the colonial situation, Kilson also recognizes these interest groups as "colonial modernizers."

The author maintains that the pattern of social stratification among Africans has been sharply affected by colonial rule. Certain regional, ethnic, tribal, and religious groups acquired skills, attitudes, and preferred positions vis-à-vis the colonial state and its expatriate groups that better equipped these groups to deal with and shape the social changes taking place in the post-colonial period. Kilson cites the kinds of factors that resulted in particular groups achieving a favored position which still benefits them. Groups who were in the areas of initial colonization gained a historical advantage over other groups; those living closest to the natural resources required for modernization gained similar advantages under colonial rule; and those groups holding political authority and power in the indigenous system secured a favored political position as a consequence of their political role in the maintenance of the colonial system.

In that part of Kilson's article reproduced in this volume, the focus of concern is the effect on African modernization and political change of the indigenous elite, the masses, and the colonial modernizers. In some respects there is an identity of interest between the indigenous and colonial modernizers; however, the extension of franchise to the masses may introduce constraints and limitations on the way in which the African elites pursue the modernization process. Kilson foresees the possibility that the modernizing elites may utilize the power of the state in order to modernize as they see fit; yet, he questions whether the African elites possess the skills and other qualifications that might justifiably warrant them to act independently of the restraints that might otherwise be imposed upon them by the masses.

Political party systems in the developing nations are relatively sensitive indicators of the discrepancy between the political "ideals" that Shils imputes to the elites and the political adaptations the societies have made to social realities. In the modernized political structures of industrialized nations political parties are most important as mechanisms for aggregating the claims and demands of diverse interest groups. While other social institutions and elements of the polity also reconcile and accommodate interest demands, it is the party system, especially in developed democratic systems, which regulates or "gives order to the performance of the aggregative function by the other structures."[3] Before a party system functions that way, however, political conditions within which there is general agreement on the "rules of the game" must develop and interest groups which are capable of articulating on behalf of their members must exist. These conditions are themselves more likely to be concomitants of industrial societies with developed polities. The absence of these conditions in the developing nations results in party systems that often do not perform well in aggregating interests, yet they do contribute to social mobilization and the modernization process.

The initial article in this chapter by Lucian W. Pye is a stimulating analytical model of transitional politics that seeks to identify the major political characteristics of developing nations. Pye has consciously stressed those characteristics that differentiate transitional from more developed polities. Notwithstanding this emphasis, many of the qualities that Pye imputes to transitional society are still to be found, usually to a lesser degree, in developed polities.[4] Yet the degree of difference is sufficiently great that there exists a basis for approaching the developing nations as a distinct category of study.

The role of political parties in the process of modernization and development is discussed by Hess and Loewenberg in their article on the Ethiopian "no-party state." While the Ethiopian situation is by no means characteristic of developing polities, by analyzing the consequences of a state without parties the authors indicate the utility of political parties as social mechanisms capable of transmitting the ideas, attitudes, and dynamics essential to mass participation in the modernization process. As Duverger had earlier observed, a state without political parties is necessarily a conservative state, and Ethiopia is no exception. Modernizing influences have nevertheless worked their way into Ethiopian society, but Hess and Loewenberg point out that the modernizers have scant opportunity for legitimate political

---

[3] See Gabriel A. Almond, "A Functional Approach to Comparative Politics," in Almond and James S. Coleman, *The Politics of the Developing Areas* (Princeton: Princeton University Press, 1960), p. 40.
[4] Alfred Diamant, "Is There a Non-Western Political Process?" *Journal of Politics*, 21, 123–127, February 1959.

participation. Elsewhere in Africa where political parties have arisen in opposition to colonial regimes, parties have been powerful forces in creating a new sense of solidarity, providing new political needs, stimulating economic organization, and legitimizing new political systems. In Ethiopia the emperor has effectively resisted political parties and, as a consequence, inhibited Ethiopian economic development. Furthermore, the repression of parties and opportunities for political expression in Ethiopia may increase the potential for political instability in the future—or assure a legitimacy crisis after the death of Emperor Haile Selassie.

The usefulness of a party system—even a one-party system—in a national campaign of social modernization can be seen in H. Clement Moore's article on the Neo-Destour Party of Tunisia. The Neo-Destour is an example of what Robert C. Tucker has elsewhere designated a "revolutionary mass-movement regime under single-party auspices," or "movement-regime."[5] Moore's description of the Neo-Destour Party, particularly its organization, warrants its classification as a "movement-regime" or, in the terminology of Moore, a "national" party. The article stresses that although there are structural similarities between the Neo-Destour Party and totalitarian parties, the Neo-Destour reflects the political values of its leader and creator, President Habib Bourguiba, whose political disposition and ideological commitments are antithetical to totalitarianism. Bourguiba is a "determined modernizer," according to Moore, "but his reformist zeal is curbed by a respect for the individual and his democratic liberties."

While the Neo-Destour is structurally authoritarian, Bourguiba has employed its cells and dominant position in Tunisian society to mobilize the energies of the population to carry out government projects and generally to inculcate a sense of citizenship among the masses. In the frame-work of the earlier article by Edward Shils, the Neo-Destour seems to represent the Tunisian elites' adjustment between their more democratic political ideals and the imperatives of modernization and nation-building. Similar to Japan in the nineteenth century, as described above by Robert Ward, Tunisia may constitute a latter-day illustration of a brand of authoritarianism being used to create the social conditions conducive to political democracy.

The final chapter of this volume examines what may be at this stage in history the overriding issue confronting the developing nations: creating and maintaining sufficient internal unity and cohesion for purposes of modernization and political development. The *latent* fissures and cleavages that existed prior to independence have now become formidable impediments to integration and unity in many countries, whereas it had earlier been assumed that modernization would eliminate or overcome these impediments. The available evidence indicates that modernization itself—at least its initial or transitional stages—intensifies the problem in numerous ways and may at times lead to what S. N. Eisenstadt calls "breakdowns of modernization."

[5] "Towards a Comparative Politics of Movement-Regimes," *American Political Science Review*, **55**, 281–289, June 1961.

Although all polities are confronted by integration problems in the course of political development, the cause of the problem often derives from a desire for a high rate of social and economic change. As Myron Weiner points out in his article on "Political Integration and Political Development," the imposition of new tasks, functions, and demands on governments are often malintegrative. He maintains, however, that depending upon the integration problem, or combination of integration problems, confronting a government there are strategies and policy choices available to political decision makers which facilitate their resolving these basic questions. Weiner's article is an attempt to identify the various integrative problems, elaborate upon their significance as they relate to holding a society and a political system together and, finally, examine the possibilities for resolving them.

W. Howard Wriggins also finds that independence does not easily lead to a viable political system but may, instead, facilitate the appearance of internal divisions. It is these impediments to unity, with specific reference to the case of Ceylon, that Wriggins describes and analyses. Communal differences are much more deeply rooted in Ceylon than in most developing nations and Wriggins finds that the communal issue is germane to most of the problems of Ceylonese unity. While in long-range terms economic development may be the overriding demand, Wriggins believes that the issue of national unity and consolidation in the more immediate future warrants equal attention in many of the developing nations.

The progress towards modernization has not only been slow but in many instances constitutional regimes have faltered and given way to authoritarian and autocratic regimes. More specifically, in the final article S. N. Eisenstadt asks what social processes have led Indonesia, Pakistan, Burma, and Sudan away from constitutionalism—or, what has precipitated the "breakdowns in their political modernization." In each of these nations Eisenstadt holds that there was empirical evidence of modernization and the existence of institutional structures generally associated with more modernized polities. However, the existence of modern political, administrative, and economic structures does not imply that they are sufficiently viable to absorb and sustain the growth and social change taking place in other institutional spheres. Although Eisenstadt describes the faltering of constitutional regimes as a "breakdown," he stresses that the process does not constitute a reversion to "traditional" social institutions. It is, more precisely, a reversion to a lower level of system capability. In his incisive analysis, Eisenstadt undertakes to explain how and why such breakdowns occur and, like Weiner and Wriggins, he sees the problem largely in terms of the strains of modernization on inadequately developed integrative mechanisms.

Chapter 13

Political Strategies of Development

SYSTEM, PROCESS, AND THE POLITICS
OF ECONOMIC DEVELOPMENT

David E. Apter

The Approach to the Problem

Economic development and technological change are among the most desired goals of political leaders in contemporary new nations. Countries which have achieved independence from colonial status since 1945—and it is to these nations that this analysis is addressed—share urgent needs in both areas. The new nations have embarked on programs which they hope will help them to ameliorate their material standards. As a result, the relationship of political development to economic development is extremely relevant. What political forms are best suited to economic growth?

Of course, the role of the government varies considerably from one new nation to another. Depending on the role of the specific government, one nation's approach to technological change and economic growth will also vary from another's. The practitioner of economic aid must have a fuller understanding of the nature of the political systems emerging in new nations, if he is to understand—and, indeed, to anticipate—the probable uses and

abuses to which economic aid will be put. Nor are such matters purely practical. Scholars, too, need to give special attention to the relationship between government and economic growth, if they are to understand both normative and analytical theories applicable to new nations.

I hope to show the relationship between politics and economics in new nations, by exploring some of the properties of systems and processes at work, so that applications of policy and ideas of politics about new nations can be seen more realistically. My focal problem centers around the political strategies used to induce technological change and economic development. I have deliberately omitted any discussion of programs of investment and capital formation, technical training, or utilization of economic and technical elites. Nor have I discussed the adaptations of outlook and ideas that are necessary for technological change and innovation. I am aware of these factors, as is everyone involved in research concerning new nations—indeed, the immensity of these problems is blinding. This makes it imperative to attempt to build new theories, ones with a general design but admitting of specific applications.

Many choices in theoretical approach are available to the observer of develop-

SOURCE. David E. Apter, "System, Process, and Politics of Economic Development," in Bert F. Hoselitz and Wilbert E. Moore, eds., *Industrialization and Society* (The Hague: UNESCO—Mouton, 1963), pp. 135–158.

441

ment in new nations. One approach can appropriately be called "behavioral." The behavioral approach examines several variables to infer, from their relationships, an explanation of individual actions, motivations, and perceptions. Principles are established determining significant roles, their allocations and linkages. However, the larger context within which action occurs is not satisfactorily dealt with.

A second common approach is *ad hoc* analysis. In the problem of development, we can assess levels of growth, especially from a comparative point of view, if we introduce three useful factors of development: (*a*) the goals of economic and social development set by political leaders and others significant in the system; (*b*) the state of technology or resources and skills available for achieving those goals; and (*c*) the degree of outside support available. This suggestive and stimulating approach is, essentially, that of W. W. Rostow, as distinct from that of W. Arthur Lewis, in discussing economic growth.[1] By determining the nature of economic growth—or insisting on a standard of goals—and evaluating the resources, human and material, made possible by the state of technology, as well as the external contributions in investment funds and technical assistance, we are enabled to indicate conditions necessary for self-sustained growth and rapid economic development.

For our inquiry, which focuses on the relationship between government and economics, neither the behavioral nor the *ad hoc* approach is entirely satisfactory. In attempting to evaluate patterns of change through examining the phenomena of development, they fail to account for the "system" needs of governments. However, these system needs are in urgent need of analysis. This is illustrated by the fact that new nations are not very stable entities, and, second, that their governments are rarely effectively institutionalized in relation to the society at large.

The alternative approach I am suggesting here is structural analysis utilizing comparative method. The concrete units of analysis are society and government. Economic development is a problem both of government and of members of society. To deal with these units in interaction, with respect to technological change and economic development, we want a theory which indicates the *properties* of the system that form the basis of the relationship between the two units. Moreover we want to indicate the processes which will result from action between systems when confronted with the problems of economic development and technological change.

I have written this long preamble because I wish to lay the foundation for what may appear an obscure way of dealing with readily discernible problems. The behavioral and the *ad hoc* approaches lend themselves to *probabilistic* theories; the third, to *systemic* theories. Each has its respective emphasis. The first two lead to an evaluation of behavior and efficiency in the development process. The structural analysis approach, as used here, leads to a theory of "properties" and relationships deriving from the needs of government—these needs having profound effects on the course of technological change. The specification of relationships is, thus, the purpose of this paper; and the problems of economic development and technological change are treated as of strategic importance for governments of new nations.

I propose to deal with these problems in two steps. First, we must specify the differences, from the range of characteristics distributed among the rapidly growing number of new nations, in the natures of political systems. Second, we must investigate the kinds of response to the problems of technological innovation that these differing systems evoke. Some of the immediate problems are (*a*) whether the role of political entrepreneurship is greater or smaller; (*b*) the degree to which reliance will be placed on state enterprise for economic development; and (*c*) the extent to which talents will accumulate in the central organs of government or will become dispersed and decentralized throughout the system. If this form of analysis proves useful—and, for the present, it must remain experimental—it should provide a more systematic basis for the three problems of growth mentioned above; namely, setting realistic goals, technology and its application, and the use of outside aid.

The discussion brings together two dimensions of analysis developed elsewhere and used independently.[2] The first dimension concerns the natures of the various authority systems that have emerged in the new nations. Three developmental types have appeared. Each type manifests characteristic mechanisms for determining goals and for applying and using available technological and other resources. I have used such types because, while many of the acts and activities in which new nations engage are ostensibly common to many or all of them—and, indeed, many of the instrumentalities and mechanisms of political and economic development are essentially similar—nevertheless, their implications for a given society differ markedly, depending upon the type of political system that is predominant in it. Hence, if we can specify a useful set of systemic properties for political systems, we shall be better able to predict the preferences of political leaders for types of entrepreneurship and economic growth. In addition, more formally, the meaning and social implications of these mechanisms will become more apparent. Our first concern, then, is to define the properties of developmental types that are sufficiently differentiated to illustrate the vast differences in the approaches to economic development in the new nations.

The second dimension concerns the processes of change within each of these types of systems. Having enlarged on the qualities of each of the types, we determine which processes are characteristic in each.

The two dimensions are structural and dynamic. The models presented here are not complete, since extremely important elements are not within the scope of this discussion. Much material has, therefore, been excluded from this paper, because the integration of the dimensions of social analysis in a larger systematic theory must always be coupled with practical field work and research—if not, it is likely to become a sterile and arid system of formal theory-building. Moreover, the integration of dimensions of social analysis inevitably results in considerable overlapping and duplication. Therefore, I believe that the process of building a general theory should consist of taking a limited series of steps, which enable us to piece together theoretical statements and propositions in a careful but necessarily tentative manner.

I should like to emphasize a point I made earlier, namely, that the new nations are different from older and more stable ones in at least one way. One distinguishing characteristic of the former is that the rules of politics and the actions of governments take place in a less institutionalized framework than in the latter. Political leaders, however popular, are acutely aware of the fact that when the institutionalization of governmental structures remains weak, they are particularly vulnerable to public whim and fancy. Hence it is useful to have a dynamic approach to the relationship of government to society.[3] This form of structural analysis has many merits. First, general technological change can be considered in relation to its effects on political organization and on the needs and structure of governments in new nations. In addition, it enables us to indicate the role that government is likely to play in technological change, in terms of reliance on political entrepreneurship and government intervention in the economic process. By examining some of the characteristics of governments in new countries, we can provide a framework for determining the levels of development goals that decision-makers will choose, the uses and applications they will make of technology, and the terms under which they will seek and apply outside aid. In other words, I am attempting here, though dealing with the fundamental system properties of governments in developing areas, to establish general guides for the analysis of more immediate empirical phenomena. We shall now turn to structural types. First I shall indicate their properties, before going on to discuss process variables and relationships.

Three developmental types have been considered here. Each represents a form of regime. We are defining them in order to examine, dynamically, the relationship of government to society. The critical question centers around the capacity of each type to absorb change and generate further innovation. All three types have emerged with lightning speed as a result of the extension of political freedom to Asia and Africa.

These types are, of course, analytical, deriving from a larger structural system of variables. They are "constructions" from typical clusterings of variables which appear frequently in the empirical universe. In that limited sense, they may be regarded as developmental profiles. They were developed primarily with respect to emerging African systems, although it is my contention that they can be applied to the governments of other new nations.[4] They are intended to be similar to Lasswell's "developmental types," the most celebrated of which was "the garrison state." Unlike Lasswell's types, which are not rooted in a wider structural base, these are derived empirically by means of a more elaborate comparative scheme.[5]

Our investigations centered around the observation that each new country in Africa faces a series of choices; in making its choices, it defines its political machinery. Some countries, e.g., Mali, Guinea, and Ghana, have chosen to mobilize their political energies and resources for a grand assault on poverty, ignorance, and backwardness. Others, like Nigeria, have tended toward some union of important constituent parts. They seek, in political

unity, a common denominator to serve all the main groups within the country. Others, e.g., Ethiopia and Uganda, represent something perhaps more rare. In them, change is filtered through the medium of traditional institutions—i.e., innovation itself is traditionalized and rendered compatible with traditional institutions.

The first type we have called a *mobilization system;* the second, a *reconciliation system*; and the third, a *modernizing autocracy*. Examples of the mobilization system include Guinea and Ghana, and, in a more extreme form, the Soviet Union and Communist China. The reconciliation system is operative in Nigeria; it has also been characteristic of the United States and other federal systems. The third, the modernizing autocracy, type may be found in Buganda, Morocco, Ethiopia, and, in its sharpest form, in Japan, particularly after the Meiji Restoration.

Each type comprises five categories: (1) patterns of legitimacy; (2) loyalty; (3) decisional autonomy; (4) distribution of authority; and (5) ideological expression.[6] We can now indicate how each of the three types of regime reflects these categories. Each is an effort to examine structurally the consequences of actual political arrangements in the politics of new nations. The crucial point on which we are examining each type is whether or not it has the capacity to absorb technological change, and, in addition, to generate new political forms.

Let me now consider the types of political systems in more detail. The mobilization system is most clearly described in Selznick's description of an "organizational weapon."[7] Characteristically, mobilization systems try to rebuild society in such a way that both the instrumentalities of government and the values associated with change are remarkably altered. In Africa, countries whose regimes are of this type incline toward the belief that, to produce "the new Africa," the structural precedents of African society must be altered, and a new system of loyalties and ideas must be created, focused around the concept that economic progress is the basis for modern society.

The characteristics of a mobilization system are as follows: (*a*) hierarchical authority; (*b*) total allegiance; (*c*) tactical flexibility; (*d*) unitarism; and (*e*) ideological specialization.[8] Party or government becomes the central instrument of change.

The reconciliation system is considerably harder to define than the first. Its outstanding characteristic is the high value it places on compromises between groups which express prevailing political objectives and views. As we are using the term, a reconciliation system evolves with the formation of a simple political unit from constituent political units which do not lose their political identity on uniting. In practical terms, reconciliation systems can include relatively loose confederations which have recognized structure or highly organized parliamentary regimes. The reconciliation system is characterized by (*a*) pyramidal authority; (*b*) multiple loyalties; (*c*) necessity for compromise; (*d*) pluralism; and (*e*) ideological diffuseness.[9]

The third type of system is the modernizing autocracy, where hierarchical authority is buttressed by traditional concepts of legitimacy. One crucial typical feature of the modernizing autocracy is its ability to absorb change as long as the system of authority is not affected by it. For example, in Uganda, the Buganda Kingdom can employ new skills, modernize the school system, and expand social-welfare activities; a civil service has replaced the patrimonial bureaucratic system while retaining intact its traditional modes of authority. The modernizing autocracy manifests a profound internal solidarity based on ethnicity or religion, by means of which support is retained for the political leaders or king who makes claims on the members of the system and controls them. Its characteristics are: (*a*) hierarchical authority; (*b*) exclusivism; (*c*) strategic flexibility; (*d*) unitarism; and (*e*) neotraditionalism.

I shall further discuss these types before going on to the second stage of this analysis, in which I shall include the consequences of economic development in each of them. As I have said, the role of the government in a country's economic development varies in terms of goals of development, the level of technology and available resources, and the degree of outside support which the country is both willing and able to enlist. The way that these aspects of economic development are handled depends largely on the nature of the political system in the given country. The three forms of political structure of new states are alternative types of systems that are different in the ways in which they cope with these facets of economic growth.

If the functioning of new nations is regarded in terms of these types, the following characteristics are discernible. In mobilization systems, the goals of economic growth are very important. Also, they tend to be unrealistic; many of them are just beyond the normal capacities of technology and resources. Consequently, the effort to achieve them requires considerable discipline. New institutions must be created for the purpose of removing all those social institutions which restrict the processes of economic development. Typically, mobilization systems are inclined toward the ideology of socialism as a contemporary expression of Puritanism. They emphasize discipline and hard work for the attainment of economic goals. This emphasis implies that economic development will re-structure society so that those roles and tasks which are functional to the establishment of a modern economic order will become the dominant ones, while older roles will be obliterated. This is why the mobilization system places great stress on militancy and party organization. Governmental enterprise becomes the major mechanism for economic growth. Correspondingly, high investments are made in education and social welfare, on the grounds that an efficient labor force is the *sine qua non* of economic development. Such systems need a powerful organizational nucleus which takes the major responsibility for the establishment and achievement of goals. They are usually "autocratic" in an organizational sense.[10]

In the reconciliation system, economic growth is more diffuse. Just as political authority is widely dispersed, so there is greater reliance on private entrepreneurship than there is in the mobilization system. Political and economic decision-making is more widespread throughout the society. For example, government shares of the gross domestic product of Nigeria represent roughly only 10 per cent compared to the government shares of Ghana, which are almost 24 per cent and rapidly rising. Politically, the reconciliation system pays far more respect to cultural separatism and local parochialism than does the mobilization system. In so far as the reconciliation type is limited in its decision-making processes by the need to find some "lowest common denominator" which will appeal to its constituent units, its progress toward goals of economic development, and the goals themselves, tend to be very moderate. The relationship between internal resources and the state of technology is closer than in the mobilization type. In the mobilization system, an effort is made to effect the quickest and closest approximation of the material cultures of the technologically advanced nations of the world. Goals are thus endowed with a symbolic quality which is lacking in both the reconciliation or modernizing autocracy systems. Contrasting examples which illustrate the differences between a reconciliation and a mobilization system (where both are concerned with economic growth) are India and Communist China. The respective strategies of development, and their consequences for the people, are vastly different in the two.[11]

The modernizing autocracy exhibits structural similarities to the mobilization type, but it is distinguished by its stability within the context of rapid economic growth. Economic goals are usually more restricted and less symbolic than those of the mobilization system. Also, they must not be insuperable obstacles to the maintenance of crucial traditional institutions. For example, in a modernizing autocracy, it may be possible to change a patrimonial chieftancy system under a king into a more rationalized civil service system; however, it would be considerably more difficult to absorb an emerging system of party politics—especially when the latter would alter the patterns of recruitment to posts of political power. Strong restraints are usually placed on changes that might lead to party politics. The modernizing autocracy may inhibit certain activities of economic development if they seem threatening to the autocratic principle of rule. In Uganda, the government of Buganda is willing to restrict foreign capital investment in commercial establishments when it feels that certain of its traditional institutions would thereby be altered. In other words, the goals of economic development are filtered through the screen of traditional institutions. To be accepted, economic goals must show some positive relationship to the existing system of authority. However, this does not prevent a great deal of modernization from taking place.[12] From this point of view, one of the intriguing aspects of Japan and Morocco—two traditional modernizing autocracies—is the alacrity with which they respond to the objectives of economic development.

Although the mechanisms of political and economic growth may seem very similar in all three types, each shows a different focus and emphasis. In the mobilization system, the problem of control is central; in its effort to transform society in order to attain economic objectives, it drives opposition underground. Local separatist tendencies must be smashed. Symbolic loyalties to the political leaders and to the state must take precedence over any others. Political leaders find that they are the managers of a society in transition and must take steps to safeguard their tenure and efficiency. Policy derives from finding a balance between the need to insure managerial success and the maintenance of political rule, on the one hand, and the actual achievement of economic goals, on the other. This is characteristic in the mobilization system. Usually, there is a government or party representative on all local development projects. He is there not only to initiate and stimulate local spontaneity but also to safeguard government or party control over the group—local groupings must not become sources of opposition.

In contrast, the spontaneous development of new groups is an important feature of the reconciliation system. The new groups may or may not contribute to the efficient achievement of economic goals; they do enlarge the degree of pluralism in the system. In the mobilization type, much of the spontaneity of local and rural development is eventually lost, because every new center of organization is usually controlled by government. Reconciliation systems not only accept opposition; in addition, the government, by catering to opposition and separatist points of view, is profoundly affected and shaped in its goals and in the methods of fulfilling those goals. In the mobilization system, potential sources of opposition are immediately attacked and either eliminated or effectively silenced. In the reconciliation system, local development more easily retains its vitality. This has important implications both for development and for democracy.[13]

The reconciliation systems are immediately concerned with the mechanics of establishing useful and acceptable economic priorities and with the means of achieving them in conformity with existing political practices. In this sense, they are far less flexible tactically than the mobilization system, while also being less doctrinaire. In reconciliation systems, the problem is to bring the goals advanced by the government into accord with the public desires. Both the consent and the support of the constituents of the national society are required. This is one reason that reconciliation systems rely heavily on outside sources of assistance. A government in such a system also prefers talent to be dispersed rather than concentrated at the center. Reconciliation systems in new nations are usually moderately socialist, and consequently extensive planning agencies are part of their governments. Nevertheless, planning is essentially of the "enabling" variety, i.e., it provides opportunities for private enterprise and local self-help by manipulating strategic sectors of the economy.[14]

In the modernizing autocracy, as we have indicated, considerable political stability is likely throughout the process of change. Less reliance on control and coercion is evident than in the mobilization system, while more efficient means of achieving goals are available than in the reconciliation system. Traditional values are not destroyed; rather, they are modified and extended. Typically, the modernizing autocracy is bureaucratic. Traditional loyalties and the bureaucracy coincide. In the modernization system, on the other hand, the civil service bureaucracy is in conflict with the party bureaucracy which, having captured the organs of state power, is inclined to consider the internal needs of the party above all others. Party eventually comes to represent the state.[15]

In each type of system, the most important issue is economic development. It is economic development which either becomes the means to rapid change or else presents the greatest threat to the prevailing system. In most new nations, there are mixed feelings about the consequences of economic development. While few disagree with the material benefits of a rising standard of living, many are bitter about the organizational consequences and the demands upon individuals that such a process involves. The mobilization system is clearly willing to ride roughshod over more parochial interests. Economic development then attains the same symbolic meaning as a national goal that freedom and independence had during the nation's colonial period. Under the banners of "freedom from want" and "increased opportunity," the population can be "mobilized" for change.

The modernizing autocracy may proceed in great leaps toward modernization. However, its periods of rapid advance must be followed by periods of digestion during which the changes effected may be absorbed into the traditional political framework.

Thus economic development produces different problems, depending upon the nature and needs of the political systems. We can now extend our analysis and attempt to indicate some of the underlying factors which determine political responses to economic change. We are concerned not only with the degree to which each of the three systems responds to the achievement of economic development, but also with the consequences of such development for the future of each system itself.

SUMMARY

All three types of systems discussed here have certain characteristics in common. Their political leaders are trying to achieve some balance between a desired level of public satisfaction, the attainment of goals of development, and the strengthening of political power. One important difference among the three types is the degree to which, in each, public satisfaction can be achieved immediately or must be postponed—a factor which has a great effect on the selection of goals. The mobilization system operates on the principle that immediate satisfaction must be sacrificed for the sake of future fulfilment. In such a system, there is a concept of forced saving in the most real sense of the term—i.e., the immediate benefits to which people aspire become limited, while postponed real gratifications through economic development become the goal of government. As a consequence, a system of government is produced in which savings for investment, in the widest sociological sense, be-

come possible. Other things being equal, we would, therefore, expect the most rapid economic growth to occur in the mobilization system.

In the reconciliation system, the goals must be moderated to conform to current demands, and the degree of forced saving is also more moderate. The degree of change is dictated chiefly by the availability of talents and resources that are widely dispersed throughout the system. If rapid technological change and economic change are to proceed, non-political means must be used to fulfill the same objectives which, in the mobilization system, are maximized through political entrepreneurship and state enterprise.

In the modernizing autocracy, it may be possible to achieve greater forced savings if the government chooses to do so. On the other hand, private sources of investment and public enterprise are likely to collaborate effectively in a close-knit relationship.

However, each type of system manifests internal conflicts and contradictions in connection with the variables listed.

To determine why each type responds in the ways generally described so far, we require a set of variables which can show the process consequences of system. Otherwise, discussion will remain at the phenomenological level, and information will be illustrative rather than explanatory. In the next section of this paper, we shall consider some process variables which apply to all three of the developmental types discussed.

In our remarks, the idea is implicit that all of the types exhibit two characteristic decisional outputs. One comprises developmental decisions; the other comprises system-maintenance decisions. Analysis of these outputs necessitates a discussion of process, and it is to the process variables that we turn for further investigation.

The Process Variables

Having described the characteristics of the three developmental types of systems in new nations, we can now undertake an analysis of the political processes characteristic of each type.

Four variables are used in this analysis. They are (*a*) *goals*, defined as operative purposes of government including economic and social development;[16] (*b*) *costs*, which are the allocations of real income which must be made with respect to the achievement of such goals; (*c*) *coercion*, or government actions to insure some specific level of conformity; and (*d*) *information*, or the knowledge available to decision-makers, on the basis of which future decisions may be made.

These process variables can now be linked to our developmental types. Then we can determine, on the basis of empirical data, the political consequences of technological change and economic development that seem characteristic.

PROCESS IN THE MOBILIZATION TYPE OF SYSTEM

A mobilization system involves government in active intervention in technological change and economic development. The organizational characteristics of government become a central feature of its activities. Organization qua organization is always somewhat autocratic; and the organizational work of the government becomes pervasive, extending over wide ranges of the social and economic life of a new nation. As a result, people are "acted upon" by an "outside" system, i.e., government. In turn, this leads to a strengthening of the hierarchical and ideological facets of control over society at large. Leadership and the state tend toward identity. Goals assume the characteristics of (*a*) inviolability, and (*b*) satisfaction postponed to a future period. Goals are thus profoundly evolutionary and often symbolic.

Hence we can assume that increasing organizational control, for the purposes of mobilization and goal achievement, inevitably runs into public conservatism. A manifestation of increasing control is

reliance on coercion to reach objectives that are established for the system. Coercion requires ideological justification. Technological change and economic development become symbolically important because they emphasize future social benefits. If developmental goals are very unrealistic, they may strain the available resources and technology within a new nation so much that mobilization systems may rely on external means to attain them—seeking to maximize their goals by political bargaining with industrialized powers or by acts of territorial expansion. The new nations have not yet indulged in the latter enterprise; but there are signs, in some mobilization systems, that agitation for territorial aggrandizement is beginning.

Third, we can assume that, as coercion increases, there is a corresponding decline in free information—or, in other words, in the information about public support and interests that is readily available to government. When coercion is increasing, the public tend to supply government with information that will please it. This decreases the reliability of information on which action may be based. It also makes it difficult for government to create subgoals proximate to public needs. Government then acts in an atmosphere of greater uncertainty. To compensate for this, government leaders are inclined to increase coercion still more to insure compliance; and a new cycle of reactions is introduced.

Such a pattern has a number of effects on economic development. First, government becomes progressively more enmeshed in investment and in seeking to control its side effects in the society. Furthermore, the costs of coercion result in diverting revenue, hitherto available for investment, into military and police activities and other punitive institutions. Third, bargaining in external relations intensifies the need for stronger standing armies and better military technology, since in any bargaining relationship between independent nations, threats to one another are inherent in any interactions. Consequently, the costs of government rise continuously, and difficulties in spending investment funds for the expansion of government enterprise are met by raising public revenues and by the intensification of the mobilization process. Simultaneously, an increasing proportion of revenue is diverted to nonproductive enterprise, i.e., to system-maintenance rather than to development.

In the mobilization system, the need for increasing governmental supervision and the effort to eliminate sources of major opposition result in a decline of cheap and valid information available to decision-makers. As this information declines, decision-makers find it more difficult to predict accurately the degree of public support that they have and the relationship of economic goals to public desires. To bridge the growing gap between the government and the people, there is an emphasis on ideological conformity. The highly centralized system of authority, in order to insure the allegiance of the people, continues to rely more and more on coercion. All voluntary organizations, trade unions, the military, and the bureaucracy must be increasingly devoted to the political leaders. The consequence is an even greater loss of free or inexpensive information, and, in extreme cases, the press and other media of public expression are controlled by the government.[17] The costs of coercion rise, and resources available for development, in part, are diverted to pay the rising expenses for the military and police. The optimal balance between economic growth and public desire becomes more and more determined by the actions necessary to secure the position of the government. In order to compensate for the diversion of funds which would ordinarily have been used for development, there is a tendency to use raw labor and "volunteer" labor for primary development. Talent accumulates at the center. The processes of administration are closely linked to the political control over economic development. Poli-

tical leaders of the second rank and administrators are fearful of being posted far from the centers of power and intrigue.

Most new mobilization systems are autocratic rather than dictatorial. For one thing, dictatorship is inefficient without a substantial technology. In addition, dictatorship produces a control problem—not only are economic resources diverted, but, more important, many of the scarce managerial skills are consumed by the military and police. Most of the new nations of Africa and Asia, however, are more concerned with utilizing these scarce talents to attain economic and social goals. Therefore, typically there is a relatively mild autocracy, in which, frequently, nominal opposition or opposition within a single party remains possible. Thus, fairly inexpensive information is available to the political leaders. They can retain a closer relationship to the public and to public needs than would be possible in a totalitarian system. A mild autocracy becomes a relatively efficient means of implementing economic development and socio-political control simultaneously, by achieving equilibrium between high goal achievement, moderate coercion, and quite cheap information. This is possible in so far as the leaders are willing to modify goals in the light of information. If leaders are fanatical or inflexible about their objectives, they rely on coercion. The optimal balance of our four variables is upset; development becomes very expensive and totalitarian. Hence autocratic mobilization systems can be regarded as more efficient than totalitarian mobilization systems.

PROCESS IN THE RECONCILIATION TYPE OF SYSTEM

In both the reconciliation system and the modernizing autocracy, the leaders are more willing to accommodate goals to public demands than are the leaders in the mobilization system. In trying to effect economic development, the mobilization system seeks to overhaul society in general through technological change. Precisely because of the ideological needs incurred by that process, the mobilization system attaches great symbolic meaning to such general goals, which become the moral basis of coercive politics.

Neither the reconciliation system nor the modernizing autocracy faces this difficulty. The modernizing autocracy derives its "morality" from tradition. The reconciliation system, when defining its objectives, is immediately concerned with gaining some agreement among its constituent units. I shall discuss this before examining process in the modernizing autocracies.

We have made several assumptions about reconciliation systems. First, in such a system, goals are based on information rather than on an image of the future. Then, too, they are high-information systems. Inexpensive information is made available to decision-makers by the variety of interest groups, voluntary associations, and political parties that express their demands to government. Third, reconciliation systems are low-coercion systems. Goals are in closer relation to resources and public desires, and government has less need to rely extensively on coercive techniques. In addition, since reconciliation systems are based upon the restrictions on government power inherent in this structural form, the government can rarely gain sufficient political consensus to enact coercive measures. Fourth, reconciliation systems cannot easily act autocratically except under very extreme circumstances, such as war.

Information is cheap because any efforts to use coercive measures would call forth expensive and strenuous opposition by local and nongovernmental groups. Acting on the basis of information rather than through coercion, the government must evolve flexible strategies that enable it to win compliance. A high proportion of available resources can be utilized for economic development. However, there is one practical limitation inherent in the

situation: a high rate of forced savings is politically impossible. The rate of capital investment is lower than that in the mobilization system. The government's efforts take the form of stimulating non-governmental development or local entrepreneurship. This may be done through providing sources of credit for private entrepreneurs, through expanding the possibilities of joint government and private enterprise through industrial development corporations and similar projects, and through encouraging outside investment.

The role of government is not organizational. The government's need is to reconcile diverse interests; it is mediating, integrating, and, above all, coordinating, rather than organizing and mobilizing. The mobilizational system fights society; the reconciliation system is a prisoner of society. Government may show that goals required by public expectations cannot, in the absence of forced measures, be achieved. The public are unwilling to sacrifice current consumption for the sake of future consumption and otherwise to modify their behavior in order to attain these goals. For this reason, while the government may be democratic, it may also break down in unfulfilment, corruption, and compromise. Thus the degree of economic development in a reconciliation system depends on the steadfast motives of the top political leaders, and on the public's determination to enforce self-discipline and to insure, through local participation in economic enterprise, a high level of development. When there are lags in the acceptance of economic goals or voluntary means of achieving them (and where, also, great cultural discontinuities may persist long after a new government has established itself), governments of the reconciliation type may be condemned to slower economic progress than would a mobilization system—at least in the short run;[18] the long-run prospects may, of course, be vastly different.

The reconciliation system must make constant efforts to find local sources of talent and engage them in the development process. When technical elites are being trained, for example, there must be a concomitant effort to maximize their services in a decentralized manner. Thus the processes of economic growth are dispersed, not only between the private and the public sectors of the economy, but also in the provinces as well as in the main center. Local decision-making and local capital investment mean a great dependence on village and local communities. Hence, rapid economic growth is possible in a reconciliation system if and only if there are extensive self-discipline, popular participation, and great civic devotion. These preconditions occur only very rarely in new nations.[19]

PROCESS IN THE MODERNIZING AUTOCRACY
TYPE OF SYSTEM

The modernizing autocracy presents a curious balance between the positions in the mobilization and reconciliation systems. First, the modernizing autocracy is able to modify its goal more easily than the mobilization system. In addition, modernizing autocracies have open to them certain coercive techniques, by traditional means, that do not result in restrictions on the flow of information.[20] Third, in so far as modernizing autocracies are autocratic, the coercive techniques available to political decision-makers have had a long tradition and are thoroughly understood by the public. Regularized means of public expression persist because, typically, modernizing autocracies have traditional limits placed on the power of decision-makers by custom and belief. Finally, the public have means for expressing their preferences about actions of government. These means are sufficiently institutionalized not to appear to government as dangerous forms of opposition within the society. The difficulty that the modernizing autocracy confronts is the possibility that changes effected in the economic sphere may eventually threaten the principle of hierarchical authority,

with consequent demands for the substantial alteration of the system.

Normally, modernizing autocracies are monarchical or bureaucratic systems of rule. The symbolic position of the ruler is heavily emphasized. Opportunities for patrimony are available to him. As economic development proceeds, larger numbers of educated and technically trained personnel are absorbed into the traditional hierarchy. Those who express the desire for greater participation in the decision-making process pose the major problem. The political, rather than the economic, consequences of technological change and development create the most serious difficulties for the modernizing autocracy.

The most important feature of the modernizing autocracy is that it is a low cost coercion system. Precedent, custom, and traditional behavioral prescriptions, having persisted through time, are central mechanisms of control over both leaders and led. At the same time, the principle of hierarchical authority and autocracy makes leaders relatively less accountable to the public than they are in the reconciliation system. Hence the leaders play an important role in innovation. Modernizing autocracies can advance technological change and require public acceptance precisely because such assertions from government are validated in the traditional patterns of authority. In so far as the government sets realistic economic goals, considerable compliance and acceptance can be assured without increasing coercive costs and, equally important, without losing cheap information. It is interesting to speculate on the reasons for this.

The typical modernizing traditional autocracy centers around a monarch with two characteristics. He embodies complete and awesome power; he is the state personified; he is the personal lord of every citizen—the relationship between king and subject is direct and immediate. From this relationship, two contrasting forms of behavior can ensue. First, the use of authority is itself acceptable. Second, it is possible for the subject to feel that he can personally lay his complaints at the feet of his king and expect remedial action in his favor. This is the reason that modernizing autocracies are low cost information systems, whereas in all other circumstances coercion and information have an inverse relationship to one another.[21]

One consequence of this set of circumstances is that modernizing autocracies can experiment with goals without paying the penalties of immediate instability. The modernizing autocracies, in distinction to the mobilization and reconciliation systems, have well-institutionalized regimes. In this, they show the greatest parallel to the historical experience of Western Europe, where, particularly in England, vast changes in economic and technological development during the nineteenth century were in accord with modifications in the political sector. Despite the magnitude of the changes, England was able to retain great stability—a factor not unrelated to the economy's ability to expand as rapidly as it did. Economic development also enabled England to change from a modernizing autocracy to a parliamentary unitary reconciliation type of system. Other examples, however, show a different pattern. Tsarist Russia was clearly a modernizing autocracy, at least after the emancipation of the serfs in 1861. But the excesses of the bureaucracy, and corruption, war, and poverty, required more effective and drastic structural reorganization than the government could provide. The Russian case can be regarded as a shift from a modernizing autocracy to a mobilization system. However, as a modernizing autocracy it sought economic development through war and expansion, as did Japan and Prussia. In these respects, the modernizing autocracies of Russia, Japan, and Germany at the turn of the century have many features in common.

The modernizing autocracies in the new nations are subject to tendencies similar to those operative in the examples given above. They can promote economic development along with stability only in the short run, because they cannot absorb the new elites sufficiently into the traditional hierarchy. The new elites become the spearhead of political reform, a situation which the modernizing autocracy can suffer only on a limited scale. (The rare exception, England, transformed the practice while retaining the form.)[22]

Conclusions

In our earlier remarks, we indicated that economic development and technological change could be viewed as a relationship between goals, resources, and outside aid. Although we did not analyze our material in terms of these three factors, they are obviously of central importance to the problem we are discussing. We must now draw them into our analysis, in order to specify the theoretical relationships which have been elicited here. The three factors can be distributed by means of a variety of institutional variables which, in effect, compose the inheritance of each new nation. Such institutional variables could be extended further, but we shall incorporate the following as most relevant: (*a*) administration; (*b*) technology; (*c*) per-capita income; and (*d*) entrepreneurship. These affect the nature of political goals. They also indicate the possibilities for development that derive from the given state of available resources and skills and the degree of structural flexibility which a new nation inherits upon independence. Although I have not discussed these factors, they are crucial as independent variables. Moreover, they are germane to any discussion of the origins of the development types. They must therefore be added to the system under discussion. If they are considered as independent variables, the theoretical system appears as shown on page 454.

We would, of course, indicate a large number of possible situations which, logically derived from the model, have

	Input		Systems and Processes		Output Government Decisions

Input

Systems and Processes

Output Government Decisions

$$\begin{bmatrix} \text{Administration} \\ \text{Technology} \\ \text{Per-capita income} \\ \text{Entrepreneurship} \end{bmatrix} \rightarrow \begin{bmatrix} \text{Mobilization} \\ \text{Reconciliation} \\ \text{Modernizing} \\ \text{autocracy} \end{bmatrix} \begin{array}{c} \text{Goals} \\ \text{Coercion} \\ \text{Information} \\ \text{Costs} \end{array} \rightarrow \begin{bmatrix} \text{Development} \\ \\ \text{System-maintenance} \end{bmatrix}$$

their counterparts in reality. We could also consider a set time period for a country, in which we evaluated the inputs, the operations of the system and process variables, and the decisional outputs, for their effect on the institutional inputs in a succeeding time period. Systemic analysis could then serve as a basis for probabilistic theories.

Limitations of space, however, preclude a more extensive discussion of this model. Nonetheless, it should now be clear that the heart of this analysis lies with the relationship between system-maintenance (politics) and development (economics). If politics is a conserving and protecting force, development must somehow strengthen and conserve the system. Hence the best test of development is a system-maintenance test.

We can now recapitulate some of the essentials of this discussion.

(*a*) The mobilization system must find the optimal balance between the achievement of forward-looking goals and the allocation of real income between coercion and information. The degree of coercion is restricted by its cost on the processes of economic growth.[23] In the mobilization system, hierarchical authority seeks not only to maintain itself but to intervene in all aspects of social life. Economic development becomes the rationale for demanding total allegiance. Tactical flexibility is essential for assuring the immediate control over problems which may emerge in the economic process; its chief characteristic is that it requires a minimum amount of public accountability.

(*b*) The reconciliation system must rely heavily on information when it defines its goals and the means of achieving them. It cannot utilize much coercion—if it does,

it will be transformed into a mobilization type of system. Its distinguishing features are its participation in different aspects of group life and its stimulation of the public to participate more fully in economic processes.

In the reconciliation system, collective legitimacy results from a representative principle shared by the entire collectivity. However, the danger of separatism, and even secession, by one or more of the constituents imposes a real limitation upon the degree of freedom the political leaders have. Since multiple loyalties exist, economic development is by no means seen in terms of the state. Instead, its perspectives tend to be transformed into special interests. Development must be diffused widely throughout the system. For example, in India, the political demands of various local interests made it necessary to construct an oil refinery in a less advantageous part of the country in order to build a refinery in the most economically desirable location.

Since compromise is innate in a reconciliation system, the pace of development is determined by the willingness of the political leaders and of the public to follow a policy of the central government. The pace of growth is never more dramatic than that which the public is prepared to accept, since policy must agree with public desires. Frequently, the result is a greater degree of superficial instability in the system, with much spontaneous conflict and expressions of bitterness among the parts. In spite of this, coercive techniques remain at a minimum; and it can be argued that the strength of the reconciliation system lies, in some measure, in the perpetuation of the conflicts themselves. Each group finds a loyalty to the system determined by parochial interests and hopes to satisfy such interests. The hypotheses of both Simmel and Gluckmann concerning the social utility of conflict are relevant here. Conflict is not necessarily destructive of the social fabric.[24] On the contrary, under a reconciliation system, conflict gives people a vested interest in the system as a whole.

(*c*) Modernizing autocracies are suspicious of advanced, dramatic programs for economic development. However, they tend to isolate those aspects of economic reforms that seem capable of being absorbed without causing too many authority problems.

In the modernizing autocracy, goals are restricted by the implications they have for the system of hierarchical authority. Those which seem to entail substantial alterations of the political framework of the society are necessarily abhorred by the government. Others, which allow the system to continue while at the same time satisfying the public—particularly with respect to expanding material standards and raising income levels—are adopted.

At the beginning of this discussion, we pointed out that many of the mechanisms of development are often similar in each of the three types. In the same sense, certain processes in the modern business enterprise in the United States and in the Soviet Union are similar. The problem of economic growth, however, poses very different problems for each kind of political system. In some, the goals of economic and technological growth become a rationale for mobilizing an entire society, and coercion is heavily used to implement mobilization. The optimal level of mobilization is reached when the costs of coercion appreciably limit the achievement of goals. The reconciliation system decides on those goals for which there is already considerable public support, so that it need employ a minimum of coercion. However, in a reconciliation government the large amount of available information may inhibit decision-makers from attaining economic growth. In the last analysis, the determination of goals, and their achievement, depend on the public willingness to work on a spontaneous and decentralized basis.[25]

The mobilization system can be efficient if it does not need to divert a large proportion of its revenues and talents to the system-maintenance sphere instead of the development sphere. In so far as it is successful in concentrating on development, it feeds out satisfactions in the social structure at large that have system-maintenance consequences. Its ability to do this is partially dependent on the urgency with which political leaders seek to develop the country and on the time which they allow for the process. If these leaders are flexible and not quick to fall back on coercive measures, they probably represent the most efficient means of creating political stability and the most rapid possible economic growth. In some mobilization systems, outside development aid may result in larger allocations of internal resources being made to system-maintenance. The dangers of this are obvious. On the other hand, suitable outside aid may effect noncoercive goal achievement without causing grave system-maintenance problems. Under such circumstances, outside aid may ultimately be the decisive factor in whether a mobilization system becomes totalitarian or democratic.[26]

An equally interesting situation occurs when the system-maintenance decisions of a modernizing autocracy become enlarged precisely beeause of the political problems posed by development achievements. As a rule, in such cases one can predict great instability for the regime, foreshadowing its change from a modernizing autocracy to one of the alternative types. Essentially, these conditions obtained in Iraq prior to the Iraqi revolution. Under such circumstances, outside developmental aid to the regime can only intensify the internal difficulties and is, therefore, ill advised.

Similar conditions obtain in a reconciliation system. If system-maintenance decisions become the major decisional burden of the government, this is a manifestation of an exceedingly unhealthy internal state; in addition it would hardly be likely that developmental decisions would help the situation. Under such circumstances, one can anticipate that, in a reconciliation type of system, there will be an increase in public expectations that is far beyond the capacity of the regime. Reconciliation systems are particularly vulnerable to this problem.

Each type of system under discussion represents a different set of relationships between goals, costs, coercion, and information. The evaluation of data about these variables should indicate the limits within which economic development and technological change can occur in each nation. Consideration of these variables should elicit the preferences which decision-makers will demonstrate by virtue of the system variables within which they must operate. It should indicate the effects that economic development will have on the systems themselves—including the transformation of one type into another.

To conclude: By means of systematic analysis of structure and process, I have attempted to provide a framework in which the study of technological innovation and economic development can be related to the politics of the developing areas. In addition, it should make it possible to draw inferences about the prospects of democracy in the context of social change.

NOTES

[1] See W. W. Rostow, *The Politics of Economic Growth* (New York, 1952); and W. Arthur Lewis, *The Theory of Economic Growth* (London, 1955).

[2] David E. Apter and Carl Rosberg, "Some Models of Political Change in Contemporary Africa," In D. P. Ray (ed.), *The Political Economy of Contemporary Africa* (Washington, D.C., 1959); and David E. Apter, "Political Development and Tension in New Nations" (unpublished background Paper for the Conference on World Tensions, Chicago, 1960).

[3] By "government," I mean here the most generalized membership unit possessing (*a*) defined responsibilities for the maintenance of the system of which it is a part; and (*b*) a practical monopoly of coercive powers. By "political system," I mean society (or other unit whose government conforms to the definition above) viewed in terms of government.

[4] The initial effort to develop these types was made in an earlier monograph, written with Professor Carl Rosberg of the University of California at Berkeley. While we share the responsibility for the development of these types, he is not responsible for their application here. See Apter and Rosberg, *op. cit.*

[5] See D. E. Apter, "A Comparative Method for the Study of Politics," *American Journal of Sociology,* November 1958.

[6] I am indebted to the participants of an informal seminar at the University of Chicago who helped derive these categories. They are Rodger Masters, Aristede Zolberg, Leo Snowiss, and Louis Cantori. Their perceptive comments were very useful during the preparation of this manuscript.

[7] Philip Selznick, *The Organizational Weapon: A study of Bolshevik Strategy and Tactics* (New York, 1952), p. 2.

[8] Although mobilization systems tend to have very pronounced ideological views on the main issues of development, in a peculiar sense such a system is less ideological than utopian—to use Mannheim's distinction between ideological and utopian thinking. In fact, in mobilization systems the party or the state will act on grounds of expediency and necessity, using ideology to give perspective and justify what appears necessary. It can be argued that opportunism remains more compelling than ideology. The most overwhelming commitment is either to the party or to the state. See Karl Mannheim, *Ideology and Utopia* (New York, 1946), pp. 49–93.

[9] See P. T. Bauer and B. S. Yamey, *The Economics of Underdeveloped Countries* (Cambridge, England, 1957), Chs. 11 and 12.

[10] The term "autocracy" is somewhat misleading. Such systems can be firmly "populist" and popular. See Donald G. MacRae "Totalitarian Democracy," *The Political Quarterly,* Vol. **31**, No. 4 (October–December 1960).

[11] See the brief discussion by C. Bettelheim, "Les exigences fondamentales d'une croissance accélérée de l'économie africaine," *Présence africaine,* June–September, 1960.

[12] See David E. Apter, *The Political Kingdom in Uganda: A Study in Bureaucratic Nationalism* (Princeton, N.J., 1961); and D. Anthony

Low and R. Cranford Pratt, *Buganda and British Overrule* (London, 1960). See also the effects of modernization in Japan, as described in the Introduction to *Kokutai No Hongi* (Cambridge, Mass., 1949).

[13] For a discussion of these problems in Guinea, see "Democracy in Guinea," *The Economist* (London), November 14, 1959.

[14] This is particularly true in those ex-colonial territories where the colonial civil service or administration had been both the planning and the administrative arm, and traditions of service and skill reside in the bureaucracy. See Ignacy Sachs, "Patterns of Public Sectors in Underdeveloped Economies," *The Indian Economic Review*, Vol. **4**, No. 3.

[15] In the reconciliation type, the bureaucracy is normally subordinate to the political arm and does not pose this problem. See D. Apter and R. Lystad, "Party, Bureaucracy and Constitutional Government," in G. M. Carter (ed.), *Transition in Africa* (Boston, 1958).

[16] An extremely difficult but important factor in goals is creativity. Although discussion of creativity is beyond the scope of this paper, a case can be made for greater creativity in the mobilization type than in the other two.

[17] For example, in Mali, the two newspapers are owned and controlled by the government and regarded as party instructional and informational sheets. The single party, the Union Soudanaise, considers the newspapers as agents of ideological communication to the local party cadres.

[18] One need only compare India and China in this regard. See the discussion of economic growth and planning in the *Report of the Commission of Enquiry on Emoluments and Conditions of Service of Central Government Employees, 1957–9* (Delhi, 1959), pp. 35–45.

[19] See the excellent discussion of this problem in Edward Shils' "Political Development in the New States," *Comparative Studies in Society and History*, **2** (1960), Part II.

[20] i.e., through religious, clan, familial, and other pressures.

[21] Both the mobilization system and the modernizing autocracy tend toward "personal" government. In the former, ideologized justifications cover up capriciousness; in the latter, custom restrains it. See Thomas Hodgkin, *Nationalism in Colonial Africa* (London, 1956), Ch. 5. See also William Kornhauser, *The*

Politics of Mass Society (Glencoe, Ill., 1959), Ch. 3.

[22] Thus the prognosis in a modernizing autocracy is political trouble. In the short run, it is a stable system. In the long run, its success in the economic field creates elites who prefer either a reconciliation or a mobilization alternative. When this occurs, economic goals may be restricted by the monarch to prevent change which he cannot control; opposing groups can easily charge the system with being feudal and archaic. Political difficulties are inherent in the system. Turkey remains one of the most interesting examples to study. There the shift to Kemalism can be described as one from a modernizing autocracy of the traditional variety to a mobilization system after the downfall of the Ottoman Empire, with a move toward a reconciliation system in the decades since the war. This has now reversed itself in an abrupt transition back to a modernizing autocracy of the secular variety. See T. Feyzioglu, "Les partis politiques en Turquie," *Revue Française de science politique*, Vol. **1**, No. 1 (January–March, 1954).

[23] If this situation persists so that coercion becomes the primary means of assuring compliance, then there may be a change from a mobilization system employing a mild autocracy to a mobilization system employing more totalitarian methods. Should this occur, then for all practical purposes coercion and information coincide, and the perfect information system is the perfect coercive system.

[24] See George Simmel, *Conflict* (Glencoe, Ill., 1955); and Max Gluckman, *Custom and Conflict in Africa* (Glencoe, Ill., 1955).

[25] An important task for the government is the crystallization of economic goals—presenting them to the public in such a way that the people respond enthusiastically to the difficulties inevitable in economic development.

There is, of course, a different but related problem of information. If information is to be effective, it must be translated into goals by efficient decision-making. If so much information is available that it cannot be "processed," decision-making suffers and the system becomes "inefficient."

[26] See Charles Wolf, Jr., *Foreign Aid: Theory and Practice in Southern Asia* (Princeton, N.J., 1960), Ch. 8. It can be maintained that the dilemma posed by the Lumumba government in the Congo about outside aid was of this nature.

ALTERNATIVE COURSES OF POLITICAL DEVELOPMENT

Edward Shils

The elites of the new states are seeking to a greater extent than ever before to create something new. Their aspirations are cast on a more drastic and more comprehensive scale even than those of the European revolutionaries who have flourished since 1789. They are working to a model, which, however vague in its details, is more elaborate and more exogenous than those which guided the formation of the modern state in Great Britain, France, Germany, and the United States. These were, of course, influenced by models drawn from outside their own territories and their own current culture. The models of the Roman Republic, of the China of the Mandarins, of the British Constitution as portrayed by Montesquieu, have played their parts in the formation of modern Western states. They were, however, only fragments accepted in isolation or as parts of a larger program which was constructed largely from elements already existent and accepted in the situation to be reformed. There was, moreover, very much in their current situation which they were prepared to accept. Even the Soviet elite, for almost the first decade of its power, had little definite idea of the form of the regime it wished to create: it wished to industrialize, it was anti-capitalistic, and it was dictatorial; but within the limits of these three determinants, it had no clear image of the future of Soviet society.

The elites of the new states, partly because of their own nature and partly because of the world situation in which the West looms so large, are in a rather

SOURCE. Edward Shils, "Alternative Courses of Political Development," *Political Development in New States* (s'Gravenhage: Mouton & Co., 1962), pp. 47–84.

different position. The elites of the new states have lying before them, not the image of a future in which no one has as yet lived or of fragments of a still living and accepted past, but rather an image of their own future profoundly different from their own past, to be lived along the lines of the already existent modern states, which are their contemporaries. Quite apart from any tendency toward doctrinairism—which is not a negligible factor—the elites of the new states are propelled by their own beliefs and sentiments, and by the structure of the contemporary world, toward a large-scale, comprehensive program for the transformation of their own societies, far beyond the political sphere. By the commitments of their past actions, by the claims on the basis of which they sought sovereignty, and by the condition of their own societies, they must orient themselves toward the realization of a quite differentiated model of a modern polity, which is already visible elsewhere in the world.

What is the predominant, visible model, the model which commands assent by its actual achievement and by the prestige of the power and ascendancy of its earthly embodiments? It is the model of a regime of *civilian rule* through *representative institutions* in the matrix of *public liberties*, those three components of a modern conception of democracy. This is the model with which the new states began their careers and from which they diverge only from a feeling of urgent necessity. Oligarchy—civilian, military, or mixed— is the alternative to which recourse is had when this necessity presses. There are also other possibilities: a traditionalistic order, monarchical, absolutistic, or feudal, resting on a basis of kinship, landownership, and religious opinion; and a modern theocracy, which exercises oligarchical powers on behalf of traditional religious values. Finally, it need not be stressed that a dictatorial communistic regime, drawing inspiration from the Soviet model and explicitly legitimating itself by Marxian doctrine, is not the least of possibilities.

Yet no regnant elite in the new states of Asia or Africa believes that its ultimate aspirations would be adequately and definitively realized in any of the latter alternatives or that any defections or variants are anything but second best. There are many critics of the regime of civilian rule, representative government, and public liberties; but few deny the validity of its principles. Although there are exponents of the other alternatives, they justify them by their greater expediency for attaining certain other goals, such as higher rates of saving and investment, or because the society is "not yet ready" for civilian rule, representative government, and public liberties. If we disregard for the moment Saudi Arabia or Yemen, where the oligarchy is traditional, even the most oligarchical of regimes, however, protests its fundamentally modern and democratic aspirations. Nor are such protestations mere hypocrisy. That vaguely limned New Jerusalem into which the rulers of the new states would take their people is conceived by them on the image of the Western states that they know— Great Britain, France, and the United States. Even the enthusiasts for the Soviet Union are subject to the attractive power of political democracy; they tend to think of the Soviet Union as a modern democratic state insofar as they think of it in an at all differentiated manner.[1]

[1] Thought about Communism and the Soviet Union in the new states is about at the level which was reached in Europe from 1925 to 1935. Communism is regarded as the same as traditionally democratic socialism, with certain qualifications which have had to be introduced because it came into life in an economically backward country, in a situation of severe

Even the most doctrinaire of politicians can scarcely be expected to have a wholly clear and unified image of the future towards which they wish to move. It cannot be expected of the elites of the new states that they should have such an image of their goal.

The rulers of the new states, although they include many intellectuals, are usually neither practicing scholars nor systematic theorists. They have not made careful studies of different types of regimes. The regime which they know best is that of the European state which formerly ruled them. Their demands for more self-government have tended generally to follow the direction of the state which was before their eyes. To some considerable extent, they remain the prisoners of their former rulers, from whom they have unquestioningly accepted much of their actual and their ideal regimes. Their hunger for modernity, the liberal auspices of their independence movements, their general tendency toward populism, make them incline toward political democracy. Their socialistic dispositions, their distant ad-

crisis, and under the leadership of tough-minded men who wish to get ahead with their tasks rather than to content themselves with the pious platitudes of Social Democrats and bourgeois reformers. Even this, however, represents a fairly high degree of sophistication, since it acknowledges some divergence from the regime of representative government and public liberty. In most instances, there is a reasonably honest unawareness of these divergences. Lenin's view that Soviet democracy is a thousand times more democratic than bourgeois democracy is widely accepted among admirers of the Soviet regimes. The number of educated persons I met in India who favored Communism while acknowledging that it is not democratic was strikingly meagre.

Knowledge about the internal affairs of Soviet states, other than the general appreciation of their industrial progress, their elimination of the rich, their racial tolerance, and their universal educational opportunity, is exceptionally slight. Nor is there any serious curiosity about what goes on there. But that is why Communism is thought, by many persons in the new states, to be another and more efficient way to democracy.

miration for the Soviet Union, their inchoate ideas about the Soviet polity, the authoritarian traditions of their own society, their proclaimed desire to find a political form in concord with the genius of their own people, their impatience with sloth and disorder, and their concern for power, make them ready to introduce substantial admixtures of oligarchy.

Their own notions are too undifferentiated, and the exigencies of life are too demanding, for them to select a single model and to strive toward it unswervingly through thick and thin. Their standards are elementary, their motives are conflicting, their situation is hard—painfully hard. They want their states to be modern; they want to be known in the larger world, among their fellow new states and among the old states, as the creators of a modern state. They need and want to keep order, they want to remain in power, and they work under immense difficulties given by external nature, by history, and by their own predilections. These considerations, against the background of the vagueness of their political principles and their perceptions, are the determinants of their direction and destiny.

In the ensuing pages we delineate certain types of regimes which might be outcomes of the interplay of a zealously pursued ideal and intractable necessity. Certain of these regimes correspond more closely to the ideals asserted by the elites of the new states. Others represent the necessities which might impose themselves if ideals fail—although these "second bests" can become ideals too. The prize of modernity is too great for an elite of a new state to renounce it out of devotion to a systematic and explicit political principle. The stony intractability of the inherited order and the resistance of tradition to ideals learned from books and teachers—however long expressed and cherished—will enforce adaptations. These adaptations will run toward concessions to the traditional order, toward the heightening of oligarchical tendencies as a means of overcoming

the refusal of the traditional order to enter the modern age, and toward the invention of new institutional arrangements through which liberal and democratic inclinations can find hitherto unknown forms of expression.

Political Democracy

COMPONENTS

By "political democracy," we mean the regime of civilian rule through representative institutions and public liberties.

At the center of this regime is a legislative body periodically elected by universal (adult or male) suffrage. This body is empowered to initiate legislation through its own individual members or committees and through the leadership of the executive branch, which might be either separately elected or selected from the members of the legislature; it is empowered to enact or reject legislation initiated by the executive. The executive is subjected to review and control through the powers of debate, enquiry, and budgetary provision, which are vested with the legislative. The executive carries out its policies through a hierarchically organized bureaucracy which is ultimately answerable to its political head or minister, under whose general guidance it operates, and who, in his turn, is answerable to the legislative.

Those who offer themselves as candidates for election as legislators do so mainly in association with or as the candidates of one of several contending parties. The party which wins the largest number of seats dominates the legislature alone, or it does so in coalition with other parties or with dissident members of other parties; or alternatively, there is a coalition of parties which together form a majority. In the presidential system, the president must work in collaboration with the majority party in the legislature.

The performance of the executive and the legislators must be subject to periodic review and assessment by the electorate, and to continuous scrutiny and criticism by the free organs of public opinion, outside the structure of government. Within the legislature, the government is subject to the scrutiny and the criticism of the minority or opposition within the legislative body, reinforced by dissident members of the majority party and independent nonparty legislators. The government is liable to dismissal through the loss of a vote of confidence in the legislative or through the loss of a regular election. In these ways, the democratic regime curbs the tyrannical and arbitrary exercise of power by the government and enforces the responsibility of the government and the legislature to certain standards of the public good of which the electorate is ultimately the judge. Essential to the organs of control and criticism already mentioned is a judiciary, independent of legislative or executive pressure, which is required for the protection of the rights of the citizenry in their relations with the government and with each other.

All branches of the regime work within the framework of a constitution which may be written or largely traditional. The conduct of the executive leadership, of the majority in the legislature, of the opposition, of the civil service, the army, and the police, as well as of the judiciary, is confined by constitutional, conventional, and legal limitations.

PRECONDITIONS

The effective and continuous functioning of the institutions of political democracy in any country, underdeveloped or advanced, depends more or less on the following conditions:

The Stability, Coherence, and Effectiveness of the Ruling Elite. The government of the day must have confidence in its own capacities and in the support which it will receive. It must therefore receive reliable support, from its parliamentary party and from the party in the country at large, as well as from its allies in the other parties (on specific issues)—sufficient to enable it to act with some measure of confidence or

at least without fear of being immediately overthrown or defeated in the legislature, or of arousing aggressive resistance or non-cooperation in the populace.

The government of the day requires the continued acknowledgment of its authority throughout most of the society. To obtain and retain that assent, it must be reasonably effective in the promulgation and execution of policy.

A fairly high degree of coherence and organization of the dominant group in the leadership of each of the parties is required. Without this effectiveness in the conduct of parliamentary business, in the regulation of the relationship between the parliamentary party and the party machinery, in the maintenance of party discipline within the legislature, and in arrangements for the harmonious succession of party leaders, it will be severely hampered. Mutual and fundamental trust is essential within the leadership of each party.

There must be political leaders who are attached to representative institutions, i.e., who feel attached to parliamentary institutions and procedures, who regard themselves as generally answerable to the electorate, who have some feeling of affinity to the nation as a whole, who have some concern for its well-being, and who regard their opponents as part of the nation and as worthy of respect. The political leaders must, despite differences in party loyalties and conflicts arising from temperament and ambition, possess a certain measure of mutual regard and solidarity. This circle of political leaders must be capable of continuous and sustained effort to keep themselves informed and to be approximately aware of the main implications of major legislative and executive actions.

The effectiveness of the political elite depends in part on the acceptance of its legitimacy by a very substantial proportion of the population, particularly by that section of the population which is politically concerned. For its legitimacy to be accepted, it must not only give an impression of a reasonable degree of competence, it must also give an impression of integrity. The regime of representative institutions will cease to find acceptance if it is generally believed that the incumbents are corrupt, i.e., that they use their power primarily for the enrichment and enhancement of themselves personally, or of their kinsmen or clients, or even of a whole class. Although the probity and disinterestedness of politicians can never be perfect, they must exist, and must be thought to exist, in considerable measure, for the regime of representative institutions to function reasonably well.

The party bureaucracy outside the legislature should not be so powerful as to turn the parliamentary party group into a mere register of the party bureaucracy's decisions. The removal of the center of gravity, to a point outside the parliament, devalues that institution in the eyes of its members and in the eyes of the public. If the public esteem for parliamentary institutions is reduced, the self-esteem and the confidence of parliamentarians are correspondingly reduced. Their capacity to act effectively, and to produce leaders capable of effective initiative, is therewith diminished.

The Practice and Acceptance of Opposition. The effective and continuous existence of political democracy requires a fairly coherent and responsible opposition to the ruling party working within the rules of the parliamentary game. This opposition should not simply interest itself in the obstruction and depreciation of the majority. It should be capable of criticizing the majority's measures on the basis of detailed and realistic information about the situation in the country and the performance of the executive. The opposition should be sufficiently coherent to control or to isolate extremists who do not wish to work within the constitutional system. The opposition must be able to resist the temptations of conspiracy and subversion, and the governing party must likewise avoid the idea that opposition is, in itself, a step in the direction of subversion.

Where the majority party is overwhelmingly larger than the combined opposition parties, there must be adequate opportunity for dissent within the majority on the floor of the parliament and not just in the party caucus—at least on certain important measures. Otherwise, the opposition becomes disheartened about parliamentary institutions, and the rank and file of the majority party become restive or demoralized.

The majority and the opposition, which is satisfied to work within the constitutional boundaries, must together form a bloc greatly preponderant *vis-à-vis* the combined "traditionalistic" and "progressivistic" extremists. Otherwise, especially in a "multiparty" system, it will be very difficult to form a majority which will be stable and which will at the same time have sufficient room for maneuver.

Adequate Machinery of Authority. This requires a competent civil service well enough trained and organized to carry out the measures taken by the legislature (or the executive leadership). It must be sufficiently detached in its own political orientations, and sufficiently loyal to any constitutional government, to make the effort to carry out the policy decided by the political elite, and sufficiently independent to be capable of offering to its political superiors detailed, matter-of-fact assessment of the measures which the government is proposing. It must have an *esprit de corps* sufficiently high, and a self-confidence strong enough, to be able to stand up to the bullying of politicians and to persist in its objectivity and matter-of-factness when it seems easier to fall in with the prejudices and passions of the political leaders.

The civil servants must be capable of working harmoniously with politicians of diverse political outlooks and of educational and social backgrounds very different from their own. It is important that the leadership of the legislative branch be able to hold its own *vis-à-vis* civil servants without, however, hamstringing them by excessive interference. The civil servants must, from their side, avoid a contemptuous attitude toward less well-educated politicians. Needless to say the civil servants should be more or less free from corruption, especially at the highest levels.[2]

The rule of law must obtain and must be recognized to obtain. There should be, therefore, a respected judiciary, independent, both subjectively and objectively, of the legislature and of the civil service, and immune to political passions, confident of its capacities, and sensitive to its responsibilities; and a legal profession which has a certain degree of professional pride and which is, in some degree, accessible to all classes of society.

There must be an adequate machinery for the protection of the constitutional order from unconstitutionally initiated changes. This would include (i) a well-disciplined police force, more or less honest and devoted to the government but not lavish or indiscriminate in the use of its powers; (ii) a competent domestic intelligence system which is able to detect and penetrate subversive bodies without randomly bullying and spying on the entire population; and (iii) a reliable military with a loyal officer corps which does not arrogate to itself the idea that it is the sole custodian of modernity and national integrity. (The civil service, police, and the army must accept a binding obligation to the prevailing civil authority.) Finally, the political leadership (especially in the Home or Interior Ministry) must not quake perpetually in fear of subversion, but it should be capable of quick and realistic action when there is an actual threat.

[2] Freedom from corruption at the highest levels is a necessity for the maintenance of public respect of government and for maintaining relations of mutual respect with the legislative branch. It is probably also necessary for the sake of efficiency and honesty throughout the service. At the lower levels, a modicum of small-scale corruption is probably not too injurious, since it introduces a certain amount of flexibility, it "humanizes" government and makes it less awesome.

The Institutions of Public Opinion. A self-confident and self-sustaining set of institutions of public opinion—i.e., press, universities, and civic and interest associations, professional bodies, trade unions, and local government bodies—must be widely spread throughout the different classes and regions of the country. This entails an autonomous set of institutions for gathering, interpreting, and diffusing information to the public, as well as to the government; it also entails the freedom of expression and association of persons and corporate bodies who can use that freedom to study the course of events and clarify and criticize alternatives of interpretation and policy. This requires, in turn, a corps of journalists, publicists, and university and college professors who are curious and well-informed on public questions, who are honest and forthright in their expression, and who have organs through which they can express themselves, without fear of serious sanctions from governmental or private bodies. There must be a group which upholds the symbols and the program of modernity, other than the class of professional army officers. This requires the existence of a modern civilian intelligentsia. It requires, in addition, a fairly numerous, moderately educated, and reasonably politically concerned section of the population (primarily middle class, but also with some peasants and working-men among them). These will constitute the reservoir from which the leaders of public opinion come, the audience for these leaders, and the resonance which will make itself audible (in a variety of peaceful ways) to legislators and administrators.

There should be a fairly dense and elaborate system of private and voluntary associations which, in addition to entering into the arena of public opinion, perform significant functions in behalf of their members, through co-operative and self-regulating internal activity, through negotiations and bargaining with other similar organizations, and through representation of their interests before the government.

These voluntary associations include: trade unions and employers' associations which have the task of protecting or aggrandizing the status of their members in their relationships with other organizations and with the government; professional associations and with the government; professional associations which promulgate and maintain standards of performance and regulate recruitment; co-operatives and private corporations which produce and distribute commodities; autonomous universities and research institutions which enable their members to teach and to learn by study and research. None of these voluntary organizations should become so powerful as to be able to hold the rest of the society to ransom.

By the performance of such functions, an "infra-structure" of decision and authority is constituted which reduces the amount of authority exercised and of decisions made by the state. By membership in such bodies, the citizenry, at least that significant section which make up the elites of the "infra-structure," become trained in the exercise of authority and the making of decisions. Even more important, they become jealous of their rights to exercise authority and to make decisions, and they become attached to the symbols of their own autonomy. This not only restricts the power of the state; but it also keeps in check tendencies toward the "politicization" of life that are inimical to the regime of civilian rule, representative institutions, and public liberties.

The Civil Order. Continuity is essential to civil order. Major and prolonged crises, i.e., insoluble problems which arouse passionate conflicts, are mortally damaging to political democracy in the new states. Even in well-established political democracies, with a fairly strong civil consensus, a major crisis, such as a severe economic depression, endangers the system. In the new states, with a very tenuous consensus, the danger of disaggregation in the presence of problems which arouse very marked disagreement and emphatic denial

of the efficacy of the existing government and of the constitutional system is all the greater. Furthermore, major crises require very strong and prompt governmental action, e.g., martial law, which necessitates the suspension of the routine institutions, and the freedoms of opposition, of expression and assembly. Emergency government destroys parliamentary control and the rule of law.

Ultimately, the institutions of political democracy must rest on a widely dispersed civility. This would embrace: (i) a sense of nationality, i.e., a firm but not intense attachment to the total community and its symbols; (ii) a degree of interest in public affairs sufficient to impel most adults to participate in elections and to follow in a very general way what is going on in the country as a whole, with a reasonable and temperate judgment of the quality of the candidates and the issues; (iii) following from this, a general acceptance and even affirmation of the legitimacy of the existing political order; (iv) a sense of their own dignity and rights, as well as their obligations, on which must rest their interest in maintaining their own private spheres, free from the arbitrary intrusions of authority; and (v) a sufficient degree of consensus regarding values, institutions, and practices to accept limits on their own self-aggrandizing tendencies. These qualities should not be intense and they need not be either equally or universally shared. They must, however, be common enough to serve as a leaven in the society at large. A society which possesses these qualities we shall call a "political society," i.e., it is one in which "polity" and "society" approximately coincide in their boundaries. Polity and society are never coterminous, even in the most advanced and best-established political democracies. In the new states, there is an even larger gap between polity and the society. Of course, the magnitude of the gap varies markedly among the new states. Some are closer to being political societies than others.

No existing state really fulfils all the

preconditions for the effective working of the regime of political democracy. In none of the advanced countries do all the politicians or journalists or trade union leaders or business leaders or the citizens measure up to the requirements of political democracy. Nonetheless, the occasional vigor of most of the press and the continuous intelligence and vigilance of an influential minority of the press, the devotion, acumen, and force of character of some of the politicians, the good sense of some of the most outstanding trade union and business leaders and a saving remnant of the citizenry, manage to keep the system going, despite continuous disequilibrating pressures. In the new states, the distance from the prerequisites of the regime of political democracy is rather greater. Deficiencies in certain of the categories are, in a few of the states, compensated for by exceptional performances in other categories. In India, for example, the outstanding qualities of the political leadership and of a few journalists, the remarkable endowment of the higher civil service, the deeply ingrained civil sense of the officer corps, as well as a fairly large reservoir of capable and civil-minded intellectuals, keep the regime as close to political democracy as a large inheritance of cultural, economic, and political obstacles permits. It is only the personal qualities of the Indian elite which compensate for the fact that India is not yet a political society.

None of the other new states is a political society either. Tribe, religion, language, and traditions of parochial hierarchy and acquiescence have stood in the way of the emergence of a civil order in practically all of the new states. The polity falls far short, in most of these countries, of coterminousness, even intermittently, with the society. Very few of the new states—perhaps Nigeria and Malaya are exceptions— have adequate compensations for their deficiencies as "political societies." Many of the new states are sovereign states only in the sense that no other state exercises sovereignty over their territory; they themselves have not yet succeeded in fully establishing their sovereignty continuously and unchallengedly over all the territory which falls within their boundaries. In many of the regimes during the early and relatively democratic phase, the politicians have not been able to establish their credentials for integrity or effectiveness. In many of them, such as Iraq, Indonesia, and the Sudan, the elites have lacked internal solidarity, not only *among* parties, but even *within* parties and cliques. Opposition has frequently been ungovernably recalcitrant and factious, and the government has shown itself correspondingly impatient with the opposition.

Under these conditions, some adaptation of the system of political democracy is made inevitable. The zealous effort of modernization, the doubts and ambivalences of the elites about political democracy, and the narrow radius of public opinion, all push in the same direction of a greater concentration of authority than political democracy would countenance.

Tutelary Democracy

There are many men of good will in the new states who, recognizing the difficulties of a system of political democracy in states which have not yet become "political societies," would wish to retain as much of the institutions of civilian rule, representative government, and public liberties as they can, while introducing, in principle and in practice, or in practice alone, modifications which could maintain an effective and stable government, modernizing the economy and the society and reinforcing and rehabilitating the feeble propensities of their people for political democracy. Some would go further; they would have a stronger executive than political democracy affords, and reduce the power of the legislature and the political parties, while attempting to retain the rule of law and public liberties. (Such a regime would be something like Bismarckian and Wilhelmian Germany). Others would maintain representative institutions while confining their powers, and those of the institutions of public opinion, within narrower bounds. They would retain all the institutional apparatus of political democracy but, recognizing the insufficiency of the cultural and social prerequisites, would attempt to keep the system going more or less democratically through very strong executive initiative and a continuous pressure from the top throughout the whole society.

The state of affairs in India leans occasionally, without deliberate intention or doctrinal preconception, toward the first alternative. The regime which President Soekarno has sought to introduce in Indonesia under the name of "guided democracy" is a more deliberate and more drastic movement to concentrate political life into a restricted elite, while keeping the form of parliamentary government and allowing the President's charisma to replace the absent civil order. The government of Burma after the transfer of power to the army in 1958 was still another approximation of tutelary democracy— perhaps the purest and most self-conscious manifestation of this type of regime hitherto known in the new states. Ceylon throughout the period of the state of emergency has also represented a form of tutelary democracy; it has made an effort to retain parts of the parliamentary regime while restricting public liberties to compensate for deficiencies in the civil order.

Tutelary democracy is a variant of political democracy which recommends itself to the elites of the new states. It does so because it is more authoritative than political democracy, and also because the institutions of public opinion and the civil order do not seem qualified to carry the burden which political democracy would impose on them. It is not the object of a theory in the way in which political democracy and totalitarian oligarchy have become theories; it is the "natural theory" of men brought up to believe in themselves as democrats, who have, for various

reasons, considerable attachment to democratic institutions and who have, for good or poor reasons, little confidence in their people's present capacity to operate democratic institutions effectively amidst the tasks of the new states. The feebleness of the "infra-structure," once the elite commits itself to the model of modernity, enjoins a certain measure of tutelary democracy, even in regimes which are fully committed to political democracy.

COMPONENTS

Tutelary democracy may retain all the institutions of political democracy, but it would adapt them all in the direction of a greater preponderance of the executive. To strengthen the discipline of the ruling party, the peaks of the executive branch of the government and of the dominant party move closer to identity than they do in a regime of political democracy. Discipline is maintained in both party and state by a strong personality or a coalition of strong personalities. Parliament, where it is retained, is much weakened in its influence, even when it retains the power to discuss, enquire, and ratify. Parliament is rendered less influential either through discouragement by the executive or through complete and disciplined domination by the party of the executive. The powers of the opposition are diminished; but it may be allowed to exist, if not in parliament, then in the press or in university circles. The press may be left free with the understanding that it will use its freedom with greater judiciousness or, alternatively, its freedom is more far-reachingly restricted. Public opinion is dominated by the executive, which speaks directly to it through the wireless which it controls and by dutiful reporting by the newspapers.

The rule of law, thanks to the survival of the liberal aspirations of many members of the elites of the new states, is one of the features of the regime of political democracy fairly likely to be retained in tutelary democracy. It has more staying power than the freedom of expression, assembly, and association, and it is less menacing to the maintenance of a minimum of public order. When it goes, then tutelary democracy turns more determinedly toward oligarchy.

PRECONDITIONS

The Stability, Coherence, and Effectiveness of Elites. In tutelary democracy, as in all other forms of government, the elite—the peak of the executive—must be effective in order to obtain and hold the assent of the ruled; to be effective it must be competent, stable, and internally coherent. Instability in the composition of the ruling elite will unsettle tutelary democracy at least as readily as it unsettles political democracy.

The political elite must be sufficiently effective, in its efforts to modernize the country, to maintain its legitimacy in the eyes of the politically interested sections of the population on whose tolerance it will depend. It must have a sufficiently good name for probity. It must be sufficiently honest so that inevitable rumors of corruption—all the more inevitable when the possibilities of the public disclosure are restricted—will not be given an obvious corroboration.

The elite of the tutelary democracy must have a firm grip on the machinery and the affections of its supporting organization. The argument for tutelary democracy is that it will provide a more disciplined and more stable regime than political democracy in a society which does not naturally incline toward consensus. If it is undisciplined and hence ineffective, and thus unable to establish its legitimacy, it will speedily move off in more oligarchical directions; alternatively, the society will become further disaggregated.

The elite in a tutelary democracy must be attached to the idea of democracy and sincerely hope, in the course of time and ultimately, to see it flourish. It will, when it coincides with the plans of the executive, permit certain institutions of political democracy to continue to operate effectively, such as parliamentary and journalistic criticism, university autonomy, etc. The attachment of the elite to democratic institutions should be such that it will be willing to renounce some of its power as the democratic capacities of the society at large grow stronger. It will, therefore, as the occasion arises, reinstate or establish anew some of the institutions of political democracy.

The Practice and Acceptance of Opposition. Because it wishes to be democratic and attempts to observe democratic forms, the elite in a tutelary democracy must minimize its use of coercive means of achieving consensus. There must be genuine trust and mutual attachment within the executive, and in relations with such formal and informal opposition as is allowed to exist in parliament and in public opinion. The opposition must not be treated by the majority as pariahs, cranks, or enemies—no more than in a regime of political democracy. The executive must, even where it allows no power to the opposition, be attached in principle to the idea of an opposition.

Opposition in a situation of powerlessness must somehow avoid its own tendencies to dissolve into a supine renegadism before the increased power of the executive, or to take refuge in unrealistic denunciation and obstruction, reaching toward subversion at its outer edge. These are the twin dangers of opposition in situations in which it is allowed a shadowy existence but is deprived of any prospect of the exercise of substantial influence.

There must be sufficient opportunities for amicable contact between the executive (majority) and the formal or informal opposition, so that the idea of a legitimate opposition is kept alive and so that the opposition retains some notion of the possibility of at least informal influence.

The Machinery of Authority. At least as much as the regime of political democracy, the regime of tutelary democracy requires a competent civil service, well enough trained and organized to carry out the measures taken by the executive, and sufficiently loyal to the executive not to wish to subvert its power or to arrogate it to itself. The civil service must be sufficiently detached, however, to accept the possibility of a new elite such as would emerge if tutelary democracy were to be transformed into political democracy. Since the parliamentary and publicistic criticism of executive policy becomes attenuated in this kind of regime, the task of the civil service to provide dispassionate and informed criticism of projected policies is all the greater.

It is important, if the regime is to be democratic as well as tutelary—no less so than in a regime of political democracy—that the civil service be respected but not regarded as "heaven-born." It must be subject to the control of the executive, and the public must have the right to appeal from its decrees or its particular decisions.

The rule of law must obtain and the decisions of the executive organs must be appealable by the citizenry. The highest officials of the executive should not be immune from legal control. The independence of the judiciary is one of the most important schools of citizenship; in a tutelary democracy, above all, its educative role is of the first order.

The regime must have at its disposal an intelligence service and police force adequate to overcome any attempt at subversion. Elites used to wielding preponderant power, and used, even where they do not seek it inordinately, to acclamation, must be able to avoid a spontaneous inclination to regard any severe criticism as disloyalty and subversion.

The leadership of the armed forces must accept the supremacy of the civilian political elite. It is very important, in a situation in which the army contains a substantial proportion of the technical elite, and in which the regime of political democracy has already been restricted and the legitimacy of the civilian political elite already strained, that professional soldiers should remain in a subordinate position and resist the temptations to further the process by arrogating to themselves the task of "modernization," in society and the state.

The Institutions of Public Opinion. The regime of tutelary democracy involves, by definition, a state of feeble public opinion, a press without strong traditions of freedom of reporting and interpretation, universities without strong traditions of independent curiosity, enquiry, and criticism, a class of intellectuals who are either compliant to authority or apolitical. It presupposes the absence of a fairly dense and elaborate "infra-structure" of private and voluntary associations. If these institutions were not lacking, the regime would not slip into tutelary democracy so readily.

The regime of limited democracy, if it is to exercise its tutelary possibilities, requires a widespread system of elementary education, a nation-wide wireless broadcasting system and, above all, the will, on the part of the elite, to stir up thought and aspirations; it must possess a parallel readiness to note and to take into account those thoughts and sentiments. The government of a tutelary democracy, in a situation of rudimentary development of the institutions and traditions of an alert and forceful public opinion, must be receptive to the first signs of such opinion once it is aroused and educated. This is, indeed, the evidence of the good faith of the tutelary elite.

The Civil Order. The regime of tutelary democracy presupposes a generally mild-mannered population, not frequently given to tumultuous manifestations, without intense political loyalties. It presupposes a general inclination to acknowledge the legitimacy of existing authority, as well as a reasonable attachment to local institutions and traditions.

Sheer apathy will enable a tutelary democracy to become an oligarchy. Fractiousness, restlessness, volatility, will force a tutelary democracy to become more oligarchical. In general, the concentration of power, coupled with the intractabilities of life in the new states, and the elite's own insistent urge for modernization, render the tutelary democratic regime more inherently unstable than either political democracy or oligarchy. Only a very skilful, self-disciplined elite with a deep immersion in liberal democratic traditions can withstand the drive toward oligarchy.

Indeed, we might even go so far as to question whether tutelary democracy is a feasible alternative, sufficiently attractive to gain the suffrage of a democratic elite experiencing difficulties in attempting to operate a regime of political democracy. As with so many other problems of the new states, very much depends on the moral and mental qualities of the political, military, and intellectual elites. If, as in India, they are sufficiently devoted to the principles of a democratic polity, then they will carry out their tutelary functions through the whole panoply of representative and liberal institutions. On the other hand, except for Burma and Lebanon, none of the regimes which have replaced political democracy in the new states, or narrowed its range of operation, has up to the present reinstated the democratic *status quo ante*. In short, our experience thus far may be interpreted as supporting the view that deliberate restrictions on the working of the institutions of political democracy traverse a road which allows no easy retracting of steps once taken.

Modernizing Oligarchies

Alarm over the gap between polity and society, and apprehension that the "reactionary mass" of the traditional society will drag down the movement toward modernity, are major motives for the espousal of forms of government which concentrate authority and seek to establish complete consensus.

Both in practice and in principle, oligarchy frequently recommends itself to those in the new states who concern themselves with the promotion of progress and the establishment of unity. Even to those with a moderate devotion to parliamentary democracy, the distance from effective democracy appears to be so great and the road so difficult, the course so full of self-imposed burdens, the procedure so inept and ineffective to solve the tasks which the elite of the society wish to undertake, that a stronger instrument than democracy is thought to be desirable. The instability of representative institutions, haste toward modernity, and fear of the "gap" which both political and tutelary democracy acknowledge and which neither can speedily overcome, seem, to some politicians, military men, and intellectuals in the new states, to be an argument for oligarchy. Oligarchy appears to many of those who stand outside it to be progressive, efficient, swift, stable, virtuous, and consensual.

Indeed, in all the new states, there is, in fact and in theory, a widespread belief in the need for a higher concentration of authority and a stronger medicine for the cure of parochialism, disunity, and apathy. In Sudan, Iraq, Egypt, and Pakistan, and among elements in Indonesia, Ceylon, and India, oligarchy is believed to be the only way to create a modern society with rational, honest administration and decisive action for social progress.

The aspiration toward "modernity," entailing, as it does in the new states, such a preponderance of public authority, would be an impetus toward oligarchy, even if the "gap" were not so great and the counterweight of traditional beliefs and practices not so heavy. Then too, inexperience with representative institutions and impatience with opposition make for oligarchy. Oligarchy is the "natural" theory of the radical "progressivists" of the new states.

Most of the oligarchical tendencies in the new states, leaving apart communism, have no well elaborated theory. There is little or no theoretical exposition of the pattern of oligarchy, civilian or military, except the general belief that it should be stable, nontotalitarian, strong, honest, and "businesslike."[3] What is presented at this point, therefore, is more of an elucidation of certain features of these regimes which purport to be strong, stable, honest, and efficient, rather than a summary of their articulated principles and aspirations.

COMPONENTS

For an oligarchical regime, military or civilian, to be "stable," etc., it must possess a well-organized elite, clique-like in structure. It must be a relatively closed group, watchful over its new members and no less watchful over aspirants to membership. If it is a civilian clique, it must possess a firm ascendancy over the military, since the latter disposes over the means of its subversion. If it is a military clique, then it may be more conciliatory toward civilians, because it needs their cooperation and because it cannot be subverted easily by a purely *civilian* clique. A military clique, too, must have a great deal of coherence, since it cannot readily avoid the danger of subversion by another military clique drawing its support from a lower level of the military hierarchy.

An oligarchical regime eliminates parliament as a deliberative organ with autonomous powers and reduces it to acclamatory and ratifying roles without the power to propose legislation, to debate it, or to revise it. At best it allows advisory functions to parliament, although it will not tolerate any parliamentary opposition. The intolerance toward opposition can be put into a legal form, through the dissolution of all political parties or the dissolution of all but one party; or it might be carried out through tampering with election results, murdering leaders and supporters of the opposition party, etc.

Modernizing oligarchies must depend on an elaborate machinery of bureaucratic administration. Civilian oligarchical elites, even when they claim to reform the

[3] As far as I know, the "theory" of Kemalism which could perform this function has few explicit proponents. The eccentric Nigerian mathematician, Dr. Chike Obe, is an exception.

obtaining structure of government, are likely to compromise with their inherited civil service and retain most of the old personnel, installing a few of the "new men" in crucial positions, and sometimes even recruiting certain senior civil servants of the old regime for posts in the cabinet. Military oligarchies, too, must utilize much of the civilian civil service, since they are not in a position to replace it by their own military bureaucracy. The desire of the oligarchies to modernize will force them to depend on the civil service to a large extent.

Oligarchical regimes are usually unwilling to tolerate an independent judiciary. An independent judiciary is part of the "slow moving" regime which they wish to replace by something more "streamlined." Moreover, newly ascendant oligarchs, insofar as they allege to care for justice at all, are usually strongly for "material justice" and against "formal justice," and the rule of law therefore suffers. Besides, a new oligarchical elite usually seeks to dissociate itself from the preceding regime by trials of "spies," "traitors," and personal symbols of a period of national degradation; for these ends, they find the rule of law and an independent judiciary inconvenient.

Oligarchies tend to arouse antagonism among both counter-oligarchs and anti-oligarchs. There is, therefore, a perpetual danger of conspiracy in a society where the criticism and opposition must be conspiratorial and are likely to be considered by the oligarchy as subversion. Hence, a stable oligarchy, military or civilian or mixed, rests heavily on the machinery of order, i.e., the police and the army. Police and soldiers will be more evident in the "political" life of an oligarchy than in political democracy or tutelary democracy.

PRECONDITIONS

A modernizing oligarchy, whether it be civilian or military, if it is to survive in a new state, requires the presence of the following conditions:

The Stability, Coherence, and Effectiveness of the Elite. Oligarchical elites, military or civilian, when they supersede a corrupt "parliamentary" or political regime, will put themselves forward as consecrated to "cleaning up the mess," redirecting the flow of national energies and resources, etc. Partly to impress their immediate followers who brought them to power, and partly to reassure themselves, they must have some striking achievements to their credit. To remain unchallengeably in power for a longer time, they will have to be able to point to some dramatic accomplishments, such as triumphs of foreign policy, marked economic progress, etc.

The oligarchical elite will have to retain a high degree of coherence to remain in power—not merely in order to legitimate itself before "public opinion" but in order to discourage divisive tendencies in the population at large, among the still surviving discredited politicians, and, perhaps most important of all, within their own ranks.

The elite must be cast in a heroic mold. It must appear to live on a level on which the self is transcended on behalf of a higher good, the good of the national society. Identification with any goal less inclusive is regarded as a falling away. Even where it does not legitimate itself by any complex ideology (as "Arab Nationalism"), it must still exemplify a very high standard of "national service" (Pakistan and Sudan). This adherence to a heroic image is necessary to the internal as well as external equilibrium of the oligarchs. Once they begin to think and act like any conventional tyrants, their subjective self-justification will falter, and the awe in which they are held by their immediate entourage and the politically interested will diminish.

If the oligarchy is to accomplish something impressive in the fiscal, economic, and technological spheres, e.g., in the execution of a land reform, or the establishment of a more equitable system of taxation, or improved irrigation, or the promotion of cooperatives, a high level of administrative efficiency and integrity will have to be attained.

The Practice and Acceptance of Opposition. In order for the oligarchy to assure its unchallenged tenure of office, opposition must be discouraged either through discrediting it by association with national enemies, or by suppressing it by coercive means, or by preventing its emergence through tension-alleviating economic and social policies. The oligarchical regime will increasingly eliminate public opposition as it progresses on the oligarchical road. Such opposition as exists must be hidden from the public eye. Nonetheless, as in all regimes, there will be opposition because opposition is inevitable. A major task of the oligarchical elite will be to detect the opposition within its own ranks and to cope with it by a combination of concessions, compromise, and suppression. Of course, an oligarchical regime might be the product of an inharmonious alliance, and the more powerful sector might not be powerful enough to suppress the less powerful sector, or it might not be able to afford to do so because it could not maintain itself in power unaided. Hence, even an oligarchical regime, although opposed in principle to opposition, might still have to allow some. Then too, sensitivity to foreign opinion, especially Western opinion, might force oligarchical regimes to tolerate a semblance of opposition in the press, even if the parliamentary opposition has been undermined or suppressed. This, however, is far from inevitable.

The Machinery of Authority. In order to justify its criticisms of its predecessor and to accredit itself before the politically relevant public, bribery, self-enrichment, and other forms of corruption among the political elite and the civil service, at least at the highest levels, must be entirely eliminated. Where corruption is found to exist in an oligarchy, it must be made the object of exemplary punishment, or it must be shown to be the product of the machinations of the "enemies."

The oligarchical elite must retain a firm hold over the security forces, i.e., the police and the army. Insofar as there is any dissatisfaction in these circles, its incumbency in office will be uncertain.

It must also maintain an efficient intelligence service to detect the loci of dissatisfaction anywhere in the society, and it must be able to act vigorously to prevent them from becoming alternative centers of power.

The Institutions of Public Opinion. The oligarchical regime presupposes a situation of feeble public opinion and rudimentary institutions of public opinion. In regimes in which modernizing oligarchies accede to power, there is little tradition of enquiry, reporting, and interpretation either in the press or in the institutions of higher education. What little there is can be suppressed without causing widespread or politically serious resentment.

Coming into a situation of a very feeble flowering of autonomous civic and interest organizations, the oligarchical elite will have either to suppress them or to organize them into para-governmental corporations, charged with responsibilities in the implementation of governmental policy, and with the privilege of demonstrating in favor of the government.

The Civil Order. The modernizing oligarchical regime does not require civility from the population. Its very existence is called for and made possible by the absence of civility. What it does require are assent and enthusiasm. The oligarchical elite is usually populistic, and it is therefore not indifferent to the public state of mind. It desires acclamation, the vociferous semblance of a unitary national will, manifested in plebiscites, demonstrations, processions, etc. Homogeneity of opinion is a desideratum of the modernizing oligarchy.

For this, sectionalism and communalism must be reduced to a minimum. Traditional ties and practices must be minimized because they block the flow of sentiments toward symbols of the nation and the elite.

The mobilized, unitary national will stands in place of public opinion. The elite deems that it will prosper best if there are no autonomous and directive public opinion and no organs of public opinion with aspirations or pretences to independence. In a modernizing oligarchy, all intellectuals are expected to serve the national ideal enthusiastically, by singing its praises (and the praises of the elite), by applying their knowledge to the tasks the elite undertakes, and by instructing the populace in the virtues of the elite and its policies.

In order for this state of intense mobilization of will to exist, there must be a widespread belief in the existence of a state of national emergency such as will justify heroic measures and call forth heroic actions. This usually entails emphasis on some external or internal enemy, the frustration of whose pernicious designs requires that complete national unity exist.

It is evident that the new states have an inclination toward oligarchy; Pakistan, Sudan, United Arab Republic, Iraq have all gone in this direction from imperfect and unstable forms of political and tutelary democracy. It is also reasonable to believe that oligarchical regimes are capable of persistence; even though the particular group of persons who rule in an oligarchy might change by co-optation or forcible displacement, the oligarchical regime has a toughness which makes it resistant to efforts to replace it by another type of regime. The question, however, is whether modernizing oligarchical elites can succeed in their efforts to modernize their societies, to rule with stability and effectiveness, and to mobilize the enthusiastic support of a politically impotent populace.

The answer is equivocal. In some respects the oligarchical elites can advance the modernization of their societies. They can improve transportation and communications, they can reform land tenure and introduce irrigation schemes and other civil engineering improvements. It is more problematic whether they can modernize the rest of the economy, particularly industrial production. Military oligarchs do not have great entrepreneurial skill; and they are not likely to be very sympathetic with private business entrepreneurs. Civilian oligarchs, other than communists, are often, despite their modernizing protestations, tied up with traditional and conservative interests and are not so likely to take radical steps to modernize their economies or to encourage vigorous and unconventional private business enterprisers to do so.

The modernization of the machinery of government and the establishment of public order definitely seem to lie within the capacities of modernizing oligarchies. They can reduce corruption in government—at least in the early period of their ascendancy—and they can, by their greater decisiveness, crush public disorders. But in the course of time, modernizing oligarchies must bow before the inheritance which they have received from the previous regime and the tensions which their own methods of ruling engender.

Nor are oligarchical elites likely to be impressively stable in their incumbency of the seats of authority. In Iraq and in the Sudan, the military oligarchy has been in recurrent danger of violent displacement from other military cliques and from communists—in Iraq, from both together. In Pakistan and in the United Arab Republic, on the other hand, the oligarchies have maintained themselves in power without serious threats of displacement by conspiratorial groups.

No oligarchy has yet succeeded in mobilizing the entire population behind its projects. It might overcome overt or organized centers of resistance, but the enlistment of enthusiastic approval seems to be the key and aspiration of modernizing oligarchies—even more than it is the desire of other types of elite. Traditional attachments are tremendously resilient and, although the external power of traditional authorities can be broken by oligarchies, there is no necessary correlation between this and the eliciting of a zealous affirmation of the modernizing oligarchical elite which supplants the traditional elite.

The factors which impede the formation of a civil order also impede the emergence of the unitary collective will, such as is sought by oligarchies. Particularism and traditionality which prevent the closure of the gap by civility also prevent its closure by propaganda or coercion. Nonetheless, a modernizing oligarchical regime is impelled to aggressive action against traditional beliefs and practices. The existence of centers of dispersed authority, modern and especially traditional, is intolerable to a modernizing oligarchy. It is a challenge which denies the claim of the oligarchy to mobilize the entire population on behalf of its modernizing program.

Totalitarian Oligarchy

Totalitarian oligarchy is oligarchy with democratic airs. It is moreover a form of oligarchy which has the advantages of a doctrine. The doctrine is the achievement of intellectuals who stand in an intellectual tradition and who have brought the doctrine to an elaborate condition. This is a considerable advantage in the new states, because it enables the party with the doctrine to attract to itself devoted educated persons, relentless in the pursuit of their goals in societies in which continuous purposiveness of effort is not common.

It shares with oligarchy the fundamental feature of being ruled by a small clique which refuses to acknowledge the legitimacy of any aspirations outside those which are contained in its own decisions. Even more than the ordinary civilian or military modernizing oligarchy, which has no clearly defined doctrine but which lives on its own *élan* and enthusiasm, totalitarianism refuses to admit the legitimacy of public opposition. Whereas civilian and military modernizing oligarchies can, *de facto*, compromise, however uncomfortably, with independent centers of power such as religious communities, kinship groups, and even local territorial authorities and private property as long as they do not aspire to be influential in the public sphere, totalitarian oligarchy, in accordance with its doctrine, seeks to dominate every sphere of life and to annul every center of previously independent authority. A totalitarian regime seeks to apply the oligarchical principle completely and unqualifiedly.

The two main forms of totalitarianism in recent history are the Bolshevist and the traditionalist (German National Socialism, Italian Fascism, Japanese nationalism. In the new states, those who orient themselves toward a totalitarian model usually have the communist or Bolshevist model in mind. No new state has yet become communist, so the picture of totalitarian oligarchy which we present will be drawn from doctrine rather than from practice. Unlike oligarchy, tutelary democracy, and even political democracy, the communist model derives from a canonical literature.

COMPONENTS

Its main components are: a strong, well-disciplined, highly coherent elite, constituting a party, bound together internally and sealed off externally by common belief in an elaborate doctrine, and a strong sense, associated with the doctrine, of an historical mission of modernizing their country as part of a worldwide movement toward an ideal of modernity. The totalitarian model is dominated by a single party rather than a clique, with its own powerful bureaucracy, which controls the party and, through the party, the bureaucracy of the state. The communist party possesses a monopoly of power and tolerates the independent existence of no other party; when it forms a "united party" with another party, it establishes a definite hegemony over its partner.

The totalitarian model dispenses with parliamentary institutions altogether except for acclamatory and ceremonial purposes.

Such parliaments as exist according to the totalitarian model have neither initiating, revising, debating, nor advisory functions. The initiation of legislation and the energy for its execution are concentrated in the governing committee of the party. There are popular elections or plebiscites; but they do not determine the composition of the elite, nor do they have even the minimal mandatory significance.

The rule of law is dispensed with and, with it, the independent judiciary as well as any idea of a law higher than the decisions of the elite of the party. This is particularly the case in "political" matters; in other spheres the rule of law or, at least, a customary practice tends to establish itself.

There is no place for public opinion as an independent instance for the judgment of the policies of the party. In its stead is an intelligentsia which seeks to legitimate all party decisions and regards them as binding for its own creative work as well as for its work in propaganda and instruction. There are no autonomous civic or interest groups —only para-party organizations.

PRECONDITIONS

The Coherence and Effectiveness of the Elite. The totalitarian elite is committed by its doctrine to large achievements. It has thus a more explicit measuring rod to remind it of its shortcomings, and is driven to strain the resources of the economy and the society to attain an ideal of modernity far from the present situation.

To do this while avoiding large-scale public dissension, the totalitarian elite must keep a very firm grasp on the machinery of order. It must enforce very strict discipline within itself and particularly over the lines which connect in with the machinery of order. Only in this way can the leading personality and his surrounding clique avoid displacement within the elite and subversion from the outside.

The Practice and Acceptance of Opposition. More than any of the other alternative models which have a chance in the new states, the totalitarian oligarchy refuses to recognize the legitimacy or even (except *post facto*) the existence of opposition. Committing itself to the denial of opposition and yet, by the strain which its modernizing program puts upon the country, necessarily arousing resentment through the society, it is in permanent danger that any intraelite opposition will be subversive of the actually dominant clique. The incumbent clique must therefore be capable of conciliating some of the opposition which might otherwise become too pronounced, and of paralyzing other opposition within the elite, by breaking up its coherence, by destroying or degrading its leaders, and by intimidating its followers.

The Machinery of Authority. An elite which imposes such heroic demands must be capable of ruthless action to enforce them. To enforce them, it requires a vast administrative apparatus. Since this apparatus, which will suffer from gigantism, overcentralization, and the pressure of urgency and overwork, will tend to be inefficient, it will require supplementary controls, such as party supervision over the governmental bureaucracy.

Partly to control this bureaucracy, partly to control the citizenry, partly to control the elite itself (outside the governing clique), an elaborate, dense, and intense police apparatus is a necessity for such a regime. The rule of law will naturally have a very fitful existence in such a regime; there will be no independence of the judiciary in cases which might in some way involve political considerations, i.e., cases which in any way could be interpreted as affecting the security of the state, in the broadest sense, or the integrity of the ideology which is associated with the state.

The Institutions of Public Opinion. The police being the chief organ for the reception of public opinion in the totalitarian regimes, and suppression being the chief response, the popular will is denied the right of expression. Nonetheless, totalitarian oligarchies are populistic; and

they therefore are impelled to claim widespread popular support for their policies. To a far greater degree than in other types of oligarchy, the totalitarian model requires the allegation of a unanimous affirmation of party decisions, arising from the alleged unity of interests of the population as a whole and the party.

Totalitarian elites are committed, by their nature and their doctrines, to the homogeneity of their societies. They will be even more distrustful of traditional elites and the practices of traditional authorities than any of the other types of modernizing elites.

There will therefore be a widely ramified machinery of organization, propaganda, and concern penetrating into every sphere of life, repressing divergences— real, incipient, and apparent—wherever it believes it discerns them and ready to apply force to a degree vastly incommensurate with the magnitude of the threat to its security.

In order to maintain and justify the state of mobilization, the totalitarian oligarchy must live in a situation of crisis or must allege that it does so. The elite's policy of imposing heroic demands on the society, in its turn, generates recurrent crises.

The Civil Order. Much more than the civilian and military modernizing oligarchies, the totalitarian elite, through its doctrine, demands a thoroughgoing mobilization of the wills of individuals behind the policies of the party. The mobilization in theory proceeds to the point at which individuality and every private interest and concern cease to exist. Civility has no occasion for birth in such a society; its place is taken by unity. The polity would become not just congruous with society— the requirement for political society— but identical with it and superior to it. Moreover, the identity will be, according to the totalitarian model, unilateral—i.e., the society will take all its lineaments from the polity; the polity will take none from the society. The result will be not a "political society" but an "ideological society."

The chances for a totalitarian oligarchy to be established in a new state are good. The model is one which is attractive to many intellectuals because it offers the prospect of rapid progress, because it offers opportunities for intellectuals to contribute to that progress, and because it promises to sweep away both the regime run by "corrupt" politicians and businessmen and the traditional order which that regime tolerates.

The chances of a totalitarian oligarchy to carry out its program in a new state, once it accedes to power, seem less favorable. Although a totalitarian elite could enforce a greater rate of savings and investment in countries as poor as most of the new states, that rate would not be so much greater than what a vigorous elite in a tutelary or political democracy or a modernizing military oligarchy could enforce. It would undoubtedly take less account of vested interests, and it could proceed more directly to its goal. In doing so, however, it would create a great deal of alienation and active hostility. To cope with this, it would require an extremely elaborate and efficient machinery of intelligence and repression. For this purpose, it would require an administrative skill which most of the new states cannot yet muster. One of the reasons for their backwardness is their deficiency in administrative skill; and it is unlikely that a totalitarian oligarchy could remedy this lack any better than any other type of modernizing regime.

Yet, if the mass of the population could not be coerced, then the modernizing program would be endangered, and with this would come disharmony within the elite and unrest in the population. Moreover, traditional orders being what they are, the totalitarian elite could not call forth from the population the unitary will which they need for their own self-legitimation. Particularistic loyalties can be suppressed; but they cannot be eradicated by drastic methods, and the effort to eradicate them could only arouse obstructions. Furthermore, many of these particularistic loyalties would find their way into the totalitarian oligarchy and would cause the same impediments to the formation of a modern regime that they cause in the alternatives to totalitarian oligarchy.

Traditional Oligarchy

The new states, whatever their earlier history, have had no recent experience of large-scale bureaucratic, traditional oligarchies. The traditional oligarchical elements which have survived into the present century led a crippled and dwarfed existence, under the toleration of foreign rulers. They have not drawn the affections of the modern sectors of their society, and, in consequence, a traditional structure of government appeals only to a small minority of those active in the public life of the new states. Although there is much sympathy and often active partisanship for the traditional culture, few would care to see an entirely traditional order maintained. There is too much belief in the desirability of a strong, vigorously modernizing state, quite highly centralized and actively interventionist, for the traditional state to find many proponents.

Traditional oligarchy is not therefore an alternative which has much chance to gain the ascendancy in any new state once it has embarked on a modernizing course, and it does not have much more chance to survive in those new states where it is now in the ascendancy. Nonetheless, below the surface of deliberate choice, traditional oligarchy is powerfully magnetic. In almost every type of regime established in the new states, some traces of traditional oligarchy will be found, because it is the proper polity of the traditional society which the modernizing elites inherit. Just as the traditional social order cannot be completely eradicated, so the traditional political order will infuse some of its ethos into any modern regime which succeeds it.

COMPONENTS

Traditional oligarchy rests on a firm dynastic constitution, buttressed by traditional religious beliefs. The ruler may be provided entirely on the basis of kinship or by a combination of kinship and choice by those qualified by kinship to participate in the process of selection. The ruler is surrounded by a palace retinue or court, consisting of persons who, through kinship or traditional clientage or through talent and the appearance of devotion to the ruler's cause, are accepted by him. The ruler's counselors are selected on the basis of kinship and personal choice.

Since there is little new legislation in traditional oligarchies, there is no need for a legislative body. New laws will be initiated by the ruler and his advisors. Since the traditional oligarchical regime undertakes few activities, its civil service will be restricted in size, and selected and maintained as a household retinue rather than as a bureaucratic apparatus.

Since the oligarchical regime has only a rudimentary apparatus of administration, it will be unable to undertake large tasks or to cope with major emergencies. Its machinery of order will be capable of dealing with only small groups of dissidents or scattered dangerous individuals.

Local kinship or territorial groups will exercise a large amount of power independently of the central government in a traditional oligarchy, maintaining their own fiscal machinery, their own machinery of order, their own judiciary. This is necessary for a traditional oligarchical order, regardless of whether it is a centralized bureaucracy or a feudal regime.

Public opinion, in the sense of legitimate, openly critical, discussion of governmental action and inaction, is absent. There might well be discussion within the court, and between the ruler and his counselors, as well as discussion with local powers. Popular participation, in discussion of issues with a scope wider than the village, is not expected.

PRECONDITIONS

Coherence and Effectiveness of the Elite. The elite will make little or no effort to modernize the country economically, educationally, or politically. Rather it will do the opposite. Should it attempt to do so, it will find its apparatus inadequate. Should it attempt to create the necessary apparatus, it will undermine its own traditional oligarchical nature.

The Practice and Acceptance of Opposition. The traditional regime being rather loose, divergent tendencies will not necessarily be oppositional or subversive. Traditional conciliar mechanisms for the resolution of conflict will be adequate for normal disagreements within the elite. The conflicts which might arise if modernized policies are pursued would be too great for the existing apparatus for the resolution of conflict. Opposition would begin to manifest itself outside the circles and scope for which the conciliar mechanisms would be adequate.

Machinery of Authority. Demands for economic, educational, or political modernization outside the ruling elite are either so slight as to be insignificant or can be controlled by the existing machinery of order. That machinery itself being rather rudimentary, the problems with which it must deal must be easily manageable if the order is not to be subverted. Where the demands for modernization become more forceful, the regime must be transformed or supplanted.

The Institutions of Public Opinion. Traditional oligarchy is incompatible with a modern intelligentsia and modern educational institutions (secondary schools and colleges), which might produce students and graduates who would become significant factors in public life. It presupposes the ascendancy of specialists in sacred texts and in the performance of rituals, and, at the base of this, a stability of religious beliefs.

The country must be sufficiently "unurbanized," so there will not emerge in the towns a large group of young men detached from their families. The "urban mob," although occasionally an instrument for the extermination of dissidence, is an extremely unmanageable tool. It can be just as destructive of traditional oligarchy as of other regimes.

The Civil Order. The traditional oligarchy presupposes a civilly indifferent population which will be unorganized outside the traditional tribal and local territorial structures.

A modern "infra-structure" would be subversive of a traditional oligarchy, partly because it would be in constant conflict with the anti-rationalism of the traditional elite. It would, furthermore, come into conflict with the traditional feudal and kinship structure on which the traditional oligarchy depends for its support.

By the primitive methods available to them for transportation and communication, as well as by virtue of their archaic fiscal procedures, they tend toward decentralization (even if nominally absolutistic). Moreover, the structures of feudal authority and kinship make for decentralization of power.

In practically every respect, a traditional oligarchy is unsuited for modernization. To become modern means to renounce its own nature; and the venturing upon a course of modernization in such a regime can only be the decision of the ruler himself who decides that he is ready to jettison much of what he has inherited. Such a possibility definitely does exist, however. A ruler might indeed decide on the modernization of his regime; and he might be able to carry it out, as long as his legitimacy is so unquestioned that even his anti-traditional decisions are accepted by his retainers and subjects. In the end, the result would be one in which the traditional regime would survive only interstitially and vestigially.

The vestigial survival of traditional oligarchy would be characteristic not only of regimes modernized by traditional rulers but by modern elites as well. The traditional order in the new states is too deeply rooted to be extirpated, even by the most repressive measures. It will constantly reassert itself in the most modernized bureaucratic structures, in modernized party systems, and in the political conceptions of modern intellectual and political elites.

AUTHORITARIANISM AS A FACTOR IN JAPANESE MODERNIZATION

Robert E. Ward

The course of political modernization in Japan raises some interesting questions with respect to the form and organization of authority in modernizing societies. . . . States which have achieved modernity

SOURCE. Excerpted from Robert E. Ward, "Political Modernization and Political Culture in Japan," *World Politics*, **15**, 569–596, July 1963; using only pp. 588–596.

may have democratic, totalitarian, or some intermediate type of political organization. The form of government does not seem to be a defining factor in mature cases of political modernization. The experience of Japan, however, makes one wonder if the same judgment applies with respect to forms of political organization in all earlier stages of the political modernization process. Is the process neutral in this respect throughout, or can one identify stages which demand authoritarian forms of government and which are antipathetic on grounds of developmental efficiency and potentiality to the introduction of democratic institutions on more than a very restricted basis? The question is of great importance from the standpoint of those who would prefer to see "backward" political systems develop along lines which are both modern and democratic. These are compatible but not necessary consequences of the developmental process. This poses the problem of how one can maximize the probability that developing polities will become both modern and democratic.

The experience of Japan alone certainly cannot provide definitive answers to either of the above questions. But neither is it irrelevant, and in circumstances where it represents the sole mature non-Western exemplar of the modernization process in all of Asia, it should be examined with unusual care and attention. The Japanese experience seems to suggest: (1) that authoritarian forms of political organization can be extraordinarily effective in the early stages of the modernization process; (2) that they need not debar the gradual emergence of more democratic forms of political organization; and (3) that some such process of gradual transition from authoritarian to democratic forms may be essential to the emergence of politics that are both modern and durably democratic. It should be emphasized again that these are no more than highly tentative hypotheses based upon the experience of Japan, but they do possess at least this much historical sanction and support. Let us then consider in a general way selected aspects of Japan's experience with the political modernization process which relate to the above three propositions.

First, authoritarian forms of political organization can be extraordinarily effective in the early stages of the modernization process. It is implied—though not demonstrable on the basis of the Japanese

experience—that democratic forms are significantly less effective and that their early introduction may in fact result in conditions that will seriously inhibit the prospects of long-term democratic development.

This contention rests primarily on observations with respect to the relationship between the political modernization process and the process of social modernization in a general or total sense. The former is not autonomous, not a goal in itself. It is instrumentally related to the larger process and goal and should serve and expedite its purposes. This larger process of modernization entails for the society concerned, especially in the critical early or "takeoff" stages, a series of shocks and strains of major proportions. It equally creates emancipations and new opportunities for some, but for major segments of the population this is apt to be a lengthy period of adjustment to new economic, social and political situations and demands. Large-scale material and psychological stresses are invariably involved. One of the routine consequences of such a situation—at least in the non-Western world of the late nineteenth and the twentieth centuries—seems to be a greatly expanded role for government. A certain and perhaps very important amount of the modernization process may still take place under private auspices, but in recent times the needs and expectations which set the standards of modernization have been so urgent and expensive that national governments have had to assume a leading and dominant role. Only power organized at this level seemed capable of massing the resources and taking and enforcing the wide-ranging and difficult decisions involved.

This primacy of government in the modernizing process is more or less taken for granted throughout the underdeveloped world today. The situation was doubtless historically different in the case of the modernization of certain Western European societies and their offshoots, but in present-day underdeveloped societies there simply are no plausible and politically viable alternatives to the primacy of government as an agent of modernization. This was also true in the Japanese case at the time of the Restoration.

The overriding problems and goals of the 1870's and 1880's in Japan were well expressed by the popular political slogan of the day—*fukoku kyōhei* (a strong and wealthy nation). This captures the essence of the complex of forces and aspirations which underlay the Restoration movement and motivated its leaders in the difficult days that followed the initial successes of 1868. The greatest and most urgent needs were for national unity and the creation of armed strength sufficient to guarantee the national security against both real and fancied dangers of foreign imperialist aggression and economic exploitation. Instrumental thereto, of course, was the creation of a strong and stable government to lead the nation along suitable paths. Fortunately for Japan, her leaders were wise enough to define these goals in broad and constructive terms. Military strength meant to them far more than a large army and navy well-equipped with Western armaments; it also meant the industrial plant to sustain and expand such a military establishment and appropriate training for the men who must staff it. National wealth came to mean a radical diversification of the predominantly agrarian economy, urbanization, systematic mass and higher education, planned industrialization, new commercial and financial institutions, and a variety of other commitments which were perceived as essential to survival and effective competitive status in a Western-dominated world. Not all of these commitments were either generally perceived or welcomed at the outset by the leadership group, but in their search for national unity, strength, and security they found themselves embarked upon a species of "modernization spiral" similar in some respects to the "inflationary spiral" of the economists. The most

intelligent and able of them adapted to the general course set by the imperatives which these goals entailed; the others were eliminated from leadership circles.

The realization of national goals of this sort did not come easily to a society such as Japan's, even given the forms of covert preparation for modernization which had characterized the later Tokugawa Period. The really critical years between 1868 and 1890 must sometimes have seemed an unending series of crises. Civil war, the threat of international war and the fact of foreign economic exploitation, a series of economic crises, inflation and deflation, the recurrent threat of samurai conspiracies against the government, the embitterment of the peasantry at the failure of the government to improve their lot, the dearth of desperately needed technical knowledge and personnel, and all of the widespread fears and tensions which attend a time of new beginnings—these were merely some of the problems which constantly confronted the new political leadership. Yet, by 1890, policies capable of dealing with all of these problems had been developed and the country was firmly embarked on the path to modernization. The foreign threats had been faced and Japan's international position was secure; the menace of civil war had been permanently liquidated; the structural vestiges of feudalism had been eliminated and the country effectively unified; the position and authority of the government had been confirmed and regularized by constitutional arrangements; the economy had been stabilized and a promising start made upon its diversification and industrialization; a system of mass compulsory education had been inaugurated and mass media of communication established; in every critical category the strength of Japan showed remarkable and promising improvements.

Under such circumstances it may be that some measure of democratic participation could successfully have been introduced into the political system. There were those who advocated such changes. The *Jiyūminken Undō* (Freedom and Popular Rights Movement), for example, called for the establishment of a national parliament, a limited suffrage, and some dispersion of political authority. Had this been attempted during these years, the results need not have been fatal to the modernization of Japan. But under conditions of more or less constant political or economic crisis, widespread popular disaffection and lack of understanding of the necessity for the sacrifices entailed by many government programs, the unpredictable qualities and perils of the country's foreign relations, and what we have learned in general of the limitations of fledgling democratic institutions in largely unprepared contexts, it is difficult to envisage the feasibility or practicality of any very significant democratic innovations at this time.

These years from 1868 to 1890, or some similar period, would seem to be a time in Japan's modernization when an authoritarian form of political organization offered distinct advantages where rapidity of response, flexibility, planning, and effective action were concerned. This is said with full appreciation of the fumbling and shortcomings of authoritarian leadership groups and irresponsible bureaucracies—including the Japanese of this period—in all of these departments. It thus assumes the availability of some at least minimally competent and unified political leadership. If this is not available—and there are obviously cases where it is not—political modernization is not a practicable proposition for the countries concerned.

In the Japanese case, however, it seems on balance highly improbable that (1) the addition of any significant or effective democratic institutions to the decision-making apparatus at such a stage of national development could have had other than deleterious effects upon the speed and decisiveness with which urgent problems were handled; and that (2) this stage of the modernization process, beset as it inevitably was by so many and such

desperate problems, would have been an appropriate time to launch so delicate an experiment as democratization.

Our second hypothesis was that the dominance of authoritarian forms of political organization in the initial stages of the political modernization process need not debar the gradual emergence of democratic forms of organization. This is not intended to imply any quality of inevitability in such a development, although in a secular sense some such tendency may exist.

In the Japanese case, no significant measures of democratization were introduced into the political system until the enactment of the Meiji Constitution in 1890, twenty-two years after the Restoration. Even then it is very doubtful if any of the authors of this document thought of their handiwork as an act of democratic innovation. It is certain that their so-called "liberal" opposition did not. Rather does it seem that the Meiji leadership group conceived of this constitution primarily as a means of regularizing the structure and operations of political authority—the absence of any rationalized or stable structure and the continual innovation and experimentation of the intervening years must have been very trying—and of further unifying and solidifying both the country and their own authority. As a consequence of this and a variety of later developments, there has been a tendency to undervalue both the degree of political change which the Meiji Constitution brought to Japan and the measure of democratic development which took place under it.

It is helpful to look at the Meiji Constitution and its attendant basic laws both in terms of the general political standards and practices of 1890 and in terms of its actual operations as well as its legal and political theory. If this is done, one will note that it makes public, explicit, and authoritative a particular theory of sovereignty and the state, and derives from this a functionally differentiated and rationally organized governmental structure; it establishes the legal status of citizens and specifies their political and civil rights and duties; it distinguishes legislative, executive, and judicial functions and, although establishing a dominant and protected position for the executive, does provide for their separate institutionalization; it specifies legal equality before the law and creates means for the assertion of popular against official rights; it establishes a restricted but expansible franchise and, in terms of this, a popularly elected house in the national legislature; it provides for some measure of decentralization in government, and renders inevitable the introduction of a much greater measure of pluralism into both the Japanese oligarchy and the political system in general.

Against the background of Tokugawa and Restoration political practices, these are notable and democratic innovations. They did not, of course, put an end to the period of authoritarian political rule in Japan. But they certainly launched a process of democratization which has continued to play a major, although usually not dominant, part in Japanese politics ever since. In this sense the history of the democratization of Japan, viewed in the light of present circumstances, is a product of erosive and catalytic agents. Much of the story is told, until 1932 at least, in terms of the erosion of the authoritarian political forms and practices characteristic of the pre-constitutional period. This process never reached the point of establishing what the contemporary West would regard as an authentically democratic political system, but, by the 1920's, the degree of pluralism, responsibility, and popular participation characterizing Japanese politics would certainly have surprised, and probably appalled, the great leaders of the Restoration Period. Between the 1920's and the 1960's there intervened, of course, the resurgence of military and ultranationalist rule, the war, and the Allied Occupation of Japan. This last acted as a catalytic agent on the submerged but still vital forms of Japanese

democracy and gave them institutional and legal advantages, authority, and prestige beyond what they could have hoped for on the basis of their own political position and strength. The consequence has been a great and apparently sudden florescence of Western-style democracy in Japan. In fact, however, the roots of this development lie deep in the political experience of post-1890 Japan.

There are two things about this gradual emergence of democratic politics from the authoritarian system of pre-1890 Japan which might have more general validity and interest. The first is that even the concession of a very carefully restricted and seemingly impotent governmental role to a popularly elected body can, over a period of time, have consequences well nigh fatal to sustained authoritarian rule. It would be hard to be optimistic about the influence or authority of the Japanese House of Representatives in terms of the provisions of the Meiji Constitution or the relevant basic laws. These faithfully reflect and implement the desire of the founders to make of the House an appealing but powerless sop to the demands of the opposition and public opinion. But the lessons to be learned from the subsequent history of the lower house are: (1) that it provides a means of institutionalizing and enlarging the role of political parties; (2) that, in modernizing circumstances, even vested powers of obstructing the smooth and effective flow of governmental decisions and actions can be critical—positive powers of initiation and control are not necessary; and (3) that in circumstances where a popularly chosen body can thus blackmail an authoritarian leadership, there is a fair possibility of forcing the latter into piecemeal but cumulative accommodations which are democratic in tendency.

The second generalization suggested by the history of democratic development in Japan relates to the conditions necessary to support an effectively authoritarian system of government. Japanese experience suggests the existence of a close relationship between effective authoritarian rule and the unity and solidarity of the oligarchy involved. The limits involved cannot be described with much precision, but authoritarian government in Japan began to disintegrate as the heretofore fairly solidary oligarchy began to split into competing cliques and factions. The probability of such rifts seems to be very high in modernizing societies. The development of role specialization and professionalization even at high levels is an essential part of the process of modernization, and this makes it hard for an oligarchy to maintain the degree of unity and cohesion feasible in revolutionary or in simpler times. Pluralism in this sense seems to be built into the process. And as an oligarchy breaks down into competing factions in this fashion, the terms of political competition in that society undergo an important change. Extra-oligarchic groups such as emergent political parties acquire new room for maneuver and new political leverages, and the ex-oligarchic cliques themselves acquire new incentives for broadening the basis of their support. Out of these altered political circumstances are apt to come new political alliances involving elements of the former oligarchy with elements of more popularly based bodies—in particular, with political parties. The total process is dilutive from the standpoint of authoritarian government and supportive of the gradual emergence of greater degrees of pluralism and democracy.

It is not intended to depict either of the foregoing generalizations on the basis of Japanese experience as controlling or inevitable. But they did occur within a fairly authoritarian context in Japan's case and there seem to be some reasons for regarding them as of more general validity. The conclusion would seem to be that an initial or early stage of authoritarian government on the path to modernization (1) does not commit a polity to long-term adherence to authoritarian forms; (2) does not necessarily make an authoritarian

course of development probable; and (3) may even contain built-in elements calculated with time and development to break down and liberalize such authoritarian forms.

Our third hypothesis is even more tentatively stated and adds up to a feeling that some such process of gradual transition from authoritarian to democratic forms may be essential to the emergence of a political system which is both modern and durably democratic. In this connection Japan's experience suggests several notions of possible interest.

First, our commonly employed systems of periodization may involve serious distortions where the history of political modernization is concerned. Thus, in Japan's case, while the feudal-modern or Tokugawa-Restoration frameworks have a plausible amount of relevance to the emergence of a modern Japanese political system, they also serve to obscure important aspects of the process. They are calculated, as is the prewar-postwar framework, to produce an overemphasis on the significance of certain dramatic and allegedly "revolutionary" events in a country's history— in this case, the Restoration or the 1945 defeat plus the Occupation. This is conducive to a dichotomous view of the political development process which seriously overstates the enduring importance of alleged discontinuities in a national history at the expense of the less dramatic but fundamentally more important continuities.

Second, if the history of the development of democracy in Japan is weighted for this distorting effect of the commonly employed categories and system of periodization, the differences in preparation, timing, and depth of democratic experience which are often held to distinguish a democratic political system in Japan from its Western analogues would perhaps seem appreciably less valid and important than is usually assumed. The two patterns of development probably have more in common than is generally recognized.

Third, if the foregoing assumptions are

valid, one is tempted to conclude that all practicing and at least ostensibly solid and durable democracies today are the products of lengthy and multifaceted evolutionary processes. In the Japanese case, if one looks only to the direct antecedents, seventy-three years intervene between the Meiji Constitution and the present. But far longer periods of preparation are involved if one looks to the less direct consequences of the introduction of mass literacy or a rationalized bureaucratic structure. In this sense it is questionable whether history provides any very encouraging examples of short-cuts to the achievement of a democratic political system.

Finally, such a train of argument suggests the importance of the relationship existing between a "modern" political system and a "democratic" political system. One hesitates to claim that all or a specific proportion of the attributes of a modern polity must be achieved before a society becomes capable of durably democratic performance or achievement, but Japan's experience at least suggests an important correlation between the two. It is hard to specify the proportions involved, but, in a rough and approximate way, one might say that perhaps only modern societies with modern political cultures . . . are practical candidates for democratization.

Chapter 14

Social Stratification and Group Politics

AGRICULTURAL ENTERPRISE AND RURAL CLASS RELATIONS[1]

Arthur L. Stinchcombe

Marx's fundamental innovation in stratification theory was to base a theory of formation of classes and political development on a theory of the bourgeois enterprise.[2] Even though some of his conceptualization of the enterprise is faulty, and though some of his propositions about the development of capitalist enterprise were in error, the idea was sound: One of the main determinants of class relations in different parts of the American economy is, indeed, the economic and administrative character of the enterprise.[3]

SOURCE. Arthur L. Stinchcombe, "Agricultural Enterprise and Rural Class Relations," *The American Journal of Sociology*, 67, 165–176, September 1961. Reprinted by permission of The University of Chicago Press. Copyright 1961 by The University of Chicago Press.

[1] James S. Coleman, Jan Hajda, and Amitai Etzioni have done me the great service of being intensely unhappy with a previous version of this paper. I have not let them see this version.
[2] This formulation derives from Talcott Parsons' brief treatment in *The Structure of Social Action* (Glencoe, Ill.: Free Press, 1949), pp. 488–495.
[3] Cf. especially Robert Blauner, "Industrial Differences in Work Attitudes and Work Institutions," paper delivered at the 1960 meeting of the American Sociological Association, in which he compares class relations and the alienation of the working class in continuous-process manufacturing with that in mechanical mass-production industries.

But Marx's primary focus was on class relations in cities. In order to extend his mode of analysis to rural settings, we need an analysis of rural enterprises. The purpose of this paper is to provide such an analysis and to suggest the typical patterns of rural class relations produced in societies where a type of rural enterprise predominates.

Property and Enterprise in Agriculture

Agriculture everywhere is much more organized around the institutions of property than around those of occupation. Unfortunately, our current theory and research on stratification is built to fit an urban environment, being conceptually organized around the idea of occupation. For instance, an important recent monograph on social mobility classifies all farmers together and regards them as an unstratified source of urban workers.[4]

[4] S. M. Lipset and R. Bendix, *Social Mobility in Industrial Society* (Berkeley, Calif.: University of California Press, 1959). The exceedingly high rate of property mobility which characterized American rural social structures when the national ideology was being formed apparently escapes their attention. Yet Lipset discusses the kind of mobility characteristic of frontiers and small farm systems very well in his *Agrarian Socialism* (Berkeley, Calif.: University of California Press, 1950), p. 33. In 1825 occupational mobility only concerned a small part of

The theory of property systems is very much underdeveloped. Property may be defined as a legally defensible vested right to affect decisions on the use of economically valuable goods. Different decisions (for instance, technical decisions versus decisions on distributions of benefits) typically are affected by different sets of rights held by different sets of people. These legally defensible rights are, of course, important determinants of the actual decision-making structure of any social unit which acts with respect to goods.

But a property system must be conceived as the typical interpenetration of legally vested rights to affect decisions and the factual situation which determines who actually makes what decisions on what grounds. For example, any description of the property system of modern business which ignores the fact that it is economically impossible for a single individual to gain majority stock holdings in a large enterprise, and politically impossible to organize an integrated faction of dispersed stockholders except under unusual conditions, would give a grossly distorted view. A description of a property system, then, has to take into account the internal politics of typical enterprises, the economic forces that typically shape decisions, the political situation in the society at large which is taken into account in economic decisions, the reliability and cost of the judiciary, and so forth. The same property law means different things for economic life if decisions on the distribution of income from agricultural enterprise are strongly affected by urban *rentiers'* interests rather than a smallholding peasantry.

It is obviously impossible to give a complete typology of the legal, economic, and political situations which determine the decision-making structure within agri-

cultural organizations for all societies and for all important decisions. Instead, one must pick certain frequent constellations of economic, technical, legal, and labor recruitment conditions that tend to give rise to a distinct structure of decision-making within agricultural enterprises.

By an "enterprise" I mean a social unit which has and exercises the power to commit a given parcel of land to one or another productive purpose, to achieve which it decides the allocation of chattels and labor on the land.[5] The rights to affect decisions on who shall get the benefit from that production may not be, and quite often are not, confined within the enterprise, as defined here. The relation between the enterprise and power over the distribution of benefit is one of the central variables in the analysis to follow, for instance, distinguishing tenancy systems from smallholding systems.

Besides the relation between productive decisions and decisions on benefits, some of the special economic, political, and technical characteristics which seem most important in factual decision-making structure will be mentioned, such as the value of land, whether the "owner" has police power over or kinship relations with labor, the part of production destined for market, the amount of capital required besides the land, or the degree of technical rationalization. These are, of course, some of the considerations Marx dealt with when describing the capitalist enterprise, particularly in its factory form. Plantations, manors, family-size tenancies, ranches, or family farms tend to occur only in certain congenial economic, technical, and political environments and to be affected in their internal structure by those environments.

[*footnote 4 continued*
the population of the United States. The orientation of most nineteenth-century Americans to worldly success was that of Tennyson's "Northern Farmer, New Style": "But proputty, proputty sticks, an' proputty, proputty graws."

[5] Occasionally, the decisions to commit land to a given crop and to commit labor and chattels to cultivation are made separately, e.g., in cotton plantations in the post bellum American South. The land is committed to cotton by the landowner, but labor and chattels are committed to cultivation by the sharecropper.

A description and analysis of empirical constellations of decision-making structures cannot, by its untheoretical nature, claim to be complete. Moreover, I have deliberately eliminated from consideration all precommercial agriculture, not producing for markets, because economic forces do not operate in the same ways in precommercial societies and because describing the enterprise would involve providing a typology of extended families and peasant communities, which would lead us far afield. I have also not considered the "community-as-enterprise" systems of the Soviet sphere and of Israel because these are as much organizational manifestations of a social movement as they are economic institutions.[6]

Systems of commercialized manors, family-sized tenancies, family smallholdings, plantations, and ranches cover most of the property systems found in commercialized agriculture outside eastern Europe and Israel. And each of these property systems tends to give rise to a distinctive class system, differing in important respects from that which develops with any of the other systems. Presenting argument and evidence for this proposition is the central purpose of this paper.

Variations in Rural Class Relations

Rural class structure in commercialized agriculture varies in two main ways: the criteria which differentiate the upper and lower classes and the quality and quantity of intraclass cultural, political, and organizational life. In turn, the two main criteria which may differentiate classes are legal privileges and style of life. And two main qualities of class culture and organization are the degree of familiarity with technical culture of husbandry and the degree of political activation and organiza-

[6] However, the origin of the *kolkhoz* or collective farm does seem to depend partly on the form of prerevolutionary agriculture. Collectivization seems to occur most rapidly when a revolutionary government deals with an agriculture which was previously organized into large-scale capitalist farms.

tion. This gives four characteristics of rural class structures which vary with the structure of enterprises.

First, rural class systems vary in the extent to which classes are differentiated by legal privileges. Slaves and masters, peons and *hacendados*, serfs and lords, colonial planters and native labor, citizen farmers employing aliens as labor—all are differentiated by legal privileges. In each case the subordinate group is disenfranchised, often bound to the land or to the master, denied the right to organize, denied access to the courts on an equal basis, denied state-supported education, and so on.

Second, rural stratification systems vary in the sharpness of differentiation of style of life among the classes. Chinese gentry used to live in cities, go to school, compete for civil service posts, never work with their hands, and maintain extended families as household units. On each criterion, the peasantry differed radically. In contrast, in the northern United States, rich and poor farmers live in the country, attend public schools, consume the same general kinds of goods, work with their hands, at least during the busy seasons, and live in conjugal family units. There were rwo radically different ways of life in rural China; in the northern United States the main difference between rich and poor farmers is wealth.

Third, rural class systems vary in the distribution of the technical culture of husbandry. In some systems the upper classes would be completely incapable of making the decisions of the agricultural enterprise: they depend on the technical lore of the peasantry. At the other extreme, the Spanish-speaking labor force of the central valley in California would be bewildered by the marketing, horticultural, engineering, and transportation problems of a large-scale irrigated vegetable farm.

Fourth, rural classes vary in their degree of political activity and organization, in their sensitivity or apathy to political issues, in their degree of intraclass communication and organization, and in their degree of political education and competence.

Our problem, then, is to relate types of agricultural enterprises and property systems to the patterns of class relations in rural social life. We restrict our attention to enterprises producing for markets, and of these we exclude the community-as-enterprise systems of eastern Europe and Israel.

Class Relations in Types of Agricultural Enterprise

THE MANORIAL OR HACIENDA SYSTEM

The first type of enterprise to be considered here is actually one form of pre-commercial agriculture, divided into two parts: cultivation of small plots for subsistence by a peasantry, combined with cultivation by customary labor dues of domain land under the lord's supervision. It fairly often happens that the domain land comes to be used for commercial crops, while the peasant land continues to be used for subsistence agriculture. There is no rural labor market but, rather, labor dues or labor rents to the lord, based on customary law or force. There is a very poorly developed market in land; there may be, however, an active market in estates, where the estates include as part of their value the labor due to the lord. But land as such, separate from estates and from manors as going concerns, is very little an article of commerce. Estates also tend to pass as units in inheritance, by various devices of entailment, rather than being divided among heirs.[7]

The manorial system is characterized by

the exclusive access of the manor lord (or *hacendado* in Latin America) to legal process in the national courts. A more or less unfree population holding small bits of land in villein or precarious tenure is bound to work on the domain land of the lord, by the conditions of tenure or by personal peonage. Unfree tenures or debts tend to be inheritable, so that in case of need the legal system of the nation will subject villeins or peons to work discipline on the manor.

Some examples of this system are the hacienda system of Mexico up to at least 1920,[8] some areas in the Peruvian highlands at present,[9] medieval England,[10] East Germany before the reconstruction of agriculture into large-scale plantation and ranch agriculture,[11] the Austro-Hungarian Empire, in the main, up to at least 1848,[12] and many other European and South American systems at various times.

The manorial system rests on the assumptions that neither the value of land nor the value of labor is great and that calculation of productive efficiency by the managers of agricultural enterprise is not well developed. When landowners start making cost studies of the efficiency of forced versus wage labor, as they did, for instance, in Austria-Hungary in the first part of the nineteenth century, they find that wage labor is from two to four times as efficient.[13] When landowners' traditional level of income becomes insufficient to compete for prestige with the bourgeoisie, and they set

---

[7] In some cases, as in what was perhaps the world's most highly developed manorial system, in Chile, an estate often remains undivided as an enterprise but is held "together in the family as an undivided inheritance for some years, and not infrequently for a generation. This multiplies the number of actual owners [but not of haciendas], of rural properties in particular" (George M. McBride, *Chile: Land and Society* [New York: American Geographical Society, 1936,] p. 139).

[8] Frank Tannenbaum, *The Mexican Agrarian Revolution* (New York: Macmillian Co., 1929), pp. 91–133.

[9] Thomas R. Ford, *Man and Land in Peru* (Gainesville: University of Florida Press, 1955), pp. 93–95.

[10] Paul Vinogradoff, *The Growth of the Manor* (London: Swan Sonnenschein, 1905), pp. 212–235, 291–365.

[11] Max Weber, *Gesammelte Aufsätze zur Sozial- und Wirtschaftsgeschichte* (Tübingen: J. C. B. Mohr, 1924), pp. 471–474.

[12] Jerome Blum, *Noble Landowners and Agriculture in Austria, 1815–1848* (Baltimore: Johns Hopkins Press, 1948), pp. 23, 68–87.

[13] *Ibid.*, pp. 192–202.

about trying to raise incomes by increasing productivity, as they did in eastern Germany, the developmental tendency is toward capitalistic plantation or ranch agriculture.[14] When the waste and common become important for cattle- or sheep-raising and labor becomes relatively less important in production, enclosure movements drive precarious tenants off the land. When land becomes an article of commerce and the price and productivity of land goes up, tenancy by family farmers provides the lord with a comfortable income that can be spent in the capital city, without much worry about the management of crops. The farther the market penetrates agriculture, first creating a market for commodities, then for labor and land, the more economically unstable does the manorial economy become, and the more likely is the manor to go over to one of the other types of agricultural enterprise.

In summary, the manorial system combines in the lord and his agents authority over the enterprise and rulership or *Herrschaft* over dependent tenants. Classes are distinct in legal status. In style of life the manor lord moves on the national scene, often little concerned with detailed administration of his estate. He often keeps city residence and generally monopolizes education. Fairly often he even speaks a different language, for example, Latin among Magyar nobility, French in the Russian aristocracy, Spanish, instead of Indian dialects, in parts of Latin America.

The pattern of life of the subject population is very little dependent on market prices of goods. Consequently, they have little interest in political issues. Even less does the peasantry have the tools of political organization, such as education, experienced leadership, freedom of association, or voting power. Quite often, as, for example, in the Magyar areas of the Hapsburg monarchy or among the Indian tribes of Latin America, intraclass communication is hindered by language bar-

[14] Weber, *op. cit.*, pp. 474–477.

riers. A politically active and competent upper class confronts a politically apathetic, backward, and disenfranchised peasantry.

FAMILY-SIZE TENANCY

In family-size tenancy the operative unit of agriculture is the family enterprise, but property rights in the enterprise rest with *rentier* capitalists. The return from the enterprise is divided according to some rental scheme, either in money or in kind. The rent may be fixed, fixed with modification in years of bad harvest, or share.[15] The formal title to the land may not be held by the noncultivator—it is quite common for the "rent" on the land to be, in a legal sense, the interest on a loan secured by the land.

This type of arrangement seems to occur most frequently when the following five conditions are met: (*a*) land has very high productivity and high market price; (*b*) the crop is highly labor-intensive, and mechanization of agriculture is little developed; (*c*) labor is cheap; (*d*) there are no appreciable economies of scale in factors other than labor; and (*e*) the period of production of the crop is one year or less. These conditions are perhaps most fully met with the crops of rice and cotton, especially on irrigated land; yet such a system of tenancy is quite often found where the crops are potatoes or wheat and maize, even though the conditions are not fulfilled. A historical, rather than an economic, explanation is appropriate to these cases.

The correlation of tenancy arrangements with high valuation of land is established by a number of pieces of evidence. In Japan in 1944, most paddy (rice) land was in tenancy, and most upland fields were

[15] But share rents in commercialized agriculture are often indicators of the splitting of the enterprise, as discussed above: it most frequently reflects a situation in which land is committed to certain crops by the landlord and the landlord markets the crops, while the scheduling of work is done by the tenant and part of the risks are borne by him.

owner-operated.[16] The same was true in Korea in 1937.[17] South China, where land values were higher and irrigated culture more practiced,[18] had considerably higher rates of tenancy than did North China.[19] In Thailand tenancy is concentrated in the commercialized farming of the river valleys in central Siam.[20] In Japan, up to World War II, except for the last period (1935–40), every time the price of land went up, the proportion of land held in tenancy went up.[21]

The pattern of family-size tenancy was apparently found in the potato culture of Ireland before the revolution, in the wheat culture of pre-World War I Rumania[22] and also that of Bosnia-Herzegovina (now part of Yugoslavia) at the same period.[23] The sugar-cane regions of central Luzon are also farmed in family-size tenancies, though this is so uneconomical that, without privileged access to the American market, cane culture would disappear.[24] It also characterizes the cotton culture of the highly productive Nile Valley in Egypt[25] and the cotton culture of the Peruvian coast.[26] This

pattern of small peasant farms with rents to landlords was also characteristic of prerevolutionary France[27] and southwest England during the Middle Ages.[28] In lowland Burma a large share of the rice land is owned by the Indian banking house of Chettyar,[29] and much of the rest of it is in tenancy to other landlords. The land-tenure system of Taiwan before the recent land reform was typical family-size tenancy.[30]

Perhaps the most remarkable aspect of this list is the degree to which this system has been ended by reform or revolution, becoming transformed, except in a few Communist states, into a system of small-holding farms. And even in Communist states the first transformation after the revolution is ordinarily to give the land to the tiller: only afterward are the peasants gathered into collective farms, generally in the face of vigorous resistance.

The system of *rentier* capitalists owning land let out in family farms (or *rentier* capitalists owning debts whose service requires a large part of farm income) seems extremely politically unstable. The French Revolution, according to De Tocqueville, was most enthusiastically received in areas in which there were small farms paying feudal dues (commuted to rent in money or in kind).[31] The eastern European systems of Rumania and parts of Yugoslavia were swept away after World War I in land reforms. Land reforms were also carried through in northern Greece, the Baltic states, and many of the succession states of the Hapsburg monarchy (the reform was specious in Hungary). A vigorous and long-lasting civil war raged in Ireland up to the time of independence,

[16] Sidney Klein, *The Pattern of Land Tenure Reform in East Asia* (New York: Bookman Associates, 1958), p. 227.

[17] *Ibid.*, p. 246.

[18] See Chan Han-Seng, *Landlord and Peasant in China* (New York: International Publishers, 1936), pp. 100–103.

[19] *Ibid.*, pp. 3–4; and Klein, *op. cit.*, p. 253.

[20] Erich H. Jacoby, *Agrarian Unrest in Southeast Asia* (New York: Columbia University Press, 1949), pp. 232–235.

[21] Ronald P. Dore, *Land Reform in Japan* (London: Oxford University Press, 1959), p. 21.

[22] Henry L. Roberts, *Rumania: The Political Problems of an Agrarian State* (New Haven, Conn.: Yale University Press, 1951), pp. 14–17; Tables IX, X, p. 363.

[23] Jozo Tomasevich, *Peasants, Politics, and Economic Change in Yugoslavia* (Stanford, Calif.: Stanford University Press, 1955), pp. 96–101, 355.

[24] Jacoby, *op. cit.*, pp. 181–191, 203–209.

[25] Doreen Warriner, *Land Reform and Development in the Middle East* (London: Royal Institute of International Affairs, 1957), pp. 25–26.

[26] Ford, *op. cit.*, pp. 84–85.

[27] Alexis de Tocqueville, *The Old Regime and the French Revolution* ("Anchor Books" [Garden City, N.Y.: Doubleday & Co., 1955]), pp. 23–25, 30–32.

[28] George Homans, *English Villagers of the Thirteenth Century* (Cambridge, Mass.: Harvard University Press, 1941), p. 21.

[29] Jacoby, *op. cit.*, pp. 73, 78–88.

[30] Klein, *op. cit.*, pp. 52–54, 235.

[31] De Tocqueville, *op. cit.*, p. 25

and its social base was heavily rural. The high-tenancy areas in central Luzon were the social base of the revolutionary Hukbalahaps during and after World War II. The Communist revolution in China had its first successes in the high-tenancy areas of the south. The number of peasant riots in Japan during the interwar period was closely correlated with the proportion of land held in tenancy.[32] Peasant rebellions were concentrated in Kent and southeast England during the Middle Ages.[33] In short, such systems rarely last through a war or other major political disturbance and constantly produce political tensions.

There are several causes of the political instability of such systems. In the first place, the issue in the conflict is relatively clear: the lower the rent of the *rentier* capitalists, the higher the income of the peasantry. The division of the product at harvest time or at the time of sale is a clear measure of the relative prerogatives of the farmer and the *rentier*.

Second, there is a severe conflict over the distribution of the risks of the enterprise. Agriculture is always the kind of enterprise with which God has a lot to do. With the commercialization of agriculture, the enterprise is further subject to great fluctuation in the gross income from its produce. *Rentiers*, especially if they are capitalists investing in land rather than aristocrats receiving incomes from feudal patrimony, shift as much of the risk of failure as possible to the tenant. Whether the rent is share or cash, the variability of income of the peasantry is almost never less, and is often more, than the variability of *rentiers'* income. This makes the income of the peasantry highly variable, contributing to their political sensitization.[34]

Third, there tends to be little social contact between the *rentier* capitalists living in the cities and the rural population. The *rentiers* and the farmers develop distinct styles of life, out of touch with each other. The *rentier* is not brought into contact with the rural population by having to take care of administrative duties on the farm; nor is he drawn into local government as a leading member of the community or as a generous sharer in the charitable enterprises of the village. The urban *rentier*, with his educated and often foreign speech, his cosmopolitan interests, his arrogant rejection of rustic life is a logical target of the rural community, whose only contact with him is through sending him money or goods.

Fourth, the leaders of the rural community, the rich peasants, are not vulnerable to expulsion by the landowners, as they would be were the landowners also the local government. The rich peasant shares at least some of the hardships and is opposed in his class interests to many of the same people as are the tenants. In fact, in some areas where the population pressure on the land is very great, the rich peasants themselves hold additional land in tenancy, beyond their basic holdings. In this case the leadership of the local community is not only not opposed to the interests of the tenants but has largely identical interests with the poor peasant.

Finally, the landowners do not have the protection of the peasants' ignorance about the enterprise to defend their positions, as do large-scale capitalist farmers. It is perfectly clear to the tenant farmer that he could raise and sell his crops just as well with the landlord gone as with him there. There is no complicated cooperative tillage that seems beyond the view of all but the

[32] Dore, *op. cit.*, p. 72 (cf. this data on tenancy disputes with the data on tenancy, p. 21).
[33] Homans, *op. cit.*, p. 119.
[34] Though they deal with smallholding systems, the connection between economic instability and political activism is argued by Lipset (*op. cit.*, pp. 26–29, 36) and by Rudolf Heberle (*Social Movements* [New York: Appleton-Century-Crofts Inc., 1951], pp. 240–248; see also Jacoby, *op. cit.*, p. 246; and Daniel Lerner, *The Passing of Traditional Society* [Glencoe, Ill.: Free Press, 1958], p. 227). Aristotle noted the same thing: "it is a bad thing that many from being rich should become poor; for men of ruined fortunes are sure to stir up revolutions" (*Politics* 1266[b]).

landlord and his managers, as there may be in manorial, and generally is in large-scale capitalist, agriculture. The farmer knows as well or better than the landlord where seed and fertilizer is to be bought and where the crop can be sold. He can often see strategic investments unknown to his landlord that would alleviate his work or increase his yield.

At least in its extreme development, then, the landowning class in systems of family-size tenancy appears as alien, superfluous, grasping, and exploitative. Their rights in agricultural enterprise appear as an unjustifiable burden on the rustic classes, both to the peasantry and to urban intellectuals. No marked decrease in agricultural productivity is to be expected when they are dispossessed, because they are not the class that carries the most advanced technical culture of agriculture. Quite often, upon land reform the productivity of agriculture increases.[35]

So family-size tenancy tends to yield a class system with an enfranchised, formally free lower class which has a monopoly of technical culture. The style of life of the upper class is radically different from that of the lower class. The lower class tends to develop a relatively skilled and relatively invulnerable leadership in the richer peasantry and a relatively high degree of political sensitivity in the poorer peasantry. It is of such stuff that many radical populist and nationalist movements are made.

FAMILY SMALLHOLDING

Family smallholding has the same sort of enterprises as does family tenancy, but rights to the returns from the enterprise are more heavily concentrated in the class of farmers. The "normal" property holding is about the size requiring the work of two adults or less. Probably the most frequent historical source of such systems is out of family-tenancy systems by way of land reform or revolution. However, they also arise through colonization of farmlands

[35] See, e.g., Dore, op. cit., pp. 213–219.

carried out under governments in which large landlords do not have predominant political power, for instance, in the United States and Norway. Finally, it seems that such systems tend to be produced by market forces at an advanced stage of industrialization. There is some evidence that farms either larger or smaller than those requiring about two adult laborers tend to disappear in the industrial states of western Europe.[36]

Examples of such systems having a relatively long history are the United States outside the "Black Belt" in the South, the ranch areas of the West, and the central valleys of California, Serbia after some time in the early nineteenth century,[37] France after the great revolution, most of Scandinavia,[38] much of Canada, Bulgaria since 1878,[39] and southern Greece since sometime in the nineteenth century. Other such systems which have lasted long enough to give some idea of their long-term development are those created in eastern Europe after World War I; good studies of at least Rumania[40] and Yugoslavia[41] exist. Finally, the system of family smallholding created in Japan by the American-induced land reform of 1946 has been carefully studied.[42]

Perhaps the best way to begin analysis of this type of agricultural enterprise is to note that virtually all the costs of production are fixed. Labor in the family holding is, in some sense, "free": family members have to be supported whether they work or not,

[36] Folke Dovring, Land and Labor in Europe, 1900–1950 (The Hague: Martinus Nijhoff, 1956), pp. 115–118. The median size of the farm unit, taking into consideration the type of crops grown on different sized farms, ranged from that requiring one man-year in Norway to two man-years in France, among the nations on the Continent.
[37] Tomasevich, op. cit., pp. 38–47.
[38] Dovring, op. cit., p. 143.
[39] Royal Institute of International Affairs, Nationalism (London: Oxford University Press, 1939), p. 106.
[40] Roberts, op. cit.
[41] Tomasevich, op. cit.
[42] Dore, op. cit.

so they might as well work. Likewise, the land does not cost rent, and there is no advantage to the enterprise in leaving it out of cultivation. This predominance of fixed costs means that production does not fall with a decrease in prices, as it does in most urban enterprises where labor is a variable cost.[43] Consequently, the income of smallholders varies directly with the market price of the commodities they produce and with variability in production produced by natural catastrophe. Thus, the political movements of smallholders tend to be directed primarily at maintenance of the price of agricultural commodities rather than at unemployment compensation or other "social security" measures.

Second, the variability of return from agricultural enterprise tends to make credit expensive and, at any rate, makes debts highly burdensome in bad years. Smallholders' political movements, therefore, tend to be opposed to creditors, to identify finance capital as a class enemy: Jews, the traditional symbol of finance capital, often come in for an ideological beating. Populist movements are often directed against "the bankers." Further, since cheap money generally aids debtors, and since small farmers are generally debtors, agrarian movements tend to support various kinds of inflationary schemes. Small farmers do not want to be crucified on a cross of gold.

Third, agrarian movements, except in highly advanced societies, tend to enjoy limited intraclass communication, to be poor in politically talented leaders, relatively unable to put together a coherent, disciplined class movement controlled from below.[44] Contributions to the party treasury tend to be small and irregular,

like the incomes of the small farmers. Peasant movements are, therefore, especially prone to penetration by relatively disciplined political interests, sometimes Communist and sometimes industrial capital.[45] Further, such movements tend to be especially liable to corruption,[46] since they are relatively unable to provide satisfactory careers for political leaders out of their own resources.

Moreover, at an early stage of industrial and commercial development in a country without large landowners, the only sources of large amounts of money available to politicians are a few urban industrial and commercial enterprises. Making a policy on the marketing and production of iron and steel is quite often making a policy on the marketing and production of a single firm. Naturally, it pays that firm to try to get legislation and administration tailored to its needs.

Fourth, small-farmer and peasant movements tend to be nationalistic and xenophobic. The explanation of this phenomenon is not clear.

Finally, small-farmer and peasant movements tend to be opposed to middlemen and retailers, who are likely to use their monopolistic or monopsonistic position to milk the farm population. The cooperative movement is, of course, directed at eliminating middlemen as well as at provision of credit without usury.

Under normal conditions (that is, in the absence of totalitarian government, major racial cleavage, and major war) this complex of political forces tends to produce a rural community with a proliferation of as-

---

[43] Wilfried Kahler, *Das Agrarproblem in den Industrieländern* (Göttingen: Vandenhoeck & Ruprecht, 1958), p. 17.
[44] I.e., as compared with polical movements of the urban proletariat or bourgeoisie. They are more coherent and disciplined than are the lower-class movements in other agricultural systems.

[45] An excellent example of the penetration of industrial capital into a peasant party is shown by the development of the party platforms on industry in Rumania, 1921–26 (Roberts, *op. cit.*, pp. 154–156). The penetration of American populists by the "silver interests" is another example.
[46] Cf. *ibid.*, pp. 337–339; and Tomasevich, *op. cit.*, pp. 246–247. The Jacksonian era in the United States, and the persistent irregularities in political finance of agrarian leaders in the South of the United States, are further examples.

sociations and with the voting power and political interest to institute and defend certain elements of democracy, especially universal suffrage and universal education. This tends to produce a political regime loose enough to allow business and labor interest groups to form freely without allowing them to dominate the government completely. Such a system of landholding is a common precursor and support of modern liberal democratic government.

In smallholding systems, then, the upper classes of the rural community are not distinct in legal status and relatively not in style of life. Social mobility in such a system entails mainly a change in the amount of property held, or in the profitability of the farm, but not a change in legal status or a radical change in style of life.[47]

A politically enfranchised rural community is characterized by a high degree of political affect and organization, generally in opposition to urban interests rather than against rural upper classes. But, compared with the complexity of their political goals and the level of political involvement, their competence tends to be low until the "urbanization of the countryside" is virtually complete.

PLANTATION AGRICULTURE

Labor-intensive crops requiring several years for maturation, such as rubber, tree fruit, or coffee, tend to be grown on large-scale capitalistic farms employing either wage labor, or, occasionally, slave labor. Particularly when capital investment is also required for processing equipment to turn the crop into a form in which it can be shipped, as for example in the culture of sugar cane and, at least in earlier times, sugar beets, large-scale capitalist agriculture predominates.

[47] The best description that I know of the meaning of "property mobility" in such a system is the novel of Knut Hamsun, *Growth of the Soil* (New York: Modern Library, 1921), set in the Norwegian frontier.

The key economic factor that seems to produce large-scale capitalist culture is the requirement of long-term capital investment in the crop or in machinery, combined with relatively low cost of land. When the crop is also labor-intensive, particularly when labor is highly seasonal, a rather typical plantation system tends to emerge. In some cases it also emerges in the culture of cotton (as in the ante bellum American South and some places in Egypt), wheat (as in Hungary, eastern Germany,[48] and Poland[49]), or rice (as on the Carolina and Georgia coasts in the ante bellum American South).[50]

The enterprise typically combines a small highly skilled and privileged group which administers the capital investment, the labor force, and the marketing of the crops with a large group of unskilled, poorly paid, and legally unprivileged workers. Quite generally, the workers are ethnically distinct from the skilled core of administrators, often being imported from economically more backward areas or recruited from an economically backward native population in colonial and semi-colonial areas. This means that ordinarily they are ineligible for the urban labor market of the nation in which they work, if it has an urban labor market.

Examples of plantation systems are most of the sugar areas in the Caribbean and on the coast of Peru,[51] the rubber culture of the former Federated Malay States in Malaya[52] and on Java,[53] the fruit-growing

[48] Weber, *loc. cit.*
[49] Victor Lesniewski and Waclaw Ponikowski, "Polish Agriculture," in Ora S. Morgan (ed.), *Agricultural Systems of Middle Europe* (New York: Macmillan Co., 1933), pp. 260–263. Capitalist development was greatest in the western regions of Poznan and Pomerania (cf. *ibid.*, p. 264). There seem to have been many remains of a manorial system (*ibid.*, p. 277).
[50] Albert V. House, *Planter Management and Capitalism in Ante-bellum Georgia* (New York: Columbia University Press, 1954), esp. pp. 18–37.
[51] Ford, *op. cit.*, pp. 57–60.
[52] Jacoby, *op. cit.*, pp. 106–108, 113.
[53] *Ibid.*, pp. 43, 45, 56–61.

areas of Central America, the central valleys of California, where the labor force is heavily Latin American, eastern Germany during the early part of this century, where Poles formed an increasing part of the labor force,[54] Hungary up to World War II, the pineapple-growing of the Hawaiian Islands,[55] and, of course, the ante bellum American South. The system tends to induce in the agricultural labor force a poverty of associational life, low participation in local government, lack of education for the labor force, and high vulnerability of labor-union and political leadership to oppression by landlords and landlord-dominated governments. The domination of the government by landlords tends to prevent the colonization of new land by smallholders, and even to wipe out the holdings of such small peasantry as do exist.

In short, the system tends to maintain the culture, legal and political position, and life chances of the agricultural labor force distinct both from the urban labor force and from the planter aristocracy. The bearers of the technical and commercial knowledge are not the agricultural laborers, and, consequently, redistribution of land tends to introduce inefficiency into agriculture. The plantation system, as Edgar T. Thompson has put it, is a "race-making situation"[56] which produces a highly privileged aristocracy, technically and culturally educated, and a legally, culturally, and economically underprivileged labor force. If the latter is politically mobilized, as it may be occasionally

by revolutionary governments, it tends to be extremist.

CAPITALIST EXTENSIVE AGRICULTURE WITH WAGE LABOR: THE RANCH

An extensive culture of wool and beef, employing wage labor, grew up in the American West, Australia, England and Scotland during and after the industrial revolution, Patagonia and some other parts of South America, and northern Mexico. In these cases the relative proportion of labor in the cost of production is smaller than it is in plantation agriculture. Such a structure is also characteristic of the wheat culture in northern Syria. In no case was there pressure to recruit and keep down an oppressed labor force. In England a surplus labor force was pushed off the land. A fairly reliable economic indicator of the difference between ranch and plantation systems is that in ranch systems the least valuable land is owned by the largest enterprises. In plantation systems the most valuable land is owned by the largest enterprises, with less valuable land generally used by marginal smallholders. The explanation of this is not clear.

The characteristic social feature of these enterprises is a free-floating, mobile labor force, often with few family ties, living in barracks, and fed in some sort of "company mess hall." They tend to make up a socially undisciplined element, hard-drinking and brawling. Sometimes their alienation from society takes on the form of political radicalism, but rarely of an indigenous disciplined radical movement.

The types of agricultural enterprise outlined here are hardly exhaustive, but perhaps they include most of the agricultural systems which help determine the political dynamics of those countries which act on the world scene today. Nor does this typology pretend to outline all the important differences in the dynamics of agricultural systems. Obviously, the system of family-sized farms run by smallholders in Serbia in the 1840's is very different from the

[54] Weber shows that, in the eastern parts of Germany during the latter part of the nineteenth century, the proportionate decrease of the German population (being replaced by Poles) was greater in areas of large-scale cultivation (*op. cit.*, pp. 452–453).
[55] Edward Norbeck, *Pineapple Town: Hawaii* (Berkeley: University of California Press, 1959).
[56] Cf. Edgar T. Thompson, "The Plantation as a Race-making Situation," in Leonard Broom and Philip Selznick, *Sociology* (Evanston, Ill.: Row, Peterson & Co., 1958), pp. 506–507.

TABLE 1.

Characteristics of Rural Enterprises and Resulting Class Relations

TYPE OF ENTERPRISE	CHARACTERISTICS OF ENTERPRISE	CHARACTERISTICS OF CLASS STRUCTURE
Manorial:	Division of land into domain land and labor subsistence land, with domain land devoted to production for market. Lord has police power over labor. Technically traditional; low cost of land and little market in land	Classes differ greatly in legal privileges and style of life. Technical culture borne largely by the peasantry. Low political activation and competence of peasantry; high politicalization of the upper classes
Family-size tenancy:	Small parcels of highly valuable land worked by families who do not own the land, with a large share of the production for market. Highly labor- and land-intensive culture, of yearly or more frequent crops	Classes differ little in legal privileges but greatly in style of life. Technical culture generally borne by the lower classes. High political affect and political organization of the lower classes, often producing revolutionary populist movements
Family small-holding:	Same as family tenancy, except benefits remain within the enterprise. Not distinctive of areas with high valuation of land; may become capital-intensive at a late stage of industrialization	Classes differ neither in legal privileges nor in style of life. Technical culture borne by both rich and poor. Generally unified and highly organized political opposition to urban interests, often corrupt and undisciplined
Plantation:	Large-scale enterprises with either slavery or wage labor, producing labor-intensive crops requiring capital investment on relatively cheap land (though generally the best land within the plantation area). No or little subsistence production	Classes differ in both style of life and legal privileges. Technical culture monopolized by upper classes. Politically apathetic and incompetent lower classes, mobilized only in time of revolution by urban radicals
Ranch:	Large-scale production of labor-extensive crops, on land of low value (lowest in large units within ranch areas), with wage labor partly paid in kind in company barracks and mess	Classes may not differ in legal status, as there is no need to recruit and keep down a large labor force. Style of life differentiation unknown. Technical culture generally relatively evenly distributed. Dispersed and unorganized radicalism of lower classes

institutionally similar Danish and American systems of the 1950's.[57] And capitalistic sheep-raisers supported and made up the House of Lords in England but supported populistic currents in the United States.

However, some of the differences among systems outlined here seem to hold in widely varying historical circumstances. The production and maintenance of ethnic differences by plantations, the political fragility of family-size tenancy, the richer associational life, populist ideology, corrupt politics of smallholders, and the political apathy and technical traditionalism of the manor or the old hacienda—these seem to be fairly reliable. Characteristics of rural enterprises and the class relations they typically produce are summarized in Table 1.

This, if it is true, shows the typology to be useful. The question that remains is: Is it capable of being used? Is it possible to find indexes which will reliably differentiate a plantation from a manor or a manor from a large holding farmed by family tenancy?

The answer is that most of these systems have been accurately identified in particular cases. The most elusive is the manor or traditional hacienda; governments based on this sort of agricultural enterprise rarely take accurate censuses, partly because they rarely have an agricultural policy worthy of the name. Often even the boundaries of

landholdings are not officially recorded. Further, the internal economy of the manor or hacienda provides few natural statistical indexes—there is little bookkeeping use of labor, of land, of payment in kind or in customary rights. The statistical description of manorial economies is a largely unsolved problem.

Except for this, systematic comparative studies of the structure and dynamics of land tenure systems are technically feasible. But it has been all too often the case that descriptions of agricultural systems do not permit them to be classified by the type of enterprise.[58] Perhaps calling attention to widespread typical patterns of institutionalizing agricultural production will encourage those who write monographs to provide the information necessary for comparative study.

---

[57] E.g., in the average size of agricultural villages, in the proportion of the crop marketed, in the level of living, in education, in birth rate, in the size of the household unit, in the intensity of ethnic antagonism, in degree of political organization and participation, in exposure to damage by military action—these are only some of the gross differences.

[58] E.g., the most common measure used for comparative study is the concentration of landholdings. A highly unequal distribution of land may indicate family-tenancy, manorial, plantation, or ranch systems. Similarly, data on size of farm units confuse family smallholding with family tenancy, and lumps together all three kinds of large-scale enterprise. A high ratio of landless peasantry may be involved in family-tenancy, plantation, or manorial systems. Ambiguous references to "tenancy" may mean the labor rents of a hacienda system, or the cash or share rents of family-size tenancy, or even tenancy of sons before fathers' death in smallholding systems. "Capitalistic agriculture" sometimes refers to ranches, sometimes to plantations and sometimes to smallholdings. "Feudalism," though most often applied to manorial systems, is also used to describe family-size tenancy and plantation economies. "Absentee landlordism" describes both certain manorial and family-size-tenancy systems.

THE POLITICAL ROLE OF THE
LATIN AMERICAN MIDDLE SECTORS

John J. Johnson

In Latin America, one of the major developments thus far in this century has been the rise to political prominence of the urban middle sectors in Argentina, Brazil, Chile, Mexico, Uruguay, and Venezuela. [1] These six republics comprise over two thirds of the total area and population and produce over three fourths of the gross product of the twenty Latin American nations. One of the major questions to be answered, perhaps in this decade, is whether or not the middle sectors can maintain their political positions in a milieu made increasingly complex by newly aroused rural working groups and by the intensification of the contest between democracy, communism, Castroism or *fidelismo*, and neutralism.

Social Groups

Nineteenth-century Latin America had a traditional middle sector of intellectuals, artists, government bureaucrats, Catholic priests, and junior officers of the armed forces. These were aligned politically with the elites and served as a buffer separating

SOURCE. John J. Johnson, "The Political Role of the Latin-American Middle Sectors," *The Annals of the American Academy of Political and Social Science*, 334, 20–29, March 1961.

[1] The terms middle sectors, middle groups, middle segments, and middle components are used in this paper rather than middle classes and middle strata, because the latter terms have come to possess essentially economic connotations in western Europe and Anglo-America. In Latin America, it has only been in recent years that income and wealth have successfully vied with learning, prejudices, conduct, way of life, and aesthetic and religious sentiments as social determinants. The terms employed herein, it is hoped, will convey the idea of middleness without paralleling any fixed criteria of middleness employed in areas outside Latin America.

the favored few from the popular masses. The modern decision-making middle groups are essentially the product of a transformation that began in the more advanced republics of Latin America between 1885 and 1915. In the three decades prior to World War I, farm hands and skilled laborers—mainly from southern Europe, investment capital—almost entirely from western Europe and the United States, and technicians and managers—primarily from Great Britain and the United States, poured into Latin America, especially into Argentina, Brazil, Mexico, Uruguay, and Chile. They played a leading role in the technological awakening of the republics and in driving them headlong on the road to semicapitalistic industrialism. Sleepy old cities became booming metropolises as administrative centers and as nexuses tieing together agricultural and mineral-producing hinterlands to overseas markets. The newly activated urban centers, with their ever-growing cultural, social, economic, and bureaucratic requirements, provided a favorable climate in which the middle sectors flourished. Today the middle groups probably constitute 35 per cent of the total population of Argentina, 30 per cent in Chile and Uruguay, 15 per cent in Brazil and Mexico, and 12 per cent in Venezuela.

Prior to World War I, "middleness" was determined almost wholly by learning and family background, and members of the middle groups were mentally much closer to the elites than they were to the working classes. After the war, the republics gave added emphasis to their material needs. This development had the effect of giving added status to the technicians, managers, and owners of modern commercial and manufacturing establishments. Thus, they acquired middle-sector standing. Meanwhile, the traditional middle groups expanded in response to the demands of education, the press, and, especially, the proliferation of posts in national, state, and municipal governments. The effect of these developments was to make the new middle groups considerably more "popular" in their origins and thinking than were the traditional middle elements.

The middle groups, in this century, have never formed a compact social layer. Their members have not had a common background of experience as there has been much movement in and about them. Some are middle sector because of their learning, others because of their wealth. Property owners are associated with persons who have never possessed property and have little prospect of ever operating their own businesses. Some take their status for granted and know where they are headed and what they want when they get there. Others are unsettled and are undergoing tensions inherent in passing from one socioeconomic group to another. Those belonging to the more settled elements ordinarily have been members so long that they have only a paternalistic interest in and a theoretical understanding of the working elements. Those who only recently have achieved middle-sector status know the lower levels of society because they have risen from them. Their feelings for those groups are likely to be highly personalized and may be highly negative.

Alliance with Labor

Diverse backgrounds have prevented the middle sectors from becoming politically monolithic. Representatives of all ideologies can be found in their ranks. This has not prevented them from gaining political pre-eminence in a major part of the Latin American area. The politically ambitious elements within the middle groups since World War I—and before

then in Uruguay—have created working arrangements with industrial laboring groups who began to expand and become articulate shortly after 1918. It was, in fact, the emergence of the urban working groups, militant, economically depressed, and unable to provide leadership from their own ranks, that offered the middle sectors an alternative to their century-long political partnership with the elite.

The various elements of the middle sectors historically have had three significant common characteristics which they have shared to a large extent with the politically conscious working groups. First, both have been overwhelmingly urban. Only Costa Rica and Argentina contain important rural middle groups, and, in Argentina, the ownership of machinery rather than land is the primary status determinant. Second, both have been, in the vast majority of cases, subject to wage worker contracts and have drawn salaries. Third, both have lacked the capabilities to take independent political action at the national level and, consequently, have been tempted to seek support wherever they can find it. Starting from this commonalty, the political leaders from the dominant segments of the middle sectors supplied at least five issues which have had lasting appeal to large numbers within their own general social categories as well as among the industrial workers. These issues related to the role of public education, industrialization, nationalism, state interventionism, and political parties in each country.

The public education issue has provided a many-edged sword for the middle-sector political leadership. Public education has been looked upon as meaning mass education, and it has always been assumed in modern Latin America that national progress and viable representative government are dependent upon an informed public. The anticlericals, whose numbers are decreasing, have seen the public school as another blow to the prestige and influence of the Catholic Church, which, for some four centuries prior to 1900, was almost the exclusive source of tutors for Latin American youths. Business men support public education—scientific rather than humanistic education—because they expect it to afford them more skilled and efficient employees. And the laborers look to the public schools to provide their offspring with opportunities they themselves did not enjoy. Thousands of public schools have been constructed. Tens of thousands of teachers have been trained. Still, about 50 per cent of the total population of Latin America over six years of age remains illiterate, and the number of illiterates is much greater than in the 1920's. There are more children in Catholic schools today than at any time in Latin American history. Efficient skilled laborers, foremen, and clerical help are still in short supply. A vast majority of middle-sector parents, including those who are politicians, when they can afford it, send their children to private schools. This constitutes, in a very real sense, an admission that public education has failed to meet its projected standards.

INDUSTRIAL POLICY

Industrialization became an obsession with the middle-sector politicians. Originally, industry meant to them light industry devoted to the production of consumer goods and semidurables, and it was promoted, in part, to help distinguish the new groups from the old, free-trade, land-oriented ruling elite. Today, industry means automobile factories and integrated iron and steel plants. The need for industrialization is accepted as a self-evident truth by all significant middle sector and urban labor components. Important and highly necessary steps have been taken in the industrial area, but numerous problems remain. Capital continues to flow into industry, often at the expense of other sectors of the economy. Industry has not resolved the problem of providing employment for those entering the labor pool, now at an estimated rate of 500,000 a year.

Nationalism

Before the middle sectors achieved political prominence after World War I, there had been only scattered appeals to nationalism. They were highly abstract appeals directed to the intellectuals. They were defensive appeals. Sometimes they stressed the protection of national boundaries, mainly against the imagined threats of the United States, and often they stressed national cultural values. In the face of the threatened collapse of France, to whom the Latin Americans looked for cultural guidance, and the emergence of "materialistic" United States, replacing Great Britain as the economic capital of the world, the new political leaders portrayed the old leaders as the tools of the foreigner, and they brought nationalism to the masses in its concrete and politically charged form. Its economic aspects were stressed more, its juridical and cultural aspects less. It sometimes served to keep out immigrants who might compete with nationals for jobs. It sometimes regulated the foreign investor to the advantage of national capitalists and workers. It sometimes protected natural resources, as, for example, petroleum in Brazil, from supposed foreign exploitation. And, at times, it has assumed a xenophobic character or an assertive posture, as, for example, when its proponents have pressed claims for control over coastal waters and submerged lands. Nationalism is currently riding a rising crest of popularity and is considered by the middle-sector leadership to be a major political ideology. It has made several of the Latin American republics more concerned with their internal problems and less responsive to their international obligations.

NATIONAL ECONOMY

The middle-sector leadership early linked itself to the doctrine of state interventionism to rise to great political heights as the doctrine gained popularity. The politicians promised to make the state directly responsible for social welfare and the expansion of the economic sector. Once in power, they wrote the states' social obligations into the national constitutions. Before World War II, several of the governments had assumed primary responsibility for the protection of various distressed elements and, in fulfillment of the state social function, had taken over the direction of the labor movement. Thus, the laborer was encouraged, if not actually coerced, to equate his own welfare with that of the party in power. Particularly since World War II, middle-sector governments have freely intervened in the industrial sphere. They have based their actions essentially upon three socioeconomic tenets: (1) Industry cannot survive without protection from outside competition; (2) Since the accrual of domestic private capital is slow, the state, with its ability to raise funds through taxation and by loans from abroad, must intercede in order to maintain the highest possible rate of industrial development at the same time that it reduces the share of private foreign capital in the economy; and (3) Solicitude for the working groups requires that the state exercise some control over prices of necessities. The contest between state capitalism and private capitalism has not been definitively decided. State capitalism has long been predominant in Uruguay. Private capitalism has remained strong elsewhere, except in the Mexican agriculture system and even there it is staging a strong comeback. Since 1958 it has been the national policy of Argentina to promote private capital at the expense of state capitalism.

NATIONAL POLITICAL FOCUS

The middle-sector leaders have fought with considerable success to substitute the organized political party for the family as the focus of political thinking. Their success probably has been due less to their political acumen than to the fact that political parties simply are better adapted to the contemporary social, economic, and cultural environment of the modern states. The family as a political entity had meaning when the electorate was limited to a small percentage of the total population. Today the political base is being broadened rapidly, and the mass voter comes from those social sectors where the family as a social unit has been the least strong. The political capabilities of the family probably have never been as effective in the cities as in the countryside: in 1925 Latin America was approximately 33 per cent urban; today it is approximately 45 per cent urban. Increased mobility has encouraged the younger generation to make associations outside the home. Women have achieved a high degree of emancipation and increasingly are able to reach rational political decisions independently of the male members of the household. Large and impersonal businesses and governments have reduced the role of the family head as a job finder, and, consequently, the sense of dependence on or obligation to him tends to weaken as the children approach voting age. The total effect has been for the post-World War I generations to transfer their allegiances to political parties, which they feel provide a common ground for those who have similar objectives based on educational and occupational interests and on social relationships outside the home.

Political Moderation

The middle sectors have been on the political stage for a half century since they first rose to power in Uruguay. With perspective it is possible to discern some of their basic long-range tendencies, to estimate their present political status, and to anticipate some of the political problems they will confront in the foreseeable future. We know, for example, that the responsibility of public office almost invariably has had a sobering effect upon them. In seeking office, they have often attacked private property, but, in power, they generally have systematically protected domestic property. They have also reserved an important segment of commerce and industry for individual initiative. They have ameliorated the age-old clerical issue. At no time since the liberation movement—1810–25—have church-state relations, as a whole, been better than at the moment. The middle groups have stood and are standing, at times almost alone, as a barrier between the worker and completely irresponsible left-wing and right-wing organizations, although it is not to be believed that they do not have extremists in their own ranks. They have often objected to the Latin American policies of the United States, and their objections are becoming louder and more frequent. But they have, with few exceptions, supported the Western powers against the Soviet bloc and have opposed any suggestion that hemispheric matters be debated in the United Nations. In brief, they have learned the art of compromise while balancing a mass of political antagonisms.

The middle groups have, thus, become stabilizers and harmonizers. They have learned the danger of dealing in absolute postulates, and their political experiences have given them a positive psychology, as opposed to the negative one so often exhibited by opposition groups.

Political Status Today

Because the middle-sector leaders have not always stayed ahead of the fires they have lighted, their political position at the present must be rated as only fair. They won the most recent national elections held in Mexico, Argentina, and Venezuela, but lost them to the right in Uruguay and Chile and to the center-right in Brazil. In Uruguay, the Nationalist Party in 1958 replaced the Colorado Party, which had controlled the government for ninety-three years, largely because of the country's failure to maintain exports at a sufficiently high level and to cope with a serious inflation. In Chile, the voters in 1958 turned to conservative businessman Jorge Alessandri, who promised to keep a firm hand on the economic area in an effort to slow down the persistent inflation that had

devalued the Chilean peso from thirty-three to the United States dollar in 1945 to a high of over 1100 to the dollar. In 1960 Brazilian voters elected to the presidency the conservative-supported but politically unpredictable Janio Quadros, whose campaign symbol was a broom with which he promised to sweep out corruption. But, as is permitted in Brazil, the voters crossed party lines and chose as vice-president the incumbent, who had associated himself with Vargas as long as that popular dictator was alive, and who subsequently sought to inherit the Vargas mantle. There is every reason to believe that recently inaugurated President Quadros will pursue essentially the same social and economic policies as did his predecessor, Juscelino Kubitschek, whose administration was successful beyond the expectations of all but the most optimistic.

Each of these defeats resulted basically from a voter discontent with the management of national affairs, rather than from a disapproval of the middle sectors' basic human welfare and economic objectives or international policies. But, now that it has appeared, opposition may become fashionable, and, if it does, there certainly is no reason to believe that it will remain a monopoly of those to the right of the middle sectors. Ironically, the opposition of the future will feed upon many of the developments and dogmas that the middle groups politicized.

EXTENSION OF SUFFRAGE

In the countries where they have been predominant, the middle sectors have been highly successful in expanding the political base. Thus, in Mexico, between 1940 and 1958, the number of voters increased over 300 per cent. In Brazil, 1,500,000 cast ballots in 1930, 9,000,000 in 1955, and approximately 12,000,000 in 1960. This achievement, if it may be so considered, was reached by enfranchising women, reducing literacy requirements, lowering the voting age, and removing property qualifications.

But the popularizing of the suffrage may, in the near future, place strains upon alliances between the middle sector and labor. When the middle-sector leadership first approached the workers, the factory employees were capable of exercising political influence far out of proportion to their number. They were militant; they could be organized on short notice, and, more often than other workers, could meet then existing literacy requirements. As long as the electorate remained relatively narrow and the income of the industrial laborers relatively low, politicians could buy their vote without placing an undue hardship upon the national economies. But the conditions have changed. Formerly, factory workers were few in number and each earned a few cents a day. A 10 per cent wage increase could mean a lot to the individual worker while being felt hardly at all by the community as a whole. Today, the number of industrial workers is vastly larger, and their wages are in dollars rather than in cents. A 10 per cent pay raise can have a national impact. Also, the expansion of the electorate to include a much larger percentage of the nonindustrial labor force has required the politicians to measure the industrial worker's share of the national income less in political terms and more in terms of his productive capacity, which has not increased outstandingly in the recent past.

POSSIBLE REALIGNMENT

A not inconceivable outcome of this situation is that the middle-sector leadership may be induced to depend less on the industrial workers and more on the nonorganized urban labor sector and the farm labor element, whose depressed conditions can be improved at relatively small cost compared with that of the organized urban industrial worker. In other words, at present, many more votes can be won in the agricultural sector than can be gained in the industrial sector at the same price to the overall economy. This would suggest that, in the near future, land reform, social reforms in rural areas, and improvement of conditions for farm workers may well be increasingly used as appeals by the middle-sector leadership. It also suggests that organized urban labor may well be left in the hands of extremist groups. There are, of course, many other possibilities, but the one above is given for purposes of indicating the extent of the political ferment in the area and its possible consequences.

The alliances between the middle sectors and industrial labor are also being altered by developments that have taken place in the ownership of industrial and commercial enterprises. When the alliances were created, a large share of industry in each country was controlled by foreign investors who did not have direct representation in government. They were made to bear directly a large portion of the original financial burdens of increased wages and other benefits awarded the workers in return for their political backing. Under such circumstances, the middle-sector politician could offer himself as a friend of the workers and as a watchdog against possible abuses from foreigners. The trend since the late 1930's, when Mexico nationalized its railroads and petroleum industry, has been for commerce and industry to become domestically controlled through either state or private ownership. As a result, the nation itself or its investing public has been called upon to carry an augmented share of the cost of gain to industrial labor. In view of this, private domestic capital increasingly has insisted that the public good really requires a concern with expanded production rather than an equalitarian distribution of income. Business men are using their legal rights and economic power to dissuade politicians who would disregard realities in currying the favor of workers. They demand that the state alert the working man to the fact that he cannot expect the same friendly consideration when he fights local interests as when he served as the protagonist against foreign rapacity. Their campaign partly explains why the position of the industrial worker has not improved significantly in the more highly developed countries of Latin America during the past decade.

The middle sectors can no longer claim an option on sponsorship of nationalism. When they first gave that ideology national stature, it was rejected by the old ruling elite, which was then the only element that contested with the middle sectors politically. But nationalism is currently embraced by all articulate elements, some of whom hold it more ardently than do the politically dominant elements of the middle sectors. In Brazil, the armed forces have become the depository of nationalism, while, according to Vice-President João Goulart, the workers there claim the authority to exercise the function of the vanguard in the nationalistic struggle in which the Brazilian people are involved. In Chile, the Communists have seized the nationalist label and are running with it. In Argentina, the extreme right, including some senior armed forces officers, vies with the Communists as the champion of nationalism. In Venezuela, both the Communists and the *fidelistas* are forcing the Betancourt government to be more nationalistic than the president would prefer or conditions would dictate. Under these circumstances it is inevitable that the middle-sector elements must periodically cast off the cloak of nationalism in which they enshrouded themselves and seek to moderate the issue, a role which will not be politically popular over the short range.

MILITARY ALIGNMENT

The armed forces have held a unique position as far as the middle-sector political leadership is concerned. When the middle sectors were still politically untried and the anarchosyndicalist-oriented labor organizations preached the end of both the military and private property, the officers of the armed forces remained faithful to the traditional ruling element. But, when the middle sectors began to

supplant the old political aristocracies and to demonstrate their basically centrist position and their worker following accepted more moderate doctrines, the military officers, who were overwhelmingly of middle sector backgrounds, ceased their traditional elitist associations and extended their support to the middle sectors. This relationship persists in all of the countries dominated by the middle sector. But there are indications that it is weakening. During the 1930's, and particularly since World War II, there has been a tendency to dip into the lower middle groups and the working groups for officer material. As this has occurred, the military's appreciation of the working man's problems and his political capabilities has grown. Today there is good reason to believe that the military establishments would accept constitutionally elected labor governments. There is, furthermore, a growing body of evidence which suggests that military officers in certain of the republics, such as Venezuela, might be reluctant to shoot down enough compatriots to stem a serious attempt on the part of either Communists or *fidelistas* to take over the government by force. This is not idle speculation. There are many in Venezuela and elsewhere in Latin America who believe that the next series of military uprisings will come when Communist or *fidelista* inspiration prompts noncommissioned officers to turn on their superiors.

OTHER FORCES

Communism and *fidelismo*, both of which are in highly dynamic and aggressive stages of their development, probably offer the greatest threat to the favorable political position of the middle sectors in the foreseeable future. Although the Communists were already operating in Latin America when the middle sectors bid for political recognition, their appearance was premature, and the middle sectors could, prior to World War II, generally ignore them. Since the war, with

Latin America in ferment and the military and scientific prestige of the Soviet Union at an all-time high, the Communists have pushed their advantage relentlessly. Their anti-United States attack wins them the support of nationalists. They direct their demagogic campaign to the still unsophisticated groups to whom the middle sectors were instrumental in giving political articulation. Because they do not operate the governments, the Communists can attack without responsibility. They can exploit the failure to improve the working man's position during the past decade and the middle sector's sometimes paternalistic attitude toward the labor movement. The *fidelistas*, whose objectives early in 1961 were indistinguishable from those of the Communists, have the advantage of being indigenous. They appeal to certain elements, especially among the students, who have been reluctant to accept Communism because of its international overtones, but whose hatred for the United States often rivals that of Castro himself.

The popularity of Communism and *fidelismo* are near their all-time highs. A considerable share of Communist and *fidelista* support comes from middle-sector intellectuals and bureaucrats, who, under past regimes, had no prospect of gaining great wealth or great power. The Cuban revolt showed them that a determined group of such people can take over a government and achieve power, at least the power to make what they regard as vital decisions about the direction and pace of social and economic change.

As this article goes to press, Venezuela, with huge foreign investments in its natural resources and a shocking inequality in the distribution of its wealth and income, seems acutely susceptible to the blandishments of both Communism and *fidelismo*. Next to Venezuela, the situation is probably most precarious in Ecuador, where all that stands between the extreme left and a takeover of the coastal area of that country is the nation's armed forces, who, as late as June 1959, suppressed riots in Guayaquil only after shooting down hundreds of Ecuadorean citizens. The armed forces of Latin America will not have the capability or the willingness to hold off the masses indefinitely. It thus becomes incumbent on the middle sectors to offer the popular elements some attractive substitutes for their present unsatisfactory and slowly changing state. On the basis of their over-all record, the middle sectors are capable of producing aggressive and imaginative leadership. But, if they do not move ahead more rapidly and with greater originality in the 1960's than they did in the 1950's, they will fail. The stakes will be large in the present decade. The political and economic alternatives will be more numerous than at any time in world history. If the middle sectors, who represent more than any other group in Latin America those values that the United States professes to cherish, are to remain politically strong, they will need help on a much larger scale than responsible elements among them previously have dared to advocate. They will also need greater freedom than they hitherto have enjoyed if they are to work out their problems in their own way.

THE MULTIPLE SOCIETY IN ECONOMIC DEVELOPMENT: MEXICO AND GUATEMALA

Manning Nash

For the anthropologist the problem of economic development and cultural change is now clearly enough delimited for an investigator to ask crucial questions. An adequate theoretical resolution of that problem area would come through a series of propositions which would give empirically relevant answers to the following questions:

1. What income-raising technology and knowledge will be adopted and how will these be fitted into the social system?
2. What kinds of persons will put into use the production-increasing innovations?
3. What series of social and cultural changes will permit the innovators, together with their new forms of production, to restructure the society and reorient the culture, so that economic development becomes a built-in feature of the ordinary operation of the society?

By detailed analyses of societies and cultures, by invoking what is known of the processes of social and cultural change, and by recourse to the growing theory of the structure and function of social systems, partial answers to these questions have been offered for many of the non-Western peoples now seeking economic betterment or having it thrust upon them.

But in the emerging conceptual apparatus for the study of culture change and economic development, some of the current notions as to the relevant dimensions of the cultural and social entity under observation have proved inadequate. Anthropologists typically analyze non-Western

peoples through a model of interpretation which yields a description of a unified whole called a culture or a society. This procedure is valid and necessary when the interest is in a series of social and cultural types forming the basis of abstraction for scientific generalization. However, it often vitiates anthropological contributions to the study of economic development and cultural change, unless supplemented by concepts and tools facilitating the interpretation of more complex social and cultural situations than the relatively small and culturally autonomous communities for which our theoretical tools have been developed.

The unit of study for economic development is a political one—the nation or, in looser terms, a country. A goodly portion of the so-called underdeveloped countries is composed of more than one cultural tradition and of diverse levels of social organization within the territorial unit over which political jurisdiction is exercised. The anthropologist who studies only one of the cultural traditions, and makes generalizations about the process of culture change and economic development for the whole country, errs conspicuously; even if the generalization is restricted to the segment under observation, the error is great, if not so egregious.[1]

I propose the use of a concept which explicitly takes into account the facts of variant cultural tradition and, at the same time, the scale of social organization as the most useful starting point for an analysis of an underdeveloped country, at least for such countries as the five "Indian" republics of Latin America. The concept suggested is that of a multiple society with plural cultures.

SOURCE. Manning Nash, "The Multiple Society in Economic Development: Mexico and Guatemala," *American Anthropologist*, **59**, 825–833, October 1957.

This concept has had some anthropological currency (Tax 1946; Beals 1953; Nash 1965b) but its employment in the understanding of the process of economic development and culture change has not yet been undertaken.[2] The utility of the concept and its research implications will be shown by reviewing some of the facts of Guatemalan and Mexican economy and society from this perspective.

As a social type, the multiple society with plural cultures is marked by the presence of at least two distinct cultural traditions, each significantly different in breadth of integration. Although the entire population of the national territory is included in a single system of political and economic bonds, only a part of the population is fully aware of the national entity, participates significantly in its cultural and social life, or has control over resources and communications of nationwide scope or impact. That part of the population which carries the national variety of culture is in fact the national society; it is scattered throughout the national territory; it is the link between the nation and other nations in the world and is the segment of the population in whom political control is vested and within which political control is contested. It is also that part of the population whose economic decisions have national repercussions.

This national political and economic segment of the multiple society is within itself divided into classes and marked by rural and urban differences. But as a social segment it is superior to those small-scale societies with different cultural traditions within the same national territory. These subordinate societies are locally organized; economic resources are small compared to the national society; political power is not vested in them; and the cultural cleavage between the national segment and its plural cultures is marked by many symbolic pointers of dress, language, occupation, custom, and perhaps even the physical features of the members.

It is plain that in Guatemala the multiple society refers on the one hand to *Ladinos* and on the other to Indians. In Mexico the chief terms of reference are to *Mexicano* as against *Indio*.[3] The two nations serve as an historical contrast, both as to the degree of persistence of a multiple society and as to different rates of economic progress.

Guatemala is a multiple society *par excellence*, with hundreds of Indian municipios each varying from the other in small and numberless ways and as a cultural tradition distinct from the Ladino society (Tax 1937). The nature of economic development and culture change in Guatemala depends not on the characteristics of the Ladino society nor on the features of the Indian society alone, but on the relations of the segments of the multiple society and the possible and probable roles each segment may or can play in the historical process. The questions which opened this paper are to be asked twice; once for the national segment, and again for the non-national segment. An understanding of economic development will emerge in the relations between these two sets of answers.

The Indian societies of Guatemala are made up of peasants who in economic organization and motivation are, and have been, receptive to changes in technology and knowledge, if such innovations are of comparative economic advantage (Tax 1953). The cultural differences between Ladino and Indian society are not matched by economic differences in type of organization, nor are the Indian economies isolated from the national economy or separate in activity or sphere (Mosk 1954; Tax 1956). Guatemalan Indian receptivity to income-raising innovation is limited then in the same way in which the limits of innovation are set in any society—by the prevailing stock of wealth, by the present command over skill and knowledge, by the estimation of worth of a new item in terms of what it displaces or replaces, by the calculation of how much trouble it is to reorient one's time, energy, and resources to use the new item in light of the rewards it offers, and by the judgment of how one looks to one's fellows by adopting the new way.

Even a cursory acquaintance with the culture of the municipios of the Western Highlands indicates that new items of technology and knowledge are subjected to estimation and calculation in a set of values and preference scales different from that of Ladino society. But the important point is that this set of different values and preference schedules does not preclude the rapid introduction of income-raising innovation or justify the appellation of "resistant to change." On the contrary, change is relatively swift and easy in Guatemalan Indian communities, if the proposed innovation is more productive within the limits of the factors enumerated earlier. The limits are apparently wide and as yet uncharted. They run the gamut from things as relatively undisturbing as a sewing machine or corn mill up to and including Central America's largest textile mill. I have reported earlier on the range and kind of changes made in a traditional Indian community in which a modern textile mill is situated, drawing almost all of its labor from the local Indian community (Nash 1955a, 1955b, 1956b).

If the cultures of the Guatemalan Indians are such as to permit a relatively wide choice among alternatives, why then is the choice not more frequently made? The answer lies, I think, in the social scale of these municipios. The units of production and consumption are households, not firms, and the household's control over resources, its capital stock, and its withholding power, in short its ability to try out something new, is perforce limited.[4] Innovations which it can undertake, almost by definition, cannot materially raise the per-capita income; and those innovations which can materially raise the income, it cannot undertake. The Indian communities, singly or severally, cannot start the self-generating process of

technological improvement and economic reorganization which can in the end lead to abundance.

The major role of taking on a comprehensive new and more productive technology is to lie, then, with some members of the national segment of the multiple society rather than with the Indian communities. But the choice of technology and its spread throughout a large part of the population depends on a proper appreciation of the nature of Indian cultures by the Ladino segment. That is to say, in the process of Guatemala's economic development it falls to the lot of Ladino society to introduce the income-increasing technique and knowledge, but unless that knowledge and technique are acceptable to and used by the Indian communities, little or no economic progress may result. As Tax has pointed out (1956), the Indians' use of the more productive coastal lands instead of the highlands would raise their standards of living and the nation's as a whole, but since in order to use the coastal land under the present system of land redistribution the Indian must move to the coast and occupy the land as a resident, few take advantage of the better land. Indians live in communities, and prefer the highlands for climatic, hygienic, and sentimental reasons. The suggestion is that Indians be allowed to use the land without having to settle there. Some of them normally do this with their own parcels of coast land and presumably would do so as easily, and to everybody's benefit, on government land. The nature of the multiple society is such that only a consideration of all segments and of their relations can lead to economically effective plan or practice, for it is primarily the role of the Indian in Guatemala to provide the bulk of the human material whose choice will decide whether the alternatives presented by Ladino society shall be fruitful.

Ladino society is frequently divided into a series of social classes which correspond rather closely to the various kinds of productive activities each social class manifests (Adams 1956; LeBeau 1956). First of all, there is a social class called upper or cosmopolitan (Wagley and Harris 1955). This class is largely urban in residence, sophisticated in style, education, consumption, and usually well travelled. It is the richest segment of Guatemala, gathering its wealth from the large coffee plantations or other export crop land, and sometimes through a large commercial establishment. Below this social class, in both wealth and status, is a segment often called the local upper class to distinguish it from the metropolitan or cosmopolitan rich and prestigeful. The local upper class is a kind of rural gentry, often with town or city residence. These are the producers of export crops or of cattle and food for internal use, on a lesser scale than the *finquero* of the large export plantation. They are the medium holders who exert political power on the local scene and are important in national politics, but their command of the factors of production is less than that of the cosmopolitans. The third social class usually named is the middle class, more recently denoted as the *masa media* (Gillin 1956). It includes persons on the social and economic scale ranging from school teachers to directors of firms, passing on the way army officers, clerks, minor government officials, and intellectual workers. The fourth social class appears to be the *clase baja*, a lower class composed chiefly in the cities of wage workers, domestics, peddlers, small scale self-employed craftsmen, and the occasional worker; in the countryside this segment includes the agricultural worker on a daily basis, the resident agricultural worker, the small merchant or shopkeeper, the few nonagricultural wage workers, the self-employed petty craftsman, and the occasional worker.

One of the four segments of Ladino society must give impetus to the process of economic development if such a process is indeed to begin and come to fruition. Which segment can and which, given good

economic reasons, is likely to do so? Not enough is known in detail about the national culture and social class system to answer this question definitively, but in broad outline the major possibilities are evident. The clase baja may be discounted either as the initiators or the carriers-through of the cultural change which will bring about economic development because it does not command sufficient economic means or organization, and it is largely illiterate, unvocal, and unrepresented politically. In a process of economic development this segment is analogous to the Indian societies and cultures in providing the human material whose choice to use the income-raising technology and knowledge is crucial.

At the other extreme, the cosmopolitans have the resources and perhaps the knowledge and political power to make economic development possible but it is unlikely that they will do so, because a major concern of large plantations is the price structure of the export market rather than problems of technological or organizational experiment and advance. Cosmopolitans can get rich and stay rich with their current technology—wasteful or inefficient as it may be—provided the world market offers them sufficient return for their product. Furthermore, it is unlikely that whatever improvements the cosmopolitans make will appeal to the members of Indian societies (whose chief economic role would be that of plantation laborers) or to the clase baja, who will also remain in the role of agricultural laborers with presumably the same levels of skill and knowledge, even if their productivity and income may rise slightly. Despite the need or desire of the cosmopolitans or the upper class for rapid, substantial economic and cultural change, they are unlikely to undertake an extensive program of change even though they command the resources and the political power to beget economic development.

The local upper class is a more promising but still an unlikely choice as a collective candidate for bringing rapid economic change to Guatemala. By and large, the rural gentry aim to expand their economic activities, especially through increasing land holdings and money crops, but the object of such expansion is to move into the social and economic role of the cosmopolitan. That is to say, successful local upper-class persons usually orient economic activity so that they may rise into the cosmopolitan segment, rather than select or implement some program which would lead to general economic change or would enlist or attract in its wake the Indian societies or the clase baja.

By a process of elimination the middle class, the masa media, remains as the only possible segment for economic development and its accompanying cultural and social reformulation. They are, I shall argue, a likely group, but the probability is of uncertain odds. The middle class is literate, politically active, socially mobile, and impoverished (Gillin 1956). Such a combination of characteristics makes them particularly susceptible to the promise of economic betterment and willing to pay the personal costs and run the social risks of rapid social change. The masa media, being poor both in personal incomes in comparison to what their tastes and aspirations consider the decent minimum and in their control over the factors of production, has no special commitment to a going technology or economic organization. They are willing to innovate economically and socially, provided the rewards accrue partly to them in terms of wealth and increased power and prestige.

Since the middle class does not make economic decisions of great scope or impact in view of their current claim on the productive mechanism, their willingness and social susceptibility to economic and cultural change can be translated into social fact and historical process only through political channels. Political power may give them control over sufficient resources to make significant cultural and economic innovation. This political

access to economic means may be achieved only if the masa media can enlist in their cause a sizeable segment of the national population, chiefly from among the clase baja and the Indian societies. Therefore, a condition of the success of the middle class in achieving political power, if indeed they ever do achieve it, is an economic program and policy which appeals to and makes adherents from the Indian society and the lower classes. The middle class, then, is a likely social segment of the multiple society to want and to seek economic development; to consider those innovations in technology and economic organization which the Indians and the clase baja will accept; and to make the necessary social and cultural changes so that economic development, necessary to their political eminence, may become a standard feature of the society.[5]

The brief argument I have here advanced appears to me logically consistent and respectful of the facts of Guatemalan culture and economy, but it has the character of a "just-so story." This may be resolved by bringing into view a neighboring multiple society, Mexico.

Mexico suggests itself for comparative purposes through the common historical experience (albeit differently paced) it shares with Guatemala: the presence of plural cultures in a multiple society and a former similarity in the class structure. It differs through the fact of recent, rapid rises in national income. Mexico of 1910 was much like Guatemala of 1940. The class system was, with some minor variation, of the four-fold variety which Guatemala now exhibits (Iturriaga 1951). A significant part of the population lived in small-scale social units manifesting different cultures, while still part of the larger political and economic national network (Basauri 1940), and of course the Indians of Mexico were culturally so similar to those of Guatemala that propositions are made about the Indians of Mesoamerica (Redfield and Tax 1952). The point need not be labored as to the social, cultural, and economic (Parra 1954) similarity of Mexico of 1910 and Guatemala of 1940, for many of those similarities persist in the two nations today.

But Mexico's economic development has been phenomenal by contrast with Guatemala's, especially in the last decade. Mexico is apparently one of the few nonindustrialized or underdeveloped countries which seems likely to "get over the hump" of transition economically and socially. The national income of Mexico more than doubled in the decade 1940–50 (IBRD 1952); output increased in every branch of production save mining; the network of roads and communication was expanded, overcoming some of the economic atomism and regionalism of the difficult topography. And some of the most isolated Indian groups and technologically backward rural dwellers have come during the past years both to feel themselves Mexicans (cf. Redfield 1930; Lewis 1951) and to use the most modern and industrial of equipment in the economy (Moore 1951).

Although it is still a relatively poor nation Mexico's rapid and substantial economic progress came in the wake of thirty years of revolution in which political control over economic resources was placed in the hands of the middle class, rather than the cosmopolitans or upper class. This segment of the population forms what is sometimes called "the new group of industrialists" (Mosk 1951) on their economic side, and the core of the "institutional" revolutionary party on their political side. This middle class segment appears to have been able to gain political control, and hence economic importance (since without implicit or explicit government blessing nothing prospers for long in Mexico), by adopting a course which appealed both to the clase baja and to the Indian populations. Their experimental attitude toward technology and economic organization was always tempered by the political consideration of not alienating the peasants and Indians upon whom their

economic success was ultimately founded. Consequently, in contemporary Mexico there is a vigorous, government-financed program for Indian betterment which sometimes yields spectacular results and makes of anthropology in Mexico an applied science (Caso et al. 1954; Villa Rojas 1955). At the same time, the government is consciously and continually seeking new technologies and ways of adapting them to Mexico, and plowing back into new investment a significant amount of profit.

I do not mean to imply that Mexican economic development is a fully understood phenomenon, or that the peculiar situation of Mexico during World War II was not of great importance, or even that Mexico will continue at the same rate in the same direction. Many parts of the picture are missing, and problems of population, internal income distribution, terrain and market, still plague Mexico.

However, I think the Mexican experience with economic development is more clearly comprehensible when viewed by means of the concept of multiple society with plural cultures. And Mexico's experience, so understood, prefigures one of the possible courses of Guatemalan development. The notion of a multiple society with plural cultures is a tool which calls attention to the diverse levels of social organization and cultural tradition, so that the anthropologist who looks at a small part of the whole does not make the error of taking the behavior of a member for the behavior of a system. It encourages the selection of strategic variables and the formulation of hypotheses which later history and cross-cultural comparison may confirm or disconfirm, rather than a listing of negative cautions which frequently have been the anthropological hallmark in the study of economic development and cultural change.

NOTES

[1] The volume prepared for the United Nations (Mead 1953) moves between descriptions of a

small segment and generalizations about a
larger whole without the apparent intervention of theoretical means of flight. Similarly,
a casebook on technological change (Spicer
1952) attempts to make suggestions about
improving the economic situation of some
14 different societies without explicit analysis
of the larger wholes in which these societies
are embedded.

[2] The notion of a multiple society with plural
cultures does not derive from formulations
aimed at solving the same problem. Boeke's
(1953) use of the "dualistic" economy in the
Indies does not apply if the country in question
is really a multiple society, and Higgins'
(1956) strictures on the dualistic theory do
much to empty that concept of meaning
anywhere. Furnivall's (1950) use of "plural
economy" lies closer to the concept of multiple
society, but does not conceive of a single
political and economic network in the same
way.

[3] Not enumerated are all the various cultural
traditions to be found in Guatemala or in
Mexico. A glance at the census shows that
there are foreigners—from the *Chinos* to the
Turcos—whose culture is different (sometimes)
from the national Hispanic-American or the
Indian. The number of such persons and their
economic and political importance is not large
enough to alter my description or the economic
development of Mexico and Guatemala.

[4] I use the household as an index to the Indian
scale of social organization and command over
the factors of production. A complete listing
of other social limitations—credit mechanisms,
storage facilities, etc.—would serve no purpose here. A detailed exposition of an Indian
economy may be found in Tax (1953).

[5] I have in mind those kinds of changes in
social structure and value system suggested by
Hoselitz (1953).

BIBLIOGRAPHY

ADAMS, R. N.
    1956 Los Ladinos de Guatemala. Gua-
        temala.
ADLER, JOHN H., E. H. SCHLESINGER AND
E. C. OLSON
    1952 Public finance and economic deve-
        lopment in Guatemala. Stanford.
BASAURI, C.
    1940 La población indígena de México.
        México.
BEALS, RALPH L.
    1953 Social stratification in Latin America.
        American Journal of Sociology,
        58, 327–339.

BOEKE, J. H.
    1953 Economics and economic policy of
        dual societies. New York.
CASO, A., SILVIO ZAVALA, JOSÉ MIRANDA,
MOISES N. GONZÁLEZ, GONZALO AGUIRRE
BELTRÁN, RICARDO POZAS A.
    1954 Metodos y resultados de la política
        indigenista. México
FURNIVALL, J. S.
    1950 Co-operation, competition, and iso-
        lation in the economic sphere. *In*
        Phillips Talbot (ed.) South Asia
        in the world today. Chicago.
GILLIN, JOHN
    1956 Cultura emergenta. *In* Integración
        Social en Guatemala. Guatemala
        City.
HIGGINS, BENJAMIN
    1956 The "dualistic theory" of under-
        developed areas. Economic Develop-
        ment and Cultural Change, **4**,
        99–115.
HOSELITZ, BERT F.
    1953 Social structure and economic
        growth. Economia Internazionale,
        6, 1–23.
INTERNATIONAL BANK FOR RECONSTRUCTION
AND DEVELOPMENT
    1951 The economic development of Gua-
        temala. Washington.
    1952 The economic development of
        Mexico. Baltimore.
ITURRIAGA, JOSÉ E.
    1951 La estructura social y cultural de
        México. México.
LE BEAU, F.
    1956 Económica agricola de Guatemala.
        In Integración Social en Guatemala.
        Guatemala City.
LEWIS, OSCAR
    1951 Life in a Mexican village: Tepoztlán
        restudied. Urbana.
MEAD, MARGARET (ed.)
    1953 Cultural patterns and technical
        change. UNESCO.
MOORE, WILBERT E.
    1951 Industrialization and labor. Ithaca,
        New York.
MOSK, SANFORD A.
    1951 Industrial revolution in Mexico.
        Berkeley.
    1954 Indigenous economy in Latin
        America. Inter-American Economic
        Affairs, **8**, 3–25.
NASH, MANNING
    1955a Cantel: the industrialization of a
        Guatemalan Indian Community.
        Unpublished Ph.D. Thesis, Chicago.
    1955b The reaction of a civil-religious
        hierarchy to a factory in Guatemala.
        Human Organization, **13**, 26–28.

1956a The recruitment of wage labor and development of new skills. Annals of the American Academy of Political and Social Science (May), 23–31.

1956b Relaciones políticas entre los indios de Guatemala. *In* Integración Social en Guatemala, Guatemala City.

PARRA, MANUEL GERMÁN
1954 La industrialización de México. México.

REDFIELD, ROBERT
1930 Tepoztlán, a Mexican village. Chicago.

REDFIELD, ROBERT, AND SOL TAX
1952 General characteristics of present-day Mesoamerican Indian society. *In* Sol Tax (ed.) Heritage of conquest. Glencoe, Free Press.

SPICER, E. H. (ed.)
1962 Human problems in technological change. New York.

TAX, SOL
1937 The municipios of the Midwestern Highlands of Guatemala. American Anthropologist, **39**, 423–444.

1946 The education of underprivileged peoples in dependent and independent territories. Journal of Negro Education, **15**, 336–345.

1953 Penny capitalism: a Guatemalan Indian economy. Institute of Social Anthropology 16. Washington.

1956 Los indios en la economia de Guatemala. *In* Integración Social en Guatemala. Guatemala City.

UNITED NATIONS, Economic Commission for Latin America
1950 Recent trends in the Mexican economy. UNESCO.

VILLA ROJAS, A.
1955 Los Mazatecos y el problema indígena de la cuenca del Papaloapan. Mexico.

WAGLEY, CHARLES and MARVIN HARRIS
1955 A typology of Latin-American subcultures. American Anthropologist, **57**, 428–451.

THE MASSES, THE ELITE, AND POST-COLONIAL POLITICS IN AFRICA

Martin Kilson

Political change among the masses (those Africans relatively untouched by modernization) is an important facet of African political change, for they are inevitably affected by the competition between African and colonial modernizers, especially—but not only—through the medium of nationalism. Unlike the emergent African bourgeoisie, the masses are generally not themselves modernizers, and thus their relationship to colonial modernizers is different. But they do desire to be modernized, or at least to rationalize or clarify the complicated and disturbing situation of partial or peripheral modernization in the midst of traditional life and ways.

When seeking *themselves* to resolve the contradictions arising from this situation, the masses, like the middle class, direct their activity to some facet of the colonial political system, and thus become conscious participants in political change. Their methods and processes, however, normally take a more violent, riotous form, often neo-traditional in structure, and lacking clear goals. This means, in turn, that political change among the masses is more difficult, more traumatic, than among the middle class.[1] (And within the masses, political change is

SOURCE. Martin Kilson, "African Political Change and the Modernization Process," *Journal of Modern African Studies*, **1**, 425–440, 1963; using only 435–440.

[1] For a detailed analysis of this process, see Martin Kilson, *Political Change in a West African State* (forthcoming).

relatively less difficult in towns or urban centres than in rural areas, since the former provide access to a more intensively modernizing environment and to the African modernizing élite.) This is revealed in the ambivalent attitude of the masses towards indigenous institutions; traditional rulers represent the authoritative unit of colonial political change nearest to the masses, who attack them as a cause of the complex political change they experience, and yet still depend upon them as the only known sources of values capable of providing the stability necessary to any people undergoing relatively rapid socio-political change. Traditional religious forms are also important in this process, being partly rejected and replaced or modified by imported religious forms, and yet simultaneously utilized as instruments for adjustment to socio-political change. Hence the politico-religious cults and messianic movements that have characterized socio-political change in Africa.[2]

As already suggested, political change among the masses becomes less difficult and traumatic only at the point where it fuses with the nationalism of the élite, thereby gaining more articulate leadership, more specific goals, and the psychological transference of aspirations and expectations to others. The nature of this élite-mass nexus, as it may be called, becomes the focal point of political change as the situation shifts from conflict between colonial and African modernizers to competition within the African community. During this shift, tribalism and other traditional or neo-traditional forces become active ingredients of African political change, affecting both the constitutional structure of the state as it moves toward independence, and the processes by which individuals and groups seek power. This occurs, of course, towards the end of the colonial period—during the decolonization of expatriate institutions—and a proper

understanding of it is, I think, crucial to an understanding of post-colonial political change.

Since the emergent African bourgeoisie is not only more deeply involved in the money economy and its social system, but also displays the political and ideological attitudes which may be expected to generate modernization, its members are therefore likely to be the power holders in the new independent state. We can also expect that the apparatus of government will be a major element in their drive for dominance in post-colonial modernization, for at no stage during the colonial era had they even begun to control the necessary elements for dominance: capital, technical skill, managerial capacity, administrative skill, and so on. Indeed, their recognition of this explains their emphasis upon the seizure of the apparatus of government as the primary instrument for competition with expatriate modernizers during the colonial era. The control of the state also becomes their main instrument in the similar competition during the post-colonial period, when the expatriates continue their monopoly of the financial, industrial, technical, and strategic ingredients of modernization, having conceded the structure of political power, but not the totality of what Dahl would call "political resources,"[3] to African modernizers. Yet the emergent African bourgeoisie—fearful of stunting further modernization in the post-colonial national society and of limiting its own progress towards dominance—has little alternative but to treat as indispensable the capital and skills of metropolitan expatriates, and in fact may at points develop a basic identity of interest with them.

It can further be expected, in view of the foregoing, that the main political conflicts during the post-colonial period will arise from competition between different segments or factions of the élite for control over the ingredients of modernization that

[2] Cf. Sylvia Thrupp (ed.), *Millennial Dreams in Action* (The Hague, 1962).

[3] Robert A. Dahl, *Who Governs?* (New Haven, Conn., 1961).

the state and its apparatus possess. Furthermore, this competition raises the problem of the likely identity of interests between expatriate capital, skills, and strategic interests, on the one hand, and at least a part of the African élite on the other hand. How far does this extend? What are its implications for the future development of the new national society? Being so inferior in their modernizing capacity, the masses will be merely peripheral to this conflict, except when middle-class factions manipulate tribalism, religion, and other socio-cultural factors for their own ends; or when the middle class as a whole *appears* incapable, as heirs to the expatriate ruling class, of satisfying the expectations and aspirations developed among the masses during the period of mature anti-colonial nationalism.

The latter problem, however, may be expected to arise only at a relatively late phase of the post-colonial period, due partly to the astute skill of the middle class in manipulating the racial aspect of nationalism to claim the allegiance of the masses and to get the masses to identify the gains of the middle class as being their own. Political parties, of course, assist in reinforcing this allegiance of the masses to their leadership, often with the important aid of the traditional ruling élite, to which most major African parties—save the few radical mass-type parties—are closely linked. They may fail to do so where there is relatively free competition among mainly middle-class-led parties; and then the tendency has been for the dominant party to preempt the political field through an authoritarian use of power, which might lead to a political dictatorship of the middle classes.[4]

What may be called the asymmetrical structure of the middle class—as a social class—also facilitates the maintenance of mass allegiance to it. By asymmetry is meant the fragmented or uneven manner in which persons enter the middle class,

without carrying their own immediate social unit along. Thus a wealthy lawyer or businessman may have a mother, father, and sundry other close kin who remain poor peasants in rural areas or depressed wage-earners in urban slums. Assuming the continuation of some traditional norms governing social relationships,[5] the lawyer or business man retains some measure of responsibility for the welfare of his poorer kin. And in this way the modern affluence of the emergent African bourgeoisie trickles down to the poorer groups, whose allegiance is thereby reinforced and their expectations of a better life in the post-colonial society strengthened.

It should be noted, further, that the gradual extension of the franchise as a filter for political pressures, in the way described above, enabled the masses eventually to secure the respect of the emergent bourgeoisie for their views and interests. Given the heavy dependence of an overwhelming proportion of African professionals, business men, etc., upon government or the political process for their existence and advancement, they have reason to pay some deference to the fact of mass enfranchisement.

There is another feature of mass enfranchisement that is relevant to post-colonial political change. The very existence of the mass franchise constitutes one of the major problems affecting the élite-mass relationship in post-colonial Africa. For, unlike the modernizing period in other countries—for example, Britain or Japan—during which the élite groups were able, for 100 years or more, to determine the nature and course of modernization free from the pressures and restraints of a mass franchise, *in the post-colonial African societies the masses are armed with the*

[4] Cf. Frantz Fanon, *Les Damnés de la terre* (Paris, 1961), pp. 118 ff., 124.

[5] This is a valid assumption. For a literary treatment of it, see Chinua Achebe, *No Longer at Ease* (London, 1960). See also Elizabeth Colson, "Native Culture and Social Patterns in Contemporary Africa," in C. Grove Haines (ed.), *Africa Today* (Baltimore, 1955), pp. 69–84.

franchise at the very beginning of the African élite's attempt to direct modernization. In Britain, for instance, only 3 per cent of adults (435,391) had a franchise in 1830—some 100 years after the commencement of the Industrial Revolution and nearly 200 years after the Civil War—and the 1832 Reform Act added only 217,386 voters to the electorate; universal manhood suffrage did not become a reality until the 1880's.[6] At the establishment of the American Republic in 1787—when American élites assumed responsibility for modernization—only 25 per cent of the adult white males were eligible to vote. White women were ineligible, as were Negro slaves and Indians, who constituted 17 out of every 100 of the population. Furthermore, a variety of restrictions on voting continued until the second half of the nineteenth century.[7] By the 1870's the structure of modernization had been laid by American élites, and the process of built-in economic growth was becoming apparent.

This situation becomes of primary concern if one assumes—as I think it valid to do—that the modernizing function is performed by élite groups mainly when their capacity to do so—and to define the direction of modernization and their own stake in it—is relatively free from restrictions and pressures by non-élite groups. Historically, this assumption is demonstrated by both capitalistic and communistic patterns of modernization; in Soviet modernization, for example, the state and its dominant party are explicitly constructed (1) to provide relative freedom for the modernizing (communist) élites from mass claims, or (2) to establish a political framework whereby the modernizing élites can bargain with the masses on terms most favorable to their own conception of modernization.[8]

Africa is unlikely to offer more favorable preconditions of modernization than Britain or Soviet Russia, and therefore one cannot expect African élites to accept the political implications for the modernization process involved in mass enfranchisement. Theoretically, they could discard the mass franchise altogether if they thought it restricted national interest—on their definition—though this would probably cause more political difficulties than it would solve. Alternatively, they could make more authoritarian the framework within which the mass franchise operates, thereby rendering it a more contrived process of mass political participation.[9] This, in fact, has already occurred to some extent in a number of independent African States, and it is likely to be an increasingly important feature of the authoritarian single-party tendencies so apparent in nearly all post-colonial African States.[10]

It is not altogether clear, however, that African modernizing élites are as justified in rejecting mass political pressures upon the modernization process as were their European counterparts. The African élites are not, for one thing, directly comparable *as modernizing elites* to their counterparts during the eighteenth and nineteenth centuries in Europe and Britain, or even in twentieth-century Russia. Having emerged in a colonial situation, the African élites are significantly lacking in capital, and in managerial, technical, scientific, and other modernizing skills. Most of these are still monopolized—as it were, neo-colonially—by expatriates; the African élites have acquired mainly political, administrative, bureaucratic, and intellectual skills, and in some states (e.g. the Congo), not much of these. In fact, for some time the governing function of African élites may not be much more than

---

[6] Charles Seymour, *Electoral Reform in England and Wales* (New Haven, Conn., 1951), p. 533.
[7] D. O. McGovney, *The American Suffrage Medley* (Chicago, 1959), pp. 16–27.
[8] Cf. Marcuse, *op. cit.*, pp. 26 ff., *passim.*

[9] Cf. Rupert Emerson, *From Empire to Nations* (Cambridge, Mass., 1960), pp. 245–246.
[10] Cf. Martin Kilson, "Authoritarian and Single-Party Tendencies in African Politics," in *World Politics* (Princeton), January 1963, pp. 262–294.

a political holding operation, maintaining a degree of political stability so that expatriate capital and skills can continue the modernization process. Liberia is the purest example, with variations on this model developing in the rest of Africa. On the other hand, the modernizing élites in eighteenth- and nineteenth-century Europe had capital and skills in their own right; even if the most modern-oriented sections of these élites were lacking in administrative or bureaucratic skills, they were able to ally themselves with the traditional or aristocratic élites who possessed them and thereby turn these skills to modern tasks.

Viewed in this context, the African élites certainly have little claim to define the modernization process, *and their stake in it*, free from the restraints of mass enfranchisement. Yet, to make such a definition is fundamentally to have the political power (including police and military power) to do so. And this the new African élites have (or have access to) and show every willingness to use.

Chapter 15

Transitional Politics and Party Systems

THE NATURE OF TRANSITIONAL POLITICS[1]

Lucian W. Pye

Compared with either traditional or modern industrial societies, the transitional societies represent a far greater diversity, for differences in their traditions are compounded by differences in the degree, intensity, and form with which they have been affected by the diffusion of the world culture. Nevertheless, the political processes of most of them seem to show a striking number of shared characteristics, accounted for, it would seem, by their common experience of breaking down traditional forms and attempting to introduce institutions and practices which originated in the now industrialized areas. As Daniel Lerner has noted, the process of modernization has a distinctive quality of its own, and the elements that make it up "do not occur in haphazard and unrelated fashion" but go together regularly because "in some historical sense they had to go together."[2]

It should therefore be possible to outline in gross terms some of the main characteristics of what might be called the transitional or non-Western political process. Since these characteristics not only represent the reactions to profound processes of social change but also define the context and the parameters for all continuing efforts at national development, such an analytical model can serve as an approach in introducing the problems of nation-building.

Our model, thus conceived, follows.[3]

1. *The political sphere is not sharply differentiated from the spheres of social and personal relations.* Among the most powerful influences of the traditional order in any society in transition is the survival of a

SOURCE. Lucian W. Pye, "The Nature of Transitional Politics: An Analytical Model," *Politics, Personality, and Nation-Building* (New Haven: Yale University Press, 1962), pp. 15–31.

[1] This chapter, in somewhat different form, first appeared as "The Non-Western Political Process," in *Journal of Politics*, **20** (August 1958), 468–486.

[2] Daniel Lerner, *The Passing of Traditional Society* (Glencoe, Ill., Free Press, 1958), p. 438.

[3] The picture of the "transitional" political process contained in this chapter is strongly influenced by George McT. Kahin, Guy J. Pauker, and Lucian W. Pye, "Comparative Politics in Non-Western Countries," *American Political Science Review*, 49 (December 1955), 1022–1041; Gabriel A. Almond, "Comparative Political Systems," *Journal of Politics*, **18** (August 1956), 391–409, reprinted in *Political Behavior: A Reader in Theory and Research*, ed. by Heinz Eulau, Samuel J. Eldersveld, and Morris Janowitz (Glencoe, Ill., Free Press, 1956); Dankwart A. Rustow, "New Horizons for Comparative Politics," *World Politics*, 9 (July 1957), 530–549, and also his *Politics and Westernization in the Near East* (Princeton, Center of International Studies, 1956).

pattern of political relationships largely determined by the pattern of social and personal relations, with the inevitable result that the political struggle tends to revolve around issues of prestige, influence, and even of personalities, and not primarily around questions of alternative courses of policy action.

The elite who dominate the national politics of most non-Western countries generally represent a remarkably homogeneous group in terms of educational experience and social background. Indeed, the path by which individuals are recruited into their political roles, where not dependent upon ascriptive considerations, is essentially an acculturation process. It is those who have become urbanized, have received the appropriate forms of education, and have demonstrated skill in establishing the necessary personal relations who are admitted to the ranks of the elite. Thus there is in most transitional societies a distinctive elite culture which, although its criteria of performance are based largely on nonpolitical considerations, is the test for effectiveness in national politics.

At the village level it is even more difficult to distinguish a distinct political sphere. The social status of the individual and his personal ties largely determine his political behavior and the range of his influence, a condition which places severe limits on the effectiveness of any who come from the outside to perform a political role, be it that of an administrative agent of the national government or of a representative of a national party. Indeed, the success of such agents generally depends more on the manner in which they relate themselves to the social structure of the community than on the substance of their political views.

Thus the fundamental framework of non-Western politics is a communal one, and all political behavior is strongly colored by considerations of communal identification.[4] In the more conspicuous

[4] Even Communist parties reflect this ten-

cases the larger communal groupings follow ethnic or religious lines. But behind these divisions lie the smaller but often more tightly knit social groupings, which range from the powerful community of Westernized leaders to the social structure of each individual village.

This essentially communal framework of politics makes it extremely difficult for ideas to command influence in themselves. The response to any advocate of a particular point of view tends to be attuned more to his social position than to the content of his views. Under these conditions it is inappropriate to conceive of an open market place where political ideas can freely compete for support on their own merits. Political discussion tends rather to assume the form of either intracommunal debate or the attempt of one group to justify its position toward another.

The communal framework also sharply limits freedom in altering political allegiances. Any change in political identification generally requires a change in one's social and personal relationships; conversely, any change in social relations tends to result in a change in political identification. The fortunate village youth who receives a modern education tends to move to the city, establish himself in a new subsociety, and become associated with a political group that may in no way reflect the political views of his original community. Even among the national politicians in the city, shifts in political ties are generally accompanied by changes in social and personal associations.

2. *Political parties tend to take on a world view and represent a way of life.* The lack of a clearly differentiated political sphere means that political parties tend to be clearly oriented not to a distinct political arena but to some aspect of the communal framework of politics. In reflecting the communal base of politics they tend to represent total ways of life; attempts to

dency; see Selig S. Harrison, "Caste and the Andhra Communists," *American Political Science Review*, **1** (June 1956).

organize parties in terms of particular political principles or limited policy objectives generally result either in failure or in the adoption of a broad ethic which soon obscures the initial objective. Usually political parties represent some subsociety or simply the personality of a particularly influential individual.

Even secular parties devoted to achieving national sovereignty have tended to develop their own unique world views: Indeed, successful parties tend to become social movements. The indigenous basis for political parties is usually regional, ethnic, or religious groupings, all of which stress considerations not usually emphasized in Western secular politics. When a party is merely the personal projection of an individual leader, it is usually not just his explicitly political views but all facets of his personality which are significant in determining the character of the movement.

Nationalist movements in particular have tended to represent total ways of life, and even after independence the tendency remains strong, because such parties are inclined to feel they have a mission to change all aspects of life within their society, even conceiving of themselves as a prototype of what their entire country will become in time. Members of such movements frequently believe that their attitudes and views on all subjects will become the commonly shared attitudes and views of the entire population.

3. *There is a prevalence of cliques.* The lack of a distinct political sphere and the tendency for political parties to have world views together provide a framework within which the most structured units of political influence tend to be personal cliques. Thus, although general considerations of social status determine the broad outlines of power and influence, the particular pattern of political relationships at any time is largely determined by decisions made at the personal level. This is the case because the social structure in non-Western societies is characterized by functionally diffuse relationships; individuals and groups

do not have sharply defined and highly specific functions and thus do not represent specific interests that distinguish them from other groupings. There is no clearly structured setting that can provide a focus for the more refined pattern of day-to-day political activities. Hence, in arriving at their expectations about the probable behavior of others, those involved in the political process must rely heavily upon judgments about personality and the particular relations of the various actors to each other. It follows that the pattern of personal associations provides one of the firmest guides for understanding and acting within the political process, and that personal cliques are likely to become the key units of political decision making in most non-Western societies.

Western observers often see the phenomenon of cliques as symptomatic of immoral and deviously motivated behavior. This may actually be the case. Considerations of motive alone, however, cannot explain either the prevalence of cliques in non-Western societies or their functions. For the fact that cliques are based on personal relations does not mean that there are no significant differences among them in their values and policy objectives. Since the members of a given clique are likely to have a common orientation toward politics, if their views were fully articulated they might constitute a distinct ideology significantly different from those of other factions.

In order to understand the workings of the political process in most non-Western countries it is necessary to analyze the character of inter-clique reactions. To ignore the importance of cliques would be comparable to ignoring the role of interest groups and elections in analyzing the behavior of American congressmen.

4. *The character of political loyalty gives political leaders a high degree of freedom in determining policies.*[5] The communal

[5] For excellent studies of this characteristic, see Myron Weiner, *Party Politics in India* (Princeton, Princeton University Press, 1957);

framework of politics and the tendency for political parties to have world views inspire a political loyalty which is governed more by a sense of identification with a concrete group than by identification with its professed policy goals. The expectation is that the leaders will seek to maximize all the interests of all the members of the group and not just seek to advance particular policies.

As long as the leaders appear to be working in the interests of the group as a whole, they usually do not have to be concerned that the loyalties of the members will be tested by current decisions. Under such conditions it is possible for leadership to become firmly institutionalized within the group without having to make any strong commitments to a specific set of principles or to a given political strategy.

Problems relating to the loyalty of the membership can generally be handled more effectively by decisions about intragroup relations than by decisions about the goals or external policies of the group. As long as harmonious relations exist within the group, it is generally possible for the leaders to make drastic changes in strategy. Indeed, it is not uncommon for the membership to feel that matters relating to external policy should be left solely to the leadership, and it may not disturb them that such decisions reflect mainly the idiosyncracies of their leaders.

5. *Opposition parties and aspiring elites tend to appear as revolutionary movements.* Since the current leadership in non-Western countries generally conceives of itself as seeking to effect changes in all aspects of life, and since all political associations tend to have world views, any new group aspiring to national leadership seems to present a revolutionary threat. The fact that the ruling party in most non-Western countries identifies itself with an effort to bring about total change in the society makes it difficult to limit the

[*footnote 5 continued*
and Keith Callard, *Pakistan: A Political Study* (New York, Macmillan, 1957).

sphere of political controversy. Isolated and specific questions tend to be transformed into fundamental questions about the destiny of the society.

In addition, the broad and diffuse interests of the ruling elites make it easy for them to maintain that they represent the interest of the entire nation. Those in opposition seeking power are thus often placed in the position of appearing to be, at best, obstructionists of progress or, at worst, enemies of the country. Competition is not between parties that represent different functional interests or between groups that claim greater administrative skills; rather, the struggle takes on some of the qualities of a conflict between differing ways of life.

This situation helps to explain the failure of responsible opposition parties to develop in most non-Western countries. For example, the Congress party in India has been able to identify itself with the destiny of the entire country to such a degree that the opposition parties find it difficult to avoid appearing either as enemies of India's progress or as groups seeking precisely the same objective as the Congress party. Since the frustration of opposition groups encourages them to turn to extremist measures, they may in fact come to be revolutionary movements.

6. *There is little or no integration among the participants due to the lack of a unified communications system.* In most non-Western societies political activities are not part of any single general process; rather there are several distinct and nearly unrelated political processes. The most conspicuous division is that between the dominant national politics of the more urban elements and the more traditional village level of politics. Those who participate in the political life of the village are not an integral part of the national politics, and they can act without regard to developments at the national level. Possibly even more significant, all the various village groups have their own separate and autonomous political processes.

This situation is a product of the communication system common to non-Western societies, where the mass media generally reach only elements of the urban population and those who participate in the national political process, and the vast majority of the people still communicate by traditional word-of-mouth means.[6] Even when the media of mass communication do reach the village through readers of newspapers or owners of radios, there is almost no "feedback" from the village level, and therefore no reflection of the vast majority of the population. Indeed, the Westerner often has less difficulty than the majority of the indigenous population in understanding the intellectual and moral standards reflected in the media of mass communication, for the media are controlled by the more Westernized elements who may be consciously seeking to relate them to the standards of the international systems of communication rather than to the local scene.

The lack of a unified communication system and the fact that there is no common political process limit the types of political issues that can arise. For example, although the non-Western societies are essentially agrarian and their industrial development is just beginning, their peoples have not been concerned with one of the issues basic to the history of Western politics: the clash between industry and agriculture, between town and countryside. The chief reason for this is that the rural elements are without a basis for mobilizing their combined strength and effectively advancing their demands on the government. It is possible that in time the rural masses, discovering that they have much in common, will find ways to mobilize their interests and so exert their full potential influence on the nation's political life. Such a development would drastically alter the national political character. In the meantime, however, the fragmented political process means that in fundamentally agrarian countries politics will continue to be more urbanized than it usually is in the industrial West. In many transitional societies one city alone dominates the politics of an entire country.

7. *New elements are recruited to political roles at a high rate.*[7] Two typical developments have caused a constant increase in the number of participants and the types of organizations involved in the political process. One is the extraordinary rise in the urban population, which has greatly increased the number of people who have some understanding about and interest in politics at the national level. A basic feature of the acculturation process which creates the subsociety of the elite is the development of attitudes common to urban life. The aspiring elites who demand to be heard generally represent a distinct stratum of urban dwellers who have been excluded from direct participation in national politics but whose existence affects the behavior of the current elite.

The other development is the more gradual reaching out of the mass media to the countryside, which stimulates a broadening awareness that, although participation in the nation's political life is formally open to all, the rural elements actually have little access to the means of influence. In some places political parties, in seeking to reach the less urbanized elements, have opened up new channels for communicating with the powerful at the nation's center which may or may not be more effective than the old channels of the civil administration. In any case, the existence of multiple channels of contact with the national government tends to increase the number of people anxious to participate in national decision making.[8]

[6] A more detailed elaboration of such a communications system is contained in the author's "Communication Patterns and the Problems of Representative Government in Non-Western Societies," *Public Opinion Quarterly*, **20** (Spring 1956), 249–257.

[7] Kahin, Pauker, and Pye, p. 1024.
[8] For an excellent discussion of this process, see Howard Wriggins, *Ceylon: The Dilemmas of a New Nation* (Princeton, Princeton University Press, 1960).

8. *There are sharp differences in the political orientation of the generations.* The process of social change in most non-Western societies results in a lack of continuity in the circumstances under which people are recruited to politics. Those who took part in the revolutionary movement against a colonial ruler are not necessarily regarded as indispensable leaders by succeeding generations; but their revolutionary role is still put forward as sufficient reason for their continued elite status. As a result, in some countries, as in Indonesia and Burma, and possibly in more acute form in most of Africa,[9] those who were not involved in the revolution feel that they are being arbitrarily excluded from the inner circle of national politics.

This problem is aggravated in societies where the population is rapidly growing because of a high birth rate. In Singapore, Malaya, and Burma, for example, over half the population is under voting age, and the median age in most non-Western countries is in the low twenties. There is thus a constant pressure from the younger generation, whose demands for political influence conflict with the claims of current leaders who consider themselves still young with many more years of active life ahead. In addition, in most of the newly independent countries the initial tendency was for cabinet ministers and high officials to be in their thirties and forties, a condition which has colored the career expectations of the youth of succeeding generations, who now face frustration if they cannot achieve comparable status at the same age.

This telescoping of the generations has sharpened the clash of views so that intellectually there is an abnormal gap in political orientations, creating a potential for extreme changes in policy should the aspiring elites gain power. Ideas and symbols deeply felt by the current leaders

[9] Cf. James S. Coleman, "The Politics of Sub-Saharan Africa," in *The Politics of the Developing Areas,* ed. by Gabriel A. Almond and James S. Coleman (Princeton, Princeton University Press, 1960).

may have little meaning for a generation which has not experienced colonial rule.

9. *Little consensus exists as to the legitimate ends and means of political action.* The fundamental fact that transitional societies are engrossed in a process of discontinuous social change precludes the possibility of a widely shared agreement as to the appropriate ends and means of political activities. At one extreme in such societies are people who have so fully assimilated Western culture that their political attitudes and concepts differ little from those common in the West. At the other extreme are the village peasants who have been little touched by Western influences. Living in different worlds, the two can hardly be expected to display a common approach toward political action.

The profound social changes in the transitional process tend to compound uncertainty, depriving people of that sense of shared expectation which is the first prerequisite of representative government. The possible and the plausible, the likely and the impossible are so readily confused that both elation and resignation are repeatedly hitched to faulty predictions. Thus in the political realm, where conscious choice and rational strategies should vie in promoting alternative human values, it becomes difficult to discern what choices are possible and what are the truly held values of the people. The resulting drift is away from realism and toward either crudely emotional appeals or toward gentle ideals that offer respectability in Western circles but are irrelevant to the domestic scene.

Some people still adhere to traditional views and conceive of politics as primarily providing opportunities for realizing status, prestige, and honor. Such views are sustained by constant demonstrations that the masses in transitional societies still derive a sense of well-being from identifying with the grandeur and glory of their national leaders. There are others, taking their cues from the colonial period, who equate government with the security of office and the dignity of clerks in the civil service. For them government is above all the ritualization of routine where procedure takes precedence over all other considerations. Still others came to their appreciation of politics out of the excitement of independence movements; they continue to expect politics to be the drama of group emotions and to despise those who would give in to the humdrum calculation of relative costs and risks. For them the politician should remain the free and unfettered soul who can stand above tedious consideration of public policies. There are also those who look to politics and government to change their society and who feel that their dreams of a new world are shared by all. Some so grossly underestimate what must be done before the fruits of modernization can be realized that their ambitions incite little sustained effort and they are quick to declare themselves frustrated. Others who accept the need to deal first with the prerequisites of development may learn that all their energies can be absorbed in distasteful enterprises without visibly advancing the ends they seek. Thus the lack of a common, elementary orientation to the goals and the means of political action reduces the effectiveness of all.

Since such diversity in orientations makes it almost impossible to identify genuine social interests, the basic function of representative politics of sensitively aggregating the diverse values of a people and translating them into public policies cannot be readily realized. Without stable groups having limited interests, the processes by which power is accumulated and directed tend to be less responsive to social needs and more responsive to personal, individual desires.

This situation has direct effects on leadership. It reinforces the tendency for the personalities of the leaders to figure more prominently and for the idiosyncrasies of their followers to be more crucial in shaping developments than the functional needs of social and economic group-

ings throughout society. Moreover, although the national leadership may appear to represent a widely shared consensus about politics, more often than not this apparent national agreement reflects only the distinct qualities of the elite subsociety. The mass of the population cannot fully appreciate the values and concepts that underlie the judgments of the elite and guide its behavior.

Lastly, since most of the groupings within the political process represent total ways of life, few are concerned with limited and specific interests. Their functionally diffuse character tends to force each group to develop its own ends and means of political action, and the relationship of means to ends tends to be more organic than rational and functional. Indeed, in the gross behavior of the groups it is difficult to distinguish their primary goals from their operational measures. Consequently, the political actors in non-Western societies tend to demonstrate quite conspicuously the often forgotten fact that people generally show greater imagination and ingenuity in discovering goals to match existing means than in expanding their capabilities in order to reach distant goals; and it is difficult to distinguish within the general political discourse of the society a distinction between discussions of desired objectives and analyses of appropriate means of political action.

10. *The intensity and prevalence of political discussion bear little relationship to political decision making.* Western observers are impressed with what they feel is a paradoxical situation in most non-Western countries. The masses seem to be apathetic toward political action, and yet, considering the crude systems of communication, they are remarkably well informed about political events. Peasants and villagers often engage in prolonged discussions on matters related to the political world outside their immediate lives, but they rarely seem prepared to translate the information they receive into action that

might influence the course of national politics.

This is a survival of the traditional pattern of behavior. In most traditional societies an important function of the elite was to provide entertainment and material for discussion for the common people, but the people did not discuss the activities of the elite in any expectation that discussion should lead to action. Now the contemporary world of elite politics has simply replaced the drama of court life and royal officialdom.

A second explanation is that one of the important factors in determining social status and prestige within the village or local community is often a command of information about the wider world; knowledge of developments in the sphere of national and even international politics has a value in itself. But skill in discussing political matters again does not raise any expectation of actual participation in the world of politics.

There is also the fact that the common people of non-Western societies often seek to keep informed about political developments only in order to be able to adapt their lives to any major changes. The experience of former drastic changes has led them to seek advance warning of any developments which might again affect their lives; but it has not necessarily encouraged them to believe that their actions might influence such developments.

11. *Roles are highly interchangeable.*[10] It seems that in non-Western societies most politically relevant roles are not clearly differentiated but have a functionally diffuse rather than a functionally specific character. For example, the civil bureaucracy is not usually limited to the role of a politically neutral instrument of public administration but may assume some of the functions of a political party or act as an interest group. Sometimes armies act as governments.[11] Even within bureaucracies

and governments individuals may be formally called upon to perform several roles.

A shortage of competent personnel encourages such behavior either because one group may feel that the other is not performing its role in an effective manner or because the few skilled administrators are forced to take on concurrent assignments. However, the more fundamental reason for this phenomenon is that in societies just emerging from traditional status it is not generally expected that any particular group or organization will limit itself to performing a clearly specified function. Under these conditions there usually are not sharply defined divisions of labor in any sphere of life. All groups tend to have considerable freedom in trying to maximize their influence.

12. *There are relatively few explicitly organized interest groups with functionally specific roles.*[12] Although there are often large numbers of informal associations in non-Western countries, such groups tend to adopt diffuse orientations that cover all phases of life in much the same manner as the political parties and cliques. It is the rare association that represents a limited and functionally specific interest. Organizations which in name and formal structure are modeled after Western interest groups, such as trade unions and chambers of commerce, generally do not have a clearly defined focus.

Groups such as trade unions and peasant associations which in form would appear to represent a specific interest are often in fact agents of the government or of a dominant party or movement. Their function is primarily to mobilize the sup-

---

[10] See Almond, "Comparative Political Systems," p. 402.

[11] On the role of armies in transitional socie-

ties, see the forthcoming study sponsored by the RAND Corporation; Dankwart A. Rustow, "The Army and the Founding of the Turkish Republic," *World Politics*, **11** (July 1959), 513–552; and Daniel Lerner and Richard D. Robinson, "Swords and Ploughshares: The Turkish Army as a Modernizing Force," *World Politics*, **13** (October 1960), 19–44.

[12] For discussions of the problems of interest articulation throughout the non-Western world, see Almond and Coleman.

port of a segment of the population for the purposes of the dominant group, and not primarily to represent the interests of their constituency. Where the associations are autonomous, the tendency is for them not to apply pressure openly on the government in order to influence the formation of public policy but to act as protective associations, shielding their members from the consequences of governmental decisions and the political power of others.

The role of the protective association was generally a well-developed one in traditional societies and in countries under colonial rule. Under such authoritarian conditions, since informal associations could have little hope of affecting the formal lawmaking process, they focused on the law-enforcing process. Since they were likely to be more successful if they worked quietly and informally to establish preferential relations with the enforcing agents of the government, each association generally preferred to operate separately in order to gain special favors. The strategy of uniting in coalitions and alliances to present the appearance of making a popular demand on the government, as is common in an open democratic political process composed of pressure groups, would have only weakened the position of all as it would have represented a direct challenge to the existing governmental elite.

The fact that this approach to political activity was a common characteristic of traditional societies and still so widely survives as a feature of the politics of societies in transition suggests the following general hypothesis:

Whenever the formally constituted lawmakers are more distant from and more inaccessible to the general public than the law-enforcing agencies, the political process of the society will be characterized by a high degree of latency, and interests will be represented by informally organized groups seeking diffuse but particularistically defined goals which will neither be broadly

articulated nor claimed to be in the general interest.

The corollary of this hypothesis would, of course, read:

Whenever the formally constituted lawmakers are less distant from and more accessible to the general public than the law-enforcing agencies, the political process of the society will be open and manifest, and interests will be represented by explicitly organized groups seeking functionally specific but universalistically defined goals which will be broadly articulated and claimed to be in the general interest.

13. *The national leadership must appeal to an undifferentiated public.* The lack of explicitly organized interest groups and the fact that not all participants are continuously represented in the political process deprive the national leadership of any readily available means for calculating the distribution of attitudes and values throughout the society. The national politician cannot easily determine the relative power of those in favor of a particular measure and those opposed; he cannot readily estimate the amount of effort needed to gain the support of the doubtful elements.

It is usually only within the circle of the elite or within the administrative structure that the national leaders can distinguish specific points of view and the relative backing that each commands. They have few guides as to how the public may be divided over particular issues. Thus, in seeking popular support, they cannot direct their appeal to the interests of particular groups. Unable to identify or intelligently discriminate among the various interests latent in the public, they are inclined to resort to broad generalized statements rather than to adopt specific positions on concrete issues; and whether the question is one of national or of merely local import, they must appear to be striving to mobilize the entire population.

The inability to speak to a differentiated public encourages a strong propensity toward skillful and highly emotional forms of political articulation. Forced to reach for the broadest possible appeals, the individual leader tends to concentrate heavily on nationalistic sentiments and to present himself as a representative of the nation as a whole rather than of particular interests within the society. This is one of the reasons why some leaders of non-Western countries are often seen paradoxically both as extreme nationalists and as men out of touch with the masses.

14. *Leaders are encouraged to adopt more clearly defined positions on international issues than on domestic issues.* Confronted with an undifferentiated public, leaders often find the international political process more clearly structured than the domestic political scene. Consequently, they can make more refined calculations as to the advantages in taking a definite position in world politics than they can in domestic politics. This situation not only encourages the leaders of some non-Western countries to seek a role in world politics that is out of proportion to their nation's power, but it also allows them to concentrate more on international than on domestic affairs. It should also be noted that in adopting a supranational role, the current leaders of non-Western countries can heighten the impression that their domestic opposition is an enemy of the national interest.

15. *The affective or expressive aspect of politics tends to override the problem-solving or public-policy aspect.* Traditional societies generally develop to a very high order the affective and expressive aspect of politics. Pomp and ceremony are basic features of their politics, and the ruling elite are generally expected to lead more interesting and exciting lives than those not involved in politics. In contrast, traditional societies do not usually emphasize politics as a means for solving social problems, questions of policy being largely limited to providing certain minimum social and economic functions and maintaining the way of life of the elite.

Although in transitional societies there is generally a somewhat greater awareness of the potentialities of politics as a means of rationally solving social problems than there is in traditional systems, the expressive aspects of politics usually continue to occupy a central place in determining the character of political behavior. The peculiar Western assumption that issues of public policy are the most important aspect of politics, and practically the only legitimate concern of those with power, is not fully accepted in non-Western politics. Indeed, in most non-Western societies the general assumption is not that those with power are committed to searching out and solving problems, but rather that they are the fortunate participants in an exciting and emotionally satisfying drama.

In part, the stress on the affective or expressive aspect of politics is related to the fact that, as we have already noted, questions of personal loyalties and identification are recognized as providing the basic issues of politics and the bond between leader and follower is generally an emotional one. In fact, in many non-Western societies it is considered highly improper and even immoral for people to make loyalty contingent upon their leaders' ability to solve problems of public policy.

There is also the fact that where the problem of national integration is of central importance, the national leaders often feel that they must emphasize the symbols and sentiments of national unity since substantive problems of policy may divide the people. It should be noted that the governmental power base of many non-Western leaders encourages them to employ symbols and slogans customarily associated with administrative policy in their efforts to strengthen national unity. The Western observer may assume that statements employing such symbols represent policy intentions when in fact their function is to create national loyalty and to condition the public to think more in policy terms.

16. *Charismatic leaders tend to prevail.*[13] Max Weber, in highlighting the characteristics of charismatic authority, specifically related the emergence of charismatic personalities to situations in which the hold of tradition has been weakened. By implication, he suggested that societies experiencing cultural change provide an ideal setting for such leaders, since a society in which there is confusion over values is more susceptible to a leader who conveys a sense of mission and appears to be God-sent.

The problem of political communication further reinforces the position of the charismatic leader. Since the population does not share the leaderships' modes of reason or standards of judgment, it is difficult to communicate subtle points of view. Communication of emotions is not confronted with such barriers, especially if it is related to considerations of human character and personality. All groups within the population can feel confident of their ability to judge the worth of a man for what he is even though they cannot understand his mode of reasoning.

As long as a society has difficulties in communication, the charismatic leader possesses great advantage over his opponents, even though they may have greater ability in rational planning. However, the very lack of precision in the image that a charismatic leader casts, especially in relation to policy, does make it possible for opposition to develop as long as it does not directly challenge the leader's charisma. Various groups with different programs can claim that they are in fact seeking the same objectives as those of the leader. For example, in both Indonesia and Burma the Communists have been able to make headway by simply claiming that they are not directly opposed to the goals of Sukarno and U Nu.

Charisma is likely to wear thin. A critical question in most non-Western societies that now have charismatic leaders is whether such leadership will become

[13] Kahin, Pauker, and Pye, p. 1025.

institutionalized in the form of rational-legal practices before this happens. This was the pattern in Turkey under Kemal Ataturk. Or will the passing of the charismatic leader be followed by confusion and chaos and possibly the rise of new charismatic leaders? The critical factor seems to be whether or not the leader encourages the development of functionally specific groups within the society that can genuinely represent particular interests.

17. *The political process operates largely without benefit of political "brokers."* In most non-Western societies there seems to be no institutionalized role for, first, clarifying and delimiting the distribution of demands and interests within the population, and, next, engaging in the bargaining operation necessary to accommodate and maximize the satisfaction of those demands and interests in a fashion consistent with the requirements of public policy and administration. In other words, there are no political "brokers."

In the Western view, the political broker is a prerequisite for a smoothly operating system of representative government. It is through his activities that, on the one hand, the problems of public policy and administration can be best explained to the masses in a way that is clearly related to their various specific interests and, on the other hand, that the diverse demands of the population can be articulated to the national leaders. This role in the West is performed by the influential members of the competing political parties and interest groups.

What is needed in most non-Western countries in order to have stable representative institutions are people who can perform the role that local party leaders performed in introducing the various immigrant communities into American public life. Those party leaders, in their fashion, were able to provide channels through which the immigrant communities felt they could learn where their interests lay in national politics and through which the national leaders could discover the social concerns of the new citizens.

In most non-Western societies, the role of the political broker has been partially filled by those who perform a mediator's role, which consists largely of transmitting views of the elite to the masses. Such mediators are people sufficiently acculturated to the elite society to understand its views but who still have contacts with the more traditional masses. In performing their role, they engage essentially in a public relations operation for the elite, and only to a marginal degree do they communicate to the elite the views of the public. They do not find it essential to identify and articulate the values of their public. Since their influence depends upon their relations with the national leadership, they have not generally sought to develop an autonomous basis of power or to identify themselves with particular segments of the population as must the political broker. As a consequence, they have not acted in a fashion that would stimulate the emergence of functionally specific interest groups.

THE ETHIOPIAN NO-PARTY STATE: A NOTE ON THE FUNCTIONS OF POLITICAL PARTIES IN DEVELOPING STATES

Robert L. Hess and Gerhard Loewenberg

The emergence of political parties performing important functions in the political system has characterized the recent history of much of the African continent.[1] The new party systems have taken various forms, including single parties with a narrow ruling elite, as in Liberia, or with mass support, as in Guinea; two-party systems where one mass party is dominant, as is the case in Kenya; and multi-party systems, as in Nigeria and Somalia. In two states, Libya and Sudan, once-flourishing political parties have been banned. Only in Ethiopia (Eritrea excluded) have there never been political parties. The Empire of the Conquering Lion of Judah can well

SOURCE. Robert L. Hess and Gerhard Loewenberg, "The Ethiopian No-Party State: A Note on the Functions of Political Parties in Developing States," *American Political Science Review*, **58**, 947–950, December 1964.

be termed a no-party state. In Ethiopia today no organization exists that would or could describe itself as a political party.

Writing in 1951, Professor Duverger concluded that "a regime without parties is of necessity a conservative regime."[2] That only a handful of partyless political systems remain today is the consequence, apparently, of the rapid pace of political modernization in the past decade. In the "non-Western" world, wherever new states have been created out of former colonial territories, the movement driving for independence has itself provided the nucleus for at least one political party and, sometimes, for more in response to the first.[3] These parties have performed a variety of functions associated with both political and economic modernization: they have provided a communications network transcending parochial boundaries, have helped to

[1] For a treatment of the development of political parties in Africa, see Thomas Hodgkin, *Nationalism in Colonial Africa* (New York, 1957) and *African Political Parties* (Penguin Books, 1961).

[2] *Political Parties* (London, 2nd ed., 1959), p. 426.
[3] Gwendolen M. Carter, *African One-Party States* (Ithaca, 1962), pp. 1–10.

organize and express the new interests, have recruited and established the new political elite, and have contributed to the legitimation of the new authorities.[4]

Political parties developed in association with economic and political modernization, not just in Asia and Africa, where parties were formed for the purpose of creating independent states, but also in Latin America, where parties grew in an independent situation. The correlation between political party development and economic modernization is not therefore limited to newly independent Africa. However, the evidence does not point to a general interdependence between the two processes.[5] In the earlier "Western" experience, in which there was a relatively slow transition to modern forms, there are notable examples of economic development without political parties. The political systems of the remaining no-party states, especially those showing signs of undergoing economic development, should therefore be viewed with special care by those interested in the relationship between economic and political change. The example of Ethiopia is particularly relevant because it is the case of a state facing the challenges of economic modernization within the framework of a traditional political system.[6]

The absence of political parties from the Ethiopian scene can be explained by the role of the Emperor and the lack of those historical factors that elsewhere stimulated the development of African political parties.

Most African political parties arose as the result of the colonial situation; in Ethiopia the "colonial" period lasted only for the brief five years of the Italian military occupation. Elsewhere, economic development in the colonial period provided one of the bases for the educational development of the personnel which later participated in political organizations; in Ethiopia the noticeable lack of economic development until recently may very well have retarded such political development. For reasons of economic underdevelopment, the rise of an African middle class through detribalization is less evident in Ethiopia than elsewhere. Political parties in other countries were aided by the development of a modern communications network by the colonial power; Ethiopia until recently had one of the poorest such systems on the continent, and strict supervision by the Government ensured that it was not used for political purposes. Elsewhere the decline of chiefly power was the result of European intervention, and a new elite, itself the creation of the Europeans, was able to take advantage of the disruption of traditional society to develop as a potential political force; in Ethiopia, however, the destruction of chiefly power came about as the result of the Emperor's consolidation of his own power and his appropriation of the authority of other traditional elements.[7] No potentially independent elite was directly involved in the process, although the Emperor did and does provide for the Western education of a growing number of closely controlled bureaucrats recruited from the traditional aristocracy and from an aristocracy of talented young men from humble origins or from ethnic minorities like the Galla. Finally, in the isolated and conservative Ethiopian social context, remarkably little attention has been paid

[4] The first three of these functions are specifically discussed by James S. Coleman in G. A. Almond and J. S. Coleman, *The Politics of Developing Areas* (Princeton, 1960), pp. 331, 336, 351, 552–556.
[5] *Ibid.*, pp. 538–544.
[6] Because they are concerned with the development of competitive party systems, Almond and Coleman, *op. cit.*, pay scant attention to Ethiopia. But see pp. 575–576. The most complete treatment of Ethiopian political development is Robert L. Hess, "Ethiopia," in Gwendolen M. Carter, ed., *National Unity and Regionalism in Eight African States* (Ithaca, 1965), 1965).

[7] A distinction should be made between the power of chiefs over clans, tribes, and larger ethnic groups and that of the village head, who has often been erroneously called chief in the literature of African exploration.

to Western organizational forms, like the mass party and modern bureaucracy, and, until very recently, to Western ideas like nationalism or democracy, while in other countries these forms and ideas have had a noticeable influence.

The impetus to modernization in Ethiopia has come not from a new elite and its political parties but from the Emperor himself as a result of his contact with Western states over the past forty years and, more recently, from his association with the new states of Africa. The emphasis in Ethiopia has therefore been on economic and administrative, but not on political modernization. Through skillful diplomacy, Haile Selassie was able, first, to preserve Ethiopia's independence except during the short period of Italian domination, and, second, to develop for Ethiopia an important role among the new African states. But these expanded relations with the world outside Ethiopia have brought his country into contact with Western technology, especially in the form of modern weapons, with Western entrepreneurs and technicians—most recently under the auspices of United States economic and military aid programs —and with Western political ideas and institutions, notably nationalism, law, and bureaucracy. Successes derived from his new international position have strengthened his domestic position, which was strong in any case because of his effective use of traditional myths of the Emperor's legitimacy. Because neither Africanization nor national independence was an issue, he faced no challenge from domestic political movements analogous to those of colonial Africa. His powerful situation permitted him to control the strongest traditional centers of authority, notably the church, the army, and the nobility, by making personal appointments within these institutional groups.

The effective transfer of authority to the Emperor was limited, however, to the regional and national level. It did not extend to the villages, where traditional authority patterns remain intact. It created no new elite structures. It left largely unchanged the linguistic, ethnic, and religious divisions of the nation. The Ethiopian economy remains the least developed in Africa. The 5 per cent literacy rate is the lowest of any African state, and per-capita income is also extremely low. Ninety per cent of the population is still in the subsistence agricultural sector of the economy. The money economy is dependent on monoculture, since coffee accounts for 45 per cent of the total value of exports. The economic development of the nation, which the Emperor seeks to promote through a series of five-year plans, is therefore taking off from a very low base and within a remarkably traditional political and social system. Whatever economic development there is may be attributed to the Emperor's initiative. But in Ethiopia there is a lack of the fervor, excitement, and enthusiasm for economic development that can be found wherever political parties in Africa have striven to mobilize the population for economic change. Although there is a sentimental attachment to the Emperor in almost all ethnic sectors of the country, it is doubtful whether the central authorities can succeed in winning the support of the rural population, which is still under the influence of traditional landlords and village heads. This raises the question of how the masses can be mobilized for economic change without political parties. More generally, how can the political functions nowadays performed by the parties in the process of economic change be performed by other structures, and with what consequences?

The absence of political parties and the existence of a traditional pattern of government have not precluded at least some political change. A new constitution was promulgated by the Emperor in 1955. While it largely confirmed the concentration of powers in his hands, it did provide for an elected Chamber of Deputies in a bicameral Parliament which also included a Senate whose 101 members are all appointed by the Emperor.

The unusual phenomenon of contested elections in a state without political parties occurred in Ethiopia in 1957 and again in 1961. The country was divided into 100 electoral districts of approximately 200,000 inhabitants on the average. Each constituency elected two deputies. Those towns with 30,000 or more inhabitants (that is, Addis Ababa and four other municipalities) were given one representative plus an additional deputy for each 50,000 inhabitants above the base figure, some measure of urban overrepresentation. Under the old constitution there had been only 72 deputies, none of whom had been popularly elected.

According to the Central Board of Registration and Election, a government agency, 491 candidates qualified to stand for the 210 seats. Candidacy required wealth of 1000 Ethiopian dollars and property ownership of twice this amount, total holdings in U.S. terms of $1200. In a nation then having a per-capita income of U.S.$56, the Chamber of Deputies was bound to consist overwhelmingly of members of the traditional nobility. There is evidence that many of the candidates were self-nominated notables who commanded local respect. Others may very well have been sponsored by the government. Despite the absence of political parties many individual candidates vigorously campaigned in competition with each other on the basis of their personal records and their positions in local society.

Of the 6,000,000 potential voters who had the necessary property qualifications in the nation of 19,000,000, slightly more than 3,000,000 registered, and apparently 80 per cent of registered voters cast their ballots in 1957. A process of selection in which over three million voters chose 210 deputies from over twice that number of candidates took place again in 1961 and will probably recur in 1965.[8] But the sole function of this

[8] For reports on the 1957 elections, see *The New*

elected Parliament has been that of legitimating the Emperor's acts.

A new elite group has not been recruited by elections. Rather it has developed among those members of traditionally privileged classes and among a new aristocracy of talent appointed by the Emperor which is participating in new or reorganized institutions created in the process of economic and administrative modernization. The establishment of the Haile Selassie I University in Addis Ababa, the legalization of the trade unions in 1962, the creation of a special palace military guard, the expansion of the bureaucracy and the judiciary, the training of army and air force officers, have all contributed to the growth, at least in the capital, of a new corps of leaders.

There has been much speculation about the aspirations of the youthful civil servants, bureaucrats, and university students who comprise a small but growing intelligentsia. In informal discussions they exhibit a general distaste for the *status quo* and often sharply criticize the distribution of political power. For them too much of Ethiopia is too far from modernization. Whether or not their impatience is a function of their age or an indication of real disaffection, they are not ardent nationalists or revolutionaries. Moreover, for Westernized youths few opportunities exist other than those in government service. For them talk has been an adequate substitute for action, and the intelligentsia are noteworthy for their political ineffectiveness. Significantly, they played no major part in the 1960 coup, and it remains to be seen how they would behave during the uncertainty of a future crisis.

During the Emperor's absence from the country in 1960, an apparently haphazard collection of members drawn from these new elites engaged in an unsuccessful coup. It gave evidence of little planning

York Times, February 19, 1957, p. 10; *ibid.*, November 2, 1957, p. 2; *Ethiopia, Facts and Figures* (Addis Ababa, 1960), pp. 10–11.

and organization, the result, basically, of the failure of communication among its participants. But it also demonstrated the existence of demands for political change and briefly challenged the myths of the Emperor's legitimacy. Significantly, during the days of the rebellion the formation of political parties was promised by its leaders, some of whom had studied in the United States. Since 1960, the process of modernization has apparently again been under the Emperor's control, and, in view of the severe penalties against free political expression, there has been no evidence of any moves to form new political organizations.

The educated elite is still very narrowly recruited. The use, primarily, of ascriptive criteria of selection preserves existing class lines and assures, if not complete loyalty to the Emperor, at least loyalty to the existing class structure. The absence of political organization has meant the lack of a ready-made communications network among the members of this elite, thus reducing its ability to take concerted political or economic action. The interests favoring change are therefore highly fragmented. If the Emperor's authority is in this way protected, it also leaves the vast majority of the population unaffected by economic change. Untouched by new political organizations, politically informed only by the government's communications monopoly and by the traditional local aristocracy, it is beyond the reach of political appeals from the new elites. But it remains also beyond the reach of economic and social changes. It is still illiterate, engaged in subsistence agriculture, governed by traditional village authorities, divided ethnically and religiously. The question of how it can be mobilized for economic purposes without being politically organized is still unanswered.

Another unanswered question concerns the chances of survival of the traditional political system when the Emperor's powers pass to a successor. Although the position of the present Emperor appears strong, it depends in part on his special international reputation, in part on the personal loyalty of his appointees, and in part on his highly personal use of legitimacy myths. Can these sources of power be transferred to a successor except through a new political organization?

Where African political parties have arisen in opposition to colonial regimes, they have developed as institutions parallel to the colonial administration, with judicial, administrative, police, education, and social welfare functions. They have provided a new set of values and given expression to new interests, in opposition to those of both the colonial regime and the traditional African milieu. They have been powerful agents for political agitation, education, and communications. In the process they have from time to time produced their cult of martyrs, their charismatic leaders, but above all they have created a new political elite. They have given Africans a new sense of solidarity, and have resolutely sought the modernization of African economies. They have given legitimacy to new political systems. In Ethiopia, however, all of these functions have been monopolized by the Emperor and an elite recruited largely by ascriptive criteria. This has placed special obstacles in the path of economic development and created prospects of ultimate political instability. The particular problems of modernization which Ethiopia faces because of the absence of political parties suggest the functions which parties usually perform in the political systems of developing states, and indicate the difficulty of finding suitable structures to substitute for them.

THE NEO-DESTOUR PARTY OF TUNISIA:
A STRUCTURE FOR DEMOCRACY?

Clement Henry Moore*

Tunisia, of all the countries in the Arab world today, seems to offer the most promising prospects for constitutional democracy. A Tunisian nation already exists, both as a historic political entity and as a people mobilized by a coherent political movement during twenty years of opposition to French domination. President Habib Bourguiba, the creator of the Neo-Destour Party, is not only the Leader needed to incarnate a new nation and decide its direction; he is also the great Educator of the public. The ideas that he communicates in his frequent and readily understood speeches are the Western political concepts and methods that the Neo-Destour assimilated more profoundly during its long struggle than any other successful Arab liberation movement. "Bourguibism" is the vision of a modern open society that respects both individual liberties and social justice. During six years of independence, despite the Algerian problem on its western frontier, Tunisia has displayed remarkable political stability. Its new Constitution, patterned on the American presidential system, has created a strong executive balanced by a National Assembly, both simultaneously elected by universal suffrage. The society seems relatively homogeneous, for the nationalist

movement displaced not only a colonial oligarchy but a traditional land-owning, governing, and religious aristocracy. All self-conscious sectors of the society have demonstrated their awareness of the need to maintain national cohesion for the sake of economic development.

The most significant factor for the future of democracy, however, may be the internal functioning of the dominant party. The Neo-Destour is the only mass party of its kind in the Arab world. Unlike Nasser's National Union, it was not manufactured by a government but was the genuine emanation of a new nation responding to a colonial situation. It was originally designed in 1934 to oppose French domination more effectively than the Destour Party[1] it replaced, by appealing to the masses as well as to the educated Tunisian elite. Though willing at times to operate within the system of a reformed French Protectorate, the Neo-Destour was never given the opportunity until 1945 to contest general elections or to exercise effective government responsibilities. For intervals adding up to almost ten years out of these two decades of opposition, most of its leaders were in prison, and only clandestine action was possible. During the rest of the time, however, public party activities were more or less tolerated, and the Neo-Destour was able to acquire an articulated structure.

Having succeeded since 1954 in capturing

SOURCE. Clement Henry Moore, "The Neo-Destour Party of Tunisia: A Structure for Democracy?" *World Politics*, **14**, 461–482, October 1961.

* The author was doing research in Tunisia for a doctoral dissertation on the Neo-Destour Party, with the aid of a grant from the Ford Foundation; the views expressed in this article are, of course, his own and not the Foundation's. They are the product mainly of extensive interviews with party officials, especially at regional and local levels.

[1] The Destour, or Liberal Constitutional, Party was founded in 1920. Its main goal, a Tunisian Constitution, is the meaning of "Destour" in Arabic. The best histories of the Tunisian nationalist movement are F. Garas, *Bourguiba et la naissance d'une nation*, Paris, 1956, and Ch.-A. Julien, *L'Afrique du Nord en marche*, Paris, 1953.

the state apparatus, the party has placed its leaders and cadres in all key positions. It tolerates the existence of two opposition parties, but one, the Communist Party, with limited activities, has little influence, while the other, the original Destour Party from which Bourguiba broke in 1933, has no activities. In the course of the independence struggle the Neo-Destour created or infiltrated a number of organizations that today group workers (UGTT), artisans and shopkeepers (UTIC), farmers (UNAT), students (UGET), youth (Neo-Destour Youth), and scouts.[2] These, together with a women's organization (UNFT) created after independence, have organizational autonomy but do not constitute independent centers of political power.

[2] The Union Générale des Travailleurs Tunisiens (UGTT) was created in January 1945 with Neo-Destour support, to provide a purely Tunisian alternative to the French Communist-dominated CGT. What is now called the Union Tunisienne des Industriels et Commerçants (UTIC) was created by the Neo-Destour in early 1946 to support the nationalist cause and to counter a similar Communist front organization. The Union Nationale des Agriculteurs Tunisiens (UNAT) was created only in 1956, but virtually all of its cadres came from the Union Générale des Agriculteurs Tunisiens, established at the same time as UTIC for similar reasons. The older organization was dissolved after some of its top leaders followed Salah Ben Youssef in 1955–56 (see text below). The Union Générale des Etudiants de Tunisie (UGET) was founded clandestinely in 1953 by Neo-Destour students in France. The Neo-Destour Youth dates back to 1936. Some of the many Tunisian scout movements were heavily infiltrated by the Neo-Destour for many years; all have since independence been combined into one organization controlled by the party. The Union Nationale des Femmes Tunisiennes (UNFT) was founded with Bourguiba's personal blessing and support in 1957. These organizations may all be treated to a varying extent as ancillary organizations of the Neo-Destour. Their structures, which complement that of the party, help to maintain national cohesion, while providing democratically elected organs for political education and leadership training. Unfortunately, for lack of space they cannot be treated in this article.

Potentially the most effective sources of political opposition, UGTT and UGET are curbed both by a genuinely felt need for national unity and by the existence within them of numbers of Destour cadres more likely in crisis to obey party discipline. Outside the party there are no representative structures whose deliberations might either overrule or give rise to important policy decisions. The National Assembly, which consists only of deputies nominated by the Neo-Destour, cannot play such a role as yet, for its deliberations are limited and take place largely within closed commissions. Tunisia's many new municipal councils, while offering a training ground for civic responsibility, have been allowed to function properly only when their elected members were local Neo-Destour candidates. Of course Tunisia has periodic elections under its new Constitution, but it has become increasingly difficult for non-Communist Independents, who might stand some chance of election, to be candidates. Hence in Tunisia today the Neo-Destour has a monopoly of political power. Bourguiba shows no intention of allowing the party gradually to induce external competition and to relinquish its political monopoly within the foreseeable future. Rather "its mission, intimately bound up with the life of the people, is permanent."[3]

Though a well-organized political party with a mass following, the Neo-Destour is neither a constitutional mass party nor a totalitarian party. The categories of Western political scientists, devised for the study of political parties in more mature political systems, cannot adequately explain Tunisia's dominant party. The Neo-Destour resembles the Congress Party of India, the CPP of Ghana, and various territorial offshoots of the RDA in French-speaking Black Africa more than it resembles European political parties. Poli-

[3] Speech by Bourguiba delivered on October 2, 1958, at an assembly of Neo-Destour cadres. See Secretariat of State for Information, *Les Congrès du Néo-Destour*, Tunis, 1959, p. 93.

tical scientists have not yet devised a generally accepted model to characterize these newer but highly structured parties.[4] However, they may be called "national" parties, and they have a number of traits in common. They all originated as elite and then as mass parties in reaction to a colonial situation. Their leaders assimilated the political culture of the colonial power, which to a greater or lesser extent constituted the ground rules of the conflict between the two. Since mass parties and universal suffrage conditioned politics in the metropolitan country, the nationalist elite had to organize similar parties, which in the West had required centuries of political evolution. During the colonial period, these parties were patterned upon metropolitan parties, usually ambiguously those of the constitutional and totalitarian Left. Indeed, the situation confronting the Left in the mother country had something in common with the colonial situation confronting the nationalists. Both found it possible to work within the capitalist or colonial system at times, but not always. But even when the nationalists were divided into two groups, they usually managed to stay within the same party for the sake of national unity. Doctrinal conflicts rarely exacerbated tactical disagreements.

Attaining independence before it had effectively mobilized and educated the most backward sectors of the society, the national party became preponderant. Its problems no longer resembled those of Socialist or Communist parties in the metropolitan country, because it no longer faced the opposition of a colonial oligarchy. Despite the absence of a generally accepted model, however, it is crucial for an evaluation of the prospects of democracy in Tunisia and a number of other new nations that the nature of the national party be clearly apprehended. These parties are not like constitutional mass parties simply because—except for the Congress Party in India—they have no effective constitutional opposition.

But it would be an even more serious mistake to confuse a party like the Neo-Destour with totalitarian parties.[5] Bourguibism is the antithesis of a totalitarian ideology, for Bourguiba recognizes that no neat doctrine or intellectual system can do full justice to the complex realities of Tunisian society. Bourguiba has confidence in Tunisia's historic destiny, but his belief in history is a youthful liberal faith unhampered by any dogma determining its outcome. He believes in reason, but only for arriving at pragmatic open solutions of his society's problems. He is a determined modernizer both of the Tunisian society and of the Tunisian economy, but his reformist zeal is curbed by a respect for the individual and his democratic liberties. He realizes that his ultimate goal of maximizing individual liberties and dignity can be achieved only through structural reforms that may in the short run curtail these liberties, but he is trying to use common sense and flexible formulas to cushion inevitable tensions as much as possible. Reason, he believes, should persuade rather than force recalcitrant sectors of the society to co-operate in the building of a new nation. The new nation for Bourguiba is a group of living individuals, not an intellectual abstraction. Bourguiba has faith in reason, but it is not a totalitarian faith because it is governed by common sense and liberal values.[6]

[4] For a documented discussion of the problem, see my article, "The National Party: A Tentative Model," *Public Policy* (Harvard Graduate School of Public Administration), **10** (1960), pp. 239–267.

[5] It will be seen that structurally the Neo-Destour somewhat resembles Communist parties. But relative emphasis upon party structure and neglect of ideologies, as exemplified by Maurice Duverger's *Political Parties* (London, 1955) and Robert Rézette's *Parties Politiques Marocains* (Paris, 1955), can be misleading, especially with regard to national parties, whose structures remain fluid.

[6] No detailed theoretical study of Bourguibism exists. But, for a discussion of some of Bourguiba's key ideas, see Roger Stephane, *La Tunisie de Bourguiba* (Paris, 1958), where the term "Bourguibism" was popularized, and

The mission of the Neo-Destour, according to its 1959 Covenant,[7] is the apparent paradox of maintaining its political monopoly, in order to preserve Tunisian independence and to modernize the economy and the society, while "working for the consolidation of a truly democratic life in which responsibilities are limited and which guarantees for individuals the enjoyment of their rights and public liberties." But the paradox, which is that of other preponderant national parties, is perhaps more apparent than real. Unlike totalitarian parties, which rule by force, the Neo-Destour is genuinely representative, for it embodies the new nation through an elite, formed by French education and united by years of resistance to French domination, that seems committed to the radical modernization of Tunisian society. National consensus has been illustrated in a number of daring innovations, such as the abolition of polygamy; the guarantee of personal and civil liberties for women; educational reform that promises eventual bilingual schooling for all children by modern French rather than traditional methods; and a massive campaign against economic backwardness and poverty, now to be spearheaded by a new super-ministry for economic planning.

Meanwhile the party is still trying to consolidate a national community in which

[*footnote 6 continued*
Gabriel Ardant, *La Tunisie d'aujourd'hui et de demain* (Paris, 1961). The best source is the collection of Bourguiba's weekly speeches since 1956, available at the Tunisian Secretariat of State for Information. For his speeches and writings before independence, see Habib Bourguiba, *La Tunisie et la France*, Paris, 1954.
[7] Political Bureau of the Neo-Destour Party, *The Covenant and Internal Statutes of the Neo-Destour*, passed by the Sixth Congress, Tunis, 1959 (published only in Arabic). I have rendered a free translation from the Arabic. In this article, political terms, whenever ambiguous, have been translated in light of the French terms that inspired their use. The internal statutes of the party passed at the Congress of 1955, along with the more rudimentary statutes of 1934 and 1937, are contained in the appendix of *Les Congrès du Néo-Destour, op. cit.*

some sectors lag behind others in political maturity. The fulfillment of this task is the essential precondition of any viable constitutional democracy in the future. It must be remembered that successful Western democracies have functioned only in the context of pre-existing national communities sharing broad purposes and agreed procedures for discovering the means of achieving these purposes. When with the rise of extremist parties these purposes and procedures were sometimes forgotten, the democracies were imperiled. By maintaining its political monopoly within the foreseeble future, the Neo-Destour may be able firmly to implant common national purposes and procedures in the minds of all Tunisian citizens, so that they acquire a coherent political culture. But this task of political education, especially when coupled with the other prime task of economic development, requires a political mechanism that can also maintain the cohesion of a growing elite. The national party appears capable of fulfilling these functions more effectively and more democratically than either a totalitarian party or an authoritarian clique composed, for instance, of army officers or of a land-owning oligarchy masked by a parliamentary system.

It must be admitted from the outset, however, that national parties like the Neo-Destour do not in their internal functioning live up to all the norms of liberal democracy. Since 1955, when the Neo-Destour took responsibility for a compromise agreement with France that did not meet all nationalist aspirations, the party has become even less democratic than it used to be in the heat of anti-colonialist combat. The former Secretary-General of the party, Salah Ben Youssef, launched a campaign against the agreement with France that by early 1956 almost developed into civil war. Though Bourguiba, with the aid of faithful political lieutenants and the UGTT, finally eliminated the Youssefist threat, the experience conclusively demonstrated that Tunisia was not ready for democratic competition even within the party. In late 1956 Bourguiba thought that Ahmed Ben Salah, then leader of the UGTT, wanted to use his trade union as the organizational base for a labor party that might challenge Neo-Destour political control. He accordingly encouraged a split within the union that eliminated Ben Salah and seriously weakened the UGTT. Though Ben Salah was subsequently appointed minister and today is in charge of Tunisia's economic planning and finance ministries, the UGTT remains firmly under Neo-Destour control. The Ben Youssef and Ben Salah stories have set the tone for prudent uniformity in Tunisian political life.

Echoing this tone, the Neo-Destour was internally overhauled in late 1958. Previously modeled on mass parties of the French Left, the Neo-Destour had consisted of cells freely elected at the local level, supervised by federations annually elected by the cells, and headed by a national congress, an interim national council, and an executive, the Political Bureau, elected by the congress. In late 1958 the federations were replaced by a smaller number of provincial offices headed by officials appointed by the Political Bureau. These party officials, called Commissioners, are not subject to criticism from the cells as the federal executives used to be at the annual federal congresses. Instead of representing the cells, the Commissioners govern them. In a sense the Neo-Destour, previously closer in structure to the French Socialist Party (SFIO), was made to resemble a Communist party, in which officials in charge of intermediate executive bodies, though in appearance elected (unanimously) at regional congresses, are in fact appointed by the central secretariat.

Bourguiba gave a number of reasons in defense of this basic change in party structure. He explained that decentralization had been necessary during the many years of clandestine activity, when national leaders were in prison. Though originally founded primarily to execute the directives of the Political Bureau, the federations had become independent centers of power when the Political Bureau could not effectively operate. During the period following independence, however, he came to feel that "We need a strong power which does not dissipate in multiple ramifications. We need cohesion and discipline to increase efficiency."[8] Furthermore, "It is indispensable that the party adapt its organization to the administrative armature of the country, so that the two structures can re-enforce one another and evolve harmoniously." The federations, rather than paralleling the new administrative structure staffed by Governors and Delegates, had been based upon the personal influence of "certain militants." "Especially those who claimed a glorious past of struggle and sacrifice have paralyzed the activity of the administration by their constant interventions." Even before the reorganization of the party, the Political Bureau had been obliged in some provinces—and notably in Tunis—to dissolve the federations.

In reality the political maturity of the party's cadres had declined disastrously after independence, for two reasons. With victory in sight by late 1954, the party was swamped with new recruits. From a membership estimated at 106,000 before July 1954,[9] the Neo-Destour had acquired roughly 325,000 members by the time of its Fifth Congress in November 1955,[10] and supposedly numbered 600,000 by 1957.[11] During these years the best cadres

[8] This and the following quotations are from Bourguiba's speech of October 2, 1958, *op. cit.*

[9] La Documentation Tunisienne, *Tunisie*, **58**, p. 22, quoted in Keith Callard's highly informative article, "The Republic of Bourguiba," *International Journal*, **16** (Winter 1960–61), p. 34.

[10] Neo-Destour Party, *The National Congress of Sfax*, Arabic ed. [Tunis, n.d.], p. 58.

[11] The unlikely figure of 600,000 was given in *Tunisie*, **58**. Today the party claims between 250,000 and 300,000 adherents, out of an adult male population of less than a million

of the party were being drained off into government jobs, where they could no longer devote the same amount of time to party activities. Cells multiplied, but lacked competent leadership. The Neo-Destour take-over of the government created problems of patronage that the federations could not always handle properly but that explained why provincial administration was sometimes "paralyzed." Arguments were sometimes bitter between members of federations and Neo-Destour government officials, nor was it always clear who governed, for was it not the party that had brought independence? Conflicts were often exacerbated by family, village, and sometimes tribal rivalries. The cumulative impact of all these factors motivated the reorganization of the party in late 1958.

Authoritarian trends in Tunisia since independence, moreover, are not surprising in light of the fundamental domestic problems, compounded by a delicate international situation, that the political system has had to handle. It would be naïve to expect the Neo-Destour, or any other ruling national party, to be internally democratic to the extent that two or more clearly defined groups would compete for power in periodic elections at successive levels within the party. The Tunisian elite is homogeneous, and for the time being is neither in need of such competition nor sufficiently large to provide a responsible alternative leadership. But the Neo-Destour may be paving the way for fuller Tunisian democracy in the future to the extent that (1) it encourages rational discussion of national and local problems; (2) it communicates to the public its democratic values and national problems; (3) it maintains its representative character by balancing the interests of the elite

and continuing to stimulate the enthusiasm of the masses; (4) it encourages wide practical participation in local politics; (5) it maintains a democratic style of elections and free criticism of authority. Negatively, too, the Neo-Destour will not have precluded a democratic future to the extent that it avoids taking a totalitarian shape. The functioning of the various organs of the Neo-Destour will be examined with these criteria in mind.[12]

The Cells

Neo-Destour cells are quite unlike Communist cells. They assemble less often and contain a larger number of members. General assemblies or information meetings usually occur at no more than three-month intervals. They lack the secrecy of Communist cell meetings, and are sometimes even open to the general public. Any Tunisian can be a cell member if he is not a member of another party, if he is committed to respect the principles of the party, if he executes its decisions and pays his dues.[13] The most important prerequisite for membership—respect for the principles of the party—does not imply the sort of conversion required by totalitarian parties, for the Neo-Destour's principles are flexible and undogmatic. Some of the party's 1000 cells have had as many as 3000 members, while most cells outside Tunis average between 100 and 400 members. The cell committee, a collectively responsible executive of from 8 to 12 cell officers elected at the annual cell assembly,[14] may meet as often as once

[footnote 11 continued]
(women in the party are still rare, except in some cities). But these figures, swollen by new recruits in some of the politically underdeveloped areas of Tunisia, may mask increasing apathy in some old party strongholds.

[12] Apart from meager newspaper reports, the only solid documentary description of the party's present structure lies in its published internal statutes. These will not be individually cited in what follows.

[13] The 1959 statutes omit the previous requirement that new members take an oath. In practice the prospective member today, at least in Tunis, needs two sponsors who are members of the party to present his name to the cell committee. The $3 annual dues are not always paid in full.

[14] The elected officers choose among themselves a President, a Secretary-General, an Assistant

a week and carry on many activities, especially in the cities. But, unlike dedicated Communists, they cannot claim a local monopoly of ideological purity and devotion. Furthermore, the Neo-Destour cell is permitted free formal and informal contacts with other cells, whereas horizontal contacts of Communist cells are kept to a fully controlled minimum. Clearly "cell" is a somewhat misleading term for the Neo-Destour to apply to what are in fact more akin to the "sections" or branches of constitutional mass parties like the SFIO.

As a result of the reorganization of the party in 1958, the Political Bureau through its Commissioners exerts significant power over the cells. Candidates for cell elections must be approved by the Political Bureau, while previously anybody could be a candidate as long as he had been a party member for at least two years.[15] The Political Bureau may suspend or dissolve any cell committee guilty of an infraction of the party's Covenant or internal statutes. The Political Bureau then delegates responsibility to an appointed commission of cell members until the convening of a general assembly of the cell, within a period in theory not to exceed six months. Before 1958, the federations could dissolve cell committees with the approval or tacit silence of the Political Bureau, but new cell elections had to be prepared within two weeks, not six months. Today even the six-month deadline is not

always respected. Nor is the principle of collective responsibility always followed by the Political Bureau, which has sometimes, under the rather flexible rules of party discipline,[16] simply removed individual trouble-makers who were misusing their cell positions. Cell committees are generally suspended or dissolved for one of two reasons: either they have been paralyzed by internal dissension, usually a function of local family rivalries, or they have been too inactive and apathetic in the execution of normal party duties. Suspended or dissolved cell committees are not an uncommon phenomenon in Tunisia today. They reflect less an overly authoritarian Political Bureau, however, than a simple lack of responsible party cadres. Within limits defined by the party's internal statutes, cell elections are genuinely democratic and follow fixed procedures understood by most members.[17]

The Political Bureau may also determine the number of cells and delimit their territorial competence. Since 1958 efforts to make the party structure parallel the

Secretary-General, a Treasurer, an Assistant Treasurer, an Orientation officer, a Youth officer, and a Social Revival officer. The Orientation officer is responsible for party propaganda within the cell's district. The Youth officer carries out the program of the Neo-Destour Youth. The Social Revival officer watches over the interests of the general public in everything from garbage collection to the building of a new mosque.

[15] But the Political Bureau does not exercise its new privilege indiscriminately. The representative of the Political Bureau who presides over the cells' general assembly may be asked to explain why a candidate was not approved.

[16] A party member or official may be punished by a warning, suspension, or expulsion from the party, if proved guilty of any of the following broad charges: (1) prejudicing interests of the party and departing from its political principles: (2) action susceptible of endangering the party or supporting one of its enemies; (3) breaking the party Covenant or internal statutes, or affecting the dignity of the party; (4) public expression of hostility toward the party or toward one of its organs. In practice the Political Bureau has a potentially formidable disciplinary arsenal, but it is a deterrent rarely employed.

[17] A few weeks before the general assembly, candidates submit their applications through the cell committee to the Political Bureau. Though the list of candidates is divulged only at the assembly, the cell members know in advance who is running for election, because prospective candidates are usually approved. At the assembly all members who have been in the party for at least nine months are electors, if they have paid a reasonable portion of their annual dues. They vote for as many candidates from the list as there are offices to fill. There are almost always substantially more candidates than offices. Voting patterns are irregular; cell elections are never blind plebiscites.

country's new administrative structure have necessitated the reduction of the number of cells from 1500 to 1000. In theory, the party now has one cell for each *cheikhat*, the government's lowest administrative division. Since these divisions are purely geographic in all parts of the country, newly regrouped cells have sometimes embraced disparate tribal fractions. Currently, however, the Political Bureau is trying to increase the number of cells in some provinces, where the necessary cadres are to be found, in order to stimulate more local initiative. There has been only one case of what appears to be outright political gerrymandering.[18]

Though the Political Bureau supervises all cell activities, local initiative is encouraged. The most recent national congress, in March 1959, passed a resolution calling for each cell to organize a local project to re-enforce Tunisia's economic and social development. The application of this resolution has of course necessitated close co-operation between the cells and higher party officials, especially when government support was needed. But most ideas came from the cells. Cells also enjoy direct contacts with local government officials. Since 1957 many elected municipal councils have been set up in villages and towns, and they are composed largely of cell officers. Often, too, the *cheikh*, though appointed by the government, will have

been the former cell president. Furthermore, the Governor's Delegate, who is the *cheikh's* superior in the administrative hierarchy, usually tries to keep on friendly terms with the cell committee, for the popular support which it represents is essential to the success of many government projects.[19] Patronage is managed through higher party levels, but cell demands and advice receive serious consideration. Local grievances voiced by the cell committee are aired either in meetings with higher party officials or in meetings grouping both party and government representatives. Consultation is constant, though the cell has few fixed prerogatives. Hierarchies lack rigidity, for virtually all provincial officials, whether in the party or in the government, are either Neo-Destour militants or former militants, brothers in the same cause.

Cell meetings, however, rarely discuss national policies. The frequent cell committee meetings, which are not public, seem to be concerned exclusively with the administration of the cell or the discussion of local problems. General meetings, held in theory once every three months, are rarely forums for the airing of national issues, though attempts to treat them thus are made from time to time by patient party officials. The annual cell assembly is almost invariably confined to a discussion, sometimes sparked by lively but orderly criticism, of the committee's activities during the year.[20] The Orienta-

[18] In Kairouan, after serious incidents on January 17, 1961, when a large crowd chanting religious slogans marched upon the Governor's office and residence to protest the transfer of a religious instructor. A re-enforced National Guard was needed to combat the mob, and a small number of people were actually killed. The incident revealed growing tension between the traditional aristocracy of the Kairouan *medina* and the governing authorities who are spearheading social revolution in the area. On February 13 and 14 the Commissioner held meetings of cell officers to explain his decision to increase the number of cells in the *medina* to 13, a surprisingly large number. On February 23 he held a meeting of party cadres to designate the new cell officers. See *Al 'Amal* (the official Neo-Destour daily newspaper), March 5, 1961, p. 3.

[19] In theory, the provincial governmental and party structures are distinct hierarchies, with horizontal contacts only between the Governor and the Party Commissioner. In principle, the Governor's Delegates have no contact with the party apparatus. But as one Delegate told me in the presence of cell officers whom I was interviewing, "We always work together in our different domains. I consult the cell about my problems, and the cell may consult me about its problems." In practice, too, Delegates are often in contact with higher party officials.

[20] But an exception to this rule that occurred in the assembly of the venerable cell grouping the artisans and businessmen of the *souks*

tion officer, in charge of propaganda, receives the party line on national and international issues from the Political Bureau. He transmits it, sometimes through an effective network of trusted militants, but it is never criticized formally in cell meetings. Party communications from above bring to mind the Neo-Destour's independence struggle; they are *mots d'ordre*, to be obeyed like the commands that launched demonstrations against colonialism. The only role permitted to cell members as such in the elaboration of national policy is their ritual agreement at assemblies to send a telegram to President Bourguiba expressing full support for all his policies at home and abroad.

The Neo-Destour cell, in short, unlike the SFIO section, is more a vehicle for the mobilization and education of the masses than a forum for discussing national issues or for proposing national policies. It is not quite democratically elected because the Political Bureau must endorse candidates, and elected officers can be easily removed by their superiors. But in reality, as in all voluntary organizations, there seems to be relatively little turnover of officers. The alternative to the Political Bureau's tutelage would not necessarily be more democratic. Intensified personality and family clashes might threaten the unity of the party, but they would not produce coherent policy alternatives emanating from the cells. Furthermore, the Political Bureau, by the diplomacy of its Commissioners, is in a position to teach diverse cell factions to tolerate one another. While the party structure allows for little cell initiative, party leaders, armed with their unambiguous powers, can afford to encourage the coherent practical initiatives that cells do take. Cell officers acquire the practical arts of democratic leadership, while their activities may in the long run be educating the public in their responsibilities as citizens.

of Tunis was related to me with pride by a higher party official.

The Provincial Offices

The substitution of appointed Commissioners for elected federation officers may not be as serious a blow as it seemed to internal democratic growth. Though elected, the old federations were essentially executive arms of the Political Bureau. Furthermore, democratic elections, far from stimulating mobility and the rise of new militants, had acted as a brake. By returning the same old militants to power over the political machines that they had created, the federations encouraged the perpetuation of a parochial leadership more apt to rest on the laurels of independence than to confront the new economic and social problems that independence had brought.

The Commissioners, on the other hand, are able to stimulate new blood by co-opting younger militants for their coordinating committees and subcommittees that assist them in working with the cells. Young school teachers and former students of French universities have thus been brought into the party apparatus, more often as unpaid militants than as paid officials. The school teachers are especially important, if the party is to take on new life by mobilizing the country for economic development. Yet, working in villages and towns where they were not born, these teachers often cannot be elected to cell committees, for most indigenous members consider them "strangers" even if they are natives of a neighboring village.

Armed with the confidence that the Political Bureau displays in him, the Commissioner is often able to obtain more for the cells under his supervision than might a democratically elected official.[21] In

[21] Though appointed, the Commissioner and his coordinating committee must effectively collaborate with the cells. In a sense they must be more representative than the Governor and his Delegates. During Ramadan in Sousse, for instance, the party officials never dared to smoke or eat in public during the daytime, because public opinion, attached to Ramadan and reflected in the cells, would not have approved. On the other hand, Tunisian

political power the Commissioner of a province ranks second only to the Governor. In constant contact with both cell leaders and the Governor, the Commissioner is able to communicate to the latter the popular demands of the former. Schools, dispensaries, public works, and patronage are accorded priority, when technically feasible, in areas where cells have built up the most political pressure. The Commissioner in large part determines these priorities, in consultation with the Governor. The parallel structure of government and party has at times resulted in serious friction between Governor and Commissioner. But knowledge of the smooth working relationship between the Secretary of the Interior (who is Assistant Secretary General of the party) and the Political Bureau has generally induced close co-operation. In the two cases since 1959 when friction became unbearable, both Governor and Commissioner were shifted. On the other hand, weak Commissioners whose choice was influenced by the Governor concerned have not lasted.

Though party statutes make no mention of any substitute for the annual federal congresses, provincial offices have developed the practice of holding regular assemblies of party cadres, roughly once every two months. These meetings are typically chaired by a member of the Political Bureau, and include the members of the co-ordinating committee, the cell officers, and some militants especially invited by the Commissioner. While there is no voting, the assembly may discuss substantive political issues. Procedure is flexible. After an opening speech by the member of the Political Bureau, scores of questions on all topics are addressed to him from the floor. There is no attempt to draw any line between a point of information and a substantive grievance. Especi-

ally in Tunis, where the cadres are politically sophisticated, such meetings can provide lucid debate on national problems. Constructive criticisms and suggestions to the Political Bureau are encouraged, and discussion can be rational, because party leaders claim no ideological monopoly. When criticized by young intellectuals of the party for lacking a "doctrine," Bourguiba is reported to have told them to go think one out and tell him about it.

While the provincial offices are formally not as "democratic" as the federations used to be, it is not certain that they cannot more effectively educate party cadres in the pursuit of democracy. By being an effective link not only between cells and the Political Bureau but between cells and the governing authorities, the Commissioner is in a position to give the cells lessons in practical responsibility. While pushing for the satisfaction of justified demands, he also explains to cells why some demands cannot be met. He assures a measure of mobility within the party and stimulates the discussion of basic government politics. Though no structures for debate exist formally at the provincial level, the informal meetings of cadres can be equally educational. Fortunately for prospects of democracy in Tunisia, the Commissioners seem to view their task as one of education toward this goal as well as simple administration of a growing party bureaucracy.

The National Council

Those who defended the reorganization of the party at the 1959 Congress pointed to the National Council as compensating for the loss of the federations. It was argued that the cells, which would henceforth directly elect a large majority of the National Council's membership, were substantially strengthened.[22]

[*footnote 21 continued*
government policy since 1960 has been to discourage observance of the month-long fast, and most high government officials in Sousse had no hesitation about smoking in public.

[22] The Director of the Political Bureau even pointed out at the 1959 Congress that cells could and should, in light of the party reorganization, give delegates specific mandates for National Council and Congress sessions.

Before independence the National Council, like its SFIO counterpart, was in fact able at times to exert important influence. Bourguiba used it as a lever upon some of his more moderate colleagues on the Political Bureau in 1938, when he was not the unquestioned Supreme Combatant which he later became. Between 1949 and 1951 the Council met frequently, and served in 1954 and early 1955 as a substitute for the Congress, which could not be convened after 1952 when the party was forced underground. Especially in 1938 and 1951, the National Council decided important tactical shifts in Neo-Destour relations with France.[23] Even after 1955, when the Council no longer met every three months as the internal statutes of the party dictated, the Political Bureau needed its agreement to a number of decisions.

After the 1959 Congress the National Council did not meet at all,[24] nor was any attempt made in the succeeding two years even to organize the election of its members by the cells. The Political Bureau's procrastination and violation of the party statutes that it itself designed had no readily observable cause. Privately party officials indicated simply that no important problems had arisen that the Political Bureau might usefully put before this

See *Le Petit Matin* (Tunis), March 5, 1959. The National Council is now theoretically composed of the members of the Political Bureau, the Commissioners, and one cell delegate for every 5000 members. Previously the National Council had consisted of the members of the Political Bureau, one delegate from each federal executive, and an equal number of members elected by the Congress. These elections were hotly contested in 1955, where 172 candidates ran for 32 seats! See *La Presse* (Tunis), November 20, 1955.
[23] See Hedi Nouira, "Le Néo-Destour," *Political Etrangère*, **19** (July 1954), 317–334.
[24] On November 17, 1961, the Director of the Neo-Destour announced that the National Council would meet sometime in February 1962 to discuss Tunisia's Three-Year Plan, which is designed to be an almost revolutionary innovation in Tunisia's social and economic life.

body. Clearly they interpreted it as being more a public forum through which party energies might be mobilized than a deliberative body that must meet regularly to check the activities of the Political Bureau. But its failure to meet regularly seems paradoxical in light of the serious efforts undertaken by the Political Bureau and its Commissioners to stimulate discussion in cadres' conferences. The fifty-odd militants whom the cells would elect would not seriously embarrass the Political Bureau in regular Council meetings, while discussions would inject a more democratic atmosphere into the party, and perhaps help to counter some signs of apathy and bureaucratization. A National Council composed of politically sophisticated Destourians might yet give the party a much-needed forum for structured debate on substantive national issues.

The Political Bureau

The Political Bureau, elected by the Party Congress, has always been the party's supreme executive organ. Statutory membership was increased in 1959 from eleven to fifteen, thus ratifying a change that the National Council had already accepted in 1957. The executive powers that the federations once held are now, somewhat increased, in the hands of the Political Bureau and the Commissioners whom it appoints. But since independence the Political Bureau superficially appears to have concentrated deliberative as well as executive powers. When Party Congresses are not in session, the Political Bureau is the party's only deliberative authority, since the National Council has lost its former importance.

Yet the Political Bureau is clearly not a form of collective leadership, despite the fiction of its collective responsibility. Elected by acclamation at Party Congresses, Bourguiba is more than a first among equals on the Bureau. The inspirational Leader, Bourguiba is also a sufficiently astute politician as not to allow any single lieutenant to become either a potential rival or an obvious successor. The Political Bureau is in practice little more than one of Bourguiba's innumerable vehicles of consultation. However, it meets regularly, once a week when Bourguiba is in town, and contains many of his principal collaborators.[25]

Apart from Bourguiba, the Political Bureau consists of five ministers, including the three most powerful (the Secretary-General of the party, who is Secretary of the Presidency; the Assistant Secretary-General, who is Secretary of the Interior; and Ahmed Ben Salah), the Governor of the Central Bank (another virtual minister), three Ambassadors, the President of the National Assembly, two trade union leaders of the UGTT, a business leader from UTIC, and the Director of the Political Bureau, who as a student was one of the founders of UGET. The last four members are especially significant for assuring that the diverse interests of the Tunisian elite be taken into consideration in all important policy decisions, thus maintaining the party's broadly representative character. Though hardly a cabinet in the British sense, in time of crisis the Political Bureau meets before Bourguiba presides over his infrequently assembled Cabinet of Ministers. The Political Bureau discusses all political problems, ranging from foreign affairs to internal economic or religious issues. Its deliberations are secret and informal, usually taking place over Bourguiba's

dinner table. However, the Political Bureau is collectively less important than it might be, because of Bourguiba's presidential style of leadership and because its three ambassadorial members, based overseas, are rarely available, while at least two others are symbols at best. The Neo-Destour Party, as an organization, does not make important decisions for a government servile to its will. Rather, as at the provincial level, party and government co-exist; neither is a dominating center of power. In practice, this means that the technicians in the administration can sometimes overrule the politicians.

But many internal party decisions emanate from four or five key members in the name of the Political Bureau. These decisions do not always affect merely the routine administration of the party. The reorganization of the party, for instance, occurred several months before the Congress had passed corresponding internal statutes. The Political Bureau may sometimes even ignore the statutes, as in its failure to convene a National Council. A speech by Bourguiba calling for a new tactical shift may provide almost the same measure of legitimacy to a decision of the Political Bureau as a Congress could provide. However, far-reaching changes in party policy usually require at least the retroactive political support, if not initiative, that only some larger body can give.

The party bureaucracy, managed for the Political Bureau by its Director, has grown since independence, though not in alarming proportions. Not including the staff of the party newspaper, the work gang "animators,"[26] janitors, and chauffeurs,

[25] In a somewhat unorthodox manner, the Political Bureau decided on November 17, 1961, after expelling one of its members from the party (Masmoudi), to co-opt Ahmed Ben Salah in his place. This decision had the salutary effect of making the Bureau's composition accord with political realities, for since January 1961 Ben Salah had become a virtual super-minister, second in some respects only to Bourguiba. Especially in the all-important economic field, the Political Bureau's discussions may therefore acquire more significance, and Ben Salah, too, may more effectively mobilize the party apparatus for his economic planning by being unequivocally a part of it.

[26] The party decided in early 1960 to create a corps of "animators" to stimulate the 150,000 unemployed unskilled workers whom the government hires at subsistence wages (including supplies of American wheat given to Tunisia) on public works projects. Unlike government foremen, the animators listen to workers' grievances, try to clear up administrative bottlenecks, and try to inculcate on the workers the idealistic notion that they are working for the good of the nation in the struggle against underdevelopment.

the bureaucracy has less than one hundred full-time officials and secretaries, spread out over Tunisia's thirteen provinces. Of course, the number would be much larger if it included the many militants holding patronage jobs in public or semi-public organizations who devote much of their time to the party. But bureaucracy is kept to a minimum, and party posts, often demanding a 70-hour week, are hardly sinecures. Aside from the Director and his Commissioners, who constitute the core of the system, the heads of the three central services for youth, orientation, and social revival keep in regular contact through the Commissioners' offices with the cell officers concerned. Unlike similar organizations affiliated with political parties in the West, the Neo-Destour Youth has no autonomy and passes no resolutions. It used to be extremely important as a device for political education and anti-colonialist agitation, and created a legion of loyal militants who after independence were able to constitute the body of the new Tunisian police force and National Guard. Today it theoretically has 80,000 members but has lost considerable dynamism,[27] because it can provide neither the excitement of a continuous independence struggle nor jobs for all the boys. The service for social revival has as its main tasks the general supervision of cell projects, the work of the party animators, and the mobilization of the masses when their cooperation is needed for the success of government projects. The party's orientation service explains national policies and the frequent speeches that Bourguiba gives. It also ensures that every public appearance of the President and other leading figures of the regime takes on the character of a mass plebiscite. In the late summer of 1961 literally thousands of meetings were organized at all levels of the party apparatus in all areas of the country to discuss the sensitive problems raised by the July Bizerte crisis and the new policy of state planning and "Neo-Destour socialism." Possibly the highly efficient apparatus of mass propaganda saved the regime after the shock of the Bizerte massacre, when Bourguiba's infallibility was disproved for many Tunisians. Certainly the apparatus strongly contributed to the widespread—if not total—acceptance of Neo-Destour socialism.

The line between administration and policy is necessarily vague. But the structure of the Neo-Destour in practice accentuates this vagueness, by allowing the more powerful members of the Political Bureau great latitude. What is perhaps more disturbing for prospects of democracy in Tunisia is the apparent absence within the ranks of the Neo-Destour of articulate doubts about its procedures at higher levels, for everyone agrees without trying to define their terms that a strong central power is needed in Tunisia today. The strongly concentrated power is moderately exercised to conciliate the various economic interests of the otherwise homogeneous elite, but anyone in the party who publicly asks basic questions about this strong central power and its possible dangers apparently runs the risk of being purged from the party.[28]

[27] The Tunisian government's *Monthly Statistics Bulletin* reported in November 1960 that only 2383 youths had been directly involved in specific Neo-Destour programs during 1959. It was perhaps these statistics that impelled Bourguiba on March 30, 1961, to devote a whole speech to the problems of youth organizations, in which he found the level of participation to be abysmal. In the summer of 1961, however, roughly 10,000 Neo-Destour youths participated as "volunteers" in the party's catastrophic campaign to force the evacuation of the French bases at Bizerte. It was said that some 3000 were killed or wounded in the one-sided four-day battle.

[28] The October 7, 1961, issue of *Afrique-Action*, a weekly paper run by Neo-Destour sympathizers, carried an editorial about personal power. It was universally attributed to Mohamed Masmoudi, the newspaper's political patron, who though a member of the Political Bureau had just been dismissed by Bourguiba from his government job as Secretary of Information. Though speaking in general terms

The Congress

The National Congress, composed of cell committee delegates, is in theory the supreme authority of the party. Since 1959 it is supposed to meet every three rather than every two years, but in fact the Neo-Destour has held only four real congresses in twenty-seven years: in 1934, 1937, 1955, and 1959. The two other ostensible congresses of 1948 and 1952 met clandestinely. Before each National Congress the cells are given at least a month in which to study the reports that the Political Bureau plans to deliver to the Congress, so that in theory basic policy issues can be intelligently discussed by Congress delegates.

In practice, the Congress is a demonstration of national solidarity rather than a forum for the articulation and structuring of differences that may divide the party. Voting is usually unanimous on resolutions. The procedure for electing the Political Bureau not only emphasizes the prestige of the Leader, who is elected separately, but mitigates divisions within the party by obliging candidates to present themselves individually on the same list rather than on separate lists. Only the popularity of diverse shifting cliques within the party can be calculated, on the basis of the number of votes received by each candidate. How-

[*footnote 28 continued*
of the type of regime headed by leaders like Bourguiba, de Gaulle, Nasser, Nkrumah, Sekou Touré, Fidel Castro, and Houphouet Boigny, the article was interpreted by the Neo-Destour as a personal attack against Bourguiba and the Tunisian system rather than an exercise in political science. On November 17, after being attacked in the Neo-Destour press and in cadres' conferences, Masmoudi was expelled from the Political Bureau and from the party. Bourguiba explained the action of the Political Bureau to the Tunisian public on the following day. He argued that Masmoudi should have expressed his opinions frankly within party organs rather than in public. Interpreting Masmoudi's article personally, Bourguiba, the other members of the Political Bureau, and many party cadres believed that Masmoudi was guilty of breaking party discipline.

ever, Congresses are democratic in two senses. The number of candidates for the Political Bureau exceeds the number of seats, so that elections are not entirely predictable. Secondly, both in Congress Commissions and in plenary, debate is apt to be extremely lively. The Congress stresses a solidarity of equals; the lowliest delegate may grill a minister with embarrassing questions and criticisms, for all are equal in their role as militants; only Bourguiba is the untouchable Father at these grand family reunions.

Decision making in the party is not democratic, but Congresses have an undeniably democratic atmosphere. In 1959 the Congress Commissions played a less important role than in 1955. On the other hand, the six-hour report delivered by the Secretary General to the Congress in 1959 was greeted with discussion and criticism that lasted into the night and continued during the following morning and afternoon sessions, before the report was unanimously accepted by the Congress. During the full day of debate, six ministerial members of the Political Bureau answered batteries of questions from the delegates. Debate covered all important government policies and many specific problems. The Congress afterward more rapidly acquiesced to the Director's report, which explained the reasons for the reorganization of the party that the Political Bureau had already executed. But on the following day the new internal statutes reflecting these changes were passed only after "laborious" discussion.[29]

Like the congresses of most mass parties with ostensibly democratic structures, the congresses of the Neo-Destour are in theory its supreme authority but in practice exert little effective power. Within limits that only the future can reveal, Neo-Destour delegates seem willing to pass any resolution that is actively supported by leaders known to have Bourguiba's blessing. But the Neo-Destour's emphasis on national solidarity, and even the automatic cheers of

[29] See *Le Petit Matin*, March 4–5, 1959.

any assembly of party members in response to the mere mention of Bourguiba's name, should not blind the observer to the democratic traditions engrained in the party. Unlike those of Communist congresses, debates and votes are not artificial displays; surprises occur,[30] though Bourguiba himself is criticized only indirectly through attacks on his ministers or close collaborators. The Neo-Destour Congress, though it may meet only four or five days every three or four years, gives party directives their legitimacy in the eyes of many militants. The give and take of plenary debate sets the tone of political behavior when the Congress is not in session. Despite its brevity, the National Congress is the Neo-Destour's most important focal point of Tunisia's new political traditions of spontaneous debate and criticism of authority.

Some conclusions emerge about the changing structure of the Neo-Destour that are significant for evaluating prospects for democracy in Tunisia. They may also help to elucidate the nature of the ruling national party, though it is dangerous to generalize from one example.

After six years of independence, the structure of the Neo-Destour has evolved clearly, and not in a liberal democratic direction. Though the cells remain relatively democratic, a handful of party leaders have effectively consolidated their control over the whole party apparatus. The mechanism increasingly has become an instrument for executing orders from above rather than a hierarchy of deliberative bodies for the articulation of representative opinion from below. An authoritarian trend has been reflected also in the increasing political monopoly that the Neo-Destour acquired after independence, when all political centers independent of party and government were eliminated. But it would be misleading to conclude that the Neo-

Destour, which resembled the SFIO on the eve of independence, is being transformed into a totalitarian party.

The Neo-Destour, even if it once formally resembled the SFIO, is clearly not and never was a constitutional mass party. In one important respect it is closer to the SFIO now than before independence. Its cells are no longer semi-clandestine centers of anti-colonial agitation; rather they are openly elected public centers of political education. But internal party democracy is even more of a myth in the Neo-Destour than in the SFIO, despite the fact that internal democracy would more readily correspond to democratic constitutional values in a preponderant party than in a party that from time to time shares governmental power and public responsibility with other parties. Apart from the triennial Congress, the Neo-Destour has no deliberative body that can effectively debate national issues and criticize the Political Bureau. It has no formal or informal structures that can channel the sporadic criticisms heard at cadres' conferences and congresses into competing policy alternatives. All important decisions are instead made by a self-perpetuating oligarchy, checked only by an amenable Congress that rarely meets.

But the Neo-Destour deviates almost equally from the Communist model. Before independence, the goal of liberation served as a substitute for ideology in capturing the minds and entire lives of the many cadres devoted to the liberation struggle. With independence, total personal engagement has withered away. Those who have remained or become devoted to the party have acquired a Bourguibist outlook, which is the negation of undiscriminating total engagement in any doctrine or organization and an acceptance of complexity and diversity, brought out by constant discussion at all party levels. Membership seems more genuinely voluntary than in totalitarian parties. The masses are not forced to join the party, and as dropping membership claims since 1958 suggest,

[30] One of Bourguiba's closest younger collaborators, for instance, was not re-elected to the Political Bureau in 1959.

membership is no longer as essential to the common man as in 1956 for the satisfaction of personal needs, such as a job or education for one's children, because the state apparatus, strengthened in 1958 at the expense of the party, tends toward greater impartiality. For the educated elite, too, party membership is no longer as essential even for a successful government career, and, conversely, opportunists in the party are discouraged by the perceptive Commissioners.

Cell activities emphasize personal initiative, not blind obedience. Horizontal contacts between cells are encouraged, not prohibited. The Neo-Destour remains a genuinely popular party, and its ideology, unlike a totalitarian one, could not justify systematic repression or vast purges. The party's leadership is open to new ideas and even to new leaders on intermediate levels, for it knows that it does not have the absolute answer to all of Tunisia's problems. If orders and most initiative come from above, the Political Bureau and its Commissioners are constantly attempting to stimulate more initiative from below and to train new cadres. Party meetings are constant experiments and retain their spontaneity, unlike Communist congresses. The Director of the Political Bureau, in charge of party administration, exerts significant power, but it belongs mainly to the older men on the Political Bureau. Intellectually rather embarrassed by its monopoly, the Neo-Destour has not made a cult of single-party dictatorship.

It is perhaps easier to conclude what the Neo-Destour is not than what it is. But some traits of this national party emerge. Maintaining a structure distinct from that of the government, the Neo-Destour is con-stantly trying to educate the population in the principles of Bourguibism, and to transform people into citizens. It maintains the cohesion of the new nation's elite. It mobilizes the energies of the population in practical projects that party and government decide upon. It acts as the link between the population and the government. It collaborates with the government in decision-making. It encourages cadres in the exercise of their local responsibilities. Despite a paternalistic structure, the Neo-Destour in fact remains representative of the nation, because its leadership strives to maintain the popularity of the party as if a powerful opposition existed.

Though not ideally democratic in structure, the Neo-Destour both in theory and in practice gives its hundreds of thousands of members and militants an effective political education. It is much more than a disseminator of government propaganda because it has a life of its own. Almost any Tunisian citizen can be a Destour militant, and one man out of every four joins the party. Congresses emphasize the equality of all militants and the right of each to criticize and to convince others of his point of view. The habitual conferences of cadres are rehearsals of congresses and teach the same lessons. The cells, tutored by generally dedicated Commissioners, encourage not only local political initiative but the general acceptance of certain democratic procedures for arriving at concrete decisions. A powerful machine that, by persuasion rather than force, is stimulating the general sharing of national purposes, the Neo-Destour also seems a training ground for possible democracy in the future, the outlines of which cannot yet be perceived.

Chapter 16

Problems of Integration and Modernization Breakdowns

POLITICAL INTEGRATION AND POLITICAL DEVELOPMENT*

Myron Weiner

It is often said of the developing nations that they are "unintegrated" and that their central problem, often more pressing than that of economic development, is the achievement of "integration." The term "integration" is now widely used to cover an extraordinarily large range of political phenomena. It is the purpose of this article to analyze the various uses of this

SOURCE. Myron Weiner, "Political Integration and Political Development," *The Annals of the American Academy of Political and Social Science*, 358, 52–64, March 1965.

* This article is a preliminary version of a portion of a study I am preparing for the Social Science Research Council Committee on Comparative Politics. The final and full version will be published in a volume entitled *The Political System and Political Development*. I want to take this opportunity to express my appreciation to the Committee for granting me permission to publish this version at this time, and to express my intellectual appreciation to my four collaborators in this study—Lucian Pye, Leonard Binder, Joseph LaPombara and James S. Coleman, not only for their comments on this manuscript and for the many ideas of theirs which found their way into these pages, but for the intellectual excitement of the entire venture. Needless to say, I alone am responsible for any errors and follies which this essay contains.

term, to show how they are related, then to suggest some of the alternative strategies pursued by governments to cope with each of these "integration" problems.

Definitions

1. Integration may refer to the process of bringing together culturally and socially discrete groups into a single territorial unit and the establishment of a national identity. When used in this sense "integration" generally presumes the existence of an ethnically plural society in which each group is characterized by its own language or other self-conscious cultural qualities, but the problem may also exist in a political system which is made up of once distinct independent political units with which people identified. National integration thus refers specifically to the problem of creating a sense of territorial nationality which overshadows—or eliminates—subordinate parochial loyalties.[1]

[1] This is perhaps the most common use of the term. For a precise view of the many attempts to define "nationality," see Rupert Emerson, *From Empire to Empire* (Boston: Beacon Press, 1960), especially Part 2: "The Anatomy of the Nation." K. H. Silvert, the editor of a collection of studies of nation-

551

2. Integration is often used in the related sense to refer to the problem of establishing national central authority over subordinate political units or regions which may or may not coincide with distinct cultural or social groups. While the term "national integration" is concerned with the subjective feelings which individuals belonging to different social groups or historically distinct political units have toward the nation, "territorial integration" refers to the objective control which central authority has over the entire territory under its claimed jurisdiction.[2]

3. The term "integration" is often used to refer to the problem of linking government with the governed. Implied in this usage is the familiar notion of a "gap" between the elite and the mass, characterized by marked differences in aspirations and values.[3] The "gap" may

[*footnote 1 continued*
alism prepared by the American Universities Field Staff, *Expectant Peoples: Nationalism and Development* (New York: Random House, 1963), suggests as a working definition of nationalism "the acceptance of the state as the impersonal and ultimate arbiter of human affairs" (p. 19). See also Karl W. Deutsch, *Nationalism and Social Communication* (New York: John Wiley and Sons, 1953) and Karl W. Deutsch and William J. Foltz (eds.), *Nation-Building* (New York: Atherton Press, 1963).

[2] For a discussion of some of the problems of territorial control in Africa see James S. Coleman, "Problems of Political Integration in Emergent Africa," *Western Political Quarterly* (March 1955), pp. 844–857.

[3] For an explanation of this use of the term integration in the literature see Leonard Binder, "National Integration and Political Development," *American Political Science Review* (September 1964), pp. 622–631. Elite-mass integration is also one of the usages in James S. Coleman and Carl G. Rosberg (eds.), *Political Parties and National Integration in Africa* (Berkeley: University of California, 1964). They use integration in two senses: "(1) political integration, which refers to the progressive bridging of the elite-mass gap on the vertical plane in the course of developing an integrated political process and a participant political community, and (2) territorial integration, which refers to the progressive reduction of cultural and regional tensions

be widest in society with a passive population and modernizing elite, but a relatively stable if frustrating relationship may exist. More often the masses are beginning to become organized and concerned with exercising influence, while the elite responds with attempts to coerce, persuade, or control the masses. It is under these conditions of conflict and often internal war that we customarily speak of "disintegration."

4. Integration is sometimes used to refer to the minimum value consensus necessary to maintain a social order. These may be end values concerning justice and equity, the desirability of economic development as a goal, the sharing of a common history, heroes, and symbols, and, in general, an agreement as to what constitutes desirable and undesirable social ends. Or the values may center on means, that is, on the instrumentalities and procedures for the achievement of goals and for resolving conflicts. Here the concern is with legal norms, with the legitimacy of the constitutional framework and the procedures by which it should operate—in short, on desirable and undesirable conduct.

5. Finally, we may speak of "integrative behavior," referring to the capacity of people in a society to organize for some common purposes. At the most elementary level all societies have the capacity to create some kind of kinship organization—a device whereby societies propagate themselves and care for and socialize their young. As other needs and desires arise within a society we may ask whether the capacity grows to create new organizations to carry out new purposes. In some societies the capacity to organize is limited to a small elite and is only associated with those

and discontinuities on the horizontal plane in the process of creating a homogeneous territorial political community" (p. 9). These two definitions correspond with our first and third definitions.

who have authority.[4] Only the state, therefore, has a capacity to expand for the carrying out of new functions. In still other societies organizational capacities are more evenly spread throughout the population, and individuals without coercive authority have the readiness to organize with others. Societies differ, therefore, in the extent to which organizational proclivities are pervasive or not, and whether organizations are simply expressive in character—that is, confined to kinship and status—or purposive.

The term "integration" thus covers a vast range of human relationships and attitudes—the integration of diverse and discrete cultural loyalties and the development of a sense of nationality; the integration of political units into a common territorial framework with a government which can exercise authority; the integration of the rulers and the ruled; the integration of the citizen into a common political process; and, finally, the integration of individuals into organizations for purposive activities. As diverse as these definitions are, they are united by a common thread. These are all attempts to define what it is *which holds a society and a political system together*. Scholars of the developing areas have groped for some such notions of integration, for they recognize that in one or more of these senses the political systems they are studying do not appear to hold together *at a level commensurate with what their political leadership needs to carry out their goals*. If each scholar has in his mind a different notion of "integration," it is often because he is generalizing from one or more specific societies with which he is familiar and which is facing some kind of "integration" problem.

[4] For an analysis of the attitudes which inhibit organized activity see Edward Banfield, *The Moral Basis of a Backward Society* (Glencoe, Ill.: Free Press, 1958). Though Banfield's study is confined to a single village in Italy, he raises the general problem of analyzing the capacities of a people to organize for common purposes.

Since there are many ways in which systems may fall apart, there are as many ways of defining "integration."

To avoid further confusion we shall use a qualifying adjective hereafter when we speak of one kind of integration problem. We shall thus speak of national integration, territorial integration, value integration, elite-mass integration, and integrative behavior and use the term integration alone when we are referring to the generalized problem of holding a system together.

Forms and Strategies

Transitional or developing political systems are generally less integrated than either traditional or modern systems. This is because these systems cannot readily perform the functions which the national leadership—or in some instances, the populace too—expects them to perform. In other words, as the functions of a system expand—or the political leadership aspires to expand the functions of the system—a new level of integration is required. When we speak of political development, therefore, we are concerned first with the expanding functions of the political system, secondly with the new level of integration thereby required to carry out these functions, and, finally, with the capacity of the political system to cope with these new problems of integration. It is necessary, therefore, that we now take a more concrete look at the kinds of expanding functions which occur in the course of political development, the specific integrative problems which these pose, and the public policy choices available to governmental elites for coping with each of these integrative problems.

NATIONAL INTEGRATION

It is useful to ask why it is that new nations with pluralistic social orders require more national integration than did the colonial regimes which preceded them. The obvious answer is that colonial governments were not concerned with national loyalties but with creating classes who would be loyal to them as a colonial power. Colonial governments, therefore, paid little or no attention to the teaching of a "national" language or culture, but stressed instead the teaching of the colonial language and culture. We are all familiar with the fact that educated Vietnamese, Indonesians, Nigerians, Indians, and Algerians were educated in French, English, and Dutch rather than in their own languages and traditions. Although the colonialist viewed the development of national loyalties as a threat to his political authority, the new leadership views it as essential to its own maintenance. Moreover, since the colonial rulers permitted only limited participation, the parochial sentiments of local people rarely entered into the making of any significant decisions of essential interest to policy makers. Once the new nations permit a greater measure of public participation, then the integration requirements of the system are higher. Moreover, the new elite in the new nations have higher standards of national integration than those of their former colonial rulers and this, too, creates new integration problems.

So long, for example, as export-import duties were imposed by a colonial ruler whose primary concern was with the impact of commercial policies upon their trade and commerce, then no questions of national integration were involved. Once these areas of policy are in the hands of a national regime, then issues immediately arise as to which sections of the country—and therefore which communities—are to be affected adversely or in a beneficial fashion by trade policies. Once educational policy is determined by national rather than colonial needs, the issues of language policy, location of educational facilities, the levels of educational investment, and the question of who bears the costs of education all affect the relations of culturally discrete groups. Finally, once the state takes on new invest-

ment responsibilities—whether for roads and post offices or for steel mills and power dams—questions of equity are posed by the regions, tribes, and linguistic groups which make up plural societies. Even if the assent of constituent groups is not necessary for the making of such decisions—that is, if an authoritarian framework is maintained —at least acquiescence is called for.

How nations have handled the problems of national integration is a matter of historical record. Clifford Geertz[5] has pointed out that public policy in the first instance is effected by patterns of social organization in plural societies. These patterns include (1) countries in which a single group is dominant in numbers and authority and there are one or more minority groups; (2) countries in which a single group is dominant in authority but not numbers; (3) countries in which no single group by itself commands a majority nor is a single group politically dominant; and (4) countries of any combination in which one or more minorities cut across international boundaries. Examples of the first group are prewar Poland (68 per cent Polish), contemporary Ceylon (70 per cent Sinhalese), and Indonesia (53 per cent Javanese). The dominant minority case is best exemplified by South Africa (21 per cent "white"). The best examples of complete pluralism with no majorities are India, Nigeria, and Malaya and, in Europe, Yugoslavia and Czechoslovakia. And finally, among the minorities which cross international boundaries, the most troublesome politically have been the Kurds, the Macedonians, the Basques, the Armenians, and the Pathans. In contemporary Africa, there are dozens of tribes which are cut by international boundaries, and in Southeast Asia there are substantial Chinese and Indian minorities.

[5] See Clifford Geertz, "The Integrative Revolution: Primordial Sentiment and Civil Politics in the New States," *Old Societies and New Nations*, ed., Clifford Geertz (New York: Free Press of Glencoe, 1963).

In general there are two public policy strategies for the achievement of national integration: (1) the elimination of the distinctive cultural traits of minority communities into some kind of "national" culture, usually that of the dominant cultural group—a policy generally referred to as assimilationist: "Americanization," "Burmanization," "detribalization;" (2) the establishment of national loyalties without eliminating subordinate cultures—the policy of "unity in diversity," politically characterized by "ethnic arithmetic." In practice, of course, political systems rarely follow either policy in an unqualified manner but pursue policies on a spectrum somewhere in between, often simultaneously pursuing elements from both strategies.

The history of ethnic minorities in national states is full of tragedy. If today the future of the Watusi in East Africa, the Hindus in East Pakistan, the Turks in Cyprus and the Greeks in Turkey, and Indians in Burma and Ceylon is uncertain, let us recall the fate of minorities in the heterogeneous areas of East Europe. Poland in 1921 had minorities totalling 32 per cent of the population. Since then 2.5 million Polish Jews have been killed or left the country and over 9 million Germans have been repatriated. Border shifts and population exchanges have also removed Ruthenian, white Russian, and Lithuanian minorities, so that today only 2 per cent of the population of Poland belongs to ethnic minorities. Similarly, the Turkish minority in Bulgaria was considerably reduced at the end of the Second World War when 250,000 Turks were forced to emigrate to Turkey in 1950, and three million Germans and 200,000 Hungarians have been repatriated from Czechoslovakia since the war. Killings, the transfers of populations, and territorial changes have made most Eastern European countries more homogeneous today than they were at the beginning of the Second World War. Yugoslavia and Czechoslovakia are the only remaining East European countries which lack a single numerically dominant ethnic group.[6]

It is sad to recount an unpleasant historical fact—that few countries have successfully separated political loyalties from cultural loyalties. The dominant social groups have looked with suspicion upon the loyalty of those who are culturally different—generally, though not always (but here, too, we have self-fulfilling prophecies at work) with good reason. Where killings, population transfers, or territorial changes have not occurred, the typical pattern has been to absorb the ethnic minority into the dominant culture or to create a new amalgam culture. Where cultural and racial differences continue in Europe or the United States, they are generally accompanied by political tensions. No wonder that so many leaders of the new nations look upon assimilation and homogenization as desirable and that strong political movements press for population transfers in Cyprus, India, and Pakistan, and are likely to grow in importance in sub-Sahara Africa. It remains to be seen whether the ideal of unity and diversity, that is, *political* unity and *cultural* diversity, can be the foundation for modern states. Perhaps the most promising prospects are those in which no single ethnic group dominates—Nigeria, India, and Malaysia. The factors at work in prewar Eastern Europe seem tragically in the process of being duplicated in many of the developing nations: the drive by minorities for ethnic determination, the unsuccessful effort by newly established states to establish their own economic and political viability, the inability of states to establish integration without obliterating cultures—and often peoples— through assimilation, population transfers or genocide, and, finally, the efforts of larger more powerful states to establish control or absorb unintegrated, fragile political systems.

[6] These figures are taken from Lewis M. Alexander, *World Political Patterns* (Chicago: Rand McNally), pp. 277–325.

TERRITORIAL INTEGRATION

The associations of states with fixed territories is a relatively modern phenomenon. The fluctuating "boundaries" of historic empires, and the fuzziness at the peripheries where kinship ties and tributary arrangements marked the end of a state are no longer acceptable arrangements in a world where sovereignty is characterized by an exclusive control over territory. In time the control over territory may be accompanied by a feeling of common nationality—our "national integration," but there must first of all be territorial integration. For most new states —and historic ones as well—the establishment of a territory precedes the establishment of subjective loyalties. A Congo nation cannot be achieved, obviously, without there being a Congo state, and the first order of business in the Congo has been the establishment by the central government of its authority over constituent territorial units. Some scholars have distinguished between the state and the nation, the former referring to the existence of central authority with the capacity to control a given territory and the latter to the extent of subjective loyalty on the part of the population within that territory to the state. There are, of course, instances where the "nation" in this sense precedes the "state"—as in the case of Israel and, according to some, Pakistan—but more typically the "state" precedes the "nation." "Nation-building," to use the increasingly popular phrase, thus presumes the prior existence of a state in control of a specified —and, in most instances, internationally recognized—territory. Territorial integration is thus related to the problem of *state-building* as distinct from *nation-building*.

Colonial rulers did not always establish central authority over the entire territory under their *de jure* control. The filling of the gap between *de jure* and *de facto* control has, in most instances, been left to the new regimes which took power after independence.

Thus, the areas under *indirect* control by colonial authorities have been placed under the *direct* control of the new governments—in India, Pakistan, Malaya, and in many areas of Africa. This process has been accomplished with relatively little bloodshed and international disturbance— although the dispute over Kashmir is an important exception—largely because the colonial regimes denied these quasi-independent pockets of authority the right to create their own armies.

The more serious problem of territorial integration has been the efforts of the new regimes to take control over border areas which were, in effect, unadministered by the colonial governments. Since both sides of a boundary were often governed by the same colonial power—as in French West Africa—or by a weak independent power—as in the Indian-Tibetan and Indian-Chinese borders—the colonial government often made no effort to establish *de facto* authority. Moreover, some of these areas are often occupied by recalcitrant tribes who forcefully resisted efforts toward their incorporation in a larger nation-state.

Some of the new governments have wisely not sought to demonstrate that they can exercise control over all subordinate authorities—wisely, because their capacity to do so is often exceedingly limited. But no modern government can tolerate for long a situation in which its laws are not obeyed in portions of its territory. As the new regimes begin to expand their functions, their need to exercise control grows. As an internal market is established, there is a need for a uniform legal code enforceable in courts of law; as state expenditures grow, no area can be exempt from the tax collectors; with the growth in transportation and communication there is a need for postal officers and personnel for the regulation in the public interest of communication and transport facilities. Finally, there is pride, for no government claiming international recognition will willingly admit that it cannot exercise authority in areas under its recognized jurisdiction, for to do so is to invite the strong to penetrate into the territory of the weak.

VALUE INTEGRATION

The integration of values—whatever else it encompasses—at a minimum means that there are acceptable procedures for the resolution of conflict. All societies—including traditional societies—have conflicts, and all societies have procedures for their resolution. But as societies begin to modernize, conflicts multiply rapidly, and the procedures for the settlement of conflict are not always satisfactory. There are societies where the right of traditional authority to resolve conflict remained intact during the early phases of modernization—Japan comes readily to mind—and were thereby able to avoid large-scale violence. But these are the exceptions. Why does the system require a new level of value integration?

First of all, the scale and volume of conflict increases in societies experiencing modernization. The status of social groups is frequently changed, even reversed, as education opens new occupational opportunities, as the suffrage increases the political importance of numbers, and as industrial expansion provides new opportunities for employment and wealth. A caste or tribe, once low in status and wealth, may now rise or at least see the opportunity for mobility. And social groups once high in power, status, and wealth may now feel threatened. Traditional rivalries are aggravated, and new conflicts are created as social relationships change.

The modernization process also creates new occupational roles and these new roles often conflict with the old. The new local government officer may be opposed by the tribal and caste leader. The textile manufacturer may be opposed by producers of hand-loomed cloth. The doctor may be opposed by a traditional healer. To these, one could add an enormous list

of conflicts associated with modernization: the conflicts between management and labor characteristic of the early stages of industrial development, the hostility of landlords to government land-reform legislation, the hostility of regions, tribes, and religious groups with one another as they find it necessary to compete—often for the first time—in a common political system where public policies have important consequences for their social and economic positions. Finally, we should note the importance of ideological conflicts so often found in developing societies as individuals try to find an intellectually and emotionally satisfying framework for re-creating order out of a world of change and conflict.

There are two modal strategies for integrating values in a developing society. One stresses the importance of consensus and is concerned with maximizing uniformity. This view of consensus, in its extreme, emphasizes as a goal the avoidance of both conflict and competition through either coercion or exhortation. A second view of the way integrative values may be maximized emphasizes the interplay of individual and group interests. Public policy is thus not the consequence of a "right" policy upon which all agree, but the best policy possible in a situation in which there are differences of interests and sentiments.

Since most developing societies lack integrative values, political leaders in new nations are often self-conscious of their strategies. In practice, of course, neither of these two strategies is pursued in a "pure" fashion, for a leadership which believes in consensus without conflict may be willing to permit the interplay of some competitive interests while, on the other hand, regimes committed to open competition often set limits as to which viewpoints can be publicly expressed.

Though movements often develop aimed at the elimination of conflict—Communists, for example, see class harmony as the culmination of a period of struggle—such movements in practice simply add another element of conflict. The problem has been one of finding acceptable procedures and institutions for the management of conflict. It is striking to note the growth of dispute-settling institutions in modern societies. When these bodies are successful, it is often possible to prevent conflicts from entering a country's political life. Here we have in mind the social work agencies, churches and other religious bodies, lawyers and the courts, labor-management conciliation bodies and employee councils, and interracial and interreligious bodies. The psychiatrist, the lawyer, the social worker, and the labor mediator all perform integrating roles in the modern society. In the absence of these or equivalent roles and institutions in rapidly changing societies in which conflict is growing, it is no wonder that conflicts move quickly from the factory, the university, and the village into political life.

A modern political system has no single mechanism, no single procedure, no single institution for the resolution of conflict; indeed, it is precisely the multiplicity of individuals, institutions, and procedures for dispute settlement that characterizes the modern political system— both democratic and totalitarian. In contrast, developing societies with an increasing range of internal conflict, typically lack such individuals, institutions, and procedures. It is as if mankind's capacity to generate conflict is greater than his capacity to find methods for resolving conflict; the lag is clearly greatest in societies in which fundamental economic and social relationships are rapidly changing.

ELITE-MASS INTEGRATION

The mere existence of differences in goals and values between the governing elite and the governed mass hardly constitutes disintegration so long as those who are governed accept the right of the governors to govern. British political culture stresses the obligations of citizens toward their government; the American political culture stresses the importance of political participation. In both, a high degree of elite-mass integration exists. At the other extreme are societies faced with the problem of internal war, and in between are many countries whose governments are so cut off from the masses whom they govern that they can neither mobilize the masses nor be influenced by them. The integration of elite and mass, between governors and the governed, occurs not when differences among the two disappear, but when a pattern of authority and consent is established. In no society is consent so great that authority can be dispensed with, and in no society is government so powerful and so internally cohesive that it can survive for long only through the exercise of cohesive authority. We need to stress here that both totalitarian and democratic regimes are capable of establishing elite-mass integration and that the establishment of a new pattern of relations between government and populace is particularly important during the early phase of development when political participation on a large scale is beginning to take place.

It is commonplace to speak of the "gap" between governors and the governed in the new nations, implying that some fundamental cultural and attitudinal gaps exist between the "elite" and the "mass," the former being secular-minded, English- or French-speaking, and Western-educated, if not Western-oriented, while the latter remain oriented toward traditional values, are fundamentally religious, and are vernacular-speaking.[7] In more concrete political terms, the government may be concerned with increasing savings and investment and, in general, the postponement of immediate economic gratification in order to maximize long-range growth, while the public may be more concerned with immediate gains in

[7] For a critique of "gap" theories of political development, see Ann Ruth Willner, "The Underdeveloped Study of Political Development," *World Politics* (April 1964), pp. 468–482.

income and, more fundamentally, equitable distribution or social justice irrespective of its developmental consequences. Often the governmental elite itself may be split with one section concerned with satisfying public demands in order to win popular support while the other is more concerned with maximizing growth rates, eliminating parochial sentiments, establishing a secular society, or achieving international recognition. The elite-mass gap also implies that communications are inadequate, that is, that the elite is oriented toward persuading the mass to change their orientation, but the feedback of political demands is not heard or, if heard, not responded to.

Perhaps too much is made of the attitudinal "gap" between governors and governed; what is more important perhaps is the attitude of government toward its citizens. Nationalist leaders out of power are typically populist. They generally identify with the mass and see in the "simple peasant" and the "working class" qualities which will make a good society possible. But once the nationalist leadership takes power and satisfies its desire for social status it tends to view the mass as an impediment to its goals of establishing a "modern," "unified," and "powerful" state. From being the champion of the masses the elite often becomes their detractor.

In all political systems, those of developing as well as developed societies, there are differences in outlook between those who govern and those who are governed. In a developed system, however, those who govern are accessible to influence by those who are governed—even in a totalitarian system—and those who are governed are readily available for mobilization by the government. In modern societies governments are so engaged in effecting the economy, social welfare, and defense that there must be a closer interaction between government and the governed.[8]

[8] Karl Deutsch has pointed out that governments of industrial societies, whether totali-

Governments must mobilize individuals to save, invest, pay taxes, serve in the army, obey laws. Modern governments must also know what the public will tolerate and must be able to anticipate, before policies are pursued, what the public reaction to a given policy might be. Moreover, the modern government is increasingly armed with sophisticated tools of economic analysis and public opinion surveys to increase its capacity to predict both the economic and political consequences of its actions. In contrast, the elites of new nations are constantly talking to the masses; it is not that they do not hear the masses, but what they hear is often so inappropriate to what they wish to do. To ban opposition parties, muzzle the press, and restrict freedom of speech and assembly does indeed close two-way channels of communication, but often this is precisely what is intended.

But whatever their fear of the masses, governmental elites in new nations cannot do without them. While the elite may be unsympathetic to mass efforts to exercise influence, the elite does want to mobilize the masses for its goals. In some developing societies an organizational revolution is already under way as men join together for increasingly complex tasks to create political parties, newspapers, corporations, trade unions, and caste and tribal associations. Governmental elites are confronted with a choice during the early stages of this development. Should they seek to make these new organizations instruments of the authoritative structures or should these organizations be permitted to become autonomous bodies, either politically neutral or concerned with influencing government? When the state is strong and the organizational structures of society weak—a condition often found in the early phases of postcolonial societies with a strong

tarian or democratic, spend a larger proportion of their GNP than do governments in underdeveloped economies, irrespective of their ideologies.

bureaucratic legacy—then government leadership clearly has such an option.[9] It is at this point that the classic issue of the relationship of liberty and authority arises, and the elite may choose to move in one direction rather than the other.

The choices made are often shaped by dramatic domestic or international crises of the moment. But they are also affected by the society's tradition of elite-mass relations. The traditional aloofness, for example, of the mandarin bureaucracy toward the Vietnamese populace and the traditional disdain of the Buddhist and Catholic Vietnamese toward the *montegnards* or "pagan" hill peoples have probably been more important factors affecting elite-mass relations in contemporary Vietnam than any strategic or ideological considerations on the part of the Vietnamese government. Similarly, the behavior of many African leaders can often be understood better by exploring the customary patterns of authority in traditional tribal society than by reference to any compulsions inherent in the development process.

In the analysis of elite-masses relations much attention is rightly given to the development of "infra-structures"— that is, political parties, newspapers, universities, and the like—which can provide a two-way communication channel between government and populace.[10] Much attention is also given to the development of a "middle strata" of individuals who can serve as links—newspapermen, lobbyists, party bosses, and precinct workers. While in the long run these developments are of great import-

ance, in the short run so much depends upon the attitude of the governmental elites, whether the elites fundamentally feel—and behave—as if they were alienated from and even antagonistic to the masses as they are, or whether the elites perceive the values of the masses as essentially being congruent to their own aims.

INTEGRATIVE BEHAVIOR

The readiness of individuals to work together in an organized fashion for common purposes and to behave in a fashion conducive to the achievement of these common purposes is an essential behavioral pattern of complex modern societies. Modern societies have all encountered organizational revolutions— in some respects as essential and as revolutionary as the technological revolution which has made the modern world. To send a missile into outer space, to produce millions of automobiles a year, to conduct research and development, to manage complex mass media all require new organizational skills. During the last few decades we have begun to understand the nature of managerial skills and the complexity of organizations— how they carry out their many purposes, how they adapt themselves to a changing environment, and how they change that environment. We know less about why some societies are more successful than others in creating men and women capable of establishing, maintaining, and adapting complex organizations for the achievement of common purposes.

The consequences of an organizational lag as an impediment to development are, however, quite apparent. The inability of many political leaders to maintain internal party and government unity in many new nations has resulted in the collapse of parliamentary government and the establishment of military dictatorships. The much vaunted organizational skill of the military has also often failed in many new nations. In Ceylon a planned military coup

[9] This theme is amplified by Fred W. Riggs, "Bureaucrats and Political Development: A Paradoxical View," *Bureaucracy and Political Development*, ed., Joseph LaPalombara (Princeton, N.J.: Princeton University Press, 1963).

[10] For a discussion of the role of infra-structures in political development, see Edward Shils, *Political Development in the New States* (The Hague: Mouton, 1962).

collapsed when several of the conspirators spoke of their plans so openly that even a disorganized civilian government had time to take action, and in many Latin American countries, and now in Vietnam, the military has proven to be as incapable of maintaining cohesive authority as their civilian predecessors.

The capacity—or lack of capacity—to organize with one's fellow men may be a general quality of societies. A society with a high organizational capacity appears to be organizationally competent at creating industrial organizations, bureaucracies, political parties, universities, and the like. Germany, Japan, the United States, the Soviet Union, Great Britain come quickly to mind. In contrast, one is struck by a generalized incompetence in many new nations where organizational breakdowns seem to be greater bottlenecks to economic growth than breakdowns in machinery. In some new countries technological innovations—such as industrial plants, railways, telegraph and postal systems—have expanded more rapidly than the human capacities to make the technologies work, with the result that mail is lost, the transport system does not function with any regularity, industrial managers cannot implement their decisions, and government administrative regulations impede rather than facilitate the management of public sector plants. Though some scholars have argued that the skill to create complex institutions will accompany or follow technological innovation, there is good reason to think that organizational skills are a prerequisite for much political and economic development. In fact, the pattern of interpersonal relations appears to be more conducive to organization-building in some traditional societies than in others. Just as the presence of entrepreneurial talents in the traditional society is a key element in whether or not economic growth occurs, so may the presence of organizational talents be an important element in whether there emerges a leadership with the capacity to run a

political party, an interest association, or a government.[11]

Surprisingly little is known about the conditions for the development of effectual political organizations. If the modernization process does produce political organizations, why is it that in some societies these organizations are effectual and in others they are not? By effectual, we mean the capacity of an organization to establish sufficient internal cohesion and external support to play some significant role in the decision-making or decision-implementing process. The multiplication of ineffectual political organizations tends to result either in a highly fragmented unintegrated political process in which government is unable to make or implement public policy, or in a political system in which the authoritative structures make all decisions completely independently of the political process outside of government. In the latter case we may have a dual political process, one inside of government which is meaningful and one outside of government which, in policy terms, is meaningless.

Some scholars have suggested that political organization is a consequence of increased occupational differentiation which in turn results from economic growth and technological change—an assumption, incidentally, of much foreign economic assistance. The difficulty with viewing political change as a consequence of social changes which in turn are the consequence of economic development is that, however logical this sequence may appear to be, in the history of change no such sequence can be uniformly found. Indeed, political organization often precedes large-scale economic change and

[11] For an attempt to relate traditional patterns of social and political relations to modern party-building, see Myron Weiner, "Traditional Role Performance and the Development of Modern Political Parties: The Indian Case," *Journal of Politics* (November 1964). The problems of party-building in a new nation are treated in my *Party-Building in a New Nation: The Indian National Congress* (in preparation).

may be an important factor in whether or not there is large-scale economic change.

In recent years greater attention has been given to the psychocultural components of political organization. Attention is given to the existence of trust and distrust and the capacity of individuals to relate personal ambition with some notion of the public good and of moral behavior. For explanations, psychologists focus on the process of primary socialization.

While psychologists focus on the working of the mind, sociologists and social anthropologists have been concerned with the working of society, and focus on the rules that effect the relationship among men—why they are kept and why they are broken. Sociologists have given attention to the complex of rules that organize social relationships, the patterns of superordination and subordination as among and between groups and individuals, how these change, and what effects they have on political and social relationships. While psychologists give attention to the primary process of socialization, sociologists and social anthropologists are concerned with the way in which the individual, during his entire life, comes to learn the rules and, under certain circumstances, to break them. It is from these two complementary views of man that we may expect the more systematic study of politically integrative and disintegrative behavior.

Conclusion

We have tried to suggest in this essay that there are many different kinds of integration problems faced by developing nations, for there are innumerable ways in which societies and political systems can fall apart. A high rate of social and economic change creates new demands and new tasks for government which are often malintegrative. The desire of the governing elite or the governed masses, for whatever reasons, to increase the functions of government are often causes of integration problems. Since modern states as well as modernizing states are often taking on new functions, it would be quite inappropriate to view integration as some terminal state. Moreover, the problems of integration in the developing areas are particularly acute because so many fundamentally new tasks or major enlargements of old tasks are now being taken on. Once the state actively becomes concerned with the mobilization and allocation of resources, new patterns of integration between elite and mass are called for. Once the state takes on the responsibilities of public education and invokes sentiments of "national" solidarity, then the integration of social groups to one another becomes an issue. And once men endeavor to create corporations, newspapers, political parties, and professional associations because they perceive their individual interests served by common actions, a new set of values is called for which provides for the integration of new structures into the political process. The challenges of integration thus arise out of the new tasks which men create for themselves.

IMPEDIMENTS TO UNITY IN NEW NATIONS: THE CASE OF CEYLON*

W. Howard Wriggins

In their search for nationhood since World War II, many peoples of Asia and Africa have discovered that independence from Western rule is only the first and perhaps the easiest step. Once the foreigner has gone, the larger problem looms of creating a viable political society. Divisions and competitive strivings held in check when outsiders controlled affairs are suddenly released. Ethnic, religious, and regional differences, that seemed less important so long as colonial administrators ruled, boil up after independence and more often than not come to dominate the loyalties and inspire the ambitions that move men in politics. To their dismay, responsible leaders find themselves heading not the homogeneous, modern nation-state they dreamed of before independence, but a congeries of separate groups. The simple, unifying purpose of the independence struggle fades away, leaving a host of contradictions and cleavages.

Indonesia is wracked by repeated resistance to Jakarta. Burma has been beset by periodic insurrection, supported in part by regional and ethnic hostility to Rangoon. The nightmare of India's Nehru is the growth of regional and linguistic differences. Imminent disintegration of the ex-Belgian Congo dramatizes the extreme case.

Are the difficulties impeding national consolidation mainly the fruit of irrespon-

sible political leadership, as ex-colonial administrators are tempted to allege? Are ill-considered linguistic and educational reforms to blame, reforms that wiser statesmanship could have avoided? What other social and political developments sharpen antagonisms and impede the building of a viable nation-state? Would more rapid economic development solve the problems of marked diversity, as the proponents of take-off aid programs often assert?

The Price of Union

No doubt repeated appeals to regional, ethnic or traditional differences stunt the growth of a sense of common nationhood. Yet political leaders usually have substantial reasons for stressing their attachment to such divisions in the body politic. Unlike the colonial administrator who preceded him, the elected politician must elicit support; he cannot impose allegiance. So long as the bulk of citizens are moved by appeals to local or traditional ties, there is no surer way of winning political backing than by demonstrating attachment to parochial loyalties. It remains an essential part of political campaigning in Scotland or Wales, as it does in Louisiana or in Maine. In Great Britain and the United States, to be sure, tacit understandings by now set bounds beyond which regional or certain other special interests cannot profitably be pressed at the expense of an overriding national interest. In new countries, the pressures for asserting regional, ethnic, or traditional values are many times greater, tacit understandings of the proper limits are not yet agreed upon, and people are little aware of a public interest that must take priority if the

SOURCE. W. Howard Wriggins, "Impediments to Unity in New Nations: The Case of Ceylon," *American Political Science Review*, **55**, 313–320, June 1961.

* This discussion develops ideas originally presented in a more detailed empirical context in the author's *Ceylon, Dilemmas of a New Nation* (Princeton University Press, 1960).

national community is to solve its problems effectively and survive.

In India, as Selig Harrison reminds us, many members of the Congress Party—and even the Communist Party—draw their strength mainly from regional or traditional interests so insistent that an over-arching identity with policies of concern to all of India in many instances is not possible. In Indonesia, many politicians and administrators feel impelled to insist upon regional interest, reenforced by traditional attachments and religious differences. Not even Sukarno can count any more upon a freely given nationwide support; he has had to reach adjustment with the army to help him hold the nation's multiplicity together. In Pakistan, differences between Urdu-speaking, moghul-influenced West Pakistan and Bengali-speaking, Hindu-influenced East Pakistan are profound. Any political man from East Pakistan who does not speak out for his region's peculiar interests is likely to lose indispensable political support at home. However understandable these political imperatives may be, it often appears that spokesmen for parochial interests press their claims excessively, disregarding the likely disruptive consequences to the whole of what they seek to achieve for the part.

In nearly all the countries of South and Southeast Asia, linguistic legislation and educational reform have had high priority. Yet governments and legislators on the side of the largest language group have persistently and seriously underestimated the strength of linguistic loyalties among minorities. In India, for example, legislation provides that Hindi shall replace English as the official language, at a pace defined by an official time-table. At the same time, the efforts to promote Hindi have sharpened minority anxieties about the larger ambitions of the Hindi-speaking segments of the population, and consolidated their loyalties to their own languages. In Malaya, Chinese are antagonized by Malay efforts to strengthen the position of Malay. In

Ceylon, Tamils have bitterly opposed efforts of the Sinhalese majority to raise the status of Sinhalese. Each such measure may promote national consolidation in the long run, but it usually favors immediately one group more than another, and changes the terms on which groups compete for opportunity, wealth, and power. Those who promote the reforms find it hard to imagine why the minorities should feel so bitter, a lack of empathy that impedes taking steps to assuage minority anxieties, or otherwise to ease what may be an unavoidable transition.

Educational reforms adopted on grounds of excellent principles—the right to universal education, for example, or the right to have children taught in the language of their parents—may have disruptive side effects which can be foreseen but are not taken seriously. A rapidly expanded school system without appropriate changes in the curriculum produces large numbers of educated citizens who are ambitious for status but for whom there are no proper jobs. Teaching children only in the vernaculars segregates them into ethnic groups from the outset and weakens communication between communities. A leadership which transcends the traditional differences such as developed, with all its inequities, under the British and to a more limited extent, under the French colonial systems is no longer produced. Neither by-product is examined with care, and sufficient counter-measures are not taken, with the result that communal awareness is heightened and competition for all-too-scarce opportunities is sharpened.

Economic development providing new opportunities and greater hope for the future would be likely to mitigate this competition in the long run, but in the politically crucial short run it does not eliminate the attachment to old divisions. At the outset, development is likely to favor those most adaptable and ready to seize new opportunities, who are often ethnic and linguistic minorities such as the Marwaris in India or aliens, like the

Chinese, in Indonesia. If this process is allowed to run its course, divisions and antagonisms are aggravated. If it is interrupted by political intervention in favor of the majority, resentments among these minorities are heightened. Improved means of communication may at first arouse more perception of group differences and sharpen conflicting ambitions.

Modernization may provoke its own reaction, as traditionalist groups organize to oppose innovation and to weaken the power of those who are responsible for it. Thus, in the short run, at least, modernization may increase group tensions. However much urbanization and industrialization may eventually free men from their traditional loyalties and make a new basis for integration possible, the transition is more likely to be immediately disruptive than to ease group relations.

The struggle for independence provokes the turning back to prewestern cultural roots. But as the early history of each country is explored, it is discovered that the ancestors of those presently engaged in common opposition to the European fought one another in bloody wars or gradual incursions upon one another's territory. When independence is finally achieved, these historical struggles take on a new urgency as groups compete for opportunity and status in the new country.

Hence, the task of national consolidation, however urgent it may be, poses very difficult problems. A close look at Ceylon's experience with relations between its majority and minority populations will illustrate these observations. The country's small size permits clearer analysis of interacting social, political, and economic factors than is possible in massive India or less organized Burma or Indonesia. Of all the new Asian countries, Ceylon seemed to have the best chance of making a successful transition to modern statehood. It began its independence most auspiciously with seasoned leadership drawn from nearly all important ethnic groups. The population was 60 per cent literate at independence. It had longer experience with nationwide elections on the basis of a universal franchise to represent single-member, territorial constituencies than any other country. Per capita GNP was higher than in any other country in the area apart from Japan. Its recent experience of relative harmony among classes and racial groups was such that there had been no insurrection, no partition, no sharp class struggle. Yet in 1956 and 1958, unprecedented riots left deep antagonisms that will be hard to soften in the future; the hitherto orderly processes of representative government were interrupted by emergency governor's rule, and the Prime Minister was assassinated.

A detailed examination of this deterioration where high hopes were entertained may shed some light on what other countries have in store. For despite their many differences, virtually all the former colonial countries on the edge of Asia share certain fundamental characteristics that complicate their search for national consolidation. First, there are fissures in the indigenous social order, often regionally defined, that separate ethnic, linguistic, and religious groups from one another. In most there are also important minorities who have come to the country within the past century, brought by European enterprisers or drawn by economic opportunities during the colonial period. Indian Tamils in Ceylon, Bengalis in Burma, Chinese in Thailand, Vietnam, and Indonesia are the legacy that must be dealt with. Both of these impediments to national unity are usually identified as "communal" differences, creating a "plural" or "mosaic" society. Second, the horizontal stratifications are no less important, dividing socioeconomic classes sharply from one another. By education, language, and culture, the leading elements are in many respects alien to the masses they must lead. The nearest analogues to this stratification in the contemporary West are perhaps to be found in Latin America, Spain, or southern Italy.

Impediments to Unity in Ceylon

THE SOCIAL STRUCTURE

The social structure of Asian countries provides an underlying element of disunity; the plural society in Ceylon is simpler than most others in the area. The majority Sinhalese community comprises nearly 70 per cent of the total population. There are two Tamil-speaking minorities: approximately 12 per cent of the population have lived on the island for many centuries; another 10 per cent are relative newcomers who arrived during the colonial period to man the tea and rubber estates and develop wholesale businesses. A Muslim minority of some 5 per cent and a Burgher community descended from mixed European and Ceylonese marriages form the balance.

The Sinhalese are largely Buddhists and speak Sinhalese, an Aryan language related to Bengali; the Tamils are Hindus who speak the Dravidian language Tamil. The Muslims, descendants of Arab traders, speak Sinhalese or Tamil and perhaps English as well, depending upon where they live. The Burghers claim English as their mother-tongue, though many speak Sinhalese too. Perhaps 8 per cent of the population are Christians, divided between Sinhalese and Tamils, though nearly all the Burghers are Christians. There are also caste groupings, less strict than in India, which need not detain us. These are the gross contours of the plural society in Ceylon.

Members of the Sinhalese and Tamil communities speak different languages, lead different lives, and follow differing family customs. Although many individuals in both communities are fully accepted within the other, the two groups hold unflattering views of each other. Their attitudes show clearly differentiated and mutually critical stereotypes. Sinhalese and Tamils consider themselves to be markedly different. Each sees in the other traits it does not admire. Group distrust lies not far beneath the surface. Each

community tends to form a network of mutual confidence and assistance when a member is faced with harm from those outside his own community. Some, though by no means all, trade unions, the Christian churches, larger business enterprises, and the public service have provided opportunities for mingling and common activity. The army, though drawing on all communities, remains small and professionalized, playing only a minor role in national integration. The communities are therefore brought together by few institutions.

Other divisions in the society complicate the fundamental Sinhalese-Tamil difference. In many ways as profound is the fissure that separates the mass of the population from the English-speaking, Western-educated elite who represent roughly 8 per cent of the total. An exact appraisal of this social distance is difficult, since the man who appears most at home in the Western offices or salons of the capital may quickly shed his Western ways when he returns to the family village. There are, of course, gradations in the degree of Westernization, from the Oxford graduate raised in an English-speaking Ceylonese family, at one extreme, to the graduate of grammar school who has learned his English after primary school, on the other. Yet the division between the trousered men who command English and the rest is a visible, striking reality, and one profoundly felt by the millions who are not part of that elite. It is significant because the distribution of wealth, opportunity, and power no longer depends alone upon family ties and family relations to the land, as in the traditional society. This is still important. But today, and for several generations already, real influence on the national stage and often wealth have depended in addition upon the acquired skills of English education and Western social ways.

Regardless of whether they were Sinhalese, Tamils, or Burghers in origin, the English-educated formed a stratum that lay across the ethnic and linguistic differences. These Tamils and Sinhalese had many close friendships that ignored communal lines. The English-educated articulated the desire for independence. Their vision usually encompassed all communities living in some degree of mutual acceptance in a gradually modernizing, unifying Ceylonese nationhood. As elsewhere in Asia, they inherited political power when the colonial rulers withdrew, in 1948.

But they were not politically homogeneous. Indeed, they competed among themselves for the opportunities of office. They were divided on political-ideological as well as religious grounds, and divisions were accentuated as their leading position in the society became less sure.

GROWING AWARENESS OF DIFFERENCES

Awareness of mutual differences has increased rather than diminished since independence. First, a cultural revival came to Ceylon only after independence, expressing the need to assert a cultural idiom distinct from Western ways. As Sinhalese and Tamils each explored their own pasts, they recalled battles won from the other; they gained a sense of inferiority or superiority toward each other. In their search, they found no common Ceylonese tradition, only separate Sinhalese and Tamil pasts. The state-wide alien rule no longer formed a common opponent uniting the different groups.

Second, an expanded educational system carried schooling to ever higher grades in the vernacular languages. More and more young people graduated from upper levels of the school system, reared entirely within one or the other vernacular culture without the unifying experience of English education.

Third, mutual understanding between the ethnic communities seemed to diminish. The vernacular press, for example, gained importance as literacy increased and as the wider masses became more actively concerned with public issues. This enhanced the distance between the Sinhalese and Tamils, since each vernacular paper tended to stress those aspects of public issues and cultural traditions which editors believed would appeal to their differentiated audiences. The press thus tended to provide contrasting and often contradictory interpretations of public problems to the different ethnic communities, hardening differences and sharpening distrust.

Fourth, with independence the Sinhalese majority expected that the Tamil and other minorities would assimilate to the Sinhalese way of life. But a sense of cultural superiority among the Tamils led them to resist the majority's effort to realize this expectation. Tamils feel a part of the capacious Indian tradition; they believe they have a culture rich in art, literature, and religious insight. Becoming part of the Sinhalese cultural world is taken to mean abandoning this great tradition. Conversely, a sense of Sinhalese cultural inferiority has made many in the majority community unusually sensitive. There are only 8 million Sinhalese in all the world. In Ceylon itself reside 2 million Tamil-speaking people; across in India there are some 28 million more. The Sinhalese are often fearful of being overwhelmed by their Tamil neighbors; the Ceylon Tamils fear being swamped by the island's majority Sinhalese. Ironically, both groups are beset with something akin to minority feelings, each oversensitive to the other's criticisms and fearful of the other's ambitions.

These differences set the stage for invidious communal comparisons. Moreover, modernization has not gone so far that an individual's professional or financial achievement is seen as his personal accomplishment. On the contrary, an individual's achievement still reflects more upon the position of his communal group. When communal differences become projected into politics, every act of members of one community is looked at for its political significance—to see, that is, whether it enhances or diminishes the relative political influence of his own community. Past political contests between communities are disinterred and over-elaborate political strategies and tactics are attributed to moves made by members of the other community that often had no political intention behind them.

Fifth, a growing awareness among the masses concerning the privileged position of the Westernized elite and a clearer cultural consciousness led to an increasing resentment against that elite. Articulate leaders of the independence movement from among the Westernized talked of welfare, of democracy, and of majority rule. But positions of control in the society were still filled by men of high birth or those fortunate enough to have been able to learn English. In a period of growing cultural self-awareness, this was not the democracy that had been preached by the leadership for many decades. The country still seemed to be ruled by an oligarchy of men alienated from indigenous traditions and cultures.

Moreover, their efforts to modernize their country, though cautious, provoked anxiety and resentment in important groups in the countryside who were among the intermediaries between the urban politicians and the rural masses. Practitioners of traditional *ayurvedic* medicine resented the resources invested in modern, Western-type medical services; Buddhist monks, keepers of the Sinhalese tradition, opposed the growing emphasis on materialistic values; vernacular teachers protested against their second-class professional status by comparison with the higher pay and respect accorded to English-speaking teachers; local officials opposed the growing influence and size of the capital's bureaucracy.

ECONOMIC COMPETITION

Awareness of economic competition increased as the population grew. The expanding school system turned out more liberal arts graduates who aspired to enter the coveted public service than the service could absorb. After an initial expansion to replace colonial officials and provide new economic and social service functions, public service hiring fell off just as more graduates began to enter the job market.

The students who could not find work form an articulate group, with time on their hands and an acute sense of grievance. They possess the skills necessary for political activity. Had there been other job opportunities, their frustrated ambitions for public service careers would not have mattered so desperately. But economic development that produced white collar jobs was disappointingly slow. The jobs they sought were not to be found in the government or elsewhere, and their liberal arts education had not fitted them for much else.

This increased the potentiality for tension between communities in part because the communal structure of Ceylon is relatively simple and readily lends itself to statistical comparisons. It was possible to argue, for example, that although the Sinhalese represented some 70 per cent of the population, they held only 60–65 per cent of the public service jobs, while the Ceylon Tamils, representing only 12 per cent of the population, held some 20 per cent of the jobs. In a time of growing unemployment in lower jobs as well, a politician could prove his devotion to the majority community by pointing the finger at the Tamils who had "usurped" more than their fair share of the best jobs.

Clearing and irrigating jungle land to be settled by peasants from the overcrowded Sinhalese and Tamil areas became a bitter apple of discord between the two communities. The land had lain under the rule of malaria, empty and desolate, until DDT made its reconquest possible. Tamils consider these new lands to be areas they have traditionally inhabited. The Sinhalese see much historical evidence to prove that Buddhist civilization once flourished before the jungle and malaria made their conquest. Both argue that settlement of peasants from the other community represents encroachment. And since political representation goes according to territorial constituencies, a significant change in the population structure of such areas would alter the balance of communal representation in the House of Representatives. Hence, even land development has sharpened group conflict.

POLITICAL IMPERATIVES

The background of political leaders and their electoral imperatives provided other potentialities for social tension.

The principal political figures have come from the Westernized elite. Broadly speaking, national electoral politics has been a struggle for office between men of this socio-economic class. Each has sought those relationships and issues that would carry influence and "project his image" across the social and linguistic gulf that separated him from the mass of voters. A convenient way of identifying himself with the voters was to demonstrate that he was more closely attached to the cultural and religious values of his constituents than his opponent, who could usually be charged with being too much like the former colonial rulers in style of life and language.

After independence, Ceylon was ruled by a coalition of moderately conservative men from the English-educated, land-owning, professional families in both Sinhalese and Tamil communities. Their support in the countryside was reenforced by the semi-feudal fact that the rural masses tended to vote the way the rural notable, landowner or employer wished. But as new men from lesser origins entered the Westernized elite, as cultural revival accented indigenous virtues often flouted by the more modern, Westernized man, as democratic ideology penetrated the countryside, the Westernized could not assume that their ruling position would continue. Their right to control affairs was bound to be tested. More direct appeals to mass sentiments often seemed the way to ensure continued political success.

Until 1956 the opposition parties were splintered, as in India, and the majority party could not be effectively challenged on the floor of the House of Representatives or at the hustings. The urban population was relatively small and underrepresented in a House designed to give greater representation to backward rural areas. Only if the opposition could undercut the government party in the countryside could it hope to displace the men who had ruled since independence.

In rural areas, between the notables and landowners who dominated national politics and the peasant and town masses, is a rural middle class of men who are prominent in their towns and villages. Buddhist monks, elected village officials, teachers skilled in the vernacular languages, practitioners of traditional *ayurvedic* medicine are such men. Opposition agitation in 1956 drew them into political activity that contributed decisively to the opposition's electoral victory that year. This agitation precipitated the elements of potential disunity into communal discord and violent conflict. The particular issue of import to them all concerned the matter of language.

Language and Politics

THE "LANGUAGE QUESTION"

It is difficult in the United States, where one language predominates, to appreciate the intensity of emotions that the "language question" can arouse. In a plural society, language distinguishes one man from his neighbor, gives him access to his own cultural tradition, is the canonical representation of his religion and the instrument for communicating about it. English had been the colonial ruler's language. Language differences had much to do with the distribution of opportunity, wealth, and political power. Widespread resentment against the airs and privileges of the English-educated, the power and aloofness of the English-speaking public service, the cultural snobbishness of the Westernized city man, made the demotion of English virtually inevitable.

As independence neared, two vexed questions of government policy toward the country's languages had to be answered. In what language should the children be taught and what should be the country's official language (or languages) of government?

After sharp and protracted debates, it was decided that Sinhalese and Tamil children should learn in their own language, while English would be taught as a second language. The policy solution was obvious enough, but the debates on the matter added to communal sensitivities. Each year they were renewed as the Opposition accused the government of not pressing ahead rapidly enough with the necessary language changeover in the higher grades of the schools. As a by-product of this decision—and significant for the long run—there would no longer be produced an island-wide elite from all communities who had passed together through the same educational experience.

ELECTORAL POLITICS

Intense feelings were provoked over the issue of the language or languages to be designated as official languages of state. Seeking to undercut the ruling coalition, the political opposition found the language question an unusually effective means for mobilizing the rural middle class in the majority community—the teachers, native physicians, the *bhikkhus* and local elected officials. Each one, for different reasons, experienced some sense of threat from Westernizing, modernizing changes or some resentment against the Westernized elite. Each rallied behind traditional communal symbols. They all believed that if Sinhalese were made the sole official language, their cultural and religious tradition would receive greater attention and their opportunities and status would be commensurately improved.

All who opposed making Sinhalese the sole official language were held to be standing in the way of legitimate—and national—aspirations. The Tamils opposed such a change and were therefore considered opponents. In the excitement of platform polemics, which were remarkably colorful and keyed to traditional allusions and indigenous fancy, many politicians made no distinction between Tamil invaders of 1000 years ago and contemporary Ceylon Tamils. Ancient antagonisms were thus revived and combined with contemporary competition for scarce opportunity and uncertain status.

Many among the Western-educated Sinhalese were generally opposed to the changes. But their will and power were sapped by two circumstances. In the first place, they feared that speaking out on behalf of moderation and a gradual transition to Sinhalese as the official language would turn the wrath of ardent Sinhalese against them, leading to the accusation that they were allies of the Tamils in a cause which they felt was all but lost already. Secondly, many experienced a growing sense of guilt that they had allowed themselves to become so alienated from their own tradition. In the name of their community's tradition, which they now sensed they had neglected, they were prepared to acquiesce in the changes even though these would seriously undermine their hitherto privileged position and risk bringing on dramatic communal difficulties.

As the Tamils saw it, to make Sinhalese the sole official language put Tamil in an inferior position and would no doubt give the Sinhalese-speaking people a competitive advantage as entrants to the public service, to teaching, university, and other desirable careers. Pride in their culture was hurt; even their status as accepted inhabitants of Ceylon seemed brought in doubt.

In the 1956 election, the Sinhalese opposition, skilfully led by Bandaranaike, was successful in displacing the formerly ruling United National Party by a landslide vote. The ruling party had been vulnerable on other counts as well, but it was primarily linguistic politics that brought it down.

ELECTORAL BY-PRODUCTS

As a by-product of the campaign, communal antagonisms were at a new high for the country. The successful Prime Minister

—like his defeated opponents—had assumed that communal antagonism could be turned up for tactical purposes and then turned down when the political need was gone. But new pressure groups organized among extremist Sinhalese and a vigorous minority of the clergy were not prepared to allow the new Prime Minister to moderate these antagonisms until their full aspirations were met. The Tamils, frightened by the upsurge of anti-Tamil sentiment, became more rigid.

Riots in 1956 followed close on the heels of the election and the debate in the House of Representatives over a language bill designed to give Sinhalese sole official standing. In the face of dramatic activities by the newly organized pressure groups, all provisions designed to safeguard Tamil interests were removed from the bill before it was submitted to debate. Starting in Colombo, vicious riots spread rapidly and over 100 were killed.

If bold political leadership, putting extremists on both sides in their place, might have cut through the fear and tension of communal intransigence, none appeared.

In 1958 more serious riots occurred. The police had become demoralized as a result of politically inspired transfers and because of restraining orders pressed upon the Prime Minister by his Marxist cabinet colleagues with political trade union interests to promote. The police were unable to restore order as rioting, looting, and burning spread. Several hundreds were killed—some say as many as 2000. In the end, 10,000 Tamils and 2000 Sinhalese sought refuge in army-managed refuge camps. When the army was finally called out, order was quickly restored. But a deeper gulf of fear now separated the minority Ceylon Tamil community from the majority Sinhalese.

As a tragic climax to these events, the Prime Minister was assassinated on his own verandah in September 1959 by a monk, a student of *ayurvedic* medicine. The case is under adjudication and there may be obscure political or even economic foundations for what at first appeared to be an act of a religious and cultural enthusiast who found the Prime Minister unable to carry out the promises he had made in the heat of political campaigning.

Conclusions

Apart from the tragedy of the hundreds killed during the riots and the assassination of the Prime Minister himself, the two rounds of communal riots left the country divided as it had not been for centuries. What conclusions can be drawn from these unhappy events?

1. The social structure of the plural society remains a stubborn social and political fact. Modernizing currents have not yet undermined the primary loyalty of the mass voters to traditional linguistic communities. A sense of Ceylonese nationhood is not yet clear.

2. Efforts to assert cultural independence from the West lead to explorations of the country's tradition. But this reaffirms diverse traditions and a past of local conflict which enlivens communal awareness and antagonisms. These differences increase after independence is achieved when the common opponent, the western ruler, no longer provides a focus for unifying antagonism.

3. Important rural middle class figures feel sufficiently threatened by modern, secular influences to be particularly susceptible to traditional appeals that have, as their by-products, profound communal implications. These men are potential intermediaries between the Westernized political leaders and opposition and the rural voters. They can therefore play an important role in politics when they are drawn into political activity, and they are by no means always carriers of modernization to the rural masses.

4. The earlier equation between education and opportunity has been disrupted and ever-higher levels of education are conducted in the vernaculars. Economic diversification and growth have not kept pace with expanding educational oppor-

tunities, resulting in a middle-class unemployment. This contributes particularly and directly to communal competition. Since the newly educated middle classes are largely trained in the vernacular languages, they identify only with their own parochial community. They do not comprehend a wider loyalty to the country as a whole, and they see their job futures in terms of their language community only.

5. Unavoidable decisions have to be made regarding the language or languages to replace English in the schools and in the government. These are bound to cause communal discord unless handled with great finesse.

6. Where a ruling elite is at a notable linguistic and cultural distance from the masses in a representative political system, those who seek to replace elected representatives may easily evoke communal and ethnic enthusiasms as a means of enlisting mass political support.

7. As one side effect of such electoral politics, communal anxieties may be greatly increased and new pressure groups develop to further press communal and religious claims. This stiffens the inflexibility of minority leaders and leaves a new government relatively little room for maneuver as it seeks an adjustment of contradictory claims.

8. A new government that is indecisive in domestic affairs and allows the vigor of the police to deteriorate unwittingly encourages extremists in both camps. Outbreaks of mob violence create further anxiety and antagonism for the future.

9. Rapid economic growth providing new opportunities to the most frustrated probably would mitigate such conflicts. In itself, however, it would not be sufficient to prevent them, and in the short run, at least, it may provide additional grounds for group antagonism.

In sum, those forces which divide, which separate one group from another grow in strength after independence—in school, in political activity and sometimes in economic life. Cultural revival enlivens the recollection of historic divisions and group conflicts; steps toward modernization arouse resistance from traditionalists who, feeling threatened, fall back on vernacular cultural values as protection. Rapidly expanding the liberal arts school system in the vernaculars at a time when the colonial administrator's *lingua franca* must be replaced produces educated unemployed, stops the creation of a nationwide elite, and provokes minority anxieties about their own future opportunities. Simultaneously, a Westernized elite at a cultural distance from the masses and not having solved important public problems, is an easy target of criticism and scorn for those who would use ethnic enthusiasm as a means of replacing the leaders who gained power at independence. As a result of such political developments, new pressure groups form around divisive, parochial purposes while new leadership may only encourage extremists if it is indecisive.

In the Ceylon setting, the Westernized elite no longer can be as self-assured as it used to be. Consolidation of ethnic communities into one nation is farther away today than it was ten years ago. The task of mending the social fabric will tax the skill and statesmanship of the new government of Mrs. Sirimavo Bandaranaike, widow of the former Prime Minister, whose electoral coalition won handsomely in June 1960. In other new countries, too, national consolidation remains one of the crucial problems of the future, demanding quite as much courage and foresight as the more familiar problems of economic development.

BREAKDOWNS OF MODERNIZATION*

S. N. Eisenstadt

I

The optimism which guided much of the concern with and many of the studies of underdeveloped areas or new nations, and which assumed that these countries were advancing—even if slowly and intermittently—towards full-fledged modernization and continuous growth, has lately given way to a much more cautious and even pessimistic view. This pessimism has been mainly due to the fact that in many new nations, where initially modern frameworks were established in different institutional fields, especially in the political one, the progress towards modernization was not only slow, but also these constitutional regimes faltered, giving way, in their place, to various autocratic and authoritarian or semi-authoritarian regimes. Indonesia, Pakistan, Burma, and Sudan are perhaps the most important recent examples of this trend.[1]

The purpose of this paper is to analyze the nature of the social processes in these countries which led to these changes, to what may be called breakdowns in their political modernization.

II

The significant characteristic of the developments in these countries is not that the "take off" from a traditional setting to modernity did not fully materialize within them.

In almost all these countries attempts were made to establish modern political and social frameworks and institutions, and many aspects or characteristics of such institutions—be they constitutions, modern bureaucratic administrations, political parties, or modern economic enterprises—were initially established. Similarly, many important indices of modernization— be they socio-demographic indices like urbanization, literacy or exposure to mass

SOURCE. S. N. Eisenstadt, "Breakdowns of Modernization," *Economic Development and Cultural Change*, **12**, 345–367, July 1964. Reprinted by permission of The University of Chicago Press. Copyright 1964 by The University of Chicago Press.

* This paper was written in 1962–63, when the author was Carnegie Visiting Professor of Political Science at the Massachusetts Institute of Technology, Cambridge, Massachusetts. The author is indebted to Professor R. N. Bellah, F. W. Frey, and M. Wiener for comments on earlier parts of this paper. Work on this problem was facilitated by a grant-in-aid from the Wenner Gren Foundation for Anthropological Research.

[1] On Indonesia see: H. Feith, *The Decline of Constitutional Democracy in Indonesia* (Ithaca: Cornell University Press, 1962); W. A. Hannah, *Bung Karno's Indonesia* (New York: American Universities Field Staff, 1961); and G. Y. Pauker, "Indonesia, Internal Developments of External Expansion," *Asian Survey*, **14**, 2 (February 1963), 69–76.

On Burma: E. R. Leach, "L'avenir Politique

de la Birmanie," *Bull Sedeis*, *Furibles*, Paris, November 1962; L. W. Pye, *Politics*, *Personality, and Nation Building* (New Haven: Yale University Press, 1962); L. Walinsky, *Economic Development in Burma, 1951–1960* (New York: Twentieth Century Fund, 1962); and John H. Badgley, "Burma, the Nexus of Socialism and Two Political Traditions," *Asian Survey*, **3**, 2 (February 1963), 89–96.

On Pakistan: K. B. Sayeed, *Pakistan, the Formative Phase* (Karachi: Pakistan Publishing House, 1960); K. J. Newman, "Pakistan's Preventive Autocracy and Its Causes," *Pacific Affairs*, **32**, 1 (March 1959), 18–34; K. B. Sayeed, "The Collapse of Parliamentary Democracy in Pakistan," *Middle East Journal*, **13**, 4 (1959), 389–406; R. Wheeler, "Pakistan, New Constitution, Old Issues," Asian Survey, **3**, 2 (February 1963), 107–116; H. Tinker, *India and Pakistan* (New York: Praeger, 1962); L. F. R. Williams, "Problems of Constitution Building in Pakistan," *Asian Review* (n.s.), **58** (July 1962), 151–160; and K. Callard, *Pakistan, a Political Study* (New York: Macmillan, 1957).

media, some diversification of the occupational structure, or structural indices like weakening of traditional frameworks, growing differentiation, the development of some modern forms of political organization like interest groups and parties—could be found, to some extent at least, continuously expanding in these societies.[2] Although large parts of these societies are still traditional in the sense of being confined to relatively close autarchic units, they are rapidly becoming "de-traditionalized" and are continuously drawn into wider, more differentiated and specialized institutional frameworks. And yet, in these societies, all these developments did not give rise to the development, especially in the political field, of viable modern institutional systems capable of absorbing continuously changing, diversified problems and demands. Many such institutional frameworks which were established in the initial period of modernization became disorganized and unable to function, giving place to the less differentiated, usually more autocratic or authoritarian regimes.

In other words, there developed in these societies several important indices of economic modernization—some changes in the relative product shares by major sectors of the economy and in per-capita real income—and of political modernization. Among these the most important were, first, the development of a highly differentiated political structure in terms of specific political roles and institutions, of the centralization of the polity, and of

development of specific political goals and orientations.

Second, political modernization here, as in general, was characterized by a growing extension of the scope of the central legal, administrative, and political activities and their permeation into all spheres and regions of the society.

Third, it was characterized by the weakening of traditional elites and traditional legitimation of rulers and by the establishment of some sort of ideological and often also institutional accountability of the rulers to the ruled, who are the holders of the potential political power. The formal expression of this process is the system of elections as it has evolved, in different ways, in most modern political systems.

Moreover, in all these spheres in the societies there also developed another crucial aspect of modernization—namely, the structural propensity to continuous change. Hence, they all faced the most crucial test of modernization, i.e., the ability to maintain "sustained" growth in the major institutional spheres and to develop an institutional structure capable of absorbing such changes with relatively few eruptions and breakdowns.

But it was exactly here that the major problems of the countries studied arise. Despite the development of the various socio-demographic and structural indices of modernization, they did not develop within them a viable institutional structure which was able to deal with the problems generated by the socio-demographic and structural changes, and at least in the political field, they changed to less differentiated, less flexible, institutional frameworks which were able to cope with a smaller range of problems.

In some of these cases, like Pakistan and perhaps Sudan, these "reversals" in the political field did not undermine the possibilities of some economic growth and may even have facilitated it. In others, like Indonesia and seemingly also Burma, the breakdown of the constitutional regime was paralleled by economic stagnation.

[2] On the concepts of modernization as used or implied in the present analysis see S. N. Eisenstadt, "Bureaucracy and Political Development," in J. LaPalombara, ed., *Bureaucracy and Political Development* (Princeton, N.J., 1963); and my *Modernization, Diversity, and Growth* (Bloomington: Indiana University, Department of Government, 1953). See also D. Lerner, *The Passing of Traditional Society* (Glencoe: Free Press, 1958).

For a pertinent economic analysis, see D. S. Paauw, "Economic Impacts in Southeast Asia," *Journal of Asian Studies*, **23**, 1 (November 1963), 69–73.

III

But although most of these societies have by now "reverted," as it were, to a level of social and especially political institutions which can be—as we shall see—seen as less flexible or differentiated than that at which they presumably started in their initial stages of modernization, yet in almost none of them did there take place a complete reversal to truly traditional types of central social institutions.

This is manifest in several interconnected ways. Although in many cases the few autocratic or authoritarian elites behave as if in the "traditional" (whether colonial, as in Pakistan, or "pre-colonial" regal, as in Burma) manner, or attempt to utilize traditional symbols and attitudes, they were not able or perhaps even willing to revert entirely to a traditional, pre-modern political structure. Some external, but still important, symbols of modernity—such as universal suffrage (even if suspended), some modern legal frameworks, were, officially at least, maintained. What is even more important is that these new rulers of elites portrayed their own legitimation in secularized, modern terms and symbols—in terms or symbols of social movements or of legal rationality and efficiency, rather than in terms of purely traditional values. This is true even in those cases, as that of Pakistan, where the emphasis on some aspects of the Islamic tradition has been relatively strong, or where, as in Indonesia, the search for new symbols or ideology was strongly couched in traditional terms.

Whatever accountability the new rulers of these societies evinced towards their subjects was not usually couched in terms of the older "religious" mandate of the ruler, but mainly in terms of more modern values or charisma in which, in principle, at least, the citizens participated or shared with the rulers. Whatever the limitations on political activities these regimes may have attempted to establish they did not abandon the idea of the citizen as distinct from the older (traditional and colonial) idea of a subject.[3]

Similarly, however anti-Western or anti-capitalist the ideologies of these regimes were, they did not entirely negate modernity. Rather, they attempted to discover or rediscover some synthesis between what they thought might be the "basic"—those undiluted by accidents of history or by materialistic orientations—values and elements of both their own tradition and those of modernity. Such attempts or formulations may have been pure utopian expressions of pious intentions without the ability or will to pay any institutional price demanded for their implementations.

Again, however actually stagnant or inefficient many of the institutional frameworks of these societies may have been before or become after the changes in their regimes, they have but rarely set themselves actively against the expansion of all of the social aspects or processes of modernization, such as education, economic development and industrialization, or rural development.

Thus we do not have here cases of non-development of modernization, or a lack of "take off" to modernization, but rather of breakdown of some (especially political) modern institutions—even if in the cases mentioned above, this breakdown took place in relatively early phases of modernization. From this point of view, these developments are not entirely dissimilar from others in the history of development of modern societies—which have been perhaps recently forgotten, although some of them did form, in their time,

---

[3] On Burma see Leach, *op. cit.*, and Badgley, *op. cit.* On Pakistan see W. I. Jennings, ed., *Constitutional Problems in Pakistan* (Cambridge: Cambridge University Press, 1958); see also the discussion between L. A. Sherwani and D. P. Singhal, "The 1962 Pakistani Constitution: Two Views," *Asian Survey*, 2 (August 1962), 9–24; and L. Binder, *Religion and Politics in Pakistan* (Berkeley and Los Angeles: University of California Press, 1961). For Indonesia see Feith, *op. cit.*, Hannah, *op. cit.*, and Pauker, *op. cit.*

foci of both public interest and of sociological analysis.

The case of the initial modernization of China, so often used as a negative example in comparison with the more successful initial modernization of Japan, comes here immediately to mind.[4] Similarly, the long history of several Latin American countries may come into the picture. Although in many of them there developed over a very long time only the very minimal structural or socio-demographic features of modernization; in other cases, as in Chile and especially in pre-Peron Argentina, an evident progress to modernization was halted or reversed.[5]

Lastly, the example of the rise of militarism in Japan and especially of Fascism and Nazism in Europe in the 'twenties and 'thirties should also be mentioned here as perhaps the most important case of breakdown of modernization, at much more advanced levels of development.[6]

In all these cases we witness the breakdown of relatively differentiated and modern frameworks, the establishment of a less differentiated framework or the development of a long series of vicious circles of underdevelopment, of blockages and eruptions often leading to institutionalized stagnation and instability and to the lack of ability to absorb continuous changes. Thus, all these developments took place within the frameworks of processes of modernization as parts of these processes. They can be seen as pathologies or breakdowns of modernization, or, as in the case of Nazism, as attempts at what might be called demodernization—but not as cases of lack of or of tardy modernization.

IV

The "external" story of all these cases is, on the face of it, relatively simple and straightforward and, in most of these cases, similar in very broad outlines, despite the great differences in detail and setting.

One basic characteristic of this story is the development of continuous internal warfare and conflict between different groups within the society, the development of extreme antagonism and cleavages without the possibility of finding any continuous and viable *modus vivendi* between them. These conflicts, the details of which have, of course, greatly varied from case to case, were also usually closely connected with continuous economic crises and, very often, with growing uncontrolable inflation. These crises, in their turn, were often fed by these very continuous conflicts and by the lack of consensus and of any clear policy of how to deal with them.

Continuous strong conflicts and cleavages over a very great variety of issues and economic deterioration and the lack of any strong acceptable leadership which could enforce legitimate authority and regulate these conflicts and problems, together with the growing corruption and

---

[4] For one of the most pertinent statements of the problem, see Marion J. Levy, Jr., "Contrasting Factors in the Modernization of China and Japan," in S. Kuznets, W. E. Moore, and J. J. Spengler, eds., *Economic Growth: Brazil, India, Japan* (Durham: Duke University Press, 1955), pp. 496–537. A recent survey is G. M. Beckman's *The Modernization of China and Japan* (New York: Harper and Row, 1963). See also Li Chien-Nung, *The Political History of China, 1840–1928*, ed. and transl. by Ssu-yu Teng and Jeremy Ingalls (Princeton: Van Nostrand, 1956),

[5] On Argentina in the 'twenties and 'thirties, see G. Pendle, *Argentina* (London: Oxford University Press, 1961), esp. Chs. 4, 5; also, A. Goletti, *La Realidad Argentina en el Siglo XX, La Politica y Los Partidos* (Mexico: Fondo de Cultura Economica, 1961), esp. Chs. 4, 5, 6. A general survey can be found also in *Argentina 1930–60*, ed. SUR (Buenos Aires, 1961), esp. P. II. See also Sergio Bagu, "La Estructuracion Economica en la Etapa Formativa de la Argentina Moderna," *Desarollo Economico*, Buenos Aires, **1**, 2 (July–September 1961), 113–129.

[6] On Japan see R. A. Scallapino, "Japan between Traditionalism and Democracy," in S. Neumann, ed., *Modern Political Parties* (Chicago: University of Chicago Press, 1956), pp. 305–354. On Germany see S. Neumann, "Germany—Changing Patterns and Lasting Problems," in *ibid.*, pp. 345–394.

inefficiency of the bureaucracy—which went beyond the scope of "traditional" corruption—have often been singled out for the explanation of the downfall of these regimes.[7]

While there can be no doubt that these explanations account at least partially for these developments, in a way, they do not go far enough. Conflicts or economic problems of what may seem as initially alarming magnitudes did probably exist and have been resolved, even if only partially, in other modern or modernizing countries. What is, therefore, of crucial importance is the fact that in the countries under consideration, these conflicts were not resolved or regulated. As a result, they spiralled into a continuous series of vicious circles which undermined the stability and continuity of the emerging modern frameworks.

V

In order to be able to explain why, in the countries studied here, these conflicts were not solved, we might attempt first to analyze the nature of some of the major developments in several institutional spheres in these societies. At this stage, this analysis will not go beyond a description of these developments and will not explore their causes. But we hope it will help to articulate the problems to be explored.

Let us start with developments in the political sphere. The most general trend that developed in this sphere in these societies was a marked discrepancy between the demands of different groups—parties, cliques, bureaucracy, army, regional groups—and the responses and ability of the central rulers to deal with these demands.

The levels of these demands were either higher or much lower (i.e., more or less

articulated) than the level of aggregation and policy making within the central institutions.[8] In most of these cases, the demands of most social groups oscillated continuously between highly articulated types of political demands, as manifest in the formation of varied interest groups and of social movements with a high level of political intensity, on the one hand, and on the other the more primitive, less articulated types, demands typified by direct pressures on the bureaucracy, as manifested in petitioning the local potentates (or bureaucracy) and central rulers and infrequent mob outbreaks.

The power position of the various groups making these varied demands has greatly increased as a result of the processes of modernization. They could no longer be suppressed and neglected, but at the same time ways of integrating them in some orderly way were found. There developed but few middle range institutional frameworks within which these varied types of political demands could become regulated and translated into concrete policy demands and policies. The leadership of the parties or of the varied movements was not able to aggregate these varied interests and political orientations in some relatively ordered way or to develop adequate policies to deal with the different demands of the major groups and with major problems to which these demands were related.

The formal institutions appropriate for such aggregation and policy formation existed in these societies in the form of central executive, administrative and legislative organs, on the one hand, and of various parties on the other, but they were not able to perform effectively such aggregation or policy formulation.

[7] For detailed description of these processes in some of these countries, see Feith, *op. cit., passim;* Callard, *op. cit.,* W. A. Wilcox, *Pakistan, The Consolidation of a New Nation* (New York: Columbia University Press, 1963) and also Chou Shun-hsiu, *The Chinese Inflation* (New York: Columbia University Press, 1963).

[8] The terms "articulation," "aggregation," etc., are used here mostly as in G. Almond and J. Coleman, eds., *The Politics of the Developing Areas* (Princeton: Princeton University Press, 1960). The various case studies presented in this book contain excellent background material and analysis for the problems discussed here.

Nevertheless, there existed within these political systems some organs—such as organs of bureaucratic administration and of local government or traditional communal units—which were able to deal with less articulated types of demands. Following the overthrow of these regimes, they became again very important foci of political processes and aggregation, as they often were in the colonial or even pre-colonial times. But during the preceding period, even their functioning was not very efficient, because they were subordinate to the more differentiated but ineffective agencies and were caught up in the various uncertainties which developed within these agencies. Hence, these organs —and especially the bureaucracy—became very often both inefficient and corrupt.[9]

Thus, the most important characteristic of the political situation in these countries has not been the mere existence of numerous conflicts or of different levels of articulation of demands, or even the lack of full coordination between these different levels—a situation which can be easily found in relatively stable traditional regimes. But in the societies studied here, because of the push to modernization, these different levels of political demands and activities were not, as in many premodern regimes, kept in relatively segregated, even if interlocked, compartments, but were brought into relatively common frameworks of political process and decision making. At the same time, within this framework adequate mechanisms and principles of aggregating them or of regulating the conflicts attendant on their development did not develop. In other words, the new values that many people wanted to realize in these societies demanded a relatively high level of coordination of individual behavior, and no structure of power and organization linking these individuals and the new, more articulated, demands and activities

[9] R. Braibanti, "Reflections on Bureaucratic Corruption," *Public Administration*, **40** (Winter 1962), 357–372.

has been created—even the older structure might have broken down.

VI

A similar picture emerges if we examine the nature and scope of what may be called eruptions and movements of protest that have developed in these societies. In terms of the contents of the symbols that have been developed or taken over by these movements, they were not necessarily different from the whole range of such symbols that had developed during different periods or stages of modernization in European, Asian, and African countries.[10] They ranged from nationalistic, anticolonial, traditionalistic, ethnic symbols through symbols of social protest or economic deprivation up to various symbols of cultural renovation coined in anti-Western terms or in terms of religious and communal revival.

They were probably—but not always and not necessarily—more extreme in the intensity of their protest than those that could be found in other, more sedate movements. But beyond this, some other more crucial characteristics of these movements and symbols stand out.[11] First was the relative closeness, separateness, and segregation of these different movements. Second was their sectarian nature, on the one hand, and their intermittency and alternation between brief periods of highly intensive eruptions and long periods of stagnation and inactivity, on the other. Third, within many such sectarian and mutually hostile movements there often developed a coalescence of different, seemingly conflicting values or social

[10] See, for a good collection of some of their ideologies: P. E. Sigmund, Jr., *The Ideologies of the Developing Nations* (New York: Praeger, 1963); and also J. H. Kautsky, "An Essay in the Politics of Development," in —, ed., *Political Change in Underdeveloped Countries* (London: Wiley, 1962), pp, 3–123.
[11] See S. N. Eisenstadt, *Essays on Sociological Aspects of Political and Economic Development* (The Hague: Mouton, 1961), where also a full bibliography is given.

orientations—such as those of traditionalism and economic development or of traditionalism and democracy. These different orientations were not usually organized or coordinated in a way which would make them meaningful, not only in terms of the momentary situation, but also in terms of some continuous activity, policy formulation, and implementation.

This was an important indicator of the lack of predisposition on the part of these various movements to become incorporated or transposed into wider frameworks, parties, or informal organs of public opinion, and of the lack of adaptation to such wider regulative frameworks. This lack of predisposition on the part of the movements was often matched by the lack of ability on the part of the ruling institutions to absorb these various symbols and orientations into their own frameworks.

As a result of these characteristics, the movements of protest and of opposition in these countries oscillated between apathy, withdrawal of the interest of wider groups and strata from the central institutions, on the one hand, and very intensive outbursts which made extreme demands on these institutions, demands for total, immediate change of the regime or of the place of any given group within this regime, on the other hand.

VII

A similar picture emerges if we analyze the characteristics of structure and processes of communication within these societies. One such characteristic has been the existence of different patterns of communication among different strata—the more traditional, closed patterns of communication within the confines of the villages, and the more differentiated, sophisticated systems of the central elites or urban groups. Second, the communicative structure in these societies was often characterized by the lack of what has been called "communicative mediators" or brokers between these different levels of communicative activities.[12] Third, it was characterized by a continuous oscillation of wide groups and strata between communicative apathy towards the central institutions of the society, on the one hand, and predilection to mob excitement and activity and succumbance to agitation, on the other hand. Fourth, there tended to develop in these societies vicious circles of oversensitivity to various mass media and the lack of ability to absorb these stimuli in some continuous and coherent way.

Thus, here, as in the political sphere, the most important characteristic is not the mere existence of different levels or types of communication—not even the relative weakness of some of the intermediary links between these different levels. Rather, the crucial characteristic of the structure of communication in these countries was the bringing together of different types of communicative behavior into a relatively common framework, exposing them to similar or common stimuli without the development among them of some stable patterns of receptivity to these stimuli.

The same situation can, of course, be found in the economic sphere proper. The major ills or economic problems of these societies were due not only to low levels of development of their economies

[12] See L. W. Pye, "Communication Patterns and the Problems of Representative Government in Non-Western Societies," *Public Opinion Quarterly*, **20** (Spring 1956), 249–257. On the structure of traditional communications, see S. N. Eisenstadt, "Communication Systems and Social Structure: An Exploratory Comparative Study," *Public Opinion Quarterly*, **19** (Summer 1955), 153–157; and —, *The Political Systems of Empires* (New York: Free Press, 1963). The most comprehensive recent work is L. W. Pye, ed., *Communication and Political Development* (Princeton: Princeton University Press, 1963), esp. the chapters by E. Shils, "Demagogues and Cadres in the Political Development of New States," pp. 64–78; H. Hyman, "Mass Media and Political Socialization, The Role of Patterns of Communication," pp. 128–149; and D. Lerner, "Towards a Communication Theory of Modernization," pp. 327–351.

and to lack of available skills or their depletion because of external events, but also, above all, to the discrepancies between the push to modernization and the institutional ability to sustained growth, between the continuous disruption of the traditional frameworks and the impossibility of finding adequate outlets in the new, modernized frameworks.

We see in all these institutional spheres a very similar situation, a situation of bringing together of different groups, of growing interdependence and mutual awareness of these different groups, but at the same time also of the lack of development of adequate new common norms which would be to some extent at least binding on these groups and which could help to regulate their new interrelationships.

VIII

This inadequate development of new integrative mechanisms has been manifest in several aspects of institutional developments and of crystallization of symbols in these societies.

One of the most important indications of this situation could be found in the development, in all institutional spheres but perhaps especially in the political one, of a sharp dissociation between what has been called solidarity makers, on the one hand, and the instrumentally task-oriented leaders and administrators, on the other hand.[13]

This distinction is not necessarily identical with that between politicians and administrators, and it may well cut across them, although, obviously, the politicians may be more prone to become "solidarity makers" while the government official may be more prone to an instrumentally

[13] See Feith, *op. cit.*, pp. 113–122; and S. N. Eisenstadt, "Patterns of Political Leadership and Support," paper submitted to the International Conference on Representative Government and National Progress, Ibadan, 1959; and E. A. Shils, *Political Development in the New States* (The Hague: Mouton, 1962), *passim*, esp. the discussion on civility.

oriented leader. Rather, it applies to two basic aspects or facets which are inherent in any political (and social) system, although they may greatly vary in their exact structural location in different political structures. The development of such a dissociation was fully described by Feith for Indonesia, but can also be found in many of the other countries studied here.[14] Truly enough, in some of the new states one of these types—especially the relatively modern, efficient administrator—might have been almost entirely lacking; but in most of the cases, cadres developed of relatively skilled people who were able to organize various administrative agencies, to develop new economic enterprises and some mechanisms or organs of organizational activity, and to attempt to establish some policies based on these rules. Many such groups or cadres came from the colonial administration; others developed as a result of economic development or programs of educational expansion.

But in most of the cases studied, the rules, injunctions, and policies developed by these cadres, leaders, or organizations were not legitimized or upheld by new common symbols and by those leaders or groups who upheld and developed these new symbols. The new symbols which were developed or upheld in these countries did not seem valid or relevant to the more mundane problems with which the rules developed by the "instrumental" cadres dealt. While some discrepancy between such different orientations is probably inherent in any political system, its extent was, in the cases discussed here, much more acute and extreme. This discrepancy could be found in all the countries studied here. Thus, for instance, in Indonesia we find that the sets of symbols and value orientations continuously developed by Sukarno and by the major parties were not only incapable of addressing themselves to the manifold problems of modernization, but negated, as it were, their existence and

[14] Feith, *op. cit.*, *passim*; and Shils, *op. cit.*, *passim*.

significance, although at the same time these problems were besetting the body politic. In Burma the mixture of symbols of Buddhism and socialism developed by U Nu, especially after the first military takeover, dealt only with the most marginal of concrete problems besetting Burmese political life.[15]

In Pakistan, the constitutional debates about the nature of the state in general and the Islamic state in particular did not greatly help the solution of the many acute administrative, economic, and political problems besetting this state in the first stages of its development.[16] In Kuomingtang China, the persistence of many traditional Confucian orientations which did not undergo an internal modernizing transformation gave rise to a mixture of "traditionalist" orientations and symbols and more extremist anti-modern or anti-Western symbols, none of which could provide adequate guidance to many of the new problems attendant on the development of modernization.[17]

The situation in some of the Latin American countries—especially in Argentina in the 'thirties—while different in details from that in the new states discussed above, exhibited several similar characteristics. There the older oligarchic elites were able to deal only to a limited extent with the new economic and political problems attendant on a continuous modernization. This limited ability of theirs and the continuously growing politizations of the broader state of the society gave rise to a continuous oscillation between repressive dictators and demagogues. Each of these tried to use different types of solidarity symbols. But what they usually had in common was the dissociation of these symbols from the various concrete economic, administrative, and political problems which were developing with continuous immigration, colonization, and economic development.[18]

[15] See Hannah, *op. cit.*; R. Butwell, "The Four Failures of U Nu's Second Premiership, *Asian Survey*, **2**, 1 (March 1962), 3–12; F. R. Von der Mehden, "The Changing Pattern of Religion and Politics in Burma," in R. K. Sakai, ed., *Studies in Asia* (University of Nebraska Press, 1961), pp. 63–74; M. Sarkiyana, "On the Place of U Nu's Buddhist Socialism in Burma's History of Ideas," in *ibid.*, pp. 58–63. See also M. M. Kitagawa, "Buddhism and Asian Politics," *Asian Survey*, **2**, 5 (July 1962), 1–12; and H. Feith, "Indonesia's Political Symbols and Their Wielders," *World Politics*, **16**, 1 (October 1963), 79–98.

[16] See Binder, *op. cit.*; and Sayeed, *Pakistan...*, *op. cit.*

[17] See, for instance, Generalissimo Chiang Kai-Shek, *Resistance and Reconstruction, Messages during China's Six Years of War* (New York: Harper), esp. pp. 84 ff., 94 ff., 155 ff.; and —, *China's Destiny and Chinese Economic History* (with notes and commentary by Philip Jaffe) (New York: Roy, 1942). See also H. R. Isaacs, *The Tragedy of the Chinese Revolution*, rev. ed. (Stanford: Stanford University Press, 1957).

[18] For Argentina within the setup of Latin America, see G. Germani, *Politica y Sociedad en Una Epoca de Transicion* (Buenos Aires: Ed Paidos, 1963), esp. Part IV; see also K. Silvert, "Liderazgo Politico y Debilidad Institutional de la Argentina," *Desarollo Economico*, **1**, 3 (October–December 1961), 155–182; and J. M. Saravia, "Argentina 1959," *Estudio Sociologico* (1959).

For broader aspects of Latin American social structures relevant for the present discussion, see Germani, *op. cit.*, Part III; K. Silvert, *The Conflict Society, Reaction and Revolution in Latin America* (New Orleans: Hauser, 1961); and also E. de Vries and M. Echavarrie, eds., *Social Aspects of Economic Development in Latin America* (Paris: UNESCO, 1963), esp. the papers by J. Lambert, "Requirements for Rapid Economic and Social Development," pp. 50–67; R. Vekemans and J. L. Segundo, "Essay of a Social Economic Typology of the Latin American Countries," pp. 67–94; J. Ahumada, "Economic Development and Problems of Social Change in Latin America," pp. 115–148; and F. Fernandes, "Patterns and Rate of Development in Latin America," pp. 187–211. See also G. Germani and K. Silvert, "Politics, Social Structure, and Military Intervention in Latin America," *European Journal of Sociology*, **2**, 4 (1961), 62–82.

For some important comparative data see T. Di Tella, "Tensiones Sociales de los Paises de la Periferrie," *Revista de Universidad de Buenos Aires*, V Epoca, Ano VI, No. 1 (1961), 49–62; F. Fernandes, *Mudanças Sociais no Brasil* (Sao Paulo: Difusao Europea do Libro, (1960); —, "Reflexoes sobre a Mudança

Similarly, in Japan in the late 'twenties and early 'thirties, the various conservative elites—whether they were the remnants of the older Meiji oligarchy or some of the conservative circles and new military groups—tried to uphold, in the face of growing problems attendant on industrialization, some of the older general symbols of patriotism and imperial loyalty, which were not adequate to deal with these new problems attendant on continuous industrialization and modernization.[19]

The rift between the different elites about the attitudes to modernity and industrialization in pre-Fascist Italy and pre-Nazi Germany is too well known to need any further elaboration or illustration here.

IX

A similar situation can be discerned in the processes of development of the new central symbols in relation to those partial groups or sectors of the society.... The various separate particularistic "primordial" symbols of local, ethnic, caste, or class groups were not incorporated into the new center of the society, and their reformation on a new level of common identification did not take place. Hence, these symbols tended to become points of structural separateness and impediments for the development of a new civil order.

It was not the mere persistence of these symbols that was of crucial importance, but rather the fact that they were not in-

corporated into the more central symbolic framework which had to be oriented towards the more differentiated and variegated problems that developed in these societies as a result of the continuous process of modernization and the growing interaction between the different groups within them. Or, in other words, no new ideology or value and symbol system developed at the center which could provide some minimal acceptable meaning and framework of answers to the varied problems stemming from the new social situation.[20]

X

If we attempt to summarize the description of the situations in the countries analyzed above, two aspects seem to stand out. First, in all the cases analyzed here, there tended to develop, in almost all the institutional spheres, a situation of growing interaction between different groups and strata of their being drawn together into new common frameworks, of growing differentiation, and at the same time of lack of adequate mechanisms to deal with the problems attendant on such internal differentiation, and on the growing interaction between the various groups. This coming together of different groups into common social frameworks may have been intermittent and unequally distributed between different groups and strata of the population. But from all these points of view, it is extremely doubtful whether it differed greatly from developments in other modernizing or modern societies at similar levels of modernization which were

[*footnote 18 continued*
Social no Brasil," *RBEP*, No. 15 (1963), 30–79; C. Furtado, *A Pre-Revoluçao Brasileira* (Rio de Janeiro: Editora Fundo de Cultura, 1962); and J. Ahumada, *Hypotheses for the Diagnosis of a Situation of Social Change: The Case of Venezuela* (Caracas: CENDES, 1963).
[19] See Scallapino, *op. cit.*; Beckman, *op. cit.*, Chs. 27, 28, 29. See also T. Ishida, *Japan's Rapid Development and Its Problems* (mimeo); and —, *The Pattern of Japanese Political Modernization*, Proceedings of the Association for Asian Studies (Philadelphia, 1963), esp. the section on "New Frontiers of Japanese Studies."

[20] See C. Geertz, "Ideology as a Cultural System," in D. Apter, ed., *Ideology and Discontent* (New York: Free Press of Glencoe, Inc., 1964); G. W. Skinner, ed., *Local, Ethnic, and National Loyalties in Village Indonesians, A Symposium* (New Haven: Yale University Southeast Asia Studies, 1959); E. A. Shils, "Primordial, Personal, Sacred and Civil Ties," *British Journal of Sociology*, **8** (1957), 130–145; and —, *Political Development...*, *op. cit.*, esp. pp. 31–37.

more successful in establishing relatively stable institutional frameworks.

The crucial problem of these societies has not been a relatively small extent of modernization, but rather the lack of development of new institutional settings, the lack of regulative mechanisms and normative injunctions upheld within strategic areas of the social structure and capable of dealing with the various problems arising in all these spheres. This situation could be described in Durkheim's terms as the non-development and non-institutionalization of the pre-contractual elements of contracts in the society. The number of "contracts," i.e., of different spheres of interaction—be they in the field of labor relations, industrial relations, or administrative practice—in which new contractual and administrative arrangements developed was very great. But adequate frameworks for the application of normative injunctions to specific situations did not develop, and many contractual arrangements were not upheld by commonly shared values and orientations.[21]

[21] The Argentine case shows the limits of continuity and stability of a society in which the precontractual elements are weak or underdeveloped from the very beginning and which did not have any strong pre-existing traditional base of solidarity.

As a result of continuous immigration and colonization in Argentina between 1890 and 1920, different, new, "relatively modern" groups—such as new planters or workers—developed. These groups tended, on the whole, to be socially and culturally rather separate. However, because of the continuous economic expansion in a colonizatory setup, they were able to continue to maintain their separate existence and mutual closeness together with continuous development, change, and modernization. Only gradually did they become interwoven into a closer framework of mutual interdependence. At the same time, the major oligarchic elites which held the ruling position in the country did not develop new symbols, institutions, and policies capable of dealing with these new problems and basically maintained the framework developed in the mid-nineteenth century, thus also impeding the full integration of these groups into new, more modern frameworks.

It was the combination of these characteristics that gave rise, in many of these cases, to what one investigator has described as the original Hobbesian state of war, i.e., to a state of internal war of all against all without the existence of any common rules which the participants could find as binding.[22]

Again, in Durkheim's terms, in all these cases there took place a failure to establish and institutionalize new levels of solidarity, to make the transition from mechanic to organic solidarity or from a level of low organic solidarity to a higher one, even though the older frameworks of solidarity were undermined by the growing differentiation and interaction between different groups and strata.

XI

The preceding discussion attempted to provide an analytic description of the developments in these societies. It does not, by itself, explain the reasons for the lack of development of the adequate integrative mechanisms in these societies. We shall attempt now to analyze some of these reasons.

This lack was not due to the lack of attempts by the rulers or the aspirants to elite positions to develop such mechanisms and policies, or to the lack of demands by various groups in the society for the development of some far-reaching social and economic policies. Manifold policies which aimed at the establishment of some regulative principles in the body politic and at the implementation of various collective goals were developed and implemented by the political elites—very often in response to various demands on behalf

It was only when, on the one hand, the interrelation between these groups became closer, and the continued economic expansion became halted, on the other, that the shaky coexistence was broken down, giving rise to long periods of conflicts and tension in the 'thirties, to the Peronist regime, and continuing later some of the same instabilities.

[22] See Sayeed, *Pakistan . . .*, *op. cit.*, esp. Chs. 14–16.

of wider groups in the society. But these policies and the demands to which they responded did not contribute to the establishment of relatively stable co-ordination in the society.

In order to be able to understand the reasons for the development of these policies and to evaluate their results, it is necessary to put them into the wider con-text of the social and political orientation of the broader social strata and of the interaction between them and the elites.

As we have seen above, all these societies were characterized by the development within them of continuous processes of social mobilization.[23] But the structure of these processes of social mobilization assumed here some special characteristics. The most important of these characteristics was that the wider social groups and strata —be they rural or urban groups, ecological or professional units—evinced a very high degree of social and cultural "closeness" and self-centeredness, however great their dependence on the groups might have become.[24]

The most important aspect of this closeness was the predominance of a purely "adaptive" attitude to the wider social setting with but little active solidary orientation to it or identification with it. This adaptive orientation could be manifest in two different, seemingly opposing but often coalescing ways. The first such way, most frequently found among various "traditional" lower- and sometimes also middle-rural and urban groups, is charac-terized by a relatively passive attitude to the wider social settings, by a great extent of rigidity in their conception of society in general and of their own place within it, in particular.

These characteristics were closely re-lated to some features of the internal structure of these groups, to a strong tendency to minimize internal differentia-tion with relatively severe sanctions against those who may have tended to break up such homogeneity, to a great weakness of flexible self-regulatory mecha-nisms within these groups, and to a very minimal ability to enter into or deal with more complex internal or external rela-tions.[25]

These characteristics had many re-percussions on the structure and activities of these groups when they were pushed into new, modernized, and differentiated urban, industrial, and semi-industrial settings. They resulted in the perpetuation of pre-vious "traditional" types of relationships, i.e., of paternalistic arrangements in industrial settings and relations in dealing with officials, politicians, or leaders of the church, in the lack of readiness to undertake responsibility or initiative in the new settings, and in general in great passivity and in small ranges of interests.[26]

Similarly, insofar as new occupational and other aspirations developed within these groups, they were focused on re-latively restricted pre-existing types or ranges of occupational and status concep-tions and images. The great propensity to academic, professional, bureaucratic, white

---

[23] K. Deutsch, "Social Mobilization and Political Development," *American Political Science Review*, **55** (September 1961), 463–515.

[24] E. R. Wolf, "Closed Corporate Peasant Communities in Meso-america and Central Java," *Southwestern Journal of Anthropology*, **12** (Spring 1957), 1–8.

[25] *Ibid.*

[26] R. M. Morse, "Latin American Cities: Aspects of Function and Structure," *Compara-tive Studies in Society and History*, **4**, 4 (July 1962), 473–494; P. Hauser, ed., *Urbanization in Latin America* (Paris: UNESCO, 1961), esp. the papers by J. F. B. Lopes, "Aspects of Adjustment of Rural Emigrants to Urban-Industrial Conditions in Sao Paulo, Brazil," pp. 234–249; and G. Germani, "Inquiry into the Social Effects of Urbanization on a Working Class Sector of Greater Buenos Aires," pp. 206–233. On a similar situa-tion in southern Italy, see Luigi Barsini, "Italy, North and South," *Encounter*, No. 105 (July 1962), 7–18; J. Mafos Mar, "Migration and Urbanization," *loc. cit.*, pp. 170–191; A. Pearse, *loc. cit.*, "Some Characteristics of Urbanization in the City of Rio de Janeiro," *loc. cit.*, pp. 191–206. See also F. Fernandes, *Mudanças Sociais no Brasil, op. cit.*, Chs. 10, 11.

collar occupations, as against more technical, business, professional occupations, which is so widely spread in many of these countries on all levels of the occupational scale, is perhaps the clearest manifestation or indication of these trends.[27]

The second major way in which this adaptive attitude to the wider social setting could be manifest was that of what may be called exaggerated, unlimited "openness" and "flexibility" and attempts to obtain within this new setting many various benefits, emoluments, and positions without any consideration of actual possibilities or of other groups in the societies. This tendency is best exemplified by some of the more active urbanized groups in Argentina and other Latin American countries.[28]

There were only relatively few groups within these societies which evinced somewhat greater and more realistic internal and external flexibility. Most important among them were some economic business communities or new professional groups, some relatively differentiated rural leadership, and some reformative religious groups. But these were, in most of the societies studied here, weak and above all relatively segregated both from the central institutions of the societies and from wider social strata.

XII

The most important structural outcome of these tendencies was that even though new types of specialized and differentiated social organizations, trade unions, or professional organizations were created both among the elite and among the broader groups of society which were drawn into new frameworks, this did not result in the creation of a viable new differentiated institutional structure.

These groups were unable to function effectively because they had to work under what may be called "false" premises, i.e., some of the prerequisites for their effective functioning did not develop in these settings. They very often exhibited characteristics of "delinquent communities," as they have been called by a student of French "retardation" or "traditionalism," i.e., communities not oriented to the attainment of their manifest goals (be they economic growth, community development, or the like), but to the maintenance of the vested status and interest positions of their members within the existing settings.[29]

Moreover, even if there tended to develop within some institutional spheres—be it in education, in the field of economic enterprises, or in the professions—either through diffusion, or through the development of specially active groups, some more stable, differentiated groups and organizations, their ability to develop and maintain their organization and activities within the wider setting was very restricted. Very often they succumbed to the pressures of the environment, becoming disorganized or transformed into "delinquent communities."[30]

These structural characteristics may also to some extent explain the nature of political activities and orientations that developed within these societies among broader groups of the society and especially the fact that monolithic aspirations, i.e., attempts to direct and control all social developments and all avenues of social and occupational mobility within them and

[27] See E. Tiryakian, "Occupational Stratification and Aspiration in an Underdeveloped Country: The Philippines," *Economic Development and Cultural Change*, **7** (1959), 431–444.
[28] I am indebted to Professor G. Germani for this information, as well as for pointing out the general significance of this type of group attitude. See G. Germani, *Politica y Sociedad*, *op. cit.*, Ch. 7.

[29] J. R. Pitts, "Continuity and Change in Bourgeois France," in *In Search of France* (Cambridge: Harvard University, Center for International Affairs, 1963), esp. pp. 254–259.
[30] F. Fernandes, "O Cientista Brasileiros o Desenvolvimento da Ciencia," *Revista Brasiliense*, No. 1 (1960), 85–121. See also F. W. Riggs, "Economic Development and Local Administration," *Philippine Journal of Public Administration*, **4**, 1 (January 1959).

to monopolize all positions of power and allocations of prestige.[31]

Secondly, but unlike, as we shall see, the case of Soviet Russia, Mexico, or Kemalist Turkey, where similar status orientations developed among the ruling elites, those in Indonesia, Burma, or Kuomingtang China were very closely connected with the development of what may be called an "ascriptive" freezing of status aspirations and symbols and with an emphasis on a very restricted range of such symbols. Most of these symbols were derived from the preceding systems—be they colonial or traditional. Moreover, only some of the symbols which existed in these societies were upheld in the new situation.[32]

Thus, political self-perception and self-legitimation of the political leaders were also to no small extent focused on the procurement through the new political frameworks of many benefits—to the collectivity as such, to the major (articulate) strata, and especially to those strata which were, as it were, deprived from sharing in these benefits in the former period.

XIII

As a result, the policies undertaken by the rulers in these societies have been characterized by continuous oscillation between the attempts at controlling all the major power positions and groups in the society and and monopolizing the positions of effective control, on the one hand, and a continuous giving in to the demands of various groups, on the other hand. Examples of such oscillating policies could be found in many important fields —be they those of public administration, education, agrarian reform, labor relations, or economic policy.[33]

In general, the various more restrictive policies in all these fields could be found in the more "traditional" countries like Pakistan or Sudan, while the policies of "giving in" to exaggerated demands of various groups could be found especially in the more modern countries like Indonesia and Burma, although both tendencies could be found, in some measure, in all these countries.

Needless to say, many such policies—especially the more repressive and regiment-

[31] See Eisenstadt, *Essays . . .*, *op. cit.*, esp. pp. 42 ff.

[32] See, for instance, Y. C. Wang, "Social Mobility in China," *American Sociological Review*, 25, 6 (December 1960), 843–855.

[33] On education policies see A. Lewis, "Education and Economic Development," *Social and Economic Studies*, 10, 2 (June 1961); J.

Roberto Moreira, *Educacao e Desenvolvimento no Brasil* (Rio de Janeiro, 1960); J. Fischer, "Universities and the Political Process in Southeast Asia," *Pacific Affairs*, 36, 1 (Spring 1963), 3–16; and H. Mint, "The Universities of Southeast Asia and Economic Development," *Pacific Affairs*, 35, 2 (Summer 1962), 116–128, For a general analysis S. N. Eisenstadt. *Education and Political Development*, Duke University Commonwealth Seminar Series 1962–63. On economic policy, see, for instance B. Glassburner, "Economic Policy Making in Indonesia, 1950–57," *Economic Development and Cultural Change*, 10, 1 (January 1962); H. O. Schmitt, "Foreign Capital and Social Conflict in Indonesia, 1950–55," *Economic Development and Cultural Change*, 10, 2 (April 1962); and J. C. Mackie, "Indonesia's Government Estates and Their Masters," *Pacific Affairs*, 34, 4 (Winter 1961–62), 337–360. On problems of bureaucratization, see Feith, *op. cit.*, esp. Chs. 7, 8, and 11; and O. Panni, "Delema da Burocratizacao no Brasil," *Boletim, Centro Latino Americano de Pesquisas em Cienciais Sociais*, 4, 3 (August 1960), 9–14: On problems of agrarian reform, see D. Felix, "Agrarian Reform and Industrial Growth," *International Development Review*, 2 (October 1960), 16–22; also T. F. Carroll, "The Land Reform Issue in Latin America," in A. Hirschmann, ed., *Latin American Issues* (New York: Twentieth Century Fund, 1961), pp. 161–201. For another interesting case study, see W. I. Ledejinsky, "Agrarian Reform in the Republic of Vietnam," in *Problems of Freedom, South Vietnam since Independence* (New York: Free Press, 1961), pp. 53–77. See "Economic Reconstruction and the Struggle for Political Power in Indonesia," *World Today*, 15, 3 (March 9), 105–114; and also D. Felix, "Structural Imbalances, Social Conflict, and Inflation: An Appraisal of Chile's Recent Anti-Inflationary Effort," *Economic Development and Cultural Change*, 8, 2 (January 1960), 113–148.

ating ones—can be found also in many other "new" and older nations; and for each concrete policy undertaken in Indonesia, Burma, or Pakistan, there could also be found an equivalent in a more stable regime. But the most important characteristic of these policies as they developed in the countries analyzed here has been not any specific detail, but rather the continuous oscillation between the repressive orientation, on the one hand, and the giving in to the various demands of many groups on the other, or the lack of development of any stable or continuous criteria of priorities.

XIV

Thus, extremely important parallels in the orientations and activities of the new elites and of large parts of the broader groups and strata within these societies can be found. Both were characterized by maintaining and developing within the new modern institutional frameworks relatively rigid and restricted social, cultural, and political orientations conceived in terms of the preceding social structure or in terms of "flexible" but unattainable goals.

Hence, there tended to develop in these cases a vicious circle of pressures on existing resources, pressures which were strongly linked to the rigidity of aspirations of these groups and were often reinforced by the policies and activities of the rulers which ultimately necessarily tended to deplete these resources. A very general result of the policies developed in such situations was to reduce available resources and to squander them. Such squandering of resources took place often because of "symbolic" or ideological reasons, and because of the attempts of the rulers to attest, in this way, to their legitimation. It usually minimized the range of maneuvering ability available to the rulers. At the same time, because of lack of any clear principles of regulation or priorities, they tended to exacerbate the level of conflict between various groups as the aspirations of them all rose while the total output of the economy remained static or even decreased.

XV

In order to be able to appreciate fully the nature of the developments in the societies discussed above, we might perhaps compare them briefly with those in countries like Mexico, Kemalist Turkey, or Meiji Japan—not to say anything about the special type of developments in Soviet Russia—where new modernizing regimes were able to deal in the initial stages of modernization with some of the problems and contradictions discussed above. There the elites were able not only to impose their policies on the wider social groups and strata, but also to draw these groups into the more differentiated institutional framework, at the same time regulating, at least to some extent, their integration within the framework.[34]

[34] The classical analysis of Japan's political modernization has been given in H. Norman, *Japan's Emergence as a Modern State* (New York: Institute of Pacific Relations, 1940). Some recent works have challenged parts of Norman's interpretation: see M. B. Jansen, *Sakamoto Ryoma and the Meiji Restoration* (Princeton: Princeton University Press, 1961); A. M. Craig, *Chosshu in the Meiji Restoration* (Cambridge: Harvard University Press, 1961); see also R. N. Bellah, *Tokugawa Religion* (Glencoe: Free Press, 1956); and —, "Values and Social Change in Modern Japan," in *Asian Cultural Studies, No. 3, Studies on Modernization of Japan* (Tokyo: International Christian University, 1962), pp. 13–57; H. Passin, "Stratigraphy of Protest in Japan," in H. Kaplan, ed., *The Revolution in World Politics, op. cit.*, pp. 112–113; R. P. Dore, *Land Reforms in Japan* (London: Oxford University Press, 1959); and see also, among many other available materials, the issue on "City and Village in Japan," of *Economic Development and Cultural Change*, **60**, 1, Part II (October 1960).

On Kemalist Turkey, see B. Lewise, *The Emergence of Modern Turkey* (London: Oxford University Press, 1961); K. H. Karpat, *Turkey's Politics, the Transition to a Multi-Party System* (Princeton: Princeton University Press, 1959); —, "Recent Political Developments in Turkey and Their Social Background," *International Affairs*, **28**, 3 (July 1962), 304–323; and F. W. Frey, "Political Development, Power,

This could be seen in some of the policies developed by these elites to deal with problems of modernization. Thus, for instance, the restructuring of the process of communication was effected in these countries by gradually linking different levels of communication and gradually incorporating them into a relatively unified system of communication. An important aspect of this process of gradual incorporation was that for a certain period of time the different levels or types of communicative patterns were kept relatively segregated, but that special interlinking mechanisms which maintained some relation to the central communicative system by the elites were gradually, but continuously, expanded.[35]

The same picture could be seen on the whole in the field of development of educational policies. Thus, in most of these countries, there was a widespread extension of primary education on the local level, side by side with the extension of special new secularized and diversified elite schools, with only a gradual extension of mobility between these levels.[36]

[*footnote 34 continued* and Communications in Turkey," in Pye, *op. cit.*, pp. 28–327.

On Mexico, see H. F. Cline, *Mexico, Revolution to Evolution* (London: Oxford University Press, 1962); R. E. Scott, *Mexican Government in Transition* (Urbana: University of Illinois Press, 1959); O. Paz, *The Labyrinth of Solitude, Life, and Thought in Mexico* (New York: Grove Press, 1961), esp. Chs. 6–8; and see also Raymond Vernon, *The Dilemma of Mexico's Development: The Roles of the Private and Public Sectors* (Cambridge: Harvard University Press, 1963).

The literature on the U.S.S.R. is of course immense, but some of the points most important from the point of view of our analysis can be found in M. Fainsod, *How Russia Is Ruled* (Cambridge: Harvard University Press, 1955); Z. K. Brzezinski, *Ideology and Power in Soviet Politics* (New York: Praeger, 1962); and J. A. Armstrong, *The Politics of Totalitarianism, The Communist Party of the Soviet Union from 1934 to the Present* (New York: Random House, 1961).

[35] See, for instance, F. W. Frey, "Political Development . . .," *op. cit.*, pp. 313–314.
[36] See F. W. Frey, "Education and Political

Third, and perhaps most important from the point of view of our discussion, has been the structuring of the processes of social mobility in these societies. In all these countries continuous processes of mobility developed which necessarily broke down the self-sufficiency of some, at least, of the traditional units and brought them into the framework of the new, more modernized institutions. This mobility was on the whole geared to realistic expanding opportunities—at least, the discrepancy between the mobility aspirations and the realities was not as great as in the other cases discussed above. The processes of mobility were here greatly connected with the development of at least some new, more differentiated status and occupational orientations and aspirations. Similarly, the processes often resulted here in a growing internal differentiation within the local—rural or urban—units, giving rise to some important changes in the structure of leadership and community participation and to growing connections between these groups and the central institution.

XVI

In all these countries the new rulers were, of course, also interested in maintaining the monopoly of power and allocation of status in their hands. But they attempted to develop and maintain such monopoly together with a growing variegation of the symbols and frameworks of status. They

Development in Turkey," in J. S. Coleman, ed., *Education and Political Development* (Princeton: Princeton University Press, 1965).

On the development of Japanese education in the Meiji period, see R. Anderson, *Japan, Three Epochs of Modern Education* (Washington: U.S. Department of Health, Education, and Welfare, Bulletin 1919); and also R. K. Hall, *Education for the New Japan* (New Haven, 1949); and H. Passin, "Education and Political Development in Japan," in Coleman, *op. cit.*

On the development of education in Mexico, see Cline, *op. cit.*, Ch. 21; and M. C. Johnston, *Education in Mexico* (Washington: U.S. Department of Health, Education, and Welfare, 1956).

also, of course, stressed the importance of the political status, but usually attempted to connect it with emphasis on new occupational, technical, and professional activities. They attempted also to minimize as far as possible various tendencies to ascriptive monopolization of upper positions by various elite and bureaucratic groups.[37]

If, however, these elites were relatively more flexible in their status orientations, they were also more cohesive and firm in the implementation of their policies; and they did not give in continuously and indiscriminately to the demands of different groups and strata within their societies. In extreme cases, like in Russia, they used coercion against these groups, but in others they attempted to direct and manipulate these demands. Some of these demands—like those for agrarian reform in Mexico—have become important symbols of the new regime. Interestingly enough, the actual policies related to these symbols did not always fully implement all the potential demands which could—and very often did—develop in connection with their symbols. Thus, for instance,

reforms that were implemented in Mexico in the field of agrarian reform were important from the point of view of the restructuring of internal arrangements of the rural communities, creating new social and economic groups within them and opening up new channels of mobility to the center. But these reforms were not on the whole allowed to block continuously the expansion of the economy by giving in to both old and new vested interests.[38]

XVII

The problem of why in Turkey, Japan, Mexico, and Russia there emerged in the initial stages of modernization elites with orientations to change and ability to implement relatively effective policies, while they did not develop in these initial phases in Indonesia, Pakistan, or Burma, or why elites with similar differences tended to develop also in later stages of modernization, is an extremely difficult one and constitutes one of the most baffling problems in comparative sociological analysis. There are but few available indications to deal with this problem. Very tentatively, it may perhaps be suggested that to some extent it has to do with the placement of these elites in the preceding social structure, with the extent of their internal cohesiveness, and of the internal transformation of their own value orientation.[39]

In most of the countries analyzed here, the new elites were mostly composed of intellectuals, and in many cases they con-

---

[37] The case of Soviet Russia is probably most instructive from this point of view. In Soviet Russia there developed, on the one hand, among many parts of the emerging elites—bureaucrats, technicians, politicians—strong tendencies to "freeze" their positions in an ascriptive way through monopolization for themselves and their families of many social, economic, and educational prerogatives. But these tendencies were countered by the attempt of the top political leaders to break up these ascriptive bases and to maintain through predominance of the party to some extent in continuous differentiation of status and power criteria. Similar tendencies and policies can be found in Kemalist Turkey, Mexico, or Meiji Japan.

See G. F. Bereday, *The Changing Soviet School* (Boston, 1960); — and Joan Petinar, eds., *The Politics of Soviet Education* (New York, 1960); Q. Anweiler, "Probleme der Schulreform in Osteuropa," *International Review of Education*, **6** (1960), 21–35; also N. K. Goncharov, "La Reforme Scholaire in U.S.S.R.," *loc. cit.*, **6** (1960), 432–442; and N. DeWitt, "Upheaval in Education," *Problems of Communism*, **8** (January 1959).

[38] On Mexican land reform see Cline, *op. cit.*, Ch. 22; J. G. Maddox, *Mexican Land Reform*, American Universities Field Staff JGM-5-57 (New York, 1957); and J. S. Herzog, *El Agrarismo Mexicano y la Reforma Agraria* (Mexico: Fondo de Cultura Economica, 1959).

[39] See Kautsky, "An Essay . . .," *op. cit.*; H. Benda, "Non-Western Intelligentsia as Political Elites," in Kautsky, *Political Change . . ., op. cit.*, pp. 235–252; and F. Mansur, *Process of Independence* (London, 1962), esp. Chs. 2 and 3.

stituted the only initially available modern elite. They had but very few internal social and ideological contacts or identifications (even if ambivalent ones) with either the bearers of pre-existing traditions or with the wider groups of the society. The modernizing orientations of these elites were focused more on the political than on the economic sphere. Surprisingly enough, they were also very often less focused on the cultural sphere, in the sense of redefinition and reformation of their own basic internal value-orientation. Consequently, they were not able to establish a strong internal cohesiveness and strong ideological and value identifications and connections with other potentially modernized groups and strata.

Similarly, the various political elites or leaders, whether the more oligarchic or more demagogic ones, in many of the Latin American countries, were also mostly dissociated, even if in a different way, from the various broader groups that were continuously coming into the society or impinging on its central institutions. The process of selection and formation of these elites was a relatively rigid and restricted one, bringing in relatively weaker elements and intensifying their alienation from the broader group, as well as their internal insecurity and lack of cohesion.[40] Similar—and even more intensive—rifts between different elites developed, as is well known, in various European countries in the 'twenties and 'thirties.

On the other hand, the elites in Turkey, Japan, and Mexico or some of the more cohesive elites in countries of later stages of modernization, however great the differences between them, had yet some contrary characteristics in common. They were not usually composed only of intellectual groups entirely alienated from the pre-existing elites and from some of the broader groups of the society, but were to

[40] See Germani, *Politica y Sociedad . . .* , *op. cit.*, Chs. 8, 9; Silver, *Liderzgo . . .*, *op. cit.*, and Fernandes, *Mudanças . . ., op. cit.*

some extent placed in secondary elite position in the preceding structure and had somewhat closer relations with many active, broader groups.

In the ideological and value spheres, they aimed at the development of a new, more flexible set of symbols and collective identity which, while not negating the traditions, would also provide some new meaning for the new processes of change. Hence, they tended, on the one hand, to be more cohesive, while at the same time to effect some internal value transformation within the broader groups and strata.

XVIII

The development of processes of social mobilization without adequate integration, of rifts between the "instrumental" and "solidarity making" leaders, and within the symbolic and ideological realism of a society, did develop in all the countries in which some breakdowns of modernization and especially of political modernization took place. They developed, as we have seen, in different phases or stages of modernization in the various new states enumerated above.

One common outcome of these processes is implicit in most of the preceding analysis—namely, the "reversal" of these regimes to what may be called a lower, less flexible level of political and social differentiation, as seen in the scope of problems with which they are capable of dealing. But, on the other hand, as has already been pointed out above, most of these less differentiated regimes have to some extent retained some of the symbols, goals, and institutional arrangements of modernity, even if they attempted to develop new ideologies and symbols.

This combination has necessarily created a potential contradiction which could develop in principle into several different directions. One such possible outcome was the institutionalization of a relatively modern system, a somewhat lower level of differentiation, albeit with some possibilities of limited institutional absorption of change, conducive to some economic growth. The other possibility is that of development of stagnative regimes with but very little capacity for absorption of change and which may either become re- latively stable or develop a system of vicious circles of eruptions, blockages, and violence. But the analysis of the conditions which may lead to any of these directions is beyond the province of this paper.

Index